KJE 27 KRA

CASEBOOK ON EU ENVIRONMENT

Casebook on
EU Environmental Law

PROFESSOR DR LUDWIG KRÄMER

·H A R T·
PUBLISHING

OXFORD – PORTLAND OREGON
2002

Hart Publishing
Oxford and Portland, Oregon

Published in North America (US and Canada) by
Hart Publishing c/o
International Specialized Book Services
5804 NE Hassalo Street
Portland, Oregon
97213-3644
USA

Distributed in the Netherlands, Belgium and Luxembourg by
Intersentia, Churchillaan 108
B2900 Schoten
Antwerpen
Belgium

Hart Publishing is a specialist legal publisher based in Oxford, England.
To order further copies of this book or to request a list of other
publications please write to:

Hart Publishing, Salter's Boatyard, Folly Bridge,
Abingdon Road, Oxford OX1 4LB
Telephone: +44 (0)1865 245533 or Fax: +44 (0)1865 794882
e-mail: mail@hartpub.co.uk
WEBSITE: http//www.hartpub.co.uk

British Library Cataloguing in Publication Data
Data Available
ISBN 1–84113–172–5 (paperback)

Typeset by Hope Services (Abingdon) Ltd.
Printed and bound in Great Britain by
Bell and Bain Ltd, Glasgow.

PREFACE

The outstanding role of European courts—the Court of Justice and the Court of First Instance—in the making of European law has often been underlined. It cannot be rated high enough, also, and in particular, when the increasing globalisation draws the attention to the activity of other international organisations and to the role which the law plays in that process. "The Court of Justice shall ensure that in the interpretation and application of this Treaty the law is observed": it would be good to read these simple words of Article 220 EC Treaty in the UN Statutes, the treaties on the World Trade Organisation or other international treaties.

This book deals with a section of the comprehensive activity in particular of the Court of Justice, which is environmental law. In environmental policy, law has a particular importance, for two main reasons: on the one hand, the environment does not have organised vested interest groups which could bring its interest to the political discussions and could defend it towards other, in particular economic interests. On the other hand, the environment (the biosphere) can well survive without humans, but humans cannot survive without the environment. In view of this, law has the task to pour the declamations, principles and orientations on environmental protection into a legal form and to guarantee the preservation of the environment as good as possible. It is at least due to the Court of Justice that despite all directives and regulations, programmes and plans, solemn declarations, charts and conventions the state of the environment deteriorates not only worldwide, but also within Europe and the European Union. Indeed, the Court has, overall, broadly interpreted the rules on the protection of the environment, deciding in favour of the environment where this was possible and innovated in order to improve the existing rules.

For this book, 50 judgments on the protection of the environment were selected. In each case, there is a short presentation of the facts and of the procedure. This part is followed by excerpts from the Court's judgment. In order to facilitate reading, intermediary titles were inserted into the judgment which were set in brackets, whenever they did not stem from the Court itself. The subsequent commentary places the judgment into the legal, environmental and political context and discusses the reasoning of the Court. The cases deal with basic issues of the EC Treaty (cases 1 to 9), horizontal legal issues (cases 10 to 18), water protection and air pollution (cases 19 to 25), products and noise (cases 26 to 32), nature protection (cases 33 to 38), waste management (cases 39 to 45) and procedural questions (cases 46 to 50).

Particular importance was given to recent judgments: 43 of the 50 judgments were made in 1996 or later; the oldest judgment comes from 1991. With one exception, judgments of 2001 and 2002 could not be incorporated any more. Also, legal developments of this period could only be mentioned in parts only.

The book addresses all persons who, in one way or the other, deal with environmental law, in particular legal practitioners, researchers, law students, academics and administrators. Its objective is to increase understanding and comprehension of the reasoning of the Court, but also of that of the European institutions and to give ideas how, with the means of law, the environment could be better protected. My professional activity as official in the department of the environment of the European Commission imposed, on many occasions, reserves in the assessment of facts. Nevertheless, I hope that readers will recognise my own opinion throughout the text.

I consider the environmental jurisdiction of the Court to be very positive and important for the environment; its weight in the political and administrative day-to-day struggle cannot easily be overestimated: the Court is an anchor in the storm, a rock in the sea of interests that are hostile to the environment. Also those commentaries which less agree with specific judgments are based on this evaluation. The reason why this book, overall, rather follows a somehow critical line lies in the fact that only a critical discussion can contribute to the creation of a European public (legal) opinion; nobody is served with base flattery. Furthermore, the critical remarks aim—and I hope that this becomes clear, too—not so much at the jurisdiction, but rather at the law, i.e. the European environmental law, as it is being formed, made, treated and applied.

It is a paradox that at present everybody within the European Union favours an appropriate protection of the environment, a sustainable development, a high level of protection and a full application of the precautionary principle: however, the devil is always in the detail. As long as the fascination lies in the sheer number of environmental regulations or court decisions and the content and application of the different environmental regulations are not examined in detail, there will be an increasing number of measures for the environment—and a slow, but progressive decrease of the protection of the environment. This book tries to make lawyers reflect on the protection of the environment.

Ludwig Krämer
Brussels,
1 July 2002

CONTENTS

TABLE OF CASES

TABLE OF TREATIES

TABLE OF SECONDARY LEGISLATION

EUROPEAN

Council

Commission Decisions

Parliament Decisions

Directives

Resolutions

UNITED KINGDOM

Statutory Instruments

1

GENERAL PRINCIPLES

---

1. THE CHOICE OF THE LEGAL BASIS

Judgment of the Court of 25 February 1999
Joined Cases C–164/97 and C–165/97

European Parliament v. *Council of the European Union*
supported by Commission of the European Communities
[1999] ECR I–1139

Facts and Procedure

In 1986, the Council adopted two Regulations, Regulation 3528/86 on the protection of the Community's forests against atmospheric pollution,[1] and Regulation 3529/86 on the protection of the Community's forests against fire.[2] Both Regulations were adopted on the basis of Articles 37 (ex Article 43) and 308 (ex Article 235) EC Treaty. In 1992, the Regulation on protection against air pollution was amended; the amending Regulation was based on Articles 37 and 175 (ex Article 130s) EC Treaty.[3] The Regulation on protection against fire was replaced by a new Regulation 2158/92, which was also based on Articles 37 and 175 EC Treaty.[4]

In 1997, the Council again amended the Regulations on protection against air pollution and fire, with the purpose of extending for a further five years the Community protection schemes. This time, however, the amending Regulations, 307/97[5] and 308/97,[6] were based on Article 37 (ex Article 43) EC Treaty alone.

The European Parliament applied to the Court of Justice in order to have Regulations 307/97 and 308/97 annulled. It argued that both Regulations should have been based on Article 175 (ex Article 130s) EC Treaty and therefore have been

---

[1] Regulation 3528/86 on the protection of the Community's forests against atmospheric pollution, [1986] OJ L326/2.

[2] Regulation 3529/86 on protection of the Community's forests gainst fire, [1986] OJ L326/5.

[3] Regulation 2157/92, [1992] OJ L217/1.

[4] Regulation 2158/92, [1992] OJ L217/3.

[5] Regulation 307/97, [1997] OJ L51/9.

[6] Regulation 308/97, [1997] OJ L51/11.

adopted by the Council under the procedure for co-operation with the European Parliament provided for in Article 252 (ex Article 189c) EC Treaty; however, since those Regulations were adopted solely on the basis of Article 37 EC Treaty, the Parliament was merely consulted.

Judgment (extracts)

[The choice of the legal basis for a Community measure]

12. ... the choice of a legal basis for a measure must be based on objective factors which are amenable to judicial review. Those factors include, in particular, the aim and content of the measure (see, for example, Case C–155/91 *Commission* v. *Council* [1993] ECR I–939, paragraph 7, and Case C–42/97 *Parliament* v. *Council* [1999] ECR I–0000, paragraph 36).

13. It is clear from the provisions of the amended regulations that the aims of the Community schemes for the protection of forests are partly agricultural since they are intended in particular to contribute to safeguarding the productive potential of agriculture, and partly of a specifically environmental nature since their primary objective is to maintain and monitor forest ecosystems.

14. In such circumstances it is necessary, in order to determine the appropriate legal basis, to consider whether the measures in question relate principally to a particular field of action, having only incidental effects on other policies, or whether both aspects are equally essential. If the first hypothesis is correct, recourse to a single legal basis is sufficient (Case C–70/88 *Parliament* v. *Council* [1991] ECR I–4529, paragraph 17, and Case C–217/94 *Parliament* v. *Council* [1996] ECR I–1689, paragraph 32); if the second is correct, it is insufficient (Case 242/87 *Commission* v. *Council* [1989] ECR 1245, paragraphs 33 to 37, and Case C–360/97 *Parliament* v. *Council* [1996] ECR I–1195, paragraph 30) and the institution is required to adopt the measure on the basis of both of the provisions from which its competence derives (Case 165/87 *Commission* v. *Council* [1988] ECR 5545, paragraphs 6 to 13). However, no such dual basis is possible where the procedures laid down for each legal basis are incompatible with each other (Case C–300/89 *Commission* v. *Council* [1991] ECR I–2867, paragraphs 17 to 21).

15. With more particular reference to the common agricultural policy and the Community environmental policy, there is nothing in the case-law to indicate that, in principle, one should take precedence over the other. It makes clear that a Community measure cannot be part of Community action on environmental matters merely because it takes account of requirements of protection referred to in Article 130r (2) of the EC Treaty (Case C–62/88 *Greece* v. *Council* [1990] ECR I–1527, paragraph 20). Articles 130r and 130s leave intact the powers held by the Community under other provisions of the Treaty and provide a legal basis only for specific action on environmental matters (see, with regard to the use of drift nets in the context of the common agricultural policy, Case C–405/92 *Mondiet* v. *Armement Islais* [1993] ECR I–6133, paragraphs 25 to 27). In contrast, Article 130s of the Treaty must be the basis for provisions which fall specifically within the environmental policy (see, with regard to waste disposal directives, Case C–155/91 *Commission* v. *Council*, cited above), even if they have an impact on the functioning of the internal market (see, with regard to a regulation on shipments of waste, Case C–187/93 *Parliament* v. *Council* [1994] ECR I–2857, paragraphs 24 to 26) or if their objective is the improvement of agricultural production (see, regarding a directive concerning plant protection products, Case C–303/94 *Parliament* v. *Council* [1996] ECR I–2943).

In this case, although the measures referred to in the regulations may have certain positive repercussions on the functioning of agriculture, those indirect consequences are incidental to the primary aim of the Community schemes for the protection of forests, which are intended to ensure that the natural heritage represented by forest ecosystems is conserved and turned to account, and does not merely consider their utility to agriculture. Measures to defend the forest environment against the risks of destruction and degradation associated with fires and atmospheric pollution inherently form part of the environmental action for which Community competence is founded on Article 130s of the Treaty.

[Trees and forestry products and the common agricultural policy]

17. Moreover, the Commission's argument that trees and forests as a whole constitute agricultural products governed by Title II of the Treaty does not appear well founded.

18. "Live trees and other plants; bulbs, roots and the like; cut flowers and ornamental foliage" appear in the list in Annex II to the Treaty, in Chapter 6, following the numbering in the Brussels Nomenclature. Since there are no Community provisions explaining the concepts contained in that annex, it is appropriate to refer to the established interpretations and the methods of interpretation relating to the Common Customs Tariff in order to interpret the annex (see Case 77/83 *CILFIT* v. *Ministero della Sanità* [1984] ECR 1257, paragraph 7). The combined nomenclature annexed to Council Regulation (EEC) No 2658/87 of 23 July 1987 on the tariff and statistical nomenclature and on the Common Customs Tariff (OJ 1987 L 256, p. 1) contains, in Chapter 6, a heading 0602 "Other live plants (including their roots), cuttings and slips; mushroom spawn", together with a subheading 0602 20 "Trees, shrubs and bushes, grafted or not, of kinds which bear edible fruit or nuts"). The first explanatory note to that chapter states that, subject to a reservation which is not relevant to this case, "this chapter covers only live trees and goods (including seedling vegetables) of a kind commonly supplied by nursery gardeners or florists of planting or for ornamental use". Thus, contrary to the Commission's contention, Annex II cannot be regarded as covering in general terms trees and forestry production even though some of those products, taken in isolation, may fall within the scope of Articles 39 to 46 of the Treaty.

19. It follows that the contested regulations do not constitute rules on the production and marketing of agricultural products.

20. The Parliament is therefore correct in its assertion that, by basing the contested regulations on Article 43 of the Treaty although Article 130s was the appropriate legal basis, the Council has infringed essential procedural requirements and undermined its prerogatives.

Commentary

I. The European Parliament as Applicant

(1) The application to the Court was made by the European Parliament, under Article 230 (ex Article 173) EC Treaty.[7] This provision distinguishes three groups which may apply to the Court of Justice (a) Member States, the Council or the Commission; (b) the European Parliament, the Court of Auditors and the European Central Bank; (c) any natural or legal person. The difference between these groups is that the first group does not need to prove any interest in bringing an action. The second group, to which the European Parliament also belongs, may act only "for the purpose of protecting their prerogatives". The third group, finally, must either be the addressee of a decision or that decision must be of "direct and individual concern" to it.[8]

(2) The present wording of Article 230(3) was introduced into the Treaty only by the Maastricht Treaty 1993. Prior to that time, the European Parliament belonged to the third of the three above-mentioned groups. The Court of Justice held in 1987[9] that the interests of the Parliament were safeguarded by the Commission's possibility, as guardian of the Treaty under Article 211 (ex Article 155) EC Treaty to bring

---

[7] Art. 230 (ex Art. 173) EC Treaty: "The Court of Justice shall review the legality of acts adopted jointly by the European Parliament and the Council, of acts of the Council, of the Commission and of the European Central Bank, other than recommendations and opinions, and of acts of the European Parliament intended to produce legal effects vis-à-vis third parties.

It shall for this purpose have jurisdiction in actions brought by a member State, the Council or the Commission on grounds of lack of competence, infringement of an essential procedural requirement, infringement of this Treaty or of any rule of law relating to its application, or misuse of powers.

The Court of Justice shall have jurisdiction under the same conditions in actions brought by the European Parliament, by the Court of Auditors and by the European Central Bank for the purpose of protecting their prerogatives.

Any natural or legal person may, under the same conditions, institute proceedings against a decision addressed to that person or against a decision which, although in the form of a regulation or a decision addressed to another person, is of direct and individual concern to the former.

The proceedings provided for in this Art. shall be instituted within two months of the publication of the measure, or of its notification to the plaintiff, or, in the absence thereof, of the day on which it came to the knowledge of the latter, as the case may be".

[8] For a discussion of this clause see the commentary to cases nos. 47 and 49, pp. 408 and 421 of this book.

[9] Court of Justice, Case 302/87, *European Parliament* v. *Rat*, [1988] ECR 5615.

an action in favour of the Parliament. Also, the Parliament's rights could be defended in preliminary rulings under Article 234 (ex Article 177); or the Parliament could itself bring an action under Article 232 (ex Article 175) EC Treaty.[10]

However, in 1990, the Court changed its attitude. It recognised that the different ways indicated of safeguarding Parliament's rights were insufficient. Therefore, it allowed an action by the Parliament in order to protect its prerogatives, in particular its right to participate in the elaboration of a legislative act according to the different provisions of the EC Treaty.[11] It was in consequence of this case law that the Intergovernmental Conference which elaborated and adopted the Maastricht Treaty in 1991 inserted the new Article 230(3) EC Treaty, which later was slightly amended by the Amsterdam Treaty in 1999.

(3) The Court was strict in the interpretation of the clause "protecting prerogatives". In 1994, it had to deal with a case where the Parliament had brought an action against the Council arguing that the legislative act in question—Regulation 259/93 on the shipment of waste[12]—should have been based on Articles 95 (ex Article 100a) and 133 (ex Article 113) EC Treaty, and not on Article 175 (ex Article 130s) EC Treaty, as decided by the Council.[13] The Court held that Article 133 EC Treaty, in the version which it had at the moment when Regulation 259/93 had been adopted, did not provide for any participation of the European Parliament in the elaboration of legislative acts. Therefore, it held the Parliament's action inadmissible, in so far as the possible omission to base the Regulation on Article 133 EC Treaty could not have infringed any of Parliament's prerogatives; it discussed the case only as regards the question whether Article 95 or 175 EC Treaty was the appropriate legal basis .

In Case C–303/94,[14] the European Parliament had invoked, among other grounds, that a Council regulation had breached Article 253 (ex Article 190) EC Treaty,[15] as it had not clearly stated the reasons on which it was based. The Court considered the application inadmissible, as Article 253 did not give any prerogatives to the European Parliament.

The whole discussion on the the role of the European Parliament as applicant under Article 230 EC Treaty is now coming to an end: the Treaty of Nice which was concluded in December 2000 in Nice (France), again amended Article 230 and

---

[10] Art. 232 (ex Art. 175) EC Treaty: "Should the European Parliament, the Council or the Commission, in infringement of this Treaty, fail to act, the Member States and the other institutions of the Community may bring an action before the Court of Justice to have the infringement established".

[11] Court of Justice, Case 70/88, *European Parliament* v. *Council*, [1990] ECR 2041.

[12] Regulation 259/93 on the supervision and control of shipments of waste within, into and out of the European Community [1993] ECR L30/1.

[13] Court of Justice, Case C–187/93, *European Parliament* v. *Council*, [1994] ECR I–2857; see for a discussion of this case p. 382 *infra*.

[14] Court of Justice, Case C–304/94, *European Parliament* v. *Council*, [1996] ECR I–2943.

[15] Art. 253 (ex Art. 190) EC Treaty: "Regulations, directives and decisions adopted jointly by the European Parliament and the Council, and such acts adopted by the Council or the Commission, shall state the reasons on which they are based and shall refer to any proposals or opinions which were required to be obtained pursuant to this Treaty".

ranged the European Parliament in the first group, next to Member States, the Council and the Commission. After ratification of this Treaty by the Member States, the European Parliament will thus have all rights which flow from Article 230 EC Treaty.

In the present case, Parliament had invoked an infringement of its prerogatives. Indeed, Article 37 (ex Article 43) EC Treaty provided for the consultation of the Parliament, whereas Article 175(1) (ex Article 130s(1)) EC Treaty provided for the co-operation of the Parliament. This presentation of the arguments was sufficient for the admissibility of the application. Whether the legal basis was in fact wrongly chosen by the Council determines the question of whether the application is well founded.

II. The Choice of a Legal Basis

(4) This judgment resumes the Court's jurisprudence concerning the choice of a legal basis in environmental matters. The choosing of a legal basis for a directive, decision or regulation in matters of environmental protection is particularly difficult, because (a) Articles 174 to 176 (ex Articles 130r to 130t) have been inserted into the EC Treaty only in 1987 by the Single European Act; (b) as the participation rights of the European Parliament differ from one legal basis to the other, there are attempts from the Community institutions to favour this or that legal basis in order to have greater or smaller participation of the European Parliament; (c) Article 175 EC Treaty[16] is followed by Article 176 (ex Article 130t) EC Treaty, which allows Member States to maintain or introduce, under certain conditions, more stringent protective measures;[17] the right for Member States for introducing such measures is quite different under other Treaty provisions.

(5) The following table shows the evolution of Parliament's participation rights, the transition from unanimity to majority decisions and the residual rights of Member States of maintaining or introducing different national legislation:[18]

---

[16] Art. 175 (ex Art. 130s) EC Treaty: "1. The Council, acting in accordance with the procedure referred to in Art. 251 and after consulting the Economic and Social Committee and the Committee of the Regions, shall decide what action is to be taken by the Community in order to achieve the objectives referred to in Art. 174.

2. By way of derogation from the decision-making procedure provided for in paragraph 1 and without prejudice to Art. 95, the Council, acting unanimously on a proposal from the Commission and after consulting the European Parliament, the Economic and Social Committee and the Committee of the Regions, shall adopt:
—provisions primarily of a fiscal nature;
—mesures concerning town and country planning, land use with the exception of waste management and measures of a general nature, and management of water resources;
—measures significantly affecting a Member State's choice between different energy sources and the general structure of its energy supply.
..."

[17] See for a discussion of Art. 176 the commentary on p. 22 *infra*.

[18] The numbering of the different Articles of the EC Treaty follows the numbering which is in force at present. "unanimity" signifies decisions taken by unanimity, "majority" decisions by majority voting.

Article EC Treaty	Participation rights of the European Parliament				Member States' residual rights
	1958	*1987*	*1993*	*1999*	
37	consultation majority	consultation majority	consultation majority	consultation majority	none
95	consultation unanimity (Art. 94)	cooperation majority	codecision majority	codecision majority	Art. 95(4 to 10)
113	none majority	none majority	none majority	none majority	none
175(1)	— unanimity	consultation majority	cooperation majority	codecision	Art. 176
175(2)	—- unanimity	consultation unanimity	consultation	Art. 176	

(6) The Court confirms that where a measure relates "principally" to a particular field of action and has only "incidental" effects on other policies, the legal basis of the "principal" field of action must be taken; if both aspects are equally essential, both legal bases must be chosen.[19] In a judgment from 1993, the Court had justified Article 175 EC Treaty as the legal basis for Directive 75/442 on waste,[20] using the terms "principally" and "ancillary".[21] When the Court had to examine whether Article 37[22] or 175 EC Treaty was the right legal basis for a ban on drift-nets, it considered that the environmental aspects played only a "contributory" role to that decision, which was "primarily" an act taken under the common agricultural policy.[23] A difference in substance between these words does not exist.

As regards the borderline between "principal" and "incidental", the Court, in a consistent body of case law, refers to the aim and the content of the legislative act in question. "Aim" is the objective of the act, as appears from its title, its recitals and the political framework within which it is adopted. "Content" refers to the different provisions of the act and again to its recitals. Though these orientations appear clear, their application in practice is sometimes doubtful.

Thus, in Case C–300/89 which concerned a directive that harmonised national programmes on the reduction of pollution for the discharge of waste from the titanium dioxide industry, both the Commission and the Council argued before the

[19] This reasoning follows that of Court of Justice, Case 165/87, *Commission* v. *Council,* [1988] ECR 5545; in Case C–300/89, *Commission* v. *Council,* [1991] ECR I–2867, the Court confirmed this reasoning, but concluded that for reasons of Parliament's right of participation, Art. 95 (ex Art. 100a) EC Treaty was alone applicable, as under a double legal basis of Art. 175—consultation procedure—and Art. 95—co-operation procedure—the Council would have to act unanimously which would undermine Parliament's rights.

[20] Directive 75/442 on waste, [1975] OJ L194/47, amended by Directive 91/156, [1971] OJ L78/32.

[21] Court of Justice, Case C–155/91, *Commission* v. *Council,* [1993] ECR I–939, para. 20.

[22] Art. 37 (ex Art. 43) EC Treaty: "The Council shall, on a proposal from the Commission and after consulting the European Parliament, acting by a qualified majority, make regulations, issue directives, or take decisions, without prejudice to any recommendations which it may also make".

[23] Court of Justice, Case C–405/92 *Mondiet* [1993] ECR I–6133, paras. 24 and 28.

Court that the "principal" objective should be decisive; however, while the Commission considered that the principal objective of the directive in litigation was the elimination of disparities of competition, the Council considered that the protection of the environment was the principal objective. The Court held that the directive at issue displayed, in equal weight, elements of both the internal market and the protection of the environment[24] and decided in favour of application of Article 95.[25] In contrast to what was stated in Case C–155/91 the principal aim of the directive in Case C–300/89 had been the internal market.[26]

In Case C–155/91, the Commission was of the opinion that the principal aim and content of Directive 75/442 were to ensure the establishment and functioning of the internal market for waste, while the Council—and in this it was followed by the Court—considered the principal aim and content to be the protection of the environment. And in the present case, the Council again was of the opinion that the environmental considerations of the Regulations were merely "incidental", while the Regulations "mainly" related to the agricultural policy. The Court did not follow this reasoning, probably because the common agricultural policy does not include a forestry policy, as will be discussed below.

(7) The reference to the principal aim of a directive or a regulation clearly has its limits, of which two are of particular importance. First, the principal aim of product-related environmental measures is doubtful: for instance, since 1988, directives on pollution emissions from cars, which led to the introduction of the catalytic converters and which were meant to fight climate change, were practically all adopted in order to protect the environment, not in order to harmonise legislation within an internal market.[27] There is little in the content of the different directives or in their recitals which even discusses the internal market issues. Yet, all these directives are based on Article 95 EC Treaty.

In the same way, restrictions on the marketing and use of asbestos, cadmium, mercury, pentachlorophenol and other dangerous substances[28] are not issued at Community level in order to ensure the establishment and functioning of the internal market, but in order to protect the environment and health. Yet, despite their aim and content, such restrictions are adopted by legislative acts which are based on Article 95 EC Treaty.

The limits to the "principal" objective of a directive become obvious in cases where a Member State restricts, for environmental reasons, the use or marketing of a product, and the Community then takes over the principles of that legislation in order to ensure the protection of the environment throughout the Community;

---

[24] Court of Justice, Case C–300/89 (n. 19 *supra*), para. 16.

[25] See for the reasons n. 19 *supra*.

[26] Court of Justice, Case C–155/91 (n. 21 *supra*), para. 20.

[27] Beginning with Directive 88/6 [1988] OJ L36/1; see also Directive 94/12 [1994] OJ L100/42.

[28] Most of these restrictions are made in the form of amendments to Directive 76/769 on the restriction of marketing and use of certain dangerous substances and preparations, [1976] OJ L262/201; until mid-2000, this Directive was amended about 20 times.

it is a fiction to argue that the principal aim of that Community measure is the establishment and functioning of the internal market.[29]

(8) Secondly, the content and in particular the recitals of a legislative act are to a large extent drafted by the Council, though the Council is also bound by the legal bases as they are laid down in the Treaty. By drafting the legal text in a specific way, the Council has a large possibility to influence its later interpretation. This is probably why the Court, in the present case, did not so much examine the content of the recitals to Regulations 307/97 and 308/97—in both Regulations, there is only one operative Article, which provides for a prolongation of the previous system and the necessary financial means as the content of these recitals very strongly referred to agricultural policy. Instead, the Court argued that measures against air pollution and fire "inherently form part of the environmental action". The same reasoning, it is submitted, will apply to product-related standards, even where they are taken in order to protect the environment: they are "inherently" part of a policy which tries to establish and maintain an internal market for products.

(9) These last years, the discussion on the applicable legal basis in environmental matters has slowed down, due to the case law of the Court which has brought considerable clarification and to the fact that the European Parliament has reached, under Article 175(1) EC Treaty, the right of codecision; thus, in particular the disputes between the application of Article 95 and 175 EC Treaty have diminished.[30]

The present situation may be summarised as follows: for environmental matters, Article 175 is the principal legal basis. Article 95 is applied only to standards for the composition and labelling of products, including bans and restrictions of use, even in those cases, where the restriction is based on environmental considerations, furthermore to air and noise emissions from products. Some exceptions to these rules exist.[31]

(10) Future conflicts are most likely to appear, where the Parliament has, until now, little or no participation rights, such as under Article 37 EC Treaty—the present case—or Article 133 (ex Article 113) EC Treaty. As mentioned above, this situation will change as soon as the Treaty of Nice, which amends the present EC Treaty, comes into force. The Council and Member States clearly appear to favour a broad use of Article 175 EC Treaty, mainly because of their rather far-reaching ability to apply national legislation under Article 176.

This underlying controversy between harmonising and national measures went so far that in summer 2000, when the Commission adopted a proposal for a directive

---

[29] A practical case of this kind is the case which is discussed on p. 33 below: Germany had prohibited a wood preservative, after numerous cases of allergy had occurred in Germany. The Community later restricted the use of that preservative for the whole of the Community: The directive in question was based on Art. 95 (ex Art. 100a) EC Treaty.

[30] For a detailed discussion see L. Krämer, *EC Environmental Law* (4th edn., Sweet & Maxwell, London, 2000), 56 *et seq.*

[31] For instance: Regulation 3093/94 on ozone-depleting substances, [1994] OJ L333/1 is based on Art. 175 EC Treaty, though it restricts the use of substances and products; Directive 80/51 on noise levels of aeroplanes, [1980] OJ L18/26, is based on Art. 80 (transport policy), while Directive 70/157 on noise levels from cars, [1970] OJ L42/16, is based on Art. 95 EC Treaty, etc.

on waste of electrical and electronic products, it split the proposal: while the bulk of the provisions was based on a text, the legal basis of which was Article 175, the provisions on the restriction of certain dangerous substances in electrical and electronic products were based on another text, the legal basis of which was Article 95 EC Treaty.[32] At the same time, the Council adopted a directive on end-of-life vehicles on the basis of Article 175 EC Treaty, though this directive also enshrined restrictions on certain dangerous substances in cars.[33] The main reason for this "new approach" probably was the attempt to reduce national measures deviating from the (future) Community provisions, as Article 95 gives fewer possibilities to Member States than Article 176 EC Treaty.

Also, the transition from unanimity to majority rules in environmental matters, Article 175(1) and 175(2) EC Treaty, is likely to create controversies. Spain had applied to the Court of Justice on the ground that the Community decision to adhere to the Convention for the protection of the Danube[34] should have been based on Article 175(2) EC Treaty, which provides for unanimous decision in the case of "management of water resources", and not on Article 175(1) EC Treaty. The Court, however, rejected that application.[35] The background to this application is that Spain has far-reaching plans for water management on the Iberian peninsula and wishes to prevent Community intervention, stirred perhaps by Portugal's complaints against these plans. In a similar way, Spain argued during the discussions on a revision of Directive 88/609 on large combustion plants[36] that this Directive significantly affected its choice between different energy sources and should therefore be based on Article 175(2), not on Article 175(1) EC Treaty.

(11) Of particular interest in the present judgment is the Court's statement that "there is nothing in the case-law to indicate that, in principle" that agricultural policy should take, as regards the legal basis, precedence over environmental policy (or vice versa). This statement, a reaction to remarks from the Council made during litigation, is limited to the "case law". It would have been preferable, had the Court replaced the words "case law" with "EC Treaty". Indeed, there is nothing in the Treaty which gives aspects of agricultural policy precedence over aspects of environmental policy—though it is clear that the political weight of agricultural policy within the Community institutions is much higher. And the same observations apply to internal market (industrial) policy with regard to environmental policy: there is no Treaty provision which allows the conclusion that the policy on the establishment and functioning of the internal market has precedence over

---

[32] Commission, Proposal for a directive on waste electrical and electronic equipment; Proposal for a directive on the restriction of the use of certain hazardous substances in electrical and electronic equipment: COM(2000)347 of 13 June 2000 [2000] OJ C365E/184.

[33] Directive 2000/53 on end-of-life vehicles, (2000) OJ L269/34.

[34] Decision 97/825, [1997] OJ L342/18.

[35] Court of Justice, Case 36/98, *Spain* v. *Council*. (2001) ECR I–779. See for a discussion of this case p. 169 *infra*.

[36] Directive 88/609 on the limitation of emissions of certain pollutants into the air from large combustion plants [1988] OJ L336/1. This Directive was based on Art. 175 (ex Art. 130s) EC Treaty, which provided, in 1988 for unanimous decisions only. Furthermore, its Arts. 3(4) and 4(2) state that amendment should be adopted unanimously.

environmental policy—though this argument is frequently heard in discussions on legal policy. The Court's statement clarifies at least that the different judgments which were issued in the past, cannot be taken to justify such an approach.

III. Forest Policy at Community Level

(12) The Court's judgment clarifies that forestry is not part of the common agricultural policy, as trees and forestry products do not normally come under the notion of "agricultural products". This notion is to be found in Article 32 (ex Article 38) EC Treaty[37] and the products meant are listed in Annex I (ex Annex II) to the Treaty. From this point, it became almost inevitable to refute the Council's argument in favour of the application of Article 37. This is also confirmed by the development of the two Regulations: as long as the Member States in Council were able to ensure the maximum of each Member State's influence, they took as the legal basis those provisions which ensured a unanimous decision, adding to Article 37 first Article 235 and then Article 130s EC Treaty. The Council turned to Article 37 as the exclusive legal basis at a moment, when the changes brought to Article 175 (ex Article 130s) EC Treaty made majority decisions unavoidable; this was a strategy which obviously did not persuade the Court.

The decisive substantive statement on forests and trees which elucidates the clause of "inherently forming part of environmental action" was made by the Advocate General who pointed out that the protection of forests and the ecological balance which they maintain were questions which interested the environment in general and not only those persons which lived from agriculture.[38]

(13) Under Article 231 (ex Article 174) EC Treaty,[39] the Court thus annulled the two Regulations 307/97 and 308/98. However, as in particular the European Parliament agreed, it declared that the annulled regulations were to "remain in force until the Council adopted, within a reasonable period, new regulations having the same subject-matter". To that extent the Commission in 1999 submitted new proposals for Regulations.[40] By the end of July 2000, these proposals had not yet been adopted.

(14) Two days after the judgment in the present case, the Council adopted a resolution on a forestry strategy for the European Union.[41] The resolution underlined

---

[37] Art. 32(1) (ex Art. 38) EC Treaty: " 'Agricultural products' means the products of the soil, of stockfarming and of fisheries and products of first-stage processing directly related to these products".

[38] Advocate General Jacobs' Opinion in Cases C–164/97 and 165/97, para. 29.

[39] Art. 231 (ex Art. 174) EC Treaty: "If the action is well founded, the Court of Justice shall declare the act concerned to be void.

In the case of a regulation, however, the Court of Justice shall, if it considers this necessary, state which of the effects of the regulation which it has declared void shall be considered as definitive".

[40] Proposal to prolong Regulation 3528/86 [1986] OJ C307/32; proposal to prolong Regulation 2158/92 [1999] OJ C307/33.

[41] Council, Resolution of 15 December 1998, OJ 1998, C56/1; see also Commission, Communication on a forestry strategy for the European Union, COM(98)649; Committee of the Regions, Opinion on the use, management and protection of forests in the European Union [1998] OJ C64/25.

that the responsibility for forest policy, under the EC Treaty, was with Member States, but stated that the Community could positively contribute to implementing a sustainable forestry and underlining the multifunctional function of forests. The strategy fixed the objectives and principles of the Community forestry strategy and asked the Commission to report after five years on the implementation of the strategy.

(15) In the present judgment, the Court left unanswered the question of the application of Article 6 EC Treaty, which reads: "Environmental protection requirements must be integrated into the definition and implementation of the Community policies and activities referred to in Article 3, in particular with a view to promoting sustainable development". If environmental requirements are to be integrated into the common agricultural policy, how can an agricultural policy be conceived which is respectful of the environment? The more a measure takes environmental requirements on board, the more it runs the risk of having to be based on Article 175 instead of Article 37. It is doubtful whether this is what Article 6 EC Treaty tried to achieve.

2. ENVIRONMENTAL PROTECTION OUTSIDE THE NATIONAL TERRITORY

Judgment of the Court of 14 July 1994
Case C–379/92

Reference for a preliminary ruling: Criminal proceedings against Matteo Peralta
[1994] ECR I–3453

Facts and Procedure

Mr. Peralta, an Italian national, was the master of a tanker registered in Italy; the shipowner is a company governed by Italian law. Early in 1990, Mr. Peralta repeatedly ordered the discharge into the sea of water which had been used to flush the tanks of his ship; these tanks had previously contained caustic soda, a harmful substance under Italian law. The discharge took place at a time when the vessel was outside the limits of Italian territorial waters.

Italian legislation from 1982 prohibited the discharge of harmful substances into territorial waters and internal maritime waters and provided furthermore that vessels flying the Italian flag were prohibited from discharging harmful substances into the sea, "even outside territorial waters".

Mr. Peralta appealed against the criminal sanctions which the Italian authorities imposed on him. The Pretore di Ravenna as the competent court stayed proceedings and referred a number of of question to the Court of Justice. In particular, he wanted to know whether Community law prevented Italy from providing for measures in order to protect the environment outside the internal territorial waters of Italy.

He was of the opinion that the Italian legislation discriminated against Italian nationals, as it treated them more severely than other nationals. He furthermore considered that Italian legislation was incompatible with international law on the environment and with Community provisions on the free circulation of goods, transport law, freedom to provide services

Judgment (extracts)

[On the question, whether the MARPOL Convention produces effects within the EC]

15. . . . the national court is asking this Court about the compatibility of the Italian legislation with the International Convention for the Prevention of Pollution from Ships, called "the Marpol Convention" (United Nations Treaty Series, Volume 1341, No. 22484). It appears to consider that this Convention produces effects in the Community legal order.

16. In so far as the Italian court raises the question of the compatibility of the Italian legislation with the Marpol Convention, it is sufficient to find that the Community is not a party to that convention. Moreover, it does not appear that the Community has assumed, under the EEC Treaty, the powers previously exercised by the Member States in the field to which the convention applies, nor, consequently, that its provisions have the effect of binding the Community (see the judgment in Joined Cases 21/72 to 24/72 *International Fruit Company and Others v. Produktschap voor Groenten en Fruit* [1972] ECR 1219, paragraph 18).

17. Whether a national provision adopted by a Member State is compatible with a convention such as the Marpol Convention is not therefore a matter on which the Court may rule . . .

23. The national court enquires about the compatibility of the Italian legislation with Article 30 in so far as it requires Italian vessels to carry costly equipment. It asks itself whether this makes imports of chemical products into Italy more expensive and therefore creates an obstacle prohibited by that article.

24. On this point, it is sufficient to observe that legislation like the legislation in question makes no distinction according to the origin of the substances transported, its purpose is not to regulate trade in goods with other Member States and the restrictive effects which it might have on the free movement of goods are too uncertain and indirect for the obligation which it lays down to be regarded as being of a nature to hinder trade between Member States (see the judgment in Case C–69/88 *Krantz* v. *Ontvanger der Directe Belastingen* [1990] ECR I–583, paragraph 11, and the judgment in Case C–93/92 *CMC Motorradcenter* v. *Pelin Baskiciogullari* [1993] ECR I–5009, paragraph 12).

25. Article 30 does not therefore preclude legislation like the national legislation in question.

[On measures taken outside the national territory]

47. . . . the difference in treatment arising under legislation such as that in question between vessels flying the Italian flag and vessels not flying the Italian flag, adversely affecting only Italian vessels, does not constitute discrimination prohibited by the Treaty since the Italian legislation cannot be applicable on the high seas to vessels not flying the Italian flag. The legislation of a Member State cannot be open to objection on the ground that it covers only vessels over which that State is entitled to exercise its jurisdiction, beyond the territorial limits of its jurisdiction.

48. Moreover, as the Court repeated in its judgment in Case 155/80 Oebel [1981] ECR 1993, paragraph 9, the application of national legislation cannot be held contrary to the principle of non-discrimination merely because other Member States allegedly apply less strict rules (see also the judgment in Case 14/68 *Walt Wilhelm and Others* v. *Bundeskartellamt* [1969] ECR 1, paragraph 13).

51. . . . legislation like the Italian legislation, which prohibits the discharge of harmful chemicals at sea, applies objectively to all vessels without distinction, whether carrying products within Italy or to other Member States. It does not make any distinction regarding services for exported products and for products marketed in Italy. It does not afford any particular advantage to the domestic Italian market, to Italian transport operations or to Italian products.

52. Mr. Peralta complains, on the contrary, of the indirect advantages enjoyed by carriers in other Member States who are not subject, on the same conditions, to the prohibition on discharging residues of caustic soda into the sea. However, in the absence of harmonization of the laws of the Member States in this field, those restrictions are merely the result of the national rules of the country of establishment to which the trader remains subject.

59. . . . Articles 3(f), 7, 30, 48, 52, 59, 62, 84 and 130r of the Treaty. . do not preclude the legislation of a Member State from prohibiting all vessels, regardless of the flag which they fly, from discharging harmful chemical substances into its territorial waters and its internal waters, or from imposing the same prohibition on the high seas only on vessels flying the national flag, or, finally, in the event of infringement, from penalizing masters of vessels, who are nationals of that Member State by suspending their professional qualification.

Commentary

I. The Protection of the Environment outside the National Territory

(1) The principal environmental question which the Court of Justice had to clarify was whether a Member State was allowed, under Community law, to protect the environment outside its own territory or territorial waters. The Court considered whether Community secondary law applied in the area which was covered by the Italian legislation and came to a negative result. Then the Court examined whether the Italian legislation was in contradiction with certain provisions of the EC Treaty.

The first provision which comes to mind and which was also mentioned by the Italian court is Article 28 (ex Article 30) EC Treaty.[42] Indeed, in a judgment which is very frequently quoted, the Court had stated that this Article affected "all trading rules.. which are capable of hindering, directly or indirectly, actually or potentially, intro-Community trade".[43] It could be argued that the prohibition on ships flying the Italian flag cleaning their tanks on the high seas would oblige them to use expensive port reception facilities for the cleaning or equip plug the ships with tanks for storing waste and waste water. This would make the import of the goods which were transported by such ships more expensive: if goods were imported into the Community by ships which were not under such an obligation and could clean their tanks on the high seas, they could be imported at a cheaper price; thus the trade between Member States could have been affected by the Italian legislation. In the same way, exports of goods which were transported by Italian ships could be more expensive, due to increased transport costs. Therefore, the Italian legislative provision could be in conflict with Article 29 (ex Article 34) EC Treaty.[44]

(2) The Court did not accept this kind of reasoning, making three arguments. First, it was of the opinion that the Italian legislation did not distinguish between the origins of the goods transported. Secondly, it held that the purpose of the Italian law was not to regulate the trade in goods between EC Member States. And, thirdly, it argued that restrictions on the free movement of goods were too "uncertain and indirect".

This reasoning is very interesting. Indeed, the above-mentioned *Dassonville* formula[45] also includes indirect effects. This formula has played and continues to play a very important role in the discussion of what kind of legislation Member States may or may not adopt under Articles 28 *et seq.* of the EC Treaty. In particular in day-to-day discussions on specific measures, the European Commission

---

[42] Art. 28 (ex Art. 30) EC Treaty: "Quantitative restrictions on imports and all measures having equivalent effect shall be prohibited between Member States".

[43] Court of Justice, Case 8/74, *Dassonville* [1974] ECR 837.

[44] Art. 29 (ex Art. 34) EC Treaty: "Quantitative restrictions on exports, and all measures having equivalent effects, shall be prohibited between Member States".

[45] Court of Justice, Case 8/74, [n. 43].

often uses the *Dassonville* formula to object to the adoption of national or regional legislation, be it trade-related or environment-related. It is therefore useful to remember that the *Dassonville* formula had referred to "trading rules", not—for instance—to environmental rules. It is true, though, that it is not altogether clear what distinguishes a trading rules from a rule which is not a trading rule, all the more as the *Dassonville* formula seems to emphasise the effect of a measure, not so much the intention to regulate a specific sector such as trade, social affairs or the protection of the environment.

(3) When the Court considers, according to the *Dassonville* formula, "all" trading rules which "indirectly" affect trade to be questionable under Article 28 EC Treaty, while in the present *Peralta* judgment some rules are considered to be "too uncertain and indirect"—this formula had already been used by the Court in earlier judgments[46]—the conclusion can only be that some national rules which affect trade are not incompatible with Articles 28 and 29 EC Treaty. The Court states as one of the conditions that the purpose of such national rules is other than the regulation of trade. It then is clear from this jurisdiction that national provisions which protect the environment may stand a fair chance of being compatible with Articles 28 and 29 EC Treaty. In the present case also, the Court left no doubt that Italian legislation was compatible with Articles 28 and 29 EC Treaty.

For Member States, though, the wording of the judgment is not easily applicable, as the differentiation between "indirect" and "too indirect", practised by the Court of Justice, leaves a considerable degree of uncertainty for them.

(4) Having examined whether the Italian legislation affects Mr. Peralta's rights under Articles 39 (ex Article 48 on the free movement of workers), 43 (ex Article 52 on the right of establishment), 49 (ex Article 59 on the freedom to provide services), the Court comes to the conclusion that Community law does not prevent Italy from protecting the environment outside its own territory and from enforcing such legislation with regard to its nationals. This seems a commonplace. However, it is quite frequently argued that Member States may protect their own environment, but that they are not entitled to go beyond their own territory. The present judgment demonstrates that the matter is not as clear cut as that.

(5) There are numerous examples of cases where Member States adopted or are adopting measures to protect the environment outside their territory; one may think of the protection of the high seas, of the ozone layer, climate change, or measures to prohibit the import of endangered species of fauna or flora, such as ivory, crocodile skins or rare animals. No Member State would be prevented, for instance, from considering mercury a substance which is dangerous for the environment and prohibiting any import of products which contained mercury. With regard to other than EC Member States, such a right would be part of that Member State's sovereign power and would be limited only by provisions of public international law—which do not, for mercury, contain specific provisions.[47]

---

[46] See Court of Justice, Cases C–69/88 *Krantz* [1990] ECR I–583, para. 11; C–93/92 *CMC Motorradcenter* [1993] ECR I–5009, para. 12.

[47] Of course, general trade rules apply.

An import ban on mercury-containing products from other Member States would have to stand the test of being compatible with Articles 28 and 30. A detailed discussion of the requirements under these provisions is found in the commentaries on the judgments no. 24, 26 and 29.[48]

(6) Another problem concerning the protection of the environment outside the national territory of a Member State was raised by a case which the European Commission had to address some years ago. The facts of the case were as follows: *corallium rubrum* is a coral which lives in the Mediterranean Sea. It is a relatively rare species. In particular in Italy and Spain, the corals are used to make jewellery which is then marketed all over the Community. Attempts to provide for international protection for *corallium rubrum*, in particular under the CITES Convention,[49] failed, also due to objections from Spain, Italy and other States bordering the Mediterranean Sea. Germany then prohibited the import of jewellery made of *corallium rubrum*. Italy considered this measure to be incompatible with Article 28 EC Treaty.

The Commission considered the German measure to be compatible with Articles 28 and 30 EC Treaty[50] and did not pursue the matter any further. As its decision not to take the matter up with the German authorities has not been published, it can only be presumed that it had accepted the argument that the German measure was justified under Article 30 (ex Article 36) EC Treaty, as it meant to protect "health and life" of *corallium rubrum* and was neither discriminating nor disproportionate. I agree with this decision,[51] which also illustrates that the provisions of the internal market do not have priority over the provisions concerning the protection of the environment. Rather, the necessity to protect the environment and that to ensure the free circulation of goods are interdependent in the sense that which objective shall prevail has to be weighed on a case-by-case basis.

(7) The *corallium rubrum* decision is exceptional. In two cases, the Court of Justice refused to accept export restrictions for goods, which were justified by the

---

[48] See pp. 207, 225 and 233 *infra*.

[49] Washington Convention on Trade in Endangered Species of 3 March 1973. The Convention is in force. The European Community is not member of the Convention, as at present, only nation States are allowed to be members. An amendment of the Convention, which was decided in Gabarone (Africa) in 1983, which would allow the membership of regional organisations, has not yet entered into force, as the amendment has not yet been ratified by a sufficient number of States. The text of the CITES Convention is reproduced in [1982] OJ L384/8.

[50] Art. 30 (ex Art. 36) EC Treaty: "The provisions of Arts. 28 and 29 shall not preclude prohibitions or restrictions on imports, exports or goods in transit justified on grounds of public morality, public policy or public security; the protection of health and life of humans, animals or plants; the potection of national treasures possessing artistic, historic or archaeological value; or the protection of industrial and commercial property. Such prohibitions or restrictions shall not, however, constitute a means of arbitrary discrimination or a disguised restriction on trade between Member States".

[51] In the meantime, *corallium rubrum* has been the subject of Community protection measures, see Directive 92/43 on the conservation of natural habitats and of wild fauna and flora [1992] OJ L206/1, annexe V ("Animal and plant species of Community interest in need of strict protection"), and Decision 98/746, [1998] OJ L358/114, which agrees to the inclusion of *corallium rubrum* in the list of protected species under the Convention on the conservation of European wildlife and natural habitats, to which the Community had adhered by Decision 82/72 [1982] OJ L38/1.

argument that the protection of the environment was less well ensured in another Member State; in the first case, France had restricted the export of used oils,[52] in the other case the Netherlands had restricted the export of waste.[53]

Some Member States allowed the export to other Member States of waste for recovery only on the condition that the recovery operation in that other Member States was protecting the environment equally well or better than in the Member State of export. The Court of Justice also considered such a clause incompatible with Article 29 EC Treaty.[54]

(8) Attention is drawn to the fact that all these cases concern either plants/animals or wastes, thus items to which the notion of "product" or "good" applies only with reservations.[55] Generally, it can be concluded that in the absence of secondary Community legislation, Member States are allowed to take measures in order to protect the environment in a third country, but that they may take measures to protect the environment in another Member State only in rather specific circumstances.

(9) It should be noted that the situation is different where the Community has adopted secondary legislation: where the Community adopted a directive to protect the environment, health and life of humans, animals or plants, a Member State may no longer have recourse to Article 30 EC Treaty and protect these objectives by way of national measures.[56] This question was raised in a case where the United Kingdom had stopped exports of live sheep to Spain on the ground that their treatment in Spanish slaughterhouses was contrary to the protection of by Directive 74/577.[57] Spain had transposed the Directive into national law, but had not laid down any penalties for breach of its provisions.

The Court held that a Member State "may not unilaterally adopt, on its own authority, corrective or protective measures designed to obviate any breach by

---

[52] Court of Justice, Case 172/82 *Fabricants raffineurs d'huiles* v. *Inter-Huile* [1983] ECR 555: "The environment is protected just as effectively when the oils are sold to an authorised disposal or regenerating undertaking of another Member State as when they are disposed of in the State of origin".

[53] Court of Justice, Case 118/86, *Nertsvoederfabriek* [1987] ECR 3883.

[54] See Court of Justice, Case C–203/96 *Dusseldorp* [1998] ECR 4075; the case will be discussed *infra*, p. 22.

[55] As regards waste, see Court of Justice, Case C–2/90 *Commission* v. *Belgium* [1992] ECR I–365, paras. 28 and 30: "waste, whether recyclable or not, should be regarded as a product . . . waste has a special characteristic. The accumulation of waste, even before it becomes a health hazard, constitutes a threat to the environment, because of the limited capacity of each region or locality for receiving it".

As regards fauna and flora species, their specific nature follows from the express mentioning of animals and plants in Art. 30 (ex Art. 36) EC Treaty. Therefore, measures to regulate trade in wastes—Regulation 259/93 [1993] OJ L30/1—and trade in endangered species Regulation 338/97 [1997] OJ L61/1—are both based on Art. 175, not on Art. 95 EC Treaty.

[56] Court of Justice, Case C–5/95, *The Queen* v. *Ministry of Agriculture* [1996] ECR I–2553, para. 18: "recourse to Art. 36 is no longer possible where Community directives provide for harmonization of the measures necessary to achieve the specific objective which would be furthered by reliance upon this provision". The Court only quotes Art. 30 (ex Art. 36) EC Treaty. However, the same reasoning will have to apply to cases, where the protection of the environment is at stake, which is not covered by the objectives mentioned in Art. 30.

[57] Directive 74/577 on stunning of animals before slaughter [1974] OJ L316/10.

another Member States of rules of Community law".[58] In such a case, thus, the Member State has to have recourse to the possibility of applying to the Court under Article 227 EC Treaty.[59]

II. *The Discharge of Pollutants into the High Sea*

(10) The cleaning of tanks at sea is regulated by a Protocol from 1978 of the London Convention for the Prevention of Pollution from Ships 1973, the so-called MARPOL Convention. The Protocol is ratified by most EC Member States.[60] In October 1986, the European Commission proposed that the Council should adhere to the Convention. However, the Council did not make the necessary decision to allow this adherence.[61]

Under the MARPOL Convention, tank washing on the high seas is permitted, subject to some conditions, the adherence to which cannot easily be controlled. Indeed, annex II to the 1978 Protocol provides: "The discharge into the sea of . . . tank washings . . . shall be prohibited, except when all the following conditions are satisfied: (a) the ship is proceeding en route at a speed of at least 7 knots in the case of self-propelled ships . . . ; (b) The procedures and arrangements for discharge are approved by the Administration . . . the concentration of the substance astern of the ship does not exceed 10 parts per million; (c) The maximum quantity of cargo discharged from each tank . . . shall in no case exceed the greater of 3 cubic metres or 1/1000 of the tank capacity in cubic meters; (d) The discharge is made below the waterline, taking into account the location of the seawater intakes; and (e) The discharge is made at a distance of not less than 12 nautical miles from the nearest land and in a depth of water of not less than 25 metres".

(11) Community law does not contain any specific provision on the washing of tanks. Directive 76/464 on pollution caused by certain dangerous substances discharged into the aquatic environment of the Community applies only to territorial waters and internal coastal waters and, furthermore, expressly excludes operational discharges from ships in territorial waters.[62] Directive 75/442 on waste exclusively applies to Community territory, too. It prohibits the "abandonment, dumping or uncontrolled disposal of waste".[63] As the residues of hydrocarbons and other materials in the tanks are undoubtedly "waste" under the definition of Directive 75/442, they are only washed away with water. This liquid is thus liquid waste and not waste water. For this reason, Directive 75/442 fully applies to the

---

[58] Court of Justice, Case C–5/95 (n. 56 *supra*), para. 20.

[59] Art. 227 (ex Art. 170) EC Treaty: "A Member State which considers that another Member State has failed to fulfil an obligation under this Treaty may bring the matter before the Court of Justice."

[60] Of the present 15 Member States, only Ireland has not ratified the 1978 Protocol: see P Sands, R Tarasofsky, M Weiss (eds.), *Documents in International Law* (Manchester University Press, Manchester—New York, 1994), Vol. IIa, p. 345.

[61] The Commission's proposal does not seem to have been published; it is mentioned in Written Question 2388/87 (Muntingh) [1988] OJ C289/33.

[62] Directive 76/464 [1976] OJ L129/23, Art. 1.

[63] Directive 75/442 in the version of Directive 91/156 [1971] OJ L78/32, Art. 4.

washing of tanks at sea, where this takes place in the territorial waters of the Community. No court ever seems to have considered such an application, but that is not surprising as it is recognised that Community environmental law is hardly known.

Recently, the Community adopted a directive on port-reception facilities for ship-generated waste and cargo residues.[64] The Directive is based on Article 80(2) EC Treaty and will become effective at the end of 2002. It will oblige ports in the Community to be equipped with reception facilities for waste and, moreover, oblige ships to pay an appropriate fee for these reception facilities, even in cases where they do not use them. Of course, this Directive will apply only to the Community, but not amend the MARPOL Convention.

(12) While the discharge[65] of pollutants essentially concerns pollutants which are dissolved in water, it does not refer to the dumping of waste, which is generally understood to be the disposal of solid waste at sea, though the terminology varies, in particular in international conventions. The Community has not adopted internal measures regarding the dumping of waste at sea.[66] Proposals for directives on this issue, made by the Commission in 1976, 1985 and 1988, failed to be adopted by the Council.[67]

The Barcelona Convention,[68] the Helsinki Convention[69] and the Paris–Oslo Convention (OSPAR)[70] all contain provisions on the dumping of waste at sea, which differ among themselves. The Community has adhered to all three Conventions. Therefore, the legal provisions of these Conventions are part of Community law.[71] This observation, however, is more theoretical than practical. Indeed, the practice is that the Commission only monitors, under Article 211 EC Treaty,[72] the application of those international conventions to which it has adhered, for which it has adopted secondary legislation which transforms the

---

[64] Directive 2000/59 on port reception facilities for ship-generated waste and cargo residues [2000] OJ L332/81.

[65] For a discussion of this notion see Court of Justice, Case C–231/97, *Van Rooj* [1999] ECR I–6355; Case C–232/97, *Nederhoff* [1999] ECR I–6385.

[66] See for details: L. Krämer, "Le déversement des déchets en mer et le droit communautaire" [1988] *Revue du Marché Commun* 328 *et seq*. The situation has not significantly changed since that publication.

[67] Commission, proposal for a directive on the dumping of waste at sea [1976] OJ C40/3; [1985] OJ C245/23; [1988] OJ C72/8.

[68] Barcelona Convention on the protection of the Mediterranean Sea against pollution, [1977] OJ L240/3; EC adhesion to the Convention: Decision 77/85, [1977] OJ L240/1.

[69] Helsinki 1974 Convention on the protection of the marine environment of the Baltic Sea area [1994] OJ L73/3; EC adhesion to the Convention: Decision 94/156 [1994] OJ L73/1; Helsinki 1992 Convention on the protection of the marine environment of the Baltic Sea [1994] OJ L157/21; EC adhesion to the Convention: Decision 94/157 [1994] OJ L73/19.

[70] Paris Convention for the protection of the marine environment in the north-east Atlantic [1998] OJ L179/3; EC adhesion to the Convention: Decision 98/392 [1998] OJ L179/1.

[71] See Court of Justice, *Opinion 1/91 on the Draft Agreement on the European Economic Area* [1991] ECR I–6079, para. 37; see also Art. 300(7) EC Treaty: "Agreements concluded under the conditions set out in this Article shall be binding on the institutions of the Community and on Member States".

[72] Art. 211 (ex Art. 155) EC Treaty: "the Commission shall: ensure that the provisions of this Treaty and the measures taken by the institutions pursuant thereto are applied".

requirements of the Convention, in the form of a regulation or a directive, into Community law. The mere decision by the Community to adhere to a convention does not yet lead to such a monitoring—which is in open contradiction to the Commission's obligations under Article 211 EC Treaty.

(13) For this reason, provisions on the dumping of waste at sea in Community law exist via the Barcelona, Helsinki and Paris–Oslo Conventions, which are part of "Community law". In practice, however, the provisions are not enforced by the Community and their application is not monitored at all. As application of international conventions on the environment is, furthermore, hardly monitored and enforced by international secretaries, bodies or agencies either, it is in practice only the EC Member States themselves which control if and to what extent they comply with the restrictions related to the dumping of wastes at sea.

(14) As regards the Brent Spar incident of 1995, where a multinational oil company wanted to dump an offshore oil platform into the Atlantic Ocean, Community law on the environment applied only in so far as the above-mentioned provision of Article 4 of Directive 75/442[73] required a previous authorisation for such dumping—which the United Kingdom had given—and such dumping did not put at risk the environment; on this question opinions differed. For the rest, United Kingdom law applied, as the installation was located in the United Kingdom's territorial waters. The United Kingdom was, under public international law, obliged not to allow this dumping.[74] Eventually, the matter was solved, as in view of massive public protestations the company abandoned its plans to dump the platform and agreed to have it dismantled on land.

(15) Generally, the Community has very deliberately omitted to adopt measures for the protection of the marine environment.[75] Member States prefer the traditional form of public international law conventions to the Commission regulatory system, as under Community law, the Commission alone has the right of introducing proposals, as the European Parliament and, hence, the public, play a greater role and as Community-wide decisions are much more easily taken at majority vote and more seriously monitored and enforced.

The conclusion of 1997, that "at present, the protection of the marine environment is not well ensured by Community law at all"[76] remains valid also today.

---

[73] Directive 75/442 (*supra* n. 63), Art. 4.

[74] See United Nations Convention of 29 April 1958, "Convention on the Continental Shelf", which has been ratified by the United Kingdom. Art. 5(5) of this Convention provides with regard to platforms: "Any installations which are abandoned or disused must be entirely removed".

[75] See last Decision 2850/2000 setting up a Community framework for co-operation in the field of accidental or deliberate marine pollution [2000] OJ L332/1which essentially aims at an exchange of information and at training only and which provides for a financial framework of 7 million Euro for the period 2000 to 2006.

[76] See L. Krämer, "Protection of the Marine Environment in Community Law", in L Krämer, *Focus on European Environmental Law* (2nd edn., Sweet & Maxwell, London, 1997), 259 *et seq.*

3. MEMBER STATES' RIGHT FOR MORE PROTECTIVE MEASURES

Judgment of the Court (Sixth Chamber) of 25 June 1998 Case C–203/96

Reference for a preliminary ruling: Chemische Afvalstoffen Dusseldorp BV and Others and Minister van Volkshuisvesting, Ruimetlijke Ordening en Milieubeheer
[1998] ECR I–4075

Facts and Procedure

The Dusseldorp company wanted to export from the Netherlands about 2. 5 million kilograms of wastes, in order to have them recovered by a company in Germany. The wastes in question consisted of oil filters, air filters, plastic and metal cans which were contaminated with oils, cloths, gloves, absorption granules and grease cartilages. Dusseldorp notified its intention to the competent Netherlands' Ministry.

In the Netherlands, a Long-term Plan for the Disposal of Dangerous Waste of 1993 was in application. This Plan contained a rule which prohibited the export of the waste in question if the intended processing abroad was not superior to the processing within the Netherlands. The Long-term Plan also attributed to a Dutch company, AVR Chemie CV, waste management functions, giving it the responsability as the sole end-processor for the incineration of dangerous waste in a revolving drum oven. Waste which could be incinerated in such an oven could be exported only by AVR Chemie.

Based on the Long-term Plan, the Ministry objected to the export of the wastes to Germany. The dispute was then referred to a Dutch court. During that litigation, it was argued that the principles of self-sufficiency and proximity, mentioned in Directive 75/442[77] (the Directive) and Regulation 259/93[78] (the Regulation) of the Community allowed a Member State to oppose shipments to other Member States not only for disposal, but also for the recovery of waste. The Dutch court submitted this question to the Court of Justice and also wanted to know whether a Member State could invoke Article 176 (ex Article 130t) EC Treaty to justify the

[77] Directive 75/442 on waste [1975] OJ L1975/39; amended by Directive 91/156 [1971] OJ L78/32.
[78] Regulation 259/93 on the supervision and control of shipments within, into and out of the European Community [1993] OJ L30/1.

export ban on waste for recovery. Furthermore, the Dutch court wanted to know whether the exclusive rights conferred on AVR Chemie were compatible with the EC Treaty.

Judgment (extracts)

[Application of Directives 75/442 and Regulation 259/93]

27. . . . first, Article 7 of the Directive provides that Member States are to draw up waste management plans in particular in order to attain the objectives set out in Articles 3,4 and 5. Of those provisions, only Article 5 refers to the principles of self-sufficiency and proximity, and then solely in respect of waste for disposal. Similarly, the seventh recital in the preamble, which refers to those principles, concerns that category of waste exclusively.

28. Secondly, the Regulation mentions those principles expressly only in the tenth recital in the preamble, which associates them solely with waste for disposal, and in Article 4(3)(a)(i) and (b), which sets out the type of measures which may be taken by the Member States and the competent authorities of dispatch and destination in order to implement them. Since it is part of Chapter A of title II of the Regulation, that provision concerns only the shipment of waste for disposal.

29. Article 7 of the Regulation, which is in Chapter B, concerning waste for recovery, and is the corresponding provision to Article 4, does not provide for the possibility of adopting measures to implement the principles of self-sufficiency and proximity.

30. It thus follows from the provisions of the Directive and the Regulation, and from the general scheme of the latter, that neither text provides for the application of the principles of self-sufficiency and proximity to waste for recovery . . .

[Application of Article 176 (ex Article 130t)EC Treaty]

35. According to Dusseldorp and the Commission, the Regulation brought about full harmonisation of the rules on shipments of waste between Member States, so that in principle the latter can object to such shipments only on the basis of that Regulation. . . .

38. Article 130t of the Treaty provides: "The protective measures adopted pursuant to Article 130s shall not prevent any Member State from maintaining or introducing more stringent protective measures. Such measures must be compatible with this Treaty. They shall be notified to the Commission."

39. It is . . . necessary to consider whether, in accordance with that provision, measures such as those adopted in the Long-term Plan for the application of the principles of self-sufficiency and proximity to waste for recovery are compatible with Article 34 of the Treaty. . . .

41. Sectoral Plan 19 of Part II of the Long-term Plan provides that export is not permitted unless the processing of oil filters abroad is superior to that performed in the Netherlands.

42. It is plain that the object and effect of such a provision is to restrict exports and to provide a particular advantage for national production.

43. ... the Netherlands Government submits, first, that the aforementioned provision of the Long-term Plan could be justified by an imperative requirement relating to protection of the environment.

44. [However,] the arguments ... concerning the profitability of the national undertaking AVR Chemie and the costs incurred by it, are of an economic nature. The Court has held that aims of a purely economic nature cannot justify barriers to the fundamental principle of the free movement of goods (Case C–120/95 *Decker* [1998] ECR I–1831, paragraph 39).

45. The Netherlands Government considers, secondly, that the contested provision of the Long-term Plan is justified under the derogation provided for by Article 36 of the Treaty concerning the protection of the health and life of humans.

46. Such a justification would be relevant if the processing of oil filters in other Member States and their shipment over a greater distance as a result of their being exported posed a threat to the health and life of humans.

47. The documents before the Court do not, however, show that to be the case. On the one hand, the Netherlands Government conceded that the processing of filters in Germany was comparable to that performed by AVR Chemie. On the other, it has not been established that the shipment of the oil filters posed a threat to the environment or to the life and health of humans.

48. It follows that the restrictions on the export of waste for recovery such as those introduced by the rules in the Netherlands were not necessary for the protection of the health and life of humans in accordance with Article 36 of the Treaty.

[Application of Article 86 (ex Article 90) EC Treaty]

58. ... AVR Chemie was designated as the sole end-processor for the incineration of dangerous waste. That undertaking can therefore be regarded as having an exclusive right within the meaning of Article 90(1) of the Treaty. ...

60. The grant of exclusive rights for the incineration of dangerous waste on the territory of a Member State as a whole must be regarded as conferring on the undertaking concerned a dominant position in a substantial part of the common market (see, to that effect, Case C–260/89 *ERT* [1991] ECR I–2925, paragraph 31).

62. ... the Netherlands Government ... in practice imposed an obligation on it (Dusseldorp) to deliver its oil filters—waste for recovery—to the national undertaking which held the exclusive right to incinerate dangerous waste, even though the quality of processing available in another Member State was comparable to that performed by the national undertaking.

63. Such an obligation has the effect of favouring the national undertaking by enabling it to process waste intended for processing by a third undertaking. It therefore results in the restriction of outlets in a manner contrary to Article 90(1) in conjunction with Article 86 of the Treaty....

67. [in order for this restriction to be justified under Article 90(2) EC Treaty], it is for the Netherlands Government ... to show to the satisfaction of the national court that that objective (to enable AVR Chemie to be economically viable) cannot be achieved equally well by other means.

Commentary

I. The Self-Sufficiency and Proximity Principles and the Recovery of Waste

(1) The Court of Justice had first of all to decide whether the principles of self-sufficiency and proximity also applied to shipments of waste for recovery. These two principles are not expressly laid down in the EC Treaty, but in secondary Community legislation: Article 5 of Directive 75/442[79] stipulates: "1. Member States shall take appropriate measures, in cooperation with other Member States where this is necessary or advisable, to establish an integrated and adequate network of disposal installations, taking account of the best available technology not involving excessive costs. The network must enable the Community as a whole to become self-sufficient in waste disposal and the Member States to move towards that aim individually, taking into account geographical circumstances or the need for specialized installations for certain types of waste. 2. The network must enable waste to be disposed of in one of the nearest appropriate installations, by means of the most appropriate methods and technologies in order to ensure a high level of protection for the environment and public health".

(2) This wording appears to be very clear: it refers only to installations for the disposal of waste, not to installations for the recovery of waste. Also, the network intended, first, "the Community as a whole" to become self-sufficient; Member States were mentioned only secondarily. Thus, at least the principle of self-sufficiency is a principle more for the Community than for Member States and it is difficult to justify restrictions on shipments of waste within the Community with this principle. In the same way, Article 5(2), which deals with the proximity principle, concerns the disposal of waste, not the recovery of waste.

(3) Regulation 259/93,[80] which deals with the shipment of waste, also was relatively clear. Its Chapter A dealt with shipments of waste for disposal and stated in Article 4(3)(a)(i): "In order to implement the principles of proximity, priority for recovery and self-sufficiency at Community and national levels in accordance with

---

[79] Directive 75/442 in the version of Directive 91/156 (n. 77 *supra*).
[80] Regulation 259/93 (n. 78 *supra*).

Directive 75/442, Member States may take measures in accordance with the Treaty to prohibit generally or partially or to object systematically to shipments of waste"; Article 4 continues to allow Member States to raise a number of objections to planned shipments of waste for disposal. In contrast to that, Chapter B of Regulation 259/93, which concerned the shipment of waste for recovery, only allowed, in Article 7(4)(a), objections to be raised against a shipment of waste for recovery based on five specific grounds, listed in that provision. The principles of self-sufficiency or proximity were not mentioned in Article 7.

(4) The wording of both Directive 75/442, Article 5, and Regulation 259/93, Article 7, was thus rather clear. The problems for the Court of Justice stemmed from two provisions: on the one hand, Article 174 (ex Article 130r) EC Treaty fixes as a principle that "environmental damage should as a priority be rectified at source". The Court of Justice had, in an earlier judgment, declared that this principle "means that it is for each region, commune or other local entity to take appropriate measures to receive, process and dispose of its own waste. Consequently, waste should be disposed of as close as possible to the place where it is produced in order to keep the transport of waste to the minimum practicable".[81]

This statement did not differentiate between "waste for disposal" and "waste for recovery"; on the contrary, the reference to the "process" of waste and the general statement that the transport of waste should be kept to the minimum practicable suggests that the Court meant its interpretation to apply to all shipments of waste, whether for disposal or for recovery.

(5) In the present case, the Court did not comment on its statement in Case C–2/90. Advocate General Jacobs did see the possible impact of the Court's remarks in Case C–2/90, but overcame the problem with two arguments:[82] (a) he argued that the principles of self-sufficiency and proximity were allowed to be achieved only in a manner compatible with Articles 28 to 30 (ex Articles 30 to 36) EC Treaty. This argument loses much of its force when the principles of self-sufficiency and proximity are derived from Article 174 EC Treaty itself, as the Court apparently did: in such a case, the principle of free circulation of goods (waste), which underlies Articles 28 to 30 EC Treaty, must be weighed against the principle of self-sufficiency/proximity which derives from Article 174 EC Treaty. The outcome of such a calculation would be everything but obvious.

(6) (b) The second argument by the Advocate General was that Case C–2/90 concerned waste for disposal and was therefore not applicable to the present case, which dealt with waste for recovery. While the argument is correct, it remains that in Case C–2/90, the Court's interpretation of Article 174 EC Treaty was general and did not refer to the specific facts of Case C–2/90.

While the arguments to set aside the Court's reasoning in Case C–2/90 do not seem convincing, I agree with the Advocate General's conclusion for the following reason: the judgment in Case C–2/90 was a highly political judgment which also

---

[81] Court of Justice, Case C–2/90, *Commission* v. *Belgium* [1992] ECR I–4431, para. 34.
[82] Opinion of Advocate General Jacobs of 23 October 1997 [1998] ECR I–4075, paras. 49 *et seq.*

came at a moment, when the Court meant to rectify the effects of its judgment in Case C–300/89,[83] which was heavily criticised by Member States as shifting the balance of power in waste management too far in favour of the Community. This explains a number of inconsistencies in the judgment in Case C–2/90[84] and justifies a narrow interpretation of it.

(7) On the other hand, both Article 7 of Directive 75/442[85] and Article 7 of Regulation 259/93[86] allow Member States to raise objections against a shipment of waste on the ground that the shipment is not in accordance with their waste management plans. Article 7 of Directive 75/442 does not differentiate between disposal and recovery operations; and Article 7 of Regulation 259/93 is expressly placed in Chapter B which deals with shipments of waste for recovery. The wording of both provisions thus does not exclude objections to recovery operations which are based on the argument that the national plan does not allow such shipments.

The Court rather interpreted the two Articles 7 expansively, concluding from the silence in both these provisions on the principles of self-sufficiency and proximity that neither Article 7 allowed objections that were based on the principles of self-sufficiency and proximity, but found it necessary to introduce three more policy-oriented arguments to justify its conclusions:[87] (a) Council resolution of 7 May 1990 on waste policy[88] specified that the objective of self-sufficiency in waste disposal does not apply to recycling; (b) the explanatory memorandum of the Commission's proposal for Regulation 259/93 explained that the principle of proximity might justify intervention with regard to waste for disposal, but not with regard to waste for recovery; (c) the recovery of waste has priority over the disposal of waste in Community waste management policy. In order to encourage such recovery, shipments of waste for recovery must be able to be made under a more flexible procedure between Member States than shipments of waste for disposal.

(8) Overall, the arguments for the Court's conclusion that the principles of self-sufficiency and proximity do not apply to shipments of waste for recovery are convincing. Allowing Member States systematically to object to shipments of waste for recovery would mean that in practice there is no difference between the provisions of Articles 4 and 7 of Regulation 259/93, though the wording of both provisions is very different.

---

[83] Court of Justice, Case C–300/89, *Commission* v. *Council* [1991] ECR I–2867.

[84] See in more detail L Krämer, *European Environmental Law Casebook* (Sweet & Maxwell, London 1993) 77 *et seq.*

[85] Directive 75/442 (n. 77 *supra*), Art. 7: "Member States may take the measures necessary to prevent movements of waste which are not in accordance with their waste management plans".

[86] Regulation 259/93 (n. 78 *supra*), Art. 7: "[Member States may object to a shipment for recovery] in accordance with Directive 75/442, in particular Art. 7 thereof".

[87] See paras. 31 to 33 of the Judgment.

[88] Council Resolution of 7 May 1990, [1990] OJ C122/2.

II. Justification of More Stringent National Measures under Article 176 (ex Article 130t) EC Treaty

(9) The Court of Justice then had to examine whether the Dutch measure to allow exports of waste for recovery to other Member States only under very restricted conditions could be justified under Article 176 EC Treaty. This provision enables Member States to adopt more stringent provisions than those adopted at Community level, provided that these measures are compatible with the other provisions of the Treaty.

It was the first time that the Court of Justice had to examine whether a national provision which deviated from provisions of Community secondary law could be justified under Article 176 EC Treaty. It would therefore have been desirable to interpret in some detail the purpose, meaning and relevance of Article 176 in the system of the Treaty. However, the Court of Justice did not do that; it omitted to examine whether the Netherlands' provision really constituted a more stringent measure; nor did it discuss the argument, advanced by Dusseldorp and by the Commission, that Article 176 EC Treaty was inapplicable, because Regulation 259/93 exhaustively enumerated in Article 7(4)(a) the objections which could be raised against shipments of waste for recovery. Both questions rank, in logic, before the question whether the national measures conform to all Treaty requirements.

(10) Whether the Netherlands' provision really is a more stringent provision under Article 176 EC Treaty is doubtful, for the following reasons: any secondary legislation, whether it is based on Article 95 (internal market) or on Article 175 (environment protection) EC Treaty, has to comply with the requirements of the EC Treaty, including its Articles 28 and 29. Regulation 259/93 thus had to strike a balance between the need to protect the environment as regards the shipment of waste and to ensure the free circulation of waste. The Community legislature adopted provisions which allowed Member States completely to ban exports and imports of waste for disposal,[89] but which allowed them to raise only some objections[90] against

---

[89] Regulation 259/93 (n. 78), Art. 4(3)(a)(i): "In order to implement the principles of proximity, priority for recovery and self-sufficiency at Community and national levels in accordance with Directive 75/442/EEC, Member States may take measures in accordance with the Treaty to prohibit generally or partially or to object systematically to shipments of waste".

[90] Regulation 259/93 (n. 78), Art. 7(4)(a): "The competent authorities of destination and dispatch may raise reasoned objections to the planned shipment:

—in accordance with Directive 75/442/EEC, in particular Art. 7 thereof, or

—if it is not in accordance with national laws and regulations relating to environmental protection, public order, public safety or health protection, or

—if the notifier or the consignee has previously been guilty of illegal trafficking. In this case, the competent authority of dispatch may refuse all shipments involving the person in question, in accordance with national legislation, or

—if the shipment conflicts with obligations resulting from international conventions concluded by the Member State or Member States concerned, or

—the ratio of the recoverable and non-recoverable waste, the estimated value of the materials to be finally recovered or the cost of the recovery and the cost of the disposal of the non recoverable fraction do not justify the recovery under economic and environnemental considerations".

shipments of waste for recovery. If these measures are compatible with Articles 28 and 29 EC Treaty—and it is clear that the Community legislature had a large degree of discretion where exactly to strike the balance, in the Regulation, between environmental and free trade in waste requirements—then the enumeration of five specific grounds to object to shipments of waste for recovery is exhaustive. There is no room for national measures to enumerate a sixth or seventh ground, as the Dutch provisions did by stipulating that the provisions of the waste processing abroad had to be superior to the processing in the Netherlands in order to be allowed: what sense would the enumeration of the four specific grounds have had if Member States could "invent" other grounds?

(11) This reasoning also becomes obvious, if one looks at the underlying philosophy of Article 7 which would read: "shipments of waste for recovery shall be permitted, unless there is objection which is justified by one of the five grounds enumerated". In contrast to that the underlying philosophy of the Netherlands' measures would be: "shipments of waste for recovery shall be permitted, unless there is objection which is justified by one of the six grounds". The Netherlands' measure is thus not a more stringent measure but another measure. However, Article 176 EC Treaty does not allow the taking of other measures.

In a previous case, which also concerned the shipment of waste, the Court had considered that the system set up by Community Directive 84/631, the predecessor of Regulation 259/93, constituted "a complete system relating to the transfrontier shipments of hazardous waste for disposal" and that this system consequently did "not imply that the Member States have powers to prohibit such transfers generally", which means that they could not adopt more stringent provisions.[91] It is significant that in that case the Court did not even find it necessary to discuss Article 130t, the predecessor of Article 176 EC Treaty, though the judgment was given in 1992, when Article 130t EC Treaty was well in force.

As mentioned, the Court in the present case did not examine this path which it had opened itself in 1992, but treated the logically second question—is the Netherlands' measure compatible with the other Treaty provisions?—before the logically prior question—whether Article 176 was of application at all.[92]

(12) Another way of consistently interpreting the meaning of Article 176 EC Treaty is to look more closely into the clause that the more stringent protective measures must be compatible "with this Treaty". This clause includes on the one hand all provisions of the Treaty itself. However, the clause also includes, on the other hand, the different directives and regulations which have been adopted by virtue of the EC Treaty, thus also secondary legislation.

It is true that this reasoning is contested in literature. However, a limitation of the clause to Treaty provisions alone does not make sense. Indeed, the Court of Justice has consistently held that Article 30 (ex Article 36) EC Treaty becomes

---

[91] Court of Justice, Case C–2/90 (n. 81 *supra*), para. 20.
[92] The Court followed in this Advocate General Jacobs, who had argued in his opinion (n. 82 *supra*), para. 74, that "none of the issues which might arise under Art. 130t need to be resolved", as Art. 29 (ex Art. 34) EC Treaty applied.

inapplicable once the Community has adopted secondary legislation, which strikes a balance between the interests protected in Article 30 and other interests.[93] If one applies this reasoning to the present case, recourse to Article 30 would be impossible, because there is Regulation 259/93. And recourse to that Regulation would be impossible if one were following the opinion of some authors, because it is secondary legislation.

In conclusion, thus, "this Treaty" also includes secondary legislation. In the present case, therefore, the Netherlands' provision had to comply also with the objection grounds of Regulation 259/93. As it did not do so, the Netherlands could not justify the provision by Article 176 EC Treaty.

III.   The Export Restriction and Article 29 (ex Article 34) EC Treaty

(13) In contrast to Article 28 EC Treaty, which applies to "any measure" which restricts the free circulation of goods, Article 29 EC Treaty applies only where on the one hand a national measure has as its object or effect the restriction of exports and, on the other hand, it thereby establishes a difference between the domestic trade and its export trade, by providing a particular advantage for national production.[94] The Court very succinctly stated that the Netherlands' measure had the "object and effect" of restricting exports and giving Netherlands' production a particular advantage and thus constituted an export restriction. It then examined whether this restriction could be justified (a) by an imperative requirement relating to the protection of the environment (Article 28, ex Article 30 EC Treaty) or (b) by the requirement to protect the health and life of humans (Article 30, ex Article 36 EC Treaty).

(14) (a) The justification of a national measure which restricts the free circulation of goods from other Member States by an imperative—or mandatory—requirement was developed by the Court since 1979, the first time in its *Cassis de Dijon* case.[95] When the Court applied it for the first time to an environmental case, it formulated it as follows: "in the absence of common rules relating to the marketing of the products in question, obstacles to free movement within the Community resulting from disparities between the national laws must be accepted in so far as such rules, applicable to domestic and imported products without distinction, may be recognized as being necessary in order to satisfy mandatory requirements recognized by Community law. Such rules must also be proportionate to the aim in view. If a Member State has a choice between various measures for achieving the same aim, it should choose the means which least restricts the

---

[93] See Court of Justice, Case C–5/95, *The Queen* v. *Ministry of Agriculture* [1996] ECR I–2553, para. 18: "recourse to Art. 36 is no longer possible where Community directives provide for harmonisation of the measures necessary to achieve the specific objective which would be furthered by reliance on this provision".

[94] Court of Justice, Case 155/80, *Oebel* [1981] ECR 1993; Case 172/82, *Raffineurs d'huiles* [1983] ECR 555; Case 237/82, *Jongeneel* [1984] ECR 483.

[95] Court of Justice, Case 120/78, *Rewe* v. *Bundesmonopolverwaltung* [1979] ECR 649.

free movement of goods . . . the protection of the environment is a mandatory requirement which may limit the application of Article 30 of the Treaty".[96]

In the present case, the Court referred to this case law, which it also applied to the Netherlands' export restriction under Article 29 EC Treaty. This is doubtful, as Article 29 is, in the Court's case law, applicable only if it creates an advantage to national products—which means that it discriminates against foreign products.[97] Thus, under its own principles, the Court should have immediately rejected the Netherlands' defence with the argument that the Netherlands' measure was not applicable "without distinction".

Instead, it rejected the application of this case law with the argument that the advantage of the Netherlands' producer to operate in a profitable manner and with sufficient material was of an economic nature, and arguments of a "purely economic nature cannot justify barriers to the fundamental principle of the free movement of goods".

But was the activity of AVR Chemie really of a "purely economic nature"? In paragraph 67 of its own judgment, the Court considered it possible that AVR Chemie had been given a task of general economic interest; the Court did not decide on this question, but was of the opinion that it was to be discussed before the national court. Supposed that in that litigation the Netherlands' government was able to prove that AVR Chemie had a task of general economic interest— would then the Netherlands' restriction of exports be capable of being justified under Article 29 EC Treaty? Certainly not, if the Court had applied the reasoning which it normally used in the context of Article 29 EC Treaty.

(15) (b) In the Court's established case law, the environmental grounds which justify a restriction on the free circulation of goods by virtue of Article 30 (ex Article 36) EC Treaty are only the health and life of humans, animals or plants. The Court could not find any threat to humans: the processing of the waste in Germany was comparable to the processing in the Netherlands, and it considered not to be proven that the shipment of the waste posed a threat to the environment or to the life and health of humans.

This last, very laconic argument that the shipment of waste does not pose a threat to the environment is again somehow surprising: indeed, the underlying assumption for the very sophisticated and complicated provisions of Regulation 259/93 was and is that the shipment of waste poses *per se* a threat to the environment. The whole system of notification of a shipment of waste to competent authorities of the Member States of dispatch, transit and destination has the purpose of ensuring tight supervision and control—these are the words of the title of the Regulation—of waste shipments, not only of wastes for disposal, but also of those for recovery. The Court seems to require a concrete threat, caused by the specific wastes in question, and does not seem to be satisfied with the abstract, general risk which the shipment of low-value material normally entails.

---

[96] Court of Justice, Case 302/86, *Commission* v. *Denmark* [1988] ECR 4607, paras. 6 and 9.
[97] See n. 94 *supra*.

IV. The Application of Article 86 (ex Article 90) EC Treaty

(16) The last question addressed to the Court was on the application of Article 86 (ex Article 90) EC Treaty,[98] a provision of competition policy. The Court was asked in essence whether the Netherlands' measure to make AVR Chemie the sole end-processor for the incineration of hazardous waste was compatible with Article 86. The Court had no doubt that, in principle, Article 86 applied and that the mono-polistic position of AVR Chemie gave that company a dominant position which contravened Article 82 EC Treaty. Whether his dominant position could be justified depended on the question whether, on balance, the Netherlands' "general economic interest" required that AVR Chemie had been entrusted the exclusive rights.

The Court did not decide this question, but requested the national court to examine it. The issue will therefore not be further discussed here. The reader is referred to the comments on page 28 *et seq*, which discuss a judgment on national measures concerning a public undertaking acting in the general economic interest.

(17) The present judgment illustrates the ongoing controversy between Member States and the Community, whether Comunity or national provisions should apply to waste management issues. There are essentially three legal instru-ments which are used in this controversy: (a) the wording of different Community directives and regulations on waste; (b) adoption of different national waste legis-lation, based on the argument that either Article 176 allows more stringent pro-tective measures or that in the absence of Community provisions national provisions are necessary; (c) adoption of national provisions, based on the necessity to act in a general economic interest (Article 86 EC Treaty).

Comunity provisions on waste are based on the assumption that wastes are mater-ials to which the rules of the EC Treaty, in particular those on the internal market, apply. The Court of Justice expressed this in the following terms: "It is common ground that waste which can be recycled and re-used, after processing if necessary, has an intrinsic commercial value and therefore amounts to goods for the purpose of applying the Treaty, and that such waste is therefore within the ambit of Article 30 et seq . . . objects which are transported over a frontier in order to give rise to commer-cial transactions are subject to Article 30, irrespective of the nature of those trans-actions. . . . the distinction between recyclable and non-recyclable waste raises a serious difficulty of practical application with regard to frontier controls, as was explained to the Court. Such a distinction is based on uncertain factors which may

---

[98] Art. 86 (ex Art. 90) EC Treaty: "1. In the case of public undertakings and undertakings to which Member States grant special or exclusive rights, Member States shall neither enact nor maintain in force any measure contrary to the rules contained in this Treaty, in particular to those rules provided for in Art. 12 and Arts. 81 to 89.

2. Undertakings entrusted with the operation of services of general economic interest or having the character of revenue-producing monompoly shall be subject to the rules contained in this Treaty, in particular to the rules on competition, insofar as the application of such rules does not obstruct the per-formance, in law or in fact, of the particular tasks assigned to them. The development of trade must not be affected to such an extent as would be contrary to the interests of the Community.

3. The Commission shall ensure the application of the provisions of this Art. and shall, where nec-essary, address appropriate directives or decisions to Member States".

change in the course of time, depending on technical progress. Moreover, whether any particular waste is recyclable or not also depends on the cost of recycling and therefore the profitability of the proposed further use, so that a decision in this connection is necessarily subjective and depends on variable factors. Therefore it must be concluded that waste, whether recyclable or not, should be regarded as a product the movement of which must not in principle, pursuant to Article 30 EEC, be impeded".[99]

(18) It cannot be contested, though, that local, regional and national authorities have responsibilities in the treatment and disposal of waste, in particular to ensure that the necessary treatment and disposal installations—landfills, incinerators, recycling plants etc. —exist and that waste is properly collected, treated and disposed of. Whether these are partly or completely tasks in the public interest which form part of the essential functions of the State as regards the protection of the environment, or whether these are, in part or in full, tasks of an economic nature which justify the application of the Treaty provisions[100] is an ongoing discussion within the Community.[101]

4. INTERNAL MARKET AND ENVIRONMENTAL PROTECTION

Judgment of the Court of 17 May 1994
Case C–41/93

France v. *Commission of the European Communities*
supported by Germany and Denmark
[1994] ECR I–1829

Facts and Procedure

Pentachlorophenol (PCP) is a chemical substance which is mainly used as a wood preservative, as an agent for the impregnation of industrial textiles, as a bactericide

---

[99] Court of Justice, Case C–2/90 (n. 81 *supra*), paras. 23 to 28.

[100] See, for a case where an undertaking had been given the task to provide for preventive anti-pollution surveillance services, Court of Justice, Case C–343/95, *Cali* v. *Servici ecologici* [1997] ECR I–1547, para. 23: "The anti-pollution surveillance . . . in the oil port of Genoa is a task in the public interst which forms part of the essential functions of the State as regards protection of the environment in maritime areas. Such surveillance is conncected, by its nature, its aim and the rules to which it is subject with the exercise of powers relating to the protection of the environment which are typically those of a public authority. It is not of an economic nature justifying the application of the Treaty rules on competition".

[101] See on this discussion also p. 331 *infra*.

in tanning and in the paper pulp industry, as a molluscide in the treatment of industrial water, and as a sterilising agent. It is recognised as being dangerous for man and the environment. Under Community legislation,[102] it is classified as a category three carcinogen, as very toxic by inhalation, toxic in contact with skin and, if swallowed, irritating to eyes, the respiratory system and skin, and dangerous for the environment, in particular the aquatic environment. PCP has been made subject to various restrictions in more than 30 countries.

In 1987, Germany notified the Commission of its intention to restrict, at national level, the use of PCP. The Commission answered that it was preparing a directive on the subject and asked the German Government to defer adopting its regulation. In 1988, the Commission submitted to the Council a proposal for a directive restricting the use of PCP. At the end of 1989, Germany adopted a regulation to restrict the use of PCP. In March 1991, the Council adopted, on the basis of Article 95 (ex Article 100a) EC Treaty, Directive 91/173 which restricted the use of "PCP and its salts and esters", but provided for less stringent requirements than the German regulation.[103]

In August 1991, Germany notified the Commission of its intention to continue to apply its national provisions instead of Directive 91/173. In December 1992, the Commission adopted a decision[104] which confirmed the German provisions. Against this decision, France applied to the Court, arguing that by taking that decision the Commission had breached the provisions of Article 95 (ex Article 100a).

Judgment (extracts)

[The procedure under Article 95(4) (ex Article 100a(4)) EC Treaty]

26. . . . where, after the expiry of the time allowed for transposing, or after the entry into force of, a harmonizing measure mentioned in Article 100a(1), a Member State intends, as in this case, to continue to apply national provisions derogating from the measure, it is required to notify the Commission of those provisions.

27. The Commission must then satisfy itself that all the conditions for a Member State to be able to rely on the exception provided for by Article 100a(4)

---

[102] Directive 67/548 on the classification, packaging and labelling of dangerous substances [1967] OJ 196/1; this Directive was amended eight times by the Council and adapted to technical and scientific progress about 25 times.

[103] Directive 91/173 amending for the ninth time Directive 76/769 relating to restrictions on the marketing and use of certain dangeroius substances [1971] OJ L85/34.

[104] The decision is not published. The Commission published a communication, which describes in detail the content of the decision [1992] OJ C334/8.

are fulfilled. In particular, it must establish wheher the provisions in question are justified on grounds of the major needs mentioned in the first subparagraph of Article 100a(4) and are not a means of arbitrary discrimination or a disguised restriction on trade between Member States.

28. The procedure laid down by that provision is intended to ensure that no Member State may apply national rules derogating from the harmonised rules without obtaining confirmation from the Commission.

29. Measures for the approximation of the provisions laid down by law, regulation or administrative action in Member States which are such as to hinder intra-Community trade would be rendered ineffective if the Member States retained the right to apply unilaterally national rules derogating from those measures.

30. A Member State is not, therefore, authorized to apply the national provisions notified by it until after it has obtained a decision from the Commission confirming them.

[The necessity to give reasons under Article 253 (ex Article 190) EC Treaty]

31. It should now be considered . . . whether the Commission decision of 2 December 1992 satisfies the requirements of Article 190 of the Treaty. . . .

34. The Court has consistently held that the obligation under Article 190 to give reasons requires that the measures concerned should contain a statement of the reasons which led the institution to adopt them, so that the Court cas exercise its power of review and so that the Member States and the nationals concerned may learn of the conditions under which the Community institutions have applied the Treaty.

35. In this case, that condition is not fulfilled. . . .

36. . . . the Commission confined itself to describing in general terms the content and aim of the German rules and to stating that those rules were compatible with Article 100a(4), without explaining the reasons of fact and law on account of which the Commission considered that all the conditions in Article 100a(4) were to be regarded as fulfilled in the case in point.

37. Consequently, the contested decision does not satisfy the obligation to state reasons laid down in Article 190 of the Treaty and must be annulled for infringement of essential procedural requirements. . . .

Commentary

I. *Article 95(4)(ex Article 100a(4)) EC Treaty in its Version Prior to 1999*

(1) Article 95(4) (ex Article 100a(4)) EC Treaty was introduced into the Treaty by the Single European Act 1987 and this judgment was the first, in which the

Court had to apply this provision.[105] Therefore, the judgment gave an opportunity to the Court to clarify a number of legal points which were unclear and very intensively discussed in legal literature.

For this reason, the Court started by analysing the procedure under Article 95(4), placed it into "its context within the scheme of the Treaty", and defined "its objective and mode of operation".[106] It found that "if the conditions which Article 100a(4) lays down are fulfilled, that provision allows a Member State to apply rules derogating from a harmonization measure adopted in accordance with the procedure laid down in Paragraph 1. As this possibility constitutes a derogation from a common measure aimed at attaining one of the fundamental objectives of the Treaty, namely the abolition of obstacles to the free movement of goods between Member States", the provision had been made subject to judicial review by the Court.

The Court did not expressly adopt the words of Advocate General Tesauro who had stated[107] that Article 95(4) (ex Article 100a(4)) EC Treaty "is intended to ensure 'reinforced' protection of certain particularly important interests and above all, to answer the preoccupations expressed by a number of countries during the negotiations leading up to the Single Act to the effect that any harmonization adopted by a majority vote might result in a diminution of the degree of protection enjoyed by such interests at national level. In other words, the provision represents a 'counterweight' to offset the relinquishment of the principle of unanimity with regard to the adoption of measures necessary for the creation and operation of the internal market, in the sense provided for in Article 100a(1)". However, it seems clear that the Court also understands the function of Article 95(4) in this way.

(2) The Court's general observation has a number of consequences. Since Article 95(4) constitutes a "derogation" from the provisions of Article 95(1) EC Treaty, it has to be interpreted narrowly. No extension, for instance, of the grounds on which that provision may be invoked—Article 30 (ex Article 36) EC Treaty, the environment or the working environment—will be possible. And normally it will be up to the Member State which applies the derogation to bring evidence that all conditions of Article 95(4) are fulfilled; the Commission has no investigative obligation.[108]

---

[105] At the time when the judgment was given, Art. 100a(4) read as follows: "If, after the adoption of a harmonization measure measure by the Council acting by a qualified majority, a Member State deems it necessary to apply national provisions on grounds of major needs referred to in Art. 36, or relating to protection of the environment or the working environment, it shall notify the Commission of these provisions.

The Commission shall confirm the provisions involved after having verified that they are not a means of arbitrary discrimination or a disguised restriction on trade between Member States.

By way of derogation from the procedure laid down in Arts. 169 and 170, the Commission or any Member State may bring the matter directly before the Court of Justice if it considers that another Member State is making improper use of the powers provided for in this article". The Amsterdam Treaty 1999 amended this provision (see n. 115 *infra*).

[106] Para. 18 of the judgment.

[107] Advocate General Tesauro, Opinion in Case C–41/93 [1994] ECR I–1829, para. 4.

[108] In the same sense see Commission Decision 99/831 [1999] OJ L329/15, para. 42; Decision 99/832 [1999] OJ L329/55, para. 34

(3) The first problem of substance for the Court was whether the "confirmation", which the Commission had to give to the German measure, was a "decision" under Article 249 (ex Article 189) EC Treaty.[109] The Commission did not seem to be of this opinion, as it did not even publish its decision, but only a communication with details of it.[110] In contrast to that, the Court left no doubt that the confirmation constituted a decision in the sense of Article 249, which allowed it then to examine whether the formal requirements for such a decision, namely to "state the reasons" on which it was based (Article 253 (ex Article 190) EC Treaty) were actually fulfilled.[111]

(4) From the binding nature of the decision and the derogatory character of Article 95(4), the Court drew the conclusion that national rules which derogated from Community rules could be put into effect only once the Commission had confirmed them. The Court explained that, otherwise, the Member States had the possibility unilaterally to apply national rules, which would make the Community legislative measures ineffective. In this way, the Court ensured coherence and cohesion of Community action, because its interpretation took away the possibility for Member States to act unilaterally and then wait, until the Commission's confirmation intervened.

(5) This interpretation of the meaning of Article 95 (4) is the decisive difference from Article 176 (ex Article 130t) EC Treaty: under that provision, Member States may act unilaterally, without first informing the Commission and without giving reasons for their action. While in the case of Article 95(4) Member States in practice will have to notify draft legislation to the Commission, Article 176 requires only the notification of the national measure once it has been taken. Therefore, the Commission's confirmation under Article 95(4) gives the green light to national legislation and is similar to an authorisation to legislate; in contrast to that, national measures under Article 176 need no green light, are therefore not "confirmed" in any way and are, at best, examined after having been adopted at national level as to their compatibility with the EC Treaty.

(6) The Court's solution that a Member State could only continue to apply derogating national legislation only after having received confirmation from the Commission was bound to create problems in cases where the confirming decision by the Commission was delayed. In such a case, two contradictory pieces of legislation co-existed, the harmonising Community legislation which was adopted under

---

[109] Art. 249 (ex Art. 189) EC Treaty: "In order to carry out their tasks and in accordance with the provisions of this Treaty, the European Parliament acting jointly with the Council, the Council and the Commission shall make regulations and issue directives, take decisions, make recommendations or deliver opinions . . . A decision shall be binding in its entirety upon those to whom it is addressed".

[110] [1992] OJ C334/8. It should be noted that the communication was published in part C of the Community Official Journal, (C stands for "Communications"); in contrast to that, part L (L stands for "*lois*" or "Legislation") contains the legally binding texts. Had the Commission considered its decision to be legally binding, it normally would have had it published in part L.

[111] In its opinion in Case C–127/97, *Burstein* v. *Bayern* [1999] ECR I–6005, Advocate General Saggio called the decision to have the character of an authorising provision of a substantive nature (*effet constitutif*) (para. 23).

Article 95(1), and the diverging national legislation which had been notified under Article 95(4) EC Treaty. The Court of Justice was called, in 1999, to decide on such a case:[112] Sweden wanted to prosecute a person who had used a colorant in a foodstuff, the use of which was prohibited under Swedish legislation, but was authorised under a Community directive from 1994. In July 1994 and November 1995, Sweden had notified under Article 95(4) that it wanted to continue to apply its national prohibition of that colorant. However, at the time of the criminal proceedings, the Commission had not yet taken a decision to confirm the Swedish provisions.

The Court of Justice confirmed its judgment in the present Case C–41/93 and stated that no Member State could, under Article 95(4) EC Treaty, apply "national rules derogating from the harmonised legislation . . . until after it has obtained a decision from the Commission confirming them". Though the Commission, by delaying a decision, "clearly" had not acted with due diligence, this did not change the principle that no unilateral application of derogating legislation was permitted. Instead of unilaterally adopting derogating legislation, a Member State had the possibility of taking legal action against the Commission for omission to act under Article 232 (ex Article 175) EC Treaty.[113] The Swedish court was thus prevented from applying the Swedish provisions in the criminal proceedings in question.

II. The New Version of Article 95 EC Treaty

(7) While the problem of co-existence of harmonised Community legislation and derogating national legislation was thus solved in law, politically there was a problem, as the Commission's reactions to Member States' notifications under Article 95(4) (ex Article 100a(4)) EC Treaty sometimes took a very long time, leaving uncertainty whether the derogating national provision or the harmonising Community provision was to apply to a specific case.[114] This problem was solved by the Amsterdam Treaty on European Union, which rearranged Article 95[115] and

---

[112] Court of Justice, Case C–319/97, *Kortas* [1999] ECR I–3143.

[113] See the wording of Art. 232 (ex Art. 175) EC Treaty on page 5, n. 10. See also Case C–5/95, *The Queen* v. *Ministry of Agriculture* [1996] ECR I–2553, where again a Member State was prevented from taken unilateral action; a reference to this case is found on page 18, n. 56. *supra*.

[114] In the case underlying Decision 99/831 (n. 108 *supra*), the Netherlands had notified their legislation on 21 January 1992; the Commission took its Decision on 26 October 1999, almost eight years later, see Decision 99/831, para. 32.

[115] Art. 95 EC Treaty (version of the Amsterdam Treaty): ". . . 4. If, after the adoption by the Council or by the Commission of a harmonisation measure, a Member State deems it necessary to maintain national provisions on grounds of major needs referred to in Art. 30, or relating to the protection of the environment or the working environment, it shall notify the Commission of these provisions as well as the grounds for maintaining them.

5. Moreover, without prejudice to paragraph 4, if, after the adoption by the Council or by the Commission of a harmonisation measure, a Member State deems it necessary to introduce national provisions based on new scientific evidence relating to the protection of the environment or the working environment on grounds of a specific to that Member State arising after the harmonisatin measure, it shall notify the Commission of the envisaged provisions as well as the grounds for introducing them.

6. The Commission shall, within six months of the notification as referred to in paragraphs 4 and 5, approve or reject the national provisions involved after having verified whether or not they are a means

in particular introduced in Article 95(6), a provision which states that, in principle, a national derogating provision is "deemed to be approved" if the Commission had not taken a decision within six months.

(8) The most important innovation introduced by this amendment of Article 95 is the fact that also new, derogating national legislation may be introduced at national level. Under the previous version of Article 95,[116] there was considerable discussion in legal literature whether the word "apply" was limited to the maintaining of existing or whether it also allowed the introduction of new legislation, though no practical case is known where this question became relevant.

The possibility of introducing new, derogating national legislation is limited to the protection of the environment or the working environment and conditional upon rather strict criteria. The obligation for the Commission to verify the compatibility of the newly introduced or maintained national legislation is specified; the new criterion that such legislation may not constitute an obstacle to the functioning of the internal market is—in this form—hardly practicable: "any national measure aiming at the establishment and operation of the internal market, constitutes in substance a measure that is likely to affect the internal market".[117] Consequently, the Commission understands this concept to prohibit national measures which have a disproportionate effect in relation to the pursued objective.[118]

As the new version of Article 95 EC Treaty is applicable only as from 1 May 1999, there is as yet no judgment from the Court on its interpretation. However, the Commission took a number of decisions under the new version.[119] In two cases, the Member States concerned applied to the Court of Justice;[120] judgments may be expected in the year 2002.

---

of arbitrary discrimination or a disguised restriction on trade between Member States and whether or not they shall constitute an obstacle to the functioning of the internal market.

In the absence of a decision by the Commission within this period the national provisions referred to in paragraphs 4 and 5 shall be deemed to have been approved. When justified by the complexity of the matter and in the absence of danger for human health, the Commision may notify the Member State concerned that the period referred to in this paragraph may be extended for a further period of up to six months.

. . ."

[116] See text of Art. 95 (ex Art. 100a), previous version, in n. 105 *supra*.

[117] Commission, Decision 99/831 (n. 108 *supra*), para. 73.

[118] *Ibid.*

[119] Decision 99/830 (sulphites, nitrites and nitrates in foodstuffs—Denmark) [1999] OJ L329/1; Decision 99/831 (PCP—Netherlands) (n. 7 *supra*); Decision 99/832 (creosote—Netherlands) (n. 108 *supra*); Decision 99/833 (creosote—Germany) [1999] OJ L329/43; Decision 99/834 (creosote—Sweden) [1999] OJ L329/63; Decision 88/835 (creosote—Denmark), [1999] OJ L329/82; Decision 99/836 (mineral wool—Germany) [1999] OJ L68/32. All Decisions concerned the continued application of existing national legislation, with the exception of Decision 99/836, which dealt with a case where new legislation was introduced.

[120] Cases C–512/99, *Germany v. Commission* (concerning Decision 99/836); C–3/00, *Denmark v. Commission* (concerning Decision 99/830).

III.   *The Restrictions on Pentachlorophenol (PCP)*

(9) As the Court's judgment annulled the Commission's decision of December 1992, the Commission had to take a new decision. This was done in September 1994.[121] In its detailed reasoning, the Commission stated that PCP was an important source of dioxins, which could cause cancer. A study of 1989 had shown that concentrations of dioxins in breast milk were highest in Belgium, Germany, the Netherlands and the United Kingdom; in Germany, the concentrations began to fall after the ban on PCP. Germany had introduced a set of measures to combat dioxin emissions. While the Decision did not give specific environmental grounds for the ban on PCP, it concluded that the ban in Germany was "justified by the specific circumstances relating to health protection and the environment in Germany".

(10) In 1996, the Commission had to decide on a Danish notification of measures concerning PCP, which were stricter than the provisions of Directive 91/173. The Commission mainly discussed the concentrations of PCP in Danish groundwater which was the principal source for the production of drinking water; "given the special circumstances" in Denmark, the measures were confirmed.[122]

In 1999, finally, the Commission decided on the Netherlands' notification to apply stricter restrictions than those laid down by Directive 91/173.[123] The Netherlands had argued that there was a problem with the general effects of PCP and the impurities contained in it on health and the environment. The Commission stated "the exceptions to the ban of PCP established in Directive 91/173 are no longer deemed to be acceptable if a sufficiently high level of health and environment protection is to be guaranteed. Therefore, it can be concluded that, although there are no specific circumstances in the Netherlands in comparison to the other Member States, the more stringent national measures can be regarded as justified."

(11) This last statement seems to indicate that the Commission will no longer require that there are "specific circumstances" in a Member State before it approves the maintaining of derogating national legislation under Article 95(4). Indeed, the wording of Article 95 provides that such specific national circumstances must exist when new derogating legislation is introduced (Article 95(5)), but not when existing national legislation is maintained (Article 94(4)).

Also in 1999, the Commission amended Directive 91/173, reducing in particular the number of exceptions. The new provisions are to be applied as from September 2000; by way of derogation, France, Spain, Ireland, Portugal and the United Kingdom were authorised to continue to apply Directive 91/173 in its original version until the end of 2008.[124]

---

[121] Decision 94/783 [1994] OJ L316/43.
[122] Decision 96/211 [1996] OJ L68/32.
[123] Decision 99/831 (n. 108 *supra*).
[124] Directive 99/51 [1999] OJ L142/22.

As regards the field of application of these Community-wide restrictions, it is necessary carefully to read the text of Directive 91/173 and its amendment. Indeed, the restrictions apply to "PCP and its salts and esters". Therefore, the restrictions do not apply to products which were treated with PCP.[125] Consequently, the Member States remain free to fix limit values for such products or to prohibit products containing or treated with PCP altogether.[126]

IV. The Statement of Reasons

(12) Article 253 EC Treaty requires that regulations, directives and decisions "shall state the reasons on which they are based". This is normally done in the recitals of a legislative act. In the present case, the Commission decision of December 1992 was not published, so that it cannot be assessed in detail. The Court interprets Article 253 in its settled case law that the statement of reasons "must show clearly and unequivocally the reasoning of the Community authority which adopted the contested measure so as to inform the persons concerned of the justification for the measure adopted and to enable the Court to exercise its powers of review. However, the statement of the reasons on which regulations are based is not required to specify the often very numerous and complex matters of fact or of law dealt with in the regulations".[127] This formula is sufficiently broad to give some discretion to the Court. In the present case, the Court was of the opinion that too little reasoning had been given.

(13) If one looks at the requirements for stating reasons for decisions under Article 95(4) which approve derogating national provisions, and compares these requirements with the general reasons stated in some Community directives or regulations, one is confronted with a remarkable discrepancy, the former being much more detailed. A good example is found in the area of PCP: Directive 99/51 amended Directive 91/173 and further restricted its use. However, a derogation from the provision of Directive 99/51 was given to France, Spain, Ireland, Portugal and the United Kingdom, until the end of 2008.

The only reason for this derogation is found in the fourth recital which states: "nevertheless, certain uses of PCP are still necessary, for technical reasons, in the oceanic maritime Member States". It is submitted that this reasoning does not comply with the requirements of Article 253; indeed, sea-going ships and maritime activities also exist in Member States such as Finland, Sweden, Denmark, Germany, the Netherlands, Italy and Greece. It appears certain that less dangerous alternatives to PCP are available.[128]

---

[125] Court of Justice, Case C–127/97 *Burstein* v. *Bayern* (n. 111 *supra*): "Council Directive 91/173 of 21 March 1991 is applicable to PCP, its salts and esters and to preparations produced from those substances, but not to products treated with those substances or preparations".

[126] See Commission, Decision 99/831 (n. 108 *supra*), para. 25.

[127] Court of Justice, Case C–27/89 [1990] ECR 1701, para. 28.

[128] See Commission Decision 99/831 (n. 108 *supra*), para. 62: "the Commission started a review programme dealing with the evaluation of the risks linked to the use of substitutes for PCP . . . This

(14) In view of this situation, a more detailed reasoning would have been necessary, under Article 253, to explain why, for technical reasons, some Member States benefitted from an eight-year derogation, in breach of the necessity to give, in an internal market, equal treatment to all Member States. Under the present wording of Directive 99/51, no court can assess why the derogation was given to some oceanic maritime States—whatever that is—but not to others.

More generally, it is not clear why a national measure which wishes to see more protective environmental provisions to be applied needs an examination under all the intricate and complicated conditions of Article 95, while a derogation from a strict Community standard which allows less stringent standards to be applied nationally may be explained in three or four words.

5. INTERPRETING EC ENVIRONMENTAL LAW

Judgment of the Court of 24 October 1996
Case C–72/95

Reference for a preliminary ruling:
Aannemersbedrijf P. K. Kraaijeveld BV and Others
and Gedeputeerde Staten van Zuid-Holland
[1996] ECR I–5403

Facts and Procedure

In 1953, huge storm-tides occurred in the Netherlands, causing the death of more than 1,800 people. In reaction to that catastrophy, a Netherlands' Law of 1958 provided for the construction of works in order to reinforce high-water protection of the land against storm-tides. Pursuant to that Law, a dyke reinforcement plan was adopted in 1990 which provided for the construction of a new dyke in an area that was owned by Kraaijeveld company and members of the Kraaijeveld family. In 1992, the plan was modified to reinforcement work on the Merwede dyke; these modifications covered Kraaijeveld's business sites and deprived the company, whose activity is related to waterways, of access to the waterways. An environment impact assessment (EIA) prior to the adoption of the plan or its modification had not been made, as Netherlands' legislation required such an EIA only when a dyke was five km or more in length, which was not the case as regards the Merwede dyke.

programme was concluded in 1998 and did result in the conclusion that in fact less dangerous alternatives were available".

The litigation which followed mainly discussed, as far as Community law was in question, whether an EIA should have been made before the 1992 modification of the plan.

Directive 85/337[129] lists the projects which come within the scope of the Directive: annex I enumerates projects which are subject to Article 4(1)[130] of the Directive, annex II projects which are subject to Article 4(2).[131] Annex II mentions in section 10(e): "Canalisation and flood-relief works" (in Dutch: "*werken in zaken kanalisering en regulering van waterwegen*", which corresponds to "works in relation to canalisation and regulation of watercourses").

The Dutch government was of the opinion that the construction or reinforcement of dykes was not covered by annex II (10)(e) of Directive 85/337. As the construction of dykes was mainly carried out only in the Netherlands, it was of the opinion that the Dutch version of Directive 85/337 was to be the only authentic language version in this case.

Furthermore, the Dutch government considered that Article 2(1)[132] of Directive 85/337 did not require an EIA to be made in this specific case, as Article 4(2) gave large discretion to Member States for projects listed in annex II to make or make not an EIA.

Judgment (extracts)

[On the interpretation of "canalisation and flood-relief works"]

28. As the case-law of the Court shows, interpretation of a provision of Community law involves a comparison of the language versions (see Case 283/81 CILFIT, cited above, paragraph 18). Moreover, the need for a uniform interpretation of those version requires, in the case of divergence between them, that the

---

[129] Directive 85/337 on the assessment of the effects of certain public and private projects on the environment [1985] OJ L175/40; amended by Directive 97/11 [1997] OJ L73/5.

[130] Directive 85/337 (n. 129 *supra*), Art. 4(1): "Subject to Art. 2(3), projects of the classes listed in Annex I shall be made subject to an assessment in accordance with Arts. 5 to 10". Directive 97/11 (n. 1 *supra*) deleted the words "of the classes".

[131] Directive 85/337 (n. 129 *supra*), Art. 4(2): "Projects of classes listed in Annex II shall be made subject to an assessment, in accordance with Arts. 5 to 10, where Member States consider that their characteristics so require.
To this end Member States may inter alia specify certain types of projects as being subject to an assessment or may establish the criteria and/or threshholds necessary to determine which of the projects of the classes listed in Annex II are to be subject to an assessment in accordance with Arts. 5 to 10". This text was amended by Directive 97/11 (n. 129 *supra*) which became effective on 14 March 1999, see n. 150 *infra*.

[132] Directive 85/337 (n. 129 *supra*), Art. 2(1): "Member States shall adopt all measures necessary to ensure that, before consent is given, projects likely to have significant effects on the environment by virtue inter alia, of their nature, size or location are made subject to an assessment with regard to their effects. These projects are defined in Art. 4". Directive 97/11 (n. 129 *supra*) added the words: "a requirement for development consent and" after the words "subject to".

provision in question be interpreted by reference to the purpose and general scheme of the rules of which it forms part (Case C–449/93 *Rockfon* [1995] ECR I–4291, paragraph 28).

29. Examination of the various language versions of point 10(e) of Annex II to the directive shows that they fall into two categories according to whether the terms employed denote the idea of flooding. The English ("canalization and flood-relief works") and Finnish ("*kanavointi- ja tulvasuojeluhankkeet*") versions are similar, whereas the German, Greek, Spanish, French, Italian, Dutch and Portuguese versions refer to canalization and regulation of watercourses, the Greek version including in addition the French term "canalisation" in brackets after the Greek term "*thieftatisis*". The Danish and Swedish versions contain only a single expression reflecting the idea of regulating watercourses ("*anlaeg til regulering af vandloeb*", "*anläggningar för reglering av vattenflöden*").

30. Given that divergence, one must go to the purpose and general scheme of the directive. According to Article 1(2) of the directive, "project" means "the execution of construction works or of other installations or schemes" and "other interventions in the natural surroundings and landscape including those involving the extraction of mineral resources". According to Article 2(1), the directive is aimed at "projects likely to have significant effects on the environment by virtue inter alia of their nature, size or location". Article 3 provides that the environmental impact assessment is to identify, describe and assess the direct and indirect effects of a project on human beings, fauna und flora, soil, water, air, climate and the landscape, material assets and the cultural heritage.

31. The wording of the directive indicates that it has a wide scope and a broad purpose. That observation alone should suffice to interpret point 10(e) of Annex II to the directive as encompassing all works for retaining water and preventing floods—and therefore dyke works—even if not all the linguistic versions are so precise.

32. Even if, as argued by the Government of the Netherlands, dyke works consist in the construction or raising of the height of embankments in order to contain watercourses and avoid flooding, works retaining a static quantity of water, rather than a running watercourse, may have a significant effect on the environment within the meaning of the directive where they are liable permanently to affect the composition of the soil, flora and fauna or the landscape. Such works must therfore fall under the directive. . . .

34. . . . the submission of the Government of the Netherlands that dykes do not fall within the scope of a Community directive because such work is specific to the Netherlands is irrelevant, since, as explained above, the criterion to be applied is the significance of the effect that a project is likely to have on the environment.

38. Since the directive provides no specific definition of "modifications to development projects", the expression must be interpreted in the light of the general scheme and purpose of the directive.

39. . . . Its purpose would be undermined if "modifications to development projects" were so construed as to enable certain works to escape the requirement

of an impact assessment although, by reason of their nature, size or location, such works were likely to have significant effects on the environment.

40. Furthermore, the mere fact that the directive does not expressly refer to modifications to projects included in Annex II, as opposed to modifications to projects included in Annex I, does not justify the conclusion that they are not covered by the directive. The distinction between a "project" and a "modification to a project", where projects included in Annex I are concerned, relates to the different systems to which they are subject under the directive, whereas such a distinction in the case of projects included in Annex II would relate to the general scope of the directive.

41. . . . in Case C–431/92 *Commission* v. *Germany* [1995] ECR I–2189, which concerned the Grosskrotzenburg thermal power station, . . . the Court held that, in order to establish whether the work envisaged should undergo an impact assessment, such projects should be assessed irrspective of whether they were separate constructions, were added to a pre-existing construction, or even had close functional links with a pre-existing construction.

42. In the light of those considerations, . . . the expression "canalization and flood-relief works" in point 10(e) of Annex II to the directive is to be interpreted as including not only construction of a new dyke but also modification of an existing dyke involving its relocation, reinforcement or widening, replacement of a dyke by constructing a new dyke in situ, whether or not the new dyke is stronger or wider than the old one, or a combination of such works.

[The discretion to provide for an EIA for projects of annex II to Directive 85/337]

48. . . . Article 2(1) of the directive refers to Article 4 for the definition of projects which must undergo an assessment of their effects. Article 4(2) allows Member States a certain discretion.

49. The interpretation put forward by the Commission—namely that the existence of specifications, criteria and threshholds does not remove the need for an actual examination of each project in order to verify that it fulfils the criteria of Article 2(1)—would deprive Article 4(2) of any point. A Member State would have no interest in fixing specifications, threshholds and criteria if, in any case, every project had to undergo an individual examination with respect to the criteria in Article 2(1).

50. . . . although the second paragraph of Article 4(2) . . . confers on Member States a measure of discretion . . . , the limits of that discretion are to be found in the obligation set out in Article 2(1) that project likely . . . to have significant effects on the environment are to be subject to an impact assessment.

51. . . . the criterion and/or the threshholds mentioned in Article 4(2) are designed to facilitate examination of the actual characteristics of any given project in order to determine whether it is subject to the requirement of assessment, not to exempt in advance from that obligation certain whole classes of projects listed in Annex II which may be envisaged as taking place on the territory of a Member State.

52. In a situation such as the present, it must be accepted that the Member State concerned was entitled to fix criteria relating to the size of dykes in order to establish which dyke projects had to undergo an impact assessment. The question whether, in laying down such criteria, the Member State went beyond the limits of its discretion cannot be determined in relation to the characteristics of projects of that nature which could be envisaged in the Member State.

53. Thus a Member State which established criteria or threshholds at a level such that, in practice, all projects relating to dykes would be exempted in advance from the requirement of an impact assessment would exceed the limits of its discretion under Articles 2(1) and 4(2) of the directive unless all projects excluded could, when viewed as a whole, be regarded as not being likely to have significant effects on the environment.

Commentary

I. On the Interpretation of Community Environmental Legislation

(1) The interpretation of Community environmental law does not differ from the interpretation of general Community law; however, as environmental lawyers often know little about Community law and Community lawyers often know little about environmental law, it may be useful to discuss interpretation rules.

Classical interpretation of legal provisions knows four approaches: the wording, the genesis, the purpose and the general scheme in which a provision is placed. In Community law, the genesis of a text is hardly ever taken into consideration. The main reason for this is that the discussions in Council, which until recently was the main producer of legal acts, are not public. Thus, normally it is not known why a specific wording was chosen. It is for this reason that the Court of Justice rarely uses documents which preceded the adoption of a legislative act in order to interpret a provision.[133]

(2) Interpretation of a legal provision first follows the wording of that provision. In that context, "it must be borne in mind that Community legislation is drafted in several languages and that the different language versions are all equally authentic. An interpretation of a provision of Community law thus involves a

---

[133] An example is Case 278/84, *Germany* v. *Commission* [1987] ECR 1, para. 17, where the Court refused to take into consideration the discussions preceding the proposal for a regulation which—according to Germany—led to a specific wording of a provision. See also Case C–203/96, *Dusseldorp* [1998] ECR I–4075, para. 31, where the Court quoted from the Commission's proposal for Regulation 259/93, using this text, however, only in support of the conclusions which it had reached without that text.

comparison of the different language versions. It must also be borne in mind, even where the different language versions are entirely in accord with one another, that Community law uses terminology which is peculiar to it. Furthermore, . . . legal concepts do not necessarily have the same meaning in Community law and in the law of the various Member States".[134] It follows from this that one and the same term may be used in Community and in national law and yet have to be interpreted differently.[135] This is a consequence of Community law being an autonomous legal order which is different and separate from the legal order of Member States and requires a uniform application of its provisions thoroughout the Community.[136] Interpretation and application of Community law therefore follow their own rules.

As the wording of Annex II 10(e) was different in the different linguistic versions, a comparison of these different versions was necessary. Because of the equal legal value of all linguistic versions, the argument of the Netherlands government, that the Dutch version of Directive 85/337, annex II 10(e) should be decisive,[137] could not be heard.

(3) The different versions of a provision are compared with the general scheme and the purpose[138] of the legal act and with Community law as a whole in order to find the correct interpretation.[139] This process led the Court to prefer a broad interpretation of "canalisation and flood-relief works" and to include in it the construction and reinforcement of dykes.[140]

---

[134] Court of Justice, Case 283/81 *CILFIT* [1982] ECR 3415, paras. 18 and 19.

[135] In Case C–449/93 *Rockfon* [1995] ECR I–4291 the Court had to interpret the notion of "establishment" and stated (para. 25): "The Court observes in this regard that the term 'establishment' as used in the Directive, is a term of Community law and cannot be defined by reference to the law of Member States".

[136] Settled case law since Case 6/64, *Costa* v. *Enel* [1964] ECR 585; see for instance Case C–287/98 *Linnster*, (2000) ECR I–6917, para. 43.

[137] Furthermore, dykes do not exist mainly in the Netherlands; probably all other Member States also have dykes. Thus the Court rightly rejected this argument.

[138] In Case 283/81 (n. 134 *supra*), para. 20, the Court had talked of "objective" and "context": "every provision of Community law must be placed in its context and interpreted in the light of the provisions of Community law as a whole, regard being had to the objectives thereof and to its state of evolution at the date on which the provision in question is to be applied". A difference in substance from the wording used in the present case does not exist.

[139] See also Court of Justice, Case C–449/93 (n. 135 *supra*) para. 28. This interpretation process may make a man out of a woman: in Case 9/79, *Koschniske* [1979] ECR 2717, the Court had to interpret the Dutch version of a Community directive, which referred to "wife" ("*diens echtgenote*"). The Court compared all other versions of the text and found that they also included husbands in the different terms which had been used. Thus, it declared that the word "wife" in the Dutch version also included husbands.

Furthermore, in case C–36/98, *Spain* v. *Council*, (2001) ECR I–779 the Court had to interpret the provision of "management of water resources" in Art. 175(2) EC Treaty, as Spain applied to the Court, arguing that by virtue of this term all water legislation would have to be adopted under Art. 175(2); the provision provides for unanimous decisions. Only the Dutch version speaks of "*quantitatief waterbeheer*" which would limit the field of application of Art. 175(2) to the management of quantitative water resources. This is probably what was intended. See for a discussion of this case p. 169 *infra*.

[140] See in contrast to that Case T–150/95 *UK Steel* [1997] OJ II–1433 (p. 110 *infra*), where the Court of First Instance refused to follow the Commission and interpret the meaning of a Community provision against its wording, but in conformity with its context and purpose (as interpreted by the Commission).

The purpose of a Community act is derived from its scope, its recitals and other elements which can be found in the adopted text. In this regard, the Court always stated that the criteria which are used for interpretation must be capable of judicial review; this can only be done by objective elements which are in the public area. For this reason the Court constantly refused to take into consideration, as regards the interpretation of a provision, declarations which one or all Member States, the Council or the Commission made in the minutes of the Council and which meant to "interpret" a provision.[141]

(4) The general scheme is first of all the legal text in which the provision in question is found. An examination takes place whether the provision is an exception to a general rule,[142] what the legal act tries to achieve, what function the provision in question has in that context, what relationship the provision has with other provisions in the same, in preceding or subsequent acts and what structure Community law wanted to give to a specific sector or aspect. In a broader context, "general scheme" includes Community law as a whole. This means that a specific provision is interpreted in line with primary and secondary Community law, including the general principles which are part of that law, such as subsidiarity, proportionality, legal security, prohibition of retroactivity, the prohibition of legitimate expectations and others.

(5) Also the fundamental rights are part of the general principles of Community law. Therefore, the Court has consistently held that Community law provisions cannot be interpreted "in such a way as to give rise to results which are incompatible with the general principles of Community law and in particular with fundamental rights".[143]

There are only a few environmental cases where questions of fundamental rights were raised by the Court. One such case is discussed on pp. 79 *et seq infra* (*Arcaro*). In another case, C–293/97,[144] British farmers sought annulment of the decisions by which United Kingdom authorities had identified some rivers as nitrate vulnerable

---

[141] See for instance Case 429/85, *Commission* v. *Italy* [1988] ECR 843, para. 9: "an interpretation based on a declaration by the Council cannot give rise to an interpretation different from that resulting from the actual wording of . . . the Directive".

[142] See for an example the Court's interpretation of Art. 95(4) (ex Art. 100a(4))EC Treaty, Case C–41/93, *France* v. *Commission* [1994] ECR I–1829 (*supra*, p. 33).

[143] Court of Justice, Joined Cases 97/87, 98/87 and 99/87, *Dow Chemical* [1989] ECR 3165, para. 9: See also para. 10: "The Court has consistently held that fundamental rights are an integral part of the general principles of law the observance of which the Court ensures, in accordance with constitutional traditions common to the Member States, and the international treaties on which the Member States have collaborated or of which they are signatories . . . The European Convention for the Protection of Human Rights and Fundamental Freedoms of 4 November 1950 . . . is of particular significance in that regard".

See also Art. 6 of the Treaty on European Union [1997] OJ C340/145: "1. The Union is founded on the principles of liberty, democracy, respect for human rights and fundamental freedoms, and the rule of law, principles which are common to the Member States.

2. The Union shall respect fundamental rights, as guaranteed by the European Convention for the Protection of Human Rights and Fundamental Freedoms signed in Rome on 4 November 1950 and as they result from the constitutional traditions common to the Member States, as general principles of Community law" . . .

[144] Court of Justice, Case C–293/97, *Standley* [1999] ECR I–2603.

zones under Directive 91/676.[145] They argued among others, that this designation infringed the fundamental property right of those owning and/or farming land to drain into surface freshwaters. The Court was of the opinion that the designation of vulnerable zones did affect the farmers' right to property. However, the system was set up, it argued, in order to protect "public health, and thus pursues an objective of general interest without the substance of the right to property being impaired".[146]

II. On the Relation between ArticleS 4(2) and 2(1) of Directive 85/337

(6) Having fixed the content of "canalisation and flood-relief works", the Court then used the above-mentioned principles of interpretation to clarify whether a modification of an Annex II project was also covered by Directive 85/337.[147] It found that the purpose and the general scheme of the Directive pleaded against the wording[148] of Annex II and in favour of such an inclusion. The key phrase is found in paragraph 39 of the judgment: "the purpose of the Directive would be undermined if some projects could escape an environmental impact assessment, though they were likely to have significant effects on the environment". Again, the purpose of the Directive is the determining factor.

(7) The Court does not discuss how a project—"modifications of annex-II projects"—that is not listed in the annexes to Directive 85/337 nevertheless can be included in its field of application. Indeed, Directive 85/337 is based on positive lists, which means that projects which are not listed in the annexes do not come under its scope. What the Court probably wanted to express is the following: the notion of "project" has to be understood as "new project" as well as "modification of an existing project", as the Directive has a broad field of application. Annex II 12 only means that modifications of Annex I projects do not systematically have to undergo an environment impact assessment, but may be subject to the same procedure as an Annex II project. The result which the Court reached seems, anyway, the right one as it does not make much sense to restrict the application of Directive 85/337, as regards the numerous projects of Annex II, only to "new" projects; modifications of existing projects may have a much greater negative impact on the environment.

(8) As regards the interrelationship between Articles 2(1) and 4(2) of Directive 85/337, the number of cases already brought before the Court of Justice where this

---

[145] Directive 91/676 concerning the protection of waters against pollution caused by nitrates from agricultural sources [1991] OJ L375/1.

[146] Court of Justice, Case C–293/97 (n. 144 *supra*), para. 56. Case C–293/97 will be discussed in detail below p. 89 *et seq.*

[147] Judgment, paras. 38 to 42.

[148] Directive 85/337 (n. 129 *supra*), Annex II no. 12: "Modifications to development projects included in Annex I and projects in Annex I undertaken exclusively or mainly for the development and testing of new methods or products and not used for more than one year". Thus, modifications of Annex II projects were not mentioned at all in the Directive.

issue was discussed[149] demonstrates the ambiguity of this relationship. The Court's reasoning may be summarised as follows: Article 4(2) gives Member States a discretionary power to decide that some projects of Annex II do not need to be the subject of an environmental impact assessment. However this discretion is limited by the fact that a specific type of projects listed in Annex II may not be excluded altogether from an EIA, and further by Article 2(1) which requires projects likely, by virtue *inter alia* of their nature, size or location, to have significant effects on the environment are to be subject of an impact assessment.

(9) The Netherlands was free to fix a limit of a particular length for dykes, below which an EIA had not to be made. However, if that limit (five km) led—*de facto*—to the result that all dykes would be exempted from the requirement of an EIA, this borderline would be too high. It remained possible for the Netherlands to demonstrate that dykes of less than five km length never could have significant effects on the environment. It seems clear, though, that such evidence is impossible to provide as in practice in sensitive natural zones, protected habitats or other vulnerable areas, such an effect could not always be avoided. Also the present case where a company was affected whose activities are linked to the use of watercourses and which risked losing access to the waterways demonstrates how exceptional it will be in practice to bring such an evidence.

(10) Article 4(2) was amended in 1997.[150] However, the ambiguity of the past is likely to continue. National, and in particular local, authorities have a tendency, for Annex II projects, to consider an environmental impact assessment unnecessary. Environmental groups, citizens' committees or individual persons often will continue to argue that in a specific case an environmental impact assessment should have been made, in particular in view of the size, location or the characteristics of the project. Disputes on the interrelationship are therefore likely to be frequent also in future.

Litigation will also be furthered by the fact that in Case C–392/96[151] the Court stated that Member States also need to take into consideration that several small Annex II projects—which individually might fall below a fixed threshhold—could have a cumulative effect. Consequently, they have to choose the criteria/threshholds for Annex II projects in a way that allows this cumulative effect to be taken into consideration.

It seems arguable whether there is really need for Article 4(2). A lot of litigation, of which the cases brought before the Court of Justice are only the tip of the iceberg, could be avoided, if Article 4(1) and (2) could be set aside. This would mean

---

[149] See in particular the following Cases: C–133/94 *Commission* v. *Belgium* [1996] ECR I–2323; C–301/95 *Commission* v. *Germany* [1998] ECR I–6135; C–392/96 *Commission* v. *Ireland* [1999] ECR I–5901; C–435/97 *WWF* v. *Bolzano* [1999] ECR I–5613.

[150] Directive 85/337 (n. 129 *supra*), Art. 4(2) in its version of the amendment by Directive 97/11 (n. 129 *supra*): "Subject to Art. 2(3), for projects listed in Annex II, the Member States shall determine through: (a) a case-by-case examination, or (b) threshholds or criteria set by the Member State whether the project shall be made subject to an assessment in accordance with Arts. 5 to 10. Member States may decide to apply both procedures referred to in (a) and (b)".

[151] Court of Justice, Case C–392/96 (n. 149 *supra*).

that projects which have a significant effect on the environment would have to undergo an environmental impact assessment before consent is given. For projects in Annex I there would be an unrebuttable presumption that they have such an impact; for projects in Annex II, the presumption would be rebuttable. Such a solution would oblige an authority which wishes to give planning consent without having made an EIA, to justify to the public why it was of the opinion that a specific project had no significant impact on the environment.

(11) One should be aware that with the Court's ruling in the present case, this solution is almost there: whenever a Member State sets threshholds or fixes criteria for the application of Annex II, that Member State is obliged to prove, in the case of litigation, that projects which remained within the threshholds/criteria never could have significant effects on the environment, i. e. on any of the assets mentioned in Article 3(2) of Directive 85/337.[152] This proof is, it is submitted, impossible. Therefore, Member States, in practice, have only the option to proceed with a case-by-case examination which is also permitted under Article 4(2) of Directive 85/337. There, in case of disputes, it would be up to the public to prove that a specific project was likely to have significant effects on the environment.

The European Union is a densely populated area with highly developed economic activity. It is difficult to see why any reasonable, cautious administration which is to achieve a high level of environmental protection would not make an evaluation of the environmental impact of any project listed in Annex II, before it gives planning consent. A proper assessment of the environmental impacts should be of much wider application than required by Directive 85/337 and its subsequent amendment.

---

[152] Directive 85/337 (n. 129 *supra*), Art. 3: "The environmental impact assessment will identify, describe and assess in an appropriate manner, in the light of each individual case and in accordance with Arts. 4 to 11, the direct and indirect effects of a project on the following factors:—human beings, fauna and flora,—soil water, air climate and the landscape,—the inter-action between the factors, mentioned in the first and second indents,—material assets and the cultural heritage".

6. MEMBER STATES OWE AN ENVIRONMENTAL RESULT

Judgment of the Court of 14 July 1993
Case C–56/90

Commission of the European Communities
v. *United Kingdom of Great Britain and Northern Ireland*
[1993] ECR I–4109

Facts and Procedure

Directive 76/160 concerning the quality of bathing water[153] was adopted at the end of 1975. It applies to all running or still fresh waters and to sea water, where either bathing is explicitly authorised or not prohibited and traditionally practised by a large number of bathers. Member States had to identify—not to designate!—the bathing waters which came under the scope of application of the Directive and then ensure that those bathing waters complied with the specific requirements of the Directive within 10 years after the Directive's notification to Member States; under certain conditions, derogations were possible.

The United Kingdom considered that water where, at some time during the bathing season, not more than 500 people were in the water, would not qualify as bathing water; where more than 1,500 people were in the water, this water would be classified as bathing water; and where the number was between 500 and 1,500, it should be decided by the authorities whether the water qualified as bathing water or not. On that basis, it identified 27 bathing waters as coming under the Directive.

In 1986 the Commission started formal proceedings under Article 226 EC Treaty against the United Kingdom, because a number of waters, among which were Southport/Formby and Blackpool, had not been identified as bathing waters and did not comply with the Directive's requirements. In 1986/87, the United Kingdom changed its criteria for "bathing water", identified 362 other waters as falling under the Directive and informed the Commission thereof; among these were the waters of Southport/Formby and Blackpool. The Commission nevertheless, in 1990 applied, to the Court.

---

[153] Directive 76/160 concerning the quality of bathing waters [1976] OJ L31/1

Judgment (extracts)

[The time limits laid down in Article 4(1) ... of the Directive]

29. The United Kingdom contends that the definition of bathing water in the second indent of Article 1(2)(a) of the directive is too imprecise to enable the Member States to identify the waters falling within its scope; consequently, that term requires further elucidation, which entails a certain discretionary power on the part of the Member States.

30. The United Kingdom maintains that in exercise of that power it laid down the criteria ... and drew up, pursuant thereto, a list of bathing waters falling within the scope of the directive. It subsequently proved necessary to review those criteria by having regard not only to the number of bathers but also to certain facilities in the bathing areas, such as toilets, changing huts, car parking areas, and to the presence of lifeguards ...

32. For reasons of legal certainty Article 4(1) ... of the directive should, in its view, be interpreted as meaning that, ... the ten-year period for ensuring that the bathing waters conform to the limit values indicated in the annex to the directive ... begin to run from the moment when the waters are identified as bathing waters within the meaning of the directive and not from the date of notification of the directive. ...

33/34. ... the directive's underlying purpose as set out in the first two recitals in the preamble thereto ... would not be attained if the waters of bathing resorts equipped with facilities such as changing huts, toilets, markers indicating bathing areas, and supervised by lifeguards, could be excluded from the scope of the directive soleley because the number of bathers was below a certain threshhold. Such facilities and the presence of lifeguards constitute evidence that the bathing area is frequented by a large number of bathers whose health must be protected.

35. The bathing areas of Blackpool and of Southport have for a long time been bathing resorts meeting the criteria mentioned above. Accordingly, as from the notification of the directive they should have been considered bathing areas within the meaning of the directive.

36. ... the time limits laid down in Article 4(1) ... of the directive ... begin to run from the date of notification of the directive.

[The nature of the obligations imposed by the directive]

40. According to the United Kingdom, the Directive merely requires the Member States to take all practicable steps to comply with the limit values ... in the United Kingdom, the necessary studies in this connection have been carried out and works are in hand which will enable the bathing waters at issue to be brought into conformity with the directive in 1995. Such works are necessarily slow, in particular because their impact on the population and the life of the town must be kept to the minimum possible. The United Kingdom adds that the Commission did not indicate to it what steps might enable it to ensure that the directive is implemented more swiftly with regard to the waters at issue.

41. That argument cannot be upheld.

42. It is clear from Article 4(1) of the directive that the Member States are to take all necessary measures to ensure that, within ten years following the notification of the directive, bathing water conforms to the limit values set in accordance with Article 3. This period is longer than that laid down for the implementation of the directive, namely two years from the date of notification (Article 12(1)), in order to enable the Member States to comply with the aforementioned requirement.

43. The only derogations from the obligation incumbent upon Member States to bring their bathing waters into conformity with the requirements of the directive are those provided for in Articles 4(3), 5(2) and 8, whose provisions are summarized above. It follows that the directive requires the Member States to take steps to ensure that certain results are attained, and, apart from those derogations, they cannot rely on particular circumstances to justify a failure to fulfil that obligation.

44. Consequently, the United Kingdom's argument that it took all practicable steps cannot afford a further ground, in addition to the derogations expressly permitted, justifying the failure to fulfil the obligation to bring the waters at issue into conformity at least with the annex to the directive.

45. The United Kingdom observes that, if the latter interpretation were to prevail, any deviation from the limit values laid down in the annex to the directive would constitute an infringement of Article 4(1) of the directive, even if the Member State concerned had taken all practicable steps to avoid such deviation.

46. Even assuming that absolute physical impossibility to carry out the obligations imposed by the directive may justify failure to fulfil them, the United Kingdom has not . . . succeeded in establishing the existence of such impossibility in this case.

47. It follows, in view of the foregoing considerations, that, by failing to take all the necessary measures to ensure that the quality of the bathing waters at Blackpool and of those adjacent to Southport confroms to the limit values set in accordance with Council Directive 76/160/EEC of 8 December 1975, the United Kingdom has failed to fulfil its obligations under the EEC Treaty.

Commentary

I. The 10-year Period for Cleaning up Bathing Waters

(1) United Kingdom had initially identified 27 bathing waters as coming under Directive 76/160 and only in 1987 designated some more waters. The Court first had to deal with the argument that the 10-year period laid down in

Article 4(1)[154] of Directive 76/160 started to run from the moment when a Member State notified a stretch of water as coming under Directive 76/160 or whether this period started from the moment when it should have notified a water. The only justification for the interpretation that the 10-year period should start with the notification which the United Kingdom gave was that of "legal certainty". The Court's answer was clear and unambiguous: the moment of entering into effect of Directive 76/160 is decisive, not the moment of notification. The Court relied on the wording of Article 4(1) and on the general objective of Directive 76/160.

This reasoning is even more convincing, if one were considering the consequences of the United Kingdom's arguments: First, a Member State would win time by not identifying bathing waters in time, as the later a water was identified the more time the Member State would have to clean it up. Secondly, a Member State could avoid the Directive's application to a specific water by not notifying it. Therefore, legal certainty rather militates against the reasoning of the United Kingdom.

(2) The most relevant point to support the Court's conclusion lies in the Directive itself: there is not one single word which would allow the interpretation that the identification (or designation or notification) of a stretch of water is constitutive for the water to come under the Directive. Rather, the Directive is built on objective criteria: as soon as there is either an authorisation to bathe or a large number of bathers, the Directive applies. For this reason, the Court also stated in paragraphs 34 and 35 of its judgment that objective criteria were capable of allowing an assessment, whether a specific water qualified as bathing water or not.

II. The Obligations under a Community Directive

(3) The United Kingdom's defence that it had taken all practical steps to comply with the Directive's requirements gave an opportunity to the Court to underline the nature and obligations of Member States under a Community directive: Member States owe a result, not an effort. They must take "all the measures necessary to ensure that the directive is fully effective, in accordance with the objective which it pursues".[155] Already the wording of Article 249 EC Treaty is entirely clear in this regard,[156] and Article 4(1) only repeats and adapts this general requirement with regard to the specificities of Directive 76/160. The question of inertia, negligence or passivity on the part of a Member State is completely irrelevant, as the

---

[154] Directive 76/160, Art. 4(1): "Member States shall take all necessary measures to ensure that, within ten years following the notification of this directive, the quality of bathing water conforms to the limit values set in accordance with Art. 3".

[155] Court of Justice, Case C–336/97 *Commission* v. *Italy* [1999] ECR I–3771 para. 19 (see p. 341 *infra*); furthermore see Case C–208/90 *Emmott* [1991] ECR I–4269, para. 18.

[156] Art. 249 (ex Art. 189) EC Treaty: "A directive shall be binding, as to the result to be achieved, upon each Member State to which it is addressed, but shall leave to the national authorities the choice of form and method".

objective result is the issue which matters. This also becomes plain if one considers the division of work between the Commission, representing the Community, and Member States: under subsidiarity aspects the Commission is not entitled to interfere with the national process of transposing a directive, for instance by suggesting a timetable or by even drafting national provisions. This is exclusively the responsibility of Member States. In the same way, it is up to Member States, whether they wish to transpose a Community directive into national law by one single legislative act or by a number of acts, whether they want to have several pieces of regional legislation or prefer one national legislative act. As the Commission is not entitled actively to influence this transposition process, it cannot either be obliged to take into consideration some or all different aspects of this process. This would bring a subjective element into the relationship between the Commission and Member States which the EC Treaty does not foresee.

(4) For the same reason, Article 226 EC Treaty allows the Commission to initiate and continue formal legal action against a Member State which does not comply with Community law. The reason why the Member State does not comply is irrelevant, except eventually in cases of "*force majeure*". Legal action under Article 226 EC Treaty is not taken against a Member State for reason of inertia or negligence, but for reason of non-compliance.

(5) It is worthwhile to re-read the United Kingdom's arguments in favour of its interpretation, which are grouped as follows:

(a) Article 4(1) lays down an obligation to use due diligence, not an absolute obligation. This provision has to be interpreted in a way that takes account of the environmental context in which the obligations are to be performed.

(b) Member States have an absolute duty to transpose a directive into internal law and to set values applicable to bathing waters.

(c) The obligation mentioned under (b) is different from the duty to reach certain results; for this latter duty, a Member State has to take only all practicable steps to ensure compliance. This follows from the fact that Directive 76/160 allows for derogations, exceptions and waivers. Also, reaching a certain result might encounter environmental and technical difficulties which may place grave obstacles in the way of compliance.

(d) Lack of compliance might be due to actions by third parties. A Member State cannot be the guarantor of observance of the law by third parties.

Apart from the fact that it is surprising to have such arguments about the nature of Member States' obligations placed in public as late as 1992,[157] the arguments may well reflect underlying considerations which are more generally held in the United Kingdom as regards obligations flowing out of Community law. Had the Court followed the United Kingdom's reasoning, this would have meant a fundamental

---

[157] The United Kingdom had used practically identical arguments in Case C–337/89, *Commission* v. *United Kingdom* [1992] ECR I–6103, which dealt with Directive 80/778 on the quality of drinking waters. See for a more general comment on this case and on the implementation of Directive 80/778 in the United Kingdom p. 185 *infra*.

change in the whole system of Community law, beyond the area of directives and reaching into Treaty law[158] and could have led to the interpretation that Community law in general does not contain obligations for Member States which go beyond the duty to take all practicable measures. Under these auspices, even the obligation to transpose a directive into internal law might not constitute an "absolute duty" any more, as each Member State could argue that the Parliamentary procedure took too long or that other circumstances prevented a transposition in time.

(6) It might be interesting to look more closely at the different defences, which Member States put forward in environmental cases, when the Commission had applied to the Court, because an environmental directive had not or not completely been transposed into national law. The following arguments were raised:

—lack of financial resources.[159]
—political problems in Northern Ireland[160]
—the necessary measures would be taken "soon".[161]
—the provisions of the directive are directly applied and existing national provisions have been interpreted in accordance with the directive.[162]
—the Commission was informed of the reasons for delayed transposition.[163]
—technical difficulties.[164]
—the repartition of concurrent powers between the federal and the regional level.[165]
—all reasonable practical measures were taken; the delay was due to particular circumstances.[166]
—an abnormal drought in part of the Member States prevented the taking of measures in the whole of that Member State.[167]
—there was no intention not to comply.[168]
—the Commission has submitted a proposal for an amendment; therefore, the existing obligations are no longer valid.[169]

---

[158] It should be noted that in the present case the United Kingdom tried to use arguments under Art. 28 (ex Art. 30) EC Treaty, in order to justify its position. It claimed that the Court had, in its judgment of "*Cassis de Dijon*" (see for that p. 30 *supra*) inserted into Art. 28 an unwritten exception to the requirement of the free circulation of goods.

[159] Court of Justice, Cases 290/89, *Commission* v. *Belgium* [1991] ECR I–2851; 42/89, *Commission* v. *Belgium* [1990] ECR 2821.

[160] Court of Justice, Case 337/89, *Commission* v. *United Kingdom* (n. 4 *supra*).

[161] Court of Justice, Cases C–190/97, *Commission* v. *Belgium* [1997] ECR I–7201; C–213/97 *Commission* v. *Portugal* [1998] ECR I–3289. For a discussion of the notion "soon", see p. 391 *infra.*

[162] Court of Justice, Case C–83/97, *Commission* v. *Germany* [1997] ECR I–7191.

[163] Court of Justice, Case C–236/96, *Commission* v. *Germany* [1997] ECR I–6397.

[164] Court of Justice, Cases C–329/96, *Commission* v. *Greece* [1997] ECR I–3749; C–282/96, *Commission* v. *France* [1997] ECR I–2929; C–71/97, *Commission* v. *Spain* [1998] ECR I–5991.

[165] Court of Justice, Cases C–347/97, *Commission* v. *Belgium* [1999] ECR I–309; C–71/97, *Commission* v. *Spain* (n. 164 *supra*); C–326/97, *Commission* v. *Belgium* [1998] ECR I–6107; C–297/95 and C–298/95, *Commission* v. *Germany* [1996] ECR I–6739 and I–6747.

[166] Court of Justice, Case C–198/97 *Commission* v. *Germany* [1999] ECR I–3257.

[167] Court of Justice, Case C–92/96, *Commission* v. *Spain* [1998] ECR I–505.

[168] Court of Justice, Case C–71/97 (n. 164 *supra*)

[169] Court of Justice, Case C–71/97 (n. 164 *supra*)

—a change of government, following elections.[170]

—many far-reaching changes had to be made since the adoption of a constitution and the accession to the EC.[171]

—other priority work.[172]

—there was no need to transpose the requirements on monitoring compliance, as national law already provides for criminal sanctions.[173]

—*force majeure*, caused by the process of institutional reform which had to be carried out over the last 30 years in order to preserve the unity of the State and the fundamental principles of a State governed on the rule of law.[174]

(7) The Court rejected all these arguments referring to its case-law according to which "a Member State may not plead provisions, practices or circumstances existing in its internal legal system in order to justify a failure to comply with the obligations and time-limits laid down in a directive".[175] In practically all of these cases, the Member State could also have invoked the argument that it had taken all practical steps to ensure compliance; then the Commission would have had the burden of proof that a Member State had not taken all such steps—which would have led to the checking of investment programmes, legislative activities, governmental, regional and local programmes and plans etc. etc.

III. Bathing Water Questions

(8) The question of delays for the bathing waters of Southport/Formby and Blackpool might be of interest. According to Community law, as the Court had confirmed in the present judgment, these bathing waters should have complied with the requirements of Directive 76/160 by end 1985. The judgment of the Court stating that the United Kingdom was in breach of its obligations was given on 14 July 1993. Subsequently, the Commission issued the following statements as regards these bathing waters:[176]

1994: "The British authorities have notified programmes aimed at bringing legislation into line with the Directive. The case is being settled".

1995: "The Member State tries to solve the problem".

1996: "The Member State is rectifying matters".

1997: "The Member State is rectifying matters"

1998: "Last verification; Blackpool will supply a clean-up report which will be examined by the Commission services".

---

[170] Court of Justice, Case C–229/97, *Commission* v. *Portugal* [1998] ECR I–6059.

[171] Court of Justice, Case C–214/96, *Commission* v. *Spain* [1998] ECR I–7661.

[172] Court of Justice, Case C–291/84, *Commission* v. *Netherlands* [1987] ECR 3483.

[173] Court of Justice, Case C–360/87, *Commission* v. *Italy* [1991] ECR I–791.

[174] Court of Justice, Case C–236/99, *Commission* v. *Belgium,* (2000) ECR I–5657.

[175] Wording from Court of Justice, Case C–214/96 (n. 171 *supra*), para. 18.

[176] Commission, Annual report on monitoring the application of Community law: 11th report (1993), [1994] OJ C154/1 (p. 173); 12th report (1994) [1995] OJ C254/1 (p. 163); 13th report (1995) [1996] OJ C303/1 (p. 177); 14th report (1996) [1997] OJ C332/1 (p. 197); 15th report (1997) [1998] OJ C250/1 (p. 194) ; 16th report (1998) [1999] OJ C354/1 (p. 181); 17th report (1999) OJ C30/1 [p. 47].

1999: "The Commission had to commence legal proceedings against United Kingdom in the Blackpool case for its failure to comply fully with the judgment in case C–56/90".

2000: "The Commission decided to send the United Kingdom an Article 228 reasoned opinion over Blackpool, where the beaches do not meet the Directive's standards".

(9) This means that 25 years after the adoption of Directive 76/160, 15 years after the date by which the bathing waters in question should have complied with that Directive and seven years after the judgment by the Court of Justice that the non-compliance constituted a breach of the United Kingdom's obligations under Directive 76/160 the bathing waters in Blackpool are still not in compliance. The procedure under Article 226 EC Treaty took, between the dispatch of the letter of formal notice and the judgment, 87 months. Since the judgment in the present case until the end of the year 2000, more than 90 months have already elapsed without the Commission applying to the Court for a second judgment. It was only at the end of 2000 that the Commission decided to apply, under Article 228 EC Treaty, to the Court for a second judgment in this case, and to ask for a daily penalty payment of 106. 800 Euros.[177]

The conclusion which can be drawn from this situation is that Community environmental law appears to be sufficient, clear and precise. However, enforcement is the weak point: where a Member State, for financial, economic or other reasons, is unwilling to ensure compliance with the environmental requirements of Community law, the mechanisms set up to ensure this compliance are simply not efficient.

(10) The Commission also brought a number of cases against other Member States to the European Court. In all these cases, the Court found against the Member State in question. In Case 72/81, the action was brought against Belgium which had not transposed the Directive into national law. Belgium defended itself with the argument that it could only transpose the Directive into national law once a constitutional reform had taken place. The Court did not accept this defence.

Case 96/81 involved the Commission and the Netherlands which had transposed Directive 76/160 by administrative circulars. The Court held that this was not sufficient.[178]

In Case 92/96 the Commission argued before the Court that a large number of Spanish inland bathing waters did not comply with the requirements of the Directive. The Court found that Spain had not fulfilled its obligation under Directive 76/160.[179]

---

[177] *ENDS Environment Daily* of 3 January 2001, p. 5; the newspaper reports on this and a German Case and concludes: "The cases appear to have more symbolic than substantive importance and neither looks likely to result in actual fines being imposed".

[178] Questions on the transposition of Community directives into national law will be discussed on p. 61 *supra*.

[179] Court of Justice, Case C–92/96 (n. 167 *supra*).

In Case C–198/97 the Court found that a number of German bathing waters did not comply with the requirements of the Directive and that some waters had not been monitored in conformity with the requirements of the Directive[180]. In Case C–307/98, Belgium was found not to have monitored inland bathing waters in Wallonia in conformity with the Directive; furthermore, some bathing waters did not comply with the Directive's requirements.[181]

As can be seen, the present Case C–56/90 is the only case which was brought before the Court and which concerned two specific bathing waters. The reason for that is that, on the one hand, there were complaints from private persons to the Commission, arguing that the bathing waters in question did not meet the Directive's requirements. And, on the other hand, the very fundamental objection which the United Kingdom had raised against its obligation under Directive 76/160 made it well worthwhile to have a statement of the Court on Member States' responsibilities under Community directives.

(11) And of the improvement of the quality of bathing water, the objective of Directive 76/160? Since 1979, the Commission published annual reports on the quality of bathing waters coming under this Directive. In its last report, which covers the 1999 bathing season,[182] it indicates that overall 11. 435 coastal zones and 4. 376 freshwater zones were sampled in 1999.[183] The results show a steady increase in the number of waters which comply with the mandatory and with the guide parameters of Directive 76/160, both for coastal and for freshwater zones. The evolution since 1995 is as follows:

Coastal zones	Number of waters sampled	% of compliance mandatory standards	% of compliance guide standards
1995	12.487	85.3	74.8
1996	12.934	91.4	81.9
1997	13.129	93.3	82.8
1998	13.218	94.6	83.8
1999	11.435	95.6	87.3
2000	11.502	96.5	88.4
Freshwater zones			
1995	5.907	51.7	38.7
1996	6.117	68.9	52.0
1997	6.180	79.8	63.5
1998	6.004	86.5	63.6
1999	4.376	90.2	66.9
2000	4.338	93.6	70.4

[180] Court of Justice, Case C–198/97, *Commission* v. *Germany* [1999] ECR I–3257.

[181] Court of Justice, Case C–307/98, *Commission* v. *Belgium*, (2000) ECR I–3933.

[182] European Commission, *Quality of Bathing Water (2000 bathing season)* (Office for Official Publications of the European Communities, Luxembourg, 2001).

[183] European Commission, *Quality of Bathing Water* (n. 182 *supra*). The indicated figures do not include France which had not provided information about the results in 2000. The figures for 1998, which did include France, were 13. 218 coastal zones and 6. 004 freshwater zones.

The United Kingdom sampled, in 2000, 551 coastal zones and 11 freshwater zones; to these figures, six coastal zones from Gibraltar have to be added. The compliance rate for coastal zones was 91.5 per cent as regards the mandatory parameters and 50.5 per cent as regards the guide parameters, thus in both cases below Community average. For the freshwater zones—the United Kingdom had identified freshwater zones for the first time in 1998, 23 years after the adoption of Directive 76/160—the compliance rates were 90.9 (coastal zones) and 54.3 (freshwater zones) per cent.[184]

In the year 2001, the Commission stated that "monitoring of bathing areas is becoming increasingly common and water quality is improving. Despite this progress, however, proceedings are still under way against roughly half the Member States, since implementation still falls far short of the Directive's requirements".[185]

(12) In 1994, the Commission made a proposal for a revision of Directive 76/160[186] which intended better to take into consideration aspects of subsidiarity and of public health. It reported, however, that Member States "preferred the Commission to start work on a new proposal rather than to pursue adoption of the 1994 proposal for revision of the directive, which had become outdated". The Commission intends to make such a new proposal in 2002.[187]

7. DIRECT EFFECT OF COMMUNITY LAW

Judgment of the Court (Sixth Chamber) of 16 September 1999
Case C–435/97

Reference for a preliminary ruling in proceedings between
World Wildlife Fund (WWF) and Others
and Autonome Provinz Bozen and Others
[1999] ECR I–5613

FACTS

The Italian airport Bolzano–St. Jacob has mainly been used, since 1925/26, for military purposes. The Italian authorities planned to transform that airport into

---

[184] European Commission, *Quality of Bathing Water* (n. 182 *supra*), p. 269.
[185] Commission, *17th Report on Monitoring the Application of Community Law* (n. 176 *supra*), p. 47.
[186] [1994] OJ C112/3; explanatory memorandum COM(94)36 of 16 February 1994.
[187] European Commission, *Quality of Bathing Water* (n. 182 *supra*), p. 14.

an airport which can be used commercially. The necessary work included the renewal and extension, to 1,400 metres, of the existing runway, construction of a control tower with air traffic control installations, construction of a departure building and of a hangar and construction of access roads and car parks.

A Law of the Autonomous Province of Bolzano of 7 July 1992 ("Law 27/92") required an environmental impact assessment to be made, as regards the extension or alteration of existing airports, when the runway had a length of 2,100 metres or more or when the thresholds referred to in Annex II to Law 27/92 were exceeded by more than 20 per cent; however, no threshholds for airport projects were set in Annex II.

Another Law of 18 January 1995 ("Law 3/95") approved a regional development plan which provided for the restructuring of Bolzano Airport; the plan requested an environment impact study to be made. That study was carried out, followed by a consultation of various bodies.

There was disagreement among the parties in the main proceedings whether an environment impact assessment (EIA) in conformity with Directive 85/337[188] ("the Directive") should have been made before development consent was given to the restructuring of Bolzano Airport.

Judgment (extracts)

[On the requirements for an alternative assessment procedure under national law]

50. . . . the national court asks essentially whether, in the case of a project requiring assessment under the Directive, Article 2(1) and (2) thereof are to be interpreted as allowing a Member State to use an assessment procedure other than the procedure introduced by the Directive.

51. . . . the national court explains that is has doubts whether the consent procedure laid down in . . . Law No 27/92 is appropriate for fully identifying the effects of the project on the environment. It states that neither noise nor the effects on the atmosphere were investigated, as Article 3 of the Directive requires, and that the public did not participate in that procedure, contrary to Article 6 of the Directive.

53. . . . where a project requires assessment within the meaning of the Directive, a Member State cannot, without undermining the Directive's objective, use an alternative procedure, even one incorporated in a national procedure which exists or is to be established, to exempt that project from the requirements laid down in Articles 3 and 5 to 10 of the Directive.

---

[188] Directive 85/337 on the assessment of the effects of certain public and private projects on the environment [1985] OJ L175/40; amended by Directive 97/11 [1997] OJ L73/5.

[On the requirements for a national legislative act exempting from an EIA]

56/57. Article 1(5) . . . exempts projects envisaged by the Directive from the assessment procedure subject to two conditions. The first requires the details of the project to be adopted by a specific legislative act; under the second, the object-ives of the Directive, including that of supplying information, must be achieved through the legislative process.

58. . . . Article 1(2) of the Directive refers not to legislative acts but to develop-ment consent. . Therefore, if it is a legislative act, instead of a decision of the com-petent authorities, which grants the developer the right to carry out the project, that act must be specific and display the same characteristics as the development consent.

59. Consequently, . . . the act must lay down the project . . . a sufficiently pre-cise and definitive manner so as to include, like development consent, following their consideration by the legislature, all the elements of the project relevant to the environmental impact assessment . . .

61. That interpretation is borne out by the sixth recital in the preamble to the Directive, which states . . . that this assessment must be conducted on the basis of the appropriate information supplied by the developer, which may be supple-mented by the authorities and by the people who may be concerned by the project.

62. It follows that the details of a project cannot be considered to be adopted by a Law, for the purposes of Article 1(5) of the Directive, if the Law does not include the elements necessary to assess the environmental impact of a project but, on the contrary, requires a study to be carried out for that purpose, which must be drawn up subsequently, and if the adoption of other measures are needed in order for the developer to be entitled to proceed with the project.

[The direct effect of Article 4(2) and 2(1) of Directive 85/337]

68. . . . the national court is essentially asking whether Articles 4(2) and 2(1) of the Directive are to be interpreted as meaning that, where the discretion conferred by those provisions has been exceeded by the legislative or administrative authorities of a Member State, individuals may rely on those provisions before a court of that Member State against the national authorities and thus obtain from the latter the set-ting aside of the national rules or measures incompatible with those provisions.

69. As regards the right of individuals to rely on a directive and of the national court to take it into consideration, the Court has already held that it would be incompatible with the binding effect conferred on directives by Article 189 of the EC Treaty (now Article 249 EC) for the possibility for those concerned to rely on the obligation which directives impose to be excluded in principle. Particularly where the Community authorities have, by directive, imposed on Member States the obligation to pursue a particular course of conduct, the effectiveness of such an act would be diminished if individuals were prevented from relying on it in legal proceedings and if national courts were prevented from taking it into consideration as a matter of Community law in determining whether the national legislature, in exercising its choice as to the form and methods for implementing the directive, had kept within the limits of its discretion set out in the directive (Case 51/76 *Verbond van Nederlandse Ondernemingen* v. *Inspecteur der invoerrechten en Accijnen* [1977] ECR 113, paragraphs 22, 23 and 24, and *Kraaijeveld*, cited above, paragraph 56) . . .

71. . . . therefore . . . Articles 4(2) and 2(1) of the Directive are to be interpreted as meaning that, where the discretion conferred by those provisions has been exceeded by the legislative of administrative authorities of a Member State, individuals may rely on those provisions before a court of that Member State against the national authorities and thus obtain from the latter the setting aside of the national rules or measures incompatible with those provisions. In such a case, it is for the authorities of the Member State to take, according to their relevant powers, all the general or particular measures necessary to ensure that projects are examined in order to determine whether they are likely to have significant effects on the environment and, if so, to ensure that they are subject to an impact assessment.

Commentary

I. The Interpretation of "Other Procedures" and "Detailed Legislation" in Directive 85/337

(1) The point of departure in this case was relatively clear: the Italian competent authorities wanted to restructure Bolzano Airport but were not keen to execute an environmental impact assessment in conformity with the requirements of Directive 85/337, probably because they were afraid that there would be too much objection of the population affected during the procedure under Article 6(2)[189] of Directive 85/337. Therefore, they provided for another procedure[190] and, furthermore, included the airport project in a plan which was adopted by (regional) legislation.[191] The Court thus had the opportunity of clarifying the meaning of different provisions of Directive 85/337 and their impact on the national provisions. In doing so,

---

[189] Directive 85/337 (n. 188 *supra*), Art. 6(2): "Member States shall ensure that:—any request for development consent and any information gathered pursuant to Art. 5 are made available to the public,—the public concerned is given the opportunity to express an opinion before the project is initiated."

[190] An alternative procedure is permitted, see Directive 85/337 (n. 188 *supra*), Art. 2(2): "The environmental impact assessment may be integrated into the existing procedures for consent to projects in the Member States, or, failing this, into other procedures or into procedures to be established to comply with the aims of this Directive".

[191] See in this context Directive 85/337 (n. 188 *supra*), Art. 1(5): "The Directive shall not apply to projects the details of which are adopted by a specific act of national legislation, since the objectives of this Directive, including that of supplying information, are achieved through the legislative process".

the Court referred more to the objectives of the Directive than to its wording, as this wording was not very precise.

(2) With regard to the alternative assessment method, the Court's conclusion are far-reaching: Article 2(2) of Directive 85/337 requires respect for the aims of that Directive. These aims can be obtained only if all elements mentioned in Article 3 of the Directive[192] are identified, described and assessed. In the case of Bolzano Airport, it appears from paragraph 51 of the judgment that the alternative assessment which the Italian authorities had undertaken did not include, according to the national court, an assessment of the air and noise impact of the airport. Now, it could well be that Law 3/95 did require an assessment study to be made which included all factors mentioned in Article 3 of Directive 85/337 and that it was just the contractor who omitted to assess the noise and air impact. The Court did not differentiate between the two cases. My understanding of its ruling is that a Member State may well choose an alternative assessment method: however, it must then scrupulously observe—in the legislation fixing the alternative method as well as in the concrete, specific assessment itself—that all elements of Article 3 of Directive 85/337 are assessed.

The same reasoning applies with regard to Articles 5 to 10 of Directive 85/337 and in particluar Article 6(2): where the public concerned[193] does not have the opportunity to express its opinion during the assessment procedure, either because the legislation excludes that possibility or because this exclusion takes place during the alternative assessment procedure, the alternative method is not valid.

(3) The Court's observations as regards the derogation for projects which are adopted by specific legislation (Article 1(5) of Directive 85/337), a provision which must be interpreted restrictively as it limits the Directive's field of application,[194] are of high relevance, too. Indeed, the Court underlines that the decision to grant planning consent must be replaced by the legislation in question. Where thus further studies are necessary after the adoption of the legislation in question, as in the present case, in particular on the direct or indirect effects of the project or where the development consent contains conditions which have not been laid down in the legislation, the legislation is to be considered as not being sufficiently detailed; then, it does not fulfil the requirements of Article 1(5). The legislative act must thus lay down "all the elements of the project relevant to the environmental impact assessment",[195] this means in practice that the legislature, before adopting the act, must examine the direct and indirect effects of the project. And the Court's

---

[192] Directive 85/337 (n. 188 *supra*), Art. 3: "The environmental impact assessment will identify, describe and assess in an appropriate manner, in the light of each individual case and in accordance with the Arts. 4 to 11, the direct and indirect effects of a project on the following factors:—human beings, fauna and flora,—soil, water, air climate and the landscape,—the interaction between the actors mentioned in the first and second indents,—material assets and the cultural heritage."

[193] It should be noted that Directive 85/337 talks in its sixth recital of "the people . . . concerned".

[194] Court of Justice, Case C–287/98, *Linster*, (2000) ECR I–6917, para. 49.

[195] Para. 59 of the Judgment.

reference to the sixth recital, though not entirely clear on this point, appears to require that also in the case of a specific act of national legislation the people concerned by the project must have the opportunity to express an opinion on the project.

This understanding was confirmed by a later judgment. In Case C–287/98, the Court interpreted the sixth recital as requiring, in the case of Article 1(5), that the legislature has available to it information equivalent to that which would be available to the competent authority in an ordinary procedure for authorising a project.[196] The minimum requirement which therefore would always have to be available is "a description of the project comprising information on the site, design and size of the project, a description of the measures envisaged in order to avoid, reduce and, if possible remedy significant adverse effects, and the data required to identify and assess the main effects which the project is likely to have on the environment".[197] The Court provides for a derogation from these provisions in cases, in particular, where several alternatives of the project were studied in detail, on the basis of information supplied which were considered by the legislature as having an equivalent environmental impact.

With this interpretation, the requirements for the application of the derogatory provision of Article 1(5) of the Directive appear rather high. The judgment might thus reduce the zeal with which Member States resorted, in the past, to this provision: the bridge on the Oeresund between Denmark and Sweden, the bridge over the Tejo at Lisbonne, motorway and railway projects for the new German *Länder* after the 1990 unification—the bigger a project is, the smaller seems to be the inclination of authorities to have an environment impact assessment made which is in line with Directive 85/337.

This judgment therefore gives powerful arguments to citizens, environmental groups and others which oppose specific projects. They may claim the full respect of Directive 85/337 and in particular of its Articles 3 and 5 to 10. And they may claim that prior to the adoption of any derogatory legislation, "all the elements" that is all direct and indirect effects of a project be examined by the legislature.

(4) The Court of Justice has not yet clearly pronounced its opinion on two aspects relating to the application of Directive 85/337. These questions are first how to interpret the requirement in Article 3 that the direct and indirect effects of a project must be "identified, described and assessed". In my opinion, this implies a written form of the impact assessment, since one cannot really "describe" the effect of a project in a non-written form. A complainant cannot find out whether all effects, including, as in the present case, noise and air impacts, have been identified and assessed, if the description is to be allowed to be made orally or in the mind of the responsible officials only.

Secondly, it is not yet clear what consequences flow from the choice of a wrong procedure, such as in the present case. This question will be discussed below.

---

[196] Court of Justice, Case C–287/98 (n. 194 *supra*), para. 54.
[197] Court of Justice, Case C–287/98 (n. 194 *supra*), para. 55.

II. The Direct Effect and the Useful Effect of Directive 85/337

(5) The most relevant parts of the judgment concern the questions of the direct effect of Directive 85/337. The Court unambiguously states that individuals may rely on the provisions of Articles 4(2) and 2(1) before a national court and thus obtain "the setting aside of the national rules or measures incompatible with it" (paragraph 71). As Articles 4(2) and 2(1) give some discretion to Member States[198] whether or not to make an environmental impact assessment for projects listed in Annex II to the Directive, this means that any individual may challenge such a decision in court on the ground that the discretion has not been exercised properly, and as long as the errors, omissions or other deficiencies are significant.[199] In such a case, the question whether the authorities erred in not making an environmental impact assessment is a question not of admissibility of the court action but of substance.

The judgment therefore makes any administrative decision on an Annex II project subject to judicial control, reducing by this the discretionary power of the administration. And where an individual can prove that significant effects of a project are likely to occur the administrative decision not to have an EIA made becomes defective.

(6) The judgment states only that individuals may rely on certain provisions of Community law before a national court. The "direct effect doctrine", which underlies this conclusion of the Court of Justice, needs some further explanation.

While Community regulations are directly applicable in all Member States, for and against individuals, directives are addressed to Member States only and oblige these Member States to reach a certain result (Article 249 EC Treaty). Member States therefore have to transpose these requirements into their national legal order. Normally, a directive does not have effects in favour or against persons before it has been transposed into the national legal order.

To this concept, the Court of Justice has made an exception. It argues that a Member State which has not or not completely or correctly transposed the provisions of a directive into national law is not allowed to invoke, as against an individual, the fact of its own omission. Therefore, where a specific provision of a directive is unconditional and sufficiently precise, an individual may rely on that provision against all local, regional or national public authorities of that Member State, if these authorities want to apply the national provision which is in contradiction with the provision of the directive in question. Furthermore, all public authorities of a Member State are obliged to set aside the provision of national law in question and to apply instead the directly applicable provision of Community law.

---

[198] See the wording of these provisions and a discussion on their discretionary effect in the discussion of the *Kraaijeveld* case, C–73/95 [1996] ECR I–5403, *supra* p. 42 *et seq.*

[199] An example of "significant" omissions might be the present case: it is clear that noise amission from the take-off and landing of aeroplanes are a very relevant effect of an airport. And the omission to let the people concerned express their opinion on the project is one of the key provisions of Directive 85/337; thus, any such omission is always significant.

(7) The core of this doctrine is the thought that a Member State shall not "profit" from its own inertia; had the Member State correctly transposed Community law, then the individual would have benefitted from the Community provision.[200] Thus, for instance, where the use of a chemical substance is authorised under Community law, but prohibited under the national legislation of a Member State, and this Member State has not yet transposed into national law the provision authorising that substance, the individual may invoke the Community provision and use the substance in question.[201] Conversely, where Community law prohibits a substance and national law authorises it, a Member State which has not yet prohibited that substance may not rely on Community law and take action against an individual; indeed, in this case the Community provision would play in favour of the Member State in question. Since, however, the doctrine is based on the idea of a sanction against an inactive Member State, it would not be of application in such a case.[202] In the same way, the doctrine could not be invoked by an individual against another individual, as it is meant to be a sanction against the Member State which has not correctly transposed Community law.[203]

(8) There is some discussion when a provision of Community law is unconditional and sufficiently precise. The Court stated in this regard that a "Community provision is unconditional where it is not subject, in its implementation or effects, to the taking of any measure either by the institutions of the Community or by Member States".[204] And "a provision is sufficiently precise to be relied on by an individual and applied by the court where the obligation which it imposes is set out in unequivocal terms".[205]

In the present case, it is perhaps doubtful whether these two conditions are really fulfilled, as Articles 4(2) and 2(1) of Directive 85/337 gave a discretionary power to Member States.[206] It is for that reason, I presume, that the Court talked of the "effectiveness" of Community law. Indeed, in the *Kraaijeveld* case,[207] the Court of Justice had used a wording which was very similar to the wording of paragraph 69

---

[200] Court of Justice, Cases 8/81, *Becker* [1982] ECR 53; 103/88, *Fratelli Costanzo* [1989] ECR I–1839; C–319/97, *Kortas* [1999] ECR I–3143.

[201] This was the situation in Case C–319/97 (n. 200 *supra*).

[202] An example of this kind is Case 80/86, *Kolpinghuis*, [1987] ECR 3982.

[203] Court of Justice, Cases C–152/84 *Marshall* [1986] ECR 723; C–91/92, *Dori* [1994] ECR I–3325; for a detailed discussion whether such a restriction is appropriate see Advocate General Lenz in Case C–91/92, para. 43 *et seq*. It seems, however, that the Court, with its judgment in the *Dori* case, had wished to bring this discussion to an end; see also Case C–192/94, *El Corte Inglés* [1996] ECR I–1281.

[204] Court of Justice, Case C–236/92, *Difesa della Cava* [1994] ECR I–484.

[205] Court of Justice, Case C–236/92 (n. 204 *supra*).

[206] See for further discussions on the direct effect doctrine L Krämer, "The Direct Effect of Community Environmental Law", in L Krämer, *Focus on European Environmental Law* (2nd edn., Sweet & Maxwell, London, 1997), 78.

[207] Court of Justice, Case C–73/95, *Kraaijeveld* (n. 198 *supra*). For a discussion of this case, see p. 42 *supra*.

of the present case.[208] In both cases, though, the Court did not use the words "direct effect", but referred to the "useful effect" (*Kraaijeveld*) or "effectiveness" (the present case). The likely reason for this wording is that the Court wanted to avoid the discussion whether a Community provision which grants a certain discretion to Member States, is really "sufficiently precise".

(9) However, the basic thought of the direct effect doctrine also applies here: as Articles 4(2) and 2(1) of Directive 85/337 provide for a very subtle balance between the necessity to make an environmental impact assessment and Member States' discretion to make or not to make such an assessment, it must be ensured that this balance is reflected in the national transposing legislation as well as in the individual administrative measure to grant development consent in a specific case. It does therefore seem that the Court talks of a "direct effect", where provisions of Community law are unconditional and sufficiently precise, but that it uses the term "useful effect" or "effectiveness" where this is not quite certain.

Be that as it may, the effect of the Court's statement in paragraph 71 of the present case is that individuals may argue before a national court that national legislation or an administrative measure has not exercised well the discretionary power of Articles 4(2) and 2(1) of Directive 85/337 and that this legislation or measure must therefore be set aside.

III. The Consequences of the Direct Effect in National Law

(10) What does it mean when the Court argues that the individual may obtain the setting aside of national legislation or national measures which do not, in a specific case, conform to the requirements of Articles 4(2) and 2(1) of Directive 85/337. "Setting aside" means that the provisions of Laws 27/92 and 3/95 could not apply to the development consent procedure for Bolzano Airport; the same would apply to any administrative decision which would not precisely follow the interpretation of Articles 4(2) and 2(1) of Directive 85/337 as determined by the Court of Justice. The Italian authorities would then have either to give a new development consent or adopt new specific legislation; in both cases, they would have to respect the Court's judgment in the present case. In practice, this leads to the conclusion that any development consent which is granted for Bolzano Airport and which does not respect Directive 85/337 as interpreted by the Court of Justice, is not valid.

---

[208] Court of Justice, Case C–72/95 (n. 198 *supra*), para. 56: "As regards the right of an individual to invoke a directive and of the national court to take it into consideration, the Court has already held that it would be incompatible with the binding effect attributed to a directive by Art. 189 to exclude, in principle, the possibility that the obligation which it imposes may be invoked by those concerned. In particular, where the Community authorities have, by directive, imposed on Member States the obligation to pursue a particular course of conduct, the useful effect of such an act would be weakened if individuals were prevented from reying on it before their national courts, and if the latter were prevented from taking it into consideration as an element of Community law in order to rule whether the national legislature, in exercising the choice open to it as to the form and methods for implementation, has kept within the limits of its discretion set out in the directive . . .".

The Court has not yet stated what would happen if a national legislature or administration nevertheless gives development consent to a project without an environment impact assessment being made first. It is well known that in Germany and in some other Member States, courts argue that there is no sanction for the breach of the provisions of Directive 85/337; thus even if an environmental impact assessment had to be made, but was in practice not made, these courts consider the development consent valid.

(11) If one thinks the doctrine of the direct effect and of the useful effect to an end, this position cannot be defended. Indeed, it is very obvious that the objectives of Directive 85/337 would be completely undermined if local, regional or national administrations could give development consent to projects without such an assessment, though this would have been necessary under Directive 85/337—including the interpretation of Articles 4(2) and 2(1) as given by the Court—and such development consent would be valid. In my opinion, the useful effect of Directive 85/337 rather requires that a development consent which is given without an environmental impact assessment that was required under Directive 85/337 must be set aside. This development consent is therefore not valid.

It is to be hoped that the Court soon finds an opportunity to clarify its ideas about this question which has very great practical importance.

(12) In a completely different context, the Court of Justice had already to decide on the consequences of a breach of Comunity law.[209] Mrs. von Colson and Kamann had applied for jobs in Germany, but had been refused those jobs, in breach of the provisions of Directive 76/207.[210] For such cases, this Directive provided that Member States had to introduce into their national legal systems such measures as were necesary to enable persons who considered themselves wronged by discrimination to pursue their claims by judicial process. German law provided for such cases that persons could obtain compensation for losses actually incurred through reliance on an expectation ("*Vertrauensschaden*"). In the specific case, that would have meant the reimbursement of the tram ticket to the two job applicants.

The Court of Justice held that it was for the Member States to determine which kind of sanctions they wanted to apply. However, any sanction had to be "such as to guarantee real and effective judicial protection" and had to have a "real deterrent effect" on the employer. Purely nominal amounts such as the reimbursement of expenses incurred "would not satisfy the requirements of an effective transposition of the directive". And "national courts are required to interpret their national law in the light of the wording and purpose of the directive in order to achieve the result referred to in the third paragraph of Article 189". In other terms, if German law excluded compensation other than the "*Vertrauensschaden*"—this point was contested—the German court had to set aside this law and provide for

---

[209] Court of Justice, Case 14/83, *von Colson and Kamann* [1984] ECR 1891.
[210] Directive 76/207 on the implementation of the principle of equal treatment for men and women as regards access to employment, vocational training and promotion, and working conditions [1976] OJ L39/40.

effective, adequate compensation with a deterring effect; and this required to go beyond purely nominal compensation.

(13) In Case 106/89, the Court expressly referred to Case 14/83 and confirmed that "the Member States' obligation arising from a directive to achieve the result envisaged by the directive and their duty under Article 5 of the Treaty to take all appropriate measures, whether general or particular, to ensure the fulfilment of that obligation, is binding on all the authorities of Member States including, for matters within their jurisdiction, the courts".[211] The Court therefore requested the national court to interpret national law against the wording of that law, if this was the only way to satisfy the requirements of Community law.[212]

For the discussion here, all will depend on whether a full and effective application of Directive 85/337 requires that a development consent which, in breach of Directive 85/337, is granted without a preceding environmental impact assessment is invalid and may only be issued once the environmental impact assessment has been made. In my opinion, it is as well that this is the case.

(14) Finally, the Court stated that where neither the direct effect or useful effect doctrine nor the Community-minded interpretation of a directive could achieve the result prescribed by a directive, "Community law requires the Member States to make good damage caused to individuals through failure to transpose a directive, provided that three conditions are fulfilled. First, the purpose of the directive must be to grant rights to individuals. Second, it must be possible to identify the content of those rights on the basis of the provisions of the directive. Finally, there must be a causal link between the breach of the State's obligation and the damage suffered".[213]

This case law, which is not relevant for the present case, is just mentioned to indicate the different options which are available for cases, where Community law and national law differ.

---

[211] Court of Justice, Case C–106/89, *Marleasing* [1990] ECR I–4135, para. 8.

[212] In the case in question, a Community directive provided for an exhaustive list of grounds for a declaration of nullity of a public limited company: Spanish law provided for supplementary grounds.

[213] Court of Justice, Case C–91/92 (n. 203 *supra*), para. 27; Joined Cases C–6/90 and C–9/90, *Francovich* [1991] ECR I–5357.

8. IMPLEMENTATION BY CIRCULAR

Judgment of the Court (Sixth Chamber) of 7 November 1996
Case C–262/95

Commission of the European Communities
v. *Federal Republic of Germany*
[1996] ECR I–5729

Facts

In 1976, the Community adopted legislation on the discharge of hazardous substances into waters.[214] This Directive provided that for specific substances of a list in Annex I the Community would subsequently fix emission limit values and quality objectives. Subsequently, the Community adopted five directives which fixed, for a number of substances, such emission limit values and quality objectives.[215] Member States had between 18 and 24 months to transpose the requirements of these directives into national law.

Germany had transposed the different directives by administrative circular. As the Commission considered the measures adopted by Germany inadequate to transpose the five directives into national law, in 1989, it started legal proceedings against Germany under Article 226 EC Treaty as regards one, and in 1992 as regards the other four directives; in 1995, it applied to the Court.

Judgment (extracts)

13/14. The Commission . . . submits that the directives at issue must be transposed in such a way as to guarantee their full application in a sufficiently clear and precise manner so that the persons concerned can ascertain the full extent of their

---

[214] Directive 76/464 on pollution caused by certain dangerous substances discharged into the aquatic environment of the Community, [1976] OJ L129/23.

[215] Directives 82/176 on limit values and quality objectives for mercury discharges by the chlor-alkali electrolysis industry [1982] OJ L81/29; 83/513 on limit values and quality objectives for cadmium discharges, [1983] OJ L291/1; 84/156 on limit values and quality objectives for mercury discharges by sectors other then the chlor-alkali electrolysis industry [1984] OJ L74/79; 84/491 on limit values and quality objectives for discharges of hexachlorocyclohexane [1984] OJ L274/11; 86/280 on limit values and quality objectives for discharges of certain dangerous substances included in List I of the Annex to Directive 76/464, [1986] OJ L181/6.

rights and, where appropriate, rely on them before national courts. So far as concerns the fixing of limit values for pollution based on directives relating to the protection of the environment, the Court has already noted the need to adopt provisions whose binding nature is undeniable.

15. In its defence, the Federal Republic of Germany notes that the Commission's complaint relates exclusively to the form of the transposition. Having regard to the case-law of the Courts, it abandons its argument that transposition by way of administrative circulars is adequate. In order to achieve transposition by way of statutory provisions, the legislative bodies are to include in the Wasserhaushaltsgesetz a provision conferring power to adopt regulations, which will enable the Federal Republic of Germany to transpose the directives at issue by means of regulations. The Federal Republic of Germany announced that such a law was to be adopted in spring 1996. However, the Federal Republic of Germany claims that, in substance, the directives at issue are already effectively transposed into German law.

16. In the present case, the Federal Republic of Germany does not deny that it has not adopted legally binding general measures to transpose the directives at issue.

17. In any event, it is settled case-law that a Member State may not plead provisions, practices or circumstances existing in its internal legal system in order to justify a failure to comply with the obligations and time-limits laid down in a directive (see, in particular, Case C–236/95 *Commission* v. *Greece* [1996] ECR I–0000, paragraph 18).

18. Since, on the expiry of the time-limits for the transposition at issue, the Federal Republic of Germany had not yet adopted measures to implement them, it must be held that, by not adopting, within the prescribed time-limits, the necessary measures to comply with the directives at issue . . . ,the Republic of Germany has failed to fulfil its obligations under those directives.

Commentary

I. *Transposing Directives by Circulars*

(1) Reading this judgment, it is surprising that this case was brought to the Court of Justice at all: the Commission had started legal proceedings against Germany on one directive as early as 1989, informing that Member State thus of its legal opinion. Germany did not really dispute the legal reasoning and admitted, during the procedure before the Court, that the case law of the Court supported the Commission's legal opinion. Furthermore, as early as 1991, the Court had issued two rather basic judgments which dealt with the transposition of Community environmental directives into national German law.[216] In both cases,

---

[216] Court of Justice, Cases C–131/88, *Commission* v. *Germany* [1991] ECR I–825 (groundwater pollution); C–361/88, *Commission* v. *Germany* [1991] ECR I–2567 (air pollution).

the Court had specified in great detail the requirements of Community law as regards the transposition of environmental provisions. The German authorities could not have had any serious doubt what the legal situation was. The opening of legal proceedings in the case of the four other directives in 1992 only confirmed the Commission's viewpoint.

As Germany was thus bound to amend its legislation anyway, its tactics can only have consisted in winning time, as it was clear that the procedure under Article 226 EC Treaty[217] would take a long time. And indeed, between the beginning of the procedure under Article 226 in the case of the four directives and the application to the Court, 34 months passed. The Court gave its judgment 15 months after the Commission's application. In total, thus, the procedure under Article 226 EC Treaty took 49 months. Germany which had not amended its legislation during that time, finally adopted legislation on 21 March 1997.[218] As the five directives had to be transposed from 1983 onwards, there was therefore a considerable gain in time until the provisions of Community law effectively appeared in the German legal order.

(2)   This procedural behaviour is not unique. At present, there is a case pending before the Court which involves the European Commission and France.[219] In that case France transposed Directive 80/778 on the quality of drinking water[220] into national law, but issued, in 1990, two ministerial circulars which allowed drinking water to be marketed which contained higher concentrations of pesticides and nitrates than allowed under Community law. France did not contest that its circulars were not compatible with the requirements of Directive 80/778. Yet, during the proceedings before the Court, it limited itself to announcing a new circular, which would repeal the older circulars.

(3)   Other cases may be mentioned: in Case 340/96,[221] the Court had to deal with legislation on drinking water in the United Kingdom which had to be enforced by the Secretary of State. However, a provision in the relevant legislation allowed the Secretary of State not to enforce that legislation when he was satisfied with an undertaking from the water company that the water would be brought into compliance with the law as quickly as possible. The Court held that the national substantive law gave the Secretary of State too much discretionary power.

---

[217] Art. 226 (ex Art. 169) EC Treaty: "If the Commission considers that a Member State has failed to fulfil an obligation under this Treaty, it shall deliver a reasoned opinion on the matter after giving the State concerned the opportunity to submit its observations.

If the State concerned does not comply with the opinion within the period laid down by the Commission, the latter may bring the matter before the Court of Justice".

[218] Bundesgesetzblatt 1997, I, p. 566.

[219] Case C–49/97, *Commission* v. *France*. The facts and the arguments of the parties in this case are taken from the Opinion of the Advocate General which was delivered on 17 September 1997.

[220] Directive 80/778 relating to the quality of water intended for human consumption OJ [1980] L229/11.

[221] Court of Justice, Case C–340/96, *Commission* v. *United Kingdom* [1999] ECR I–2023; this judgment will be discussed further on p. 185 *infra*.

Directive 80/68 on the protection of groundwater[222] provided among other things that an authorisation was necessary for the artificial enrichment of groundwater; such authorisation could be given only if there was no risk of pollution of the groundwater. The Netherlands had not transposed this last requirement and defended themselves before the Court, saying that authorisations would anyway be given only if there was no risk of groundwater pollution.[223] The Court, however, did not accept this defence and insisted on the necessity to have this phrase also transposed into national law. In Case C–131/88, Germany was criticised because its legislation provided for an authorisation of discharges into the groundwater, whereas Community law provided for a ban on such discharges. Germany argued that authorisations for discharges would not be granted; however, the Court insisted that the ban should be reproduced in German law.[224]

(4) The general preference for administrative measures rather than legislative provisions which is at the basis of all these actions is relatively easily understandable: in almost all Member States, the protection of the environment is, to a very large extent, in the hands of the administration, which takes, every day, numerous decisions and measures to authorise or to restrict, to permit, to accept or to tolerate. "The administration" is not an abstract, but consists of human beings which exercise, through their decisions, considerable influence on the behaviour of economic operators, individuals or others, and, at the same time, on the environment. The normal interest of an administration cannot be to see itself narrowed down in its discretionary power by legal provisions which are also binding upon the administration itself. Indeed, discussions with economic operators on the conditions to be put into a permit or conditions under which a discharge is allowed are less discretionary when there is a legal requirement that such and such limit must be respected or provision applied.

(5) The struggle on power has long gone beyond the problems of transposing, implementing and enforcing Community environmental law. For about ten years, Community environmental law has been drafted in a way which provides for large discretionary power of local, regional or national authorities to apply it. The best example of this is Directive 96/61[225] which provides that installations must use, as regards emissions into the air, water and soil, the "best available techniques" to prevent such emissions. However, it is up to the administration to determine in any specific case what the best available technique is. And this will not only lead to a rather limited degree of equal conditions for installations of the same kind in the Community, but also to an increased bargaining on the part of economic operators, who will be looking for the site with the least burdensome conditions.

---

[222] Directive 80/68 on the protection of groundwater against pollution caused by certain dangerous substances, [1980] OJ L20/43.

[223] Court of Justice, Case 291/84, *Commission v. Netherlands* [1987] ECR 3483.

[224] Court of Justice, Case C–131/88 (n. 216 *supra*).

[225] Directive 96/61 concerning integrated pollution prevention and control [1996] OJ L257/26.

II. *The Case Law on Transposing Directives by Circulars*

(6) As regards the transposition of Community environmental provisions, the case law of the Court of Justice is quite clear: Community directives must be transposed into national law in a way that guarantees "the full application of the directive in a sufficiently clear and precise manner so that, where the directive is intended to create rights for individuals, the persons concerned can ascertain the full extent of their rights and, where appropriate, rely on them before the national courts".[226]

It is not sufficient that a Member State *de facto* does not apply a provision which is contrary to Community law or, inversely, applies a provision of Community law without having transposed it into national law; this also applies where a provision of Community law has direct effect,[227] where, in other words, a citizen may invoke a (non-transposed) provision of Community law in court. Indeed, the Court is of the opinion that such a situation does not give sufficient legal certainty to persons. Therefore, it "has consistently held that the incompatibility of national legislation with Community provisions, even provisions which are directly applicable, can be finally remedied only by means of national provisions of a binding nature which have the same legal force as those which must be amended. Mere administrative practices, which by their nature are alterable at will by the authorities and are not given the appropriate publicity, cannot be regarded as constituting the proper fulfilment of obligations under the Treaty (see Case C–334/94 *Commission* v. *France* [1996] ECR I–1307, paragraph 30). Accordingly, the provisions of a directive must be implemented with unquestionable binding force and with the specificity, precision and clarity required in order to satisfy the requirements of legal certainty".[228]

Whenever a Community environmental provision intends to create rights and obligations for individuals, this provision must therefore be transposed into national law. This applies first of all to all emission limit values which are fixed, as an individual polluter may not exceed such limit values.[229] This furthermore applies to quality standards (quality objectives) which provide that a specific concentration

---

[226] Court of Justice, Cases C–59/89, *Commission* v. *Germany* [1991] ECR I–2607; C–14/90, *Commission* v. *France* [1991] ECR I–4331; see also Case C–197/96, *Commission* v. *France* [1997] ECR I–1489.

[227] On the direct-effect doctrine see p. 67 *supra.*

[228] Court of Justice, Case C–197/96 (n. 216 *supra*), paras. 14 and 15; see also Cases C–131/88 (n. 216 *supra*), para. 61; C–361/88 (n. 216 *supra*), para. 16; C–339/87, *Commission* v. *Netherlands* [1990] ECR 851, para. 25.

[229] Court of Justice, Case C–14/90 (n. 216 *supra*); Case C–361/88 (n. 216 *supra*), para. 16: "the obligation imposed on Member States to prescribe limit values not to be exceeded within specified periods and in specified circumstances, . . . is imposed 'in order to protect human health in particular'. It implies, therefore, that whenever the exceeding of the limit values could endanger human health, the persons concerned must be in a position to rely on mandatory rules in order to be able to assert their rights. Furthermore, the fixing of limit values in a provision whose binding nature is undeniable is also necessary in order that all those whose activitiesare liable to give rise to nuisances may ascertain precisely the obligations to which they are subject".

of pollutants in the air, the water or the soil may not be exceeded; in such a case, the permit for the emitting individual is influenced by this quality standards, which the emittant—together with other emittants—may not exceed. Here, the same reasoning as for limit values applies.

(7) Next, procedural requirements which intend to give rights to individuals need to be expressly transposed into national law.[230] This applies, for instance, to provisions on the content of a permit and on conditions in it, the application for an authorisation, the necessity of a study to be undertaken, the consultation of the public, the necessity to report to authorities etc. Finally, all provisions of Community law which are accessory to these aforementioned provisions, such as definitions, also need to be expressly transposed, as otherwise the notions of Community law could not be fully understood.[231]

(8) However, the obligation to transpose a Community provision into national law is not limited to those provisions which create rights and obligations for individuals. In Case 186/91,[232] the Court considered that the obligation, laid down in Directive 85/203,[233] to consult with other Member States prior to the fixing of concentration values for nitrogen dioxide in the air also needed to be transposed into national law as, otherwise, local or regional authorities might not be aware of their obligations.

In Case C–237/90,[234] the Court had to decide on a provision in Directive 80/778 on the quality of drinking water[235]. That provision allowed Member States to grant, under certain conditions, derogations from the requirements of the Directive; the Member States had to inform the Commission of these derogations. Germany had sub-delegated this ability to grant derogation to the *Länder*. The Court held that in such a case, Germany had to introduce a provision into its national law which asked the *Länder* to inform the German government of the derogations granted, in order to allow Germany to comply with its obligations under the Directive towards the Commission. The general obligation of the *Länder* which flowed from the system of a federal State, was not enough.

In view of these interpretations, the obligation to provide for an explicit transposition into Member States' law exists in my opinion also where a Member State

---

[230] See for instance, Court of Justice, Case C–131/88/n. 216 *supra*), para. 61: "the procedural provisions of the directive lay down, in order to guarantee effective protection of groundwater, precise and detailed rules which are intended to create rights and obligations for individuals. It follows that they must be incorporated into German law with the precision and clarity necessary in order to satisfy fully the requirement of legal certainty".

[231] To give an example: Directive 76/464 (n. 214 *supra*) fixes limit values and quality objectives for the discharge of dangerous substances into water. In Directive 80/779 on air quality limit values and guide values for sulphur dioxide and suspended particulates [1980] OJ L229/30, the notion "limit values" corresponds to the notion "quality objectives" in Directive 76/464.

[232] Court of Justice, Case 186/91, *Commission v. Belgium* [1993] ECR I–851.

[233] Directive 85/203 on air quality standards for nitrogen dioxide, [1985] OJ L87/1, Art. 11: "Where a Member State intends to fix, in a region near the border with one or more other Member States, values for concentrations of nitrogen dioxide in the atmosphere . . . it shall hold prior consultations with the Member States concerned".

[234] Court of Justice, Case C–237/90, *Commission v. Germany* [1992] ECR I–6103.

[235] Directive 80/778 (n. 220 *supra*).

is obliged, by virtue of a Community provision, on the one hand to adopt a clean-up plan or a management plan, on the other hand to establish a report on the implementation of a directive or regulation. The Court has not had to decide these issues.

(9) In the case of clean-up or management plans, individuals will be affected by such plans, in seeing obligations established, rights to see the content of the plan respected when individual decisions are taken in pursuance thereof etc. They are therefore entitled to know that there is a legal obligation for the Member State in question to establish a plan; this knowledge also allows them to participate in the discussions on the elaboration of the plan and influence its outcome. As the environment is not the property of the administration, the elaboration of a plan and its content cannot be left exclusively to the administration, but requires that all affected individuals have the chance to participate. The transposition of the Community obligation to make a plan thus creates legal certainty about the meaning, the impact and possible content of the plan.

(10) Reports on the implementation of a Commuinity directive are first of all to be established by the administration which has this obligation under Community law. However, implementation reports also inform individuals about the application of the Directive, the measures taken and to be taken, the future intentions, the account of the monitoring of the different provisions etc. Disposing of this kind of information allows individuals as well as companies to participate in the legal and political discussion whether the Directive in question had established the right balance between environmental and other—economic, public, leisure etc. —interests, whether a strengthening or any other revision of the Directive is necessary or opportune, whether specific areas have received special protection and whether that was appropriate, whether the national report was established at all or whether some political pressure on the Member State's government on the part of its own citizens is necessary to establish such a report, etc. The obligation to establish an implementation report is therefore not just an internal matter between the Commission's and the Member State's administration, but part of ensuring that citizens are capable of participating in the discussion on the appropriate amount of environmental protection within the European Union.

Where a Community provision exclusively concerns relations between the Member State and the Commission without affecting individuals, transposition into national law is not necessary. This concerns for instance a provision in Directive 75/442[236] which requests Member States to inform the Commission of any draft legislation to promote prevention, recycling or recovery of waste.[237]

(11) In the present case, the different Community directives which Germany had not transposed fixed emission limit values and quality standards (quality objectives) for a number of pollutants. As economic operators are obliged to

---

[236] Directive 75/442 on waste [1975] OJ L194/47; amended by Directive 91/156 [1971] OJ L78/32.
[237] Court of Justice, Case 380/87 [1989] ECR 2491.

respect these values, there could be no reasonable doubt about the obligation on Germany to transpose the requirements of the different directives into national law.[238]

9. COMMUNITY ENVIRONMENTAL LAW AND CRIMINAL LAW

Judgment of the Court (Fourth Chamber) of 26 September 1996
Case C–168/95

Reference for a preliminary ruling: Criminal proceedings
against Luciano Arcaro
[1996] ECR I–4705

Facts

Mr. Arcaro is the proprietor of an undertaking whose main activity is the working of precious metals. The Italian authorities prosecuted him for discharging cadmium from his plant into the River Bacchiglione, without having applied or obtained an authorisation for doing so.

Italian law differentiates between "new" and "existing" plants. For existing plants, no emission limit values for cadmium discharges have yet been fixed and the obligation to have an authorisation for cadmium discharges exists only once such emission limit values have been fixed. Mr. Arcaro's plant is an existing plant under Italian law.

The Italian court asked the Court of Justice, among others, whether it would be possible directly to apply Community directives against Mr. Arcaro, or "what other method of procedure may be adopted under a correct interpretation of Community law to achieve the elimination from national legislation of provisions which are incompatible with those of Community law, where the direct application of the latter would result in impairment of the citizen's legal position".

---

[238] Directive 76/464 (n. 214 *supra*), the "mother directive" of the five directives in question, is further discussed on p. 177 *infra*.

Judgment (extracts)

[The direct effect of a directive in criminal matters]

32. . . . Article 3 of Directive 76/464 is to be interpreted as making any discharge of cadmium, irrespective of the date on which the plant from which it comes commenced operation, subject to the issue of a prior authorisation.

33. . . . the national court wishes to ascertain in substance whether, in the absence of full transposition by a Member State within the time allowed of Directive 76/464, and therefore of Article 3 thereof, and of Directive 83/513, a public authority of that State may rely on that Article 3 against an individual, although this may impair that individual's position.

35. Having regard to a situation such as that with which the main proceedings are concerned, it is not necessary to examine whether Article 3 of the Directive is unconditional and sufficiently precise.

36. The Court has made it clear that the possibility of relying, before a national court, on an unconditional and sufficiently precise provision of a directive which has not been transposed exists only for individuals and only in relation to "each Member State to which it is addressed". It follows that a directive may not by itself create obligations for an individual and that a provision of a directive may not therefore be relied upon as such against such a person . . . The Court has stated that this case-law seeks to prevent a Member State from taking advantage of its own failure to comply with Community law.

37. In the same line of authority the Court has also ruled that a directive cannot, of itself and independently of a national law adopted by a Member State for its implementation, have the effect of determining or aggravating the liability in criminal law of persons who act in contravention of the provisions of that directive.

[Community law and national criminal law]

39. . . . the national court essentially seeks to ascertain, whether, upon a correct interpretation of Community law, there is a method of procedure allowing the national court to eliminate from national legislation provisions which are contrary to a provision of a directive which has not been transposed, where the latter provision may not be relied on before the national court.

40. It should be observed first of all that there is no such method of procedure in Community law.

41. It should be added that the Member States' obligation, arising under a directive to achieve the full result envisaged by the directive and their duty, under Article 5 of the Treaty, to take all appropriate measures, whether general or particular, to ensure fulfilment of that obligation, are binding on all the authorities of Member States including, for matters within their jurisdiction, the courts. It follows that, in applying national law, the national court called upon to interpret that law is required to do so, as far as possible, in the light of the wording and purpose of the directive in order to achieve the result pursued by the directive and thereby comply with the third paragraph of Article 189 of the Treaty.

42. However, that obligation of the national court to refer to the content of the directive when interpreting the relevant rules of its own national law reaches a limit where such an interpretation leads to the imposition on an individual of an obligation laid down by a directive which has not been transposed or, more especially, where it has the effect of determining or aggravating, on the basis of the directive and in the absence of a law enacted for its implementation, the liability in criminal law of persons who act in contravention of that directive's provisions.

Commentary

I. Direct Effect and Criminal Law

(1) The case, which was the basis of this judgment, is simple as well as scandalous: Community legislation requires Member States to introduce legislation that cadmium discharges into waters must be authorised and must be kept within certain limits that were fixed at Community level.[239] This legislation has been effective since 1985 as regards cadmium discharges and since the late 1970s as regards authorisations. Italy introduced national legislation only for new plants. Thus, the great majority of cadmium discharging plants may do so without any prior authorisation, any necessity to respect limit values and any sanction. And also Mr. Arcaro could not be prosecuted, as his criminal action, committed about 10 years after the entry into effect of the Community legislation, was not a criminal offence under Italian law.

Italy had been condemned by the Court of Justice in 1990, because it had not completely transposed Directive 83/513 into national law.[240] In 1992, it adopted new legislation;[241] the European Commission considered this legislation to be satisfactory without taking the fact that the numerous existing installations were not covered by this new legislation up with the Italian authorities.[242]

---

[239] Directive 76/464 on pollution caused by certain dangerous substances discharged into the aquatic environment of the Community [1976] OJ L129/23; Directive 83/513 on limit values and quality objectives for cadmium discharges [1983] OJ L291/1.

[240] Court of Justice, Case C–70/89, *Commission* v. *Italy* [1990] ECR I–4817.

[241] Decree no. 133 of 27 January 1992 on industrial discharge of dangerous substances into the aquatic environment, *Gazzetta Ufficiale* no. 41, Supplement 34, of 19 February 1992.

[242] The Commission's *Ninth Annual Report on Monitoring the Application of Community Law (1991)* [1992] OJ C250/1, indicates on p. 122 that the Commission had issued a reasoned opinion under Art. 228 (ex Art. 171) EC Treaty against Italy, because that country had not followed the Court judgment in Case C–70/89 (n. 240 *supra*). The *Tenth Annual Report on Monitoring the Application of Community Law (1992)* [1993] OJ C233/161 mentions that this case was filed and the *Eleventh Annual Report* (1993) [1994] OJ C154/1, lists on p. 171 the Court judgments which Italy had not yet

(2) In an attempt to find a way of nevertheless applying Italian criminal law against Mr. Arcaro, the Italian court first asked the Court of Justice whether it was possible to apply the doctrine of "direct effect".[243] The answer from the Court of Justice was clear and consistent with its settled case law: the direct application of Community directives in Member States can exceptionally be accepted in favour of an individual, not against an individual.[244] But in no case may Community law be used against or to the detriment of an individual. The reason for this is that "this case-law seeks to prevent a Member State from taking advantage of its own failure to comply with Community law".[245]

(3) One might well argue whether it is really an advantage for Italy that environmental pollution is, contrary to what Community law provides, possible without a penal sanction and whether it is not a disadvantage that environmental impairment may not be sanctioned by Italian courts. However, the Court's case law on direct effect does not look at general interest questions, but merely at the question whether the direct application of Community law which is not transposed by public authorities would bring the individual citizen into an advantageous or disadvantageous position.

In my opinion, one could and should consider allowing a direct application of untransposed Community law in all cases where important assets of general Community interest—human rights, environmental protection—would be impaired by the omission to apply Community law. Human rights and environmental protection do not stop at national frontiers, and it is not really clear why they should be prevented from national legal orders to deploy their full effect— perhaps not so much in criminal law for reasons which will be discussed in a moment, but rather in administrative law.

II. *Community Environmental Law and Criminal Law*

(4) The national court then wanted to know whether any other possibility existed of applying Community law within the Italian legal order and thus allowed the prosecution of Mr. Arcaro. The Court of Justice again referred to earlier jurisprudence which provided for interpretation of national law in the light of Community legislation.[246] As the Court could not proceed to such interpretation of Italian law itself—this is the responsability of the national court—it referred only to the general principles of interpretation.

However, the Court drew a clear limit: all interpretatian of Italian law must stop where it would lead to a criminal sanction against Mr. Arcaro without a correspond-

implemented. Case 70/89 does not figure on that list. This can only mean that the reasoned opinion was no longer pursued against Italy.

   [243]   See for a discussion of the "direct effect" of directives p. 67 *supra*.
   [244]   Court of Justice, Cases C–91/92 *Dori* [1994] ECR I–3325; 192/94 *El Corte Inglés* [1996] ECR I–1281; see also p. 67 *supra*.
   [245]   Para. 37 of the judgment.
   [246]   Court of Justice, Cases C–106/89, *Marleasing* [1990] ECR I–4135; Case C–334/92, *Wagner Miret* [1993] ECR I–6911; C–91/92, *Dori* (n. 244 *supra*); see also p. 47 *supra*.

ing provision in Italian criminal law. This statement made in paragraph 42 of the judgment is just another description of the general principle "*nullum crimen sine lege*", a principle which is laid down in Article 7 of the European Convention on Human Rights.[247] Human rights are general principles of law and the Treaty on European Union requires the Community institutions to respect these human rights.[248] In concrete terms this means, according to the Court of Justice, that Community law provisions may not be interpreted in such a way as to give rise to results which are incompatible with these human rights.[249] Already for this reason, the Court was not prepared to accept any interpretation of Community law provisions which could have enabled the Italian court to pronounce a penal sanction against Mr. Arcaro.

(5) The EC Treaty does not cover criminal law. It is only very exceptionally that the Treaty talks of "penalty" and, when it so does, it rather refers to "penalty payment".[250] Article 229 provides that regulations "may give the Court of Justice unlimited jurisdiction with regard to the penalties provided for in such regulations"—which implies that such penalties may be fixed. However, environmental regulations never made use of that: Regulation 880/92 on the eco-label prohibits false or misleading advertising or the use of labels or logos which may lead to confusion, but does not contain any provision on sanctions at all.[251] Regulation 2455/92 on the export or import of dangerous chemicals does not provide for any provision on sanctions at all.[252] Regulation 1836/93 on the eco-audit scheme requests Member States to provide for appropriate legal provisions for cases where the Regulation is not respected,[253] without clarifying the nature of such provisions. Regulation 3093/94 on the substances that deplete the ozone layer provides that Member States shall lay down sanctions to be applied for breach against that

---

[247] European Convention for the Protection of Human Rights and Fundamental Freedoms, signed in Rome on 4 November 1950, Art. 7: "1. No one shall be held guilty of any criminal offence on account of any act or omission which did not constitute a criminal offence under national or international law at the time when it was committed. Nor shall a heavier penalty be imposed than the one that was applicable at the time the criminal offence was committed.

2. This Art. shall not prejudice the trial and punishment of any person for any act or omission which, at the time when it was committed, was criminal according to the general principles of law recognised by civilised nations".

[248] Treaty on European Union [1997] OJ C340/145, Art. 6(2): "The Union shall respect fundamental rights, as guaranteed by the European Convention for the Protection of Human Rights and Fundamental Freedoms signed in Rome on 4 November 1950 and as they result from the constitutional traditions common to the Member States, as general principles of Community law".

[249] Court of Justice, Joined Cases 97–99/87, *Dow Chemical* [1989] ECR 3165.

[250] See Art. 83 which allows regulations or directives in the area of competition policy to make provision for "penalty payments"; Art. 228 which allows the Court of Justice to impose a "penalty payment" on a Member State.

[251] Regulation 880/92 on a Community eco-label award scheme [1992] OJ L99/1.

[252] Regulation 2455/92 concerning the export and import of certain dangerous chemicals [1992] OJ L251/13.

[253] Regulation 1836/93 allowing voluntary participation by companies in the industrial sector in a Community eco-management and audit scheme [1993] OJ L168/1, Art. 16: "Member States shall take appropriate legal or administative measures in case of non-compliance with the provisions of this Regulation".

Regulation.[254] Regulation 259/93 on the shipment of waste provides that the Member States shall "prohibit and punish illegal traffic" of waste,[255] but does not give any further detail. Only Regulation 338/97 on trade in endangered species is more specific: its provision on sanctions enumerates the infringements of the Regulation for which "appropriate" sanctions must be introduced.[256]

(6) As regulations hardly contain any criminal sanction, it comes as no surprise that environmental directives do not provide for sanctions at all. In the different directives, Member States are just asked to take the necessary steps in order to transpose the requirements of the directive into national law.[257] This does not mean, though, that Member States are not obliged to adopt criminal sanctions in order to ensure the complete application and enforcement of a Community directive. The Court of Justice has specified these requirements in a landmark decision of 1989,[258] where it stated: "where Community legislation does not specifically provide any penalty for an infringement or refers for that purpose to national laws, regulations and administrative provisions, Article 5 of the Treaty requires the Member States to take all measures necessary to guarantee the application and effectiveness of Community law.

For that purpose, whilst the choice of penalties remains within their discretion, they must ensure in particular that infringements of Community law are penalized under conditions, both procedural and substantive, which are analogous to those applicable to infringements of national law of a similar nature and importance and which, in any event, make the penalty effective, proportionate and dissuasive.

Moreover, the national authorities must proceed, with respect to infringements of Community law, with the same diligence as that which they bring to bear in implementing corresponding national laws".

(7) These words of national sanctions being "effective, proportionate and dissuasive" since then have become the standard formula used to describe the obligation of

---

[254] Regulation 3093/94 on substances that deplete the ozone layer [1994] OJ L333/1, Art. 19: "Each Member State shall determine the penalties to be imposed in the event of any failure to comply with this Regulation or with any national measures taken to implement it".

[255] Regulation 259/93 on the supervision and control of shipments of waste within, into and out of the European Community [1993] OJ L30/1, Art. 26(5).

[256] Regulation 338/97 on the protection of species of wild fauna and flora by regulating trade therein [1997] OJ L61/1, Art. 16: "1. Member States shall take appropriate measures to ensure the imposition of sanctions for at least the following infringements of this Regulation: (a)–(m) . . . 2. The measures referred to in para. 1 shall be appropriate to the nature and gravity of the infringement anmd shall include provisions relating to the seizure and, where appropriate, confiscation of specimens".

[257] A recent example is Art. 18 of Directive 99/31 on the landfill of waste [1999] OJ L182/1, which reads: "1. Member States shall bring into force the laws, regulations and administrative provisions necessary to comply with this Directive not later than two years after its entry into force. They shall forthwith inform the Commission thereof.

When Member States adopt these measures, they shall contain a reference to this Directive or shall be accompanied by such reference on the occasion of their official publication. The methods of making such a reference shall be laid down by the Member States.

2. Member States shall communicate the texts of the provisions of national law which they adopt in the field covered by this Directive to the Commission".

[258] Court of Justice, Case 68/88, *Commission* v. *Greece* [1989] ECR 2965.

Member States as regards sanctions.[259] The problem is that the European Commission does not monitor, under Articles 211[260] EC Treaty, whether Member States have provided for effective, proportionate and dissuasive sanctions when they transpose a directive into national law. There is not one single environmental case where the Commission took legal action against a Member State under Article 226 EC Treaty,[261] because that Member State had not adopted appropriate sanctions.

III. Community Co-operation in Criminal Matters

(8) The great majority of criminal matters come under Title VI of the Treaty on European Union which provides for co-operation between Member States. The procedure for judicial co-operation differs from the procedure set up under the EC Treaty on a number of points; the most important of these are:

—The right of initiative for action is with any Member State and with the European Commission, whereas in the EC Treaty the Commission has a monopoly of making proposals (Article 34(2) of the Treaty on European Union);

—Generally, the European Parliament's role is purely consultative (Article 39 of the Treaty on European Union);

—There is only a rather limited judicial control by the Court of Justice (Article 35 of the Treaty on European Union)

—According to Article 34 of the Treaty on European Union, decisions may take the following form:

(a) common positions, "defining the approach of the Union to a particular matter";

(b) framework decisions, which "shall be binding upon the Member States as to the result to be achieved but shall leave to the national authorities the choice of form and methods". The Treaty adds that such framework decisions "shall not entail direct effect". Obviously, the jurisdiction of the Court of Justice which is so largely based on the concept that citizens in the European Union shall also derive rights from directives and other provisions of EC law was considered too favourable to citizens;[262]

(c) other decisions, which also "shall be binding and shall not entail direct effect";

---

[259] Treaty on European Union [1997] OJ C340/145. Title VI has the heading: "Provisions on Police and Judicial Cooperation in criminal matters".

[260] Art. 211 (ex Art. 155) EC Treaty: "In order to ensure the proper functioning and development of the common market, the Commission shall:—ensure that the provisions of this Treaty and the measures taken by the institutions pursuant thereto are applied; . . .".

[261] Art. 226 (ex Art. 169) EC Treaty: "If the Commission considers that a Member State has failed to fulfil an obligation under this Treaty, it shall deliver a reasoned opinion on the matter after giving the State concerned the opportunity to submit its observations.

If the State concerned does not comply with the opinion within the period laid down by the Commission, the latter may bring the matter before the Court of Justice".

[262] On the direct effect case-law see p. 47 *supra.*

(d) conventions, i. e. treaties of public international law. These conventions enter into force once they have been ratified by half of the Member States.

(9) The Council of Europe worked out, between 1991 and 1998, a draft "Convention on the protection of the environment through criminal law". This draft Convention met limited enthusiasm of the Contracting Parties of the Council of Europe. As the EC Member States realised that it would be desirable to have a common basic set of rules on criminal sanctions for environmental impairment within the European Union, before the Union was enlarged to States from Central and Eastern Europe, Denmark in September 1999 submitted the proposal for a Council framework decision in order to combat serious environmental crimes.[263] The proposal took up large parts of the Council of Europe's draft Convention. It defined "serious environmental crime"[264] and suggested to having made punishable under criminal law. Legal persons were to be held criminally responsible and close co-operation among Member States was foreseen.

The European Parliament supported in general terms the Danish initiative.[265] The Council discussed the Danish initiative and changed its heading into "relating to the protection of the environment by criminal law". As a legal basis, the Council considered Articles 29, 31(e) and 34(2)(b) of the Treaty on European Union. By the end of the year 2001, no final decision has been taken. The Commission was of the opinion that measures to protect the environment through criminal sanctions, could validly be based on Article 175(1) EC Treaty. It therefore proposed, in 2001, a directive with this objective[265a], and announced its intention to apply to the Court of Justice, should the Council adopt the Danish framework decision.

(10) At present, judicial co-operation in criminal matters is possible in the following areas:[266]

(a) facilitating and accelerating cooperation between competent ministries and judicial or equivalent authorities of the Member States in relation to proceedings and the enforcement of decisions;
(b) facilitating extradition between Member States;
(c) ensuring compatibility in rules applicable in the Member States, as may be necessary to improve such cooperation;
(d) preventing conflicts of jurisdiction between Member States;
(e) progressively adopting measures establishing minimum rules relating to the constituent elements of criminal acts and to penalties in the fields of organised crime, terrorism and illicit drug trafficking.

---

[263] [2000] OJ C39/4.
[264] Art. 1: "acts or omissions, under aggravating circumstances and in breach of national environmental legislation, consisting in (a) pollution of air, water, soil or subsoil resulting in substantial damage to the environment or a clear danger thereof, or (b) storage or disposal of waste or similar substances resulting in substantial damage to the environment or presenting an obvious risk thereof".
[265] [1992] OJ C191/1.
[265a] (2001) OJ C180E/238.
[266] Treaty on European Union (n. 259 *supra*), Art. 31 (ex Art. K. 3).

Thus, environmental crime is not mentioned in this provision. The Danish proposal might be grouped under letters (c) or (d), but will certainly need some amendments in order to be adopted.

For the rest there is some activity on the part of the Council to combat organised crime. In 2000 the Council adopted an "act on the prevention and control of organised crime: a European Union strategy for the beginning of the new millennium".[267] The act does not give any precise legal basis but was "adopted pursuant to Title VI" of the Treaty on European Union. It contains 39 recommendations to combat organised crime; however, no legal definition seems to exist so far of that term; it is not clear whether illegal activities related to waste shipments, discharging, incineration dumping or landfilling could come under the term "organised crime".

Furthermore, the Commission recently drafted a communication on the "mutual recognition of final decisions in criminal matters", where it listed the problems and reflected on possibilities for solving them within the context of the European Union.[268]

(11) All these forms of co-operation only signal that the solution for punishing the act committed by Mr. Arcaro is exclusively found in Italian law. Member States do not seem to wish to protect the environment by criminal law provisions set up at Community level.

I maintain that at the moment where one really considers the protection of the environment to be in the general interest of the Community, the case law of the Court of Justice could—and should—be extended in order also to consider the requirement for an authorisation to discharge pollutants into the environment to be of direct effect, wherever this is foreseen under EC law. This direct effect would not be capable of contravening criminal law and in particular the principle of *ne bis in idem*. But it could apply in administrative law and lead to the possibility of addressing an administrative sanction against Mr. Arcaro, such as an administrative fine or the withdrawal of the licence to operate the plant. Indeed, when cadmium discharges are polluting the River Bacchiglione, it is not the Italian State "which takes advantage of its own failure", as the Court of Justice formulated. Rather, it is a choice between the right of Mr. Arcaro to damage a general interest, his right to pollute thus, and the right of all Italian citizens to see their environment adequately protected.

It is to be hoped that the Court of Justice finds some opportunity adequately to weigh individual against general interests, when the protection of the environment is at stake.

---

[267] [2000] OJ C124/1
[268] Commission, COM(2000)495 of 26 July 2000.

2

HORIZONTAL PROBLEMS

---

10. A RIGHT TO POLLUTE?

Judgment of the Court (Fifth Chamber) of 29 April 1999
Case C–293/97

*Reference for a preliminary ruling: The Queen v. Secretary
of State for the Environment and Ministry of Agriculture,
Fisheries and Food, ex parte H.A. Standley and Others and
D.G.D. Metson and Others*
[1999] ECR I–2603

Facts and Procedure

In 1991, the Community adopted Directive 91/676 concerning the protection of waters against pollution caused by nitrates from agricultural sources.[1] This Directive asked Member States to identify waters which were "affected by pollution and waters which could be affected by pollution" (Article 3(1)) and to "designate as vulnerable zones all known areas of land in their territories which drain into the waters identified . . . and which contribute to pollution (Article 3(2))". The Directive provided in Annex III that for such vulnerable zones the methods of farming agricultural land had to be regulated and that action programmes had to be elaborated which had to ensure that "the amount of livestock manure applied to the land each year, including by the animals themselves, shall not exceed a specific amount per hectare". That annual amount of manure was specified as an amount which contained 170 kilogrammes of nitrogen.

The United Kingdom authorities subsequently identified, amongst others, the rivers Waveney, Blackwater and Chelmer as surface waters affected by nitrate pollution and designated the areas in East Anglia which drain into those waters as vulnerable zones under Directive 91/676. These decisions were challenged by Mr. Standley and Mr. Metson, farmers in East Anglia, and by other persons who owned or farmed land in that area. They were of the opinion that the Directive

---

[1] Directive 91/676 [1991] OJ L375/1.

allowed Member States to take such measures only once they had established the extent to which the pollution of water was effectively caused by nitrates from agricultural sources. Otherwise Directive 91/676 would be invalid, because it infringed several legal and environmental principles and also their fundamental property rights.

Judgment (extracts)

[The necessity to establish the extent of pollution caused by nitrate from agriculture]

29. . . . it should be observed that, when the Member States identify waters affected by pollution in accordance with article 3(1) of the Directive, they are to apply the criteria laid down in Annex I. Under paragraph A. 1 of that annex, surface freshwaters, in particular those used or intended for the abstraction of drinking water, must be identified as waters affected by pollution when they contain, or could contain. . more than the concentration of nitrates laid down in Directive 75/440.

30. It does not follow from the wording of that provision that the Member States are required to determine precisely what proportion of the pollution in the waters is attributable to nitrates of agricultural origin or that the cause of such pollution must be exclusively agricultural.

[The breach of environmental principles and of fundamental rights]

42. The applicants in the main proceedings argue, first, that the identification of waters which exceed that threshhold because of the presence of nitrates of non-agricultural origin (Article 3(1) of the Directive), the designation as vulnerable zones of agricultural zones of agricultural land which drains into those waters even though that land accounts for only part of the concentration of nitrates (Article 3(2)) and the establishment of an action programme which imposes on farmers alone responsability for ensuring that the threshhold is not exceeded (Article 5) give rise to disproportionate obligations on the part of the persons concerned, so that the Directive offends against the principle of proportionality.

43. Second, they submit that the Directive infringes the polluter pays principle laid down in Article 130r(2) of the EC Treaty, on the ground that farmers alone bear the cost of reducing the concentration of nitrates in waters to below the threshhold of 50 mg/l even though agriculture is acknowledged to be only one of the sources of those nitrates, while the other sources escape all financial burden.

44. Third, they maintain that the Directive is contrary to the principle under which environmental damage should as a priority be rectified at source, a principle which is to be read in conjunction with the polluter pays principle, as is clear from

Article 130r(2) of the EC Treaty. Contrary to the first of those principles, the consequence of the interpretation placed on the Directive by the respondents in the main proceedings is that, instead of the nitrate pollution of waters from atmospheric deposition, which originates principally from industry and transport, being prevented or reduced at source, farmers are required to bear the entire burden of preventing or reducing nitrate pollution of surface freshwaters.

45. Finally, they submit that the right to property is infringed by imposing on farmers the entire responsability for, and economic burden of, reducing nitrate concentrations in the waters concerned when others are the major or substantial causes of those concentrations.

46/50. So far as concerns the principle of proportionality, ... the Directive contains flexible provisions enabling the Member States to observe the principle of proportionality in the application of the measures which they adopt. It is for the national courts to ensure that that principle is observed.

51. As regards the polluter pays principle, suffice it to state that the Directive does not mean that farmers must take on burdens for the elimination of pollution to which they have not contributed.

52. As has been pointed out ... the Member States are to take account of the other sources of pollution when implementing the Directive and, having regard to the circumstances, are not to impose on farmers costs of eliminating pollution that are unnecessary. Viewed in that light, the polluter pays principle reflects the principle of proportionality.

53. The same applies to breach of the principle that environmental damage should as a priority be rectified at source, since the arguments of the applicants in the main proceedings are indissociable from their arguments relating to the breach of the principle of proportionality.

54. As regards infringement of the right to property, the Court has consistently held that, while the right to property forms part of the general principles of Community law, it is not an absolute right and must be viewed in relation to its social function. Consequently, its exercise may be restricted, provided that those restrictions in fact correspond to objectives of general interest pursued by the Community and do not constitute a disproportionate and intolerable interference, impairing the very substance of the rights guaranteed.

55. It is true that the action programmes which are provided for in Article 5 of the Directive and are to contain the mandatory measures referred to in Annex III impose certain conditions on the spreading of fertiliser and livestock manure, so that those programmes are liable to restrict the exercise by the farmers concerned of the right to property.

56. However, the system laid down in Article 5 reflects requirements relating to the protection of public health, and thus pursues an objective of general interest without the substance of the right to property being impaired.

57. While the institutions and the Member States are bound by the principle of proportionality when pursuing such an objective, the Directive does not ... offend against that principle ...

Commentary

I. *Directive 91/676 on Nitrate Pollution of Waters Caused by Agriculture*

(1) The judgment is one of the first which deals with the problems of Directive 91/676, a Directive to protect the environment against nitrate pollution from agricultural activity. At the same time it demonstrates the difficulties of putting into environmental reality the Treaty's provision that "environmental protection requirements must be integrated into the definition and implementation of the Communities policies and activities".[2]

The Directive's approach is rather clear: where surface freshwater in a Member State contains or could contain more than 50 mg per litre of nitrates, Member States had to take measures in order to improve the water quality by reducing the amount of "livestock manure" that was applied to the land. As the maximum amount of manure which could be brought on the land which drained to the polluted freshwater was limited to 170 kilogrammes of nitrogen, the Directive had the effect that the quantity of livestock in vulnerable zones had to be limited; in practice, thus, intensive stock farming was made more difficult.

(2) It was thus not surprising that Directive 91/676 met particular difficulties in most Member States and was objected to by many farmers. Mr. Standley and his farmer colleagues tried to use legal proceedings to fight their case.[3] They were in particular of the opinion that Directive 91/676 concerned only those waters where the nitrate concentration of 50 mg per litre was caused by agricultural activity. For that reason, before any water could be identified under Directive 91/676, the responsible Member State would first have to determine to what extent the different polluters had contributed to the nitrate concentration in waters.

The problem in the Directive's wording was that Member States had to identify those waters which were "affected by pollution" or which could be affected by pollution if action were not taken[4] and that "pollution" only referred to agricultural sources.[5] Thus, the applicants argued, nitrate concentration in waters which came from other sources could not be considered to constitute "pollution"; where the threshhold of 50 mg per litre was not exclusively reached by nitrates from agricultural sources, the waters were not polluted and could not be

---

[2] EC Treaty, Art. 6.

[3] The case, which led to the present request for a preliminary ruling, is published in [1998] *Journal of Environmental Law* 92, with an analysis by S Elworthy, at p. 103

[4] Directive 91/676 (n. 1 *supra*), Art. 3: "1. Waters affected by pollution and waters which could be affected by pollution if action pursuant to Art. 5 is not taken shall be identified by the Member States in accordance with the criteria set out in Annex I.

2. Member States shall . . . designate as vulnerable zones all known areas of land in their territories which drain into the waters identified according to paragraph 1 and which contribute to pollution".

[5] See Directive 91/676 (n. 1 *supra*), Art. 2: "For the purpose of this Directive: (j) 'pollution': means the discharge, directly or indirectly, of nitrogen compounds from agricultural sources into the aquatic environment."

identified. As a consequence thereof, the land which drained into such waters could not be designated as a vulnerable zone.

(3) The Court of Justice was not of the opinion that only those waters could be identified where the 50 mg per litre-threshhold was caused by agricultural activity alone. It used three principal argument for that reasoning: first, it saw the ident-ification of waters, the designation of vulnerable zones and the establishment of action programmes under Article 5[6] as "a process". As, however, Article 3(2) requested the designation of vulnerable zones already, where agricultural sources "contributed" to pollution and also the action programmes had to consider other than agricultural sources,[7] the Court found that also the identification of waters had to consider other sources.

The second argument came from a provision in the Directive which allowed Member States to designate the whole of their territory as a vulnerable zone. The Court argued that this provision clarified that nitrate reduction action pro-grammes also had to be established where the nitrate concentration from agricul-tural sources was less than than 50 mg per litre. The third argument finally came from the Directive's objective: the Court argued that if only those waters were identified where agricultural sources alone caused the nitrate contamination this would lead to the exclusion of "numerous cases where agricultural sources make a significant contribution to the pollution, a result which would be contrary to the Directive's spirit and purpose". To these arguments, the Court added that nitrate pollution was harmful to human health, irrespective of whether it had been caused by agricultural or industrial sources.

(4) It is difficult to consider that a different interpretation of Article 3 would have been more reasonable. The Directive does not contain any provision on how the exact sources of nitrate concentration could be established. Some pollution of this kind certainly comes from the air, but to what extent agriculture contributes to such inputs from the air is impossible to measure. Mr. Standley's reasoning would thus have made it largely impossible to apply the Directive at all.

(5) Almost all Member States had considerable problems with the transposition of Directive 91/676 into national law and its practical application.[8] The Directive should have been transposed into national law by the end of 1993; by the end of 1994, only Denmark and Luxemburg had done so. At the end of 1996, infringement proceedings under Article 226 EC Treaty were running against at the end of 1997 against 13, and at the end of 1999, against seven Member States, namely Belgium,

---

[6] Directive 91/676 (n. 1 *supra*) Art. 5: ". . . Member States shall, for the purpose of realising the objectives specified in Art. 1, establish action programmes in respect of designated vulnerable zones."

[7] Directive 91/676 (n. 1 *supra*), Art. 5(3): "Action programmes shall take into account: (a) available scientific and technical data, mainly with reference to respective nitrogen contributions originating from agricultural and other sources."

[8] See Commission, The implementation of Council Directive 91/676/EEC concerning the protec-tion of waters against pollution caused by nitrates from agricultural sources, COM(97)473 of 1 October 1997; Court of Auditors, Special Report 3/98 concerning the implementation by the Commission of EU policy and action in the field of water pollution [1998] OJ C191/1.

Germany, Spain, Italy, Austria, the United Kingdom and Luxemburg;[9] the Court of Justice had ruled against Spain and Italy which had not transposed the Directive into their national laws.[10]

(6) At the end of 1999, the Court of Justice found that the United Kingdom had breached its obligations under Directive 91/676.[11] The following omissions were found: (a) the United Kingdom had only identified such surface waters under Article 3 of Directive 91/676 which were intended to be used for the abstraction of drinking water, whereas the Directive contains no such limitation; (b) the United Kingdom had identified, under Article 3, only groundwater which was intended for human consumption, whereas Directive 91/676 contains no such limitation; (c) by the end of 1995, the United Kingdom had not designated vulnerable zones under Article 5 for Northern Ireland. In early 1999, three such zones were designated; however, this designation was again based on the erroneous assumption that only waters were to be designated which were used for the abstraction of drinking water; (d) the United Kingdom had not established action programmes for vulnerable zones, contrary to the requirements of Article 5 of Directive 91/676.

The United Kingdom had not contested the reproaches made by the Commission and acknowledged that it was in breach of its obligations under Directive 91/676. It explained that it had initially interpreted the scope of Directive 91/676 differently, as applying only to water which was used for the production of drinking water. In this context, it should be noted that the beginning of the formal procedure under Article 226 EC Treaty, on 21 October 1996, obviously had not led the United Kingdom, prior to the Court's judgment, to correct its "different" interpretation of the Directive.

(7) The United Kingdom adopted, in 1996, a scheme that provided financial assistance to investment in new or improved farm waste facilities, the Farm Waste Grant (Vulnerable Zones) Scheme. The scheme provided for an aid rate of 25 per cent of eligible expenses. In the year 2000, the aid rate was increased to 40 per cent; the overall amount made available was 7. 2 million Euro. The scheme which will run till 2003, was approved by the Commission under Articles 87 and 88 EC Treaty.[12]

II. *Fundamental Rights and Legal Principles*

(8) The discussion on the infringement of legal principles and fundamental rights raises a number of rather important issues. The Court has consistently held that provisions of Community law could not be interpreted in such a way "as to

---

[9] Commission, *Monitoring the Application of Community Law, 14th Report* (1996) [1997] OJ C332,p. 1 (p. 185); *17th Report* (1999), COM(2000)92 of 23 June 2000, Vol. I, p. 72.

[10] Court of Justice, Case C–71/97 *Commission* v. *Spain* [1998] ECR I–5991; Case C–195/97, *Commission* v. *Italy* [1999] ECR I–1169.

[11] Court of Justice, Case C–69/99, *Commission* v. *United Kingdom*, (2000) ECR I–10979.

[12] [2000] OJ C258/4.

give rise to results which are incompatible with the general principles of Community law and in particular with fundamental rights".[13] The fundamental rights are considered to be general principles,[14] whose observance is ensured by the Court. Other legal principles are, for instance, the principles of subsidiarity, of proportionality, and of the protection of legitimate expectations.

(9) The Court's interpretation of the fundamental right to property, which the applicants in the main proceedings in the present case claimed to have been infringed by the Directive's provisions is a model of the Court's general approach to fundamental rights. The Court repeats earlier findings by stating that the right to property forms part of the general principles of Community law. Then it states that it is not an absolute right, but must "be viewed in relation to its social function". While the right to property may not be infringed, the exercise of this right may be restricted, provided that the "very substance of the right is guaranteed", that the restrictions pursue an objective of general interest and that the restrictions are proportional.[15] This approach allows the Court to weigh the pros and cons of the disputed Community measures.

The reasoning is made rather quickly, one might even think hastily. Indeed, it takes four lines to find that the restrictions provided for in Annex III to the Directive impair the right to property of the farmers concerned. In one supplementary phrase (paragraph 56), the Court then states that these restrictions pursue an objective of general interest and do not impair the substance of the right to property. And also the respect of the principle of proportionality is argued with one phrase (paragraph 57).

(10) It is not clear why the Court stated that Directive 91/676 pursued the objective of protecting "public health" instead of stating that the objective pursued was the protection of the environment. Since 1985, the Court has recognised that the protection of the environment is a general interest of the Community.[16] And the Court's wording is not backed by Directive 91/676 itself. Indeed, the third recital of the Directive mentions the "environmental risk",[17] recital six indicates the necessity to protect "human health and living resources and aquatic ecosystems" and Article 1 indicates as the Directive's objective the reduction and prevention of water pollution. The notion of "public health"—which is different from human health![18]—does not appear in the Directive. And nobody has ever argued

[13] Court of Justice, Joined Cases 97/87, 98/87 and 99/87, *Dow Chemical* [1989] ECR 3165, para. 9; see also Case C–22/94, *Irish Farmers* [1997] ECR I–1809, para. 27.

[14] See the discussion on p. 42 *supra*.

[15] See also Court of Justice, Cases 44/79, *Hauer* [1979] ECR 3727, para. 17; 265/87, *Schräder* [1989] ECR 2237, para. 15; C–280/93, *Germany* v. *Council* [1994] ECR I–4973, para. 78.

[16] The first judgment was in Case 240/83, *ABDHU* [1985] ECR 531, para. 13: "The directive must be seen in the perspective of environmental protection, which is one of the Community's essential objectives"; see also Case 302/86, *Commission* v. *Denmark* [1988] ECR 4607, para. 8.

[17] Directive 91/676 (n. 1 *supra*) 3rd recital: ". . . while the use of nitrogen-containing fertilizers and manure constitutes an environmental risk, excessive use of fertilizers constitutes an environmental risk".

[18] The wording of the EC Treaty is not very elucidating: Art. 30 mentions the "protection of health and life of humans"; Art. 94(3) mentions "health" next to "safety, environmental protection and consumer protection". Title XIII, which consists of Art. 152 alone, is called "public health". Art. 152(1)

that the eutrophication of waters, one of the consequences of nitrate pollution, is a problem of public health. The Court's terminology is all the more surprising as Article 174 EC Treaty expressly indicates the the objectives of environmental policy include the protection of human health.

(11) In substance, the restriction on holding cattle on land beyond a certain quantity limits the property rights,[19] but cannot seriously be considered to be a partial expropriation; it might already be doubtful whether the value of the farm land is not increased by such a measure—at least in the long term. The Court's basic statement that the right to property is affected but not infringed is thus correct.[20] And the statement that the restricting measures are proportional also seems correct. Indeed, less far-reaching measures which have the same effect to reduce nitrate pollution in vulnerable areas are not easily imaginable.

It is clear that farmers are likely to contest any measure which restricts their right to produce agricultural products, be these measures based on environmental considerations or other the pursuit of other objectives. Thus, for example, in Case C–22/94, Irish farmers had unsuccessfully attempted to have Community measures on milk quotas set aside, arguing that their right to property was affected;[21] and in Case C–186/96, a German farmer challenged some Community measures intended to remedy the surpluses on the milk market, again arguing that his right to property had been impaired; the Court considered the measures appropriate and proportional.[22] In the Netherlands, some courts considered the restriction of the possibility to hold products a form of expropriation which was

reads: "A high level of human health protection shall be ensured in the definition and implementation of all Community policies and activities.

Community action . . . shall be directed towards improving public health, preventing human illness and diseases, and obviating sources of danger to human health. Such action shall cover the fight against the major health scourges, by promoting research into their causes, their transmission and their prevention, as well as health information and education.

The Community shall complement the Member States' action in reducing drugs-related health damage, including information and prevention".

According to Art. 153(1), the consumer protection policy "shall contribute to protecting the health, safety and economic interests of consumers". Art. 174 finally indicates as one of the objectives of Community environmental policy is the contribution to "protecting human health".

In view of this terminology, it becomes even more mysterious why the Court stated that eutrophication of waters pursues the protection of public health.

[19] See also the provision on property rights in the European Convention on Human Rights and Fundamental Freedoms 1950, Art. 1 of the First Additional Protocol: "Every natural or legal person is entitled to the peaceful enjoyment of his possessions. No one shall be deprived of his possession except in the public interest and subject to the conditions provided for by law and by the general principles of international law.

The preceding provisions shall not, however, in any way impair the right of a State to enforce such laws as it deems necessary to control the use of property in accordance with the general interest or to secure the payment of taxes or other contributions or penalties".

[20] In Case T–170/00, *Förde-Reederei* v. *Council* judgment of 20 February 2002, not yet reported, the applicants claimed compensation because Council Directive 92/12 ended the possibility to make tax-free sales of goods on board of ferry-boats within the Community. The Court of First Instance rejected the application, without discussing the ownership of property.

[21] Court of Justice, Case C–22/94, *Irish Farmers' Association* [1997] ECR I–1809, paras. 26 to 31.

[22] Court of Justice, Case C–186/96, *Demand* [1998] ECR I–8529, paras. 40 to 42.

only allowed against compensation.[23] Transferred to the present case this would mean that there is a (fundamental) right of farmers to pollute; therefore, it is to be welcomed that the Court rejected Mr. Standley's arguments which creates legal certainty.

(12) As regards the principle of proportionality, the Court did not give a definition. Some elements of what the proportionality principle means are to be found in Article 5 EC Treaty which states: "Any action by the Community shall not go beyond what is necessary to achieve the objectives of this Treaty". In Case C–359/92 , the Court stated that "the principle of proportionality requires that measures taken by the Community institutions should be appropriate to achieve the objective pursued without going beyond what is necessary to that end".[24] The legal, political, economic, social and environmental arguments in favour of or against a measure must therefore be weighed against each other; but the Community legislature has a large amount of discretion as regards the decision on what is appropriate, and the Court has most frequently refrained from putting its own discretion in the place of those of the Council and Parliament.

(13) In the present case the Court looked into the provisions of Directive 91/676 and the various possibilities which were given to Member States to take account of local and regional characteristics of the vulnerable zones, to adapt the action programmes and to use the codes of good agricultural practice, and concluded that the proportionality principle had been observed. Thus, here in the Court's judgment, neither can be interpreted as to give farmers a right to pollute.

III. Environmental Principles (Article 174(2) EC Treaty)

(14) While it is clear from the Court's different judgments that Community secondary law may not breach the general legal principles of fundamental rights it remains to be discussed whether the environmental principles that are mentioned in Article 174(2) EC Treaty[25] are principles of the same nature, in the sense that Community legislation may not infringe them. Doubts in this regard come from the vagueness of these principles: the prevention principle requires the prevention of environmental impairment or damage, though it is clear that any human activity—even the breathing of humans—"affects" the environment in one way or the other. How far would preventive measures have to go in order not to impair this principle? It is submitted that this cannot be known with the necessary legal certainty.

[23] See C W Backes, *Duurzame groei?* (Kluwer, Deventer, 2000), p. 42.

[24] Court of Justice, Case C–359/92, *Germany v. Council* [1994] ECR I–3681, para. 44; see also Case C–174/89, *Hoche* [1990] ECR I–2681, para. 19; Joined Cases 177/99 and 181/99 (2000) ECR I–7013, para. 43.

[25] Art. 174(2) EC Treaty: "Community policy on the environment shall aim at a high level of protection taking into account the diversity of situations in the various regions of the Community. It shall be based on the precautionary principle and on the principles that preventive action should be taken, that environmental damage should as a priority be rectified at source and that the polluter should pay".

(15) In the same way the polluter pays principle is unclear: already the wording of the different language versions of the Treaty[26] shows considerable differences: while the English version states that the polluter should pay, the Danish version states that the polluter shall pay; the French version mentions the polluter-payer-principle and the German text calls this principle the "principle of causation". It remains open what a polluter is, whether he shall pay or should pay, for which kind of impairment he should pay, to whom he should pay and how much he should pay. These few remarks may be sufficient to demonstrate that the content and the limits of the polluter pays principle are not precise. Therefore, it seems almost impossible to declare any legal provision contrary to the polluter-pays principle.[27]

(16) In the present case, the Court affirms that the Directive "does not mean that farmers must take on burdens for the elimination of pollution to which they have not contributed" and continues to state that the polluter pays principle "reflects the proportionality principle". It is arguable whether these affirmations are correct: suppose the nitrate pollution of a river exceeds 50 mg per litre, 50 per cent of which stems from industrial sources and 50 per cent from agricultural sources. Annexe III(2) of Directive 91/676 then requests Member States to limit the quantity of cattle per hectare, though it is admitted that they have a certain discretion of calculation.[28] This means that there are restrictions imposed on farmers which are in part caused by industrial pollution—and in economic terms one might well argue that farmers are held responsable for pollution which is (in part) caused by industry.

These observations do not mean that the Court's conclusions are disapproved of. Rather they wish to demonstrate that it does not seem possible to draw specific conclusions from the polluter pays principle. This is all the more so, as the percentage to which one or the other source contributes to the pollution of water—or, more generally, of the environment—can in most cases not really be determined with sufficient precision; such percentage changes from day to day, from water stretch to water stretch, from one vulnerable zone to the other.

(17) Similar considerations apply to other general principles, such as the one that requests that environmental damage be rectified at source. This, in Case C–2/90, the Court interpreted Articles 28 and 30 (ex Articles 30 and 36) EC Treaty

---

[26] See p. 42 *supra* on the interpretation of Community law.

[27] See for more details: L Krämer, "The 'Polluter Pays' Principle in Community Law. The Interpretation of Article 130r of the EEC Treaty", in L Krämer, *Focus on European Environmental Law*, (Sweet & Maxwell, London, 1992), p. 244.

[28] Directive 91/676 (n. 1 *supra*), Annex III: "Measures to be included in action programmes . . . (2) These measures will ensure that, for each farm or livestock unit, the amount of livestock manure applied to the land each year, including by the animals themselves, shall not exceed a specific amount per hectare.

The specified amount per hectare be the amount of manure containing 170 kg N. However, (a) for the first four year action programme Member States may allow an amount of manure containing up to 210 kg N; (b) during and after the first four year action programme, Member States may fix diferent amounts from those referred to above. These amounts must be fixed so as not to prejudice the achievement of the objectives specified in Art. 1 and must be justified on the basis of objective criteria, for example:—long growing seaons,—crops with high nitrogen uptake,—high net precipitation in the vulnerable zone,—soils with exceptionally high denitrification capacity . . ."

in a case which concerned Belgian import restrictions on waste; the Court found these restrictions well founded. It then justified its conclusion by stating that "the principle that environmental damage should as a priority be rectified at source . . . means that it is for each region, commune or local entity to take appropriate measures to receive, process and dispose of its own waste. Consequently waste should be disposed of as close as possible to the place where it is produced in order to keep the transport of waste o the minimum practicable".[29] A similar approach was taken when the Court applied the prevention principle of Article 174 EC Treaty in a case where it discussed Community measures to impose an export ban on British beef because of mad cow disease. It used the principle to justify a specific Community measure.[30]

And this seems to be the significance of the different principles in Article 174: they constitute guiding principles for political or legislative decisions and may be used—as a sort of *leitmotif*—to explain or justify a decision which was taken. But they cannot really be used in order declare a Community measure void, because it contradicts one of these principles. Thus, the opinion that for instance the principle that environmental damage should be rectified at source would require Community legislation to be based on emission limit values rather than on quality standards cannot be based on a corresponding requirement in Article 175 EC Treaty.

In the present case, the Court did not discuss the legal significance of the principles laid down in Article 174(2) EC Treaty. It satisfies itself with the conclusion that they express the proportionality principle which was not impaired in this case.

---

[29] Court of Justice, Case C–2/90, *Commission* v. *Belgium* [1992] ECR I–4431, para. 34. See also Case C–203/96, *Dusseldorp* [1998] ECR I–4075, where the Court again discusses the shipment of waste, disallows national restrictions to such shipments and does not even mention the principle that environmental damage should be rectified at source (see p. 22 *supra*).

[30] Court of Justice, Case C–180/96, *United Kingdom* v. *Commission* [1998] ECR I–2265, paras. 99–100: "Where there is uncertainty as to the existence or extent of risks to human health, the institutions may take protective measures without having to wait until the reality and seriousness of those risks becomes fully apparent. That approach is borne out by Art. 130r(1) of the EC Treaty, according to which Community policy on the environment is to pursue the objective inter alia of protecting human health. Art. 130r(2) provides that that policy is to be based in particular on the principles that preventive action should be taken and that environmental protection requirements must be integrated into the definition and implementation of other Community policies".

It seems that the Court could also have mentioned the precautionary principle next to or instead of the prevention principle.

11. ENVIRONMENT AND TRANSPORT

Judgment of the Court of 26 September 2000
Case C–205/98

Commission of the European Communities v. *Austria*
[2000] ECR I–7367

Facts and Procedure

The Brenner motorway links Innsbruck in Austria to Verona in Italy; the Austrian parts ends at the Brenner pass on the frontier with Italy. It is one of the very few motorways which cross the Alps and is predominantly used by goods vehicles of over 12 tonnes. As Switzerland, Austria's neighbour country, had for decades practised a policy which promoted Alpine transit by rail and as road traffic generally increased considerably after 1945, citizens along the Brenner motorway more and more frequently complained about noise levels, air pollution, traffic congestion and other environmental impairment. The Austrian government therefore adopted a number of measures to reduce such effects, amongst others, by raising road tolls on the Brenner motorway.

In 1993, the Council adopted Directive 93/89 on tolls for the use of certain infrastructures.[31] When Austria acceded to the European Union on 1 January 1995, no specific transitional provisions for this Directive were agreed. In 1995, the Court of Justice annulled Directive 93/89[32] on the ground that it had been adopted without proper consultation of the European Parliament, but preserved its effect pending the adoption of a new directive;[33] this new directive was adopted in 1999.[34]

In July 1995 and February 1996, Austria raised the toll rates for use of the Brenner motorway; it introduced three levels of toll, for full journeys, partial journeys and

---

[31] Directive 93/89 on the application by Member States of taxes on certain vehicles used for the carriage of goods by road and tolls and charges for the use of certain infrastructures [1993] OJ L279/32.

[32] Court of Justice, Case C–21/94, *European Parliament* v. *Council* [1995] ECR I–1827.

[33] Art. 231(2) EC Treaty only gives the Court the possibility "if it considers it necessary, state which effects of the regulation which it has declared void shall be considered as definitive". The wording of this provision restricts its application to regulations. For the first time in 1992, the Court applied Art. 231(2) by analogy to a directive, Case C–295/90, *European Parliament* v. *Council* [1992] ECR I–4193, justifying this by reason of legal certainty. In Case C–21/94 (n. 32 *supra*), no specific reason was given. Presumably, the Court also considered reasons of legal certainty to be important, as the raising of tolls and user charges by Member States without a legal basis in Community law might have raised objections from the point of view of freedom of transport.

[34] Directive 1999/62 on the charging of heavy goods vehicles for the use of certain infrastructures [1999] OJ L187/42.

short journeys. The money raised was attributed to a finance company Asfinag, which was controlled by the Austrian State. Asfinag was required to construct, plan, operate, maintain and finance Austrian motorways and express highways, including, but not limited to, the Brenner motorway.

The Commission was of the opinion that the Austrian provisions discriminated against goods vehicles over 12 tonnes from other Member States, that the tolls collected were not used exclusively to cover the costs of constructing, operating and developing the Brenner motorway and that therefore the Austrian measures were not compatible with Article 7(b)[35] and (h)[36] of Directive 93/89. The Austrian Government saw no discrimination in the measures adopted and was of the opinion that it was not obliged to use the money raised by the tolls for the maintenance of the Brenner motorway only.

As no solution could be found for these differences, the Commission applied, on 29 May 1998, to the Court of Justice.

Judgment (extracts)

[Discrimination of hauliers from other Member States]

62. . . . the Commission . . . criticises the Republic of Austria for having, through the two tariff changes at issue, set tolls in such a manner that they give rise . . . to discrimination indirectly based on the nationality of the haulier . . . in that those changes for the most part affect vehicles registered in the other Member States.

63. . . . it must be recognised . . . that, for the purposes of establishing the existence of discrimination indirectly based on the nationality of hauliers, the registration of vehicles constitutes, as the rules on the carriage of goods by road in the European Union stand at present, a valid criterion in so far as vehicles registered in a Member State are, as a rule, operated by economic operators of the same Member State . . .

65. . . . it is clear . . . that the effect of the two tariff changes at issue is substantially to increase the toll rates only for vehicles with more than three axles following the full intinerary on the Brenner motorway . . . the fact that the increases at issue result, in part, from the abolition of reduced tariffs in no way detracts from that finding.

---

[35] Directive 93/89 (n. 31 *supra*), Art. 7: "Member States may maintain or introduce tolls and/or introduce user charges in accordance with the following conditions: . . . (b) Without prejudice to Art. 8(2)(e) and Art. 9, tolls and user charges may not discriminate, directly or indirectly, on the grounds of the nationality of the haulier or or of origin or destination of the vehicle;".

[36] Directive 93/89 (n. 31 *supra*), Art. 7: "Member States may maintain or introduce tolls and/or introduce user charges in accordance with the following conditions: . . . (h) Toll rates shall be related to the costs of constructing, operating and developing the infrastructure network concerned".

66. Thus, as from 1 February 1996, the toll rates for vehicles with more than three axles following the full itinerary has increased, as compared with the situation obtaining before 1 July 1995, by 150% where they travel by day and by 283% for journeys by night. In the case of low-noise low-pollution vehicles, the increase is 130% for travel by day and 360% for travel by night. In contrast, vehicles with up to three axles, whatever the itinerary followed, have not been affected by the increases at issue, and nor have vehicles with more than three axles which do not complete the full itinerary on the Brenner motorway, save for the minor change . . . regarding the journey from Matrei/Steinach to the Brenner frontier post . . .

67. It must also be observed that . . . about 84% of vehicles with more than three axles, 99% of which follow the full itinerary on the Brenner motorway, are not registered in Austria.

69. . . . it is necessary to verify whether . . . vehicles not registered in Austria, the great majority of which are affected by the contested increases, are in a situation comparable to that of vehicles registered in Austria, the great majority of which have not been affected by those increases.

75. . . . for the purposes of the comparison, account must be taken of the partial itineraries actually used by vehicles with more than three axles for transport operations similar to that undertaken on the full itinerary . . . In contrast, the journeys which are not of interest or are of a purely incidental interest for carriage operations . . . cannot be taken into account for the purposes of the comparison.

76. . . . any inequality of treatment will stem from the fact that a majority of the vehicles in the favoured group is represented by vehicles registered in Austria, whilst the majority of the vehicles making up the disfavoured group, which represent 99% of the total traffic of vehicles with more than three axles, is constituted by vehicles not registered in Austria.

79. . . . it must be held that, in the case of vehicles with more than three axles carrying goods, there is a difference of treatment between, on the one hand, those following the full itinerary, of which the great majority are not registered in Austria, and, on the other hand, those which, being in a comparable situation, follow the partial itineraries . . . the vast majority of which are registered in Austria.

81. That finding is confirmed by an examination of the legislative background to the two tariff changes at issue. The resolution of the regional Parliament of the Land of Tyrol, of 17 May 1995, which gave rise to those tariff changes, emphasised the need to protect "domestic hauliers" ("*heimischen Frächter*") from the "drastic charges" deriving from those tariff changes.

90. . . . the tariff differences . . . cannot be justified on grounds relating to environmental protection or by considerations based on national transport policy.

91. According to the first and second recitals in the preamble to the Directive, elimination of distortions of competition between transport undertakings in the Member States calls for both the harmonisation of levy systems and the establishment of fair mechanisms for charging infrastructure costs to hauliers, and those objectives can be achieved only in stages. According to the 10th recital, until technically and economically more appropriate forms of levy are in place, distortions of competition between transport undertakings of the Member States may be attenuated by the possibility of retaining or introducing tolls . . . The 11th recital makes it clear, in that respect, that it is important, in particular, for tolls and user charges not to be discriminatory.

92. It is clear from those considerations that the Community legislation, whilst aware of the fact that the removal of distortions of competition in the area of carriage of goods by road can be achieved only in stages, clearly expressed its intention to achieve that objective, in so far as it is indispensable for the proper functioning of the internal market, and decided, to that end, in particular to harmonise certain aspects of the rules on tolls and user charges.

93. That explains why, in the area covered by the Directive, the Community legislature did not wish to allow States to derogate from the rules laid down therein except on the grounds, and in accordance with the conditions, laid down in the Directive.

94. Thus, exemptions from or additional reductions in vehicle charges must be authorised by the Council and be based on grounds of specific policies of a socio-economic nature or linked to that State's infrastructure (Article 6(5)(a) of the Directive).

95. On the other hand, neither the recitals in the preamble to the Directive nor the provisions of the Directive contemplate the possibility of relying on grounds relating to policies on national transport or environmental protection in order to justify tariff arrangements which give rise to indirect discrimination within the meaning of Article 7(b) of the Directive. No other provision of the Directive allows derogations from the non-discrimination rule when toll rates are fixed.

99. . . . it must be concluded that the intention of the Community legislature, in adopting the Directive, was to prohibit tariff differences based, directly or indirectly, on the nationality of hauliers or the origin or destination of the vehicle specifically with regard to the fixing of toll rates, without permitting any derogations in that regard.

[The use of the tolls for maintaining the Brenner motorway]

130. It must be observed first that . . . the "infrastructure network concerned" within the meaning of Article 7(h) of the Directive refers only to the section of the infrastructure for the use of which the toll is paid.

131. If the Austrian Government's argument were accepted, Member States would be able, through the financing arrangements chosen, to evade the requirement of a link between toll rates and the costs of construction, operation and development of the section in question and Article 7(h) of the Directive would thus to a large extent be rendered ineffectual.

133. If the thesis put forward by the Austrian Government were accepted, the result would be that vehicles with a total gross laden weight of 12 tonnes or more would contribute to financing the entire motorway network funded by Asfinag by

means of the toll paid for use of the Brenner motorway and at the same time through the user charges to which they are liable for using Austrian motorway infrastructures in general.

134. As regards the Austrian Government's argument that the requirement of a direct link between toll rates and costs associated with the infrastructure concerned would give rise to successive decreases in toll rates on heavily used motorways which, by reason of the subsequent increase in traffic, would have more and more damaging effects on, in particular, the environment, it need only be pointed out that, if such a consequence were to ensue, it would be the result of a mechanism intentionally created by the Community legislature, upon which it would then, if necessary, be incumbent to take appropriate measures to remedy the situation.

135. As regards, second, the allegation that there is no link between the contested increases and the costs relating to the Brenner motorway, it must be pointed out . . . that an examination of the income and expenditure of the company Alpen Strassen for the previous financial years, and of the forecasts for 1995 to 1997, shows that, when the contested measures were adopted, the forecasts of the Austrian authorities themselves showed that the tolls charged on the Brenner motorway already exceeded by more than 150% the costs of construction, operation and developmentof the same motorway, even if the effects of the increase in the toll rates brought about by the abovementioned measures were disregarded.

136. In those circumstances, the two tariff changes at issue cannot be regarded as being linked to the cost of the infrastructure network concerned within the meaning of Article 7(h) of the Directive. . .

Commentary

I. National Environmental Measures and Discrimination

(1) The judgment, pronounced by the full Court of Justice, is one of those decisions which deal with the integration of environmental requirements into other policies. Article 6 EC Treaty is clear in this regard: "Environmental protection requirements must be integrated into the definition and implementation of the Community policies and activities referred to in Article 3, in particular with a view to promoting sustainable development". Austria tried to protect the population, in particular in Tirol, which lived next to the Brenner motorway, by increasing the tolls,[37] i. e. the economic costs for the users of the motorway. However, it was confronted with the provisions of Directive 93/89 which had been adopted, it is true,

---

[37] Directive 93/89 (n. 31 *supra*) Art. 2: "For the purposes of this Directive . . . 'toll' means payment of a specific amount for a vehicle travelling the distance between two points on the infrastructure referred to in Art. 7(d); the amount shall be based on the distance travelled and on the category of the vehicle".

prior to Austria's accession to the European Union (1 January 1995), but which Austria had accepted during the accession negotiations, without asking for a derogation or a transition period.

The judgment indicates, in conformity with the request by the European Commission, two breaches of Community law, discrimination against non-Austrian hauliers and non-respect of the obligation to use the income from the tolls exclusively for the maintenance of the Brenner motorway.

(2) It is difficult to object to the Court's findings on discrimination. As clearly appears from the figures quoted in paragraph 66 of the judgment, Austria had considerably increased the tolls for the full journey of the Brenner motorway, but hardly increased the tolls for partial and short journeys. As the full journey was almost exclusively used by non-Austrian hauliers, and the partial or short journeys in the main by Austrian hauliers (see the figures in paragraph 67), the Court concluded that this differentiation constituted an indirect discrimination of foreign hauliers.

And it appears from the Court's statement in paragraph 81 that this differentiation was intended: the Austrian legislature deliberately introduced the differentiation in order to avoid Austrian hauliers also having to pay the increased tolls.

(3) The principle of non-discrimination[38] is a basic principle of EC law. It is not only found in Article 7(b) of Directive 93/89[39] and in Article 7(4) of Directive 1999/62,[40] which replaced Directive 93/89, but also in Article 12 EC Treaty[41] and, in the Title on Transport, in Articles 72[42] and 75[43] EC Treaty. And, indeed, it does not make sense to create an internal market, where state frontiers are no longer economic frontiers and then allow, be it only in the area of transport, a differentiated treatment of economic operations according to the nationality of the operators.

Austria could have avoided the criticism of discrimination on grounds of nationality if it had introduced the same tolls for full, partial and short journeys. For economic, social or other reasons, it decided not to do so.

[38] See para. 70 of the present judgment (not reproduced here): "According to the settled case-law of the Court, discrimination can arise only through the application of different rules to comparable situations or the application of the same rules to different situations (see, in particular, Case C–279/93 *Schumacker* [1995] ECR I–225, para. 30)".

[39] Directive 93/89, Art. 7(b) (n. 35 *supra*).

[40] Directive 1999/62 (n. 34 *supra*), Art. 7(4): "Tolls and user charges may not discriminate, directly or indirectly, on the grounds of the nationality of the haulier or the origin or destination of the vehicle".

[41] Art. 12 EC Treaty: "Within the scope of application of this Treaty, and without prejudice to any special provisions contained therein, any discrimination on grounds of nationality shall be prohibited".

[42] Art. 72 EC Treaty: "Until the provisions referred to in Art. 71(1) have been laid down, no Member State may, without the unanimous approval of the Council, make the various provisions governing the subject on 1 January 1958 or, for acceding States, the date of their accession less favourable in their direct or indirect effects on carriers of other Member States as compared with carriers who are nationals of that State".

[43] Art. 75 EC Treaty: "1. In the case of transport within the Community, discrimination which takes the form of carriers charging different rates and imposing different conditions for the carriage of the same goods over the same transport links on grounds of the country of origin or of destination of the goods in question shall be abolished . . .".

And the Court was quite adamant: environmental reasons could not justify any such discrimination. Directive 93/89 did not provide for such a possibility and the Court was of the opinion that the grounds on which derogations could be allowed were exhaustively enumerated in Directive 93/89 itself.

(4) The Austrian Government had argued that the environmental problems of the local population did not stem from Austrian vehicles which used the partial or short journeys, but rather from the fact that many vehicles of more than 12 tonnes chose the Brenner motorway itinerary instead of the route via Switzerland in order to carry goods from Germany and Northern Europe.[44] This argument would, provided it were correct—and there is little objective element to dispute that it is indeed correct—justify differentiated toll rates for the full and for partial or short journeys. However, the Court relied on the argument that Directive 93/89 did not allow to differentiation or discrimination between national and non-national hauliers for environmental reasons and, thus, rejected this argument.

(5) Article 6 EC Treaty[45] cannot help either in such a case. It requires environmental requirements to be integrated into other Community policies. This is different from integrating environmental requirements into individual legislative texts. A Community transport policy, seen as a whole, could well be considered to take into consideration environmental requirements, without each individual legislative measure having to incorporate these requirements. Article 6 EC Treaty is thus much more a policy provision to orient the Community in the different sectors of EC policy, rather than a legal requirement which would need application and respect within the context of each individual measure of a specific policy sector. Article 6 thus has a limited capacity to impose the consideration of environmental requirements.

The Court gave this conclusion expression by stating that the "legislature"—in other words the Council—had decided, when adopting Directive 93/89, that no grounds other than those expressly mentioned in that Directive could justify a derogation from the provisions of Directive 93/89. The Court did not even discuss the possibility of applying Article 6 EC Treaty in this specific case—and it appears from the foregong that it was right in that.

(6) In substance, could Austria really hope to reduce traffic across the Alps via the Brenner motorway by increasing toll rates and thus avoiding "detour traffic"? This must be doubted. Indeed, Switzerland had adopted a bundle of measures to reduce transit traffic by road, for instance by limiting heavy vehicles to 28 tonnes, while Austria and the EC allowed 44 tonnes; by offering railway transport to heavy goods vehicles etc. In order really to be able to compete with the environmentally friendly Swiss transport policy, Austria would thus have had to do much more than just increase toll rates.

---

[44] See para. 89 of the present judgment (not reproduced here), where the Austrian government argued that the difference of tariffs is "essential to combat, by means of the contested increases on the full itinerary, the phenomenon of 'detour traffic' ('*Umwegtransit*'), whereby 30 to 40% of vehicles with more than three axles carrying goods from Germany and Northern Europe to Italy, and vice versa, make a detour through Austria in order to benefit from lower tariffs than those applied, in particular, in Switzerland".

[45] See the wording of Art. 6 EC Treaty in para. 1 of the commentary, *supra*.

Still, in order to reduce transport via the Brenner motorway by 30 to 40 per cent, the bundle of measures to be taken would have been so comprehensive and the price increase so considerable that socially such measures could hardly be seen by car and other vehicle drivers to be acceptable. The answer to the problem of environment caused by traffic can thus probably only lie in a strategic policy which tries to introduce long-term policy objectives and goals thorough a long, continuous process during which traffic is progressively reduced, railway transport improved, production and consumption methods changed etc.

(7) A similar measure to the Austrian one had been tried, in 1990, by Germany. Germany had introduced legislation by which it imposed a tax on the use of roads which was payable on all heavy goods vehicles of more than 18 tonnes, regardless of their place of registration, and which used federal motorways outside built-up areas. However, at the same time Germany had considerably lowered motor vehicle tax which applied, of course, only to motor vehicles registered in Germany.[46] At the request of the Commission, the Court of Justice declared such legislation incompatible with the discrimination prohibition of Article 72 EC Treaty,[47] as only German carriers had a benefit.[48] In practice, thus, the German approach—increase of road use fees with reductions for German carriers—had the same bias as the Austrian approach in the present case.

II. The Use of the Income from the Tolls

(8) The Court rightly interpreted Article 7(h) of Directive 93/89 in a sense that the money raised from tolls was to be used for the maintenance and construction of that road where the toll was raised. The contrary position from the Austrian government that such money could be used for those roads for which the responsible financing company is in charge, is unacceptable; as the Court argued in paragraph 131 of the judgment, such an interpretation would have enabled Austria to charge Asfinag with all Austrian roads and in this way use the money from the tolls from the Brenner motorway for all Austrian roads. This cannot have been the sense of Article 7(h).

The second argument raised by the Austrian government carries more environmental weight: if the tolls from the Brenner motorway could be used only for the construction and operation of the Brenner motorway, then the tolls would decrease the more trucks used the motorway and pay tolls. However, Article 7(h) indicates that the tolls are raised for construction and maintenance purposes, not for purposes of deterring, for environmental reasons, the use of the Brenner motorway. Had the tolls also had such an environmentally motivated deterrent purpose, then this would have had to be expressed more clearly in that provision.

---

[46] *Gesetz über Gebühren für die Benutzung von Bundesfernstrassen mit schweren Lastfahrzeugen* of 30 April 1990, Bundesgesetzblatt I, p. 826.

[47] Art. 72 EC Treaty (n. 42 *supra*).

[48] Court of Justice, Case C–195/90R, *Commission* v. *Germany* [1990] ECR I–3351 (interim measures); Case C–195/90, *Commission* v. *Germany* [1992] ECR I–3141.

(9) The conclusion thus is that Directive 93/89 contained no provision which allowed tolls to be raised or toll rates to be increased for environmental purposes. When adopting this Directive, the Community simply had not forged Directive 93/89 as a tool for environmental protection.

III. *Integrating the Environment into the Common Transport Policy*

(10) Directive 1999/62,[49] which was adopted after the annulment of Directive 93/89 by the Court of Justice,[50] tried to introduce some environmental considerations into the systems of tolls and user charges. Member States were allowed to vary the toll rates according to the emissions of the vehicles.[51] Furthermore, Member States were allowed to use part of the amount of the toll or the user charge for the general transport network:[52] Finally, Austria received some satisfaction for its local transport: it may permanently "exempt from the Austrian user charge the stretch of motorway between Kufstein and Brenner".[53] Whether these rather modest measures really constute a method of reducing transport by (high) toll rates or user charges, must be seriously doubted.

(11) In 1992, the Community concluded an international Treaty with Austria on the reduction of transport by heavy goods vehicles, in pursuance of which the Community adopted a regulation on ecopoints.[54] When Austria acceeded to the Community on 1 January 1995, the ecopoint system was incorporated into the Accession Treaty.[55] The Protocol promoted in general terms rail and combined transport, without providing for specific measures. As regards road transport, it was agreed that the nitrous oxide emissions from heavy goods vehicles of more than 7.5 tonnes crossing Austria should be reduced, until 2003, to 40 per cent of their amount in 1991. For that year, the total of nitrous oxide emissions was established at 23. 306. 580 g/kWh. For each gramme, an ecopoint was fixed and for each heavy goods vehicle crossing Austria the nitrous oxide emissions had to be determined and established in an official document. Furthermore, each heavy goods vehicle had to be equipped with an official ecopoint card, the points of which then were counted during the crossing of Austria. While thus, for instance, in 1995 16. 710. 818 ecopoints were allowed to be used by crossing vehicles (71. 7% of the ecopoints used in 1991), this figure was to be progressively reduced and was to reach

---

[49] Directive 1999/62 (n. 34 *supra*).

[50] See p. 100 *supra.*

[51] Directive 1999/62 (n. 34 *supra*), Art. 10: "Member States may vary the rates at which tolls are charged according to (a) vehicle mission classes, provided that no toll is more than 50% above the toll charged for equivalent vehicles meeting the strictest emission standards . . .".

[52] Directive 1999/62 (n. 34 *supra*); Art. 10(2): "Neither shall this Directive prevent the Member States from attributing to environmental protection and the balanced development of transport networks a percentage of the amount of the user charge, or of the toll, provided that this amount is calculated in accordance with Art. 7(7) and (9)".

[53] Directive 1999/62 (n. 34 *supra*), Art. 7(2)(iii).

[54] See Convention on the Transit of the Alps between Austria and the Community [1992] OJ L373/6; Regulation 3637/92 [1992] OJ L373/1

[55] Accession Treaty, Protocol No. 9 [1994] OJ C241/361.

9. 321. 531 in 2003.[56] Article 11(5) of Protocol 9 states: "At the end of the transitional period, the 'acquis communautaire' in its entirety shall be applied". The transitional period is the period between 2001 and 2003, so that the ecopoint system will expire on 31 December 2003. In a policy decision of end 2001, the European Council granted Austria a prolongation of the system till 2006. After that the number of heavy goods vehicles crossing Austria will be unlimited.

The Protocol also contained a clause, according to which only a specific number of truck journeys should take place. When this number was exceeded by more than 8 per cent, a "penalty clause" should enter into effect and cut the traffic levels in order to balance the total number of journeys. However, when such a situation occurred in 2000, no reduction in traffic took place. It was therefore only logical that the Commission proposed, at the end of the year 2000, to have this penalty clause abolished.

(12) Viewed from the environmental point, the ecopoint system is likely to decrease the nitrous oxide emissions in Austria from foreign heavy goods vehicles. To what extent nitrous oxide emissions from Austrian heavy goods vehicles and the total increase in passenger cars and buses has increased since Austria's accession to the European Union due to general traffic increase is not known. Anyway, the ecopoint Protocol addresses only the nitrous oxide emissions, but neither other emissions nor noise or traffic congestion, so that its environmental benefit for the persons living along the Brenner motorway must have remained limited. As it was set up as a transitional measure, its efficiency is limited.

(13) A Commission White Paper of 1992[57] pleaded for the adoption of strict standards for exhaust emissions, energy consumption and noise emissions, as well as standards on technical controls for cars and environmental impact assessments for infrastructure plans and projects, including cost-benefit analyses. It pleaded for the promotion of public transport, bicycles and electric cars, the reduction of private car use and the transport of land use for transport infrastructure projects. In 1995, an action programme for the years 1995–2000 was published.[58]

At the centre of Community transport policy are attempts to increase car production, to create a more efficient transport infrastructure—motorways, roads, railway lines, airports etc. and to adopt stricter standards on vehicle emissions and fuel composition. Forecasts for the year 2010 show increases of 40 per cent in passenger road traffic and of 50 per cent in freight transport (compared to 1994/95).[59] At present 150 million people per year cross the Alps, 83 per cent by road and 17

---

[56] See the corrected figures for the years 2000 to 2003 in Regulation 2012/2000 [2000] OJ L241/18.

[57] Commission, White Paper on a Community Strategy on Sustainable Mobility, COM(92)494 of 2 December 1992.

[58] Commission, The Common Transport Policy—Action programme 1995–2000, COM(95)302 of 12 July 1995.

[59] European Environmental Agency, *Environment in the European Union at the Turn of the Century* (Office for Official Publications of the European Communities, Copenhagen, 1999), p. 66.

per cent by railway. Within the next 20 years, passenger transport in the Alps is expected to increase by 50 per cent and freight transport by 100 per cent.[60]

What a strategic, long-term transit transport policy could achieve, is shown by the example of Switzerland, where about 15 per cent of freight transport is done by road and 85 per cent by railway. In contrast to that, freight transport by road achieves 65 per cent in Austria and even 75 per cent in France.[61]

(14) In 1999, the Community and Switzerland concluded a Convention on land transport which will require Switzerland progressively to increase, until 2005, the admitted overall weight of trucks up to 40 tonnes[62] (at present 28 tonnes) and which provides, overall, for more liberalisation in land transport; heavy good vehicles of up to 34 tonnes have been allowed to travel in Switzerland since 1 January 2001. In contrast to that, the measures aiming at a reduction of road transport do not appear to have played an improtant role in the Convention. The Convention yet has to be ratified by both sides.

12. ENVIRONMENTAL AID TO INDUSTRY

Judgment of the Court of First Instance (Fifth Chamber) of 25 September 1997 Case T–195/90

UK Steel Association v. Commission of the European Communities, supported by Grand Duchy of Luxembourg; and Arbed SA, interveners
[1997] ECR II–1433

Facts and Procedure

The applicants attacked a Commission Decision of 31 December 1994,[63] taken under the Treaty establishing the European Coal and Steel Community (ECSC Treaty), by which the Commission decided not to raise objections against a decision by the Luxembourg government to grant an of 91. 950. 000 Luxembourg francs to

---

[60] European Environmental Agency (n. 59 *supra*) p. 381 which continues: "two-thirds of the Alps population suffer from trafic noise. In Tyrol 87% of high ozone levels are caused by traffic and the 1980s lead concentration in mother's milk close to the Brenner motorway exceeded other regions by seven times. . . Other traffic-caused impacts are fragmentation of untouched areas, deterioration of recreation areas, and socio-economic, double-edged effects such as better accessibility to mountains or changing competition betweenc mountains and low-lands".

[61] Figures from E Brandt, "Verkehrspolitik und transeuropäische Netze", in M Röttinger and C. Weyringer (eds.), *Handbuch der europäischen Integration* (2nd edn., Manz, Vienna, 1996), pp. 931 *et seq.*

[62] For 2001 and 2002, 300.000 trucks of up to 40 tonnes may pass through Switzerland; for 2003 and 2004, this figure is 400. 000 trucks. See Regulation 2888/2000 on the distribution of permits for heavy goods vehicles travelling in Switzerland [2000] OJ L336/9.

[63] The Commission Decision is not published. Its essential parts are reproduced in Commission notice 94/C 400/02 [1994] OJ C400/10.

ARBED SA, a Luxembourg steel company. This aid represented 15 per cent of the sum which Arbed had committed to spending on environmental protection in connection with the construction of a new electrical steel plant in Esch-Schifflange (Luxembourg). The new steel plant was to replace existing plants, which did not comply with the new Luxembourg environmental protection standards.

The applicant considered the aid to be incompatible with Commission Decision 3855/91/ECSC,[64] the so-called Fifth Steel Aid Code, which was applicable when the contested decision was adopted. The preamble to that Decision explained the purpose of the Decision;[65] its Article 3 stated: "1. Aid granted to steel undertakings for bringing into line with new statutory environmental standards plants which entered into service at least two years before the introduction of the standards may be deemed compatible with the common market . . .".

The applicant was of the opinion that the aid which Luxembourg gave to ARBED was incompatible with Community law, as only environmental investments in existing plants were eligible for such aid, not investments in new plants.

The Commission asked the Court to dismiss the application. It was of the opinion that it was possible, under Decision 3855/91, to grant aid to firms which, instead of simply adapting existing plant more than two years old, opt to replace it by new plant meeting the new standards. It admitted that it had, in 1995, submitted a proposal to the Council to get the Council's agreement for amending Article 3, with the aim of adapting environmental aids in the steel sector to the rules which applied in other economic sectors.[66] The general rules on environmental aids which were applicable when Decision 38/55/91 had been taken, did not provide for aid given to new plants.[67] However, these rules had been amended

---

[64] Commission Decision 3855/91/ECSC establishing Community rules for aid to the steel industry [1991] OJ L362/57.

[65] See in particular Part I of the preamble, 4th para., according to which the aim of the rules is " not to deprive the steel industry of aid for research and development or for bringing plants into line with the new environmental standards", and Part II of the preamble which states: "In order to ensure that the steel industry and other industries have equal access to aid for research and development, in so far as this is permitted by the Treaties, the compatibility of these aid schemes with the common market will be assessed in the light of the Community ramework on state aid for research and development. As the provisions on aid for environmental protection are identical to those contained in the framework on state aid in environmental matters, they have not been changed. If the rules laid down by these two general frameworks were changed substantially during the term of validity of this Decision, a proposal for an amendment would be presented".

[66] Commission Communication: "Request for Council assent and consultation of the ECSC Committee, pursuant to Art. 95 ECSC Treaty, concerning a draft Commission decision amending Art. 3 of the Steel Aid Code", SEC(95)315 of 14 March 1995; the proposal seems to have not been published.

This Communication stated: "Art. 1: Art. 3 of Decision 3855/91/ECSC is replaced by the following: Aid for environmental protection. Aid for environmental protection may be deemed compatible with the common market if it is in compliance with the rules laid down in the Community guidelines in force on state aid for environmental protection".

[67] The Community framework on state aid in environmental matters had first been adopted in 1974, then renewed in 1980 and extended in 1987. These frameworks had not been published. However, extensive extracts had been quoted in Commission, *Fourth Report on Competition Policy 1974* (Brussels–Luxembourg, 1975), para. 175; *Tenth Report on Competition Policy 1980* (Brussels–Luxembourg, 1980), paras. 222 *et seq.*; *Sixteenth Report on Competition Policy 1986* (Brussels–Luxembourg, 1986), paras. 259 *et seq.*

in 1994 and stated since then that in certain circumstances, firms which decided to replace existing plant more than two years old by new plant meeting new environmental standards may receive aid in respect of that part of the investment costs that did not exceed the cost of adapting the old plant.[68]

The Commission was of the opinion that in the light of this evolution, Article 3(1) of Decision 3855/91 should be interpreted as also allowing State aid to new plants.

The Court of First Instance annulled the Commission's Decision to allow the granting of aid.

Judgment (extracts)

87. It is necessary to examine whether the assumption underlying the contested decision, that Article 3(1) of the Fifth Code allowed aid to be granted for replacing existing plant by new facilities meeting environmental protection standards, is correct in the light of the wording, context and purpose of that article.

88. As regards wording, Article (1) refers only to "bringing into line with new ... standards plants which entered into service at least two years before the introduction of the standards". A purely literal interpretation of Article 3(1) therefore excludes any investment not intended to bring facilities already in service into line with new standards by, for example, replacing them by new facilities, even if they meet the environmental protection standards.

89. The Commission expressly found in the contested decision that in this case existing plant was not being adapted but was being replaced by new facilities. It has submitted, however, that an interpretation of Article 3(1) in the light of its context and purpose leads to the conclusion that such a possibility is consistent with Article 3(1).

90. That reasoning must therefore be examined to determine whether it is well founded.

91. On the basis of the principle set out in Part II of the preamble to the Fifth Code, that the steel industry and other industries must have equal access to aid for environmental protection, the contested decision states, in the third paragraph of the section entitled " The Commission's assessment" that the same provisions of Community legislation regarding aid for environmental protection should be generally applicable to all firms, whether steel firms or not.

92. It goes on to note, in the fourth paragraph of that section, that the Community guidelines on State aid for environmental protection ... of ... 1994, expressly stipulate that firms which, instead of simply adapting existing plant more than two years old, opt to replace it by new plant meeting the new standards may receive aid in respect of that part of the investment costs that does not exceed the cost of adapting the old plant.

---

[68] Commission, Community guidelines on state aid for environmental protection [1994] OJ C72/3.

93. Finally, in the fifth paragraph of the same section, the contested decision notes that it would seem quite feasible to extend this general principle, as laid down in the EC guidelines, to the steel aid code provided that it does not run counter to the wording of the Article 3 of the Fifth Code, and concludes in the ninth paragraph that the aid in question is compatible with the common market.

94. That reasoning cannot be upheld.

95. Firstly, the Fifth Code introduced rules which allow aid to be granted to the steel industry in a limited number of specified cases, and Article 1(1) thereof posits the principle that such aid may be deemed Community aid and therefore compatible with the orderly functioning of the comon market only if it satisfies the provisions of Articles 2 to 5. The compatibility of aid must therefore be assessed in the light of those provisions.

96. Secondly, the automatic application of the EC guidelines to the steel sector is not provided for in the Fifth Code. Such automatic application cannot be inferred from the principle stated in the preamble to the Fifth Code, that the steel industry and other industries must have equal access to aid for environmental protection. That preamble merely notes that the rules governing aid for environmental protection laid down by the two frameworks were identical at the time when the Fifth Code was adopted. However, the second paragraph of Part II of the preamble . . . states that it would be necessary to present a proposal for an amendment to the Fifth Code if the rules laid down by the two general frameworks were changed substantially during the term of validity of the fifth Code. The application of the EC guidelines to the steel sector is therefore not automatic.

97. Thirdly, the EC framework in force when the Fifth Code was adopted—the EC framework adopted in 1980 and extended in 1987—was in fact amended in 1994. The penultimate paragraph of point 3. 2. 3. A of the new guidelines provides for the possibility of granting aid for investment intended to replace existing plant by new plant. That possibility was not expressly provided for in the 1987 EC framework, which was in force when the Fifth Code was approved.

98. The eventuality envisaged in the second paragraph of Part II of the preamble to the Fifth Code has therefore occurred, since the rules laid down by the 1987 EC framework were changed substantially by the 1994 EC guidelines during the terms of validity of the Fifth Code. Consequently, application to the ECSC sector of the principle established by the new 1994 EC guidelines was conditional on the presentation of a proposal for the amendment of the Fifth Code to bring it into line with the new guidelines.

99. A proposal for such an amendment was in fact presented by the Commission on 14 March 1995 . . . , after the adoption of the contested decision. That proposal was specifically intended to amend Article 3 of the Fifth Code. At point 5 of the proposal, the Commission noted that the new 1994 EC guidelines on State aid for environmental protection differed in at least five major aspects from the former guidelines and thus from the Fifth Code. Among those five aspects, it specifically mentioned the possibility provided for in the penultimate paragraph of 3. 2. 3. A of the new EC guidelines of granting aid in certain circumstances to firms which, instead of simply adapting existing plant more than two years old, opt to replace it by new plant meeting the new standards. The presentation of that proposal confirms . . . that the Commission considered it necessary to amend Article 3 of the Fifth Code in order to be able to apply the principle contained in the EC guidelines to the ECSC sector, and therefore contradicts the Commission's interpretation of Article 3(1) of the Fifth Code in the contested decision. The Commission cannot, therefore, claim that the proposal for an amendment was intended solely to increase the transparency of the Fifth Code, without, however, modifying its substance and meaning. . . .

101. In the light of all the foregoing, it is clear that Article 3 of the Fifth Code does not provide for the possibility of granting aids to firms which, instead of simply adapting existing plant, opt to replace it by new plant meeting the new environmental standards. Consequently, the assumption in the contested decision, that it is possible to extend that provision of the EC guidelines to the steel aid code because it does not contradict the wording of Article 3 of the Fifth Code, must be rejected, since it does run counter to the clear wording of that article.

Commentary

I. State Aid Given to the Construction of a New Steel Plant

(1) In itself, the present judgment deals only with the problem of interpreting a provision of Community law; however, at the same time it illustrates the integration of environmental requirements into other policies, in this case industrial policy.

Decision 3855/91[69]—to which the Court permanently refers as the "Fifth Code"—provides that Member States may grant State aid to existing steel installations in order to allow them to comply with new environmental standards. Luxembourg wanted to grant state aid not for an existing, but for a new plant. The Commission, asked under Article 67 ECSC Treaty to agree to this aid, was of the opinion that the wording of Decision 3855/91 could be set aside, because the purpose and context of that Decision allowed state aid to be granted also for new steel installations.

The Court of First Instance did not agree with this legal interpretation, but decided that the wording of Decision 3855/91 should prevail. Indeed, Article 3 of Decision 3855/91 is anything but ambiguous: "Aid granted to steel undertakings for bringing into line with new statutory environmental standards plants which entered into service at least two years before the introduction of the standards may be deemed compatible with the common market". Thus, in order to receive aid, a plant had to have entered into service two years before the introduction of the standards. This wording definitely excludes aid granted for the construction of a new plant.

---

[69] Decision 3855/91 (n. 64 *supra*).

(2) The Commission rather put the emphasis on the purpose and system for granting state aid to steel undertakings and used a number of reasonings which will be discussed here one by one.

First, the Commission argued that the 1994 Community guidelines on state aid for environmental protection allowed for state aid to be given to firms which decided to replace existing plant more than two years old by new plant meeting new environmental standards, provided that the aid was limited to that part of the investment costs that did not exceed the cost of adapting the old plant.[70] The Commission was of the opinion that the provisions of these 1994 guidelines were to apply to its contested Decision, as this Decision was taken after the adoption of the guidelines.

However, the individual Decision of 31 December 1994 with regard to ARBED was based on Commission Decision 3855/91 and at the time when that Decision of 1991 was adopted, the 1987 guidelines on environmental aid applied, not those of 1994. And the 1987 guidelines did not provide that environmental aid could also be granted to the construction of new steel plants, but referred only to existing plants.[71]

(3) The second argument used by the Commission was that Decision 3855/91 had automatically been adapted to the new environmental guidelines of 1994, without there being a necessity expressly to amend it. The Court also rejected that argument, referring to the wording of Part II of the preamble which expressly stated that Decision 3855/91 would have to be amended, should there be any significant change in the rules on environmental aid.[72] And the Commission itself had presented, in March 1995, thus after the contested Decision of 31 December 1994 had been taken, a proposal to the Council amending Decision 3855/91,[73] in which it had suggested the amendment of Article 3 of Decision 3855/91 in order to adapt it to the new rules on environmental aid;[74] the Council, though, had not agreed to this proposal.

---

[70] Commission, Guidelines on state aid for environmental protection [1994] OJ C72/3, s. 3.2.3.A.

[71] The wording of the 1987 guidelines was, to that extent, the same as in Art. 3 of Decision 3855/91 (n. 64 *supra*), which is reproduced in para. 1 *supra*.

[72] Decision 3855/91 (n. 64 *supra*), preamble, part II: "In order to ensure that the steel industry and other industries have equal access to aid for research and development, in so far as this is permitted by the Treaties, the compatibility of these aid schemes with the common market will be assessed in the light of of the Community framework on state aid for research and development. As the provisions on aid for environmental protection are identical to those contained in the framework on state aid in environmental matters, they have not been changed. If the rules laid down by these two general frameworks were changed substantially during the term of validity of this Decision, a proposal for an amendment would be presented".

[73] Commission, Request for Council assent and consultation of the ECSC Committee, pursuant to Art. 95 of the ECSC Treaty, concerning a draft Commission decision amending Art. 3 of the Steel Aid Code, SEC(95)315 of 14 March 1995.

[74] Commission (n. 73 *supra*): "Art. 1: Art. 3 of Decision 3855/91 ECSC is replaced by the following: 'Aid for environmental protection. Aid for environmental protection may be deemed compatible with the common market if it is in compliance with the rules laid down in the Community guidelines in force on state aid for environmental protection' ".

(4) The Court therefore concluded that as Decision 3855/91 itself requested an express amendment if the environmental aid guidelines had changed, such express amendment could not be substituted by an automatic adaptation to amended environmental aid guidelines.

The Commission further argued that it was one of the basic aims of Decision 3855/91 to ensure that the steel industry had access to the same state aids as other industries[75] and that this aim allowed the application of the 1994 rules on environmental aid to the steel industry as soon as they were applied to other industries. It is clear, though, that this argument, which was also rejected by the Court, does not carry much weight, since Decision 3855/91 could have provided for an automatic application of the rules on environmental aid, but had instead expressly provided for an amendment, if new rules on environmental schemes came into force. The Court was therefore rather short in rejecting that argument.

(5) Neither did the Court accept the Commission's argument that Article 3(1) of Decision 3855/91 should be interpreted broadly. It mainly argued that as Decision 3855/91 "constitutes a derogation from Article 4 of the ECSC Treaty, it must be interpreted strictly".[76]

As thus in 1994 environmental aid could not, under the Community rules in force at that time, be given to the construction of new steel plants, the Court of First Instance annulled the Commission Decision of 31 December 1994. Subsequently, the Commission adopted a new decision, by which it declared the aid given by Luxembourg to ARBED incompatible with Article 4(c) of the ECSC Treaty and ordered Luxembourg to claim the aid back from ARBED.[77]

II. Environmental Aid and Community Law and Policy

(6) As mentioned, Article 4(c) of the ECSC Treaty prohibits state aid for the coal and steel industry. However, such state aid was frequently granted by Member States, practically since the begin of the ECSC Treaty in 1952. In 1980, for the first time specific provisions for aids to the steel industry were fixed at Community level,[78] and since then, this practice has continued.[79]

---

[75] Decision 3855/91 (n. 64 *supra*), preamble, part I: "the aim of the rules laid down . . . is firstly not to deprive the steel industry of aid for research and development or for bringing plants into line with new environmental standards".

[76] Para. 114 of the Judgment. Art. 4(c) of the ECSC Treaty provides: "The following are recognized as incompatible with the common market for coal and steel and shall accordingly be abolished and prohibited within the Community, as provided in this Treaty: . . . (c) subsidies or aids granted by States, or special charges imposed by States, in any form whatsoever".

[77] Commission Decision K(1998) 1764 [1999] OJ L45/51.

[78] Commission, Decision 257/80/ECSC, establishing Community rules for specific aids to the steel industry [1980] OJ L29/5 (the so-called "first steel aid code").

[79] See Commission, Decision 2496/96/ECSC establishing Community rules for state aid to the steel industry [1996] OJ L338/42 (the so-called "sixth steel aid code").

The EC Treaty, which entered into effect in 1958, repeated the principle of the prohibition of state aids,[80] but was wise enough expressly to allow specific categories of aids,[81] which were enumerated in Article 87(2) and (3) EC Treaty; furthermore, Article 87 EC Treaty was placed in the chapter on competition policy, which meant that a state aid became relevant under Community law to the extent that it distorted or threatened to distort competition. Since the early 1970s, the Commission has published guidelines or framework communications on aid in specific sectors—car sector, textiles, research, regional aid etc.—which are, in law, non-binding instruments, but which limit the Commission's discretion to approve or disapprove aid granted by Member States. The decision by the Commission to approve or disapprove a specific state aid[82] is, however, based on the provisions of the Treaty, not on the guidelines.

The total amount of state aid given in the Community is considerable. Between 1994 and 1998, its annual average amount was 93 billion Euro.[83] Environmental aid formed only a small part of this aid (0.65 per cent); it developed as follows: 1994 473.8 million Euro, 1995 506.1 million, 1996 536.7 million Euro, 1997 544.3 million and 1998 732.1 million Euro.[84] The biggest per centage of all state aid for environmental projects was given in Denmark (15.11 per cent), followed by the Netherlands (2.73 per cent), Sweden (2.52 per cent) and Austria (2.19 per cent). In Ireland and Portugal, no state aid constituted environmental aid, in Greece (0.01 per cent), the United Kingom (0.05 per cent) and Italy (0.12 per cent) the percentage was insignificant.[85]

(7) The "Community guidelines on state aid for environmental protection" of early 2001 entered into effect in February 2002 and are applicable till end 2007.[86] They apply to aid that is given to protect the environment "in all sectors governed by the EC Treaty". It aims at satisfying a double imperative: (a) ensure the competitive functioning of markets, while promoting the completion of the single market and increased competitiveness in firms; (b) ensure that the requirements of

---

[80] Art. 87 (ex Art. 92) EC Treaty: "1. Save as otherwise provided in this Treaty, any aid granted by a Member State or through State resources in any form whatsoever which distorts of threatens to distort competition by favouring certain undertakings or the production of certain goods shall, insofar as it affects trade between Member States, be incompatible with the common market".

[81] As regards the notion of aid, see Court of Justice, Case 30/59, *Steenkolenmijnen* [1961] ECR 1: "A subsidy is normally defined as a payment in cash or in kind, made in support of any undertaking, other than the payment by the purchaser or the consumer for the goods or services which it produces. An aid is a very similar concept, which, however, places emphasis on its purpose and seems especially devised for a particular objective which cannot normally be achieved without outside help. The concept of aid is nevertheless wider than that of a subsidy because it embraces not only positive benefits such as subsidies themselves, but also interventions which, in various forms, mitigate the charges which are normally included in the budget of an undertaking and which, without therefore being subsidies in the strict sense of the word, are similar in character and have the same effect".

[82] As regards the rules for the application of state aid (Art. 87 EC Treaty) see Regulation 659/99 [1999] OJ L83/14.

[83] Commission, Fourth survey on state aid in the European Union. COM(2000) 205 of 11 April 2000, para. 10 and p. 110.

[84] Commission (n. 83 *supra*), p. 110.

[85] These percentage figures refer to the annual average 1996–1998.

[86] (2001) OJ C37/3.

environmental protection are integrated into the definition and implementation of competition policy. Internalisation of costs is seen as a priority objective. The Commission states that in general, "the pollutor pays principle and the need for firms to internalise the costs associated with protecting the environment would appear to militate against the granting of State aid". Therefore, "aid is not justified in the case of investments designed merely to bring companies into line with new or existing Community technical standards"; small and medium-sized companies (SMEs) might justify a derogation from this principle. Also, where more stringent standards are applied than fixed by the Community, aid may be granted. Aid may be granted on the basis of Article 87(3)(c) or, exceptionally, Article 87(3)(b) EC Treaty.[87] [88] The guidelines provide for the possibility to grant aid

(a) in the form of investment aid. Aid for the investment in land, buildings, plant and equipment and in the adaptation of production methods with a view to protecting the environment may be given in order to improve on the Community standards applicable up to 30 per cent of the investment costs; where energy saving investments are made, the aid may be up to 40 per cent. Specific rules are given for SMEs, investment in renewable energy (up to 100 per cent) and for aid in regions which are eligible for national regional aid. Also, specific rules are made for the rehabilitation of polluted industrial sites (aid up to 100 per cent of the costs, plus 15 per cent of the cost of the work) and the relocation of firms established in a designated natural habitat.

(8) Practical examples are the Commission's decision to allow the United Kingdom to grant an environmental aid of up to 30 per cent for the construction of a sludge treatment plant in Birmingham by Jaguar and Ford; the Commission found that this plant would reduce polluting discharges far beyond (between 50 and 87 per cent reduction) the existing standards.[89] Also the environmental aid which Mercedes-Benz obtained from France for the construction of the "Smart" car plant in Hambach-Saargemünd did not meet objections from the Commission.[90] In contrast to that, the Commission partly refused to consider aid which Germany had granted to Volkswagen for its plant in Mosel and Chemnitz as environmental aid. The Commission argued that the strict air pollution standards were aimed at by all Community car producers and were therefore not really supplementary requirements.[91]

---

[87] See, however, as an example of an aid approved under Art. 87(3) (a) the aid granted to the waste treatment plant Broerius Abfallverwertung in Germany, Commission, *XXVIIth Report on Competition Policy* (1997) (Brussels–Luxembourg, 1998), p. 263.

[88] Art. 87(3) (ex Art. 92(3)) EC Treaty: "The following may be considered to be compatible with the common market: (a) aid to promote the economic development of areas where the standard of living is abnormally low or where there is serious underemployment; (b) aid to promote the execution of an important project of common European interest or to remedy a serious disturbance in the economy of a Member State; (c) aid to facilitate the development of certain economic activities or of certain economic areas, where such aid does not adversely affect trading conditions to an extent contrary to the common interest; . . ."

[89] Commission (undated), Communication [1996] OJ C311/15.

[90] Commission (undated), Communication [1996] OJ C391/11.

[91] Commission, Decision 96/666 [1996] OJ L308/46, para. XII.

The Commission accepted investment aid of 30 per cent granted by Italy to a plant which was situated in a residential area and where the investment had reduced the discharge of sludge by 40 per cent, water consumption by 50 per cent furthermore noise emissions and transport.[92]

In recent years, state aid to invest in renewable energies has become more frequent. Examples are aid given to a Swedish plant for investment in energy from biomass, water and wind;[93] an aid scheme in the Netherlands aimed at stimulating the use of electricity generated from renewable energy sources (13. 5 million Euro per year);[94] a scheme in Germany to grant aid for projects which used energy-saving standards and renewable energy[95] and the Commission's decision not to raise objections against the introduction of an energy tax on electricity and mineral oil in Germany.[96]

(9) (b) Aid to SMEs for advisory/consultancy services in the environmental field

(c) Operating aid which covers aid for management of waste and aid in the energy-saving field. This category also covers temporary reduction of environmental taxes and charges; thus, the Commission approved a Danish system to introduce a CO_2 tax but to exempt industries with a large energy use[97] and a system introduced by the Netherlands to introduce a groundwater and waste tax, but to provide for exemption of certain industrial activities.[98]

(d) Operating aid for the combined production of electric power and heat. Normally, measures which aim at inciting final consumers to purchase environmentally friendly goods cannot be considered to be state aid, unless there are specific financial advantages for certain industrial undertakings, for instance because only one undertaking is manufacturing that product. It is for this reason that Community directives on car emissions contain a specific clause which restricts the possibility to grant financial incentives to consumers for the purchase of environmentally friendly cars:[99] as all car producers technically could produce such cars, such an incentive would not constitute, under Article 87 EC Treaty, a state aid.

(10) Different forms of aid for one and the same project can be cumulated: Thus, for instance, the Commission did not raise objections to state aid granted by Austria to the undertaking BMW Steyr which was to enable the undertaking to modernise and extend its activity of constructing motors and which consisted of aid for research and development, environmental aid, training aid, innovation aid and regional aid.[100]

---

[92] Commission (undated), Communication [1995] OJ C294/11.

[93] Commission, *XXVIIth Report on Competition Policy* (n. 87 *supra*), p. 265.

[94] Commission *XXVIIIth Report on Competition Policy* (1998) (Brussels–Luxembourg, 1999), p. 255.

[95] [2000] OJ C266/5.

[96] Commission, *XXIXth Report on Competition Policy* (1999) (Brussels–Luxembourg, 2000), para. 253.

[97] Commission, *XXV Report on Competition Policy* (Brussels–Luxembourg, 1996), p. 246 *et seq.*

[98] Commission (n. 97 *supra*), p. 247

[99] See, for instance, Directive 94/12 [1994] OJ L100/42 Art. 3: Tax incentives "shall apply to all new vehicles offered for sale on the market of a Member State which comply in advance with the requirements of Directive 70/220, as amended by this Directive; they shall be terminated with effect from the mandatory application of the emission values laid down in Art. 2(3) for new motor ehicles; for each type of motor vehicle, they shall be for an amount lower than the additional cost of the technical solutions introduced to ensure compliance with the values set and of their installation on the vehicle".

[100] Commission (undated), Communication [1998] OJ C12/5.

In general, it seems that the Commission tends to be generous in approving environmental aid given by Member States. The cases where aid for national projects aiming at strengthening the environment is refused are exceptional and concern either cases where the environmental cover rather concerns measures with another objective, such as regional policy, protectionism or distortion of competition; and this might well have been the underlying rationale of the Decision in the present *ARBED* case.

13. ENVIRONMENTAL TAXES

Judgment of the Court of 2 April 1998
Case C–213/96

Reference for a preliminary ruling: Outokumpu Oy
[1998] ECR I–1777

Facts and Procedure

Outokumpu Oy is a Finnish company which principally sells electricity to its daughter companies in Finland. In 1995, it concluded a contract with a Swedish company for the purchase of electricity from Sweden. The Finnish authorities asked Outokumpu Oy to pay a tax which was charged in Finland on certain energy sources and was based on legislative Act 1473/94.

The Finnish legislation varies the amount of the tax according to the energy source (coal, lignite, peat, natural gas, electricity produced by nuclear power or by water power, pine oil). It exempts electrictiy produced in small generators, electricity produced from certain industrial waste, electricity generated from peat if the production is no higher than 25.000 megawatt per year and electricity produced by nuclear or water power in Finland which is then exported from Finland. The rate of duty on imported electricity was calculated to correspond to the average tax rate of electricity produced in Finland, but without taking into consideration the tax reductions provided for in the legislation for some energy sources.

Outokumpu Oy appealed to a Finnish court as it was of the opinion that the Finnish tax was incompatible with Community law. The Finnish court referred the case to the Court of Justice for a preliminary ruling, asking whether it was compatible with Community law for a Member State to levy duty on imported electricity at a flat rate when the duty on electricity generated within that State is imposed at various rates, depending essentially on the production method and prompted by environmental concerns.

Judgment (extracts)

29. . . . an excise duty of the kind at issue in the main proceedings constitutes internal taxation within the meaning of Article 95 of the Treaty, not a charge having equivalent effect to a customs duty within the meaning of Articles 9 and 12.

30. As regards the compatibility of such a duty with Article 95 of the Treaty, it is settled case-law, first, that in its present state of development Community law does not restrict the freedom of each Member State to establish a tax system which differentiates between certain products, even products which are similar within the meaning of the first paragraph of Article 95 of the Treaty, on the basis of objective criteria, such as the nature of the raw materials used or the production processes employed. Such differentiation is compatible with Community law, however, only if it pursues objectives which are themselves compatible with the requirements of the Treaty and its secondary legislation, and if the detailed rules are such as to avoid any form of discrimination, direct or indirect, against imports from other Member States or any form of protection of competing domestic products.

31. Article 95 of the Treaty therefore does not preclude the rate of an internal tax on electricity from varying sources according to the manner in which the electricity is produced and the raw materials used for its production, in so far as that differentiation is based, as is clear from the actual wording of the national court's question, on environmental considerations.

32. As the Court stated in case 302/86 *Commission* v. *Denmark* [1988] ECR 4607, paragraph 8, protection of the environment constitutes one of the essential objectives of the Community. Moreover, since the entry into force of the Treaty on European Union, the Community's task includes the promotion of sustainable and non-inflationary growth respecting the environment (Article 2 of the EC Treaty) and its activities include a policy in the sphere of the environment (Article 3(k) of the EC Treaty).

33. Furthermore, as the Advocate General observes in paragraph 58 of the Opinion, compatibility with the environment, particularly of methods of producing electrical energy, is an important objective of the Community's energy policy.

34. However, on the question whether differentiation such as that which characterises the tax system at issue in the main proceedings is compatible with the prohibition of discrimination in Article 95 of the Treaty, the Court has consistently held that that provision is infringed where the taxation on the imported product and that on the similar domestic product are calculated in a different manner on the basis of different criteria which lead, if only in certain cases, to higher taxation being imposed on the imported product . . .

35. That is the case where, under a system of differential taxation of the kind at issue in the main proceedings, imported electricity distributed via the national network is subject, whatever its method of production, to a flat-rate duty which is higher than the lowest duty charged on electricity of domestic origin distributed via the national network.

36.   The fact that electricity of domestic origin is in some cases taxed more heavily than imported electricity is immaterial in this connection since, in order to ascertain whether the system in question is compatible with Article 95 of the Treaty, the tax burden imposed on imported electricity must be compared with the lowest tax burden imposed on electricity of domestic origin . . .

37.   The Finnish Government raises the objection that in view of characteristics of electricity, the origin and consequently the method of production of which cannot be determined once it has entered the distribution network, the differential rates applicable to electricity of domestic origin cannot be applied to imported electricity. It submits that in those circumstances application of a flat rate, calculated so as to correspond to the average rate levied on electricity of domestic origin, is the only logical way of treating imported electricity in an equitable manner.

38.   The Court has already had occasion to point out that practical difficulties cannot justify the application of internal taxation which discriminates against products from other Member States . . .

39.   While the characteristics of electricity may indeed make it extremely difficult to determine precisely the method of production of imported electricity and hence the primary energy sources used for that purpose, the Finnish legislation at issue does not give the importer the opportunity of demonstrating that the electricity imported by him has been produced by a particular method in order to qualify for the rate applicable to electricity of domestic origin produced by the same method.

40.   Moreover, the Court has already held that although in principle Article 95 of the Treaty, does not require Member States to abolish differences which are objectively justified and which national legislation establishes between internal taxes on domestic products, it is otherwise where such abolition is the only way of avoiding direct or indirect discrimination against the imported products . . .

41.   In the light of the foregoing considerations, the answer must be that the first paragraph of Article 95 of the EC Treaty precludes an excise duty which forms part of a national system of taxation on sources of energy from being levied on electricity of domestic origin at rates which vary according to its method of production while being levied on imprted electricity, whatever its method of production, at a flat rate which, although lower than the highest rate applicable to electricity of domestic origin, leads, if only in certain cases, to higher taxation being imposed on imported electricity.

Commentary

I. The Finnish Ecotax on Electricity

(1) The Court first had to establish whether the Finnish levy came under Article 25 (ex Article 12)[101] or under Article 90 (ex Article 95) EC Treaty.[102] To that extent, it has stated in settled case law that any pecuniary charge which is imposed unilaterally on goods[103] by reason of the fact that they cross a frontier comes under Article 25 (ex Article 12) EC Treaty. However, if the charge forms part of a general system of internal duties which apply systematically to categories of products according to objective criteria applied without regard to the origin of the product, the charge falls within the scope of Article 90 (ex Article 95) EC Treaty.[104] The difference is, thus, whether the pecuniary charge applies to imported products alone or whether it applies to both imported and domestic products. As the Finnish legislation establishes a system of general internal taxation on electricity and also covers domestic electricity, Article 90 applies.

(2) As there is no Community legislation on the taxation of electricity or energy sources generally, Member States are free to establish tax systems as they consider appropriate; of course, though, they have to respect the provisions of the EC Treaty, including Article 90. This provision applies as a *lex specialis* to tax systems,[105] which may therefore not be assessed under Article 28 (ex Article 30) EC Treaty.[106] In particular circumstances, Article 28 EC Treaty may be applicable.[107]

Article 90(1) prohibits any direct or indirect discrimination of imported products. This provision has continuously been applied by the Court of Justice in a very strict manner: whether the different fiscal treatment of imported and domestic products was the effect of different rates, of different methods of calculation or due to other circumstances, the Court prohibited the national measures, as soon as in theory or in practice it discovered a different treatment. In the present case, the

---

[101] Art. 25 (ex Art. 12) EC Treaty: "Customs duties on import and exports and charges having equivalent effect shall be prohibited between Member States. This prohibition shall also apply to customs duties of a fiscal nature".

[102] Art. 90 (ex Art. 95) EC Treaty: "No Member State shall impose, directly or indirectly, on the products of other Member States any internal taxation of any kind in excess of that imposed directly or indirectly on similar domestic products.

Furthermore, no Member State shall impose on the products of other Member States any internal taxation of such a nature as to afford indirect protection to other products".

[103] Electricity is a product under the provisions of the EC Treaty: see Court of Justice, Cases C–393/92, *Almelo* [1994] ECR I–1477; C–158/94, *Commission* v. *Italy* [1997] ECR I–5789.

[104] Court of Justice, Cases 78/76 *Steinike and Weinlig* v. *Germany* [1977] ECR 595; 32/80, *Kortmann* [1981] ECR 251; C–90/94, *Haahr Petroleum* [1997] ECR I–4085.

[105] Court of Justice, Cases 74/76, *Iannelli and Volpi* [1977] ECR 557; C–78–83/90, *Compagnie Commerciale de l'Ouest* [1992] ECR I–1847.

[106] Art. 28 (ex Art. 30) EC Treaty: "Quantitative restrictions on imports and all measures having equivalent effect shall be prohibited between Member States".

[107] Commission, Environmental taxes and charges in the single market, COM(97)9 of 26 March 1997; for a discussion of such a case see p. 251 *infra*.

lowest rate of tax for electricity produced in Finland was 0 per cent; imported electricity was taxed according to a flat rate which, logically, was higher than 0 per cent. There were thus cases where imported electricity was charged at a higher rate than electricity that was produced in Finland.

(3) However, the problem here was that the product in question was electricity. Electricity cannot be stored; therefore, once it enters the electricity grid one can no longer distinguish whether it is produced from nuclear or water power, from coal, oil or wind. "For that reason, it is common ground that it is not just difficult but impossible to identify the source, and hence the method of production, of imported electricity".[108]

Finland had expressly wished to differentiate between the tax rates for electricity according to the methods of production, in order to promote environmentally friendly methods of energy production. Indeed, Finnish Law 1473/94 imposes very heavy rates of tax on electricity produced from heavy fuel oil and coal to very low rates of tax on hydroelectric. This was possible for domestic production, but, as mentioned, impossible for imported electricity. Applying the lowest rate of tax for imported electricity would not make sense, since such a policy only would incite electricity import and thus not reach the desired political effect of promoting environmentally friendly methods of energy production. The question was, therefore, whether Finland had to abandon its differentiation of the rates of tax according to the method of production, as it could not establish the same differentiation for imported electricity; or whether Finland could form an average rate of tax (flat-rate) for imported electricity.

(4) Finland took the view that for the abovementioned reasons the different way of taxing domestic electricity and imported electricity was the only way of linking environmental considerations and the taxation of electricity. The Court of Justice, however, did not share that point of view. It took the line that environmental protection considerations did not justify any differentiated treatment of domestic and imported electricity. It repeated earlier judgments that there was discrimination as soon as the duty on imported electricity was higher, be it only in certain cases, than the lowest duty charged on electricity of domestic origin.[109] It considered the difficulty of determining the origin of imported electricity as a practical difficulty and then referred to earlier judgments according to which practical difficulties could not justify a discrimination of imported products.[110] The Court saw itself the consequence of its interpretation: the Finnish tax legislation on electricity (Law 1473/94) would have to be abolished in order to avoid discrimination against imported electricity.

(5) What is interesting is that Finland had expressly invoked environmental reasons for its legislation. The Advocate General had taken up these arguments and considered that, despite the earlier judgments on the interpretation of Article

---

[108]   Advocate General Jacobs, Opinion in the present Case C–213/96, para. 59.

[109]   Court of Justice, Case C–152/89, *Commission* v. *Luxembourg* [1991] ECR I–3141.

[110]   Court of Justice, Cases C–152/89 (n. 109 *supra*); C–375/95, *Commission* v. *Greece* [1997] ECR I–5981.

90, the environmental considerations could justify a different method of calcula-tion for domestic and imported electricity, provided that the flat rate of tax for imported electricity was correctly calculated. The Court of Justice mentioned, it is true, environmental aspects in paragraphs 31 to 33 of its judgment. However, these arguments were used in an abstract way only. When Article 90 (ex Article 95) EC Treaty itself was discussed, the word "environment" no longer appeared.

(6) In other terms, the principles of interpretation of Article 90 EC Treaty, developed in other than environmental cases, prevailed also in a situation where national legislation expressly—and in an objectively verifiable way—tried to pro-mote the production of electricity in an environmentally favourable manner. There was no attempt by the Court to weigh the diverging interests in question—on the one hand the objective to avoid tax discrimination of imported electricity, "if only in certain cases" (paragraph 34 of the judgment), on the other hand the objective to make a prudent and rational use of natural resources (Article 174 EC Treaty) and to promote alternative energies in order to fight climate change—and to come to a balanced solution. The specificity of the present case—the impossi-bility of identifying the method of production only exists for electricity, the national legislation without doubt pursues an environmental objective—could and should have allowed the Court at least to discuss the environmental concerns. Instead, the Court invoked the formal aspect of discrimination, "if only in certain cases" and with that argument finished the discussion.

(7) This way of proceeding ignores that at the time of the judgment Article 174(2) EC Treaty was in force, which provided that environmental requirements had to be integrated into the definition and implementation of other Community policies.[111] It does not comment on the fact that in the interpretation of Article 28 EC Treaty the Court has long since established that obstacles to the free circulation of goods must be accepted in so far as they are necessary to attain mandatory requirements recognised by Community law and that the protection of the envir-onment is such a mandatory requirement.[112] It is true that, in principle, only such national environmental provisions may be considered mandatory requirements, which are "indistinctly applicable" to domestic and imported products. However, the Court did not attach too much importance to the question of discrimination against an environmental measure, when it considered a specific outcome of a case desirable.[113] The present judgment seems to stop the discussion on environmen-tal issues as soon as it has reached the point that different treatment between domestically produced and imported electricity is established. From an environ-mental point of view it is regrettable that Member States may not differentiate, as regards electricity, according to the method of production.

---

[111] See now Art. 6 EC Treaty: "Environmental protection requirements must be integrated into the definition and implementation of the Community policies and activities referred to in Art. 3, in par-ticular with a view to promoting sustainable development".

[112] See in particular Case 302/86, *Commission* v. *Denmark* [1988] ECR 4607.

[113] See in particular Case C–2/90, *Commission* v. *Belgium* [1992] ECR I–4431, where the question of discrimination was not even discussed by the Court.

(8) It can only be speculated why the Court adopted such a conservative attitude which was fully in line with earlier considerations, but which did not take into consideration the specific environmental concerns. One issue may be that France which is potentially an exporter of electricity produces much of its electricity from nuclear energy. The political consequences of charging electricity at a higher rate just because it came from nuclear power plants could be considerable and might have influenced the arguments by the Court. However, that remains speculation.

In a judgment of 13 March 2001, Preussen Elekton AG, not yet reported, the Court considered that a German scheme on the promotion of wind energy was compatible with Community law, though that system was limited to German producers and thus contained elements of discrimination of non-German producers of wind energy.

II. Ecotaxes at National and Community Level

(9) The general interpretation of Article 90 EC Treaty, as developed by the Court of Justice in this and several other judgments,[114] may be summarised as follows: Member States are, in principle, free to choose the system of taxation which they consider most suitable; the system which is applied to domestic products constitutes the point of reference for determining whether products of other Member States are taxed more heavily than domestic products; Article 90 is not respected if a product from another Member State is more heavily charged than a domestic product.

The Community actively promoted the use of environmental taxes and charges in its fifth environmental action programme, but was probably thinking more of such taxes at Community than at national level.[115] Within Member States, the use of environmental taxes has considerably increased over the recent years[116] and there seems to be almost consensus among experts that such taxes can be a very efficient tool to change behaviour. Their main advantage is seen in:

—the effect of bringing the costs of environmental pollution and other costs of using the environment (use of water, resources etc.) to the price of the goods or services,
—creating an incentive to avoid the tax by using a product that is not taxed or using less of the taxed product.

---

[114] Court of Justice, Cases 106/84, *Commission* v. *Denmark* [1986] ECR 833; 196/85, *Commission* v. *France* [1987] ECR 1597; C–47/88, *Commission* v. *Denmark* [1990] ECR I–4509; C–132/88, *Commission* v. *Greece* [1990] ECR I–1567; C–113/94, *Casarin* [1995] ECR I–4203.

[115] Fifth Community environmental action programme [1993] OJ C138/5, para. 7.4: "In order to get the prices right and to create market-based incentives for environmentally friendly economic behaviour, the use of economic and fiscal instruments will have to constitute an increasingly important part of the overall approach. The fundamental aim of these instruments will be to internalise all external environmental costs incurred during the whole life-cycle of products from source through production, distribution, use and final disposal, so that environmentally-friendly products will not be at a competitive disadvantage in the market place vis-à-vis prdoucts which cause pollution and waste".

[116] See *European Environmental Agency, Environmental Taxes: Implementation and Environmental Effectiveness* (Office for Official Publications of the European Communities, Copenhagen, 1996).

—reducing the costs of pollution control.

—encouraging innovation.

—raising revenues.

(10) At Community level, the Commission made, in 1991, a proposal for the Community-wide introduction of a combined carbon dioxide energy tax, in order to fight climate change.[117] The proposal was based on Articles 93 and 175(2) EC Treaty, which both require unanimous decisions. This unanimity could not be reached, since a number of Member States opposed and continue to do so, for fundamental reasons, the adoption of taxes and charges at Community level. The Commission therefore amended its proposal and suggested[118] that Member States remained free to decide whether they wanted to introduce a CO_2 energy tax; where they so decided, they had to comply with certain conditions fixed in the proposal. Nevertheless, unanimous agreement in Council was not reached.

Prior to 1991, the Commission had already proposed, when it suggested the introduction of lead-free petrol in the Community, to have different levels of tax for leaded and unleaded petrol.[119] This proposal had been rejected;[120] subsequently such tax differences were introduced in some Member States, with the effect that when it was decided, in 1998, to phase out regular leaded petrol,[121] Italy, Spain and Greece, which had not adopted tax (price) differentiation measures, requested—and obtained—derogation periods.

(11) In view of the obvious political difficulties linked with the adoption of environmental taxes at Community level, the Commission has not yet made other proposals for the introduction of such an eco-tax.[122] Several directives, in particular in the waste area, provide for the possibility of adopting economic measures at Community level; however, such provisions do not have any legal value.

---

[117] [1992] OJ C196/1.

[118] COM(95)172 of 10 May 1995.

[119] [1984] OJ C178/5

[120] Directive 85/210 concerning the lead content of petrol [1985] OJ L96/25.

[121] Directive 98/70 which replaced Directive 85/210 [1998] OJ L350/58.

[122] See the Commission's resumé in Communication: Europe's environment: what directions for the future? The global assessment of the European Community programme of policy and action in relation to the environment and sustainable development, "Towards sustainability", COM(99)543 of 24 November 1999, para. 6.1: "At the Community level, many of the Directives issued by the Commission allow for tax incentives to encourage early implementation (such as those on vehicle emissions and fuel quality). However, the adoption of EU-wide measures, such as a CO_2 tax or an energy products tax, on the other hand has been disappointing. The institutional set-up (need for unanimous agreement in the ECOFIN Council) has prevented any real progress".

14. PREVENTION OF INDUSTRIAL ACCIDENTS

Judgment of the Court (Sixth Chamber) of 17 June 1999
Case C–336/97

Commission of the European Communities v. *Italy*
[1999] ECR I–3771

Facts and Procedure

Directive 82/501 on the major-accident hazards of certain industrial activities[123] required Member States to ensure that industries which were covered by that Directive took measures to prevent major accidents. Member States had to comply with the requirements of Directive 82/501 by early 1984.

Italy transposed Directive 82/501into Italian law in May 1988.[124] The Commission took the view that the Directive had not been fully implemented in Italy. Thus, it started formal action under Article 226 EC Treaty[125] against Italy in November 1992 and sent, in November 1995, a reasoned opinion and applied in September 1997 to the Court. It argued that Italy had not fulfilled its obligations under Article 7(1) and (2)[126] of the Directive, by omitting to draw up emergency plans outside the establishments affected by the Directive and by not making the necessary controls and inspections.

The Court found that Italy had failed to fulfil its obligations under the Directive.

---

[123]   Directive 82/501 [1982] OJ L230/1

[124]   *Decreto del Presidente della Repubblica n. 175 of 17 May 1988 attuativo della direttiva n. 82/501 relativi ai rischi di incidenti rilevanti connessi con determinate attivitá industriali,* Gazzetta Ufficiale no. 127 of 1 June 1988, p. 1.

[125]   Art. 226 (ex Art. 169) EC Treaty: "If the Commission considers that a Member State has failed to fulfil an obligation under this Treaty, it shall deliver a reasoned opinion on the matter after giving the State concerned the opportunity to submit its observation.

If the State concerned does not comply with the opinion within the period laid down by the Commission, the latter may bring the matter before the Court of Justice".

[126]   Directive 82/501 (n. 123 *supra*), Art. 7: "1. The Member States shall set up or appoint the competent authority or authorities who, account being taken of the responsability of the manufacturer, are responsible for . . . ensuring that an emergeny plan in drawn up for action outside the establishment in respect of whose industrial activity notification has been given . . .

2. The competent authorities shall organise inspections or other measures of control proper to the type of activity concerned, in accordance with national regulations".

Judgment (extracts)

18. The Italian Republic contends that, in order to transpose those provisions of Directive 82/501 properly, the Member States merely have to appoint the competent authorities responsible for ensuring that the emergency plans for action are drawn up and organising the relevant inspections and measures of control. It argues that, although it is an objective of Directive 82/501 to ensure that emergency plans are actually drawn up and that inspections and controls are in fact carried out, those tasks cannot in themselves constitute specific obligations imposed on the Member States by the directive; rather, they are merely a logical consequence of its application in practice.

19. In that connection, it should be borne in mind that, under the first paragraph of Article 10 EC (ex first paragraph of Article 5), the Member States are to take all appropriate measures, whether general or particular, to ensure fulfilment of the obligations arising out of the Treaty or resulting from action taken by the institutions of the Community. Such action includes directives which, pursuant to the third paragraph of Article 249 EC (ex third paragraph of Article 189), are binding as to the result to be achieved upon each Member State to which they are addressed. Under the Court's case-law, that obligation implies, for each Member State to which a directive is addressed, adopting, within the framework of its national legal system, all the measures necessary to ensure that the directive is fully effective, in accordance with the objective which it pursues . . .

20. According to Article 1 of the directive . . . the purpose of the directive is, inter alia, to ensure that the necessary measures are adopted to prevent major accidents caused by certain industrial activities, and to limit the consequences of any such accidents.

21. To that end, Directive 82/501 not only provides for obligations which the Member States are under a duty to impose on manufacturers, such as those arising under Articles 3, 4 and 5, but also imposes certain obligations on the Member States directly, such as those in Article 7(1) and Article 7(2) which are at issue here.

22. In addition, under Articles 4 and 5 of Directive 82/501 the obligations imposed by the directive on manufacturers are expressly intended to contributeto the fulfilment of the Member States' obligations under Article 7.

23. First, it is in order to enable the competent authorities appointed by the Member States pursuant to Article 7 of Directive 82/501 to draw up emergency plans for action outside the establishment referred to in the third indent of Article 7(1), that the second indent of Article 5(1)(c) requires the information relating to possible major-accident situations which manufacturers are to notify to those authorities to include any details necessary to enable such plans to be prepared.

24. Secondly, it is for the purposes of the inspections and controls referred to in Article 7(2) of Directive 82/501 that Article 4 imposes on manufacturers to prove to the competent authorities of the Member States at any time that they have identified existing major-accident hazards and adopted the measures referred to in that provision.

25. Accordingly, the objective pursued by Directive 82/501, namely to prevent major accidents and limit their consequences by means of the measures favoured by the directive, would be in danger of being seriously compromised if it were open to the Member States merely to set up or appoint the competent authorities for drawing up emergency plans for action outside the establishments and organising ispections and measures of control, without ensuring that those plans and inspections were actually completed.

26. According to the Italian Republic's reply to the reasoned opinion, which post-dates the time-limit within which it was to comply with its obligations under Directive 82/501, only 110 out of a total of 443 emergency plans for action outside the establishments had been drawn up as at that date.

27. Furthermore, whilst the Italian Republic stated in its defence that the number of industrial establishments which were notified to the competent authorities under Directive 82/501 and should accordingly have been inspected or subject to other measures of control only amounted to 391 instead of 710, the figure which it gave in its letter of 14 January 1992, it acknowledged at the same time that only 220 establishments had in fact been inspected.

28. In those circumstances, it is appropriate to allow the Commission's action and declare that, by failing to ensure that emergency plans are drawn up for action outside the establishments in respect of whose industrial activity notification has been given pursuant to Article 5 of Directive 82/501, and by failing to organise inspections or other measures of control proper to the type of industrial activity concerned, in breach of the third indent of Article 7(1) and Article 7(2) of the directive, the Italian Republic has failed to fulfil its obligations thereunder.

Commentary

I. *The Application of Directive 82/501 by Italy*

(1) Directive 82/501 was the Community's legislative reaction to a serious industrial accident which had occurred in 1976 in Seveso (Italy), where some 600 people had to be evacuated from their homes and about 2,000 were treated for dioxin poisoning. Directive 82/501 took some inspiration from provisions which then existed for nuclear installations. It concerned industrial sites where certain dangerous chemicals were processed. For those sites which came under the Directive, undertakings had to inform the authorities of the chemicals which were used and of the safety and emergency plans which they had put in place. According to Article 7(1), the authorities had to "ensure that an emergeny plan is drawn for action outside the establishment", in order to ensure proper information and protection of the adjacent population. Furthermore, they had to inspect the sites or

take other control measures in order to ensure that the industrial companies had really taken all necessary measures under the Directive (Article 7(2)).

(2) When the Commission published its first report on the application of Directive 82/501,[127] the Italian regulatory measures had just been adopted and could not yet been taken in consideration. In 1992, eight years after the Directive became applicable, Italy informed the Commission that it had identified 210 sites—with about 710 establishments or depots—which came under the Directive, but that neither did the emergency plans according to Article 7(1) exist nor had the inspections and controls under Article 7(2) of the Directive been carried out.[128] In 1997, 13 years after the Directive became applicable, it informed the Commission that 110 emergeny plans for action outside the establishments had been drawn up, whereas 443 plans should have been adopted; furthermore, 179 establishments had been inspected.[129] In its defence before the Court, Italy indicated that only 391 establishments—instead of 710, as stated earlier—had to be inspected and that 220 inspections had been made.[130] Finally, in the Commission's report on the application of Directive 82/501 in the years from 1994 to 1996,[131] which was based on information from the Member States, Italy indicated that emergency plans for action outside the establishment existed for 190 sites whereas there were 430 sites which came under the Directive. 40 inspections were made in 1994 and 179 in 1996.[132]

(3) The least one can say about these figures is that the number of establishments, according to the statement of the Italian authorities themselves, decreased constantly from 710 in 1992 to 391 during the procedure before the Court (1998/9). This sheds some light on the reliability of the figures. And it is easily understandable that the Court did not enter into a discussion of those figures, but preferred to state rather succinctly, that , in any case, Italy had not complied with its obligations.

(4) In the same way, the Court was rather short in rejecting the argument that the Directive provided for tasks for Member States, but not for—legally binding—obligations. Indeed, who other than the Italian authorities, at local, provincial, regional or national level, could draw up emergency plans for a major industrial accident? Who else could inspect the companies which came under the terms of the Directive? Arguing, as Italy implicitly did in paragraph 18 of the judgment, that the "application in practice" was not a legal obligation for Member States would lead to the conclusion that Member States could limit themselves to transposing a directive into the national legal order, without concern for its daily application. The Court rightly rejected this reasoning and stated that Member States must take

---

[127] Commission, report on the application of Directive 82/501, COM(88)261 of 18 May 1988.
[128] Para. 11 of the present judgment.
[129] Para. 15 of the present judgment.
[130] Para. 27 of the present judgment.
[131] Commission, Report on the application of Directive 82/501 between 1994 and 1996 [1999] OJ C291/1.
[132] Commission (n. 131 *supra*), para. 4. 2. 8.

"all the measures necessary to ensure that the directive is fully effective".[133] This corresponds to the consistent case law of the Court[134] which may be summarised by the statement that Member States are obliged to ensure a result, not an effort.[135]

(5) It should be clear, though, that there are limits to the enforcement of the obligations which Member States have. Though the Commission has, under Article 211 EC Treaty, to ensure "that the provisions of this Treaty and the measures taken by the institutions pursuant thereto are applied", it has no enforcement mechanisms available to it to ensure proper application. The only means at the Commission's disposal are the provisions of Articles 226 *et seq.* EC Treaty, i. e. the application to the Court of Justice.[136] However, it would not be effective for the Commission to bring an action before the Court under Article 226 EC Treaty if a Member State had, in one specific year, made too few inspections, did not draw up all emergency plans or update them or failed to comply with other obligations; as in environmental matters, on average, the procedure under Article 226 EC Treaty takes four to five years,[137] and as this procedure ends at best with a Court judgment stating that a Member State has failed to fulfil its obligations, there is little deterrent effect which this procedure would have on Member States.

(6) Therefore the frequency of inspections and other control measures to be made under Directive 82/501 remains largely in the responsibility of Member States; the same is true for the updating of emergency plans and other obligations. Where a Member State so wishes, Directive 82/501 enables it to take and enforce rather effective accident prevention measures. However, where a Member State is less inclined to pursue a vigurous accident prevention policy, Community law is not efficiently able to force it to do so. This statement is probably correct for the whole of Community environmental law.

(7) There is only one other case in which Directive 82/501 was discussed by the Court. In 1992, the Court gave judgment in a case which involved the Commission and Netherlands; the Commission reproached the Netherlands for not having transposed several provisions of Directive 82/501 into Dutch law.[138] There were 15

---

[133] Para. 19 of the present judgment; emphasis added.

[134] See Court of Justice, Cases C–56/90, *Commission* v. *United Kingdom* [1993] ECR I–4109 (see the discussion of this case on p. 52 *supra*); C–208/90, *Emmott* [1991] ECR I–4269.

[135] See also Advocate General Jacobs, para. 14 of his Opinion in the present case: "the idea that Member States may wash their hands of the matter once the competent authorities are in place would run counter to the whole body of case-law to the effect that Member States may not escape responsability for complying with their obligations under a directive on the ground that the task has been delegated to domestic authorities . . . or that the failure to comply was caused by the action or inaction of some other, even independent, agency of the State . . ."

[136] See, in contrast to Art. 211 EC Treaty, Art. 83(2) (ex Art. 87(2)) EC Treaty which provides in the area of competition: "The regulations and directives referred to in para. 1 shall be designed in particular: (a) to ensure compliance with the prohibitions laid down in Art. 81(1) and in Art. 82 by making provision for fines and periodic penalty payments; (b) to lay down detailed rules for the application of Art. 81(3), taking into account the need to effective supervision on the one hand, and to simplify administration to the greatest possible extent on the other . . .". The Community made extensive use of these provisions, in particular by Regulation 17 of 1962 [1962] OJ 13/204.

[137] See for more more details on this issue pp. 154 and 420 *infra*.

[138] Court of Justice, Case C–190/90 [1992] ECR I–3265.

different pieces of law in the Netherlands which were intended to transpose that Directive, the oldest one dating from 1934; they concerned worker protection, measures to combat accidents and their consequences and environmental protection. The Court finally found that the Netherlands had properly transposed Article 3—obligation for the manufacturer to take measures necessary to prevent major accidents—and Article 4 of Directive 82/501—obligation for the manufacturer to prove to the competent authorities that they have identified the accident hazards and adopted the appropriat safety measures.

In contrast to that the Netherlands had not transposed the provisions providing that:

—manufacturers inform the competent authorities of the competent person on the spot from whom the authorities may seek assistance in the event of an accident (Article 5(1)(c) third indent);
—manufacturers inform the persons liable to be affected by a major accident of the safety measures taken and on correct behaviour in the case of an accident (Article 8(1));
—manufacturers immediately inform, in the case of a major accident, the competent authorities and deliver information on the details of the accident, the emergency measures taken and the measures taken to prevent any recurrence of such an accident.

II. The Substitution of Directive 82/501 by Directive 96/82

(8) Directive 82/501 was completely reviewed and replaced by Directive 96/82,[139] which largely maintained the structure and concept of Directive 82/501. The new Directive also aims at preventing major industrial accidents which involve dangerous substances and limiting the consequences thereof. It concerns establishments where dangerous substances are present in quantities that are laid down in an annex. The operator of the establishment has to produce a safety report which gives details of the establishment, the dangerous substances present, possible major risks of accidents and the management systems available. This last requirement is justified by the fact that "analysis of the major accidents in the Community indicates that the majority of them are the result of managerial and/or organizational shortcomings". Establishments must furthermore have an internal emergency plan and must inform the public authorities in such a way that these are able to draw up an external emergency plan. Persons—inside and outside the establishment—who are likely to be affected by an accident must be informed of the safety measures and of the requisite behaviour in the event of an accident. After an accident, the operator has to provide comprehensive information to the authorities on the accident and on the measures taken to prevent recurrence.

---

[139] Directive 96/82 on the control of major-accident hazards involving dangerous substances [1997] OJ L10/13.

Finally, the Directive provides for detailed rules on the inspection of the establishments by competent authorities and introduces national and Community reporting provisions.

(9) Between 1984 and 1993, a total of 178 accidents have been notified to the Commission under Directive 82/501. The total number of accidents which came under this Directive during that time-span, was estimated between 700 and 800.[140] Any estimation on how many accidents have been prevented by virtue of the provisions of both directives, is obviously not possible.

(10) The Directive does not cover pipelines—the estimated length of oil, gas and chemical pipelines in the Community is about 200.000 km—transport activities, military establishments, hazards created by ionising radiation,[141] mines, quarries, boreholes and waste landfills. When thus in April 1998 an accident occurred in a mine in Aznalcóllar (Spain) which caused serious environmental damage, it was found that Directive 96/82 did not apply. The same conclusion was reached when in January 2000 mining activity caused serious environmental damage in Baia Mare (Roumania);[142] and when in spring 2000 an exploding fireworks plant set a residential quarter in Enschede (Netherlands) in flames, the Directive's application was doubtful, as the exact quantity of the dangerous substances was not known. These incidents made the Community authorities consider a review of Directive 96/82, in order also to have other risks included in its realm. It is to be hoped that this consideration will lead to better results than the announcement made shortly after the nuclear accident at Chernobyl in 1986, where the Commission committed itself to making a proposal for accident prevention provisions in nuclear installation,[143] but omitted to do so.

(11) The accident-prevention scheme set up by the Community co-generated the International Convention on Transboundary Effects of Industrial Accidents signed in Helsinki on 17 March 1992, to which the Community adhered in 1998.[144]

---

[140] K Rasmussen, *The Experience with the Major Accident Reporting System from 1994 to 1993* (Luxembourg, 1995); C Kirchsteiger (ed.), *Lessons Learnt from Accidents* (EUR 17733) (Ispra, 1998).

[141] This provision means that nuclear installations which process dangerous substances which reach the Directive's threshholds are covered by the Directive.

[142] It is obvious that Directive 96/82 could not apply as Roumania was not a member of the EC: However, the accession negotiations had already started when the accident occurred and Roumania had been invited to adapt its environmental legislation to the requirements of Community law—which included Directive 96/82.

[143] Commission, Fourth environmental action programme [1987] OJ C328/1 paras. 4. 3. 8 and 4. 6. 4.

[144] Decision 98/685 [1998] OJ L326/1; the Convention is reproduced *ibid.*, p. 3.

15. ACCESS TO ENVIRONMENTAL INFORMATION

Judgment of the Court (Sixth Chamber) of 17 June 1998
Case C–321/96

Reference for a preliminary ruling in the proceedings between
W. Mecklenburg and Kreis Pinneberg—Der Landrat
[1998] ECR I–3809

Facts and Procedure

Mr. Mecklenburg and the county (Kreis) Pinneburg disagreed about the right of access to information relating to the environment.

Kreis Pinneberg prepared planning approval for the construction of a road. Mr. Mecklenburg asked the Kreis to send him a copy of the statement of views which the competent countryside protection authority had issued with regard to the planning approval of the road. The Kreis refused, arguing that the statement of views was not information relating to the environment, but rather an assessment of available information. Also, it considered that the planning approval procedure was a "procedure" under Article 3(2) of Directive 90/313,[145] which allowed the competent authority to refuse access to information.

During the administrative appeal procedure, Mr. Mecklenburg could not obtain a more positive decision by the administration; thus, he introduced court proceedings. The administrative court rejected his application. On appeal, the appeal court asked the Court of Justice for a preliminary ruling whether the statement of views of a "subordinate contryside protection authority" which participated in development proceedings as a representative of public interests was a measure which, under Directive 90/313, gave individuals the right of access to information, i.e. to seeing that statement; furthermore, the appeal court asked whether the proceedings of an administrative authority were "preliminary investigation proceedings" in the meaning of Directive 90/313.

---

[145] Directive 90/313 on the freedom of access to information on the environment [1990] OJ L158/56.

Judgment (extracts)

[Information relating to the environment]

19. It must be noted in the first place that Article 2(a) of the directive includes under "information relating to the environment" any information on the state of the various aspects of the environment mentioned therein as well as on activities or measures which may adversely affect or protect those aspects, "including administrative measures and environmental management programmes". The wording of the provision makes it clear that the Community legislature intended to make that concept a broad one, embracing both information and activities relating to the state of those aspects.

20. Secondly, the use in Article 2(a) of the directive of the term "including" indicates that "administrative measures" is merely an example of the "activities" or "measures" covered by the directive. As the Advocate General pointed out in paragraph 15 of his Opinion, the Community legislature purposely avoided giving any definition of "information relating to the environment" which could lead to the exclusion of any of the activities engaged in by the public authorities, the term "measures" serving merely to make it clear that the acts governed by the directive included all forms of administrative activity.

21. In order to constitute "information relating to the environment for the purposes of the directive", it is sufficient for the statement of views put forward by an authority, such as the statement concerned in the main proceedings, to be an act capable of adversely affecting or protecting the state of one of the sectors of the environment covered by the directive. That is the case, as the referring court mentioned, where the statement of views is capable of influencing the outcome of the development consent proceedings as regards interests pertaining to the protection of the environment.

22. Accordingly, the reply to the first question is that Article 2(a) of the directive is to be interpreted as covering a statement of views given by a countryside protection authority in development consent proceedings if that statement is capable of influencing the outcome of those proceedings as regards interests pertaining to the protection of the environment . . .

[Access to information relating to preliminary investigation proceedings]

24. It should be noted that under the third indent of Article 3(2) of the directive national law may permit requests for information relating to "matters which are, or have been, sub judice, or under enquiry (including disciplinary enquiries), or which are the subject of preliminary investigation proceedings".

25. Since that is a derogation from the general rules laid down by the directive, Article 3(2), third indent, may not be interpreted in such a way as to extend its effects beyond what is necessary to safeguard the interests which it seeks to secure. Furthermore, the scope of the derogations which it lays down must be determined in the light of the aims pursued by the directive ...

26. As far as the aims of the directive are concerned, the principle of freedom of access to information is laid down in Article 1 thereof. The seventh recital in the preamble to the directive emphasises the fact that the refusal to comply with a request for information to the environment may, however, be justified "in certain specific and clearly defined cases".

27. As regards the interests the protection of which the third indent of Article 3(2) of the directive serves to secure, the exceptions provided for therein relate to information held by a public authority relating, first, to matters which are the subject of legal proceedings, next, to matters which are the subject of enquiries (including disciplinary enquiries) and, lastly, to matters which are the subject of "preliminary investigation proceedings". It is thus clear, as the Advocate General pointed out in paragraph 23 of his Opinion, that that exception covers exclusively proceedings of a judicial or quasi-judicial nature, or at least proceedings which will inevitably lead to the imposition of a penalty if the offence (administrative or criminal) is established. Viewed in that context, therefore, "preliminary investigation proceedings" must refer to the stage immediately prior to the judicial proceedings or the enquiry.

28. That interpretation is borne out by the history of the directive. Article 8(1) of the proposal for a directive submitted by the Commission on 31 October 1988 (OJ 1988 C 335, p. 5) allowed for an exception to the right of access to information where exercise of that right might be prejudicial "to the secrecy of procedures brought before the courts". It was as a result of the opinion given by the Economic and Social Committee on 31 March 1989 (OJ 1989 C 139, p. 47, point 2. 6. 1), which proposed the inclusion of a reference to the confidentiality of "investigative proceedings", that the term "preliminary investigation proceedings" was added to the proposal for a directive.

29. Lastly, it is settled case-law that the need for a uniform interpretation of Community directives makes it impossible for the text of a provision to be considered, in case of doubt, in isolation; on the contrary, it requires that it be interpreted and applied in the light of the versions existing in the other official languages ... The German word at issue, *Vorverfahren*, should therefore be compared, not only with the terms instruction *préliminaire*, *azione investigativa preliminare*, *investigación preliminar* and *investigacao preliminar* in French, Italian, Spanish and Portuguese, but also with "preliminary investigation proceedings" in the English version, *opsporingsonderzoeken* in Dutch and *indledende undersoegelser* in Danish. As the Advocate General pointed out in paragraph 25 of his Opinion, comparison of the various language version shows that the "preliminary investigation proceedings" referred to by the directive must be linked to the activities which precede contentious or quasi-contentious proceedings and which arise from the need to obtain proof or to investigate a matter before the procedural phase properly so-called has even begun. However, "preliminary investigation proceedings" does not cover all acts of the administration which are open to challenge in the courts.

30. In the light of those considerations the reply to the second question is that the term "preliminary investigation proceedings" in the third indent of Article 3(2) of the directive must be interpreted as including an administrative procedure such as that referred to in Paragraph 7(1)(2) of the *Umweltinformationsgesetz*, which merely prepares the way for an administrative measure, only if it immediately precedes a contentious or quasi-contentious procedure and arises from the need to obtain proof of or to investigate a matter prior to the opening of the actual procedure.

Commentary

I. The Interpretation of Directive 90/313

(1) This was the first judgment which concerned Directive 90/313 on the freedom of access to information on the environment.[146] Already the title of the Directive is revealing, as the access to information is called a "freedom", which brings this right into the context of a fundamental right.[147] This intention is confirmed by the seventh recital in the preamble which states that it is "necessary to guarantee to any natural or legal person . . . free access to available information on the environment".[148] Having mentioned this general "guarantee" to free access to information, the eighth recital mentions that "in certain specific and clearly defined cases" access to information may be refused.

Article 1 of the Directive states that the Directive's objective is "to ensure freedom of access to . . . information";[149] Article 3(1) requests Member States to make information on the environment available.[150] And only then does there follow, in Article 3(2), an enumeration of the grounds which allow—not require!—the refusal of access to information.

(2) The Directive itself thus lays down the classical principle of rule and exception to the rule: normally, access to information shall be available, and only in exceptional circumstances shall there be a possibility of refusing such access. As regards the interpretation of the Directive's provisions, it follows from this struc-

---

[146] Directive 90/313 (n. 145 *supra*).

[147] See also Commission Written Questions 210/92 and 211/92 (Telkämper) [1992] OJ C317/14, which also considers the right under Directive 90/313 to be a "fundamental right" (*Grundrecht*).

[148] It is to be noted that the 7th recital adds that the access shall be guaranteed to any person "throughout the Community"; however, the provisions of the Directive itself do not contain this limitation. In such a case, the wording of the provisions of Directive 90/313 must prevail over the recitals.

[149] Directive 90/313 (n. 145 *supra*), Art. 1: "The object of this Directive is to ensure freedom of access to, and dissemination of, information on the environment held by public authorities and to set out the basic terms and conditions on which such information should be made available".

[150] Directive 90/313 (n. 145 *supra*), Art. 3(1): " Save as provided in this Art., Member States shall ensure that public authorities are required to make available information relating to the environment to any natural or legal person at his request and without his having to prove an interest".

ture that the ground for refusal must be interpreted narrowly. The Court clearly refers to these interpretation rules in paragraphs 19 and 25 of its judgment.

The first question which was put to the Court has considerable practical relevance. Indeed, in procedures for town and country planning or for development consent the responsible administration frequently has to request the opinion of another administration.[151] And it makes a considerable difference whether such an opinion may be kept internal and thus more or less confidential, or whether the opinion is public, may be discussed and questioned and thus be the subject of democratic controversies.

(3) The Court interpreted the notion of "information relating to the environment" broadly. Reading the wording of Article 2(a) of Directive 90/313,[152] it is difficult to reach another conclusion. Where the pros and cons of road construction are discussed, it is very relevant to know what the administration which is, as in the main proceedings in the present case, specifically charged to take care of nature protection aspects, has to say as regards the existence of important habitats or biotopes, of species of fauna or flora, of the likely effects of the road on the landscape, soil, groundwater etc. The argument of Kreis Pinneberg that the opinion only constituted the evaluation of facts that were already known by Mr. Mecklenburg is a pure fiction and was rightly rejected by the Court: how can an individual citizen know of all these aspects by himself—and, at a later stage, possibly also about the risk to soil and groundwater, noise impacts and other elements.

The Court's interpretation of Article 2(a), based on the wording and on the purpose of that provision, clarifies that statements made by administrations in an administrative procedure generally come under the notion of "information relating to the environment". The interpretation of this notion is therefore not limited to administrations concerned with nature protection and their statements. The decisive criterion is whether the statement is capable of influencing the outcome of the main proceedings as regards the protection of the environment.

(4) The Court's answer to the second preliminary question is of particular importance for Germany. Indeed, in Germany, any administrative act or other decision may be the subject of an administrative procedure, where a higher administrative administration re-examines the legality and opportunity of the administrative decision. Germany had transposed Article 3(2), last indent, of Directive 90/313[153] in Article 7(1) of its *Umweltinformationsgesetz*,[154] by stating:

---

[151] As regards environmental impact assessments, Directive 85/337 on the assessment of the effects of certain public and private projects on the environment [1985] OJ L175/40, even imposes in Art. 6(1) on Member States the obligation to ensure that those administrations which have "specific environmental responsabilities" are given the opportunity to express their opinion on the request for development consent.

[152] Directive 90/313 (n. 145 *supra*), Art. 2(a): " 'information relating to the environment' shall mean: any available information in written, visual, aural or data-base form on the state of water, air, soil, fauna, flora, land and natural sites, and on activites (including those which give rise to nuisances such as noise) or measures adversely affecting, or likely so to affect these, and on activites or measures designed to protect these, including administrative measures and environmental management programmes".

[153] See the wording of that provision in para. 24 of the judgment.

[154] *Gesetz zur Umsetzung der Richtlinie 90/313 über den freien Zugang zu Informationen über die Umwelt*, BGBl. 1994, I–1490.

"There shall be no right [to freedom of access to information on the environment] . . . 2. during the course of legal proceedings, criminal enquiries or an administrative procedure, as regards information received by the authorities in the course of such proceedings . . .". This provision thus excluded access to information on the environment for all information which the administrative authorities received in the course of administrative proceedings. German legal writers were almost unanimous in considering the provision on administrative procedures contrary to Directive 90/313, but were not successful in changing the legislation.

(5)   The Court of Justice again examined first the objective of Article 3(2), third indent, of Directive 90/313, then the way in which this provision was incorporated into the Directive, and finally the wording of the provision in the different languages. It concluded that the German transposition was too broad and opened too large possibilities for refusing access to information. Its interpretation restricted the notion of "preliminary investigative proceedings" to judicial or quasi-judicial proceedings. Thus, the German legislation which held "administrative procedure" to be the same as "preliminary investigative proceedings" (*Vorverfahren*) of the Directive, was held to constitute an incorrect transposition.

The Court did not discuss the fact that the German administrative proceedings normally are called "*Widerspruchsverfahren*", whereas the German wording of Directive 90/313 refers to "*Vorverfahren*". Thus, the German *Umweltinformationsgesetz* itself had stretched the Directive's wording, by associating "*Vorverfahren*" with "*Widerspruchsverfahren*", thus with administrative proceedings generally. Anyway, the Court's interpretation cannot be but applauded, since it restricts the field of application of the exception clause to the strict necessary.

(6)   The judgment in the present case was given on 17 June 1998. On 9 September 1999, the Court again had to deal with the question whether the German interpretation of "preliminary investigative proceedings" (*Vorverfahren*) was correct, as the Commission had brought an action against Germany with the argument that Germany had not properly transposed Directive 90/313 into national law. Germany repeated the arguments which had been advanced in the present case. The Court—again the Sixth Chamber—did not spend much time on the dispute but simply referred to its judgment in the present case and therefore held that Germany had not complied with its obligations under the Directive.[155]

In Case C–217/97, the Court also had the opportunity to clarify some other notions of Directive 90/313. First, it rejected the Commission's opinion that individuals also had a right of access to information on the environment which is held by courts, criminal prosecution authorities and disciplinary authorities. The Court was of the opinion that the Commission had not proven that those bodies, outside the information obtained in the exercise of their judicial, enquiring or disciplinary activity, held any information relating to the environment; Germany was therefore not obliged to grant access to information held by such authorities.

---

[155]   Court of Justice, Case C–217/97, *Commission* v. *Germany* [1999] ECR I–5087.

This part of the judgment surprises somehow. At least, courts and the other bodies have statistics which may show how many prosecution procedures had started, how many cases were actually brought to the courts, what the severity of sanctions was, how often persons were acquitted in environmental cases, how often public authorities took disciplinary action against passive or permissive officials:[156] such data are evidence of how well a law is enforced, applied in practice and respected. It must be regretted that the judgment in Case C–217/97 has missed the opportunity to clarify matters in this context.

(7) The Court further held that Germany had not transposed the clause which entitled a person to obtain information in part, where this is possible.[157] The Court also clarified that Germany had not correctly transposed the Directive by charging a fee also in cases where the access to information was refused.[158] In contrast to that, the Court considered the transposition concerning the amount of fees to be correct, stating expressly that it had not to judge whether the application in practice led to excessive charges. On this last point some complaints should be mentioned which revealed that access to information was sometimes charged at up to 10.000 Deutschmark in Germany.

Until October 2000, the two cases mentioned were the only cases submitted to the Court of Justice;[159] it may not be altogether an accident that they both concerned Germany. Indeed, during the discussions of Directive 90/313 in Council, Germany opposed the adoption of the Directive for several months, objecting in particular that individuals should have access to information relating to the environment without "having to prove an interest",[160] and arguing that such a provision was contrary to German "information tradition". This tradition, it was argued, provided that a right to information existed only where individuals could demonstrate a justified interest in obtaining that information. Germany feared an avalanche of requests by individuals and only gradually found that its apprehensions were not justified. However, the delayed transposition of Directive 90/313 into national law, the extended possibilities of refusing access to information, the high costs which were charged for granting access are all expressions of this traditional attitude.

In July 2001, eleven years after the adoption of Directive 90/313, Germany adopted legislation in order to bring its national law in line with Community law.[160a]

---

[156] See as an example Case C–168/95 (*supra* p. 79), where one might have wished to see criminal or disciplinary action taken against the responsible persons for the state of law and its application in Italy.

[157] Directive 90/313 (n. 145 *supra*), Art. 3(2), second subpara.: "Information held by public authorities shall be supplied in part where it is possible to separate out information on items concerning the interests referred to above".

[158] Directive 90/313 (n. 145 *supra*), Art. 5: "Member States may make a charge for supplying the information, but such charge may not exceed a reasonable cost".

[159] Three more cases were pending at that time before the Court, Case C–189/99 *Commission* v. *Spain* [1999] OJ C226/26; Cases C–402/99, *Commission* v. *Belgium* [1999] OJ C6/31 and C–29/00, *Commission* v. *Germany* [2000] OJ C149/23.

[160] Directive 90/313 (n. 145 *supra*), Art. 3(1) (n. 150 *supra*).

[160a] Gesetz of 27 July 2001, BGBL I, p. 1950.

II. Access to Information, an Emerging Fundamental Right

(8) Directive 90/313 does not apply to Community institutions. When the Commission submitted its proposal for a directive in 1988, it announced that it would take other initiatives with the objective of applying the principle of free access to information relating to the environment to the Community bodies.[161] Until the end of 2000, no such decision has been proposed. More generally, Council,[162] Commission,[163] the European Parliament[164] and other institutions and bodies[165] undertook, in the 1990s, to grant access to documents which they held. These initiatives were not limited to the environmental sector, but referred to all sectors of policy. In a considerable number of cases, the possibility of accessing to documents in particular of the Council and of the Commission was subject of litigation before the Court of Justice and the Court of First instance.[166]

In August 2000, the Council amended its earlier decisions on public access to Council documents.[167] Against these Decisions, the European Parliament brought an action under Article 230 EC Treaty arguing that since the entry into force of the Amsterdam Treaty on 1 May 1999 and its new Article 255, the Council was no longer competent to take such decisions which had rather to be taken by way of codecision between the European Parliament and the Council.[168]

(9) Of the different court cases, Case T–105/95 may be specifically mentioned, as it concerned environmental issues. The applicant, the World Wide Fund for Nature, requested "access to all Commission documents relating to the Mullaghmore project and in particular to the examination whether structural funds may be used for the project". The Mullaghmore project was the construction of an interpretative centre for visitors at Mullaghmore (Ireland), which

---

[161] Commission, COM(88) of 28 November 1988.

[162] Council Decision 93/731 on public access to Council documents [1993] OJ L340/43; see also Code of Conduct (93/730) concerning public access to Council and Commission documents [1993] OJ L340/41.

[163] Commission, Decision 94/90 on public access to Commission documents [1994] OJ L46/58.

[164] European Parliament, Decision 97/632 on public access to documents [1997] OJ L263/27.

[165] See for instance European Investment Bank, Provisions concerning access to documents of the Bank [1997] OJ C243/13; European Environmental Agency, Decision on public access to documents [1997] OJ C282/5.

[166] Court of Justice, Case C–58/94, *Netherlands v. Council* [1996] ECR I–2169; Court of First Instance, Cases T–194/94, *Carvel v. Council* [1995] ECR II–2765; T–105/95, *World Wide Fund for Nature v. Commission* [1997] ECR II–313; T–124/96, *Interporc v. Commission* [1998] ECR II–231; T–610R, *Carlsen and others v. Council* [1998] ECR II–485; T–83/96, *v.d. Wal v. Commission* [1998] ECR II–545; T–174/95, *Svenska Journalistförbundet v. Council* [1998] ECR II–2289; T–92/98 *Interporc v. Commission* [1998] ECR II–3521; T–188/97, *Rothmans v. Commission* [1999] ECR II–2463; T–14/98, *Hautala* [1999] ECR II–2489; T–309/97, *Bavarian Lager* [1999] ECR II–3217; T–188/98, *Kuijer*, [2000] ECR II–1959; T–123/99, *IT Corporation v. Commission*, [2000] ECR II–3269; T–20/99, *Denkavit v. Commission*, [2000] ECR II–3011.

[167] Decision 2000/527 and Decision 2000/23 [2000] OJ L212/9.

[168] See [2000] OJ C355/15.

would, according to the applicants, damage important fauna and flora habitats.[169] The Commission refused access to the documents, arguing in particular that the documents had served to assess whether formal proceedings against Ireland should be started under Article 226 EC Treaty. The Court of First Instance found that the Commission had not, under Article 253 EC Treaty,[170] justified its refusal in a sufficiently differentiated manner and thus annulled the Commission's decision to refuse access to the documents. The case was solved by a later decision of an Irish court which did not allow the Mullaghmore project to go on.

(10) The Amsterdam Treaty amending the Treaty on European Union introduced a new Article 255 into the EC Treaty, giving each natural or legal person residing in a Member State a right of access to the European Parliament, Council and Commission documents; detail will be fixed by a Council and European Parliament measure which must be adopted by May 2001.[171] A regulation in this area was adopted by the Community in 2001 which gives large access to documents held by the three institutions. It does not contain specific rules on access to environmental information.[172]

(11) The proposal gives a right of access to documents of the Council, the European Parliament and the Commission. It covers documents drawn up by these institutions or received by them from third parties and which are in their possession. "Document" shall mean "any content whatever its medium (written on paper or stored in electronic form or as a sound, viual or audiovisual recording", but not including "discussion documents, opinions of departments and . . . informal messages". Access to documents shall be refused where disclosure could significantly undermine the protection of the public interest; privacy and the individual; commercial and industrial secrecy or the economic interests of a person; or confidentiality of a third party having supplied the document. It may be expected that the proposal will be adopted during the year 2001.

(12) In 1998, the United Nations (Economic Commission for Europe) opened for signature the Aarhus Convention on access to information, public participation

---

[169] See for more details of the project Court of First Instance, Case T–461/93, *An Taisce and WWF v. Commission* [1994] ECR II–733, where an application against a decision of the Commission not to start formal proceedings against Ireland was rejected as inadmissible. The appeal agains this judgment was rejected: Court of Justice, Case C–325/94P [1996] ECR I–3727.

[170] Art. 253 (ex article 190) EC Treaty: "Regulations, directives and decisions adopted jointly by the European Parliament and Council, and such acts adopted by the Council or the Commission, shall state the reasons on which they are based and shall refer to any proposals or opinions which were required to be obtained pursuant to this Treaty".

[171] Art. 255 EC Treaty: "1. Any citizen of the Union, and any natural or legal person residing or having its registered office in a Member State, shall have a right of access to European Parliament, Council and Commission documents, subject to the principles and conditions to be defined in accordance with paras. 2 and 3.

2. General principles and limits on grounds of public or private interests governing this right of access to documents shall be determined by the Council, acting in accordance with the procedure referred to in Art. 251 within two years of the entry into force of the Treaty of Amsterdam.

3. Each institution referred to above shall elaborate in its own Rules of Procedure specific provisions regarding access to its documents".

[172] Regulation 1049/2001, [2001] OJ L145/43.

in decision-making and access to justice in environmental matters".[173] The Convention was signed by the European Community and all its Member States, though with some delay by Germany;[174] it entered into force in autumn 2001. The Convention is, as regards its structure, modelled on Directive 90/313. It makes access to environmental information available to "the public"[175] upon request, without an interest having to be stated. For the rest, it extends the definitions of "information relating to the environment" and "public authority" with regard to the definitions of Directive 90/313, provides for further details on the form in which the information has to be made available, shortens the deadlines for the administrations' reactions and restricts the possibility to refuse access to information.

The Community is proparing to adhere to the Convention. As regards the provisions of the Convention relating to access to information,[176] the Commission submitted, in summer 2000, a proposal for a directive on access to information[177] which is intended to replace, after its adoption, Directive 90/313 and to provide for—minor—adjustments, in order to make the new text fully compatible with the provisions of the Aarhus Convention; at the same time, the Commission published a report on the application of Directive 90/313 in the Member States.[178]

---

[173] See in particular United Nations (Economic Commission for Europe), *The Aarhus Convention: an Implementation Guide* (United Nations, New York–Geneva, 2000).

[174] While the Community and 14 Member States signed on 25 June 1998, Germany signed on 21 December 1998.

[175] Under Art. 2(4) of the Convention, the public means one or more natural or legal persons.

[176] See for a discussion of the provisions on access to justice L Krämer, "The Citizen in the Environment—Access to Justice" [2000] *Environmental Liability* 127.

[177] Commission, (2000) OJ C337E/156.

[178] Commission, Report on the experience gained in the application of Council Directive 90/313 on freedom of accession to information on the environment. COM(2000)400 of 29 June 2000.

16. THE IMPACT ON THE ENVIRONMENT OF PROJECTS

Judgment of the Court (Fifth Chamber) of 21 September 1999
Case C–392/96

Commission of the European Communities v. *Ireland*
[1999] ECR I–5901

Facts and Procedure

Directive 85/337[179] requires Member States to make an environmental impact assessment in certain cases, before planning consent for certain projects is given. Ireland transposed this Directive into national law by two legislative measures[180] which it notified to the Commission.

The Commission was of the opinion that Ireland had not transposed Directive 85/337 correctly. On 13 October 1989 and 7 November 1991, it sent letters of formal notice to Ireland, based on Article 226 EC Treaty. As it was not satisfied with the Irish reply, it sent, on 28 April 1993, a reasoned opinion. The Irish reply to the reasoned opinion was not considered sufficient by the Commission which applied, on 5 December 1996, to the Court of Justice.

Judgment (extracts)

58. ... the infringement alleged by the Commission is Ireland's incorrect transposition of Article 4(2) of the Directive through the use of threshholds which have the effect that all the characteristics of a project are not taken into consideration when it comes to determining whether the project is to be the subject to an impact assessment. Certain projects likely to have significant effects on the environment may thus escape the assessment requirement because they do not reach the threshholds set.

---

[179] Directive 85/337 on the assessment of the effects of certain public and private projects on the environment [1985] OJ L175/40; amended by Directive 97/11 [1997] OJ L73/5.

[180] European Communities (Environmental Impact Assessment) Regulations, Statutory Instruments 349 of 1989, amended by European Communities (Environmental Impact Assessment) (Amendment) Regulations, Statutory Instruments 101 of 1996; Local Government (Planning and Development) Regulations, Statutory Instruments no. 25 of 1990; Local Government (Planning and Development) Regulations 1994.

59. So, the alledged infringement has to do with the way in which the Directive has been transposed into Irish law and not with the actual result of the application of the transposing legislation.

60. In order to prove that the transposition of a directive is insufficient or inadequate, it is not necessary to establish the actual effects of the legislation transposing it into national law: it is the wording of the legislation itself which harbours the insufficiencies or defects of transposition.

61. There is, therefore, nothing to prevent the Commission from demonstrating that transposition is defective or insufficient without waiting for the application of the transposing legislation to produce harmful effects.

62. Since the Directive forms part of Community environmental policy, which, as pointed out in the first preamble to the Directive, consists in preventing the creation of pollution or nuisances at source rather than subsequently trying to counteract their effects, the opposite conclusion would be even more justified in this case.

63. It does not therefore matter that the evidence adduced by the Commission in support of its action consists of mere complaints which have not yet been investigated.

64. As far as the objection to threshholds is concerned, although the second subparagraph of Article 4(2) of the Directive confers on Member States a measure of discretion to specify certain types of projects which are to be subject to an assessment or to establish the criteria or threshholds applicable, the limits of that discretion lie in the obligation set out in Article 2(1) that projects likely, by virtue inter alia of their nature, size or location, to have significant effects on the environment are to be subject to an impact assessment . . .

65. Thus, a Member State which established criteria or threshholds taking account only of the size of projects, without also taking their nature and location into consideration, would exceed the limits of its discretion under Articles 2(1) and 4(2) of the Directive.

66. Even a small-scale project can have significant effects on the environment if it is in a location where the environment factors set out in Article 3 of the Directive, such as fauna and flora, soil, water, climate or cultural heritage, are sensitive to the slightest alteration.

67. Similarly, a project is likely to have significant effects where, by reason of its nature, there is a risk that it will cause a substantial or irreversible change in those environmental factors, irrespective of its size.

68. In order to demonstrate that Ireland has failed to fulfil its obligation in this regard, the Commission has put forward several convincing examples of projects which, whilst considered solely in relation to their size, may none the less have significant effects on the environment by reason of their nature or location.

69. The most significant example is afforestation because, when carried out in areas of active blanket bog, it entails, by its nature and location, the destruction of the bog ecosystem and the irreversible loss of biotopes that are original, rare and of great scientific interest. In itself, it may also cause the acidification or eutrophication of waters.

70. It was however necessary, and possible, to take account of factors such as the nature or location of projects, for example by setting a number of threshholds corresponding to varying project sizes and applicable by reference to the nature or location of the project.

71. Ireland's explanation that other environmental protection legislation, such as the Habitats Regulations, made it unnecessary to assess afforestation, land reclamation or peat extraction projects carried out in environmentally sensitive location must be dismissed. Nothing in the Directive excludes from its scope regions or areas which are protected under other Community provisions from other aspects.

72. It follows that, by setting, for the classes of projects covered by points 1(d) and 2(a) of Annex II to the Directive, threshholds which take account only of the size of projects, to the exclusion of their nature and location, Ireland has exceeded the limits of its discretion under Articles 2(1) and 4(2) of the Directive.

73. As regards the cumulative effect of projects, it is to be remembered that the criteria and/or threshholds mentioned in Article 4(2) are designed to facilitate the examination of the actual characteristics exhibited by a given project in order to determine whether it is subject to the requirement to carry out an assessment, and not to exempt in advance from that obligation certain whole classes of projects listed in Annex II which may be envisaged on the territory of a Member State.

74. The question whether, in laying down such criteria and/or threshholds, a Member State goes beyond the limits of its discretion cannot be determined in relation to the characteristics of a single project, but depends on an overall assessment of the characteristics of projects of that nature which could be envisaged in the Member State concerned.

75. So, a Member State which established criteria and/or threshholds at a level such that, in practice, all projects of a certain type would be exempted in advance from the requirement of an impact assessment would exceed the limits of its discretion under Articles 2(1) and 4(2) of the Directive unless all the projects excluded could, when viewed as a whole, be regarded as not being likely to have significant efects on the environment.

76. That would be the case where a Member State merely set a criterion of project size and did not also ensure that the objective of the legislation would not be circumvented by the splitting of projects. Not taking account of the cumulative effect of projects means in practice that all projects of a certain type may escape the obligation to carry out an assessment when, taken together, they are likely to have significant effects on the environment within the meaning of Article 2(1) of the Directive.

77. In order to demonstrate that Ireland has failed to fulfil its obligation in this regard, the Commission has also provided various examples of the effects of the Irish legislation as drafted.

78. Ireland has not denied that no project for the extraction of peat, covered by point 2(a) of Annex II to the Directive, has been the subject of an impact assessment, although small-scale peat extraction has been mechanised, industrialised and considerably intensified, resulting in the unremitting loss of areas of bog of nature conservation importance.

79. As regards initial afforestation, covered by point 1(d) of Annex II to the Directive, such projects, encouraged by the grant of aid, may be implemented in proximity to one another without any impact assessment at all being carried out, if they are conducted by different developers who all keep within the threshhold of 70 ha over three years.

80. The Commission has also cited the example of land reclamation projects, covered by point 1(d) of Annex II to the Directive, whose cumulative effect is not taken into account by the Irish legislation. Nor has it been disputed that much land clearance has taken place in the Burren without a single impact assessment being carried out, although it is an area of unquestionable interest. Limestone pavement, which is characteristic of the area, has been destroyed, as have vegetation and archaeological remains, giving way to pasture. Considered together, those interventions were likely to have significant environmental effects.

81. As regards sheep farming in particular, the Commission has proved that, again encouraged by the grant of aid, this has grown in an unrestrained fashion, which is a development which may have adverse environmental consequences. However, it has not demonstrated that sheep farming as practised in Ireland constitutes a project within the meaning of Article 1(2) of the Directive.

82. It follows from all of the foregoing that, by setting threshholds for the classes of projects covered by point 1(d) and 2(a) of Annex II to the Directive without also ensuring that the objective of the legislation will not be circumvented by the splitting of projects, Ireland has exceeded the limits of its discretion under Articles 2(1) and 4(2) of the Directive . . .

Commentary

I. The Transposition of Environmental Impact Requirements into Irish Law

(1) The judgment is one of the numerous judgments[181] which the Court of Justice has given on the interpretation of Directive 85/337. A considerable part of

---

[181] Directive 85/337 (n. 179 *supra*) was discussed in the following cases: C–313/93, *Commission* v. *Luxembourg* [1994] ECR I–1279; C–396/92, *Bund Naturschutz* [1994] ECR I–3717; C–431/92, *Commission* v. *Germany* [1995] ECR I–2189; C–133/94, *Commission* v. *Belgium* [1996] ECR I–2323; C–72/95 *Kraaijeveld* [1996] ECR I–5403 (see also *supra* p. 42); C–321/95P *Greenpeace* v. *Commission* [1998] ECR I–1651 (see p. 403 *infra*); C–81/96, *Haarlemmerliede* [1998] ECR I–3923; C–301/95 *Commission* v. *Germany* [1998] ECR I–6135; C–150/97, *Commission* v. *Portugal* [1999] ECR I–259; C–435/97, *WWF* [1999] ECR I–5613; C–392/96, *Commission* v. *Ireland* [1999] ECR I–5901 (the present case); C–287/99, *Linster*, (2000) ECR I–6917.

Attention is drawn to Case T–585/93, *Greenpeace* v. *Commission* [1995] ECR II–2205, where Directive 85/337 should have been, but was in fact not, discussed: see p. 403 *infra*.

the litigation turns on the question of Member States' discretion whether they make an environmental impact assessment before giving planning consent for a specific project: Directive 85/337 provides in Article 2: "Member States shall adopt all measures necessary to ensure that, before consent is given, projects likely to have significant effects on the environment by virtue inter alia of their nature, size or location are made subject to an assessment with regard to their effects. These projects are defined in Article 4". Article 4 stipulates: "1. . . . projects of the classes listed in Annex I shall be made subject to an assessment . . . 2. Projects of the classes listed in Annex II shall be made subject to an assessment . . . where Member States consider that their characteristics so require".

Thus, for projects in Annex I, an environmental impact assessment always has to be made; for projects in Annex II, Member States have a discretion to decide whether they make such an assessment. To limit this discretion, Directive 85/337 makes two provisions: on the one hand, Member States "may establish criteria and/or threshholds" in order to determine which of the projects listed in Annex II have to undergo an impact assessment(Article 4(2) second subparagraph). On the other hand, Article 2 requires an impact assessment where a project is likely to have significant effects on the environment.

(2) These provisions do not completely clarify the interdependency between Articles 2 and 4 of Directive 85/337. Fortunately enough, the Court's judgments have considerably contributed to interpreting both provisions. In Case C–435/97,[182] the Court clarified that the individual citizen may submit before a court that an environmental impact assessment was not made but should have been made. In Case C–72/95,[183] the Court clarified that Article 2 is the key provision, by stating that a project which is likely to have significant effects on the environment should not be allowed to "escape" the requirement of an impact assessment, just because it is listed in Annex II. In Case C–431/92, the Court pointed out that also the amendment of an Annex II project required an environmental impact assessment where the conditions of Article 2 were fulfilled.[184] Other decisions, where this core function of Article 2 appeared, were cases C–133/93[185] and C–301/95;[186] in these cases the Court decided that Member States were not entitled to exclude altogether classes of Annex II projects from the requirement of an environmental impact assessment, as this would make it impossible correctly to apply Article 2 of Directive 85/337.

---

[182] Case C–435/97, *WWF* (n. 181 *supra*), para. 71; see for a discussion of Case C–435/97 p. 61 *supra*.

[183] Case C–72/95, *Kraaijeveld* (n. 181 *supra*), para. 39; see for a discussion of Case C–72/95 p. 42 *supra*.

[184] Case 431/92, *Commission* v. *Germany* (n. 181 *supra*). Annex II no. 12 is—to say the least—confusing in this regard, as it only mentions amendments of Annex I projects, but is silent on Annex II-projects: "[Have to undergo an environment impact assessment at the discretion of Member States] Modifications to development projects included in Annex I and projects in Annex I undertaken exclusively or mainly for the development and testing of new methods or products and not used for more than one year".

[185] Case C–133/93, *Commission* v. *Belgium* (n. 181 *supra*).

[186] Case 301/95, *Commission* v. *Germany* (n. 181 *supra*).

(3) The present judgment further clarifies that the fixing of a threshhold for projects which come under Annex II is not sufficient to satisfy the requirements of Article 2. Indeed, as the Court put it, also small projects which remain within the limits of the threshhold fixed may have significant effects on the environment. Member States which fix threshholds will therefore also have to incorporate a general clause into their national legislation that a project which has, due to its nature or its location, significant effects on the environment will have to undergo an environmental impact assessment. The same follows from the cumulative effect of projects which may, seen together, have a strong negative impact on, for instance, a natural habitat, while they remain, each taken for itself, within the fixed threshholds. There must, therefore, always be a general clause which incorporates Article 2 of the Directive into national legislation.

(4) On this point, though, the judgment is not altogether clear: in paragraph 59 of its judgment, the Court states without any ambiguity that the infringement which is the subject matter of the litigation between Ireland and the Commission "has to do with the way in which the Directive has been transposed into Irish law and not with the actual result of the application of the transposing litigation". Examining the (correct) transposition of a Community provision into national law is a legal-logical operation: it is certain that such an examination cannot consider all theoretical possibilities and must keep some semblance of reality. However, the Court has very frequently stated that the object of litigation of a dispute about correct transposition is completely different from the object of litigation where the application in practice is in question. It is for that reason that a Member State cannot justify itself, in a case where the correct transposition was in question, by arguing that in practice Community law was respected.[187]

(5) But if this is the case, why then does the Court mention that the Commission has put forward "several convincing examples" (paragraph 68), "various examples of the effects" (paragraph 77), "proved" that a measure had negative consequences (paragraph 81), and why has the Court limited its judgment to the finding that the splitting of projects of points 1(d) and 2(a) of Annex II may be contrary to Article 2 of the Directive? Clearly, such a splitting of projects may also occur with other projects of Annex II. And obviously, any project of Annex II, if developed in a highly sensitive zone such as a particularly vulnerable habitat, may have a significant effect on the environment—as the Court itself stated in paragraph 66 of its judgment.

The only logical conclusion is thus that any project of Annex II may, in specific circumstances, have significant effects on the environment. For this reason, the Member States must incorporate into their national legislation a clause that

---

[187] See para. 60 of the present judgment: "In order to prove that the transposition of a directive is insufficient or inadequate, it is not necessary to establish the actual effects of the legislation transpsong it into national law: it is the wording of the legislation itself which harbours the insufficiencies or defects of transposition".

See also Court of Justice, Case C–83/97, *Commission* v. *Germany* [1997] ECR I–7191; Case C–217/97, *Commission* v. *Germany* [1999] ECR I–5087; in that last case, it was the Commission which wished to deduce from a specific practice an incorrect transposition—an attempt which the Court rejected.

requires national, regional or local authorities to make an environmental impact assessment where such significant effects are likely, by virtue in particular of the size, the nature or the location of the project. The criteria or threshholds alone are therefore never sufficient. And in pursuance of the judgment in Case C–435/97,[188] at the same time, any citizen may argue at any time before a national court that the conditions of Article 2 of Directive 85/337 are fulfilled, even though the criteria or threshholds that were fixed by national legislation have been respected.

II. Town and Country Planning and Environmental Impact Assessments

(6) Directive 85/337 was the first Community environmental measure which directly affected town and country planning, by requiring an environmental impact assessment before development consent for a project was given and by ensuring that environmental organisations and the "public concerned", thus the individual citizen, had a right to make their voices heard during the planning process. The Community competence for taking such measures comes from Article 175(1) EC Treaty, as appears clearly from the wording of Article 175/2).[189] Directive 85/337 concerned those projects which were listed in either its Annex I or Annex II. Such "projects" include motorways and roads, ports and airports, plants and other infrastructure projects. The Court rightly pointed out that the grazing of sheep was not mentioned in Annex I or II of the Directive and could thus not be considered to be a "project". Seen from a Community-wide perspective, this public participation which frequently broke the monopoly of local or regional bodies rather arbitrarily to decide on the realisation as well as on the siting of projects, has brought considerable democratic elements to the planning procedure.

(7) There were, in my eyes, four main weaknesses of Directive 85/337: (a) the Directive did not require the developer to study alternatives to his project.[190] Directive 97/11 which amended Directive 85/337[191] has remedied this aspect and has since 1999, required in Article 5(3) that the developer submit information which contains an outline of the main alternatives studied by him. It will have to

---

[188] Case C–435/97, *WWF* (n. 181 *supra*); for a discussion of Case C–435/97 see p. 61 *supra*.

[189] Art. 175 (ex Art. 130s) EC Treaty: "1. The Council, acting in accordance with the procedure referred to in Art. 251 and after consulting the Economic and Social Committee and the Committee of the Regions, shall decide what action is to be taken by the Community in order to achieve the objectives referred to in Art. 174. 2. By way of derogation from the decision-making procedure provided for in para. 1 and without prejudice to Art. 95, the Council, acting unanimously on a proposal from the Commission and after consulting the European Parliament, the Economic and Social Committee and the Committee of the Regions, shall adopt: . . .—measures concerning town and country planning, land use with the exception of waste management and measures of general nature, and management of water resources . . ." Environmental impact assessment provisions are certainly "measures of general nature".

[190] Directive 85/337 (n. 179 *supra*), Annex III (2): The developer has to provide information which contains "where appropriate, an outline of the main alternatives studied . . .".

[191] Directive 97/11 (n. 179 *supra*).

be seen whether indeed most realistic and least impairing alternatives will be studied, so that the decision-taking authority is really presented with alternative options for the project.

(b) The authorities which have to give planning consent are not obliged in any way to respect the results of the environmental impact assessment in the sense that they must take measures to minimise the negative environmental effects of the project.[192] The wording of Article 8 rather allows them to take them into consideration, which means that they think of these effects and then forget about them. This leads in practice to the situation that often there is a policy decision taken on the realisation of a specific project, then an environmental impact assessment is made and then the project is realised as originally planned.

(8) This weakness is linked to the third issue: (c) very often, a town and country plan or any other local, regional or national plan decides on the realisation of a project—a motorway, an airport, or another infrastructure project, but also a waste incinerator, a landfill etc.—and the actual development consent procedure only ratifies what was politically decided long before. In an attempt to remedy this, the Community made a proposal for a directive "on the assessment of the effects of certain plans and programmes on the environment."[193] This Directive will have to be applied as of 2003. It is therefore too early to assess whether the principal plans for town and country planning will really be subject to an environmental impact assessment.

(9) (d) The fourth problem is only now solved: Directive 85/337 does not indicate what happens, if development consent is given, but without an environmental impact assessment having been made in breach of the requirements of Directive 85/337 and its transposing legislation, or when there were significant deficiencies in the impact assessment procedure. Member States' administrations and courts sometimes tend to minimise the relevance of such omissions or deficiencies and consider the development consent procedure nevertheless as valid. In contrast to that, the only consequence of an omitted environmental impact assessment or of an assessment which is deficient to a significant degree must be to declare the development consent procedure invalid. Only this "sanction" can ensure that environmental impact assessment procedures are being taken seriously and not only as an onerous and unwelcome burden. The Court of Justice has not yet decided on this question.

(10) The cases decided by the Court can be divided into two groups. A first group concerns questions related to the transposition of the Directive into national law: some judgments dealt with the issue that a Member State had not transposed the Directive at all,[194] or had omitted to transpose it completely.[195] A

---

[192] Directive 85/337 (n. 179 *supra*), Art. 8: "The results of the consultations and the information gathered pursuant to Arts. 5, 6 and 7 must be taken into consideration in the development consent procedure".

[193] Directive 2001/42 [2001] OJ L197/30.

[194] Court of Justice, Case C–313/93, *Commission* v. *Luxembourg* (n. 181 *supra*).

[195] Court of Justice, Cases C–133/94 *Commission* v. *Belgium* (n. 181 *supra*); C–301/95, *Commission* v. *Germany* (n. 181 *supra*).

"transposition" question was also the problem whether Directive 85/337 which entered into effect on 3 July 1988 should apply to projects which were, in one way or the other, initiated before that date. The Court decided that the Directive should not apply where the development consent procedure was initiated prior to 3 July 1988, even where the decision on the project was taken at a later time.[196] The Court argued that, as the Directive did not provide for transition periods, this interpretation was the only way to ensure on the one hand legal certainty and on the other hand the safeguarding of effectiveness of Directive 85/337. Where, however, an earlier development consent, given prior to 3 July 1988, had not been made use of and now a new consent was needed, an environmental impact assessment was necessary.

Some Member States had delayed in transposing Directive 85/337 and the Court had to decide whether they were entitled to provide for an environmental impact assessment only from the day on which the national transposing legislation became effective. The Court judged that the date of 3 July 1988 was decisive and that Member States were not allowed to apply the Directive only from a later date.[197] The Court did not see any retroactive effect in this decision.

(11) A second group of judgments concerns the question whether for a specific project an environmental impact assessment should have been made.[198] Frequently, such questions came, by way of a preliminary request, from a national court.

(12) In 1991, the United Nations opened for signature the "Convention on Environment Impact Assessment in a transboundary context"[199] which was largely based on the model of Directive 85/337. The Community and its Member States—with the exception of France, Germany and Ireland—have adhered to this Convention. The Convention takes into consideration in particular the transnational effects of a project, which affects or may affect the environment in another State, and also contains provisions on the co-operation of contracting parties in such cases.

Also deserving of mention is the Aarhus "Convention on access to information, public participation in decision-making and access to justice in environmental matters" which again was elaborated under the auspices of the United Nations and opened for signature in 1998. The Community and all its Member States signed this Convention. In 2001, the Commission proposed an amendment of Directives 85/337 and 96/61 in order to align these Directives, as regards public participation, to the requirements of the Aarhus Convention.[199a]

---

[196] Court of Justice, Case C–396/92, *Bund Naturschutz* (n. 181 *supra*), para. 32; Case C–81/96, *Haarlemmerliede* (n. 181 *supra*), para. 23.

[197] Court of Justice, Cases C–396/92, *Bund Naturschutz* (n. 181 *supra*); C–301/95, *Commission* v. *Germany* (n. 181 *supra*); C–150/97, *Commission* v. *Portugal* (n. 181 *supra*).

[198] Court of Justice, Cases C–431/92, *Commission* v. *Germany* (n. 181 *supra*), which concerned a power plant; C–72/95, *Kraaijeveld* (n. 181 *supra*), which concerned the construction of a dyke; C–81/96, *Haarlemmerliede* (n. 181 *supra*)which concerned the construction of a port and an industrial zone; C–435/97, *WWF* (n. 181 *supra*) which concerned the construction of an airport.

[199] Convention signed at Espoo (Finland) on 25 June 1991.

[199a] (2001) OJ C 154E/123.

17. ENVIRONMENTAL REPORTING

Judgment of the Court (First Chamber) of 12 December 2000
Case C–435/99

Commission of the European Communities v. *Portugal*
[2000] ECR I–11179

Facts and Procedure

Several directives in the water sector provided that Member States should report on their implementation to the Commission at regular intervals.[200] These reporting requirements were, in 1991, consolidated in Directive 91/692[201] which provided that, in the water sector, Member States should send in their reports concerning the years 1993 to 1995 at the latest by 30 September 1996.

As the Commission had not received these reports, it started formal proceedings and applied, in November 1999, to the Court.

Judgment (extracts)

15. It is not disputed that the reports on the implementation of Directives 76/464, 78/659, 80/68, 83/513, 84/156, 84/491 and 86/280 did not reach the Commission within the prescribed period and that, consequently, the Commission's action in that connection must be regarded as well founded.

---

[200] The following directives are to be mentioned which all were the subject of the present judgment: Directive 76/464 on pollution caused by certain dangerous substances discharged into the aquatic environment of the Community [1976] OJ L129/23; Directive 78/176 on waste from the titanium dioxide industry [1978] OJ L54/19; Directive 78/659 on the quality of fresh waters needing protection or improvement in order to support fish life [1978] OJ L222/1; Directive 80/68 on the protection of groundwater against pollution caused by certain dangerous substances [1980] OJ L20/43; Directive 82/176 on limit values and quality objectives for mercury discharges by the chlor-alkali electrolysis industry [1982] OJ L81/29; Directive 83/513 on limit values and quality objectives for cadmium discharges [1983] OJ L291/1; Directive 84/156 on limit values and quality objectives dor mercury discharges by sectors other than the chlor-alkali industry [1984] OJ L74/49; Directive 84/491 on limit values and quality objectives for discharges of hexachlorocyclohexane [1984] OJ L274/11; Directive 86/280 on limit values and quality objectives for discharges of certain dangerous substances included in List I of the Annex to Directive 76/464 [1986] OJ L181/16.

[201] Directive 91/692 standardising and rationalising reports on the implementation of certain directives relating to the environment [1991] OJ L377/48.

16. As to the report on the implementation of Directive 78/176, which was sent to the Commission with the Portuguese Government's defence, it must be borne in mind that it is evident from the case-law of the Court of Justice that, in proceedings under Article 226 EC, the question whether a Member State has failed to fulfil its obligations must be determined by reference to the situation prevailing in that Member State at the end of the period laid down in the reasoned opinion and that the Court cannot take account of any subsequent changes . . . In the present case, it has been established that, at the end of that period, the report had not been provided.

17. The argument of the Portuguese Government that it was not required to submit a report on the implementation of Directive 78/176 on account of its particular situation, namely that there is no waste from the titanium dioxide industry on Portuguese territory (an argument which the government itself contradicted by subsequently sending the report), must in any event be rejected. As the Advocate General observes in point 16 of his Opinion, the provision at issue binds all Member States in the same way and, if none of the activities referred to in Directive 78/176 are carried out in the territory of a Member State during the period under consideration, that State must indicate that fact in its report, which it may not dispense with under any circumstances.

Commentary

I. Reporting Requirements in EC Environmental Law

(1) In this case, the Court of Justice had an easy time: for most directives, Portugal did not deny that it had not submitted reports. Only the reports on Directives 80/68 on groundwater and 78/176 on waste from titanium dioxide were at question. As regards the report on the groundwater Directive, the Court referred to settled case law, according to which only those national factual elements could be taken into consideration which had been submitted before the end of the period that was fixed in the Commission's reasoned opinion; it was not disputed that Portugal had not done so and thus the Commission's complaint was well founded.

(2) As regards Directive 78/176, Portugal had argued that it was not under an obligation to report, as there was no production of titanium dioxide in Portugal and thus no waste either. However, this argument is clearly erroneous: Directive 78/176 requires Member States to proceed with waste from titanium dioxide industry in a specific manner: And it could well happen that France or another EC Member State or a third country producing titanium dioxide had brought its TiO_2 waste to Portugal, for instance for reasons of cost or ease of transport. The Court was thus quite right in requiring a report from Portugal or at least an official statement that no waste from titanium dioxide production occurred in Portugal or was shipped to, treated or disposed of in Portugal.

(3) The interest of this case lies in the fact that it is the first case under the reporting Directive[202] which was dealt with by the Court. It is true that the Court had already, in 1990, given a judgment against Belgium for not having made the necessary reports under different Community environmental directives.[203] However, there was no way of avoiding the procedure in the present case against Portugal.

Reporting requirements under Community environmental law might be looked at more closely. Since the adoption of Community environmental directives and regulations which started in 1975, it has been a rather frequent practice to require Member States to send at regular intervals reports to the Commission concerning the implementation of the directive in question. The Commission was normally asked to publish a report on implementation, based on Member States' information. Early environmental directives provided that the publication of a Community report should depend on the consent of Member States. Progressively, however, this conditions was abandoned.

(4) Frequency of reporting, indications of the content of the report and other details varied from one directive to another. Also the practice of Member States and of the Commission varied; some Member States did not report, others reported with delay; the content of the national reports frequently was not comparable. Often, the number of national reports to be sent to the Commission was considered an excessive bureaucratic burden. The Commission sometimes published a Community-wide report without having received national reports from all Member States; sometimes it took the absence of some reports as a reason for not publishing a Community report at all.

(5) In order to improve a situation which was generally considered not to be satisfactory, Directive 91/692 was adopted which tried ot harmonise and rationalise the reporting system. The Directive introduced:

—a standard period of three years for the national reports;
—the making of national reports based on a questionnaire which had previously been agreed between Member States and the Commission, in order to supply information that was comprehensive, consistent and comparable;
—the elaboration of one consolidated national report for each different sector, such as water, air, waste or nature, instead of reports per individual directive;
—specific three-year periods for which the national reports were to be made;
—specific dates by which national consolidated reports had to be sent to the Commission: this date was 30 September of the year following the three-year period;
—specific dates by which the Commission had to publish the Community-wide report per sector: this date was 30 June of the year following the receipt of the national reports.

---

[202] Directive 91/692 (n. 201 *supra*).
[203] Court of Justice, Case C–162/89, *Commission* v. *Belgium* [1990] ECR I–2391.

One directive was exempted from this system, Directive 76/160 on the quality of bathing waters.[204] It was thought that the reports on the quality of bathing waters were of so much public interest that an annual report would be more appropriate.[205]

(6) On the different water directives, the Commission adopted questionnaires in 1992.[206] Member States were asked to send in their national reports which had to cover the period 1993 to 1995, by 30 September 1996, and the Commission planned to publish its Community-wide report on 30 June 1997. However, the first Community-wide report was published only in 2000,[207] thus, at a time when the second report should already have been published. On air directives, where the reporting time was 1994 to 1996 and where a Community-wide report should have been published in 1998, no such report has been published by the end of 2000. The same applies to nature protection. In the chemicals sector, only one directive came under the provisions of Directive 91/692, which was Directive 82/501 on the prevention of chemical accidents; the Commission published a report on the implementation of that Directive in 1999.[208] In the waste sector—reporting time 1995 to 1997, publication of a Community-wide report foreseen in 1999—a report was published in January 2000.[209] As the present judgment deals with the reports in the water sector, the following discussion will mainly concentrate on this.

(7) The overall balance of the reporting Directive 91/692 is not very positive: no sectoral report established completely. For two important sectors, there are no reports at all. The reports which were made are not really consolidated reports on a specific sector, but rather concentrate on the individual directives. This may be the fault of Directive 91/692 itself, as the system of questionnaires which are established for each individual directive rather suggests answers to the different questions—and this inevitably leads to directive-specific reports, not to consolidated reports.

(8) In the water report, the Commission did not indicate when the different national reports had come in; it mentioned only that "many returns were only submitted in 1997".[210] And no information at all was given why the Commission report was made only in 2000. Portugal was, next to Luxembourg, the only

[204] Directive 76/160 [1976] OJ L31/1.

[205] Furthermore, on a number of directives, Member States were not able to agree that regular reports were to be made. Examples are Directives 85/337 on the assessment of the effects of certain public and private projects on the environment and 90/313 on access to environmental information.

[206] Commission Decision 92/446 [1992] OJ L247/6; amended by Commission Decision 95/337 [1995] OJ L200/34.

[207] Commission, *The Standardised Reporting Directive; a Synthesis Report on the First Application of Standardised Reports from Member States from 1993 to 1995* (Office for Official Publications of the European Communities, Luxembourg, 2000).

[208] Commission, Report on the application of Directive 82/501 between 1994 and 1996 [1999] OJ C291/1.

[209] Commission, Report on the implementation of Community waste legislation for the period 1995 to 1997. COM(1999)752 of 10 January 2000.

[210] Commission (n. 207 *supra*), p. 5.

Member State which had not sent in any information on water directives at all; this is parallel to the findings in the waste report, where the Commission stated that Portugal had not reported on three of the four directives on which it should have reported.[211]

An analysis of the answers from Member States to the water questionnaires shows the following table:[212]

Percentage of questions contained in the questionnaires adopted under Directive 91/692 for which at least some information was provided by Member States for the period 1993 to 1995 (no judgment is made of how complete or how good the information was)

Directive	Number of questions	BE	DK	DE	EL	ES	FR	IRL	IT	LUX	NL	PO	UK
Drinking water (80/778)	12	53	67	83	75	75	100	83	83	0	92	0	83
Groundwater (80/68)	10	40	60	90	20	0	100	90	0	0	80	0	90
Surface water (75/440)	13	33	100	92	100	0	100	0	100	0	62	0	100
Measurement Method (79/869)	4	25	75	100	0	0	100	0	100	0	100	0	100
Dang. substances (76/464)	33	48	52	39	52	0	70	30	0	0	58	0	34
Titanium dioxide (78/176)	8	29	100	0	0	0	100	0	0	0	100	0	75
Fishwater (78/659)	13	56	0	100	0	0	8	100	85	0	77	0	42
Shellfish water (79/923)	13	15	23	77	62	100	8	0	23	—	77	0	92

It follows from this that for only one Directive, Directive 80/778 on the quality of drinking water, more than half of all questions were answered on average. And only five of the 12 Member States—Denmark, Germany, France, Netherlands and the United Kingdom—answered more than half of all questions.

(9) The Commission tried to explain the problem of data collection in the following words:[213] "It has to be recognised that the reporting of data is not a popular

---

[211] Commission (n. 207 *supra*) p. 4.

[212] Commission (n. 207 *supra*), p. 6. Only eight of the 14 directives which come under Directive 91/692 are examined. Austria, Finland and Sweden did not have a reporting requirement, as they had acceded to the Community only in 1995.

[213] Commission (n. 207 *supra*), p. 5.

activity. There are many who like to receive data but do not wish to be originators. Even those that like to receive, are really only interested if what they receive arrives in precisely the form that they want, and everybody's wants are different. One reason why people dislike originating data is that they see the task as extra, and, to them, unnecesaary work. They have all the information but strongly resent having to copy it out onto special report forms. To overcome this resentment it has become standard practice to allow those who generate data, to use copies of their normal working documents,to pass on the data, thus avoiding onerous copying. While this makes life easier for originators, it often complicates the work of those in the subsequent stages of the data chain. Data that need to be amalgamated will often arrive from the various different sources in widely different formats. Frequently also, the units of measurement used differ from place to place, and do not conform to the units required for reporting under The Reporting Directive. It is against this human, real life background that the implementation of The Reporting Directive has to be judged. The objective sounds simple, but to reach it requires many different stages of handling of millions of individual items of information, originatng from thousands of individual sources, spread over 15 countries employing some 18 languages".

(10) The difficulties of information gathering under Directive 91/692 may be summarised as follows:

(a) Member States do not report in time, delaying the establishment of an EC-wide report;

(b) The questionnaires are based on individual directives, and do not favour a consolidated report for the whole sector;

(c) Co-operation between different national departments—agriculture, industry, energy, transport etc.—is at present insufficient and improvement would be of paramount importance for the environmental sector;

(f) The questionnaires are drafted in such a way that Member States have to report mainly on the legal transposition of a directive rather than on its application and enforcement in practice;

(e) Where a Member State finds that the monitoring was not done well, or was incomplete or showed negative results which could be interpreted as a breach of the requirements of the specific directive, there will be a temptation to hide these facts, for instance by omitting the incriminating data from the reporting programme;

(f) Sampling or measurement sometimes, and for a variety of reasons, simply is not done;

(g) The sampling points, sampling methods, points where the sample must be taken and other factors may change from one year to the next and thus make the reporting data unusable;

(h) Most questions in the questionnaires aim at receiving information on the transposition and on the general or specific administrative measures that were taken in order to comply with the requirements of a specific directive.

There is very little information collected on the monitoring of national law, the enforcement of directives, the functioning of the directives in practice etc. This has as a consequence that the inormation transmitted to the Commission often does not reflect the ecological, economical and administrative reality within Member States.

Hitherto, these deficiencies have at best been identified, but no review procedure on reporting has been started.

II. Length of Procedure in Environmental Cases

(11) The judgment is also of interest because the formal proceedings under Article 226 EC Treaty[214] against Portugal in the present case started on 30 June 1998 and the judgment was given on 12 December 2000. This is a remarkably short period. I examined the judgments issued in the years 1992 to 1999 and it may be worthwhile to mention the main results of the findings, as regards delays.[215]

Average length of litigation before the Courts in months (in brackets the number of environmenal cases):

Legal basis	1992–1994	1995–1997	1998–1999
Article 226	22 (14)	14 (30)	20 (37)
Article 230	14 (9)	20 (5)	29 (2)
Article 234	18 (6)	16 (15)	23 (17)

However, if one includes the pre-Court litigation under Article 226 EC Treaty, the figures become rather different.

Length of litigation according to Article 226 EC Treaty between the dispatch of the letter of formal notice till the judgment of the Court

	Number of cases	Average duration of litigation
1992–1994	14	57
1995–1997	30	47
1998–1999	37	68

---

[214] Art. 226 (ex Art. 169) EC Treaty: "If the Commission considers that a Member State has failed to fulfil an obligation under this Treaty, it shall deliver a reasoned opinion on the matter after giving the State concerned the opportunity to submit its observations.

If the State concerned does not comply with the opinion within the period laid down by the Commission, the latter may bring the matter before the Court of Justice".

[215] See for a full report L Krämer, "Die Rechtsprechung der EG-Gerichte zum Umweltrecht 1998 und 1999" [2000] *Europäische Grundrechte Zeitschrift* 265; this article follows earlier reports on the same subject: for the period 1992 to 1994, see [1995] *Europäische Grundrechte Zeitschrift* 45 and the period 1995 to 1997 [1998] *Europäische Grundrechte Zeitschrift* 309.

(12) This means in practice that in 1998 and 1999, the average duration of a procedure under Article 226 EC Treaty was 68 months, thus five and a half years; and it is only small consolation that in previous periods, the time-span was shorter (47 and 57 months respectively). The long duration must inevitably act as a very strong deterrent for the Commission from starting proceedings and bringing matters before the Court: At the same time, the temptation for Member States to reckon that any breach of the obligations under Community directives will take four years or more before it is condemned by the Court, and thus may be remedied during that procedure, is very considerable.

The main origin of these lengthy procedures is the decision-making procedure, during the pre-litigation phase, within the Commission.[216] Few efforts have been undertaken so far to accelerate the procedures; the present case demonstrates that quicker procedures are possible and it can only be hoped that this case serves as a model for shortening the delays in environmental lititgation before the European Courts.

18. INTERNAL MARKET REPORTING

Judgment of the Court (Sixth Chamber) of 16 September 1997
Case C–279/94

Commission of the European Communities v. *Italy*
[1997] ECR I–4743

Facts and Procedure

In 1992, Italy adopted Law 257/92 laying down rules concerning the cessation of the use of asbestos.[217] The Law provided a complete prohibition on the extraction, importation, exportation, marketing and production of asbestos, asbestos products and products concerning asbestos. As regards the concentration of asbestos fibres at the working place, the Law fixed certain limits which were not to be exceeded.

The Commission was of the opinion that Italy had failed to notify the draft Law to the Commission, as required by Directive 83/189 as amended.[218] Article 8(1) of

---

[216] See L Krämer [2000] *Europäische Grundrechte Zeitschrit* (n. 215 *supra*), p. 267; for a more detailed discussion of this question see p. xx *infra*.

[217] Law No 257 of 27 March 1992 laying down rules concerning the cessation of the use of asbestos, Gazzetta Ufficiale, Ordinary Supplement No 87 of 13 April 1992, p. 5.

[218] Directive 83/189 laying down a procedure for the provision of information in the field of technical standards and regulations [1983] OJ L109/8; this Directive was amended by Directive 88/182

this Directive provided that the Member States should immediately communicate to the Commission any draft technical regulation. As its discussion with the Italian Government did not lead to a solution, the Commission brought the present action.

Judgment (extracts)

30. As far as Article 1(2) of Law No 257/92 is concerned, that provision prohibits the extraction, importation, exportation, marketing and production of asbestos, asbestos products and products containing asbestos after a period of one year after the date of entry into force of the Law. Such a provision, in prohibiting the marketing and use of asbestos, constitutes a technical regulation which the Italian Government ought to have notified in accordance with the first subparagraph of Article 8(1) of the Directive.

31. As regards Article 3 of Law No 257/92, paragraph (1) lays down in particular limits for concentrations of inhalable asbestos fibres at workplaces where asbestos is used, processed or disposed of. Paragraph (2) lays down limits, procedures and analytical methods for the measurement of pollution of the environment by asbestos. Paragraph (3) empowers the Minister for for Health to update or amend paragraphs (1) and (2). Paragraphs (4) and (5) amend or repeal previously existing limits.

32. Article 8 of Law No 257/92 provides that the classification, packaging and labelling of asbestos and products containing asbestos are to be governed by Law No 256/74, as amended and supplemented by Decree 215/88.

33. It should be recalled that when the Commission applies to the Court for a declaration that a Member State has failed to fulfil its obligations under the Treaty, the Commission itself must adduce evidence of the alleged infringement . . .

34. According to Article 1, point 5 of the Directive, however, a "technical regulation" is to be understood as meaning "technical specifications, including the relevant administrative provisions, the observance of which is compulsory, *de iure* or *de facto*, in the case of marketing or use in a Member State". According to Article 1, point 1, of the directive, a "technical specification" is a specification contained in a document which lays down the characteristics required of a product such as levels of quality, performance and safety. Article 3(1) of Law No 257/92 lays down limits for the concentration of inhalable asbestos fibres at workplaces. Since this does not define a characteristic required of a product, it does not in principle fall within the definition of a technical specification and consequently cannot be regarded as a technical regulation which has to be notified to the Commission pursuant to the first subparagraph of Article 8(1) of the Directive . . .

[1988] OJ L81/75. In 1998, thus after the present judgment was given, the Directive and all its subsequent amendments were consolidated by Directive 98/34 [1998] OJ L204/37.

36. Although the Commission asserts that Article 8 of Law No 257/92 constitutes a new technical regulation . . . it must be concluded that it has not supported this assertion with any evidence. Consequently, the Commission's argument on this point must be dismissed . . .

38. As regards the Italian Government's obligation to notify the full text of Law No 257/92, including the provisions which do not constitute technical regulations, it must be observed that, according to the last sentence of the first subparagraph of Article 8(1) of the Directive, the Member States must also communicate to the Commission the text of the basic legislative or regulatory provisions principally and directly concerned, should knowledge of such a text be necessary to assess the implications of the draft technical regulation.

39. It is apparent from the foregoing that many provisions of Law No 257/92 do not constitute technical regulations within the meaning of Article 1, point 5 of the Directive or even basic legislative or regulatory provisions which principally and directly concern the technical regulation contained in that Law, within the meaning of the first subparagraph of Article 8(1) of the Directive.

40. However, the aim of the last sentence of the first subparagraph of Article 8(1) of the Directive is to enable the Commission to have as much information as possible on any draft technical regulation with respect to its content, scope and general context in order to enable it to exercise as effectively as possible the powers conferred on it by the Directive.

41. Only full communication of Law No 257/92 could enable the Commission to evaluate the exact scope of any technical regulations contained in that Law which, as its title indicates, concerns the cessation of the use of asbestos.

42. However, the mere fact that all the provisions contained in Law No 257/92 are notified to the Commission does not prevent the Italian Republic from bringing into force immediately, and therefore without waiting for the results of he examination procedure provided for by the Directive, the provisions which do not constitute technical regulations.

43. Consequently, it must be declared that, in adopting Law No 257/92 without having notified the draft Law to the Commission, the Italian Republic has failed to fulfil its obligations under the first subparagraph of Article 8(1) of the Directive.

Commentary

I. The Standstill Directive 98/34

(1) The judgment limits itself to the question whether the Italian Law 257/92 which prohibits the production and marketing of asbestos should have been notified, in draft form, to the European Commission. It does not mention in one word the two questions which are more important: (a) what is the consequence of the omission to notify the draft Law; (b) was Italy entitled to ban the marketing and

use of asbestos? It was, of course, the Commission which deliberately limited the subject-matter of the litigation, for reasons which will be discussed below.

The Court held that the prohibition on marketing and using asbestos constituted a technical regulation under Directive 83/189 and should therefore have been notified, in draft form, to the Commission (paragraph 30).

(2) Directive 83/189 and its subsequent amendments were, in 1998, repealed by Directive 98/34 which consolidated all previous texts and amendments in one single text.[219] As regards the discussion of this notification Directive hereafter, the most recent wording of Directive 98/34 will be used.

(3) Originally, Directive 83/189 was conceived as promoting European industrial standardisation; this explains that Articles 2 to 7 refer to this industrial standardisation and establish provisions for better co-operation at Community level. The notification of national legislation in draft form was, in the beginning, considered to be an accessory measure to this co-operation in standardisation which meant to cover those cases where a technical standard was given a more general application by means of an administrative provision.[220] This is the reason why the Directive, when it was adopted in 1983, did not mention the words "legislation", "regulation" or a similar expression. Rather quickly, however, the control of national legislation which affected, directly or indirectly, the free circulation of products became a prominent, if not the prominent, feature of the Directive. This accentuation of the control of national legislation was mirrored in the progressive fine-tuning given to the notion of "technical regulation" which now reads:[221] "[technical regulations are] technical specifications and other requirements, including the relevant administrative provisions, the observance of which is compulsory, *de iure* or *de facto*, in the case of marketing or use in a Member State or a major part thereof, as well as laws, regulations, or administrative provisions of Member States, except those provided for in Article 10, prohibiting the manufacture, importation, marketing or use of a product.

De facto technical regulations include:

—laws, regulations or administrative provisions of a Member State which refer either to technical specifications or other requirements or to professional codes or codes of practices which in turn refer to technical specifications or other requirements and compliance with which confers a presumption of conformity with the obligations imposed by the aforementioned laws, regulations or administrative provisions,

—voluntary agreements to which a public authority is a contracting party and which provide, in the public interest, for compliance with technical specifications or other requirements, excluding public procurement tender specifications,

---

[219]   Directive 98/34 (n. 218 *supra*); amended by Directive 98/48 [1998] OJ L217/18.

[220]   In law, an industrial standard normally is a recommendation issued by the standardisation organisation and addressed to its members, inviting them to follow the provisions of that standard.

[221]   Directive 98/34 (n. 218 *supra*), Art. 1 no. 9.

—technical specifications or other requirements which are linked to fiscal or financial measures affecting the consumption of products by encouraging compliance with such technical specifications or other requirements; technical specifications or other requirements linked to national social-security systems are not included . . ."

(4) It is obvious that this text tries, as far as possible, to include any national measure; for this reason also, the exclusion of measures laid down by local authorities which was contained in the original text of the Directive[222] was subsequently deleted. This broad application is re-enforced by the notion of "other requirements" which constitute, according to Article 1 no. 3 of the Directive "a requirement . . . imposed on a product for the purpose of protecting, in particular consumers or the environment, and which affects its life cycle after it has been placed on the market, such as conditions of use, recycling, reuse or disposal, where such conditions can significantly influence the composition or nature of the product or its marketing".

These broadly drafted provisions include, in practice, any product-related environmental measure elaborated at national level, with the exemption of some measures of fiscal nature. Directive 98/34 thus allows the Commission to gain a rather complete insight into Member States' planned measures in all areas related to products or production processes.

(5) Where a Member State elaborates any national provision which comes under the realm of Directive 98/34, that Member State is obliged, under Article 8 of Directive 98/34, to communicate the draft to the Commission. This communication has to be accompanied by the text of the basic legislative or regulatory provisions "should knowledge of such text be necessary to assess the implications of the draft" (Article 8(1)); also this text has been considerably refined during recent years.[223]

The communication to the Commission has the consequence that the adoption of the draft technical regulation has to be postponed by three months. This delay is six months where the Commission or another Member State—all Member States receive the draft technical regulation sent to the Commission—delivers a detailed opinion within three months where it is argued that the draft may create

---

[222] This exclusion is mentioned in para. 3 of the present judgment (not reproduced here).

[223] See also the most recent addition: "Where, in particular, the draft seeks to limit the marketing or use of a chemical substance, preparation or product on grounds of public health or of the protection of consumers or the environment, Member States shall also forward either a summary or the references of all relevant data relating to the substance, preparation or product concerned and to known and available substitutes, where such information may be available, and communicate the anticipated effects of the measure on public health and the protection of the consumer and the environment, together with an analysis of the risk carried out as appropriate in accordance with the general principles for the risk evaluation of chemical substances as referred to in . . . Regulation 793/93 . . . or . . . Directive 67/548 . . .".

The term "where such information may be available" may very easily be omitted in the political discussions with a Member State.

obstacles to the free circulation of goods. And where the Commission announces its intention to propose or adopt a Community legislative text on the subject-matter, the adoption of the national text must be postponed by 12 months. Finally, if the Council adopts a common position on the subject-matter, the period of standstill is extended to 18 months.[224]

(6) The pressure to see the draft national environmental measure being criticised by other Member States—sometimes by practically all, such as was the case in autumn 2000, when Denmark banned lead from almost all products and processes—is a considerable deterrent, all the more as also within the Member State which plans the measure objections from vested interest groups is frequent. There is, however, another way to ensure full compliance with the notification and standstill provisions of Directive 98/34; this is due to the interpretation which the Court of Justice gave to that Directive. Indeed, in 1996, the Court decided that, where a Member State adopts a national measure without having previously notified it under Directive 98/34, this provision is unenforceable against private persons and in particular economic operators; national courts are obliged not to apply the national measure in question.[225] This "sanction", which follows from the direct effect of the Directive's provisions, is very effective since penalties or other sanctions which are possibly pronounced under the national measure are also not valid. And where a lack of notification leads to the unenforceability of national legislation several years later—as happened recently in the Netherlands—the necessity of reviewing administrative and judicial measures several years later may create considerable difficulties.

(7) *De facto*, Directive 98/34 has replaced an information standstill agreement in environmental matters which was adopted in 1973 in the form of a gentlemen's agreement.[226] The Commission's announcement in 1987 that it intended to draft legislation on a standstill procedure in environmental matters[227] was never realised.

Directive 98/34 affects numerous environmental measures; measures which fix quality standards for the air or water normally do not come under the field of application of the Directive: likewise, nature protection measures are normally not affected. In the same way, measures on the storage of products or on industrial installations are normally not notifiable. In contrast to that measures concerning waste aspects of materials clearly come under Directive 98/34. Where they are not product-related, Directive 75/442 on waste requires them nevertheless to be notified to the Commission; however, in such a case, there is no standstill procedure following this notification.

---

[224] See for details of these standstill provisions Directive 98/34 (n. 218 *supra*), Art. 9.

[225] Court of Justice, Case C–194/94 *Security International* v. *Signalson* [1996] ECR I–2201.

[226] Agreement of the representatives of the Governments of the Member States meeting in Council on information for the Commission and for the Member States with a view to possible harmonisation throughout the Communities of urgent measures concerning the protection of the environment [1973] OJ C9/1; amended [1974] OJ C86/2.

[227] Fourth environmental action programme [1987] OJ C328/1, para. 2. 1. 7.

II. Asbestos Products in the Internal Market

(8) As the Commission had not applied to the Court of Justice to assess the Italian ban on asbestos, there was no judgment on this question. However, the asbestos ban is a good example of Community product policy. It has well known for several decades that asbestos is carcinogenic. After having adopted a number of directives on the protection of persons at their work-place, the Community adopted in 1983 a directive which provided for a ban on most asbestos fibres;[228] however, as a concession to the asbestos industry, the Community accepted that the remaining asbestos products were not to be labelled with the Community warning symbols for dangerous products which were orange,[229] but with a label in black and white and the letter "a", the symbol organised by the industry. As Directive 76/769 and Directive 83/478 were both based on Article 94 (ex Article 100) EC Treaty, Member States were in principle prevented from deviating from the provisions of Directive 83/478 which had allowed the marketing and use of chrysotile asbestos.

(9) However, as asbestos was capable of being substituted, over the years nine Member States decided to provide for a total ban on asbestos, including Italy by Law 257/92. The Commission recognised that such a total ban distorted competition within the Community and was incompatible with Article 28 EC Treaty.[230] Instead, however, of taking action against those nine Member States under Article 226 EC Treaty, in order to have the Court of Justice pronounce the incompatibility of the different national measures with EC law, the Commission either remained passive or, as in the present case, used the "back door" of a breach of Directive 98/34 (ex Directive 83/189) to embarass Member States.

This legally most unsatisfactory situation found its solution only in 1999, when the Community adopted a further amendment to Directive 76/769 and accepted a total ban on all asbestos products.[231]

(10) While asbestos may thus progressively disappear from the market, it should be noted that asbestos waste will continue to cause problems. A directive from 1987 contains some rather rudimentary provisions on asbestos waste.[232] However, Member States are divided on whether asbestos waste is to be considered to be hazardous waste or not, which is relevant for its disposal in landfills for non-hazardous or hazardous waste.[233] In order to facilitate landfilling, the majority of Member State appears to favour a classification as non-hazardous. The Community is likely to decide on this question in mid-2002.[234]

---

[228] Directive 83/478 amending Directive 76/769 relating to restrictions on the marketing and use of certain dangerous substances [1983] OJ L263/33.

[229] These symbols were introduced by Directive 67/548 on the classification, packaging and labelling of dangerous substances [1967] OJ L196/1.

[230] Commission, answer to Written Question P–591/96 (Féret) [1996] OJ C183/39.

[231] Directive 1999/77 [1999] OJ L207/18.

[232] Directive 87/217 on the prevention and reduction of environmental pollution by asbestos [1987] OJ L85/40.

[233] Directive 1999/31 on the landfill of waste [1999] OJ L182/1.

[234] See Decision 2000/532 on a Community waste list, [2000] OJ L226/3, no 170601 where asbestos-containing material is, at present, classified as hazardous.

3

WATER AND AIR*

---

19. MAJORITY DECISIONS IN WATER LAW

Judgment of the Court of 30 January 2001
Case C–36/98

Spain v. Council of the European Union
Supported by France, Portugal, Finland and
Commission of the European Communities
(2001) ECR I–779

Facts and Procedure

On 24 November 1997, the Council adopted Decision 97/825 concerning the conclusion of the Convention on co-operation for the protection and sustainable use of the River Danube.[1] The Council based this Decision on Article 175(1) (ex Article 130s(1)) EC Treaty,[2] together with Article 300(2) and the first subparagraph of (3).[3] Spain was of the opinion that the Decision should have been adopted on the basis of Article 175(2) (ex Article 130s(2)) EC Treaty, which

---

* For further judgements discussing environmental aspects of water pollution see cases in sections 2 (*Peralta*), 6 (*UK Bathing Waters*), 8 (*Water Discharges*) and 9 (*Bacchiglione*), all in chapter 1 *supra*; sections 10 (*Standley*) and 17 (*Portuguese Reports*) in chapter 2 *supra*, and section 46 (Air Pollution and Water Law) in chapter 7 *infra*. For further judgements discussing air pollution questions see the cases in section 1, chapter 1 *supra* (Forests and the Environment), section 11, chapter 2 *supra* (Bremner Motorway) and section 47, chapter 7 *infra* (Air Pollution and Water Law)

[1] Decision 97/825 concerning the conclusion of the Convention on cooperation for the protection and sustainable use of the river Danube [1997] OJ L342/18.

[2] Art. 175(1) (ex Art. 130s(1)) EC Treaty: "The Council . . . shall decide what action is to be taken by the Community in order to achieve the objectives referred to in Art. 174".

[3] Art. 228 EC Treaty was amended and renumbered as Art. 300 by the Treaty of Amsterdam which entered into force in May 1999. At the time of the Council Decision 97/825, the previous version applied, which reads as follows: Art. 228(2): "Subject to the powers vested in the Commission in this field, the agreements shall be concluded by the Council, acting by a qualified majority on a proposal from the Commission. The Council shall act unanimously when the agreement covers a field for which unanimity is required for the adoption of internal rules . . .". Para. 3 concerned the participation of the European Parliament in decision-making.

requires unanimous decisions.[4] It therefore applied, under Article 230 (ex Article 173) EC Treaty, to the Court of Justice.

Judgment (extracts)

[The scope of Article 130s(1) and of Article 130s(2) of the Treaty]

46. It . . . follows from the very wording of those two provisions that Article 130s of the Treaty in principle constitutes the legal basis of acts adopted by the Council in order to attain the objectives referred to in Article 130r of the Treaty. On the other hand, Article 130s(2) of the Treaty was drafted in such a way that it is to apply where the measures to be adopted concern matters indicated therein, such as the management of water resources.

47. As regards the concept of "management of water resources", it follows from the consistent case-law of the Court that an interpretation of a provision of Community law involves a comparison of the language versions (see Case C–72/95 *Kraaijveld and Others* v. *Gedeputeerde Staten van Zuid-Holland* [1996] ECR I–5403, paragraph 28).

48. In the present case, it should be observed that the use in the French version of the word "*hydrauliques*", which means "relating to the flow and distribution of water", implies that what is referred to in the second indent of the first subparagraph of Article 130s(2) of the Treaty is the management of water resources in their physical dimension and tends to support the interpretation advocated by the Council and the interveners. The Dutch version ("*kwantitatief waterbeheer*") is comparable, in that it uses terms which imply the management of water in its quantitative, as opposed to its qualitative aspects. The German ("*der Bewirtschaftung der Wasserressourcen*"), Spanish ("*la gestión de los recursos hídricos*"), Italian ("*la gestione delle risorse idriche*"), Portuguese ("*gestão dos recursos hídricos*"), Finnish ("*vesivarojen hoitoa*"), Swedish ("*förvaltning av vatten-resurser*"), Danish ("*forvaltning af vandressourcerne*"), English ("management of water resources"), Irish ("*bainisteoireacht acmhainní uísce*") and Greek ("*ti diaxírisi ton idátinon póron*") versions may cover not only the quantitative aspects of the management of water but also qualitative aspects.

49. In the case of divergence between the language versions of a Community measure, the provision in question must be interpreted by reference to the purpose and general scheme of the rules of which it forms part (see in particular, in that regard, Case C–420/98 *W.N.* [2000] ECR I–2847, paragraph 21).

---

[4] Art. 175(2) (ex Art. 130(2)) EC Treaty: "By way of derogation from the decisionùmaking procedure provided for in para. 1 and without prejudice to Art. 95, the Council, acting unanimously on a proposal from the Commission and after consulting the European Parliament and the Economic and Social Committee, shall adopt:—provisions primarily of a fiscal nature;—measures concerning town and country planning, land use with the exception of waste management and measures of a general nature, and management of water resources;—measures significantly affecting a Member State's choice between different energy sources and the general structure of its energy supply".

50. In that regard, it should be pointed out first of all that it is clear from the objectives of Community policy on the environment and from a reading of Article 130r in conjunction with Articles 130s(1) and (2) of the Treaty that the inclusion of the "management of water resources" in the first subparagraph of Article 130s(2) of the Treaty is not intended to exclude any measure dealing with the use of water by man from the application of Article 130s(1) of the Treaty.

51. Next, apart from the measures concerning the management of water resources, the second indent of the first subparagraph of Article 130s(2) of the Treaty refers to measures relating to town and country planning and to land use with the exception of waste management and measures of a general nature. These are measures which, just like those based on Article 130s(1) of the Treaty, are intended to attain the objectives referred to in Article 130r of the Treaty, but which regulate the use of the territory of the Member States, such as measures relating to regional, urban or rural management plans or the planning of various projects concerning the infrastructure of a Member State.

52. The territory and land of the Member States and their water resources are limited resources and the second indent of the first subparagraph of Article 130s(2) of the Treaty therefore refers to the measures which affect them as such, that is measures which regulate the quantitative aspects of the use of those resources or, in other words, measures related to the management of limited resources in its quantitative aspects and not those concerning the improvement and the protection of the quality of those resources.

53. That interpretation is borne out by the fact that waste management and measures of a general nature are excluded from the application of the second indent of the first subparagraph of Article 130s(2) of the Treaty. Measures of a general nature are, for example, measures which, whilst relating generally to town and country planning and land use in the Member States, do not regulate the performance of specific infrastructure projects or, although imposing certain limits on the way in which land may be used in the Member States, do not regulate the use to which the Member States plan to put their land.

54. Furthermore, the measures referred to in the three indents of the first subparagraph of Article 130s(2) of the Treaty all imply the involvement of the Community institutions in areas such as fiscal policy, energy policy or town and country planning policy, in which, apart from Community policy on the environment, either the Community has no legislative powers or unanimity with the Council is required.

55. It follows from a consideration of those various factors, taken together, that the concept of "management of water resources" does not cover every measure concerned with water, but covers only measures concerning the regulation of the use of water and the management of water in its quantitative aspects.

[The legal basis on which the Convention was adopted]

59. If examination of a Community measure reveals that it pursues a twofold purpose or that it has a twofold component and if one of these is identifiable as the main or predominant component, whereas the other is merely incidental, the act must be based on a single legal basis, namely that required by the main or predominant purpose or component . . .

60. As regards the purpose of the contested decision, although the Convention which it approves also refers to the regulation of the use of the waters of the catchment area of the river Danube and the management of those waters from a quantitative aspect, it is clear from the recitals to the contested decision and from the preamble to the Convention that the principal purpose of the Convention is the protection and improvement of the quality of those waters.

74. It follows from that examination that, according to its aim and its content, the primary purpose of the Convention is the protection and improvement of the quality of the waters of the catchment area of the river Danube, although it also refers, albeit incidentally, to the use of those waters and their management in its quantitative aspects.

75. It follows from the foregoing that internal Community rules corresponding to the provisions of the Convention are adopted on the basis of Article 130s(1) of the Treaty. The Council was therefore correct to take the first sentence of Article 228(2) and the first subparagraph of Article 228(3) of the Treaty as the basis for approving the Convention.

Commentary

I. Article 175 (1) and (2) EC Treaty

(1) The judgment clarifies a legal controversy which is of considerable relevance to Community water law. It intervenes at a time when, at a political level, a solution was found to that problem; however, it may well be that information on the imminent judgment and its content had influenced that political decision itself.

(2) When the Single European Act which entered into effect in 1987 introduced an environmental chapter into the EC Treaty (Articles 130r to 130t), all decisions in the environmental area had to be taken unanimously. The Maastricht Treaty on European Union which entered into effect 1993 introduced, in Article 130s(1) (now Article 175(1)) EC Treaty, majority decisions in the environmental sector. However, it added a second paragraph to Article 130s according to which decisions in certain areas had to be taken unanimously. And among these areas was "management of water resources". The dispute in the

present case was on the question whether Decision 97/825, which approved the conclusion of the "Convention on cooperation for the protection and sustainable use of the river Danube", was to be taken unanimously under Article 175(2) (ex Article 130s(2)) EC Treaty, as Spain argued, or whether it came under Article 175(1) (ex Article 130s(1)) EC Treaty as the Council argued. This was due to the fact that Article 228(2) EC Treaty which has since been amended, provided that for the conclusion of international agreements the Council could normally decide by a qualified majority; however, the Council had to act unanimously "when the agreement covers a field for which unanimity is required for the adoption of internal rules".

(3) The Court started its analysis with a comparison of applications of the Article and found, not surprisingly, that they diverged. The Dutch version of Article 175(2) EC Treaty mentioned "quantitative management of water resources" ('*kwantitatief waterbeheer*') and the Court was of the opinion that the French version also used words which "tend[ed] to support" the opinion that Article 175(2) covered the quantitative aspects of water management; all the other linguistic versions of the Treaty did not differentiate between "quantitative" and "qualitative", but used neutral terminology which could apply to both.

(4) There is little to add to the Court's linguistic interpretation. It might be relevant to note that Article 175(2) EC Treaty did not use the words "water legislation", though it used the words "waste legislation". This is an indication that it was not intended to bring the totality of water legislation into Article 175(2), but only parts of it. Then the differentiation between "quantitative" and "qualitative" may become reasonable, though past Community secondary legislation does not really distinguish between the two areas and it may be doubtful whether such a distinction is really practicable: indeed where the reduction of discharge of pollutants is decided—a measure which falls into the "qualitative" area—the availability of the water for drinking water purposes of for agricultural use is increased—and certainly the question of how much water may be used for such purposes comes into the area of "quantitative" management of resources. It is probably for this reason that past Community environmental action programmes which contained a reference to the management of water resources included both quantitative and qualitative aspects.

(5) Having found divergencies between the language versions, the Court examined the "purpose and general scheme" of Article 175 EC Treaty. It found that the different other aspects mentioned in the second indent of Article 175(2)—town and country planning, land use—referred to the use of the territory of the Member States and that the territory and land of Member States, as well as their water resources, were a limited resource. The second indent, according to the Court, shows an intention to safeguard the unanimity rule to decisions on such limited resources and therefore refers only to quantitative, but not to qualitative aspects. The Court consolidates this conclusion by interpreting the exclusion cases in the second indent of Article 175(2), the position of this Treaty provision in the general system of the Treaty and the fact that, anyway, the Community was obliged to

reach a high level of environmental protection which made it unnecessary to give to each Member State a right of veto in order to ensure this objective in the water sector (paragraphs 53 to 56 of the judgment).

(6) The Court's conclusion—only quantitative measures are covered by the unanimity requirement of Article 175 (2) EC Treaty—is certainly to be approved of, and legal authors seem almost unanimous in favour of this result. It would not really be understandable why the resource "water" would have to be regulated by the Community by unanimous decisions, but why other, equally important, resources—waste, fauna and flora, energy (in its environmental aspects) and even air—could be regulated by way of majority decisions.

(7) On several occasions, primary and secondary Community law takes into consideration this argument of the Court that the use of a limited physical resource should be decided upon by unanimity. Thus, for the establishment and development of trans-European networks (Articles 154 *et seq.*), the Community shall elaborate guidelines. These guidelines are, according to Article 156 EC Treaty, decided by way of majority decisions. However, Article 156 EC Treaty also states: "Guidelines and projects of common interest which relate to the territory of a Member State shall require the approval of the Member State concerned". This means, for instance, that the Community could not decide, by qualified majority, to build a new motorway between Germany and Italy which crossed the Austrian territory, without Austria approving of this project. Similar examples could be given in respect of high-speed railways, energy pipelines and other measures.

(8) Another example can be found in Directive 92/43 on fauna and flora habitats.[5] This Directive has the objective of establishing a Community list of Special Areas of Conservation which form a coherent "European ecological network" (Natura 2000). The areas entering this list are taken from national lists which each Member States establishes according to provisions laid down in Article 4 of Directive 92/43. Where a specific area has not been inserted into a national list, but the Commission is of the opinion that it should have been inserted, a dispute settlement procedure is started. The final arbiter is the Council which, however, has to decide by unanimity (Article 5(3) of Directive 92/43).

(9) Generally, it should be indicated that Community environmental legislation does not oblige Member States to realise infrastructure projects or other installations. Where a Member State decides to have no waste incineration installations, no nuclear energy installations, no motorways, airports or high-speed railways, it is free to take such a decision; the Community does not interfere with this. Rather, Community provisions apply in those cases where any such project is to be realised, by fixing conditions for its planning, construction and operation. The only exception to this is Directive 91/271 on urban waste water[6] which provides for waste water treatment for urban agglomerations. Even here, though, it is not a

---

[5] Directive 92/43 on the conservation of natural habitats and of wild fauna and flora [1992] OJ L206/7.
[6] Directive 91/271 concerning urban waste water treatment [1991] OJ L135/40.

specific type of installation that is required, but rather a specific form of treatment of waste water; as long as the requirements of the Directive are attained, Member States are free to resort to whatever form of water treatment they wish.

(10) Article 175(2) EC Treaty was amended by the Treaty of Nice, which will still have to be ratified by all 15 Member States before it becomes effective. As regards "management of water resources"; the word "quantitative" was added. In the interpretation which was given to the present Article 175(2) by the Court in the present judgment, this means only a clarification which will contribute to preventing future litigation.

(11) Much more important is, for the future development of the Community, the deletion of the words "and measures of a general nature" in the second indent. This deletion is not to be commented on in detail here. However, there are voices in the legal literature which argue that the obligation to designate natural habitats under Directives 79/409[7] and 92/43[8] is such a general measures.[9] If this opinion were held correct, such Directives would, in future, have to be adopted by unanimity, as the deletion of the words "measures of a general nature" can be understood only in the sense that such measures come under Article 175(2) as soon as they concern town and country planning or land use. However, I do not share this interpretation and am rather of the opinion that such measures are general environmental measures which belong to Article 175(1) EC Treaty.

(12) The Court went on to examine whether the Danube Convention concerned qualitative or quantitative aspects of water resource management and found that it contained elements of both. It then applied its theory of "centre of gravity",[10] without calling it that. Rather, the Court mentioned the "main or predominant purpose or component" as opposed to "incidental" (paragraph 59), "principal purpose" (paragraph 60), "primarily concerned with" (paragraphs 62 and 67), "primary purpose" as opposed to "incidentally" (paragraph 74). Little has to be added to that. The Court is certainly right in its finding that the Sofia Convention in question did not try to regulate the use of the water resources of the Danube river and that its intention was to promote co-operation among riparian States and the States in the catchment area of the river on the one hand, the improvement of water quality on the other hand.

II. Transboundary Water Management

(13) The fact that Spain applied to the Court in this case and that Portugal supported the Council is not a pure accident. Indeed, for a number of years Spain has been preparing a huge national water plan which has the main objective to divert

---

[7] Directive 79/409 on the conservation of wild birds [1979] OJ L103/1.

[8] Directive 92/43 (n. 5 *supra*).

[9] See, for instance, A Epiney, *Umweltrecht in der Europäischen Union* (C Heymann, Cologne, Köln, Berlin, Bonn, Munich, 1997), p. 58; W Frenz, *Europäisches Umweltrecht,* (Beck, Munich, 1997), para. 86.

[10] See on that theory p. 1 *supra*.

water from the north of Spain, where it is abundant, to the dry parts of southern Spain. As several big Spanish rivers end on Portuguese territory, such plans are most likely to affect Portuguese interests in the content of the planned Spanish activities. And Portugal may hope to find support within the Community, should Spain ever wish, in the future, to act unilaterally; if Spain had to agree to any measure adopted at Community level on water issues, it would have had a powerful right of veto which might have allowed it to steer the orientation of Community water policy into a direction that was in line with Spanish interests.

(14) In the past, the scarcity of water resources was not a considerable problem in the Community. In the 1960s and 1970s, France and the Netherlands had diverging opinions on the use of the Rhine river which was polluted by French potassium mines to an extent that the water could not easily be used by Dutch farmers. There was a basic decision not to bring this kind of issue under Community law, as both the Netherlands and France preferred intergovernmental co-operation via bilateral agreements or via the Rhine Commission.

(15) The Community thus kept itself away from such issues and it has hitherto been not involved in practice in the management of river systems (Rhine, Elbe, Oder, Danube). The fact that the Community has adhered to the different conventions concerning these rivers[11] has not changed this situation: while in law, the different conventions became Community law with the Community's adherence to them, the Commission, in contradiction to its obligations flowing from Article 211 EC Treaty,[12] does not monitor the application of these conventions by the contracting States that are also Community Member States. Whether this abstention can in future be pursued remains to be seen: the enlargement of the Community towards the east will create considerable new problems, for the Vistula, the Balkan region and elsewhere. At the same time will the upcoming climate change and the increased use of water lead to more controversies among States, including Member States. The new Community water Directive,[13] which is likely to influence the water policy and management of all present and future Member States to a considerable degree, may be a good first step to reconsidering the transboundary management of water by the Community.

---

[11] Apart from Decision 97/825 (n. 1 *supra*) which is the subject of the present judgment see Decision 77/586 to adhere to the Bonn Convention for the protection of the Rhine against chemical pollution [1977] OJ L240/35; Decision 90/160 to adhere to the Regensburg Agreement on co-operation and management of water resources in the Danube basin [1990] OJ L377/28; Decision 91/598 to adhere to the Magdeburg Convention on the International Commission for the protection of the Elbe [1991] OJ L321/25; Decision 1999/257 to adhere to the Wroclaw Convention on the International Commission for the protection of the Oder against pollution [1999] OJ L100/20.

[12] Art. 211 (ex Art. 155) EC Treaty: "... the Commission shall ... ensure that the provisions of this Treaty and the measures taken by the institutions pursuant thereto are applied".

[13] Directive 2000/60 establishing a framework for Community action in the field of water policy [2000] OJ L327/1.

20. PROGRAMMES TO REDUCE WATER POLLUTION

Judgment of the Court (Sixth Chamber) of 11 November 1999
Case C–184/97

Commission of the European Communities v. *Germany*
[1999] ECR I–7837

Facts and Procedure

Directive 76/464 on the discharge of dangerous substances into water was adopted in 1976.[14] It introduced permit requirements for all such discharges. The dangerous substances were classified into two categories: list I[15] comprised substances which were selected mainly on the basis of their toxicity, persistence and bioaccumulation. List II[16] contained other, less dangerous substances. For substances in List I the Directive provided for the fixing of Community-wide emission limit values and quality standards. For List II substances, Member States were requested to establish programmes for the reduction of water pollution.[17] Member States were allowed to take more stringent measures than those provided for under Directive 76/464 (Article 10 of that Directive).

As the Commission was of the opinion that Germany had not established the programmes which were required under Article 7(1) of Directive 76/464, it

---

[14] Directive 76/464 on pollution caused by certain dangerous substances discharged into the aquatic environment of the Community [1976] OJ L129/23.

[15] Directive 76/464 (n. 14 *supra*) Annex: "List I contains certain individual substances which belong to the following families and groups of substances, selected mainly on the basis of their toxicity, persistence and bioaccumulation . . .".

[16] Directive 76/464 (n. 14 *supra*), Annex: "List II contains:—substances belonging to the families and groups of substances in List I for which the limit values referred to in Art. 6 of the Directive have not been determined,—certain individual substances and categories of substances belonging to the families and groups of substances listed below, and which have a deleterious effect on the aquatic environment . . .".

[17] Directive 76/464 (n. 14 *supra*) Art. 7: "1. In order to reduce pollution of the waters . . . by the substances within List II, Member States shall establish programmes in the implementation of which they shall apply in particular the methods referred to in paras. 2 and 3. 2. All discharges into the waters . . . which are liable to containany of the substances within list II shall require prior authorisation by the competent authority in the Member State concerned, in which emission standards shall be laid down. Such standards shall be based on the quality objectives, which shall be fixed as prodided for in para. 3. 3. The programmes referred to in para. 1 shall include quality objectives for water; these shall be laid down in accordance with Council directives, where they exist. 4. . . . .

5. The programmes shall set deadlines for their implementation. 6. Summaries of the programmes and the results of their implementation shall be communicated to the Commission. 7. . . . .".

applied to the Court. However, it limited its application to those 99 substances which belonged to List I, but had not been regulated at Community level.

Judgment (extracts)

22. The Commission alleges that the German Government . . . did not adopt programmes including quality objectives. .

24. . . . the German Government contends that it has in fact adopted measures of that kind by laying down, on the basis of Article 7a of the Wasserhaushalts-gesetz, uniformly applicable limit values for emissions in the case of all List I and II substances . . .

26. . . . in the German Government's view, the structure of the directive is such that, once limit values for emissions have been put in place, ensuring their observance results in full implementation of the directive which then no longer requires programmes to be drawn up of quality objectives to be laid down under Article 7 of the directive.

27. As regards the need for programmes to be drawn up in respect of the substances at issue, it should be noted that even if they are List I substances the Council has not yet determined emission limit values, as provided for in Article 6 of the directive. Those provisions are therefore to be provisionnally treated as List II substances governed by Article 7 of the directive . . .

28. Under that provision the Member States are required, inter alia, to adopt programmes which include both water quality objectives and a requirement that any discharge of substances in List II be subject to prior authorisation laying down emission standards calculated on the basis of those quality objectives.

29. Accordingly, the laying down by a Member State of limit values for emissions of List II substances is not sufficient to exempt that Member State from drawing up the programmes provided for in Article 7 of the directive.

30. In addition, those programmes, contrary to the German Government's assertions, are necessary because where the Council has not laid down limit values for emissions of List I substances, they constitute the sole means of verifying that the Member States have adopted measures under the directive to combat water pollution.

33. As regards more specifically the need to lay down quality objectives, the German Government maintains that the implementation, by laying down limit values for emissions, of a system of protection analogous to that provided for in Article 6 of the directive exempts it from the requirement to lay down such objectives.

34. That argument cannot be upheld. Whilst Article 6(2) of the directive requires the Council to lay down the quality objectives for list I substances, Article 7(3) of the directive imposes the same obligation on Member States in regard to List II substances. The Community legislature therefore attaches particular importance to the laying down of quaaality objectives for all the substances referred to in the directive.

36. Furthermore, as the Commission has rightly observed, programmes including quality objectives are also necessary to cover cases of pollution by substances emanating from diffuse sources.

39. Although it is true that the Council's fixing of emission limit values is intended to eliminate water pollution by List I substances, the elimination is not likely to be brought about by the mere fixing of limit values; in the end . . . it is entirely dependent on the level at which they are fixed.

40. Accordingly, the German Government's argument that it may br inferred from the directive itself that the method of emission limit values constitutes in itself a more stringent instrument than the programmes referred to in Article 7 must be rejected as unfounded.

55. In accordance with the Court's case-law, programmes to be drawn up under Article 7 of the directive must be specific . . .

56. It has also been held that what is specific to the programmes in question is the fact that they must embody a comprehensive and coherent approach, covering the entire national territory and providing practical and coordinated arrangements for the reduction of pollution caused by any of the substances in List II which are relevant in the particular context of the Member State concerned, in accordance with the quality objectives fixed by those programmes for the waters affected. They differ, therefore, both from the general hygiene programmes and from overall ad hoc measures designed to reduce water pollution . . .

57. The Court also added that the quality objectives fixed by those programmes on the basis of analyses serve as a point of reference for calculating the emission standards specified in the prior authorisations.

58. Consequently, neither general rules nor ad hoc measures adopted by a Member State which, though comprising a wide range of water-protection standards, none the less do not lay down quality objectives relating to a given watercourse or area of water cannot be deemed to constitute a programme within the meaning of Article 7 of the directive.

Commentary

I. *Planning of Pollution Reduction of Waters*

(1) Directive 76/464 is one of the oldest water directives of the Community and the first which addressed discharges, principally from industry, of pollutants into water. No wonder that it was heavily contested between and among Member States, the Commission and Member States and economic operators. In the early 1990s, the Commission largely abandoned the monitoring of the Directive and undertook to establish a new water framework directive which was finally adopted in 2000 and which is to be implemented in future decades.

Thus, the present judgment almost comes as an afterthought. It is part of a series of infringement procedures which the Commission had, in the early 1990s, initiated under Article 226 EC Treaty against all[18] Member States and which concerned the Directive's Article 7, the obligation for Member States to set up programmes for the pollution of waters by List II substances. By the end of 2001, the Court had given judgments against Luxembourg,[19] Italy,[20] Spain,[21] Belgium,[22] Germany,[23] Greece[24], Portugal[25] and Netherlands.[25a]

(2) In the present case, Germany argued in particular that it had adopted more stringent measures than those required by Directive 76/464, by adopting emission limit values at national level also for those List I substances for which the Community had not adopted EC-wide emission-limit values. However, while Article 12 of Directive 76/464 indeed does allow Member States to adopt more stringent environmental protection provisions—the same possibility which is now laid down in Article 176 EC Treaty—the Court rejected the German argument, stating that the fixing of emission limit values for pollutants is not a more stringent measure, but another measure. And in fact one must wonder whether the German argument before the Court was motivated by tactical procedural considerations or whether Germany had simply misunderstood the whole concept of Directive 76/464.

(3) For List II substances, the main obligation for Member States is laid down in Article 7: Member States shall establish pollution reduction programmes for waters. These programmes must contain quality objectives for the different (national) waters. And the national authorisations granted for the discharge of List II substances into the water have to contain emission limit values (or emission standards, in the terminology of Directive 76/464). These emission limit values for the individual discharger have to be aligned so that the—previously fixed—quality objectives are not exceeded.

(4) The essential difference from the fixing of emission limit values for the individual dischargers alone is that the total quantity of pollutants which enter the water may well be so high that the pollution of the receiving water is increased and not, as required by Article 7, reduced. The reason for such a potential increase may either be the low level at which the individual emission limit values are fixed or it may be due to the great number of individual dischargers. Thus, emission limit

---

[18] Commission, 9th annual report on monitoring application of Community law—1991 [1992] OJ C250/161 and 12th annual report on monitoring application of Community law—1994 [1995] OJ C254/49. Some procedures were stopped at a later stage.

[19] Court of Justice, Case C–206/96, *Commission* v. *Luxembourg* [1998] ECR I–3401.

[20] Court of Justice, Case C–285/96, *Commission* v. *Italy* [1998] ECR I–5935.

[21] Court of Justice, Case C–214/96, *Commission* v. *Spain* [1998] ECR I–7661.

[22] Court of Justice, Case C–207/97, *Commission* v. *Belgium* [1999] ECR I–309.

[23] Court of Justice, Case C–184/97, *Commission* v. *Germany* [1999] ECR I–7837 (the judgment discussed here).

[24] Court of Justice, Case C–384/97, *Commission* v. *Greece* [2000] ECR I–3823.

[25] Court of Justice, Case C–261/98, *Commission* v. *Portugal*, (2000) ECR I–5905.

[25a] Court of Justice, Case C–152/98, *Commission* v. *Netherlands* Judgment of 10 May 2001, not yet reported.

values alone do not necessarily reduce pollution of the receiving water. Rather, the overall quality of the receiving water needs to be determined and fixed by way of (binding) quality standards.

(5) Germany had thus simply applied another system, not a more stringent system. From the German point of view, this was logical. Indeed, when Directive 76/464 was adopted in 1976, the United Kingdom was the only Member State to plead for the fixing of Community-wide quality objectives, whereas the other eight Member States of that time were in favour of EC-wide emission limit values. As by that time the Directive, based on Articles 100 and 235 (now Articles 94 and 308) EC Treaty, required unanimity among Member States a compromise was finally found which provided, as regards List I substances, for the EC-wide elaboration of emission limit values and quality objectives, and as regards List II substances for the provisions laid down in Article 7. The Community decision was thus to have, quality objectives fixed for List II substances, and this not at EC level, but rather at the level of Member States.

(6) The only point which Germany could invoke was the fact that List II also contained substances which belonged, as regards their classification, to List I. Indeed, the Commission had out of the some 4,000 substances which were said to be discharged into Community waters made a first list of priorities which comprised some 1,500 substances. Out of this list, a second priority list of List I substances which contained 129 substances was formed and submitted to the Council. The Council stated in a Resolution that the list of 129 substances would serve the Community as a basis for further work on the implementatiuon of the Directive, and noted that the Member States recognised the list of 129 substances as a provisional basis for any national measures to combat pollution of water by those substances when applying the measures provided for in the Directive.[26]

Later, three further substances were added to that list. Of the whole list, 18 were, between 1982 and 1990, the subject of Council directives laying down emission limit values and quality objectives. For 15 others, the Commission submitted a proposal for a directive to the Council[27] on which the Council has not—yet—decided. This brings the total number of List I substances on that priority list, for which EC-wide limit values had neither been adopted nor proposed by the Commission, to 99 substances—the number for which the Commission had asked Germany in the present litigation to fix quality objectives.

(7) The Court did not accept Germany's defence that the Commission could have made proposals for a directive with regard to these 99 substances also. Indeed, Article 7 of the Directive is unconditional. If the German argument were correct, then the inclusion of List I substances in List II would have made no sense at all, as the possibility of making legislative proposals existed right from the beginning.

The Court therefore rightly refused to examine whether the Commission could have made legislative proposals for the 99 substances, and why it did not. The

---

[26] Council, Resolution of 7 February 1983 [1983] OJ C46/17.
[27] Proposal for a Council directive [1990] OJ C55/7.

Commission has never publicly declared why it stopped, after 1991, making proposals for emission limit values and quality objectives for List I substances.[28] Nor do there seem to exist resolutions from the Council or the European Parliament to request a standstill of this work; on the contrary, until 1991, all public statements by all Community institutions pointed towards an acceleration of the work on List I substances.[29]

That being the case: the Court satisfied itself with the formal arguments that Article 17 had laid down independent obligations for Member States, so that any omission to act under Article 6 could not affect the obligations flowing from Article 7. There is no doubt that this argument is legally correct.

(8) The third argument from the German government consisted in stating that its legislation was rather detailed and constituted, for that reason, a "programme" for the reduction of water pollution in the sense of Article 7 of Directive 76/464. The Court had already discussed a similar argument raised in another case by Belgium.[30] In that case, the Court had stated that the different pieces of legislation did not constitute "comprehensive and coherent programmes for pollution reduction, based on studies of the waters affected and setting quality objectives". They rather constituted *ad hoc* measures; this was not sufficient to qualify them as programmes under Article 7 of Directive 76/464.

(9) In the present litigation against Germany, the Court largely repeats, in paragraphs 55 to 57, the arguments made in the previous case. The programmes had to be specific, comprehensive and coherent, cover the entire national territory and provide "practical and coordinated arrangements for the reduction of pollution" and provide for quality programmes for the relevant national waters. As the German legislation did not lay down quality objectives, it could not be considered to constitute a programme for the quality of German waters.

(10) Generally, legislation is different from a programme. A programme is a bundle of measures of reaching an objective and must contain a timetable for its implementation.[31] The administration and, if appropriate, private groups and

---

[28] Perhaps some of the political thinking of the Commission in the early 1990s is reflected in the following Statement, which stems from the Commission. European Community Water Policy, COM(96)59 of 21 February 1996, Annex 1. 1. 4: "The procedure for producing daughter directives for the List I substances has proved burdensome and slow, whilst the performance of most Member States in producing reduction programmes for List II substances has been negligible. The Directive has also been criticised for not considering the ever growing list of substances of potential concern and for not addressing cumulative toxic effects. Many of these criticisims are answered by the proposed Integrated Pollution Prevention and Control Directive (IPC), though controls of some sort will still be required for those industries not covered by the IPC".

Then, at least at the drafting of this para. (1996) it was thought that the IPPC Directive—Directive 96/61 [1996] OJ L257/26—would substitute Directive 76/464. As Directive 96/61 never addressed questions of cumulative effects or the growing number of dangerous substances, the conclusion must be that the Commission anticipated, in 1991, deregulation and decentralisation as regards the discharge of dangerous substances.

[29] See for more details L Krämer, "Protecting the Marine Environment in Community Law" in L Krämer, *Focus on European Environmental Law*, (Sweet & Maxwell, London, 1997), ii, 259 *et seq.*

[30] Court of Justice, Case C–207/97 (n. 22 *supra*), paras. 38 to 46.

[31] See also Directive 76/464 (n. 14 *supra*), Art. 7(5).

bodies must act to realise the objectives of the programme. I would not rule out that a legislative measure may also contain all these elements; then it may have to be considered to be a "programme" in the sense of Article 7. However, typically a legislative measure lays down general measures and targets to be reached, but does not indicate which water quality of a given watercourse or lake or coastal water has to be reached within which specific time-period. The Court's evaluation of the German legislation is thus fully approved.

Thus, the Commission won in all the aspects of its application.

II. Directive 76/464, its Monitoring and its Evolution

(11) The other cases decided so far by the Court all ended with the Court's statement that the Member State in question had not complied with its obligation under Article 7 of Directive 76/464. In Case C–206/96[32], the Luxembourg government argued that the 99 substances in question were not discharged into waters in Luxembourg, so that no programme had to be elaborated. However, during the oral proceedings before the Court, Luxembourg agreed that at least some of the 99 substances were discharged in Luxembourg. In Case C–285/96, Italy did not defend itself before the Court so that the Court, in conformity with Article 94(2) of its Rules of Procedure, made a judgment of default.

In Case C–214/96,[33] Spain defended itself with the argument that since its accession to the European Community in 1986, it had had to deal with so many far-reaching changes in its administration that it had not elaborated programmes. That argument was rejected by the Court.[34] The Court held, furthermore, that quality objectives had been set neither by Spain nor by its regions for those waters, which come under their responsibility.

In Case C–207/97,[35] Belgium, apart from the argument that its legislation constituted a programme, raised the argument that the list of 99 substances, based on the Council Resolution of 7 February 1993,[36] had no binding force. The Court agreed with that, but held nevertheless that Article 7 contained a clear legal obligation for Member States to set quality objectives for all List I substances which had not been the subject of Community emission limit values and quality objectives.

In Case C–384/97,[37] the Court found that Greece had adopted some *ad hoc* measures to reduce water pollution, but that these measures did not constitute a comprehensive and coherent programme for reducing pollution, were not based on studies of the waters affected and did not set quality objectives.

---

[32] Court of Justice, Case C–206/96 (n. 19 *supra*).
[33] Court of Justice, Case C–214/96 (n. 21 *supra*).
[34] See on this defence of "internal circumstances" p. 58 *supra*.
[35] Court of Justice, Case C–207/97 (n. 22 *supra*).
[36] See on that list p. 181 *supra*.
[37] Court of Justice, Case C–384/97 (n. 24 *supra*).

(12) In Case C–261/98,[38] Portugal argued that it had made serious efforts to fully comply with the requirements of Article 7,[39] though it admitted that full compliance had not yet been reached. The Court found that Portugal had neither laid down quality objectives for the 99 substances nor set deadlines for their implementation. It therefore held that the different Portuguese documents submitted did not constitute a programme under Article 7 of Directive 76/464.

Apart from these cases, the Court of Justice found against Greece, because it had not, for Lake Vegorrítis and the Gulf of Pagasaí, set up programmes for the reduction of water pollution.[40] The Court considered that some general environmental programmes could not be considered programmes under Article 7, but was confronted with the admission by the Greek government that its different legislative and regulatory measures could not be regarded as programmes in the sense of Article 7 of Directive 76/464.

(13) At the end of 2000, the European Parliament and the Council adopted the new Water Framework Directive.[41] Under its Article 21(2), Directive 76/464 will be repealed 13 years after the entry into effect of Directive 2000/60. Article 21(3)(b) provides: "For the purposes of Article 7 of Directive 76/464, Member States may apply the principles for the identification of pollution problems and the substances causing them, the establishment of quality standards, and the adoption of measures, laid down in the Directive". As this book is on judgments of by the Court of Justice, it does not seem appropriate to discuss in detail the new provisions of Directive 2000/60. It should be noted, however, that the obligation to set up programmes for the reduction of water pollution and to fix quality objectives has existed since 1976 and has still not yet been implemented. And in view of this new Directive it does not seem very likely that the Commission will sue, under Article 228 EC Treaty, any Member State for not having complied with a Court judgment as regards the obligations under Article 7 of Directive 76/464. In any case, the instrument of planning in Community environmental legislation should seriously be considered in the light of the experience of Article 7.

---

[38] Court of Justice, Case C–261/98 (n. 25 *supra*).

[39] See on the argument that "serious efforts" had been taken to comply with Community law p. 52 *supra*.

[40] Court of Justice, Joined Cases C–232/95 and C–233/95, *Commission* v. *Greece* [1998] ECR I–3343.

[41] Directive 2000/60 establishing a framework for Community action in the field of water policy [2000] OJ L327/1.

21. THE BATTLE ON DRINKING WATER

Judgment of the Court (Fifth Chamber) of 22 April 1999
Case C–340/96

Commission of the European Communities v. *United Kingdom of Great Britain and Northern Ireland*
[1999] ECR I–2023

Facts and Procedure

In 1980, the Council adopted Directive 80/778 on the quality of drinking water.[42] Member States had five years in order to bring their drinking water up to the quality requirements of Directive 80/778, but could, under certain conditions, ask for an extension of that time.

In 1992, the Court of Justice found that the United Kingdom had failed to fulfil its obligations flowing from Directive 80/778 by not having ensured that all drinking water in the United Kingdom complied with the Directive's requirements.[43]

In 1991, the United Kingdom amended its drinking water legislation. The new Water Industry Act 1991 required water suppliers to supply to premises for domestic or food production purposes only water which complied with the water purity standards of the Water Industry Act, which transposed the Directive into national law. Section 18 of the Act provided that where water was supplied that did not comply with the purity requirements, the Secretary of State had to make a— provisional or final—enforcement order which specified what the water company had to do in order to supply water that complied with the purity requirements.

However, under section 19(1) of the Act, the Secretary of State was not required to make an enforcement order in relation to any water company if he was satisfied that the company in question had given an undertaking to take all such steps as it appeared to him to be appropriate for the company to take for the purpose of securing or facilitating compliance with the relevant rules.

The Commission was of the opinion that this mechanism did not completely comply with the requirements of Directive 80/778 and applied to the Court.

---

[42] Directive 80/778 relating to the quality of water intended for human consumption [1980] OJ L229/11.

[43] Court of Justice, Case C–337/89, *Commission* v. *United Kingdom* [1992] ECR I–6103: "by failing, first, to implement in the regulations applicable in Scotland and Northern Ireland and, as regards water used in the food industry, also in Engalnd and Wales Council Directive 80/778/EEC . . . and, secondly, to ensure that the quality of water supplied in 28 supply zones in England conforms to the requirements of the directive concerning nitrates, the United Kingdom has failed to fulfil its obligations under the EEC Treaty . . .".

Judgment(extracts)

15. . . . the United Kingdom acknowledged that breaches of individual standards for certain of the water-quality parameters in the Directive had occurred and were in some cases still occurring. It further accepted that the Directive required it to ensure that all supplies of drinking water in the United Kingdom met the requirements of the Directive at all times. On the other hand, the United Kingdom Government did not in any way accept the Commission's contention that the system of undertakings contained in the Act constituted a failure to enforce the standards of the Directive.

24. The United Kingdom Government contends that the Commission has not succeeded in establishing that the failings recorded result from the systematic acceptance of undertakings given by the water companies.

25. It notes in this regard that the monitoring of certain pesticides became technically possible only in the mid-1980s. Thus, it was not possible to confirm non-compliance with the Directive's requirements in regard to herbicides until 1989, and the companies did not at that time have the technical knowledge which would have enabled them to adopt immediately the appropriate methods of treatment. The United Kingdom adds that, in certain cases, compliance with the requirements of the Directive necessitated significant construction work, public consultation and environmental impact assessments. Where relevant, it was also necessary to install alternative systems of domestic water supply.

26. The United Kingdom Government also argues that the water companies are best placed to identify the measures required for compliance with the Directive, and, consequently, that undertakings constitute, for the purpose of attaining the desired result, a more expeditious and efficacious procedure than that of enforcement orders. Moreover, national courts have already recognised the advantages which recourse to undertakings has over recourse to enforcement orders.

27. It must be pointed out that . . . Member States must, in order to secure the full implementation of directives in law and not only in fact, establish a specific legal framework in the area in question. In the case of the mechanism of undertakings which is at issue in the present proceedings this has not been achieved.

28. As may be seen from paragraphs 7 and 8 of the present judgment, while the Act sets out the procedure to be followed for issuing an enforcement order and requires the Secretary of State to specify the measures necessary to ensure that the water in question is brought into compliance with the Directive's requirements within as short a time as possible, that is not the case with regard to the system of undertakings provided for under section 19 of the Act, since that provision authorises the Secretary of State to accept an undertaking on the sole condition that it contains such measures as it appears to him for the time being to be appropriate for the company to take in order to secure or facilitate compliance with the standards in question.

29. The Act thus does not specify the matters to be covered by the undertakings, in particular the parameters to be observed in respect of derogations, the programme of work to be carried out and the time within which it must be completed, and, where appropriate, the information to be given to the population groups concerned.

30. It follows that the Act does not set out a specific legal framework in the sense contemplated in the case-law cited above.

31. The conclusion that the method of undertakings does not meet the requirements of Community law is not affected by the United Kingdom's argument that the Commission approved the system of undertakings, in particular in a letter dated 16 May 1989. The Court has consistently held that the Commission may not, except where such powers are expressly conferred upon it, give guarantees concerning the compatibility of specific practices with Community law. In no circumstances does it have the power to authorise practices which are contrary to Community law . . .

32. It must therefore be held that, by accepting undertakings from water companies for the purpose of ensuring that water complies with the requirements of the Directive, without the conditions governing the acceptance of such undertakings being specified in the Act, the United Kingdom has failed to fulfil its obligations under the Treaty and under the Directive. . .

Commentary

I. Drinking Water in the United Kingdom and Court Procedures

(1) This is an astonishing judgment! The Court does not quote one single provision of Directive 80/778 in order to support its conclusion that the United Kingdom has not complied with its requirements under that Directive; thus, one might ask what the proceedings were about. The reader should remember that: in 1992, the Court found in Case C–337/89 that the United Kingdom had not complied with its requirements under Directive 80/778, because it did not supply drinking water to consumers and users which conformed to that Directive.[44] It would thus have been normal for the Commission to take action, under Article 228 (ex Article 171) EC Treaty, against the United Kingdom, because that Member State had not complied with the first judgment of the Court; and the version of Article 228 EC Treaty which has been in force since 1 May 1993 provides that the Court may, in such cases, fix a penalty payment against the defaulting Member State.[45]

---

[44] See the tenor of the judgment in Case C–337/89 in n. 43 *supra*.

[45] Art. 228 EC Treaty (version since 1 May 1993): "1. If the Court of Justice finds that a Member State has failed to fulfil an obligation under this Treaty, the State shall be required to take the necessary measures to comply with the judgment of the Court of Justice. 2. If the Commission considers that the Member State concerned has not taken such measures it shall, after giving that State the opportunity to

Instead, the Commission engaged in a battle, whether the system of undertakings which the United Kingdom had set up was an appropriate method of complying with the Directive. Even if the Court had "accepted" the legislative measures adopted by the United Kingdom, what would have been the result for drinking water in the United Kingdom? The United Kingdom accepted that it had not complied with its obligations under Directive 80/778.[46] Then it is not really clear why the Commission did not even apply, be it in addition to its other applications, for a penalty payment.[47]

(2) Where a Community directive provides for obligations for Member States, it requires them to achieve a certain result within a certain time-limit. Member States cannot be heard about internal considerations, difficulties or other defences.[48] As regards Directive 80/778 on drinking water, its basic requirement is laid down in Article 7(6) which reads: "Member States shall take the steps necessary to ensure that water intended for human consumption at least meets the requirements specified in Annex I"; Annex I specifies the different parameters which are to be respected. Article 19 states that the "Member States shall take the necessary measures to ensure that the quality of water intended for human consumption complies with this Directive within five years of its notification". Thus in mid-1985, the obligation to reach a specific result was clear and unambiguous.

(3) From this requirement, Article 9 allowed a derogation for reasons of the nature and structure of the ground and for exceptional meteorological conditions[49]; Article 10 allowed for temporary derogations in the event of emergencies[50] and Article 20 allowed for longer transition periods than 1985 to apply in exceptional cases and for population groups to be geographically defined.[51]

---

submit its observations, issue a reasoned opinion specifying the points on which the Member State cocerned has not complied with the judgment of the Court of Justice. If the Member State concerned fails to take the necessary measures to comply with the Court's judgment within the time-limit laid down by the Commission, the latter may bring the case before the Court of Justice. In so doing it shall specify the amount of the lump sum or penalty payment to be paid by the Member State concerned which it considers appropriate in the circumstances. If the Court of Justice finds that the Member State concerned has not complied with its judgment it may impose a lump sum or penalty payment on it".

[46] See in particular para. 15 of the present judgment.

[47] It is true that the procedure under Art. 226 EC Treaty which led to the present judgment began in 1991, thus prior to the new provision of Art. 228 EC Treaty in the version of the Maastricht Treaty. However, the substance of that provision existed also prior to the entry into effect of the Maastricht Treaty, which took place in 1993. The only significant new element added to Art. 228 by the Maastricht Treaty was that a penalty payment could be decided against the Member State concerned.

[48] See in more detail p. 57 *supra*.

[49] Directive 80/778 (n. 42 *supra*), Art. 9: "1. Member States may make provision for derogations from this Directive in order to take account of: (a) situations arising from the nature and structure of the ground in the area from which the supply in question emanates . . . (b) situations arising from exceptional meteorological conditions".

[50] Directive 80/778 (n. 42 *supra*), Art. 10: "1. In the event of emergencies, the competent national authorities may, for a limited period of time. . . allow the maximum admissible concentrations shown in Annex I to be exceeded".

[51] Directive 80/778 (n. 42 *supra*), Art. 20: Member States may, in exceptional cases and for geographically defined population groups, submit a special request to the Commission for a longer period for complying with Annex I. This request, for which grounds must be duly put forward, shall set out the difficulties experienced and must propose an action programme with an appropriate timetable to

Already in Case C–337/89 the United Kingdom had argued "that the directive does not impose an obligation to achieve a result but merely requires Member States to take all practicable steps to comply with the standards laid down".[52] And the Court had stated quite soberly that "the defendant's claim that it took all practicable steps to secure compliance cannot justify . . . its failure to comply with the requirement to ensure that water intended for human consumption at least meets the requirements of Annex I of the directive".[53]

(4) Nothing thus would have prevented the Commission from starting its second proceeding against the United Kingdom under Article 228 EC rather than again Article 226 EC Treaty. For such an initiative, the Commission would have had all the more reasons as, during the parliamentary preparation of water legislation in 1989, an amendment to the Bill had suggested fixing the final delay of compliance with the requirements of Directive 80/778 until 1 September 1993; however, the United Kingdom government itself had set aside this amendment which was subsequently not introduced into United Kingdom legislation.[54] Instead, the different, subsequent pieces of water legislation which were also marked by the attempt to privatise the water industry in the United Kingdom did not contain any time-limit for compliance. Nor did the different "undertakings" which were subsequently submitted by the water services to the Secretary of State and which were, in part, the subject-matter of the present judgment of the Court of Justice systematically contain an indication of when compliance with the standards of Directive 80/778 would be reached.

(5) The key phrases of the Court's judgment in the present case are to be found in paragraphs 28 and 29, where the Court indicates that the Water Industry Act did not specify the content of the undertakings "in respect of derogations, the programme of work to be carried out and the time within which it must be completed". Suppose, the Water Industry Act had contained such specification: would then the application of the Commission have to be rejected? It is submitted that not, because the United Kingdom either had to comply with the requirements of Directive by 1985 or follow the conditions and procedures of Article 9, 10 or 20— which it did not. This test clearly reveals, in this author's opinion, the political character of the whole procedure under Article 226 EC Treaty in the present case.

The judgment of the Court does not indicate how many undertakings were made and accepted, and this silence seems rather remarkable. The Opinion of Advocate General Mischo indicates that they were "very frequent" and that, in

be undertaken for the improvement of the quality of water intended for human consumption. The Commission shall examine these programmes, including the timetables. In the case of disagreement with the Member State concrned, the Commission shall submit appropriate proposals to the Council".

[52] Court of Justice, Case C–337/89 (n. 43 *supra*), para. 18.

[53] Court of Justice, Case C–337/89 (n. 43 *supra*), para. 25.

[54] See for details N Haigh (ed.), *Manual of Environmental Policy: the EC and Britain* (Longman, in association with the Institute for European Environmental Policy, London, looseleaf), p. 4.4–6; I Bache and D McGillivray, "Testing the Extended Gatekeeper: the Law, Practice and Politics of Implementing the Drinking Water Directive in the United Kingdom" in J Holder (ed.), *The Impact of EC Environmental Law in the United Kingdom* (John Wiley, Chichester, 1997), 147 *et seq.*

contrast, the number of enforcement orders was so small that no comparison between the accepted undertakings and the enforcement orders could be made.[55] Haigh states that all 10 water service companies made such general undertakings.[56] As to these general undertakings which covered the whole area served by the respective company numerous specific undertakings for specific supplies and/or for specific parameters have to be added, it seems legitimate to conclude that the system of undertakings was in reality that which applied in the United Kingdom and that the possibility for the Secretary of State to have recourse to enforcement orders was rather theoretical.

(6) Where dates for final compliance were given, these extended until the year 2000, thus about 10 years into the future. And here another feature of the present judgment and its pre-litigation procedure becomes apparent: the Commission started the procedure under Article 226 EC Treaty in September 1991 and issued a Reasoned Opinion in June 1993; then it took until October 1996 before it applied to the Court. The Court gave its judgment in April 1999. The whole procedure thus took about 90 months, out of which 61 refer to the administrative procedure under Article 226. This long delay in the whole procedure had as a consequence that the United Kingdom, while not contesting as against the Commission that some standards of the Directive were not respected at some places in the United Kingdom, could continue its—or the water service companies'—investment programme for the cleaning up of drinking water, without having to negotiate and agree with the Commission or the whole of the Community on the speed and volume of such investments—as Article 20 of Directive 80/778 expressly provided for!

(7) In other terms: only after this second judgment by the Court has there been some sort of legal clarity about the United Kingdom's obligations under Directive 80/778, 19 years after the Directive's adoption. Instead of commencing clean-up in 1980 in order to comply with the Directive, such investments essentially started 10 years later. And the judgment in the present case made the Commission forget to ensure—in the extreme even by recourse to Article 228 EC Treaty—that compliance with the 28 zones which had been the subject-matter of the Court's judgment in Case C–337/89 really took place.

Seen from that angle, the present judgment came late and was not really capable of imposing compliance with Community law on the United Kingdom. And is has not yet happened elsewhere in environmental law that the Commission obtained a judgment from the Court of Justice under Article 226 EC Treaty and then began a new procedure under that same Article, because the Member State concerned had, in the meantime amended its legislation.

[55] Court of Justice, Case C–340/96 (the present case), Opinion of Advocate General Mischo, paras. 45 and 55.

[56] N Haigh (n. 54 *supra*) p. 4.4.10.

II. Planning the Drinking Water Improvement via Community-wide Planning

(8) Does drinking water in the United Kingdom conform to the requirements of Directive 80/778 at least by now, the end of 2001? The answer is that the Commission has no reliable information on that. Directive 80/778 does not provide for any requirement for Member States to report on its application. Such an obligation was introduced only in 1991 by Directive 91/692.[57] The first report under that Directive was to cover the period 1993–1995; it was published, with three years' delay, in 2000[58] and does not contain any information on drinking water quality, though the Commission announces that it will, in future, publish more information on the quality of drinking water in the Community.

(9) In view of this scarcity of information, it is not surprising that the Court of Justice, apart from the two cases against the United Kingdom, had only few cases to decide which concern drinking water: most, if not all, Member States progressively put the necessary legislation into place. And the Commission is not informed in detail on the practical application of drinking water legislation, the quality of drinking water or possible cases of non-respect of certain maximum admissible concentrations.[59]

(10) The first judgment concerned a case in Italy.[60] In Piemonte, the competent authorities had authorised drinking water to contain a concentration of atrazina up to 1 microgramm per litre, thus 10 times the concentration which was provided for as the maximum admissible concentration in Directive 80/778. The Italian judge wanted to know whether such a regulation could be based on Article 10 of the Directive which allowed derogations in emergency situations.[61] The Court found that an emergency situation was a stuation where the competent authorities had to face sudden difficulties with drinking water supply which could not be solved otherwise than by derogations. Such derogations had to be limited in time and could not constitute an unacceptable risk to public health.

(11) In a judgment against Belgium, the Court found that water from private sources of supply was excluded from the scope of Directive 80/778.[62] Furthermore it stated that a Member State could apply, under Article 20 of the Directive, for a longer period of transition only as long as the original period of transition was

---

[57] Directive 91/692 standardising and rationalising reports on the implementation of certain Directives relating to the environment [1991] OJ L3777, p. 48.

[58] Commission, *The Directive on Standardising Reports. A Comprehensive Report on the First Standardised Reports by Member States, Covering the years 1993–1995* (Office for Official Publications, Luxembourg, 2000), p. 11.

[59] See also Commission, 16th annual report on monitoring the application of Community law—1998 [1999] OJ C354/52: "Although the Commission continues to receive many complaints concerning incorrect implementation of this Directive, not all of them result in infringement proceedings as the burden of proof is on the Commission and complainants often have problems obtaining evidence".

[60] Court of Justice, Case C–228/87, *Pretura unificata Torino* v. *X* [1988] ECR 5099.

[61] Directive 80/778 (n. 42 *supra*), Art. 10 (n. 50 *supra*).

[62] Court of Justice, Case C–42/89, *Commission* v. *Belgium* [1990] ECR I–2821.

running, i.e. until 17 July 1985. Afterwards, the Member State only had the option of recourse to Article 10 of Directive 80/778. Finally, the Court of Justice stated that the drinking water in Verviers contained too much lead and that Belgium could not invoke the cost and complexity of the construction of a treatment station in order not to comply with the lead parameters.

(12) In a judgment against Germany,[63] the Court again had to deal with the interpretation of Article 10 of Directive 80/778. It repeated its previous conclusions that Article 10 applied only in the case of a sudden, unforseen event. Economic considerations could not justify the use of this provision to authorise derogations. Indeed, Germany had used Article 10 in order to justify the exceeding of the levels for nitrates or pesticides, which principally stem from normal agricultural activity, thus not an "emergency event".

An application to the Court based on the fact that the French government had issued circulars in which it asked provincial and local administrations to ignore the exceeding of certain parameters,[64] in particular for nitrates and pesticides, was not pursued, since France had withdrawn the two circular in question.[65]

(13) Overall, the Commission was quite positive about the effects of Directive 80/778.[66] Since 1994, a revision of that Directive has been started which led, in 1998, to the adoption of a new directive. As from the year 2003, Directive 80/778 will be superseded by this new Directive 98/83 on the quality of water for human consumption.[67] This new Directive will cover all water "regardless of its origin and whether it is supplied from a distribution network, from a tanker, or in bottles or containers"; water from an individual supply normally remains exempted and other waters may be exempted by Member States. Drinking water must be wholesome and clean and comply with certain minimum requirements laid down in parameters. The number of parameters has decreased and Member States have greater flexibility to grant derogations. The monitoring provisions have been extended and remedial measures been made more explicit. Overall, the structure and concept of Directive 80/778 have been maintained and the main standards (pesticides, nitrates, heavy metals) have remained untouched or (for lead) even made more severe.

(14) In view of this new text, it is more than unlikely that the Commission will, in the foreseeable future, initiate proceedings against the United Kingdom under Article 228 EC Treaty, because the judgments of the Court of Justice of 1992 and 1999 have not been complied with.

[63] Court of Justice, Case C–237/90, *Commission* v. *Germany* [1992] ECR I–5973.

[64] Case C–49/97, *Commission* v. *France* [2000] ECR II–0051.

[65] Commission 15th annual report on monitoring the application of Community law—1997, [1998] OJ C250/62.

[66] Commission, Communication: "European Comunity Water Policy", COM(1996)59 of 21 February 1996, p. 25: "The impact of this Directive has been significant and it is generally recognised that it has been the driving force behind the overall improvement in drinking water quality which has taken place in the Community over the past decade. The Directive has provided governments and water suppliers with a stable and predictable base for their investment programmes, and can now expect to receive water complying with explicit Community-wide quality standards".

[67] Directive 98/83 on the quality of water intended for human consumption [1998] OJ L330/32.

22. WASTE WATER TREATMENT IN BRUSSELS

Judgment of the Court (Sixth Chamber) of 6 July 2000
Case C–236/99

Commission of the European Communities v. *Belgium*
[2000] ECR I–5657

Facts and Procedure

Directive 91/271 was adopted in 1991.[68] It required Member States to ensure that for waste water which discharges into sensitive river basins, collection systems were established at the latest by 31 December 1998 for agglomerations of more than 10,000 population equivalent.[69] Such sensitive areas had to be identified by 31 December 1993. Member States also had to ensure that water in agglomerations of more than 15,000 population or equivalent underwent at least secondary treatment[70] before discharging.

Member States were given the possibility, in exceptional cases and for geographically defined population groups, to submit a special request to the Commission for a longer period than to 31 December 2000; however, they then had to justify their request, explain the technical difficulties which they had experienced and to submit an action programme and a timetable (Article 8).

Furthermore, by 31 December 1993 Member States had to establish a programme for the implementation of Directive 91/271 and subsequently submit information on it to the Commission (Article 17); they could incorporate the eventual action programme under Article 8 into this general programme.[71]

---

[68] Directive 91/271 concerning urban waste water treatment [1991] OJ L135/40.

[69] Directive 91/271 (n. 68 *supra*), Art. 5: "2. Member States shall ensure that urban waste water entering ollecting systems shall before discharge into sensitive areas be subject to more stringent treatment than that described in Art. 4, by 31 December 1998 at the latest for all discharges from agglomerations of more than 10. 000 p.e. . . . .".

[70] Water management distinguishes three levels of treatment: primary treatment is treatment by physical and/or chemical process involving settlement of suspended solids or other equivalent processes. Secondary treatment is treatment by a process generally involving biological treatment with a secondary settlement or equivalent process. Tertiary treatment is treatment (additional to secondary treatment) of the nitrogen (nitrification–denitrification) and/or phosphorous and/or of any other pollutant affecting the quality or a specific use of the water: microbiological pollution, colour etc. wording taken from: Commission, COM(98)775 of 15 January 1999, p. 9).

[71] Directive 91/271 (n. 68 *supra*), Art. 17: "1. Member States shall by 31 December 1993 establish a programme for the implementation of this Directive. 2. Member States shall by 30 June 1994 provide the Commission with information on the programme . . ."

Belgium designated the Senne, the river into which the waste water of the Brussels agglomeration is discharged, as a sensitive area under Directive 91/271. In May 1996 it informed the Commission that it envisaged, for the Brussels agglomeration, the construction of two waste water treatment plants, one north and one south of Brussels. Water collection and treatment for the Brussels agglomeration would be starting at the end of 2003. It referred to budgetary constraints and asked for an extension of the period for transposition of Directive 91/271. The programme was also offically transmitted in July 1996; at the same time, Belgium asked for an extension of the time-limit laid down in the Directive.

The Commission was of the opinion that this programme did not comply with the requirements of Directive 91/271 and commenced, in May 1998, formal proceedings under Article 226 EC Treaty.

Judgment(extracts)

20. It should be observed at the outset that the Kingdom of Belgium acknowledges that it did not transpose the directive, and in particular Article 17, within the prescribed period.

21. While it admits that it has failed to fulfill the obligation laid down in Article 17 of the directive, the Belgian Government claims in its defence, first, that the difficulties created by the process of institutional reform which it has to carry out over the last 30 years in order to preserve the unity of the State and the fundamental principles of a State founded upon the rule of law constitute exceptional circumstances which explain and justify the problems experienced by the Brussels-Capital Region. Those circumstances constitute a case of force majeure, since they give rise to exceptional difficulties which are beyond the control of the Kingdom of Belgium.

22. In that regard, it should be pointed out that the difficulties to which the Belgian Government refers are of a purely domestic nature, since they result from its political and administrative organisation and, accordingly, do not constitute a case of *force majeure.*

23. Furthermore, according to settled case-law, a Member State may not plead situations in its internal legal order, including those resulting from its federal organisation, in order to justify a failure to comply with the obligations and time-limits laid down in a directive . . .

24. The Belgian Government cannot therefore plead that situation in order to justify its failure to meet the obligations arising under the directive.

25. Next, the Belgian Government states that following the Brussels-Capital Region's letter of 28 May 1996 in which the Belgian authorities asked the Commission for an extension of the period prescribed for transposition of the directive, the Commission was required, pursuant to Article 5 of the EC Treaty (now Article 10 EC), to take account of any difficulties experienced by that

Member State. It claims that the Commission should, accordingly, have either proposed an amendment of the directive in order to extend the period specified therein or delayed bringing an action for failure to fulfil obligations.

26. It must be pointed out that unless a directive has been amended by the Community legislature for the purpose of extending the periods prescribed for implementation, the Member States are required to comply with the periods originally laid down.

27. Since no such amendment was made, and having regard to the fact that the Belgian Government relies in its defence on an alleged case of *force majeure*, that argument raised by the Belgian Government cannot justify its failure to comply with the obligations laid down and the time-limits prescribed in the directive.

28. Second, it should be pointed out that under the system established by Article 226 EC the Commission enjoys a discretionary power as to whether it will bring an action for failure to fulfil obligations and it is not for the Court to judge whether that discretion was wisely exercised . . .

29. It follows that the Belgian Government was not entitled to require the Commission to delay bringing the present action for failure to fulfil obligations.

30. Last, the Belgian Government maintains that the Commission was also required, under Article 10 EC, to state the reasons for its refusal to grant its request for an extension of the period laid down in the directive.

31. It should be pointed out that, although Article 8 of the directive allows the national authorities to submit a request to the Commission for a longer period for complying with Article 4 of the directive, the Belgian Government stated in the observations which it submitted to the Court that it had never sought application of that provision in its favour in order to justify the request for a longer period for implementing the directive referred to in the communication of the purification programme of 28 May 1996.

32. As regards the argument alleging an infringement of Article 10 EC, it suffices to state that in any event the fact that the Commission failed to state the reasons for refusing to extend the period prescribed in the directive does not justify the Kingdom of Belgium's failure to comply with the obligations laid down therein.

33. Since the implementation programme communicated to the Commission by the Kingdom of Belgium did not comply with the time-limits laid down in the directive for completion of the urban waste water collection and treatment systems in the Brussels-Capital Region, the action brought by the Commission must be held to be well founded.

34. Consequently, it must be held that by communicating to the Commission a programme for the implementation of the directive which does not comply with that directive as regards the Brussels-Capital Region, the Kingdom of Belgium has failed to fulfil its obligations under Article 17 of the Directive.

Commentary

I. Waste Water Treatment in Brussels

(1) The judgment does not raise new or surprising legal aspects. Belgium had not taken the necessary measures to transpose Directive 91/271 on urban waste water into national law, as far as the Brussels agglomeration was concerned. In order to justify its delay, it invoked constitutional reforms, the cost and complexity of the investments in Brussels for a waste water treatment plant; together, these grounds constituted, in Belgium's opinion, a case of *force majeure* or, in English, an act of God. The Court of Justice rejected the existence of a case of *force majeure*.

(2) "*Force majeure*" is a concept of law which essentially pleads that unforeseeable circumstances beyond the sphere of influence of a party made the fulfilment of legal obligations impossible. While most national legal orders of Member States recognise such a concept, it has never been expressly recognised as a legal principle which applies generally in Community law. Following a number of judgments by the Court of Justice, the Commission issued, in 1988, a non-binding interpretative note on this notion.[72] The Court of Justice was of the opinion that the concept of "*force majeure* is not identical in the different branches of law and the various fields of application".[73]

(3) In the area of Article 226 EC Treaty which concerns, among other things, the complete and correct transposition of the requirements of a directive into national law and its effective application, the Court of Justice has always been extremely reluctant to recognise, on the part of a Member State, a case of "*force majeure*",[74] though in one specific case it discussed this question in some detail.[75]

(4) In the present case, Belgium had argued that the constitutional status of the Brussels Region had been fixed by legislation only in 1988. The overall budget of the Region was 65,000,000,000 Belgian francs, out of which 1,800,000,000 Belgian francs were allocated to environmental purposes.[76]

However, Belgium did not really try to explain why it submitted the programme for the Brussels agglomeration, which it was obliged to elaborate until the end of 1993 and to submit by June 1994, only in May/July 1996. The constitutional reform which was finished in 1988 did not affect the existence of administration which was responsible for waste water in Brussels. Furthermore, the attribution, by the Brussels Region, of a rather limited budget for environmental purposes is not unchangeable: it might require a political decision by the Brussels budgetary

---

[72] Commission, Notice C(88)1696 on *force majeure* in agricultural matters [1988] OJ C259/10.

[73] Court of Justice, Case 4/68, *Schwarzwaldmilch* [1968] ECR 377.

[74] See the different examples on p. 57 *supra*.

[75] Court of Justice, Case 101/84 [1985] ECR 2629. In that case, Italy had not supplied the Commission with certain statistical data and defended itself with the argument that all its files had been destroyed in the transport ministry as a result of a terrorist bomb attack. This fact was proven. However, the Court argued that Italy was no longer entitled to invoke this circumstance several years later, as it could have reconstituted its files.

[76] See Advocate General Jacobs' Opinion in the present case, paras. 27 and 28.

authority to spend more money on environmental issues. But such a decision is always possible. Also, declaring that the construction of a waste-water treatment station is an "environmental" project is not the only or consequent classification that could have been made. One might also imagine that the construction is financed or co-financed under the heading of water supply services, infrastructure projects which the Brussels budget may contain. Finally, as the Advocate General pointed out in his Opinion, it is not clear why the Belgian State did not financially assist the Brussels Region, be it for a period of time and with reimbursable credits.

(5) It must rather be assumed that Belgium and/or the government of the Brussels Region did not set aside early enough the necessary financial means for the construction of waste water treatment plants for the Brussels region and that this was the main reason for the delay. There seems not to have been any planning which envisaged finishing the necessary works for Brussels in 1998; rather, right from the beginning, the Belgian authorities calculated the year 2003 as the date to begin to comply with the Directive's requirements, not to comply fully with them!

(6) The problems of the River Senne are not new. For decades, if not centuries, the river has been used to discharge untreated waste water in particular from the Brussels agglomeration, to the North Sea.[77] And Belgian authorities at local, regional or national level have, it appears, never made any serious effort to equip Brussels with a modern, performing sewer system. It is this evolution which led to the fact that Brussels is, together with Milan in Italy, the only big agglomeration within the European Community which will not be able to keep the deadline for complying with the Directive's requirements.[78]

II. Implementation of Directive 91/271 on Urban Waste Water

(7) Directive 91/271 is the only environmental directive which obliges Member States to build specific infrastructure projects (waste water treatment installations). Whether Member States build waste incinerators, large combustion plants, nuclear installations, motorways, airports or ports—Member States remain autonomous whether they want the specific type of installations or not. In contrast, Directive 91/271 imposes the obligation to provide for the collection and secondary treatment of urban waste water for all agglomerations of more than

---

[77] See C Baudelaire, "Une eau salutaire"

"Joseph Delorme a découvert
Un ruisseau si clair et si vert
Qu'il donne aux malheureux l'envie
D'y terminer leur triste vie.
—Je sais un moyen de guérir
De cette passion malsaine
Ceux qui veulent ainsi périr:
Menez-les au bord de la Senne.
'Voyez' dit ce Belge badin

Qui n'est certes pas un ondin—
'La contrefacon de la Seine'.
'Oui' lui dis-je 'une Seine obscène!'
Car cette Senne, à proprement
Parler, où de tout mur et de tout fondement
L'indescriptible tombe en foule
Ce n'est guères qu'un excrément
Qui coule."
(About 1865).

[78] Commission, Implementation of Directive 91/271; COM(98)775 of 15 January 1999, p. 26.

2,000 population equivalent.[79] For 14 Member States—Italy had not, by 1999, transmitted any information on its urban waste water management—this represented 17,351 agglomerations of more than 2,000 population equivalent and meant that about 40,000 waste treatment instalations had to be built.[80]

(8) Furthermore, by the end of 2000 biodegradable industrial waste waters from plants which belong to the sector listed in the Directive have to respect the established conditions before they are discharged. Also, the Directive provides for monitoring of those discharges, phases out the disposal of sludge to surface waters and contains a number of other obligations for Member States.

(9) Member States had to make, and did make, considerable investments for collecting systems as well as for the treatment plants. The Commission indicated that the overall investment made and planned until 2005 was 130 billion Euro,[81] out of which about half (64 billion Euro) were made in Germany.[82] The Commission calculated that this meant an average cost of 0. 43 Euros per cubic metre of water consumed.

Evaluation and forecasts of 1993–2005 investments in collecting systems and treatment plants in billion Euro—value 1994/95[83]

Member State	Collecting system	Treatment plants	Total
Belgium	1.77	2.14	3.90
Denmark	2.40	1.70	4.10
Germany	35.30	28.87	64.17
Greece (1993–2000)	0.44	0.73	1.17
Spain	4.70	6.15	10.87
France	8.02	4.02	12.04
Ireland	0.49	1.14	1.63
Luxembourg	0.00	0.27	0.27
Netherlands	1.10	1.83	2.93
Austria	7.67	2.12	9.80
Portugal	1.46	0.94	2.40
Finland	1.00	0.55	1.55
Sweden	1.40	1.50	2.90
United Kingdom	2.78	9.74	12.53
Total (14 Member States)	68.53	61.70	130.26

[79] Commission (n. 78 *supra*), p. 5: "The population equivalent is a unit of measurement of organic biodegradable pollution representing the average load of that pollution produced by one person in one day; in the directive it is fixed at 60 grammes of BOD 5(five-day biochemical oxygen demand) per day".

[80] Court of Auditors, Special Report 3/98 concerning the implementation by the Commission of EU policy and action in the field of water pollution [1998] OJ C191, paras. 3 and 5.

[81] Commission (n. 78 *supra*), p. 22. Investment figures for Italy are not included; for Greece the planned investments between 2001 and 2005 are not included either: The figures are based on information from Member States.

[82] When the Commission made the proposal, these costs were estimated at 40 to 60 billion Euros; in 1998, the Court of Auditors (n. 80 *supra*), paras. 3 and 5, estimated the necessary costs at 201 billion Euros for nine Member States. These figures may show the value and at the same time the limits of cost-benefit-analyses.

[83] Commission (n. 78 *supra*), p. 24.

(10) The Commission had applied to the Court of Justice, because Greece,[84] Germany[85] and Italy[86] had not taken the necessary measures completely to transpose the Directive into national law. Neither Germany nor Italy were heard with the argument that the Regions (*Länder*) were responsible for taking the necessary measures; as in the present case, the Court held that such aspects concerned the internal situation of a Member State which did not constitute a valid defence. In 1999, the Commission reported that Germany had, in the meantime, adopted the necessary legislation, but that it had decided to take action under Article 228 EC Treaty against Italy, because Italy had still not complied with the first judgment; furthermore, the Commission stated that formal proceedings under Article 226 EC Treaty against Greece and Spain continued.[87]

These actions are necessary and useful. However, it seems almost sure that, in the present case, planning for the Brussels region will not be accelerated by the Court's judgment against Belgium, which means that Belgium will only start in 2003 to collect and treat urban waste water in the Brussels region.

23. QUALITY OF FISH WATER AND SHELLFISH WATER

Judgment of the Court (Fifth Chamber) of 12 December 1996
Case C–298/95

Commission of the European Communities v. *Germany*
[1996] ECR I–6747

Facts and Procedure

Directive 78/659 on the quality of fresh waters needing protection or improvement in order to support fish life[88] was adopted on 18 July 1978. It requested Member States, within two years to designate fresh waters which needed protection or improvement to support fish life.[89] Member States had then to establish

---

[84] Court of Justice, Case C–161/95, *Commission* v. *Greece* [1996] ECR I–1979.

[85] Court of Justice, Case C–297/95, *Commission* v. *Germany* [1996] ECR I–6739.

[86] Court of Justice, Case C–302/95, *Commission* v. *Italy* [1996] ECR I–6765.

[87] Commission, Sixteenth annual report on monitoring the application of Community law—1998 [1999] OJ C354/52.

[88] Directive 78/659 on the quality of fresh waters needing protection or improvement in order to support fish life [1978] OJ L222/1.

[89] Directive 78/658 (n. 88 *supra*), Art. 4: "1. Member States shall, initially within a two year period following the notification of this Directive, designate salmonid waters and cyprinid waters".

programmes in order to reduce pollution and to ensure that designated waters conformed, within five years, to the 14 physical and chemical standards laid down in the Directive.[90] They had to sample the waters according to specific provisions fixed in the Directive. On the implementation of the Directive, they had to inform the Commission.

Directive 79/923 on the quality required for shellfish waters,[91] adopted on 30 October 1979, is constructed in a similar way. Member States had to designate, within two years, those waters to which the Directive was to apply.[92] Then they had to establish programmes in order to reduce pollution and to ensure that the designated waters conformed, within six years, to the 12 different standards laid down in the Directive.[93] They had to sample the waters and to regularly report to the Commission.

The Commission was of the opinion that Germany had neither transposed the different standards in the two Directives into national law nor established programmes for fishwaters and shellfish waters. Since Germany and the Commission were of different opinions whether such measures were necessary, the Commission applied, on 15 September 1995, to the Court.

Judgment(extracts)

[The setting of binding standards for fishwaters and shellfish waters]

13. . . . Germany does not deny that transposition of Article 3 of Directives 78/659 and 79/923, which, under the division of State powers, is the responsibility of the Laender, has not yet been accomplished in Germany by means of binding legislation but points out that transposition is under way. The executive authorities of the Laender, which must be empowered by the legislatures to adopt transposing

[90] Directive 78/659 (n. 88 *supra*), Art. 3: "1. Member States shall, for the designated waters, set values for the parameters listed in Annex I, in so far as values are listed in column G or in column I".

Art. 5: "Member States shall establish programmes in order to reduce pollution and to ensure that designated waters conform within five years following designation in accordance with Art. 4 to both the values set by the Member States in accordance with Art. 3 and the comments contained in columns G and I of Annex I".

[91] Directive 79/923 on the quality required for shellfish waters [1979] OJ L281/47.

[92] Directive 79/923 (n. 91 *supra*), Art. 1: "This Directive concerns the quality of shellfish waters and applies to those coastal and brackish waters designated by the Member States as needing protection or improvement in order to support shellfish . . . life and growth and thus to contribute to the high quality of shellfish products directly edible by man".

Art. 4: "1. Member States shall, initially within a two-year period following the notification of this Directive, designate shellfish waters".

[93] Directive 79/923 (n. 91 *supra*), Art. 3: "1. Member States shall, for the designated waters, set values for the parameters listed in the Annex, in so far as values are given in column G or column I . . .".

Art. 5: "Member States shall establish programmes in order to reduce pollution and to ensure that designated waters conform, within six years following designation in accordance with Art. 4, to both the values set by the Member States in accordance with Art. 3 and the comments contained in columns G and I of the Annex".

legislations, have already been so empowered in six out of the sixteen Laender. A draft standard regulation transposing Directive 78/659 has also been drawn up for the Laender.

15. . . . one of the purposes of the directives at issue is to protect human health through the monitoring of the quality of waters which support, or could support, fish suitable for human consumption, such as salmon, trout, pike or eel, mentioned in Article 1(4) of Directive 78/659, or shellfish "directly edible by man" in the words of Article 1 of Directive 79/923.

16. In those circumstances, it is particularly important that directives should be transposed by measures which are indisputably binding. In all cases where non-implementation of the measures required by a directive could endanger human health, the persons concerned must be in a position to rely on mandatory rules in order to be able to assert their rights. .

17. In the present case, even if the amounts of residue permitted in foodstuffs are, under other national legislative provisions, subject to limit values, the Federal Republic of Germany has failed to demonstrate that, in the event of non-implementation of the measures required by Directives 78/659 and 79/923, consumption of fish or shellfish will not present any danger for human health.

18. In all events, as regards the procedural difficulties relied upon by the German Government to explain the delay in transposing Directives 78/659 and 79/923, it is sufficient to recall that, as the Court has held repeatedly, a Member State may not plead provisions, practices or circumstances existing in its internal legal system in order to justify a failure to comply with the obligations and time-limits laid down in a directive . . .

19. It must accordingly be held that, by failing to adopt within the periods prescribed all the measures necessary to comply with Article 3 of Directives 78/659 and 79/923, the Federal Republic of Germany has failed to fulfil its obligations under the Treaty.

[The establishment of pollution reduction programmes]

22. It must be held, first, that Article 5 of Directives 78/659 and 79/923 lays down an obligation for Member States to establish programmes in order to reduce pollution and to ensure that the designated waters conform, within respectively five and six years following their designation, to both the values set for the parameters indicated in the respective annexes and the notes contained in columns G and I thereof.

23. . . . Directives 78/659 and 79/923 set out, in their respective annexes, some 14 and 12 precise physical and chemical parameters for which Member States set values. Article 6 of each of those directives also determines, for the purpose of implementing Article 5, the percentages of samples which must comply with those values in order for the designated waters to be regarded as satisfying the directives' requirements.

24. It follows clearly from the wording of Article 5 of Directives 78/659 and 79/923 as well as from the detailed arrangements for monitoring water quality laid down by those directives that Member States have an obligation to establish specific programmes in order to reduce pollution of fresh waters and shellfish waters within five and six years respectively.

25. As regards Directive 78/659, general water-purification programmes, such as those relied on by the German Government, cannot therefore be regarded as constituting an adequate transposition of Article 5.

26. It should also be stressed that the objective of reducing water pollution caused by effluent pursued by such general programmes does not necessarily correspond to the more specific objective of Directive 78/659, which is to improve the quality of fresh waters in order to support fish life.

27. As regards Directive 79/923, the fact that shellfish waters meet the requirements of the directive, as the German Government claims, likewise cannot exempt it from the obligation to establish specific programmes in accordance with Article 5 of that directive.

28. The results notified by the German Government relate only to samples taken in the Land of Lower Saxony in 1991 and provide no evidence whatever that the shellfish waters in the Laender concerned meet the requirements of Directive 79/923.

29. In any event, the fact that samples in a single Land at a particular time meet the requirements of Directive 79/923 cannot release a Member State from the obligation under Article 5 of that directive to establish specific programmes applicable to all designated shellfish waters with the aim of reducing pollution in those waters within six years.

Commentary

I. Monitoring Application of the Two Directives by the Commission

(1) The judgment stating that Germany had not transposed the most significant parts of both Directives 78/659 and 79/923 was given in 1996, 16 and 15 years after this transposition should have been completed. This is an astonishingly long time and it may be worthwhile to examine more closely how implementation and the monitoring of application of these Directives have developed since their adoption by the Council.

As in all environmental directives, Member States had to inform the Commission of the national provisions which they adopted in the field governed by the two Directives.[94] Furthermore, they had to inform the Commission about the designated waters and to send, five (Directive 78/659) or six years (Directive

---

[94] Directive 78/659 (n. 88 *supra*), Art.17, Directive 79/923 (n. 91 *supra*), Art. 15.

79/923) after the initial designation of waters and at regular intervals thereafter, "a detailed report to the Commission on designated waters and the basic features thereof".[95] The Commission was to publish the information obtained.

(2) In 1987, the Court of Justice was asked whether the provisions of Directive 78/659 could be used in criminal proceedings against a person, though they had not yet been transposed into national law.[96] In conformity with earlier judgments, the Court answered in the negative.[97]

In 1988, the Court had to decide on an application by the Commission which was of the opinion that Italy had not complied with its obligation under Directive 78/659.[98] Italy defended itself with the argument that it had designated waters in the Bolzano region. The Court found that this was not enough and that Italy had not even fixed values for the mandatory parameters.

In 1994, the Court delivered a second judgment against Italy, because it had still not complied with the judgment of 1988.[99] The Court did not fix a penalty against Italy, because the relevant Treaty provision of Article 228 (ex Article 171) had just entered into force; however, this had not yet been the case when the Commission had applied to the Court, so that the Commission had not requested to fix a penalty payment.

(3) In 1997, the Court of Justice found that Italy had not complied with its obligations under Directive 79/923, as it had not designated all shellfish waters which the Directive required, had not established programmes and had not fixed values for the designated waters.[100]

In its reports on monitoring the application of Community legislation, the Commission reported in 1993 that too few waters had been designated under both Directives and, furthermore, that the transposition measures had not always been adopted in a legally binding form.[101] In 1994, it reported that problems in Italy with fishwaters continued, though a second procedure against Italy was pending; procedures under Article 226 EC Treaty were also mentioned against Greece.[102] The procedure against Greece was stopped the next year.[103] In 1996, new cases were reported against France and Belgium as regards Directive 78/659.[104] In 1998, the case against Belgium was stopped; new proceedings against the United Kingdom was mentioned and it was reported that proceedings against France and

---

[95] Directive 78/659 (n. 88 *supra*), Art. 16; the same wording is in Directive 79/923 (n. 91 *supra*), Art. 14.

[96] Court of Justice, Case 14/86, *Pretore di Salò* v. *X.* [1987] ECR 2545.

[97] For more details on the effects of a directive in national law see p. 42 *supra*.

[98] Court of Justice, Case C–322/86, *Commission* v. *Italy* [1988] ECR I–3995.

[99] Court of Justice, Case C–291/93, *Commission* v. *Italy* [1994] ECR I–859.

[100] Court of Justice, Case C–225/96, *Commission* v. *Italy* [1997] ECR I–6887.

[101] Commission, 10th annual report on monitoring the application of Community law—1992 [1993] OJ C233/56.

[102] Commission, 11th annual report on monitoring the application of Community law—1993 [1994] OJ C154/48 and 98.

[103] Commission, 12th report—1994 [1995] OJ C254/95.

[104] Commission, 13th report—1995 [1996] OJ C303/159.

Spain—which had not been mentioned earlier—had been closed.[105] In 1999, the Commission reported that Italy had made "considerable progress" and that the United Kingdom had transmitted new measures.[106]

(3) In 1995, the Commission published a report on the state of application of Directives 78/659 and 79/923.[107] As regards Directive 78/659, it reported that the initial designations of waters was generally late.[108] Member States did not all report on their waters.[109] The Commission report is silent on the question whether all fishwaters were designated by Member States[110], on the national programmes and, in particular, whether the waters complied, five years after designation with the requirements of Directive 78/659.

(4) As regards Directive 79/923, the Commission report does not give a general assessment of the Directive's application, but only a summary report of the situation in Member States. Thus, Belgium has designated one shellfish water and not transmitted a report; nothing is decided about any clean-up programme. The number of designated shellfish waters in Denmark is not indicated; the clean-up plans seem to be part of general water quality plans. In Germany, five shellfish waters were designated in one region; no report has been transmitted and nothing was mentioned about clean-up programmes. Greece listed 47 shellfish waters, but did not report. The Commission's report is silent on clean-up programmes. Spain also designated 47 shellfish waters and sent a report in 1991. The Commission's report is silent on clean-up programmes. France designated 82 waters and reported in 1990. Nothing is said about clean-up programmes. Ireland designated two waters and reported on them; no clean-up programme is mentioned. Italy has not designated waters. The Netherlands designated seven waters and extensively reported on them. No clean-up programmes were mentioned. Portugal was on the point of designating 17 waters; no report was sent. There is no mention of a clean-up programme. The United Kingom designated 29 shellfish waters and reported on them in 1988. There is no mention of clean-up programmes.

(5) In 1996, the Commission issued a Communication on water policy in which it also commented on the different water directives.[111] On Directive 78/659, it stated that it gives Member States "discretion in the designation of Fish Waters

---

[105] Commission, 15th report—1997, [1998] OJ C250/62 and 173.

[106] Commission, 16th report—1998 [1999] OJ C354/52.

[107] Commission, *Quality of Fresh Water for Fish and of Shellfish Water. Summary Report on the State of Application of the Directives 78/659 and 79/923* (Office for Official Publications of the European Communities, Luxembourg, 1995).

[108] Commission (n. 107 *supra*) p. 9: Belgium 1987, Germany 1990, Denmark –, Greece 1990, Spain 1990, France 1986, Ireland 1980, Italy 1981, Luxembourg 1982, Netherlands 1984, Portugal –, United Kingdom 1980. As can be seen from the mention of Italy, the "initial designation" does not mean complete designation, as the Court stated, in 1988, that Italy had designated waters only in the Bolzano region. The indications show that at best Ireland and the United Kingdom had complied with their obligations in time.

[109] Commission (n. 107 *supra*), p. 9: no report was received from Belgium, Denmark, Spain, France, Italy and Portugal.

[110] In Case C–225/96 (n. 100 *supra*), the Court had found—for Directive 79/923—that Member States were obliged to designate all waters.

[111] Commission, European Community water policy, COM(96)59 of 21 February 1996, p. 23.

and therefore is implemented very differently across the Community"; it announced that it would be repealed. On Directive 79/923, it commented that many, if not all, of the comments on the Fish Water Directive also applied to the Shellfish Water Directive.

Finally, the Commission issued a synthesis report on water for the years 1993 to 1995.[112] For Directive 78/659, Denmark, Greece, Spain, Luxembourg and Portugal, for Directive 79/923 Ireland and Portugal did not provide information. The report lists a considerable number of omissions, exceeding of the fixed limit values etc. and is completely silent on the existence and the success of the different clean-up programmes. One almost has the impression that the existence of such programmes is a taboo subject.

(6) If one looks at these different judgments, publications, reports and statements it seems clear that monitoring of the application of Directives 78/659 and 79/923 is neither systematic nor consistent. No Member State other than Germany has been prosecuted because of lack of clean-up programmes. The Commission has not systematically collected information on the transposition of both Directives, on the programmes established and on the values set. The Commission has not established regular reports on the implementation of the Directives and taken action under Article 226 EC Treaty, where omissions or deficiencies appeared. The number of designated waters varies considerably from one Member State to the other. Reporting obligations have not always been complied with. The setting of values does not appear to be systematic in Member States; nor does the respect of the fixed values to be general.

Generally, it seems that the applications to the Court have some element of arbitrariness and do not treat Member States on equal terms.

II. Binding Transposition Provisions to Protect the Environment

(7) All this does not explain why, in the present case, the Commission applied to the Court only in September 1995, though there had not been legally binding provisions in Germany, no programmes and no binding values. One important reason for this delay is the fact that the principle, which the Court of Justice repeated in paragraph 16, was, for the first time, stipulated by the Court in 1991. In that first decision which concerned Directive 80/68 on groundwater,[113] the Court stated: "The directive at issue in the present case seeks to protect the Community's groundwater in an effective manner by laying down specific and detailed provisions requiring the Member States to adopt a series of prohibitions, authorization schemes and monitoring procedures in order to prevent or limit discharges of ertain substances. The purpose of those provisions of the directive is thus to create rights and obligations for individuals. It should be pointed out that

[112] Commission, *The Standardised Reporting Directive; A Synthesis Report on the First Application of Standardised Reports from Member States, from 1993 to 1995* (Commission, Luxembourg, 2000), p. 30 *et seq.*
[113] Directive 80/68 on the protection of groundwater against pollution caused by certain dangerous substances [1980] OJ L20/43.

the fact that a practice is consistent with the protection afforded under a directive does not justify failure to implement that directive in the national legal order by means of provisions which are capable of creating a situation which is sufficiently precise, clear and open to permit individuals to be aware of and enforce their rights . . . in order to secure full implementation of directives in law and not only in fact, Member States must establish a specific legal framework in the area in question".

In this judgment, thus, the Court did not examine whether there was a risk to human health. It satisfied itself with the conclusion that Directive 80/68 created rights and obligations for individuals. The health aspect appeared only in later judgments.[114]

(8) This jurisprudence from 1991 presumably was the point of departure for the Commission to start, in 1992, formal proceedings against Germany under Article 226 EC Treaty, as it opened the possibility of forcing Germany to live up to the commitments which it had accepted when agreeing to the adoption of the two Directives. However, the question then must be raised whether specific and formal legislation would also have been required for the transposition of the two Directives, if the references to human health in the recitals and some provisions of the two texts had not been made. It is submitted that the result would have been the same. Indeed, it is not clear how the fixing of standards, the obligation to sample according to the detailed specifications of the Directives and the requirements to reach a specific quality of fishwaters and shellfish waters within a specific period could be reached without specific national legislative measures. In other terms: the same reasoning which the Court applied to the protection of human health must apply to the protection of the environment as such: where a directive is detailed and specific in its attempt to protect the environment, the transposing legislation must equally be deteiled and specific.

(9) This is also necessary where Community environmental law requires Member States to elaborate management plans or programmes or—as under Directives 79/659 and 79/923—clean-up plans or programmes. Such plans or programmes are not just a request addressed to the national, regional or local administration. Rather, citizens have rights to be informed about them and to participate in their elaboration. They have to orient their behaviour according to such programmes, see permits or licences granted or refused, see budgets attributed or oriented according to such plans etc. It may be regretted, therefore, that the Court accentuated the health aspect of both Directives which allowed it to omit discussion of the obligation, for a Member State, to transpose a directive by means of binding provisions, where the directive "only" aimed at the protection of the environment.

(10) Finally, it should be mentioned that the new water framework directive[115] provides in Article 21(2) that Directives 78/659 and 79/923 will be repealed 13

---

[114] Court of Justice, Case C–361/88, *Commission* v. *Germany* [1991] ECR I–2567, para. 16; Case C–59/89, *Commission* v. *Germany* [1991] ECR I–2607, para. 19; Case C–58/89, *Commission* v. *Germany* [1991] ECR I–4983, para. 14.
[115] Directive 2000/60 on establishing a framework for Community action in the field of water policy [2000] OJ L327/1.

years after its entry into force; as the Directive entered into force at the end of 2000, this will thus take place in 2013. It will be interesting to see to what extent the Commission will enforce the application of both Directives in all Member States in the same way. If Member States were getting the impression, as regards enforcement of Community environmental law, that all animals are equal but that some animals are more equal, this would necessarily have serious repercussions on the credibility of the Commission and its environmental policy.

24. OZONE-DEPLETING SUBSTANCES

Judgment of the Court of 14 July 1998
Case C–284/95

Reference for a prliminary ruling between
Safety Hi-Tech Srl and S. & T. Srl
[1998] ECR I–4301

Facts and Procedure

The Community has adhered to the Vienna Convention for the protection of the ozone layer and the Montreal Protocol on substances that deplete the ozone layer.[116] The Community has also adhered to the second amendment of the Montreal Protocol of 1992.[117] In order to fulfil its commitments under international law, the Community adopted, in 1994, Regulation 3093/94[118] which replaced earlier regulations. Article 5(1) of that Regulation stated that the use of hydrofluorocarbons (HCFCs) was prohibited as from 1 June 1995, except certain specific uses which were expressly enumerated. There was no such general prohibition in the Regulation for halons.

Safety Hi-Tech is the manufacturer of a product "NAF S III" which is composed of HCFCs and used for firefighting. In July/August 1995, it sold a quantity of the product to S.&T. Subsequently, S.&T. refused to accept delivery of the goods, arguing that the marketing and use of HCFCs for firefighting had been prohibited, since 1 June 1995, by virtue of EC Regulation 3093/94.[119] Safety Hi-Tech appealed

---

[116] Decision 88/540 [1988] OJ L297/8; the Vienna Convention and the Montreal Protocol are printed as an annex to the Decision.

[117] Decision 94/68 [1994] OJ L33/1.

[118] Regulation 3093/94 on substances that deplete the ozone layer [1994] OJ L333/1.

[119] Regulation 3093/94 (n. 118 *supra*).

to an Italian court for payment of the purchase sum. It argued that Regulation 3093/94 was invalid as it was in breach of Community law, in particular as regards the following aspects:

—a complete ban on HCFC was illegal as, on the one hand, such ban did not take into consideration the protection of the environment as a whole and aimed at protection of only part of it, i.e. the ozone layer; other products which had a much higher negative environmental impact such as halons, had not been banned;

—a complete ban on HCFC was disproportionate;

—a complete ban on HCFC was contrary to Article 28 (ex Article 30)[120] EC Treaty.

Judgment (extracts)

[The ban on HCFCs]

21. . . . the Regulation, including Article 5 thereof, is intended to implement the commitments given by the Community under the Vienna Convention and the Montreal Protocol and the second amendment thereto.

22. It is settled law that Community legislation must, so far as possible, be interpreted in a manner that is consistent with international law, in particular where its provisions are intended specifically to give effect to an international agreement concluded by the Community . . .

23. By virtue of Article 2(3) of the Vienna Convention, the parties to that convention may adopt more severe domestic measures provided that they are intended, having regard to scientific evaluations, to promote the use of substitutes that are less harmful to the ozone layer.

24. To that end, the sixth recital in the preamble to the Regulation indicates that, in the light of scientific evidence in particular, it is appropriate in certain cases to introduce control measures which are more severe than those of the second amendment to the Montreal Protocol.

25. It is in order to attain that objective that Article 5 of the Regulation prohibits the use of HCFCs.

26. That general prohibition, which applies with effect from 1 June 1995, is, however, subject to a series of exceptions exhaustively listed in Article 5(1) of the Regulation . . .

28. It is clear from those provisions that the use of HCFCs for firefighting is not provided for by the Regulation, as from 1 June 1995.

---

[120] Art. 28(ex Art. 30) EC Treaty: "Quantitative restrictions on imports and all measures having equivalent effect shall be prohibited between Member States".

30. . . . in so far as the release of HCFCs into commercial channels is a step preparatory to the use of such substances and has no aim other than their use . . . , it must be concluded that, because the use of HCFCs has been totally prohibited since 1 June 1995, the marketing of them for firefighting must also be regarded as prohibited from that date.

[Compatibility of the ban with Article 174(ex Article 130r) EC Treaty]

35./36. Article 130r of the Treaty . . . sets a series of objectives, principles and criteria which the Community legislature must respect in implementing environmental policy.

37. However, in view of the need to strike a balance between certain of the objectives and principles mentioned in Article 130r and of the complexity of the implementation of those criteria, review by the Court must necessarily be limited to the question whether the Council, by adopting the Regulation, committed a manifest error of appraisal regarding the conditions for the application of the Treaty.

38. It is therefore necessary to verify, whether, having regard to its objective, the Regulation was adopted in breach of Article 130r of the Treaty.

39./40. Hi-Tech . . . submits that the Regulation, by authorising the use of other substances, such as halons, does not take account of two other fundamental parameters for environmental protection, namely the HCFCs Global Warming Potential (hereinafter "GWP") and their Atmospheric Lifetime (hereinafter "ALT"), factors which should be taken into account together with the Ozone Depletion Potential (hereinafter "ODP"). According to Hi-Tech, if all factors were taken into consideration, HCFCs would be found to be much less harmful than halons. Consequently, the Regulation, by taking account only of the ODP and laying down only measures to combat depletion of the ozone layer, did not ensure protection of the environment as a whole, as required by Article 130r of the Treaty, but only of part of it.

41. It must first be observed that the lack of any prohibition on the use of other substances, even if assumed to be illegal, could not in itself affect the validity of the prohibition on the use of HCFCs.

42. As to the complaint concerning the failure to take account of the GWP and the ALT of HCFCs, it must be borne in mind that Article 130r(1) of the Treaty provides, among other objectives of Community environmental policy, for the protection and improvement of the quality of the environment.

43. . . . Article 130r is confined to defining the general objectives of the Community in the matter of the environment. Responsability for deciding what action is to be taken is conferred to the Council by Article 130s. Moreover, Article 130t states that the protective measures adopted jointly pusuant to Article 130s are not to prevent any Member State from maintaining or introducing more stringent protective measures compatible with the Treaty.

44. It does not follow from those provisions that Article 130r(1) of the Treaty requires the Community legislature, whenever it adopts measures to preserve, protect and improve the environment in order to deal with a specific environmental problem, to adopt at the same time measures relating to the environment as a whole.

47. . . . according to High-Tech, by authorising the use of halons, which display a much higher ODP than HCFCs and therefore represents a much greater threat to the ozone, the Regulation failed to ensure a high level of environmental protection . . .

48. As far as that requirement is concerned, it must be observed that the Regulation ensures a high level of protection. It is clear from the fourth and fifth recitals in its preamble that, in the light of scientific evidence and with a view to fulfilling the Community's obligations under the Vienna Convention and the second amendment to the Montreal Protocol, the purpose of the Regulation is to lay down measures to control, in particular, the use of HCFCs. The sixth recital, moreover, states that, in the light of scientific evidence in particular, it is appropriate in certain cases to introduce control measures which are more severe than those in the second amendment to the Protocol. By prhibiting, in Article 5(1) of the Regulation, the use of HCFCs and thereby adopting a more stringent measure that that deriving from its international obligations, the Community legislature did not infringe the requirement of a high level of protection . . .

50. Lastly, Hi-Tech considers that, by not prohibiting the use orf other substances also intended for firefighting, including hydrofluorocarbons and perfluorocarbons, the Regulation did not take account of the available scientific and technical data, as required by Article 130r(3) of the Treaty, because those substances, the GWP and ALT of which are considerable, are more damaging to the environment than HCFCs, the ODP, GWP and ALT for which are regarded as acceptable.

53. It is precisely in order to take account of the available scientific and technical data that Article 5(6) of the Regulation, dealing with the use of HCFCs, provides that the Commission may, in the light of technical progress, add to, delete items from or amend the list of prohibited uses.

54. In addition, it is clear from the case-file in the proceedings before the national court that, when the Regulation was adopted, there were, from the scientific point of view, alternatives to the use of HCFCs, involving recourse to products less harmful to the ozone layer, such as water, powder and inert gases.

56. High-Tech also considers that the prohibition on the use, and hence the marketing, of HCFCs for firefighting is disproportionate in relation to the aim of environmental protection.

58. In view of the objective of the Regulation, which is to protect the ozone layer, it must be held that the means employed. . . namely the prohibition on the use, and hence the marketing, of HCFCs for firefighting, was suitable for the purpose of attaining that objective. In view, however, of the fact that other substances that are equally, or indeed more harmful to the ozone layer, such as halons, are authorised for firefighting, it is necessary to determine whether that prohibition exceeds the limitations inherent in observance of the principle of proportionality.

59. It need merely be recalled that . . . halons display an extinguishing capability which is not otherwise available, particularly in dealing with fires in small spaces, and are of extremely low toxicity, whereas, to achieve the same result, a larger quantity of HCFCs would be needed, entailing a greater toxic impact.

[The ban on HCFCs and the free circulation of goods under Article 28 (ex Article 30) EC Treaty]

63. It is settled law that the prohibition of quantitative restrictions and of all measures having equivalent effect applies not only to national measures but also to measures adopted by the Community institution . . .

64. Environmental protection . . . is an imperative requirement which may limit the application of Article 30 of the Treaty.

66. . . . a prohibition on the use and marketing of HCFCs which is designed to protect the ozone layer cannot be regarded as disproportionate to the aim pursued.

67. It must therefore be stated that consideration of the question referred has disclosed no factor of such a kind as to affect the validity of Article 5 of the Regulation.

Commentary

I. The Partial Ban on HCFCs

(1) On the same day, when the judgment in Case C–284/95 was delivered, the Court gave a second judgment in a case which involved Mr. Bettati and Safety Hi-Tech and was based on essentially the same facts.[121] The Advocate General's Opinion was joined in the two cases and the reasoning of the Court was very largely identical. The two judgments may therefore be commented upon together.

The two judgments belong to the very few which the Court of Justice has issued on air emissions. The reaons for this low number will be discussed below.[122] Discussions on ozone depletion and climate change are almost non-existent before the Court. Its interpretation of the relevant provisions of Regulation 3093/94 leaves very little room for criticism.

(2) The Court was not asked in these two cases which had been brought before it under Article 234 EC Treaty[123] whether Regulation 3093/94 was rightly based on

---

[121] Court of Justice, Case C–341/95, *Bettati* v. *Safety Hi-Tech* [1998] ECR I–4355.

[122] See p. 215 *infra*.

[123] Art. 234 (ex Art. 177) EC Treaty: "The Court of Justice shall have jurisdiction to give preliminary rulings concerning: (a) the interpretation of this Treaty; (b) the validity and interpretation of acts of the institutions of the Community and of the ECB; (c) the interpretation of the statutes of bodies established by an act of the Council, where those statutes so provide.

Where such a question is raised before any court or tribunal of a Member State, that court or tribunal may, if it considers that a decision on the question is necessary to enable it to give judgment, request the Court of Justice to give a ruling thereon.

Where any such question is raised in a case pending before a court or a tribunal of a member State

Article 175 (ex Article 130s) EC Treaty or whether it should not have been based on Article 95 (ex Article 100a) EC Treaty instead. The Regulation deals with ozone-depleting substances and restricts or bans their marketing and use. Ozone-depleting substances are products in the sense of Article 28 EC Treaty. And for almost all restrictions of bans on products, the Community legislature has taken Article 95 (ex Article 100a) EC Treaty as the legal basis, as the restriction or prohibitiion of such substances and products affects their circulation within the internal market. The purpose of banning or restricting products—the protection of agricultural plants or animals,[124] prevention of damage to the environment,[125] protection of health and safety of consumers[126]—did not play a role. I am, generally, of the opinion that provisions which regulate products must, in law, be based on Article 95 and not on Article 175 EC Treaty.[127]

(3) The Court's arguments as regards the ban on HCFCs, while halons were not banned, are convincing from the legal point of view. Indeed, the Community would have had problems if it had also banned halons in the same way as HCFCs, as there were substitute products available for HCFCs, but not for (all uses of) halons. The two products therefore have different characteristics and it must be left to the Council's discretion which of these characteristics it choses for regulating the substances.[128] Therefore, the argument of Safety Hi-Tech that the Community should have regulated the different ozone-depleting substances not only according to their Ozone Depletion Potential, but also according to their Global Warming Potential and their Atmospheric Lifetime, is not very realistic: it must be left to the legislature how it wishes to cut the cake, which means which criteria to select. And a taking into consideration of all three characteristics of a substance would only raise new disputes about which ponderation would have to be given to each of them.

(4) Apart from this, Safety Hi-Tech was correct in its technical statement: the Ozone Depleting Potential of halon ranges from 6.0 to 12.0, while the Ozone Depleting Potential of HCFCs ranges from 0.012 till 0.086.[129] Generally, the reader

---

against whose decision there is no judicial remedy under national law, that court or tribunal shall bring the matter before the Court of Justice".

[124] See for instance Directive 79/117 on the prohibition of marketing and use of certain plant protection products [1979] OJ L33/36.

[125] See for instance Directive 85/210 on the lead content of petrol [1985] OJ L96/25; Directive 91/157 on batteries [1991] OJ L78/38.

[126] See for instance Directive 76/769 on the restriction of marketing and use of certain substances or preparations [1976] OJ L262/201; Directive 76/768 on cosmetics [1976] OJ L262/169.

[127] See in more detail L Krämer, *EC Environmental Law* (4th edn., Sweet & Maxwell, London, 2000), p. 56 *et seq.*

[128] In this context, it is not quite clear why the Court compares the two substances HCFCs and halons under the heading of "proportionality". Indeed, in other cases, the Court had ruled that the question of treating equal cases alike and unequal cases not alike was a problem of discrimination, not of proportionality: see p. 105 *supra.*

[129] European Environmental Agency, *Environment in the European Union at the Turn of the Century* (Office for Official Publications of the European Communities, Luxembourg, 1999), p. 101, table 3. 2. 1. The Ozone Depleting Potential gives the impact of an emission of one kilogramme of the substance on the depletion of stratospheric ozone.

will have to take care not to gain a false impression from the judgment: the production of halons in the European Community has stopped since 1994, while the production of HCFCs which was pushed by the chemical industry from the 1980s in order to serve as a substitute for chlorofluorocarbons (CFCs), has considerably increased since then,[130] will start to be reduced from 2008 onwards and will stop only in 2026. At present, halons contribute to about 9 per cent of the total effect of ozone depleting substances, HCFCs only to about one percent.[131]

II. The Fight Against Ozone Depletion—Probably a Success Story

(5) Ozone depletion in the stratosphere is reported to have considerable environmental and health effects[132]. Overall, there is prudent optimism that the reduction of production and use of ozone depleting substances which has taken place over the last 20 years and which will continue, could lead to the full recovery of the ozone layer in about 50 years, though the ozone layer is likely to be in its most vulnerable state in the 20 years to come.

Until now, the Global Warming Potential of a substance has not been considered in international discussions—which mainly are held in the framework of the Montreal Protocol—which have concentrated on the Ozone Depleting Potential. Whether this will have to be changed remains to be seen: for instance, the hydrofluorocarbons (HFCs), mentioned in paragraph 50 of the judgment, have been developed largely as alternatives to CFCs and HCFCs when these were progressively outphased under the Montreal Protocol. However, hydrofluorocarbons which were in the meantime taken up by the Kyoto Protocol on climate change as one of the greenhouse gases, have a Global Warming Potential of 11.700—which means that they are 11.700 times more powerful than carbon dioxide (CO_2).[133] Their production and use will therefore have to be carefully controlled.

(6) Community measures on ozone depleting substances started in 1980. The Council adopted a decision which froze the production capacity of CFC–11 and CFC–12.[134] In 1988, the Community adhered to the Vienna Convention on the

---

[130] See European Environmental Agency (n. 129 *supra*), p. 102, table 3. 2. 2: production of HCFCs in the European Community in 1989 was 61. 2 kilotonnes (12 Member States), and in 1996 102 kilotonnes.

[131] European Environmental Agency (n. 129 *supra*), p. 101. The Agency states at p. 103: "The concentration of halons (the major anthropogenic bromine compounds used as fire extinguishers) is still increasing . . . Whilst the production of halons was phased out in developed countries in 1994, the continuing increase in concentration is probably caused by emissions from halons in existing applications, mostly in developed countries and from newly produced halons in developing countries".

[132] European Environmental Agency (n. 129 *supra*), p. 108: "A thinning of the ozone layer will tend to increase the amount of ultraviolet radiation reaching the earth's surface . . . The result can be damage to human health, including skin cancer, eye cataracts, and suppression of the immune system. Marine and terrestrial ecosystems can also be affected by ultraviolet radiation . . . , and there is evidence of reduced production of phyto plankton, the basis of the ocean's food chain, in the Antarctic during ozone hole conditions".

[133] L Krämer (n. 127 *supra*) p. 224.

[134] Decision 80/372 concerning chlorofluorocarbons in the environment [1980] OJ L90/45; Decision 82/795 [1982] OJ L329/29, defined "production capacity" and improved data collection.

protection of the ozone layer and to the Montreal Protocol to that Convention[135] and adopted a regulation on certain CFCs.[136] This regulation was replaced in 1991;[137] a new regulation then came in 1994[138] and, finally, another one in 2000.[139] All measures aimed at progressively reducing or stopping the production, marketing and use of ozone depleting substances, in part well in advance of the requirements of the different obligations under the Montreal Protocol. This relative success story for the Community and worldwide is probably due to the fact that the number of ozone depleting substances is rather limited, that the Montreal Protocol was also ratified and implemented by the United States which have a considerable impact on environmental behaviour worldwide, and that the economic impact of substituting ozone depleting substances was limited.

(7) Apart from the present case, there is only one other case in which the EC provisions on ozone depleting substances were discussed, in substance, before the Court. In Case T–336/94, the company Efisol SA applied to the Court for financial compensation, as the Commission had refused to grant it a licence to import 1,800 tonnes of CFCs from Russia and Ukraine.[140] The Court of First Instance dismissed the application. It found that the Commission had given an import quota of 1,800 tonnes of CFC–11 to Efisol in 1994,[141] on the assumption that the CFCs would be used as "feedstock in the manufacture of other chemicals". However, "feedstock uses" in the context of Regulation 541/91[142] are those manufacturing processes that result in the complete consumption (destruction, decomposition etc.) of the controlled substances. The production of polyurethane foam, for which Efisol intended to use the CFCs was not such a feedstock use so that no quota should have been attributed to Efisol and no import licences could be issued. As the company had made incorrect declarations as to the intended use of the CFCs when it asked for obtaining an import quota, it could not rely on legitimate expectations to obtain import licences.

---

[135] Decision 88/540 (n. 116 *supra*).

[136] Regulation 3322/88 concerning the control on certain chlorofluorocarbons and halons which deplete the ozone layer [1988] OJ L297/1.

[137] Regulation 594/91 on substances that deplete the ozone layer [1991] OJ L67/1.

[138] Regulation 3093/94 (n. 118 *supra*).

[139] Regulation 2037/2000 on substances that deplete the ozone layer [2000] OJ L244/1.

[140] Court of First Instance, Case T–336/94, *Efisol SA v. Commission of the European Communities* [1996] ECR II–1343.

[141] Commission, Decision 94/84 [1994] OJ L42/20.

[142] Regulation 594/91 (n. 137 *supra*).

25. AIR QUALITY STANDARDS

Judgment of the Court of 30 May 1991
Case C–59/89

Commission of the European Communities v. *Germany*
[1991] ECR I–2607

Facts and Procedure

Directive 82/884[143] was adopted in 1982. It intended to protect humans against the risk of lead poisoning[144] and fixed, for that purpose, a limit value for lead in the air—"2 micrograms Pb/m3 expressed as an annual mean concentration" (Article 2). After a transitional period, this concentration of lead in the air was not to be exceeded on the territory of Member States. Article 3 required Member States to identify areas of risk and then to establish plans for the progressive improvement of the air in such areas.[145] Member States were obliged to bring into force the laws, regulations and administrative provisions necessary in order to comply with the Directive within two years.

Germany informed the Commission that the Directive was transposed into German law by virtue of a law of 15 March 1974[146] and a general administrative provision to implement the Law of 1974 (technical circular);[147] this technical circular was subsequently amended on several occasions. In 1986, a maximum value of 2 micrograms Pb/m3 was inserted in that technical circular.

The Commission was of the opinion that Germany had not taken the necessary measures to transpose the Directive into national law, but had only adopted general administrative provisions. The Commission was of the opinion that these general provisions did not really constitute rules of law and applied to the Court.

---

[143] Directive 82/884 on a limit value for lead in the air [1982] OJ L378/15.
[144] Directive 82/884 (n. 143 *supra*), Art. 1: "1. This Directive shall fix a limit value for lead in the air specifically in order to help protect human beings against the effects of lead in the environment. 2. This Directive shall not apply to occupational exposure".
[145] Directive 82/884 (n. 143 *supra*) Art. 3: ". . . 2. Where a Member State considers that the limit value fixed in Art. 2(2) may be exceeded in certain places . . . , it shall inform the Commission thereof. 3. The Member States concerned shall . . . forward to the Commission plans for the progressive improvement of the quality of the air in such places . . .".
[146] *Gesetz zum Schutz vor schädlichen Umwelteinwirkungen durch Luftverunreinigungen, Geräusche, Erschütterungen und ähnliche Vorgänge (Bundesimmissionsschutzgesetz)*, BGBl. 1974, I, p. 721.
[147] *Technische Anleitung zur Reinhaltung der Luft* (TA Luft), 1974.

Judgment (extracts)

[The absence of binding legal provisions to transpose Directive 82/884]

18. It should be borne in mind ... that, according to the case-law of the Court ..., the transposition of a directive into domestic law does not necessarily require that its provisions be incorporated formally and verbatim in express, specific legislation; a general legal context may, depending on the content of the directive, be adequate for the purpose provided that it does indeed guarantee the full application of the directive in a sufficiently clear and precise manner so that, where the directive is intended to create rights for individuals, the persons concerned can ascertain the full extent of their rights and, where appropriate, rely on them before the national courts.

19. In that respect, it should be pointed out that the obligation imposed on the Member States to prescribe a limit value which must not be exceeded in specified circumstances, laid down in Article 2 of the directive, is imposed, according to Article 1, "specifically in order to help protect human beings against the effects of lead in the environment". It does not apply, however, to occupational exposure. Except in that case the obligation implies, therefore, that whenever the exceeding of the limit valuesd could endanger human health the persons concerned must be in a position to rely on mandatory rules in order to be able to assert their rights. Furthermore, the fixing of a limit value in a provision the mandatory nature of which is undeniable is also necessary in order that all those whose activities are liable to give rise to nuisances may ascertain precisely the obligations to which they are subject.

20. It should first be observed, however, that the limit value of 2 micrograms/m3 is to be found only in the technical circular "air" and that the latter has only a limited area of application.

21. Contrary to the contention of the Federal Republic of Germany, that circular does not apply to all plant ...

22. The area of application of the circular is ... the immediate neighbourhood of well-defined buildings or plant, while the directive has a wider scope of application, which concerns the entire territory of the Member States. The general nature of the directive cannot, therefore, be satisfied by a transposition which is expressly confined to certain sources of the exceeding of the limit value which it lays down and to certain measures to be adopted by the administrative authorities.

23. Nor, secondly, is the concern to enable individual to assert their rights satisfied in the sphere of application of the circular itself, namely plant for which a licence is required. The Federal Republic of Germany and the Commission differ on the question of the extent to which, in German academic legal writing and case-law, technical circulars are being recognized as being binding in nature. The Commission was able to refer to judicial decisions denying the binding nature of such circulars, in particular in the sphere of tax law. The Federal Republic of

Germany, for its part, referred to a line of decision recognizing that binding nature in the field of nuclear energy. It must be stated that, in the particular case of the technical circular "air", the Federal Republic of Germany has not pointed to any national judicial decision explicitly recognizing that that circular, apart from being binding on the administration, has direct effect *vis-à-vis* third parties. It cannot be claimed, therefore, that individuals are in a position to know with certainty the full extent of their rights in order to rely on them where appropriate, before the national courts or that those whose activities are likely to give rise to nuisances are adequately informed of the extent of their obligations.

24. It follows from the foregoing considerations that it is not established that Article 2(1) of the directive has been implemented with the unquestionable binding force, or with the specificity, precision and clarity required by the case-law of the Court in order to satisfy the requirement of legal certainty.

[The absence of obligations to set up clean-up plans]

25. The Commission charges the Federal Republic of Germany with having failed to adopt the appropriate measures for ensuring that the limit value prescribed by the directive is actually observed, as required by Article 3 of the directive . . .

28. . . . the fact that a practice is in conformity with the requirements of a directive may not constitute a reason for not transposing that directive into national law by provisions capable of creating a situation which is sufficiently precise, clear and transparent to enable individuals to ascertain their rights and obligations . . . in order to secure the full implementation of directives in law and not only in fact, Member States must establish a specific legal framework in the area in question.

33. . . . the competent authorities of the Laender have to implement plans for the protection of the air only when they find the existence of effects which are harmful to the environment . . . the law on protection against pollution does not specify the threshold beyond which effects on the environment may be found to be harmful. The technical circular "air" imposes obligations on the administrations only in the event of well-defined acts and in respect of specific plant. There are, therefore, no general and mandatory rules under which the administrative authorities are required to adopt measures in all cases where the limit values of the directive are likely to be exceeded.

34. It follows that Article 3 of the directive has not been transposed into the internal legal system in such a way as to cover all the cases capable of arising and that the national rules do not have the binding nature necessary in order to satisfy the requirement of legal certainty.

Commentary

I. Air Quality Standards and Individual Rights

(1) In environmental policy of Member States, administrative circulars have a long tradition. The present judgment, adopted on the same day as the judgment in Case C–361/88,[148] which concerned the transposition into German law of Community air quality standards on sulphur dioxide and suspended particulates, clarified that Community air quality standards, also aimed at the protection of persons and could therefore not be transposed into national law by administrative circulars. The core of the Court's argument is that the administrative circulars referred to by Germany only were binding on the administration but did not entitle individual persons to rely on them before national courts. Therefore, they do not give the necessary legal certainty to individuals as regards the individuals' rights and obligations flowing out of the Community provisions on air quality. The Court repeated these arguments in three cases against France, which had also transposed Community air quality directives into national law by administrative circulars.[149]

(2) This aspect is relevant, as the second part of the Court's judgment in the present case concerning the fact that the German circular, the *"Technische Anleitung Luft"*, did not cover the whole of German territory but was limited to places around industrial installations, could have relatively easily been remedied by the German authorities which could have extended the circular's field of application to the whole of Germany. And this aspect did not play any role at all in the three cases mentioned above against France, where the administrative circulars did cover the whole of the national territory.

(3) Also in other cases, the Court requested that the transposition of a Community directive into national law was made in the form of a binding piece of legislation, as soon as the Community provision also intended to protect the life and health of humans.[150] Hitherto, however, there has been no express Court decision which requires the transposition of Community environmental law provisions into national law by binding measures, where the Community measure aims at the protection of the environment as such and not specifically at the protection of human health. Examples of such measures could be, for instance, the

[148] Court of Justice, Case C–361/88, *Commission* v. *Germany* [1991] ECR I–2567.

[149] Court of Justice, Cases C–13/90, *Commission* v. *France* [1991] ECR I–4327 concerning Directive 82/884 (n. 143 *supra*); C–14/90, *Commission* v. *France* [1991] ECR I–4331 concerning Directive 85/203 on limit values for nitrogen dioxides in the air [1985] OJ L87/1; C–64/90, *Commission* v. *France* [1991] ECR I–4335 concerning Directive 80/779 on limit values and guide values for sulphur dioxide and suspended particulates in the air [1980] OJ L229/30.

[150] See Court of Justice, Cases C–131/88, *Commission* v. *Germany* [1991] ECR I–825 (protection of groundwater); C–58/59, *Commission* v. *Germany* [1991] ECR I–4983 (quality of surface water); C–298/95, *Commission* v. *Germany* [1996] ECR I–6747 (fishwater and shellfish water), see also p. 207 *supra*; C–262/96, *Commission* v. *Germany* [1996] ECR I–5729 (discharges of pollutants into water).

establishing of recovery or recycling targets,[151]the introduction of collection systems for packaging waste, batteries[152] or end-of-life vehicles.[153]

(4) However, there is no serious doubt that also in cases where the protection of the environment alone is in question Member States are obliged to adopt binding transposition measures and are not allowed to satisfy themselves with administrative circulars. The Court of Justice has consistently held that mere administrative practices or measures which could, by their very nature, be amended at the discretion of the administration do not constitute proper implementation of the obligations which derive for Member States out of Article 249 EC Treaty.[154]

II. Enforcing the Application of Air Pollution Legislation

(5) Community legislation on air pollution offers a picture which is, from the legal point of view, not satisfactory. It may be subdivided into provisions on installations, composition and emission standards of products and quality-related emission standards. As regards installations, Community legislation adopted, in 1984, Directive 84/360 on air emissions from industrial installations,[155] an approach which was based on unenforceable provisions: new installations had to comply with "the application of the best available technology, provided that the application of such measures does not entail excessive costs";[156] furthermore, Member States had to "implement policies and strategies, including appropriate measures, for the gradual adaptation of existing plants . . . to the best available technology".[157] This loose terminology led to the consequence that the criterion of "best available technology not entailing excessive costs" was understood by everybody in a different way and did not have any significant impact on Member States' authorisation practice. Yet, when Directive 96/61[158] was adopted in 1996 it took over this concept, in arguing that a plant should be authorised according to the best techniques; however, this notion included also the specific economic situation of plants. At present, voluminous documents are elaborated at the Community level of what constitutes the best technique; as, however, these documents are not binding, techniques change relatively quickly and changes in technologies are not easy to make in existing installations, it is difficult to see how they

---

[151] See, for instance, Directive 94/62 on packaging and packaging waste [1994] OJ L365/10.
[152] Directive 91/157 on batteries [1991] OJ L78/38.
[153] Directive 2000/53 on end of life vehicles [2000] OJ L269/34.
[154] Court of Justice, Case C–83/97 *Commission* v. *Germany* [1997] ECR I–7191(fauna and flora habitats' designation); Case C–242/94 *Commission* v. *Spain* [1995] ECR I–303. In Case C–334/89 *Commission* v. *Italy* [1991] ECR I–93, the Court indicated that the protection of endangered bird species was a task that was necessary to protect the common Community heritage and therefore required the adoption of precise and specific transposition measures by Member States.
[155] Directive 84/360 on the combating of air pollution from industrial plants [1984] OJ L188/20.
[156] Directive 84/360 (n. 155 *supra*), Art. 4.
[157] Directive 84/360 (n. 155 *supra*), Art. 13.
[158] Directive 96/61 concerning integration of pollution prevention and control [1996] OJ L257/26.

will lead to any significant reduction on air emissions in a foreseeable time. No Court judgment was ever given on bad application of Directive 84/360 by any Member State.

(6) Directive 88/609 on large combustion plants[159] provided for emission limit values and some design requirement for new plants; for existing plants, national emission ceilings were introduced for sulphur dioxide and nitrogen oxides, which were to be reached by 1998 and 2003. No formal action was ever started by the Commission, because a new or existing plant did not comply with the Directive's requirements. This is not surprising, since the monitoring of application of an overall reduction in the emission of pollutants is impossible in practice. The monitoring of emissions stemming from the different incinerators that are covered by Community legislation follows the same pattern: as measuring methods and frequencies are not fixed, such monitoring has never led to the begin of any action against any Member State under Article 226 EC Treaty or to a judgment by the Court of Justice. In 2001, this Directive was replaced by Directive 2001/80 which is structured in the same way.[159a]

(7) Product-related standards at Community level which concern air pollution are largely limited to cars and fuels. They need not be addressed here in detail. Suffice it to mention Directive 85/210 on lead in petrol[160] which started to introduce, at Community level, the use of lead-free petrol. However, the relevant provision of Article 3(1)[161] is again drafted in terms which are unenforceable and allowed each Member State to introduce lead-free petrol at a speed which it thought fit. This led to the situation that, when the Community wanted, as from 1 January 2000, to move to the ban on leaded petrol, Italy and Spain asked for—and obtained—a derogation, as they had not organised their market in a way that allowed the transition to unleaded petrol for all cars. Of course, there never was any action against any Member State for not respecting Article 3(1) of Directive 85/210. As regards cars, the introduction of the catalytic converter and of lead-free petrol has reduced, since the end of the 1980s, air pollution from lead and also led to a considerable reduction of air emissions from the individual car—while it is true that overall air pollution from transport is increasing, due to road transport increase.

(8) The legal situation of the enforceability of Community air quality standards is worst. Next to those three directives on sulphur dioxides, lead and nitrogen oxides which were mentioned above,[162] Directive 92/72 on ozone is to be mentioned.[163] These four directives fix quality standards which shall not be exceeded in the territories of Member States. However, Community provisions on measuring

---

[159] Directive 88/609 on the limitation of emissions of certain pollutants into the air from large combustion plants [1988] OJ L336/1.

[159a] Directive 2001/80, [2001] OJ L309/1.

[160] Directive 85/210 on the lead content of petrol [1985] OJ L96/25.

[161] Directive 85/210 (n. 160 *supra*), Art. 3: "1. ... Member States shall take the necessary measures to ensure the availability and balanced distribution within their territories of unleaded petrol from 1 October 1989 ...".

[162] See nn. 143 and 149 *supra*.

[163] Directive 92/72 on air pollution by ozone [1972] OJ L297/1.

stations,[164] methods and frequency and sanctions for exceeding the concentrations were either drafted in extremely general terms or—as regards sanctions—not drafted at all. The exceeding of the concentration values of ozone in the air only creates information or warning obligations for Member States; there is no obligation to provide for pollution abatement measures or for ensuring that there is no repetition.

(9) Again, no action against Member States was ever started for breach of the quality standards for any of the four directives. In particular, there has been no judgment because of the exceeding of limit values in cities such as Athens,[165] Thessaloniki, Milan, Bilbao or others; the reason for this is most probably that the Commission has no evidence of the actual concentrations of pollutants in the air of those cities. The only source of information is the Member States; and results of measurements very largely depend on the number of measurement stations, the exact place and method of measuring and other factors, where Community legislation either gives Member States a large amount of flexibility or does not address these questions at all.

(10) It is submitted that in view of the present state of integration and the great number of aspects left to Member States, Community legislation on air quality standards is not enforceable. Where a Member State wishes to comply with that legislation and the measures provided therein, air quality standards give a useful indication of where to go and on which measures to concentrate. However, where a Member State is, for whatever reason, unwilling or unable to comply with the standards, there is hardly a possibility of enforcing Community air quality standards. This means that in practice and as regards their effects Community air quality directives are more guidelines than binding pieces of legislation.

This situation is reflected in the Court's judgments on air pollution provisions: overall, there have been, between 1976 and 2000, only 12 judgments on air pollution issues. With the exception of four cases that concerned product-related issues,[166] these cases[167] concerned the total or partial absence of transposing

---

[164] Directive 82/884 (n. 143 *supra*) provides in Art. 4 that sampling stations are installed and operated "where individuals may be exposed continually for a long period" and where Member States consider that the concentration value is "likely not to be observed". See also Directive 80/779 (n. 149 *supra*), Art. 6 and Directive 85/203 (n. 149 *supra*), Art. 6 on measuring stations. This led to the situation that in 1990, the United Kingdom had 26 measuring stations for lead and 12 for nitrogen oxides, while, for instance, Netherland had 21 for lead and 60 for nitrogen oxide: and Germany 142 for lead and 372 for nitrogen oxide, see Commission, COM(95) 372 of 26 July 1995.

[165] Athens has for about 20 years practised a policy which tries to reduce the high air pollution and recognises itself that more needs to be done. Yet, legally it is seen to be in compliance with its obligations under Community environmental law.

[166] Court of First Instance, Cases T–336/94, *Efisol* [1996] ECR II–1343; C–329/95, *VAG Sverige* [1997] ECR I–2675 (see p. 260 *infra*); C–284/95, *Safety Hi-Tech* [1998] ECR I–4301 (see p. 207 *supra*); C–341/95, *Bettati* [1998] ECR I–4355.

[167] Court of Justice, Cases 92/79, *Commission* v. *Italy* [1980] ECR 1115; C–361/88 (n. 148 *supra*); C–59/89, the present case; C–13/90 (n. 149 *supra*); C–14/90 (n. 149 *supra*); C–64/90 (n. 149 *supra*); C–186/91 *Commission* v. *Belgium* [1993] ECR I–851; C–320/99, *Commission* v. *France*, (2000) ECR I–10453.

Community provisions into national law; the application of Community air pollution legislation in practice is not an issue of concern for the Commission.

(11) The legal situation is not likely to change. As regards air emissions from installations, Directive 96/61[168] will apply in future, which gives local, regional and national authorities considerable flexibility as regards the fixing and monitoring of standards. Those installations which do not fall under that Directive will continue to come under Directive 84/360.[169] Air quality standards have been based on a new set of directives,[170] which will replace the four existing air quality directives. However, they do not change the substance of the present approach, but rather increase flexibility for the authorising and monitoring national authorities.

(12) In the mid–1990s, the Community engaged in an Auto Oil Programme which aimed at reducing emissions from transport. In long discussions with car manufacturers and the oil industry, measures for emissions from passenger cars, light commercial vehicles and the composition of petrol and diesel fuels were agreed upon, which were subsequently put into legislation.[171] These measures, which are all emission-oriented, rather confirm that the legal approach on quality standards is not a promising and successful approach. The perspective for the year 2010 of air emissions is positive: a considerable reduction of pollution emissions into the air is predicted.[172] Whether this is enough will have to be seen.[173]

(13) The picture is less sunny. Air pollution problems include "damage to flora and fauna, decomposition of materials, buildings, historical monuments, weather and climatic changes, as well as health risks mostly associated with inhalation of gases and particles . . . Some of these (health) effects can be acute and reversible, while others develop gradually into irreversible chronic conditions. Low-level exposure to a complex of pollutants in air, water, food, consumer products and buildings may be affecting overall quality of life or significantly contributing to asthma, allergies, food poisoning, some cancers, neuro-toxicity and immune-suppression. Particulate air pollutants possibly cause, per year, 40,000 to 150,000

---

[168] Directive 96/61 (n. 158 *supra*).

[169] Directive 84/360 (n. 155 *supra*).

[170] Directive 96/62 on ambient air quality assessment and management [1996] OJ L296/55 (framework directive); Directive 1999/30 relating to limit values for sulphur dioxide, nitrogen dioxide and oxides of nitrogen, particulate matters and lead in ambient air [1999] OJ L163/41; a proposal for a new directive on tropospheric ozone concentrations was made [2000] OJ C56E/40 and adopted in early 2002.

[171] Directive 98/69 [1998] OJ L104/32 (car emissions); Directive 98/70 [1998] OJ L40/52 (lead in petrol).

[172] European Environmental Agency, *Environment in the European Union at the Turn of the Century* (Office for Official Publications of the European Communities, Luxembourg, 1999), pp. 146 *et seq*; 327 *et seq.*

[173] See, for instance, European Environmental Agency (n. 172 *supra*), p. 151: "To attain ambient ozone concentrations at a level below which adverse effects on human health and ecosystems are unlikely: European-wide emission reduction of 80% or more will be needed. Even with major improvements in current technologies, this will hardly be achievable and large changes in societal behaviour would be needed".

deaths in adults in EU cities";[174] material damage of sulphur dioxide emissions alone is estimated at 13. 5 billion Euros per year.[175]

(14) This brings the discussion back to the possibility for the individual to rely on the respect of limit values in court. As mentioned, the values in Directive 92/72 must not be respected by Member States, but only create information and warning obligations. And the new Directive 1999/30[176] fixes the limit values which shall not be exceeded, in a way that the individual person or an environmental group cannot gain certainty, whether it is exceeded or at risk to be exceeded or not. Indeed, the limit value for lead is drafted as follows:

—annual limit value for the protection of human health
—averaging period: calendar year
—limit value 0.5 microgram/m^3
—margin of tolerance: . . .
—date by which limit value is to be met: . . .

The notion of "averaging period" is not defined. Seen in the context of Annex IV, the limit value must be understood as being, on average of a calendar year, 0.5 micrograms.

As regards the other limit values, the situation is even less clear: the limit value for sulphur dioxide is subdivided into an hourly limit value for the protection of human health, a daily limit value for the protection of human health and a limit value for the protection of ecosystems. The hourly limit value for human health is "not to be exceeded more than 24 times a calendar year", the daily limit value for human health may not be exceeded more than three times a calendar year, and the limit value for ecosystems is an average value for the calendar year. For nitrogen oxides and particulate matters the drafting of Directive 1999/30 is similar.

(15) How then shall an individual person—assuming that he lives in Athens—under these cicumstances apply to a court and require measures against air pollution, because the limit value is at risk to be exceeded? That person would need closely to follow the measuring results, list the different results of the different measuring stations and try to construct its case. Directive 1999/30 does not give any remedy to such persons, but limits itself—as the air quality directives mentioned above[177]—to require Member States to establish and monitor pollution reduction plans. However, these plans have not worked in the last 20 years and it will be interesting to see whether they will be effective in the future.

The subject of individuals' rights under air quality standards cannot be exhaustively discussed here. Probably things will change only at the moment when

---

[174] European Environmental Agency (n. 172 *supra*), p. 324.

[175] European Environmental Agency (n. 172 *supra*), p. 152; the text continues: "This probably underestimates the cost of the damages if the enhanced corrosion levels resulting from the combined exposure to O$_3$ and acydifying compounds were to be considered".

[176] Directive 1999/30 (n. 170 *supra*); Annex I to this Directive fixes the limit value for sulphur dioxide, Annex II for nitrogen dioxide and oxides of nitrogen, Annex III for particulate matter and Annex IV for lead.

[177] Directive 80/779 (n. 149 *supra*); Directive 82/884 (n. 143 *supra*); Directive 85/203 (n. 149 *supra*).

a court awards to persons who live in an area where limit values are exceeded, damages for bodily injury, for pain and suffering and/or for economic damage. Until then, air quality limit values will be—at best—a tool for the administration, but not an instrument to protect individual persons from damage.

4

PRODUCTS AND NOISE*

26. DANGEROUS CHEMICALS IN THE COMMUNITY

Judgment of the Court of 11 July 2000
Case C–473/98

Reference for a preliminary ruling in the proceedings between
Kemikalieinspektionen and Toolex Alpha AB
[2000] ECR I–5681

Facts and Procedure

Toolex Alpha AB is a Swedish manufacturer of machine parts which are used in the production of compact discs. It uses trichloroethylene to remove residues of grease produced during the manufacturing process.

Trichloroethylene is classified, under Directive 67/548,[1] as a category 3 carcinogen with the indications R 40 (toxic) and R 52/53 (harmful to the environment).[2] Directive 76/769[3] does not contain provisions on the marketing and use of trichloroethylene. Trichloroethylene underwent a risks evaluation pursuant to Regulation 793/93.[4] According to that evaluation it is appropriate to limit the risks to which workers and consumers are exposed, and to which the population in general is exposed. An evaluation of the risks to the environment also led to the finding that there is a possibilitiy of contamination of plant-life.

* For further judgments discussing product issues, see cases in s. 4, chap. 1 *supra* (*Pentachlorphenole*), ss. 13 (*Outokumpu*) and 18 (*Asbestos*) of chap. 2 *supra*.

[1] Directive 67/548 on the classification, packaging and labelling of dangerous substances [1967] OJ 196/1.

[2] See para. 5 of the present judgment (not reproduced below): "Trichloroethylene is classified as a category 3 carcinogen, with the indications R 40 (toxic) and R 52/53 (harmful to the environment). Carcinogens are divided into three categories, category 3 containing the least dangerous of them. R 40 indicates 'possible risks of irreversible risks' and R 53 that the substance 'may cause longterm adverse effects in the aquatic environment' respectively".

[3] Directive 76/769 relating to restrictions on the marketing and use of certain dangerous substances and preparations [1976] OJ L262/201.

[4] Regulation 793/93 on the evaluation and control of the risks of existing substances [1993] OJ L84/1.

In 1991, Sweden adopted a regulation[5] which prohibited, for industrial use, the sale, transfer or use of chemical products composed wholly or partially of trichloroethylene, but allowed for general exemptions where they are justified on specific grounds, and individual exemptions where there are special reasons for doing so. The provisions for granting such exemptions were further specified in a national measure, which was last amended in 1997.[6]

Toolex applied for permission to continue the use of trichloroethylene. This application was rejected. As the dispute was not solved, the matter was brought to a Swedish court which referred the matter to the Court of Justice for a preliminary ruling.

Judgment (extracts)

25. ... whilst Article 36 of the Treaty allows the maintenance of national restrictions on the free movement of goods, justified on grounds which constitute fundamental requirements recognised by Community law, recourse to Article 36 is not possible where Community directives provide for harmonisation of the measures necessary to achieve the specific objective which would be furthered by reliance upon that provision ...

26. Thus, ... it is necessary first to establish whether the Member States are still entitled to regulate the industrial use of trochloroethylene ...

27. The Commission submits that the classification and marketing directives, together with the risks evaluation regulation, create a set of Community rules on trichloroethylene which is commensurate with stringent safety requirements and is sufficiently well developed to render any national prohibition on the use of the substance superfluous.

28. The Court does not share that view.

29. The classification directive covers a very clearly defined field, namely the notification, classification, packaging and labelling of dangerous substances. As regards the use of such substances, the classification directive merely requires that their packaging bear safety recommendations designed to inform the general public of the particular care that should be taken when handling the substance in question. It does not harmonise the conditions under which dangerous substances may be marketed or used, which are the very matters that fall within the purview of national legislation such as that in issue in the main proceedings.

30. Given that the marketing directive, in itself, does no more than state certain minimum requirements, as is plain from Article 2 thereof ... , it clearly presents no obstacle to the regulation by the Member States of the marketing of substances that do not fall within its scope, such as trichloroethylene.

---

[5] *Förordningen om vissa klorerade lösningsmedel*, 1991:21.
[6] *Kemikalieinspektionens föreskrifter om undantag fraan förbud i förordningen* (1991:1289) *om visse klorerade lösningsmedel*, KIFS 1995:6, amended by KIFS 1997:3 and KIFS 1998:8.

31. Nor, finally, does the risks evaluation regulation, in itself, preclude the Member States from exercising such a power. Its objective is to establish a procedure for evaluating the risks associated with existing substances and identifying priority substances which, because of their potential effects on man and the environment, require immediate attention at Community level. Although it is intended to assist in the management of such risks at Community level, the risks evaluation regulation neither imposes obligations nor harmonises rules on the use of substances in general or trichloroethylene in particular.

32. Whilst, under Article 11(3) of the risks evaluation regulation, it is for the Commission to propose Community measures within the framework of either the marketing directive or another appropriate Community instrument on the basis of the results of a risks evaluation carried out and strategy recommended in accordance with that regulation, the fact remains that is has not yet exercised that power with regard to trichloroethylene.

35. It should first be observed that national legislation such as that at issue in the case in the main proceedings constitutes, in principle, a measure having an effect equivalent to a quantitativerestriction within the meaning of Article 30 of the Treaty.

36. On the one hand, the general prohibition on the industrial use of trichloroethylene is likely to bring about a reduction in the volume of trichloroethylene imported.

37. On the other hand, although individual exemptions may be granted by the competent national authority, the concept of a measure having an effect equivalent to a quantitative restriction also applies to the obligation imposed upon economic operators to apply for exemption or a dispensation from a national measure which itself amounts to a quantitative restriction or measure having equivalent effect . . . Moreover, it is clear from the written obsevations and from the submissions made at the hearing that any exemptions granted are merely temporary and that the long-term objective of the Swedish legislature is still to remove trichloroethylene from industrial use enitrely.

38. Second, it should be borne in mind that the health and life of humans rank foremost among the property or interests protected by Article 36 of the Treaty. . .

39. On this point there has been no suggestion that national legislation, such as that in issue in the case in the main proceedings, which aims to prohibit absolutely the industrial use of trichloroethylene, might be based upon any considerations other than the protection of the health and life of humans or the protection of the environment. Moreover, it is clear from the classification of trichloroethylene under the classification directive that it is acknowledged at Community level that the substance is dangerous.

However, national rules or practices having, or likely to have, a restrictive effect on the importation of products are compatible with the Treaty only to the extent that they are necessary for the effective protection of the health and life of humans. A national rule or practice cannot therefore benefit from the derogation provided for in Article 36 of the Treaty if the health and life of humans may be protected just as effectively by measures which are less restrictive of intra-Community trade . . .

45. Taking account of the latest medical research on the subject, and also the difficulty of establishing the threshhold above above which exposure to trichloroethylene poses a serious health risk to humans, given the present state of research, there is no evidence in this case to justify a conclusion by the Court that national legislation such as that at issue in the case in the main proceedings goes beyond what is necessary to achieve the objective in view . . .

46. In particular, the system of individual exemptions, granted subject to conditions, established by the Swedish regulation appears to be appropriate and proportionate in that it offers increased protection for workers, whilst at the same time taking account of the undertakings' requirements in the matter of continuity.

47. First, exemption is granted on condition that no safer replacement product is available and provided that the applicant continues to seek alternative solutions which are less harmful to public health and the environment. Those requirements are compatible with the "substitution" principle which emerges, *inter alia*, from Council Directive 89/391/EEC of 12 June 1989 on the introduction of measures to encourage improvements in the safety and health of workers at work (OJ 1989 L 183 p. 1) and Council Directive 90/394/EEC of 28 June 1990 on the protection of workers from the risks related to exposure of carcinogens at work (Sixth individual Directive within the meaning of Article 16(1) of Directive 89/391/EEC) (OJ 1990 L 196 p. 1) and which consists in the elimination or reduction of risks by means of replacing one dangerous substance with another, less dangerous substance.

48. Second, the concern to avoid causing disruption to an undertaking where there is no alternative solution does not justify the grant of an exemption unless exposure to trichloroethylene is at acceptable levels.

49. In light of the foregoing considerations, national legislation which lays down a general prohibition on the use of trichloroethylene for industrial purposes and establishes a system of individual exemptions, granted subject to conditions, is justified under Article 36 of the Treaty on grounds of the protection of health of humans.

Commentary

I. *Community Legislation on Chemicals*

(1) The judgment clarifies a legal situation which was largely undisputed among academic legal researchers, but does not seem to have been clear in the political area. Otherwise, it is not explainable why the European Commission made the statement that is mentioned in paragraph 27 of the judgment. However, this statement illustrates, from the legal point of view, the Community policy on substances and products: the attempt to stop and to prevent any Member State

initiative on the restriction or phasing-out of the marketing and/or use of products. This would be acceptable on the condition that the Community itself were taking the necessary steps to restrict or prohibit, for the whole of the Community, the marketing of products and substances which are, in the broad sense, dangerous to humans and/or the environment.

(2) However, such a Community policy exists only in rudimentary form. Perhaps the most obvious aspect of this is the fact that this "substitution principle" which the Court of Justice mentions in paragraph 47 of its judgment as an "emerging principle" exists, at present, only in the area of worker protection.[7] There is no attempt at the Community level systematically to reduce the marketing and use of dangerous substances (heavy metals, carcinogens etc.), wherever they can be reduced by less dangerous substances. As such a substitution principle is part of Swedish environmental policy, it is not surprising that these different approaches must, sooner or later, conflict with each other.

(3) The Court of Justice is very short and precise as regards the analysis of existing Community legislation: there is no provision in Community legislation which regulates the marketing and use of trichloroethylene. Directive 76/769[8] contains an Annex on substances and preparations the use of which is restricted or banned Community-wide. However, that Annex constitutes a positive list of restrictions which means that those substances which are not on that list are not restricted. Of course, restrictions of substances and products are not exclusively regulated in Directive 76/769; directives on food and pharmaceutical, cosmetics, pesticides, batteries, petrol and diesel all contain—widely dispersed, it is true—restrictions on certain substances. Yet, these measures are anything but systematic. And none of them generally regulates trichloroethylene.

(4) A certain attempt was made, under Regulation 793/93,[9] at least to evaluate the human and environmental risks of existing chemical substances. However, the experience with that Regulation is not encouraging: the Guidance document for making the risk assessment has about 700 pages.[10] No wonder that the risk assessment for individual substances takes at present three to four years. And the risk assessment in itself does not automatically lead to legislative initiatives on the part of the Commission or Member States to restrict the marketing or use of a substance which has found to be presenting a risk.

(5) This problem may perhaps be illustrated by the risk assessment for cadmium: In order to become eligible for a risk assessment, the substance must be inserted in a Community priority list, which was the case for cadmium.[11] Belgium

---

[7] The proposal for a 6th Community environmental action programme, COM(2000)31 of 24 January 2001, now mentions that there should be a new principle in Community environmental policy, the substitution principle.

[8] Directive 76/769 (n. 3 *supra*).

[9] Regulation 793/93 (n. 4 *supra*).

[10] Commission, *Technical Guidance Document in Support of Commission Directive 93/67 on Risk Assessment for New Notified Substances and Commission Regulation 1488/94 on Risk Assessment for Existing Substances*, parts I to IV (Commission, Luxembourg, 1996).

[11] Commission Regulation 143/97 [1997] OJ L25/13, nos. 2 and 3.

as the reporting Member State produced, after roughly four years, a provisional report which had about 800 pages. However, on eight of the nine sub-chapters which Belgium had examined, the conclusion was that further research would be necessary before a risk assessment was possible. The draft report was then discussed with other Member States with the result that by mid–2002 a risk assessment for cadmium still does not exist. And this example concerns a substance which is probably the best researched environmental pollutant of all and on which as early as in 1987 the Commission had announced an action programme to substitute cadmium whenever technically possible,[12] and on which the Council, in 1988, had adopted a resolution approving the strategy and expressly repeated that cadmium be substituted whenever this was technically possible.[13]

(6) The Court's conclusion on the assessment of secondary Community legislation is clear: apart from the provisions on the classification, packaging and labelling under Directive 67/548, there are no Community provisions on trichloroethylene. The Commission's argument on a "set of Community rules" (paragraph 27 of the judgment) is dismissed without great discussion; the same applies to the opinion that national legislation is superfluous. This Commission opinion does not sufficiently consider that, where the Community does not protect the environment by Community-wide provisions it cannot prevent Member States from doing so. And it cannot be the Community's assessment to decide whether such national measures are superfluous or not: in environmental matters, Member States may do whatever they want, and are limited only by the EC Treaty and secondary Community legislation which is derived from that Treaty.

II. Justification of the National Measure under Article 30 EC Treaty

(7) As such secondary legislation does not exist for trichlorothylene, the Court's assessment of the Swedish measure was made against the yardstick of Article 30 (ex Article 36) EC Treaty.[14] In this assessment, the Court concentrated on the criterion "protection of health and life of humans", though the classification of trichloroethylene, under Directive 67/548, was both "toxic" and "harmful to the environment". However, as Article 174(1) EC Treaty expressly mentions that Community environmental policy also contributes to the protection of human health, the Court's concentration on the health aspects must be seen as including also the environmental aspects.

---

[12] Commission, Environmental pollution by cadmium. Proposal for an action programme, COM(87)165 of 21 April 1987.

[13] Resolution of 25 January 1988 [1988] OJ C30/1.

[14] Art. 30 (ex Art. 36) EC Treaty: "The provisions of Arts. 28 and 29 shall not preclude prohibitions or restrictions on imports, exports or goods in transit justified on grounds of public morality, public policy or public security; the protection of health and life of humans, animals or plants; the protection of national treasures possessing artistic, historic or archaeological value; or the protection of industrial and commercial property. Such prohibitions or restrictions shall not, however, constitute a means of arbitrary discrimination or a disguised restriction on trade between Member States".

(8) The point of departure for the Court was the undisputed fact that trichloroethylene is dangerous, a point which the Court elaborates once more in some detail (paragraphs 38 and 39). One may wonder whether this elaboration is really necessary, as the Community legislature had already stated that trichloroethylene was dangerous, by classifying it as "toxic" and "harmful to the environment" in Directive 67/548.

(9) The main emphasis of the Court's examination under Article 30 EC Treaty was whether the Swedish measure was proportionate. Here the Court examines the question whether the measure was really necessary, i.e. whether measures could have been adopted instead that are less restrictive on intra-Community trade. In practice, though, the Court elaborates on the same adverse health effects of trichloroethylene that had helped it to classify the substance as dangerous (toxic).

(10) The Court does not really examine less far-reaching measures such as a warning label with instructions for use, or a special permit for undertakings which wish to use trichloroethylene. It does not discuss either whether a ban on a carcinogen of class 3, the class of the least dangerous carcinogens, is really necessary— all the more so as many other EC Member States obviously have not prohibited the use of that substance. And the Court does not discuss why the substance is prohibited only for industrial use and not also for private use; this differentiation might at least give an indication that the Swedish authorities did not consider a total prohibition to be necessary.

(11) Yet, I am of the opinion that the Court was right in not addressing these different aspects. Indeed, its statement in paragraph 40 that the least restrictive means must be taken is slightly misleading: Member States have a considerable amount of discretion as regards the means they take in order to protect life and health of their citizens. They have to assess the risk which stems from the substance, the different medical and scientific findings, the exposure of workers and other parts of the population. They must decide whether—and to a large extent to what degree—they want to take into consideration the precautionary principle, and if and to what extent the substitution principle which the Court approvingly mentions in paragraph 47 of its judgment shall be applied in the regulatory context. The Court could, for instance, not hold against Sweden that other Member States have limited their action on trichloroethylene to a strict permit requirement: Sweden alone decides whether it wishes to have this known carcinogen on its market and in its environment.

In conclusion: the decision to restrict or prohibit a substance or a product is the result of complex economic, political, technical, environmental considerations. And it is submitted that a substance which is known to be dangerous may always be banned by a Member State under Articles 28 and 30 EC Treaty, without this being considered to be a disproportionate measure. This is what the Court of Justice declared in earlier judgments: in Case C–293/94 the Court stated that "in the absence of harmonising rules, it is for the Member States to decide on their intended level of protection of human health and life and on whether to require prior authorisation for the marketing of such products".[15] This formula was also used in earlier and later judgments.[16]

(12) In its evaluation of proportionality, the Court considers "the latest medical research on the subject" and the difficulty of establishing a threshold for the substance—which is the same difficulty as for any carcinogen—and is of the opinion that the Swedish measure does not go beyond what is necessary. In that it mentions in particular the system of allowing individual exemptions to be granted (paragraphs 46 to 48), which apparently offers sufficient flexibility to take care of the specific situations of different undertakings.

(13) The judgment is of considerable importance for Community product policy. Indeed, the number of substances and preparations which are banned or restricted in their use under Commuity legislation, and in particular under Directive 76/769, is very limited; and where a substance is regulated in that Directive, the derogations, exceptions and transition periods are numerous. Confronted with the clarifications in the present judgment, Member States may now pursue an active product policy at national level, for instance by systematically reducing the presence of toxic substances, substances which are harmful to the environment or which fulfil other characteristics. The Court's judgment also allows an active national policy of substituting dangerous substances by substances which present less danger for humans or for the environment. Such a substitution policy exists at present in Sweden, but does not exist at Community level.

As long as Member States ensure the necessary flexibility by providing for the possibility of granting an exception in specific cases, their national legislation will hardly be capable of being attacked. Under Directive 98/34,[17] any such national regulation will have to be notified to the Commission in the draft stage in order to allow an assessment of its impact on the circulation of goods within the Community. However, this is a formal requirement which leads to a standstill for the national legislation for several months only.[18]

[15] Court of Justice, Case C–293/94, *Brandsma* [1996] ECR I–3159, para. 11.

[16] See Cases 272/80, *Biologische Producten* [1981] ECR 3277, para. 9; C–125/88, *Nijman* [1989] ECR I–3533, para. 12; C–400/96, *Harpegnies* [1998] ECR I–5121, para. 33. See also p. 242 *infra*.

[17] Directive 98/34 laying down a procedure for the provision of information in the field of technical standards and regulations [1998] OJ L204/37.

[18] See for more details on the procedure under Directive 98/34, p. 161 *supra*.

27. BIOTECHNOLOGY—POLICY AND LAW

Judgment of the Court of 21 March 2000
Case C–6/99

Reference for a preliminary ruling between
Greenpeace France and Others v. Ministère de
l'Agriculture et de la Pêche and Others
[2000] ECR I–1651

Facts and Procedure

This judgment concerns the placing on the market of genetically modified maize.

Directive 90/220[19] has the objective of approximating Member States' legislation and protecting human health and the environment as regards the deliberate release of genetically modified organisms ("GMOs") into the environment, as well as the placing on the market of products which contain or consist of GMOs intended for subsequent deliberate release into the environment. It requires Member States to take all appropriate measures in order to avoid adverse effects on human health and the environment from such releases. On the placing on the market of products containing GMOs, the Directive contains detailed provisions.

The manufacturer or the Community importer must notify the competent authority of the Member State in which such a product is to be placed on the market for the first time of his intention and add the necessary information on the product (Article 11). The competent authority must then carry out a risk assessment; after that, it shall either inform the manufacturer that it rejects the proposed release or forward the dossier to the European Commission with a favourable opinion (Article 12). The Commission has the obligation to forward the dossier to all other Member States. If no objection from another Member State is received within 60 days, the competent authority that received the original notification shall give its written consent to the manufacturer. If an objection is raised by another Member State, the Commission shall take a decision by way of a committee procedure.[20]

---

[19] Directive 90/220 on the deliberate release into the environment of genetically modifed organisms [1990] OJ L117/15; amended by Directive 94/15 [1994] OJ L103/20 and Directive 97/35 [1997] OJ L169/72.

[20] This committee procedure is laid down in Art. 21 of Directive 90/220: "The Commission shall be assisted by a committee composed of the representatives of the Member States and chaired by the representative of the Commission. The representative of the Commission shall submit to the committee a draft of the measures to be taken. The committee shall deliver its opinion on the draft . . . The opinion shall be delivered by . . . majority . . . The Commission shall adopt the measures envisaged if they are

Where the Commission takes a favourable decision, the competent authority that received the original notification shall give consent in writing to the manufacturer, eventually accompanied by specific conditions of use, and shall inform the other Member States. The product may then be used throughout the Community (Article 13).

Where a Member State receives new information on a product that has received written consent to be put on the market, it may provisionally restrict or prohibit the use and/or sale of that product on its territory. It shall inform the Commission and the other Member States of such action. Then, the Commission shall take a decision within three months.[21] There is a specific procedure for such a decision.[22]

France had received a request to place on the market genetically modified maize "with the combined modification for insecticidal properties conferred by the Bt-endotox gene and increased tolerance to the herbicide glufosinate ammonium". It forwarded the dossier to the Commission, together with a favourable opinion. Other Member States raised objections. The Commission submitted a favourable proposal for a decision to the committee set up under Directive 90/220. The committee did not deliver an opinion. Therefore, the Commission referred the case to the Council. The Council did not take a decision. The Commission thus decided that "the French authorities shall give consent to the placing of the market" of the genetically modified maize and attached some conditions to that decision.[23]

Subsequently, France adopted, on 4 February 1997, a decree authorising the placing on the market of the genetically modified maize. On 5 February 1998 it adopted a decree modifying the official list of plant species and varieties grown in France. The purpose of this decree was to authorise the marketing of seeds of certain varieties of genetically modified maize.

Greenpeace and others attacked the decree of 5 February 1998 before the French Conseil d'Etat, arguing that it was unlawful. They argued in particular that this decree was based on the decree of 4 February 1997 which was in itself unlawful, as the procedure followed by the French authorities before the dossier had been forwarded to the Commission had been irregular. The Conseil d'Etat had doubts whether Article 13(4)[24] of Directive 90/220 gave any discretion to Member States

---

in accordance with the opinion of the committee. If the measures envisaged are not in accordance with the opinion of the committee, or if no opinion is delivered, the Commission shall, without delay submit to the Council a proposal relating to the measures to be taken. The Concil shall act by qualified majority. If, on the expiry of a period of three months . . . the Council has not acted, the proposed measures shall be adopted by the Commission".

[21] Directive 90/220 (n. 19 *supra*), Art. 16: "1. Where a Member State has justifiable reasons to consider that a product which has been properly notified and has received written consent under this Directive constitutes a risk to, human health or the environment, it may provisionally restrict or prohibit the use and/or sale of that product on its territory. It shall immediately inform the Commission and the other Member States of such action and give reasons for its decision. 2. A decision shall be taken on the matter within three months in accordance with the procedure laid down in Art. 21".

[22] Directive 90/220 (n. 19 *supra*), Art. 21 (n. 2 *supra*).

[23] Commission, Decision 97/98 [1997] OJ L31/69.

[24] Directive 90/220 (n. 19 *supra*), Art. 13(4): "Where the Commission has taken a favourable decision, the competent authority that received the original notification shall give consent in writing to the notification so that the product may be placed on the market".

to refuse consent to the manufacturer and therefore referred to the Court of Justice in order to know whether arguments submitted by Greenpeace could still be heard.

Judgment (extracts)

[Community or national authorisation on the marketing of genetically modified products]

28. . . . whilst another wording might have made it more explicit that the Member States' powers were circumscribed, the fact remains that both the use, in the French version of Article 13(2) and (4) of Directive 90/220, of the present indicative and the construction in the sentences in that provision indicate clearly and unequivocally that the Member State concerned is obliged to give its consent.

29. Furthermore, the meaning and content of that provision are reflected in other language versions of Directive 90/220, in particular in the English version ("The competent authority. . . shall give its consent in writing").

30. Consequently, having regard to the terms of Article 13(2) and (4) of Directive 90/220, that provision places the Member State concerned, in the cases there referred to, under an obligation to issue its consent in writing.

33. . . . for the purposes of implementing a Community procedure for authorising the placing on the market of products containing GMOs, the Community legislature, in . . . Directive 90/220, has provided for close cooperation between the Commission and the competent authority of the Member State in which the product is to be placed on the market for the first time.

39. . . . the procedure for authorising the placing on the market of a product containing GMOs, envisaged in Directive 90/220, comes into operation only at the end of a procedure during which the national authorities have adopted a favourable opinion on the basis of the examination provided for in Article 12(1) of the directive and have thus had the opportunity fully to exercise their own powers to assess the risks which the release of products containing GMOs entails for human health and the environment.

40. . . . the applicants in the main proceedings argue that an interpretation of Article 13(2) and (4) of Directive 90/220 to the effect that the Member States' powers are circumscribed would be contrary to the precautionary principle.

41. It must be pointed out in this regard that, according to the eighth recital of the preamble to Directive 90/220, the directive establishes "harmonised procedures and criteria for the case-by-case evaluation of the potential risks arising from the deliberate release of GMOs into the environment". According to the ninth recital, such a case-by-case evaluation of the potential risks should always be carried out prior to a release.

42. As is clear from paragraph 39 above, it is to that end that the competent national authorities have a power of assessment for the purpose of ensuring that the notification referred to in Article 11 of the directive is in conformity with its requirements, giving particular attention to the assessment of the risks arising from the placing on the market of products containing GMOs for the environment and human health, as provided for in Article 12(1) of Directive 90/220 and as mentioned in the third recital.

43. As regards the competent authorities of the other Member States, Article 13(2) and (3) of Directive 90/220 provides that these may raise objections before the competent authority concerned gives its consent to the notification.

44. Next, observance of the precautionary principle is reflected in the notifieer's obligation . . . immediately to notify the competent authority of new information regarding the risks of the product to human health or the environment and the authority's obligation . . . immediately to inform the Commission and the other Member States about this information and, secondly, in the right of any Member State, provided for in Article 16 of the directive, provisionally to restrict or prohibit the use and/or sale on its territory of a product which has received consent where it has justifiable reasons to consider that it constitutes a risk to human health or the environment.

45. It must be added that the system of protection put in place by Directive 90/220 . . . necessarily implies that the Member State concerned cannot be obliged to give its consent in writing if in the meantime it has new information which leads it to consider that the product for which notification has been received may constitute a risk to human health and the environment.

[Irregular national procedures, leading to the Community decision]

49. . . . when the Commission has taken a "favourable decision" under Article 13(4) of Directive 90/220, the competent authority which forwarded the application with a favourable opinion to the Commission, must . . . issue the "consent in writing". . . .

50. Such an obligation presupposes that . . . the competent national authority has forwarded the dossier to the Commission with a favourable opinion and has thus initiated the Community phase of the procedure . . .

51. Thus, the decision of the competent authority is the prerequisite for the Community procedure and, in the absence of any indication to the contrary from another Member State . . . may even determine its outcome.

53. . . . it is for the national courts to decide on the regularity of the examination of the notification . . . and on the consequences which any irregularities in the conduct of that examination might have on the legality of the decision taken by the competent authority . . . to forward the dossier to the Commission with a favourable opinion.

54. It should also be observed that, where the administrative implementation of a Community decision is a matter for the national authorities, the judicial protection guaranteed by Community law affords individuals the right to challenge, indirectly, the legality of that decision before the national court and to ask it to refer questions to the Court of Justice for a preliminary ruling on the validity of that decision. In such a case, the Court of Justice alone has competence to declare a Community act to be invalid . . .

55. . . . where the national court finds that, owing to irregularities in the conduct of the examination of the notification by the competent national authority to forward the dossier with a favourable opinion to the Commission . . . , that court must refer the matter to the Court of Justice for a preliminary ruling if it considers that those irregularities are such as to affect the validity of the Commission's favourable decision, setting out the reasons for which it believes that the decision must be held to be invalid and, if necessary, ordering suspension of application of the measures for implementing that decision until the Court of Justice has ruled on the question of validity . . .

56. Should the Court of Justice hold that the Commission's favourable decision is unlawful, the conditions for the issue of the consent in writing by the competent authority laid down in Article 13(2) and (4) of Directive 90/220 would not be fulfilled and the consent in writing would therefore not have been validly given or could not be validly given.

Commentary

I. *The Interdependency of National and Community Administration in Biotechnology*

(1) Biotechnology is a new technology which is heavily contested in the Community. The present case on which the Court had to give a preliminary ruling and the circumstances surrounding it are a good illustration of this ongoing controversy. The Court of Justice only had to add one part to this mega-puzzle of ecological and economic, national and Community, legal and political interests; however that part was very important and helped clarifying the situation. Apparently, the Court followed the suggestion by Advocate General Mischo.[25] It set aside the political aspects of the case and limited itself to answer the two questions which the French Conseil d'Etat had put; it did not go into the question of assessing the validity of the procedure at national level nor that of Decision 97/98, issued by the Commission,[26] as it had not been asked to do so.

(2) The company Ciba-Geigy, which became in the meantime Novartis Seeds, had asked the French authorities to obtain the authorisation to market genetically modified maize. The application was examined and the French authorities were of the opinion that the conditions for authorising the marketing of the maize were

---

[25] Opinion of Advocate General Mischo in Case C–6/99 [2000] ECR I–1651, para. 24.
[26] Decision 97/98 (n. 23 *supra*).

fulfilled. In conformity with Directive 90/220, they thus sent the application to the Commission in order to obtain the agreement to market the maize Community-wide. After an intricate procedure, which will be commented in a moment, the green light was given by Decision 97/98. The French authorities then took the necessary steps to make the marketing of the genetically modified maize in France possible. One of these national decrees was then attacked in court and led to the intervention of the Court of Justice.

The Court of Justice was asked whether the "green light" which Commission Decision 97/98 had given to France meant that the French authorities had to allow the marketing or whether they had some discretion and could also refuse authorisation. This was politically delicate, since the Government had changed in France since the first favourable opinion was given; in the meantime, a Secretary of State from the Green Party was in charge of the environmental file, who was known to have little sysmpathy for genetically modified products.

(3) The Court of Justice held that Decision 97/98 did not leave France any discretion, but that it had to authorise the marketing of the genetically modified maize (paragraphs 25 to 47). The resoning seems convincing. Indeed, the French authorities had made up their minds as regards the application for marketing, by adopting a "favourable opinion" and sending the file to the European Commission. They even had had, twice—during the committee procedure at Commission level and during the voting procedure in Council—the political possibility of changing their minds. The wording and also the purpose of the authorisation procedure under Directive 90/220 is just, to allow the national decision to gain Community-wide acceptance, as the Court of Justice quite rightly allows.

(4) The precautionary principle cannot be of help either, contrary to what Greenpeace argued. The Court explained in great detail that this principle has been inbuilt into the whole procedure under Directive 90/220 (paragraphs 41 to 46). Then it is not possible, where this procedure has been followed, to argue nevertheless that, in the name of the precautionary principle, the decision which was reached should be set aside. The precaution which needs to be taken lies in the procedure itself and is not independent of the legal provisions.

(5) The Court then had to say what should happen if new elements appeared which made the original national procedure that had led to the transmission of the dossier to the Community and to the favourable opinion of the French authorities irregular. The Court was of the opinion that first of all the French authorities had to assess whether there had indeed been any irregularities and to what extent such irregularities affected the decision to transfer the dossier to Brussels (paragraph 53). However, the Court was aware that, on the one hand, too much time might have elapsed so that this first part of the national procedure—provided it was capable of being attacked at all[27]—could no longer be attacked. Therefore, it stated that individuals might also tackle the "second" national decision, i.e. the one

---

[27] National procedural rules may vary on whether the decision to transfer the dossier to the Community level and the issuing of a favourable opinion are independent decisions which may be attacked in court and who shall have standing in such cases.

which definitely grants authorisation to market the product, and this also on the "indirect" (wording in paragraph 54) ground that the first national decision was irregular or unlawful. If the national court found new grounds on the irregularity of the first national decision, it may resort to the procedure provided for in Article 16 of Directive 90/220.[28] Should at this stage the validity of Community Decision 97/98 become doubtful, the national court would have to refer the case, under Article 234 EC Treaty, to the Court of Justice which "alone has competence to declare a Community act to be invalid" (paragraph 54).

In this way, the Court of Justice solved the interdependence between national and Community decision-making under Directive 90/220 and, as mentioned, its decision seems to be unassailable.

II. Genetically Modified Products on the Community Market

(6) However: the legal rules are one thing, the political issues are another. When France had transferred the dossier to the Commission with its favourable opinion, 13 Member States objected to a favourable Community decision. This was different with the Commission: the Commission came to the conclusion that the putting into circulation of the genetically modified maize would not constitute a risk for human health or the environment. It therefore submitted a proposal to the Committee that had been set up under Directive 90/220. The Committee voted. In order to amend the Commission proposal, the Committee would have to have been unanimous.[29] This was, of course, impossible, as France, which had submitted the dossier, was on the side of the Commission.

(7) Thus, the Committee did not deliver an opinion, and the Commission proposal for a positive decision went to the Council.[30] The Council voted on the proposal; however, under Article 250 EC Treaty, the Council needed unanimity in order to amend the Commission's proposal. As France remained on the side of the Commission, this unanimity was not reached. The right to take a decision then fell back to the Commission—which followed its own proposal and after consulting its scientific committees for animal nutrition, for food and on pesticides,[31] issued the favourable Decision 97/98.

---

[28] Directive 90/220 (n. 19 *supra*), Art. 16: "1. Where a Member State has justifiable reasons to consider that a product which has been properly notified and has received written consent under this Directive constitutes a risk to human health or the environment, it may provisionally restrict or prohibit the use and/or sale of that product on its territory. It shall immediately inform the Commission and the other Member States of such action and give reason for its decision. 2. A decision shall be taken on the matter within three months in accordance with the procedure laid down in Art. 21".

[29] See Art. 250 EC Treaty: "1. Where, in pursuance of this Treaty, the Council acts on a proposal from the Commission, unanimity shall be required for an act constituting an amendment to that proposal".

[30] See for details of the procedure Directive 90/220, at Art. 21; that provision is largely reproduced in n. 20 *supra*.

[31] These scientific committees have been set up since the late 1960s, in order to assist the Commission in progressively building up a Community scientific opinion. In 1997, the Commission co-ordinated the different scientific committees by two decisions: Decision 97/404 [1997] OJ L169/85 and Decision 97/579 [1997] OJ L237/18.

(8) Several Member States were not in agreement with that decision, in part also because they were principally opposed to the placing on the market of genetically modified products. Thus, they invoked Article 16 of Directive 90/220,[32] argued that the safety provisions had not sufficiently been respected and prohibited the marketing of the maize that had been approved by the Commission, on their territory; nothing indicated that such measures were considered to be provisional and no new safety element was presented. France itself was doubtful whether it should definitely authorise the marketing of the genetically modified maize. As Greenpeace and other applicants tackled several French decrees in court and the Conseil d'Etat had provisionally suspended the marketing in the course of one of these judicial actions, France agreed to have the present case sent to the Court of Justice in order to obtain a preliminary ruling. This confirmed doubts about the safety of genetically modified products. The Commission, without taking a formal decision, did not take legal action under Article 226 EC Treaty against those Member States which had prohibited the marketing of the maize in question. *De facto*, thus, a moratorium was established within the Community,[33] whereby no genetically modified food product would be placed on the market before the Court of Justice had given its preliminary ruling and before the review of Directive 90/220 was finished.[34]

(9) When the Court had given its ruling in the present case, the French Conseil d'Etat was called on to decide on the substance of the case in France. In November 2000 it ruled that the procedures prior to the transmission of the dossier to the European Commission did not contain any significant irregularity and that thus the manufacturer was allowed to market his product in France.

(10) The *de facto* moratorium concerned genetically modified food products which were to be placed on the market within the Community. However, imports raised another problem. Indeed, in particular in the United States of America, the production of genetically modified maize, soya and other products is widespread. Authorisations in the USA concern in part modifications which are not authorised by the Community. As the widespread objection of European consumers to genetically modified food was well known and as the USA exports large quantities of maize and soya to the Community for agricultural and food industry use in particular, the USA refused to separate genetically modified products from products that were not genetically modified. And the omission, by the Community, completely to apply the provisions of Directive 90/220 led to the situation that genetically modified products also entered the Community—without anybody knowing with certainty in what quantities.

Controls under Directive 90/220 are, among other provisions, foreseen by Article 4(3) which reads: "Member States shall ensure that the competent authority organizes inspections and other control measures as appropriate, to ensure compliance with this Directive". The Directive authorises the marketing only of

---

[32] See the text of Art. 16 (n. 21 *supra*).
[33] See Advocate General Mischo, Opinion in the present case [2000] ECR I–1651 para. 22.
[34] As regards this review, see below para. 13 of this commentary.

those genetically modified products which have expressly been authorised. Thus, Member States are, under Article 4(3), under the obligation to examine in particular imports from the United States in order to ensure that the imports do not lead to the marketing of genetically modified products which have not been authorised by the Community.

However, Member States satisfy themselves, under Article 4(3), with random checks which make the discovery of genetically modified products dependant from hazard.[35]

(11) A systematic examination of imports from the United States would certainly slow down the shipment of products and thus affect trade. In law, however, such measures are certainly allowed. And the refusal from the United States to contribute to a smoother commercial relationship by separating non-modified and modified products considerably contributes to this situation. Anyway, the import from the United States without systematic controls leads to the present situation that genetically modified products are, via processing in the food chain, almost omnipresent in European food.

(12) This leads to the general observation that the legal provisions of Directive 90/220 do not and cannot decide in the place of politicians; whether genetically modified products shall be marketed in the Community or not is a policy decision. No labelling or other information measure will be capable of replacing this political decision. Leaving the choice to the consumer and allowing him, via labelling, to take or reject genetically modified products means *de facto* that the marketing of such products on a large scale is accepted: food in schools, canteens and restaurants, special offers, combined food such as pizzas and many other food parts simply cannot be labelled in all details. Letting the consumer decide yes or no to genetically modified food approaches hypocrisy, as the decision was taken earlier.

(13) In 1996, the Commmission published a report on the review of Directive 90/220[36] and made, in 1998, a proposal for a directive amending Directive 90/220 which was finally adopted in 2001.[37] The original Commission's idea prudently to facilitate the marketing of genetically modified products was not too strictly pursued, as public opinion was more and more opposed to biotechnology for food products altogether and more and more governments accepted that genetically modified food—in contrast to genetically modified medicine—was not a desirable technology to promote. The new directive follows, in its structure, the model of Directive 90/220, but considerably increases the precautionary and safeguard measures. It is to take effect as of 17 October 2002. Whether it will lead to a new start for biotechnology technology is not clear.

The future of biotechnology is thus as yet uncertain. However, one thing is evident: in the discussion on the introduction of this technology within the European Community, the basic principles of free circulation of goods, consumer health and

---

[35] Occasional checks of a shipload of some 100,000 tonnes of a product will normally not result in discovery of less than 1,000 of tonnes of genetically modified products.

[36] Commission, COM(96)630 of 10 December 1996.

[37] Directive 2001/18 [2001] OJ L106/1.

safety and the need to ensure a high level of environmental protection are bluntly set aside. Either there will be a political decision against biotechnology in the food area or, through non-decision, economic forces will ensure that biotechnology progressively enters the Community market. Personally, I remain convinced that neither the Community nor the world generally is in need of genetically modified food and that there is need for a political decision in this area. It would be ridiculous to leave such a decision with long and far-reaching consequences to the market which would only create new dependencies: between the strong and the weak, it is freedom which suppresses and it is regulation which makes free.[38]

28. PESTICIDES IN THE ENVIRONMENT

Judgment of the Court (Sixth Chamber) of 17 September 1998
Case C–400/96

Reference for a preliminary ruling: Criminal proceedings against Jean Harpegnies
[1998] ECR I–5121

Facts and Procedure

Jean Harpegnies is a Belgian farmer. He was accused by the Belgian authorities of having placed on the market pesticides which had not previously been approved and of having manufactured, imported or packaged such products without first being authorised for that purpose. Belgian legislation prohibits plant protection products which have not previously been approved by the minister responsible for agriculture from being marketed.[39]

Community legislation in the area of pesticides essentially consists of Directive 91/414 on plant protection products[40] and of Directive 98/8 on biocidal products.[41] Directive 98/8 had not yet been adopted when the proceedings against Mr. Harpegnies started.

The Belgian court asked the Court of Justice whether the Belgian legislation, in so far as it requires authorisation by the Belgian authorities of plant protection products marketed in another Member State, is compatible with the provisions of Article 28 (ex Article 30) EC Treaty.

---

[38] La Rochefoucauld *entre les forts et les faibles, c'est la liberté qui supprime et c'est la loi qui libère.*
[39] Royal Decree of 5 June 1975 on the storing, marketing and use of pesticides and plant protection products.
[40] Directive 91/414 concerning the placing of plant protection products on the market [1991] OJ L230/1; in its judgment, the Court of Justice calls this Directive "the Directive".
[41] Directive 98/8 concerning the placing of biocidal products on the market [1998] OJ L123/1.

Judgment (extracts)

12. . . . the national court's question seeks to ascertain, in substance, whether Article 30 of the Treaty precludes legislation of a Member State under which a plant protection product must be authorised before it is placed on the market of that State even when that product has already been authorised by the competent authorities of another State.

13. A preliminary point to be noted is that the national court has not described precisely the products covered by the question asked. It is apparent from the documents in the main proceedings that various brands of product are involved.

21. Since it is not made clear what type of product is at issue in the main proceedings, the question raised should be answered as if those proceedings were concerned with both pesticdes and biocidal products.

23. First, with regard to pesticides, to which the Directive applies, one of the principal objectives of the Directive is to lay down uniform rules governing the conditions and procedures for the authorisation of plant protection products.

24. In order to achieve that objective, the Member States are required under Article 3(1) of the Directive to ensure that plant protection products covered by the Directive are not placed on the market in their territory without first having been authorised by the competent authority . . .

25. While Article 8 of the Directive provides for transitional measures and derogations, the prior authorisation required by the Directive remains mandatory even where the pesticide in question has been authorised, in accordance with the Directive, by the competent authority of another Member State.

26. The answer to the first part of the question must therefore be that the Directive requires prior authorisation, granted pursuant to either Article 4 or Article 8, to be obtained from the competent authority of each Member State in which a pesticide covered by the Directive is placed on the market.

27. As regards biocidal products, the Directive does not apply to such products and there are no harmonised rules at Community level covering either their production or their marketing.

28. The compatibility of legislation such as that in the main proceedings must therefore be assessed by reference to Article 30 of the Treaty.

29. Under Article 30 quantitative restrictions on imports and all measures having equivalent effect are prohibited in trade between Member States. The Court has consistently held that all trading rules enacted by Member Staters which are capable of hindering, directly or indirectly, actually or potentially, intra-Community trade are to be considered as measures having an effect equivalent to quantitative restrictions (see, in particular, Case 8/74 *Procureur du Roi* v. *Dassonville* [1974] ECR 837, paragraph 5). However, Article 36 of the Treaty provides that Article 30 is not to preclude prohibitions or restrictions on imports justified, inter alia, on grounds of the protection of human health, provided that those prohibitions or

restrictions do not constitute a means of arbitrary discrimination or a disguised restricion on trade between Member States.

30. A legal provision of a Member State prohibiting biocidal products which have not been previously authorised from being marketed, acquired, offered, put on display or sale, kept, prepared, transported, sold, disposed of for valuable consideration or free of charge, imported or used, constitutes a measure having an effect equivalent to a quantitative restriction within the meaning of Article 30 of the Treaty . . .

31. It is therefore necessary to establish whether national legislation such as that in the main proceedings may be justified in the light of the derogations referred to in Article 36 of the Treaty.

32. Since biocidal products are used to combat organisms harmful to human or animal health and organisms liable to damage natural or manufactured products, they inevitably contain dangerous substances . . .

33. It is settled case-law that, in the absence of harmonising rules, it is for the Member States to decide on their intended level of protection of human health and life and on whether to require prior authorisation for the marekting of such products. . .

34. Nevertheless, the principle of proportionality which underlies the last sentence of Article 36 of the Treaty requires that the power of the Member States to prohibit imports of products from other Member States should be restricted to what is necessary to achieve the objectives of protection being legitimately pursued . . .

35. As the Court has previously held . . . , whilst a Member State is free to require a biocidal product which has already received approval in another Member State to undergo a fresh procedure of examination and approval, the authorities of the Member States are nevertheless required to assist in bringing about a relaxation of the controls existing in intra-Community trade and to take account of technical or chemical analyses or laboratory test which have already been carried out in another Member State . . .

36. The answer to the second part of the question must therefore be that national legislation which prohibits a biocidal product not previously authorised by the competent authority from being placed on the market constitutes a measure having an effect equivalent to a quantitative restriction within the meaning of Article 30 of the Treaty which is justified under Article 36 of the Treaty, even if that product has already been authorised in another Member State, provided that technical or chemical analyses or laboratory tests are not unnecessarily required when the same analyses and tests have already been carried out in that other Member State and their results are available to the competent authorities of the importing Member State or can, at their request, be made available to them.

Commentary

I. The Authorisation of Pesticides in EC Law

(1) Pesticides in Community terminology are subdivided into agricultural (plant protection products) and non-agricultural (biocidal products) pesticides. About 20,000 agricultural pesticides with some 700 active substances are thought to be used within the Community. As the Court of Justice did not know exactly whether the pesticides found with Mr. Harpegnies were agricultural pesticides or biocidal products, it decided to examine the legal situation alternatively.

Directive 91/414 on plant protection products was proposed by the Commission in 1976 and, based on Article 37 (ex Article 43) EC Treaty, adopted by the Council in 1991. It regulates the placing on the market of plant protection products. The Directive differentiates between plant protection products which have to be authorised by the individual Member States and the active substances for such products which are authorised by the Community. A plant protection product may be authorised to be placed on the market only if it contains an active substance that is listed in Directive 91/414 and is thus authorised Community-wide; extensive transition periods ensure that the product may continue to be marketed, even where Community authorisation of the active substance is not yet finished.

(2) The authorisation of a plant protection product is valid for the Member State for which it was requested.[42] However, Article 10 provides that Member States are also obliged to authorise a pesticide that was authorised in another Member State on their own territory, provided the "relevant agricultural, plant health and and environmental (including cimatic) conditions" are comparable in the regions concerned. The applicant has to demonstrate this comparability.

The legal situation as fixed by Directive 91/414 was thus so clear that the Court of Justice could be rather short (paragraph 25); and the only surprise is that the Court did not expressly mention Article 10, where it is specifically mentioned that a plant protection product which is authorised in one Member State nevertheless needs an authorisation in other Member States.

(3) The Court then examined whether the result would be different if the pesticide in question had been a biocidal product. At the time of the case, Directive 98/8 was not yet in force so that this examination had to be made under the provisions of Articles 28 and 30 EC Treaty.

(4) For biocidal products, the Court had already had to decide a similar case.[43] In that case, Mrs. Brandsma, the head of a supermarket in Belgium, was charged by the Belgian authorities with having sold a biocidal product that had been authorised

---

[42] Directive 91/414 (n. 40 *supra*), Art. 3: "1. Member States shall prescribe that plant protection products may not be placed on the market and used in their territory unless they have authorised the product in accordance with this Directive".

[43] Court of Justice, Case C–293/94, *Brandsma* [1996] ECR I–3159.

in the Netherlands, but not in Belgium; the Court was asked whether Belgium was entitled to make the marketing of that biocide in Belgium dependant on an authorisation by the Belgian authorities, to which the Court answered in the positive.[44]

(5) In the present case, the Court first referred to the famous "*Dassonville* formula" which had been established in 1974 and which stipulates that any national measure which is capable of hindering "directly or indirectly, actually or potentially, intra-Community trade" must be considered as incompatible with Article 28 EC Treaty.[45] This formula has been, and still is, extensively used in the discussions between Community insitutions and the Member State, whether there is use or abuse of powers in favour of the free circulation of goods. And when questions came up whether national measures which aim at the protection of the environment where justified under Article 28 EC Treaty, the Commission frequently referred to the *Dassonville* formula in order to argue that such measures were not legal.

(6) In its environmental jurisprudence, the Court of Justice was much more reserved. In the first case, where it had to assess the compatibility of a national measure in favour of the environment, Case C–302/86, the *Danish Bottles* case,[46] it used another string of arguments. The Court had developed, in a judgment of 1979, the so-called "*Cassis-de-Dijon*" doctrine, which stated that in the absence of Community rules relating to the marketing of of products, obstacles to free movement within the Community resulting from disparities between the national laws must be accepted in so far as such rules, applicable to domestic and imported products without distinction, may be recognised as being necessary in order to satisfy mandatory requirements recognised by Communty law, where such rules were proportionate to the aim in view.[47] The Court did not refer to the *Dassonville* formula, but used the *Cassis-de-Dijon* formula to state that "the protection of the environment is a mandatory requirement which may limit the application" of Article 28 EC Treaty.[48]

(7) Since then, the Court has referred, in environmental cases, to the *Dassonville* formula at its discretion, but not systematically. In the present case, the Court used that formula and then examined whether there was a justification under Article 30 (ex Article 36) EC Treaty. This was possible, since the justification for such a measure was related to health and safety of humans, animals or plants, items that were expressly mentioned in Article 30. But it would have clearly been more difficult to use these grounds, if the national measure had consisted in something other than the protection of health and safety.

(8) Anyway, the Court did not go into theoretical considerations. It first stated that it was for Member States to decide which degree of protection of humans or

---

[44] This jurisdiction is in line with earlier judgments of the Court, see Cases 94/83, *Heijn* [1984] ECR 3263; 125/88, *Nijman* [1989] ECR 3533.

[45] Court of Justice, Case 8/74, *Dassonville* [1974] ECR 837, para. 5.

[46] Court of Justice, Case 302/86, *Commission* v. *Denmark* [1988] ECR 4607,

[47] Court of Justice, Case 120/78, *Rewe* v. *Bundesmonopolverwaltung* [1979] ECR 649.

[48] Court of Justice, Case 302/86 (n. 46 *supra*), para. 9.

the environment they wanted to fix at national level. This clarifies that, for instance, instead of providing for an obligation for a biocidal product to be authorised, Member States could also provide for a total prohibition or—in the opposite—only for some labelling requirements. The proportionality principle does not interfere in this question, as otherwise it would never be possible for a Member State to prohibit the marketing of a product.

(9) It is only when a Member State decides to subject a biocidal product to an authorisation procedure that the subsequent considerations of the Court of Justice apply: the Member State is fully entitled to require a second authorisation of the product, even where it has already been authorised by another Member State.

Member States are thus hardly restricted in their action. However, in view of the proportionality principle, they will have to avoid the repetition of chemical analyses or laboratory tests which were made in another Member State—to the extent, of course, that the conditions in that other Member State are more or less equivalent. This requirement was first laid down by the Court in 1981.[49] It has since been introduced, in a slightly modified version, into Article 10 of Directive 91/414[50] which deals with the mutual recognition of authorisations of plant protection products that were authorised in another Member State, and in a somehow modified form in Article 13 of Directive 98/8.[51]

(10) This Directive will in future be applicable to biocidal products, of which some 15,000 are thought to exist on the Community market. The structure of Directive 98/8 is very similar to that of Directive 91/414. Active substances are authorised by the Community and will be inserted into a positive list which will form part of Directive 98/8. The different Member States will remain responsible for authorising biocides, on the basis of common principles which are laid down in Directive 98/8. A recognition of authorisations pronounced in another Member State is foreseen.[52]

In the present case, therefore, it did not really matter whether there was Community legislation—as in the case of plant protection products Directive 91/414—or not (yet)—as in the case of biocidal products, in view of the nature of the rights of Member States; in both cases Belgium was entitled to require an authorisation for the pesticide and to prohibit the marketing or use of any pesticide that had not had such an authorisation.

---

[49] Court of Justice, Case 272/80, *Biologische Producten* [1981] ECR 3277.

[50] Directive 91/414 (n. 40 *supra*), Art. 10: "1. At the request of the applicant . . . a Member State to which an application is made for the authorization of a plant protection product already authorized in another Member State must:—refrain from requiring the repetition of tests and analyses already carried out in connection with the authorization of the product in that Member State . . . and—. . . also authorize the placing of that product on the market in its territory . . .".

[51] Directive 98/8 (n. 41 *supra*).

[52] Directive 98/8 (n. 41 *supra*): Art. 4: "1. . . . a biocidal product that has already been authorised or registered in one Member State shall be authorised or registered in another Member State within 120 days, or 60 days respectively, of an application being received by the other Member State, provided that the active substance of the biocidal product is included in Annex I or IA and conforms to the requirements thereof . . .".

II. Maintaining or Introducing more Protective National Measures

(11) This result is specific to the present case. Different provisions of the EC Treaty contain rules that lead to different possibilities for Member States to maintain or introduce environmental provisions at national level; of course, this applies in particular in those areas where Community legislation has been adopted. The two main provisions in this relation are, on the one hand, Article 176 EC Treaty[53] and, on the other hand, Article 95(4) to (9) EC Treaty.[54]

(12) Article 176 EC Treaty allows Member States to maintain or introduce more protective national measures when a Community provision was based on Article 175 EC Treaty. The national more protective measures must be compatible with the EC Treaty; and as all Community directives and regulations are based on the EC Treaty, the national measures must, of course, also be compatible with secondary Community law.

Of particular importance as regards the compatibility requirement are, of course, Articles 28 and 30 EC Treaty, in the form which these Treaty provisions have received through the jurisprudence of the Court of Justice. In any case, the national measures may not constitute a means of arbitrary discrimination or a disguised restriction on trade between Member States and may not be disproportionate to the aim which is pursued. As mentioned in the present case (paragraph 33), though, Member States have a considerable amount of discretion under Articles 28 and 30 to decide on the level of protection which they wish to ensure; and this discretion also applies where a national measure is examined as to whether it is compatible with Article 176 EC Treaty.

Up to now, the Court has only in one case given an interpretation of Article 176 EC Treaty, and this even in an *obiter dictum*. This case is discussed elewhere in this book.[55]

---

[53] Art. 176 EC Treaty: "The protective measures adopted pursuant to Art. 175 shall not prevent any Member State from maintaining or introducing more stringent protective measures. Such measures must be compatible with this Treaty. They shall be notified to the Commission".

[54] Art. 95 EC Treaty: ". . . (4) If, after the adoption by the Council or by the Commission of a harmonisation measure, a Member State deems it necessary to maintain national provisions on ground of major needs referred to in Art. 30, or relating to the protection of the environment or the working environment, it shall notify the Commission of these provisions as well as the grounds for maintaining them. (5) Moreover, without prejudice to para. 4, if, after the adoption by the Council or by the Commission of a harmonisation measure, a Member State deems it necessary to introduce national provisions based on new scientific evidence relating to the protection of the environment or the working environment, on grounds of a problem specific to that Member State arising after the adoption of the harmonisation measure, it shall notify the Commission of the nevisaged provisions as well as the grounds for introducing them. (6) The Commission shall, within six months of the notifications as referred to in paras. 4 and 5, approve or reject the national provisions involved after having verified whether or not they are a means of arbitrary discrimination or a disguised restriction on trade between Member States and whether or not they shall constitute an obstacle to the functioning of the internal market".

[55] Court of Justice, Case C–203/96, *Dusseldorp* [1998] ECR I–4075; see for a discussion of this case p. 22 *supra*.

(13) Compared to Article 176 EC Treaty, the possibility for a Member State to maintain or introduce more protective national legislation is very considerably reduced where the Community measure is based on Article 95 EC Treaty. Indeed, Article 95(4) to (6) lays down the following conditions:

Maintaining national legislation	*Introducing national legislation*
—to satisfy one of the major needs of Article 30, or the protection of the environment or the working environment	—necessity to introduce a measure related to the protection of the environment or the working environment
—no arbitrary discrimination	—new scientific evidence
—no disguised restriction on trade	—a problem specific to the acting Member State
—no obstacle to the functioning of the internal market.	—problem arose after the adoption of the harmonising measure
	—no arbitrary discrimination
	—no disguised restriction of trade
	—no obstacle to the functioning of the internal market.

(14) The possibility of introducing more protective national measures even in cases where the Community harmonising measure was based on Article 95 EC Treaty was introduced by the Treaty of Amsterdam which entered into effect on 1 May 1999. There is no Court judgment yet on this issue. And it is submitted that the conditions for such national measures are so severe that there will hardly ever be cases of this kind.[56]

The Commission was confronted with a number of requests for introducing more protective national legislation. Until the end of the year 2000, all such applications were rejected. In one case, the affected Member States applied to the Court; this case has not yet been decided.[57]

(15) Even the possibility of maintaining more protective national legislation in the case where the Community legislation had been based on Article 95 is more of a theoretical than of a practical nature. Since the introduction of that provision, very few cases have ever become relevant, and in no case had the Court of Justice brought out a judgment which discussed in detail the compatibility of a national legislation with Article 95(4). The first case where the Court did discuss Article 95(4) (ex Article 100a(4)) EC Treaty was a case where the Commission had not adequately justified its decision to allow the national legislation to be maintained;[58] this case and questions around Article 95(4) to (8) are discussed elsewhere in this book.[59]

---

[56] See also H Sevenster, "The environmental guarantee after Amsterdam: does the emperor have new clothes?" (2000) 1 *Yearbook of European Environmental Law* 291 *et seq.*

[57] Cases C–512/99, *Germany* v. *Commission,* concerning Commission Decision 99/836 [1999] OJ L68/32.

[58] Court of Justice, Case C–41/93, *France* v. *Commission* [1994] ECR I–1829. This case is discussed in detail on p. 33 *supra.*

[59] See p. 33 *supra.*

Also the second case did not require a substantive discussion of Article 95(4) EC Treaty by the Court:[60] Sweden had applied to be allowed to maintain its national legislation under Article 95(4); however, at the moment when the legislation in question became relevant under Swedish law, the Commission had not yet decided on this request. The Court held that Member States were allowed to continue to apply their national legislation only after having received a corresponding Commission decision.[61]

(16) It is likely that the question of Member States' rights under Article 95 EC Treaty will become more important in future, as a possible enlargement of the Community will make Community-wide agreements on restrictions of use of substances or products at a high level of environmental protection less easy.

Where Community legislation is based on provisions other than Article 175 or 95 EC Treaty, there is no possibility for Member States to maintain or introduce more protective environmental measures. An analogous application of these provisions via the "integration" provision of Article 6 EC Treaty[62] is not possible, for the reason that it would not be possible to decide whether Article 95(4) to (9) or 176 EC Treaty should apply.

(17) The question of Member States' rights under Articles 175/176 EC Treaty on the one hand, under Article 95 EC Treaty on the other hand, is of considerable practical importance. In 1997, the Commission proposed a directive on end of life vehicles, which the Council adopted in 2000.[63] This Directive was based on Article 175 EC Treaty, though it contains provisions which provide for a ban on certain heavy metals—cadmium, lead, mercury, chromium VI—in the manufacture of new cars. When the Commission submitted, in 2000, a proposal for a directive on end of life electrical and electronic products,[64] it decided to split the proposal into two and to base those parts which dealt with the prohibition of certain heavy metals and other substances on Article 95 EC Treaty. The principal reason for this split was that the Commission did not want Member States, once the proposal adopted, to maintain or introduce more protective environmental measures under the conditions of Article 176 EC Treaty. The Commission was afraid that such a possibility would lead to difficulties for the free circulation of electrical and electronic products, as Member States might be tempted to set new environmental conditions for the production of such goods. The Council and the European Parliament have not yet decided whether they will adopt two directives on such products or

---

[60] Court of Justice, Case C–319/97, *Kortas* [1999] ECR I–3143.

[61] See now, however, Art. 95(6) EC Treaty, introduced by the Treaty of Amsterdam with effect from 1 May 1999: if the Commission has not taken a decision within six months, "the national provisions . . . shall be deemed to have been approved".

[62] Art. 6 EC Treaty: "Environmental protection requirements must be integrated into the definition and implementation of the Community policies and activities referred to in Art. 3, in particular with a view to promoting sustainable development".

[63] Directive 2000/53 on end of life vehicles [2000] OJ L269/34.

[64] Commission proposal for a directive on waste electrical and electronic equipment; proposal for a directive on the restriction of the use of certain hazardous substances in electrical and electronic equipment, COM(2000)347 of 13 June 2000.

whether they will merge the two texts—which then would lead to the application of Article 175 EC Treaty.[65]

29. ECO-LABELS ON PRODUCTS

Judgment of the Court (Fifth Chamber) of 20 March 1997
Case C–13/96

Reference for a preliminary ruling in the proceedings between
Bic Benelux SA and Belgian State
[1997] ECR I–1753

Facts and Procedure

When Belgium, in the early 1990s, reformed its constitutional structure and established a federal system, the government of that time needed, in order to obtain the necessary majority for the constitutional changes, the support of the Belgian environmental political party. However, that party requested, as compensation, the introduction of environmental taxes in Belgium, which were thus provided for in 1993.[66] Environmental taxes[67] were in particular introduced for drink packages, batteries, pesticides, papers and certain disposable articles,[68] and also disposable razors. The legislation required that those articles for which an environmental tax

---

[65] See for a detailed discussion of these legal questions M Onida, "Challenges and Opportunities in EC Waste Management: Perspectives on the Problem of End of Life Vehicles" (2000) 1 *Yearbook of European Environmental Law* 253 *et seq.*

[66] *Loi du 16 juillet 1993 visant à achever la structure fédérale de l'Etat* [1993] Moniteur belge 17013.

[67] Art. 369 of the Law of 16 July 1993 (n. 66 *supra*): "*Pour l'application de la présente loi, on entend par: 1° écotaxe: taxe assimilée aux accises, frappant un produit mis à la consommation, en raison des nuisances écologiques qu'il est réputé générer . . .*" (For the application of the present law, environmental tax shall mean: a tax assimilated to excise duty, applicable to a product which has been released on to the market, on account of the environmental impairment which that product is deemed to generate; the judgment translated, in paras. 3 and 26 and in the tenor, "nuisance" with "damage").

[68] Art. 369 of the Law of 16 July 1993 (n. 66 *supra*): "*7° objet jetable: objet conçu pour une utilisation unique ou pour une série limitée d'utilisations et qui perd sa valeur d'usage, soit après une utilisation unique, soit après une série limitée d'utilisations, soit parce qu'un de ses éléments est usé, vidé ou déchargé, et qu'il ne peut être, selon le cas, soit remplacé, soit rempli, soit rechargé*" (article designed to be used either once or a limited number of times and which loses its usefulness either after being used once or a limited number of times, or because one of its essential parts has been used, destined or exhausted and cannot be replaced, refilled or recharged).

had to be paid had to be marked with a distinctive sign.[69] A ministerial order laid down details for the distinctive sign.[70]

Bic Benelux SA, which marketed disposable razors in Belgium, began legal action against the Belgian provisions on environmental taxes. It was of the opinion that the ministerial order was not valid as it had not been, prior to its adoption by Belgium, notified to the European Commission in accordance with the requirements of Community legislation. Bic was of the opinion that the Belgian measures should have been notified to the Commission under Directive 83/189,[71] as that Directive was applicable to the kind of marks specified by the Belgian legislation. That Directive requires all national technical regulation which consists of technical specifications,[72] to be sent, in draft form, to the Commission. This notification triggers a Community procedure during which the national measure is examined with regard to the question whether it creates obstacles to the free circulation of goods within the Community.

The Belgian Conseil d'Etat decided to stay proceedings and to ask the Court of Justice, whether Directive 83/189 was applicable to the Belgian legislation in question.

Judgment (extracts)

14./15. The Conseil d'Etat . . . decided to . . . submit the . . . question to the Court . . . whether an obligation to affix specific distinctive signs to products which are subject to a tax levied on them on account of the environmental damage which they are deemed to cause, such as that laid down in . . . the Ministerial Order, constitutes a technical specification within the meaning of Directive 83/189 and whether the national enactment introducing it is a technical regulation within the meaning of the same Directive.

[69] Art. 391 of the Law of 16 July 1993 (n. 66 *supra*): "To ensure that the collection of environmental tax is monitored and consumers are informed, all containers or products subject to one of the environmental taxes provided for by this Law must be clearly marked by a distinctive sign indicating either that environmental tax is payable and the amount of such tax . . .".

[70] *Arrêté ministériel* of 24 December 1993 *relatif au régime des produits soumis à l'écotaxe* [1993] Moniteur belge 28903.

[71] Directive 83/189 laying down a procedure for the provision of information in the field of technical standards and regulations [1983] OJ L109/8; amended by Directive 88/182 [1988] OJ L81/75 and by Directive 94/10 [1994] OJ L100/30. In 1998, thus after the present judgment was delivered, the Directive was consolidated by Directive 98/34 [1988] OJ L204/37. This last Directive was then amended by Directive 98/48 [1998] OJ L217/18.

[72] Directive 83/189 (in the version applicable at the time of the judgment), Art. 1: "1. Technical specification: a specification contained in a document which lays down the characteristics required of a product such as levels of quality, performance, safety or dimensions, including the requirements applicable to the product as regards terminology, symbols, testing and test methods, packaging, marking or labelling, and the production methods and procedures . . . 5. Technical regulation: technical specifications, including the relevant administrative provisions, the observance of which is compulsory, de jure or *de facto*, in the case of marketing or use in a Member State or a major part thereof, except those laid down by local authorities".

19. . . . There is no basis in Directive 83/189 for an interpretation limiting its application to national measures capable of harmonization only on the basis of Article 100a of the Treaty. The aim of that Directive is, by preventive monitoring, to protect the free movement of goods, which is one of the foundations of the Community. Such monitoring is necessary since technical regulations covered by the Directive are capable of hindering, directly or indirectly, actually or potentially, intra-Community trade in goods. Such hindrances may arise from the adoption of national technical regulations even if those regulations do not duplicate markings affixed in the Member State of origin and irrespective of the grounds on which they were adopted.

20. Consequently, the fact that a national measure was adopted in order to protect the environment or that it does not implement a technical standards which may itself constitute a barrier to free movement does not mean that the measure in question cannot be a technical regulation within the meaning of Directive 83/189.

21. Nor are the definition of "other requirement" introduced by Directive 94/10, and the reference therein to protecting the environment, of any relevance as regards the meaning to be given to "technical specification", since the new provision concerns only requirements other than technical specifications.

22. In the Commission's submission, the mandatory marking of products subject to environmental tax, which is intended to ensure that the collection of environmental tax is monitored, must be regarded as a fiscal accompanying measure, and thus as a fiscal measure comparable to national provisions requiring tax strips to be affixed to products subject to excise duty. The Commission submits that, in the absence of any express provision, Directive 83/189, which was applicable at the material time, cannot be applied to fiscal measures . . .

23. . . . first, the marking requirement in issue in the main proceedings constitutes, according to the definition given in Article 1(5) of Directive 83/189, a *de jure* technical regulation in that its "observance . . . is compulsory . . . in the case of marketing" of the product concerned and that it is, according to the definition given in Article 1(1), a technical specification, since the enactment defines "the characteristics required of a product such as . . . the requirements applicable to the product as regards . . . marking or labelling".

24. Second, the marking in issue is intended to inform the public of, *inter alia*, the effects of the products on the environment, and the Belgian Government has confirmed the importance to be attached to that aspect of the rules governing marking. The aim of the tax, which is to protect the environment, is thus reinforced by the marking, which, like other environmental labelling, whether linked to an environmental tax or not, reminds consumers of the harmful effects of the products in question on the environment.

25. Since the marking requirement in issue can in no way be regarded as exclusively a fiscal accompanying measure, it does not therefore constitute a requirement linked to a fiscal measure . . .

26. Consequently, the answer to be given is that an obligation to affix specific distinctive signs to products which are subject to a tax levied on them on account of the environmental damage which they are deemed to cause, such as that laid down in Articles 11 and 18 of the Ministerial Order, constitutes a technical specification within the meaning of Directive 83/189, and the national enactment introducing it is a technical regulation within the meaning of the same Directive.

Commentary

I. Fiscal Marks on Products

(1) Reading this judgment, one wonders perhaps where the relevant point is; at first glance, it may be quite irrelevant for the environment whether the distinctive sign which Belgian legislation imposed on products for which an environmental tax had to be paid comes under Directive 98/34 (ex Directive 83/189)[73] or not. The effect of the judgment becomes obvious only if the content of Directive 98/34 (ex Directive 83/189)[74] itself and the Court's interpretation of this Directive are taken into consideration. Directive 98/34 requests Member States to notify, in draft form, all technical regulations which practically includes all product- or process-related environmental provisions.[75]

(2) In a judgment of 1996, the Court found that a breach of the obligation to notify renders the technical regulations inapplicable so that they may not be

---

[73] Directive 98/34 (n. 71 *supra*).

[74] For the sake of simplicity, this commentary will refer only to Directive 98/34, even though, at the time of judgment, Directive 83/189 and not 98/34 was of application.

[75] See, as regards the notion of "technical regulation", n. 72 *supra*; the notion has since been fine-tuned: under Directive 98/34 (Art. 1(9)) it reads as follows: " 'technical regulation', technical specifications and other requirements, including the relevant administrative provisions, the observance of which is compulsory, de jure or *de facto*, in the case of marketing or use in a Member State or a major part thereof, as well as laws, regulations or administrative provisions of Member States . . . prohibiting the manufacture, importation, marketing or use of a product".

De facto technical regulations include:—laws, regulations or administrative provisions of a Member State which refer either to technical specifications or other requirements or to professional codes or codes of practice which in turn refer to technical specifications or other requirements and compliance with which confers a presumption of conformity with the obligations imposed by the aforementioned laws, regulations or administrative provisions,—voluntary agreements to which a public authority is a contracting party and which provide, in the public interest, for compliance with technical specifications or other requirements, excluding public procurement tender specifications,—technical specifications or other requirements which are linked to fiscal or financial measures affecting the consumption of products by encouraging compliance with such technical specifications or other requirements; technical specifications or other requirements linked to national social-security systems are not included".

See also Art. 1(2) and (3): " 'technical specification', a specification contained in a document which lays down the characteristics required of a product such as levels of quality, performance, safety or dimensions, including the requirements applicable to the product as regards the name under which the product is sold, terminology, symbols, testing and test methods, packaging, marking or labelling and conformity assessment procedures . . .

'other requirements', a requirement, other than a technical specification, imposed on a product for the purposes of protecting, in particular, consumers or the environment, and which affects its life cycle after it has been placed on the market, such as conditions of use, recycling, reuse or disposal, where such conditions can significantly influence the composition or nature of the product or its marketing".

enforced against individuals.[76] The Court based this conclusion on the fact that Articles 8 and 9 of Directive 98/34 are precise and unconditional[77] and must therefore be interpreted as meaning that individuals may rely on them before national courts.[78] The Court compared the procedure established by Directive 98/34 (ex Directive 83/189) with a simple information procedure—such as the procedure under Directive 75/442[79]—and underlined that the aim of Directive 98/34 was not simply to inform the Commission, but to eliminate or restrict obstacles to trade, to inform other Member States of technical regulations envisaged by a State, by way of introducing a standstill period following the notification to give the Commission and other Member States time to react and to propose amendments for lessening restrictions to the free movement of goods arising from the envisaged measure, and to grant the Commission time to propose a harmonising directive. The Court concluded that breach of the obligation to notify constituted a substantial procedural defect with the effect that the technical regulations in question were inapplicable to individuals. Where an individual correctly relies on the breach of such an obligation before a national court, that court must decline to apply a national technical regulation which has not been notified.

(3) This judgment had very considerable effects. Thus, the Dutch government identified some 330 regulations which had been adopted in the Netherlands without having been notified to the Commission and on which sanctions, fines, administrative sanctions could now no longer be based, as the regulations were inapplicable.[80] And it may well be that even at present a number of environmental provisions of Member States which have not been notified under Directive 98/34, are in fact not either enforceable by the national authorities.

(4) In the present case, the validity of the Belgian environmental tax provisions depended thus on the question whether they constituted a technical provision in the sense of Directive 98/34 or not. The Court was of the opinion that the measure was a technical provision in the sense of Directive 98/34 and I agree with this conclusion. Indeed, what the provisions do is to divide products into those which carry the mark (sign, label) "environmentally taxed" and those which do not carry

---

[76] Court of Justice, Case C–194/94, *CIA Security International SA* v. *Signalson* [1996] ECR I–2201.

[77] Directive 98/34 (n. 71 *supra*), Art. 8: "... Member States shall immediately communicate to the Commission any draft technical regulation ... ;they shall also let the Commission have a statement of the grounds which make the enactment of such a technical regulation necessary, where these have not already been made clear in the draft ...".

Art. 9: "1. Member States shall postpone the adoption of a draft technical regulation for three months from the date of receipt by the Commission of the communication referred to in Art. 8(1) ...".

[78] See on this direct effect doctrine p. 42 *supra*.

[79] Directive 75/442 on waste [1975] OJ L194/47, as amended by Directive 91/156 [1991] OJ L78/32, Art. 3(2): "Except where Council Directive 83/189/EEC of 28 March 1983 laying down a procedure for the provisions of information in the field of technical standards and regulations applies, Member States shall inform the Commission of any measures they intend to take to achieve the aims set out in para. 1. The Commission shall inform the other Member States and the committee referred to in Art. 18 of such measures"; as regards the interpretation of this provision (direct effect declined) see Court of Justice, Case 380/87, *Cinisello Balsamo* [1989] ECR 2491.

[80] See Commission, The operation of Directive 98/34 from 1995 to 1998, COM(2000) 429 of 7 July 2000, para. 97.

this mark. The mark is intended to inform consumers–buyers–users that the product which bears such a mark is environmentally less friendly than others. In this way the use and consumption of products without a mark will be favoured as it is hoped that the mark will help to make a reflected choice between the different products on the market. The mark is also necessary to convey the message about environmental performance to the consumer; the price of a product alone would not be informative enough, as on the one hand, for instance, no real price comparison between disposable razors and other razors can be made, and on the other hand the manufacturer might counterbalance the price effect of the environmental tax by reducing his own profit, so that the price which would be visible for the consumer would not show any difference from the situation before the introduction of the environmental tax.

(5) This different effect on products distinguishes the Belgian provision for example from the fiscal sign which is to be found on cigarette packs: all cigarette packs bear this mark and cigarettes which are bad or less bad for human health are not differentiated. In contrast to that, the Belgian measure expressly aims at selecting products which cause environmental impairment, taxing them and obliging them to bear a mark which makes the environmental tax visible to everybody, conveying in practice the information that the product impairs the environment. There is thus a clear intention to inform consumers and to induce them to change their behaviour by buying products which are environmentally more friendly (and are thus not taxed).

II. Eco-labelling at National and Community Level

(6) The fact that the Belgian provisions come under the procedural requirements of Directive 98/34 does not mean that they could not be introduced into Belgian law. Belgium would be obliged only to respect the procedure of that Directive: notify the provisions in draft form to the Commission and wait for the end of the standstill period. Whether these provisions are compatible with Community law depends on the EC Treaty and on secondary legislation. As regards the EC Treaty, it must be noted that the provisions of harmonising tax provisions are laid down in Articles 90 to 93, and not in Articles 28 to 30 EC Treaty: the very fact that there is a special chapter on tax provisions in the EC Treaty means that these provisions are *leges speciales* to the provisions on the free circulation of goods. This is often argued about or forgotten, in particular by legal writers who are close to vested interests, but is confirmed by the Court of Justice.[81]

---

[81] Court of Justice, Cases 74/76, *Iannelli and Volpi* [1977] ECR 557; C–78–83/90, *Compagnie Commerciale de l'Ouest* [1992] ECR I–1847.

(7) At present, there is no Community harmonisation of environmental taxes under Article 93[82] or Article 175(2)[83] EC Treaty. The Commission made, in 1991, a proposal for a directive on the Community-wide introduction of a combined CO_2 energy tax.[84] The proposal was based on Articles 93 and 175(1) EC Treaty, which both required, at that time, unanimous decisions in Council. This unanimity could not be reached since a number of Member States, in particular United Kingdom, opposed for fundamental reasons the fixing of taxes and charges at Community level. The Commission therefore amended its proposal in the sense that Member States remained free to decide whether they wanted to introduce a CO_2 energy tax; where they so decided, they were asked to comply with certain conditions fixed in the proposal.[85] By the end of 2001, this proposal had not yet been adopted and seems to be no longer relevant.

(8) Therefore, as regards the Belgian measure, Article 90 EC Treaty is the relevant provision. The essential difference between Articles 90[86] and 28 EC Treaty is that Article 90 prohibits national measures which are discriminating, whereas Article 28 prohibits discriminating or disproportionate measures.[87] In view of that it is not surprising that even the Commission tries to bring as many national provisions as possible under Article 28 instead of Article 90.[88] As Belgium is free to introduce taxes on whatever product or process it wants, the introduction of an environmental tax is compatible with Community law, as there is not the slightest sign of any direct or indirect discrimination of products from other Member States.

(9) This also applies to the distinctive mark which was introduced on disposable razors. The Court seems to consider this mark as having to be examined under Article 28 EC Treaty, as it alludes, in paragraph 19 of the judgment, to the *Dassonville* formula which is the formula for examining the compatibility of

---

[82] Art. 93 EC Treaty: "The Council shall, acting unanimously on a proposal from the Commission and after consulting the European Parliament and the Economic and Social Committee, adopt provisions for the harmonisation of legislation concerning turnover taxes, excise duties and other forms of indirect taxation to the extent that such harmonisation is necessary to ensure the establishment and the functioning of the internal market . . .".

[83] Art. 175(2) EC Treaty: ". . . the Council, acting unanimously on a proposal from the Commission and after consulting the european Parliament, the Economic and Social Committee and the Committee of the Regions, shall adopt:—provisions primarily of a fiscal nature; . . .".

[84] [1992] OJ C196/1.

[85] Commission, COM(95)172 of 10 May 1995.

[86] Art. 90 EC Treaty: "No Member State shall impose, directly or indirectly, on the products of other Member States any internal taxation of any kind in excess of that imposed directly or indirectly on similar domestic products.

Furthermore, no Member State shall impose on the products of other Member States any internal taxation of such a nature as to afford indirect protection to other products".

[87] The prohibition of discriminating or disproportionate measures under Art. 28 (and 30) EC Treaty does not follow from Art. 28 EC Treaty itself, but has been developed by the Court of Justice, in particular on the basis of Art. 30(2) EC Treaty which reads: ". . . [national] prohibitions or restrictions shall not, however, constitute a means of arbitrary discrimination or a disguised restriction on trade between Member States".

[88] See Commission, Communication on environmental taxes and charges in the Single Market, COM(97)9 of 26 March 1997.

national measures with Article 28 EC Treaty.[89] However, again it must remain the responsibility of Belgium whether it wishes to inform its citizens of the different environmental impact of the products which are on the Belgian market. It seems clear that individuals are more easily oriented to buying environmentally friendly products, if they are informed—be it by means of a mark—which these environmentally products are. In my opinion thus, the strengthening of the environmental tax effects by the introduction of a mark is neither discriminating nor disproportionate and therefore—once the procedural provisions of Directive 98/34 have been respected—legal.

(10) The Community has introduced quite a number of eco-marks and eco-labels, without having developed, though, a coherent system for environmental labelling. A labelling award scheme of 1992,[90] which provided for the voluntary participation of producers and introduced a flower as an eco-logo, was reviewed in 2000;[91] until the end of 2000, only about 250 products had been awarded this label. This limited success may also be due to the co-existence of the Community and national eco-labels.

Regulation 2092/91 introduced the notion "organic" for agricultural products that stem from organic farming.[92] Dangerous chemical substances and preparations must bear symbols which characterise the substance or preparation as "toxic", "dangerous" etc., or as "dangerous for the environment".[93] Directive 91/157 introduces a label for the separate collection of batteries.[94] For electrical household appliances a mandatory environmental label was introduced which indicates the energy and water consumption, the performance and the noise level.[95] Overall, it is difficult to assess to what extent such labels really managed to influence consumer behaviour.

III. The Notification Directive 98/34

(11) As regards Directive 98/34, it has already been mentioned that it has a very wide field of application; it therefore has *de facto* replaced an informal standstill agreement in environmental matters which was agreed in 1973 in the form of a gentlemen's agreement;[96] the Commission's announced intention in 1987 to

---

[89] See the text of this formula on p. 243 *supra*.

[90] Regulation 880/92 on an eco-label award scheme [1992] OJ L99/1.

[91] Regulation 1980/2000 [2000] OJ L237/1.

[92] Regulation 2092/91 on organic production of agricultural products and indications referring thereto on agricultural products and foodstuffs [1991] OJ L198/1.

[93] Directive 67/548 [1967] OJ L196/1 as subsequently amended (chemical substances); Directive 99/45 [1999] OJ L200/1 (chemical preparations).

[94] Directive 91/157 on batteries and accumulators containing dangerous substances [1991] OJ L78/38.

[95] Directive 92/75 on the conservation of energy and other resources by household appliances [1992] OJ L297/15, and subsequent individual directives.

[96] Agreement of the representatives of the Governments of the Member States meeting in Council on information for the Commission and for the Member States with a view to possible harmonisation throughout the Communities of urgent measures concerning the protection of the environment [1973] OJ C9/1.

draft legislation on a standstill agreement in environmental matters[97] was never realised.

(12) The amount of draft legislation received by Member States under Directive 98/34 is very high: it was 439 in 1995, 523 in 1996, 900 in 1997 and 604 in 1998.[98] As regards industrial standardisation, the situation is even more expressive, as the following table shows; it reflects the number of new standardisation activities started each year at national level, at European and international level.[99]

New standardisation activities started each year

Year	National activities	European activities	International activities	Total
1991	2193	5887	2130	10210
1992	2286	5014	3252	10552
1993	2128	2466	1860	6454
1994	1630	1985	1454	5069
1995	1913	2091	1190	5194
1996	1593	1643	1223	4459
1997	1427	2270	1116	4813
1998	1546	1684	958	4188
Total	14716	23040	13183	50939

This means in clear terms that more than 70 per cent of all industrial standardisation of these years was made at European or international level. Since industrial standards are practically written by economic operators, the figures show that these economic operators clearly go towards the larger rather than the national market, to a great extent even for globalisation. Compared to that activity, the combined national and Community legislation is very small. These figures clearly demonstrate that the argument of excessive quantities of EC legislation—be it general or be it environmentally orientated legislation—is a myth, and one might speculate whether this is not a deliberately launched myth in order to promote further legislative deregulation.

(13) The sectors concerned by national legislative initiatives are telecommunications (17.3 per cent); agriculture and foodstuffs (17.2 per cent), mechanical engineering (16.6 per cent), transport (16.1 per cent) and building and construction (12.1 per cent). The number of notification in the sector "environment—packaging" was 155, which is about 6.2 per cent of all notifications. The

---

[97] Fourth environmental action programme [1987] OJ C328/1, para. 2.1.7.

[98] Commission (n. 80 *supra*), para. 6.19.

[99] Commission (n. 80 *supra*), para. 6.1. It should be noted that CEN (Comité Européen de Normalisation) and CENELEC (Comité Européen de Normalisation Electrotechnique) goes slightly beyond the membership of EC Member States; furthermore, the Commission points out that the figures could be overestimated, as in some cases, national activities might be linked to European or international activities.

breakdown shows 65 "environment—packaging" notifications from Netherlands, 14 from Belgium, 11 from Austria, 10 from Denmark and Germany, nine from France, seven from Finland, six from Sweden, four from Portugal, the United Kingdom, Italy and Greece, three from Ireland and two from Spain.[100] The four Cohesion Fund Member States—Ireland Portugal, Greece and Spain—thus notified only 13 draft texts, while the first four Member States notified 100 texts: a clear indication that ranking of environmental concerns is also influenced by the economic development.

30. TOTAL HARMONISATION AND THE ENVIRONMENT

Judgment of the Court (Fifth Chamber) of 29 May 1997
Case C–329/95

*Reference for a preliminary ruling in administrative proceedings
brought by VAG Sverige AB*
[1997] ECR I–2675

Facts and Procedure

Community Directive 70/156 which was subsequently amended several times, introduced a procedure for Community type-approval for cars.[101] According to that procedure, applications for Community type-approval are to be submitted by the car manufacturer to the approval authority of a Member State. The application must be accompanied by an information folder and provide for information on compliance with each of the some 40 separate Community directives which harmonise technical rules for instance for tyres, window glass, seats, brakes etc. The approval authority examines the car type and the information received. If it finds compliance with the existing technical rules, it must issue an approval certificate which states that the vehicle type in question conforms to the particulars in the information folder and meets the technical requirements of all the relevant separate directives. The type-approval certificate is then delivered to the applicant car manufacturer. On that basis, the manufacturer has to issue a certificate of conformity for each vehicle in the series,

---

[100] Commission (n. 80 *supra*), paras. 6.21 to 6.24; the high figures for the Netherlands are in part due to the "backlash" in 1997 which led to 32 notifications that year.
[101] Directive 70/156 on the approximation of the laws of the Member States relating to the type-approval of motor vehicles and their trailers [1970] OJ L42/1.

certifying thereby that the vehicle conforms to the approved vehicle type. The registration, sale or entry into service in a Member State of a new car may take place only where the car is accompanied by a certificate of conformity.[102]

If a Member State finds that a vehicle or parts of a vehicle which is accompanied by a valid certificate of conformity poses a serious risk to road safety, that Member State may refuse the putting into circulation of that car for a period of maximum six months.[103]

VAG Sverige AB is the general agent in Sweden for Audi and Volkswagen cars. In May 1995, it wanted to register a new car in Sweden which was accompanied by a certificate of conformity. The Swedish authority refused the registration, as under Swedish law a national certificate was necessary in addition to the Community certificate of conformity.

Where a car already has a certificate of conformity under Community law, this certificate is converted into the national certificate without any additional tests. However, in order to obtain the Swedish certificate of conformity, the manufacturer has, furthermore, to choose, for each car type an "engine family", that is to say a category of vehicles with a similar engine, and must submit the necessary information on the car to the competent authority, which then issues the national certificate of conformity. Also, to obtain the Swedish certificate, an annual payment of 32.330 Swedish kronor per engine family is to be made, plus approximately 200 kronor per vehicle sold.

Furthermore, the Swedish certificate of conformity is linked to a system of vehicle control and manufacturers' responsibility. Under Swedish legislation, any manufacturer or importer into Sweden of cars is obliged to repair without charge vehicles which are found in an official test[104] not to comply with the air emission rules; this obligation ceases to exist where a private vehicle is older than five years or has travelled more than 80,000 kilometres. Where there is a serious defect, the manufacturer may be required to change some parts of the anti-pollution system at his own expense or even to recall all vehicles of the same time.

VAG Sverige AB's application was refused, as it had not chosen an engine family and thus did not possess a valid national certificate of conformity. When VAG Sverige AB appealed to a Swedish court, that court asked for a preliminary ruling on the compatibility of the Swedish system with Community law.

---

[102] Directive 70/156 (n. 101 *supra*), Art. 7: "1. Each Member State shall register, permit the sale or entry into service of new vehicles on grounds of their construction and functioning if, and only if, they are accompanied by a valid certificate of conformity . . .".

[103] Directive 70/156 (n. 101 *supra*), Art. 7(3): "If a Member State finds that vehicles, components of separate technical units of a particular type are a serious risk to road safety although they are accompanied by a valid certificate of conformity or a properly marked, then that State may, for a maximum period of six months, refuse to register such vehicles or may prohibit the sale or entry into service in its territory of such vehicles, components or separate technical units. It shall forthwith notify the other Member States and the Commission thereof, stating the reasons on which its decision is based. If the Member State which granted type-approval disputes the risks to road safety notified to it the Member States concerned shall endeavour to settle the dispute. The Commission shall be kept informed and shall, where necessary, hold appropriate consultations for the purpose of reaching a settlement".

[104] The exhaust emission tests are made horizontally, according to the different engine families.

Judgment (extracts)

17. ... the national court is asking essentially whether Directive 70/156 must be interpreted as precluding national legislation under which motor vehicles covered by a valid Community type-approval certificate cannot be registered unless a national certificate is produced attesting to their conformity with national requirements concerning exhaust emissions.

18. It is clear from Article 7(1) and (3) of Directive 70/156 that a Member State may refuse to register a vehicle with a valid Community type-approval certificate only if it finds that the vehicle is a serious risk to road safety. Moreover, this refusal may last no longer than six months and the Member State taking such a decision must forthwith notify the other Member States and the Commission.

19. Save in those highly specific circumstances, Directive 70/156 does not provide for any possibility of refusing to register new vehicles covered by a valid Community type-approval certificate.

20. It must be held that national rules such as those at issue in the main proceedings do not satisfy the conditions governing derogation laid down in Article 7(3). Refusal to register under the national rules is linked to considerations of protection of the environment and not to reasons relating to road safety.

21. The Swedish Government points out, however, that, during the negotiations concerning the accession of the Kingdom of Sweden to the European Union, the representatives of the European Union stated that in the absence of any Community provisions on manufacturers' liability, the Kingdom of Sweden could maintain its system if it complied with the directives concerning product liability and safety.

22. It must be noted, however, that nothing in the Act concerning the conditions of accession of the Kingdom of Norway, the Republic of Austria, the Republic of Finland and the Kingdom of Sweden and the adjustments to the Treaties on which the European Union is founded (OJ 1994 C 241, p. 21) exempts the Kingdom of Sweden from compliance with Directive 70/156 or postpones its application in this regard. Annex XII, which details the transitional measures relating to the environment referred to in Article 112 of the Act of Accession, does not in fact mention the Directive.

23. Moreover, it should be borne in mind that declarations recorded in minutes are of limited value, since they cannot be used for the purposes of interpreting a provision of Community law where no reference is made to the content of the declaration in the wording of the provision in question and the declaration therefore has no legal signifcance (Case C–292/89 *Antonissen* [1991] ECR I–745, paragraph 18).

Commentary

I. *Total Harmonisation and National Environmental Measures*

(1) In view of the clear wording of Article 7 of Directive 70/156,[105] it is difficult to see how the Court could have come to a different decision, when it based itself on that Directive. The Swedish measures clearly had an objective to ensure the minimisation of air pollution from cars: This has nothing to do with road safety and Article 7 of the Directive allows Member States to deviate from the Community system of type-approval only for reasons of road safety.

This part of the judgment is thus not in dispute. And in the same way there is nothing to object to the Court's findings on declarations which had been made during the accession process of Sweden to the Community: as Directive 70/156 is not mentioned as among those directives or regulations, for which Sweden has been given a derogation, it has to comply with the Directive's requirements from the date of accession, i.e. from 1 January 1995.

(2) The subject-matter starts becoming more interesting when one looks into the substantive law of environmental protection: Directive 70/156 has been adopted on the basis of Article 94 (ex Article 100) EC Treaty.[106] The question then is whether Article 95(4) EC Treaty[107] could be applied, which allows a Member State to maintain national environmental legislation which is more stringent than the Community legislation. This consideration is, of course, hypothetical, as Sweden never had had recourse to the procedure under Article 95(4) EC Treaty.

(3) Obviously, that provision applies, according to its wording, only to such measures which were based on Article 95(1) EC Treaty. However, it could be considered to apply this provision by analogy to those directives which were adopted on the basis of Article 94 EC Treaty. This could all the more be justified as Sweden acceded to the Community only in 1995 and thus had not agreed to the system set up by Directive 70/156. The national Swedish measure aims at reducing air pollution and constitutes thus an environmental measure. It cannot either seriously be argued that such a measure contradicts Article 95(6), as neither arbitrary discrimination nor a disguised restriction on trade between Member States nor an obstacle to the functioning of the internal market[108] is visible.

---

[105] Directive 70/156, Art. 7 (n. 102 *supra*).

[106] Art. 94 (ex Art. 100) EC Treaty: "The Council shall, acting unanimously on a proposal from the Commission and after consulting the European Parliament and the Economic and Social Committee, issue directives for the approximation of such laws, regulations or administrative provisions of the Member States as directly affect the establishment or functioning of the common market".

[107] Art. 95(4) (ex Art. 100a(4)) EC Treaty: "If, after the adoption by the Council or by the Commission of a harmonisation measure, a Member State deems it necessary to maintain national provisions on grounds of major needs referred to in Art. 30, or relating to the protection of the environment or the working environment, it shall notify the Commission of these provisions as well as the grounds for maintaining them".

[108] As regards this last criterion, see L Krämer, *EC Environmental Law* (4th edn., Sweet & Maxwell, London, 2000), p. 101: The clause that there may not be an obstacle to the functioning of the internal market "is only meaningful when it is completed by a word such as 'inadequate' or 'inappropriate'. This

(4) In my opinion therefore, Sweden could have used Article 95(4) EC Treaty and had its national measures approved. Proponents of the common market would probably object to this interpretation and argue, as it seems the Court has implicitly done, that Directive 70/156 provides for a total harmonisation of the rules on type-approval of cars and that a total harmonisation which tries to create uniform EC-wide rules is incompatible with derogating national rules. However, this argument overlooks Article 6 EC Treaty,[109] which has existed, in essentially the same wording, since 1987 in the environmental chapter of the EC Treaty. One might have expected, since the insertion of this integration principle into the EC Treaty, that Community legislation on type-approvals for cars would consider environmental aspects; this would have been possible, for instance, by adding to the case of road safety which could justify measures at national level (Article 7(3) of Directive 70/156) as new case for justifying national measures on environmental grounds. But—one is almost tempted to state, of course—nothing has been undertaken in this regard at Community level.

(5) The Community type-approval system and the some 40 technical directives which are linked to it, apply only to new cars.[110] Hitherto, now, there has been no legislation which requires technical standards to be complied with in the use of cars. In particular, when the Community introduced the catalytic converter for cars, it made this converter mandatory for new cars. But nothing was provided for the retrofitting of existing cars or the continued proper functioning of catalytic converters in use. As catalytic converters are mandatory only for all new cars since 1 January 1993, it will take until 2005 or later before all cars without a catalytic converter have disappeared from the roads of the Community.

Thus, Sweden would have been able to maintain its system of manufacturers' responsibility for exhaust emissions, if the system were not linked to the issuing of the certificate of conformity for new cars, but organised in another way, for instance combined with the regular technical control of cars during use. The environmental result—ensuring that cars which are less than five years old or have travelled less than 80,000 kilometres comply with exhaust emission provisions, and this free of charge for users—could be reached in the same way.

---

would mean that, in each individual case, the Commission would have to weigh up the protection of the environment against seeing the internal market function properly. Thus, a national measure must be proportional to the objective pursued by it". This interpretation is now shared by the Commission, see Decision 1999/832 [1999] OJ L329/25.

[109] Art. 6 EC Treaty: "Environmental protection requirements must be integrated into the definition and implementation of the Community policies and activities referred to in Art. 3, in particular with a view to promoting sustainable development".

[110] See, for instance, Directive 70/220 on measures to be taken against air pollution by emissions from motor vehicles [1970] OJ L76/1, Art. 2: "No Member State may refuse to grant EEC type-approval . . . of a vehicle on grounds relating to air pollution by gases from positive ignition engines of motor vehicles . . .".

II. *Producer Responsibility in Sweden and the EC*

(6) This leads to the substance of the Swedish legislation: it introduced a system of producer responsibility for air emissions from cars. The originality of this system consists of making the producer responsible for exhaust emissions from cars continuing to be in conformity with national or Community air pollution legislation. This result is reached by a number of measures: first, the car user does not have to pay for adjusting the exhaust system during the first five years of the car's lifetime; this gives a supplementary incitement to car users to accept control of exhaust emissions and to take their cars back to the trader, if there is a need. Secondly, car manufacturers finance the system of general, horizontal controls of cars of the same type which allows these systematic controls to be made. And this avoids charging the taxpayer with the financing of the control system.

(7) Of course, car manufacturers have the ability to charge car purchasers with the costs of the adjustments of cars and of the control system. However, this seems better than having the system financed by the taxpayer as, in environmental matters, the polluter shall pay[111] and not the taxpayer. And while it may be doubtful whether the car producer or the car user should be considered as the polluter,[112] it is more equitable to charge either of them than the taxpayer, who is in no way the cause of air contamination by cars.

As such, the Swedish system is a concept to reduce air emissions during the average lifetime of catalytic converters of cars. Where the Swedish authorities find such a system appropriate for their country to combat air pollution, it seems well conceived and appropriate in order to realise the concept of producer responsibility. It can only be hoped that ways are found to maintain the system in function.

(8) The concept of producer responsibility[113] is relatively recent in Community environmental law and policy. It appeared for the first time in a Commission document on waste management strategy of 1996,[114] where, under the heading "producer

---

[111] See Art. 174(2) EC Treaty: "Community policy on the environment . . . shall be based on the principle(s) . . . that the polluter should pay".

[112] Council Recommendation 75/436 regarding cost allocation and action by public authorities on environmental matters [1975] OJ L194/1 (Annex, para. 3) was of the opinion that this question could be decided as a matter of discretion in one or the other way: after the definition of "pollution chain" as being pollution from several consecutive causes, the text gives the following example: "in cases of environmental pollution by motor vehicles exhaust fumes, not only the user of the vehicle but also the manufacturer of the vehicle and of the fuel are responsible for causing atmospheric pollution" and then concludes: "in the case of pollution chains, costs could be charged at the point at which the number of economic operators is least and control is easiest or else at the point where the most effective contribution is made towards improving the environment, and where distortions of competition are avoided".

[113] It is significant that the Court's judgment speaks, in paras. 10 and 21, of "manufacturers' liability" and not of producer responsibility. Normally, in Community legal terminology, liability is the (financial) responsibility for precise, specific damage which has occurred, which can be expressed in a sum of money, against which insurance can be taken out etc. In contrast to that, producer responsibility indicates the political and managerial responsibility for economic behaviour, which requires a strategy to improve environmental performance and prevent environmental impairment.

[114] Commission, Communication on the review of the Community strategy for waste management, COM(96)399 of 30 July 1996.

responsibility", it is stated: "Considering the life cycle of a product from manufacture until the end of its useful life, producers, material suppliers, trade, consumers and public authorities share specific waste management responsibilities. However it is the product manufacturer who has a predominant role. The manufacturer is the one to take key decisions concerning the waste management potential of his product, such as design, conception, use of specific materials, composition of the product and finally its marketing. The manufacturer is therefore able to provide the means not only to avoid waste by a considered utilisation of natural resources, renewable raw materials or non-hazardous materials, but also to conceive products in a way which facilitates proper re-use and recovery. Marking, labelling, the issue of instructions for use and of data sheets may contribute to this aim".

(9) Producer responsibility in this context means that the concept of the nineteenth century "let the buyer beware" (*caveat emptor*) is no longer valid. The twentieth century has seen the progressive development of producers' obligations after the marketing of a product, such as fair and non-misleading advertising, labelling requirements, obligations to provide for instructions for use, obligations to give warnings, to check the marketed products for potential side-effects, propensity to cause accidents, obligations to call back to modify the product etc. And as regards waste management with its first policy priority of preventing waste generation, the responsibility of the manufacturer concerns also the phase when the product has come to the end of its useful life. The producer must ensure that as few hazardous materials as possible are in the product in order to facilitate its recycling, recovery or safe disposal. He is obliged to design and conceive the product in a way that recycling and recovery are made easier etc.

(10) Aspects of producer responsibility in legislation are found, for the first time, in Directive 2000/53 on end-of life vehicles:[115] among others, Member States must ensure that "economic operators set up systems for the collection of all end-of life vehicles" (Article 5(1)); that "the delivery of the vehicle to an authorised treatment facility . . . occurs without any cost for the last holder and/or owner as a result of the vehicle's having no or a negative market value" (Article 5(4)), and that "producers meet all, or a significant part of, the costs of the implementation of this measure and/or take back end-of life vehicles . . ." (Article 5(4)).

(11) In the proposal for directives on end-of life electrical and electronic products, which is at present under discussion in the Council and the European Parliament, the Commission repeated the relation between the polluter pays principle of Article 174 EC Treaty and producer responsibility.[116] It then stated: "The proposal for a WEEE Directive seeks to extend the traditional role of producers by making them responsible for the management of electrical and electronic products at end-of-life. The creation of a link between the producers and waste management

---

[115] Directive 2000/53 on end-of life vehicles [2000] OJ L269/34.
[116] Commission, Proposal for a directive on waste electrical and electronic equipment; proposal for a directive on the restriction of the use of certain hazardous substances in electrical and electronic equipment, COM(2000)347 of 13 June 2000.

contributes to an improved product design with a view to facilitating recycling and disposal of products once they reach their end of life".[117]

(12) Consequently, the proposal provides that "producers set up systems to provide for the treatment of WEEE" (Article 5(1)); that "producers provide for the collection of WEEE from holders other than private households" (Article 4(3)); that "producers set up systems to provide for the recovery of separately collected WEEE" (Article 6(1)); that after five years "Producers provide for the financing of the collection of WEEE from private households deposited at collection facilities. . . as well as of the treatment, recovery and environmentally sound disposal of WEEE (Article 7(2)) etc.

As yet, the Community and the Commission have not begun to provide for producer responsibility in legislative texts other than on waste issues. For future years, the Commission plans to develop an environmentally oriented integrated product policy. It remains to be seen to what extent the concept of producer responsibility which is a modernised form of the polluter pays principle, will be made concrete or whether it will become—as the polluter pays principle during the last 30 years of Community environmental legislation and policy—a slogan for Sunday speeches and a paper tiger in the environment.

31. PRODUCTS AND NATURE PROTECTION

Judgment of the Court (Sixth Chamber) of 13 July 1994
Case C–131/93

Commission of the European Communities v. *Germany*
[1994] ECR I–3303

Facts and Procedure

In 1989, a provision was introduced into German legislation which made the importation of all species of live crayfish subject to the grant of a licence. Such a licence could be granted only for research or teaching purposes.[118] The importation of live crayfish for commercial purposes, in particular for restocking private pools or for consumption, was prohibited. However, the Bundesamt für Ernährung und Forstwirtschaft could, on application, grant a derogation where

---

[117] Commission (n. 116 *supra*), para. 4.3.
[118] *Erste Verordnung zur Änderung der Verordnung zum Schutz wildlebender Tier- und Pflanzenarten,* Bundesgesetzblatt 1989 I, p. 1525.

the application of the prohibition "would, contrary to the legislature's intention, lead to excessive hardship".[119]

A number of undertakings in Germany which had specialised in the importation of crayfish argued that this legislation led to a drop in their profits to an extent that their economic existence was threatened. For that reason, the Bundesamt granted, on a transitional basis, import licences for crayfish; these licences were given for a period of six months at a time. Undertakings which benefitted from such a derogation had to indicate the precise quantity imported, the country of origin and the name of the species concerned. Furthermore, they had to sell the imported crayfish only to final purchasers, but not to wholesalers or retailers; the purchasers had to take all adequate measures of precaution and disinfection, so as to prevent imported crayfish from being released into the wild and ensure that the water used to keep the crayfish was disinfected before being disposed of.

Between 1989 and 1993, import licences relating to a total quantity of 961,400 kg of crayfish were granted.

The Commission was of the opinion that the German rules in question were incompatible with Articles 28 (ex Article 30) and 30 (ex Article 36) EC Treaty. Germany considered that the import ban was indispensable for providing effective and lasting protection against crayfish plague (aphanomycosis) and for preserving their genetic identity.

Judgment (extracts)

9. . . . the German measure in question has the effect of impeding intra-Community trade in that it prohibits imports for commercial purposes of live freshwater crayfish from another Member State or from a non-member country in free circulation in the Community.

12. . . . Article 30 of the Treaty precludes the application to intra-Community trade of national legislation which maintains a requirement, even as a pure formality, for import licences or any other similar procedure, and a measure adopted by a Member State does not escape that prohibition simply because the competent authority enjoys a discretionary power to grant derogations.

13. Since the German Government has sought to justify its rules on the importation of live freshwater crayfish by referring to considerations concerning the protection of the health and life of animals and the preservation of native species, it is. . . necessary to consider whether the rules in question fall within the powers which Member States have for achieving those objectives.

17. It is not disputed that the purpose of the national measure in question is to protect the health and life of native crayfish so that the measure is accordingly covered by the exception provided for in Article 36 of the Treaty.

---

[119] *Gesetz über Naturschutz und Landschaftspflege*, Bundesgesetzblatt 1987 I, p. 889, Art. 31(1).

18. However, rules restricting intra-Community trade are compatible with the Treaty only in so far as they are indispensable for the purposes of providing effective protection for the health and life of animals. They cannot therefore be covered by the derogation provided for in Article 36 if that aim may be achieved just as effectively by measures having less restrictive effects on intra-Community trade.

19. The question to be examined, therefore, is whether the German restrictions in question satisfy the principle of proportionality as so expressed.

20. In this regard, the Federal Government submits that a total ban on importing live freshwater crayfish was the only way of effectively protecting native crayfish against aphanomycosis since not only animals from non-member countries but also species originating from other Member States are capable of carrying the crayfish plague virus. Furthermore, the rules in question were necessary to limit as much as possible the proliferation of non-indigenous species in natural stretches of water in Germany so as to protect the genetic identity of local populations of crayfish against faunal distortion which occurs upon the introduction in national territory of animals of the same species but of different origin. The prohibition of importation of live freshwater crayfish is, in its view, also justified by Article 15 of Council Regulation (EEC) No. 3626/82 of 3 December 1982 on the implementation in the Community of the Convention on International Trade in Endangered Species of Wild Fauna and Flora (OJ 1982 L 384, p. 1).

21. That argument must be rejected forthwith.

22. As the Commission has rightly pointed out, Article 15(1) of Regulation No 3626/82 expressly provides that if a Member State, for the purpose, in particular, of conserving native species, maintains or takes stricter measures than those provided for by that regulation, it must comply with the Treaty and, in particular, Article 36 thereof.

23. It is not disputed that the total import ban in force in the Federal Republic of Germany constitutes a measure which is stricter than those provided for by Regulation 3626/82.

24. As far as the prevention of the risks of crayfish plague and of faunal distortion is concerned, the Commission submits that this objective could have been achieved by measures having less restrictive effects of intra-Community trade.

25. For example, instead of simply prohibiting imports of all species of live freshwater crayfish, the Federal Republic of Germany could have confined itself to making consignments of crayfish from other Member States or already in free circulation in the Community subject to health checks and only carrying out checks by sample if such consignments were accompanied by a health certificate issued by the competent authorities of the dispatching Member State certifying that the product in question presented no risk to health, or instead confined itself to regulating the marketing of crayfish in its territory, in particular by subjecting to authorisation only the restocking of national waters with species likely to be carrying the disease and restricting release of animals into the wild and restocking in areas in which native species are to be found.

26. However, the Federal Government has not convincingly shown that such measures, involving less serious restrictions for intra-Community trade, were incapable of effectively protecting the interests pleaded.

27. Moreover, the conditions which importers are required to observe under the authorization system applied by the German authorities so as to mitigate the harshness of the import ban laid down by the Federal legislation, which require the traders concerned to comply with all health measures, to use imported crayfish in a way which prevents them from being released into the environment and to ensure that the water in which they are kept is disinfected, show that the defendant Government itself considers that those means, less restrictive of intra-Community trade than a total import ban, are sufficient for achieving the objective of native crayfish against crayfish plague and faunal distortion.

28. It follows that the Commission's complaint is well founded.

Commentary

I. Import Ban for Crayfish and Articles 28/30 EC Treaty

(1) The Court had to assess a measure which was perhaps a protectionist measure, but for which evidence was not easy to establish. Germany had forbidden the import of live European crayfish including such crayfish which came from non-European countries, but which were already in free circulation within the Community. The Commission had accepted that the importation of crayfish from third countries—in particular from North America, where the crayfish plage (*aphanomycosis*) was widespread, could indeed pose a problem and had therefore limited its case against Germany to the breach of intra-Community rules on free trade, thus Articles 28 (ex Article 30)[120] and 30 (ex Article 36) EC Treaty.[121] Nevertheless, the case remained delicate, as the German regulation had been based on a provision of nature protection, the Regulation on the Protection of Species (*Bundesartenschutzverordnung*).

(2) And while with products in general, the provisions on the free circulation of goods and the interdependency between Articles 28 and 30 EC Treaty are relatively clear, animals and plants, under the EC Treaty, are not automatically to be treated as "products" or goods: this follows in particular from Article 30 EC Treaty, which allows restrictions on the free circulation rules, if such restrictions

---

[120] Art. 28 (ex Art. 30) EC Treaty: "Quantitative restrictions on imports and all measures having equivalent effect shall be prohibited between Member States".

[121] Art. 30 (ex Art. 36) EC Treaty: "The provisions of Arts. 28 and 29 shall not preclude prohibitions or restrictions om imports, exports or goods in transit justified on grounds of . . . the protection of health and life of humans, animals or plants . . . Such prohibitions or restrictions shall not, however, constitute a means of arbitrary discrimination or a disguised restriction on trade between Member States".

are necessary to protect the health and life of animals and plants. It would be unthinkable to have in Article 30 EC Treaty a provision which allowed the restriction of the free circulation of goods in order to protect precious or rare products.

(3) Furthermore, it is principally for this reason that Community measures on trade in endangered species are based on Article 175 EC Treaty, not on the internal market provision of Article 95;[122] the same applies to practically all fauna and flora measures taken by the Community. Only measures on genetically modified organisms follow the provisions on the internal market,[123] as in this area of biotechnology the borderline between life and non-life has been set aside.

The Court did not have difficulty in finding that the German import ban was a measure having an equivalent effect on imports to quantitative restrictions. This fact was undisputed and is hardly arguable, all the more 50 as the wording of Article 30 EC Treaty demonstrates that also prohibitions on grounds of animal or plant protection come under Article 28 EC Treaty.

(4) The big question was, therefore, whether the German measure could be justified by virtue of Article 30. On this point, the Court accepted that the measures were intended to protect German fauna, as appears clearly from paragraph 17 of the judgment. However, the existence of an objective enumerated in Article 30 EC Treaty is not sufficient to justify a national measure, where such a measure is either discriminating or disproportionate; both these criteria are taken from Article 30, second sentence.[124]

(5) The Court does not examine the discriminating character of the German measure. A measure is discriminating when it treats national producers or traders better than foreign producers or traders. This principle would be applicable in the present case if the situations of German crayfish "producers" (fishermen, farmers) and other EC producers were comparable. The Commission had not argued that the German measure was discriminating[125]—but in fact they were, as becomes clear when one reads a provision of German law which was quoted by the Advocate General,[126] but not taken up by the Court itself. That provision allowed German owners or holders of crayfish to release them into the wild if they obtained an authorisation for doing so; foreign owners or holders could not do this, due to the import prohibition. Nor is it very obvious why an import of crayfish could be allowed by way of derogation, but on condition that there was no sale to wholesalers or retailers.

---

[122] See in particular Regulation 338/97 on trade in endangered species [1997] OJ L61/1; this Regulation replaced Regulation 3626/82 which is mentioned in para. 20 of the judgment.

[123] See also p. 233 *supra*.

[124] Art. 30 EC Treaty (n. 121 *supra*).

[125] See Advocate General van Gerven, Opinion in the present case [1994] ECR I–3303, para. 16.

[126] Advocate General van Gerven (n. 125 *supra*), para. 15, quoting Art. 20d(2) of the *Bundesnaturschutzgesetz* (n. 119 *supra*): "Animals and plants of non-regional origin ('*gebietsfremde*') may be released into the wild or grown in the wild only with authorisation from the authority having competence under the laws of the Land. This rule does not apply to the growing of plants for agricultural or forestry purposes. Authorisation shall be refused if the risk of distortion of native flora or fauna or a threat to the existence or propagation of native species of plants and animals or population of such species cannot be excluded".

(6) The Court concentrated on the question whether the import ban was proportionate and examines, which measures Germany could have taken that were less restrictive for the intra-Community trade. It mentioned (paragraphs 25 and 27):

(a) making health checks on the consignments of crayfish;
(b) making checks by sampling if the consignment was accompanied by a health certificate issued by the Member State of dispatch;
(c) regulating the marketing of crayfish in Germany;
(d) impose import conditions to crayfish importers.

(7) These examples contradict to a certain extent the Court's assertion made in paragraph 16 of the judgment that it is "for the Member States to decide upon the level which they wished to protect the health and life of animals". If the Court's extensive interpretation of the proportionality principle[127] were correct, practically never could a prohibition of a substance or a product be decided at national level. Indeed, one may always think of a system of authorisation, of health checks and tight controls which could in theory reach a system equivalent to a prohibition. But such reasoning overlooks that Member States have a discretionary power to decide which type of monitoring and control they want to introduce. Already the system of sanctions—civil law, administrative or criminal—leads to such different approaches in the monitoring and control systems that the Court adhering to its own proportionality test, would—in any given case—have to tackle most national systems with the argument that they go further than the least restrictive system.

(8) It is submitted that the proportionality principle is used by the Court when the Court wishes to reach a certain result. If one looks at the arguments used in Cases C–473/98 and C–389/96[128] and compares them with the present case, one finds that the reasoning is not made with the same stringency: in those cases where the Court considered the national measure proportionate, it did not give a list of possibilities for less restrictive measures as it did in the present case.

Measures (a) and (b) mentioned above in paragraph 6 of this commentary are rather theoretical. Indeed, one might wonder whether the requirement of systematic health checks of crayfish to be brought to Germany would really be a recommendable measure. The instauration of health control stations—the crayfish are alive!—the cost of controls and the administrative arrangements appear to be quite complicated. The same applies to health certificates issued in other Member States: is it really for the German authorities to check, before taking national measures, whether all other Member States issue health certificates, whether these are reliable, whether there is abuse of such certificates etc?

(9) The possibility mentioned under (c) above seems, in contrast, convincing as far as the release of crayfish into the wild or the restocking of waters is concerned:

---

[127] See in more detail on this principle p. 97 *supra*.
[128] Court of Justice, Case C–473/98, *Kemikalieinspektionen* [2000] ECR I–5681 (p. 225 *supra*); C–389/96 *Aher-Waggon* [1998] ECR I–4473 (p. 275 *infra*); C–67/97 *Bluhme* [1998] ECR I–8033.

it is not necessary to ban the import of crayfish from other Member States, as the German legislation itself proves.[129] However, protection against the crayfish plague cannot be assured by such a less restrictive measure, so that the reasoning would have to go back to the reasoning under (a) or (b) above.

(10) In my opinion, only the last argument carries the Court's reasoning: if it is possible for the German authorities to grant derogations from the import ban for almost one million kg of crayfish, then it is not really convincing that for the rest there should be an import ban. This argument seems all the stronger as the possibility of granting a derogation, under the German nature protection legislation, was not really drafted to ensure the survival of undertakings which had specialised in the import of crayfish.[130] If this provision of the *Bundesnaturschutzgesetz* can be stretched to apply to the eight to 10 German specialised undertakings—these seem to be all undertakings in Germany in this business—then it is not clear why the same conditions for import cannot apply to other persons who want to trade in living freshwater crayfish.

In summary, thus, authorisations of imports of crayfish with rather strict conditions as regards health-related infection prevention measures and strict conditions regarding releases of crayfish into the wild are concerned, appear to reach the same result of protection than the import ban. Therefore, the Court's conclusion is convincing.

II. Import Bans and the Protection of Biodiversity

(11) Attention is drawn to the fact that Community environmental law does not contain provisions to protect the local, regional or national fauna and flora. Such measures are left entirely to Member States—and it is obvious that only some Member States have taken such measures which are not even very efficient.

(12) In 1998, the Court had to give a preliminary ruling in another case where the question was raised whether a national legislative measure to protect indigenous species was compatible with the Treaty and in particular with its Articles 28 and 30.[131] The facts of the case were as follows: Danish legislation[132] prohibited the keeping on the island of Laesoe of bees other than those of the subspecies *apis mellifera mellifera* (Laesoe brown bee). Mr. Bluhme was prosecuted for keeping on Laesoe bees other than the subspecies in question. He argued the the prohibition on keeping certain bees at Laesoe was in conflict with Article 28 EC Treaty.

(13) The Court once more applied the *Dassonville* formula[133] according to which all measures capable of hindering intra-Community trade, whether directly

---

[129] See the provision quoted in n. 126, *supra*, which provides for a licence.

[130] See *Bundesnaturschutzgesetz* (n. 119 *supra*), Art. 31: "On application, derogation from the prohibitions of this law may be granted, if (1) the application of an individual provision would, in the individual case, lead to excessive hardship, contrary to the legislature's intention and in so far as it is compatible with the objectives of nature protection and land conservation . . .".

[131] Court of Justice, Case C–67/97 (n. 128 *supra*).

[132] *Bekendtgoerelse No. 528 om biavl paa Laesoe* of 24 June 1993.

[133] The clause was first used in Case 8/74, *Procureur du Roi* v. *Dassonville* [1974] ECR 837, para. 5.

or indirectly, actually or potentially, constituted measures having equivalent effect to quantitative restrictions and concluded that the prohibition on keeping bees at Laesoe fell under Article 28 EC Treaty; the fact that the prohibition concerned only a very small part of Denmark was of no relevance.

When the Court then examined whether such a measure could be justified by virtue of Article 30 EC Treaty, it had to overcome the difficulty that Mr. Bluhme argued that there was no subspecies *apis mellifera mellifera* which was genetically distinct and unique to the island of Laesoe. The Court considered that "measures to preserve an indigenous animal population with distinct characteristics contribute to the maintenance of biodiversity by ensuring the survival of the population concerned. By so doing, they are aimed at protecting the life of those animals" and were thus capable of being justified under Article 30 EC Treaty. It then continued: "From the point of view of such conservation of biodiversity, it is immaterial whether the object of protection is a separate subspecies, a distinct strain within any given species or merely a local colony, as long as the populations in question have characteristics distinguishing them from others and are therefore judged worthy of protection either to shelter them from a risk of extinction that is more or less imminent, or, even in the absence of such a risk, on account of a scientific or other interest in preserving the pure population at the location concerned".

(14) This argument is convincing, though in the specific case Mr. Bluhme just had argued that the Laesoe brown bee did not have distinguishing characteristics. It seems that the Court should better have left the question, whether that subspecies existed to the national court, as the Court of Justice had been asked only for a preliminary ruling.

As regards the question of proportionality, the Court stated: "As for the threat of the disappearance of the Laesoe brown bee, it is undoubtedly genuine in the event of mating with golden bees by reason of the recessive nature of the genes of the brown bee. The establishment by the national legislation of a protection area within which the keeping of bees other than Laesoe brown bees is prohibited, for the purpose of ensuring the survival of the latter, therefore constitutes an appropriate measure inrelation to the aim pursued". The Court of Justice also found that the approach to establish protected areas for certain species was already practised by Community law, in particular by means of the special protection areas in the Directive on wild birds[134] and the special conservation areas in Directive 92/43.[135]

(15) Again, I would not argue about the Court's conclusions, which are convincing. However, the examination of the proportionality of the import prohibition leaves some questions open, such as: is there really a need to protect the Laesoe brown bee? Cannot this be done by intensified research and artificial breeding of the bee? Does that bee occur in other parts of Denmark? Is any interest to

---

[134] Directive 79/409 on the conservation of wild birds [1979] OJ L103/1.
[135] Directive 92/43 on the conservation of natural habitats and of wild fauna and flora [1992] OJ L206/7.

preserve an "animal pure population at the location concerned" capable of justifying import restrictions, as the Court seems to imply? What if such an interest were of an economic nature, given the Court has held that Article 30 EC Treaty can only be evoked in order to protect interests of non-economic nature?

The examination of the proportionality principle remains an intricate issue.

32. COMMUNITY NOISE POLICY AND LAW

Judgment of the Court (Fifth Chamber) of 14 July 1998
Case C–389/96

Reference for a preliminary ruling in the proceedings between
Aher-Waggon GmbH and Germany
[1998] ECR I–4473

Facts and Procedure

The company Aher was the owner of an aeroplane which it had bought, in 1992, in Denmark and which had been registered in that Member State since 1974. The aeroplane had a sound level of 72. 2 dB(A) for its maximum take-off weight. In 1986, Germany had introduced, by way of legislation, maximum permitted noise levels of 69 dB(A) for the aeroplanes in question.

In order to be allowed to be used in a Member State, an aeroplane must be registered in that Member State.[136] However, when Aher asked to have the plane registered in Germany, it got a negative answer, on the ground that the plane exceeded the noise emission limits in force in Germany.

Community Directive 80/51[137] which is based on Article 80(2) (ex Article 84(2) EC Treaty,[138] fixes noise emission limits for subsonic aircraft;[139] the permissible

---

[136] Directive 80/51 on the limitation of noise emissions from subsonic aircraft [1980] OJ L18/26; amended by Directive 83/206 [1983] OJ L117/15, Art. 3: "1. Each Member State shall ensure that all civil propeller-driven aeroplanes with a maximum certificated take-off mass not exceeding 5. 700 kg and all civil subsonic jet areoplanes if they do not fall within one of the categories set out in Volume I of Annex 16/5, but use areodromes situated in any Member State, are certificated in accordance with requirements which are at least equal to the applicable standards specified in Part II, Chapter 2 or 6 of Volume I of Annex 1615 when being newly registered in its territory".

[137] Directive 80/51 (n. 136 *supra*).

[138] Art. 80 (ex Art. 84) EC Treaty: "1. The provisions of this Title shall apply to transport by rail, road and inland waterway. 2. The Council may, acting by a qualified majority, decide whether, to what extent and bywhat procedure appropriate provisions may be laid down for sea and air transport".

[139] Directive 80/51 (n. 136 *supra*), Art. 1: "Each Member State shall ensure that any civil subsonic jet or propellor-driven aeroplane registered in its territory and falling within one of the categories set out

noise level for the type of plane which was owned by Aher was 73 dB(A). The Directive allows Member States to fix more stringent requirements.[140] Thus, Aher's aeroplane complied with the Directive's noise limits, but not with the more stringent requirements in German law.

During the litigation before the German courts, Aher submitted that aeroplanes of the same type as its own were registered in Germany and therefore allowed to be used in that country. The German authorities argued that these other aeroplanes had been registered in Germany before the national legislation had been strengthened. The German Bundesverwaltungsgericht, the supreme administrative German court, asked the Court of Justice whether the German provisions were compatible with Community law and in particular with Article 28 (ex Article 30) EC Treaty.

Judgment (extracts)

14. . . . the national court essentially asks whether Article 30 of the Treaty precludes national legislation which makes the first registration in national territory of aircraft previously registered in another Member State conditional upon compliance with stricter noise standards than those laid down by the Directive, while exempting from those standards aircraft which obtained registration in national territory before the Directive was implemented.

15. It should be noted at the outset that the Directive merely lays down minimum requirements, as is shown by the words "in accordance with requirements which are at least equal to the applicable standards" which appear in Article 3(1). The Directive thus allows the Member States to impose stricter noise limits.

16. Nevertheless, it is necessary to consider whether a Member State which, like the Federal Republic of Germany, has introduced stricter noise limits has, in exercising that power, infringed other provisions of Community law, in particular Article 30 of the Treaty. Even though the Directive is based on Article 84(2) of the Treaty, which enables the Council to adopt appropriate provisions for air transport, it is settled case-law that that provision canot be interpreted as excluding air transport from the general rules of the Treaty.

---

in Volume I (Aircarft Noise) of Annex 16 to the Convention on international civil aviation, as applicable from 26 November 1981, in accordance with Amendment 5, (hereinafter referred to as Annex 16/5) may not be used in the territory of Member States unless it has granted noise certification on the basis of satisfactory evidence that the aeroplane complies with requirements which are at least equal to the applicable standards specified in Part II, Chapters 2,3,5, or 6 of Volume I of Annex 16/5".

It is submitted that this text is hardly readable and, due to its references to the annexes to the international convention on civil aviation, not understandable. It seems a model of how legislation should not be drafted.

[140] There is neither a recital nor an express provision in Directive 80/51 which indicates that Member States may maintain or introduce more restrictive measures. The minimum character of Directive 80/51 follows from the use of the words "at least" in Art. 1 (see n. 139 *supra*), 2, 3 (see n. 136 *supra*), 5 and 7.

17. In that regard, it is settled case-law that any measure capable of hindering, directly or indirectly, actually or potentially, intra-Community trade constitutes a measure having an effect equivalent to a quantitative restriction.

18. National legislation of the kind at issue in the main proceedings restricts intra-Community trade since it makes the first registration in national territory of aircraft previously registered in a Member State conditional upon compliance with stricter noise standards than those laid down by the Directive, while exempting from those standards aircraft which obtained registration in national territory before the Directive was implemented.

19. Such a barrier may, however, be justified by considerations of public health and environmental protection of the kind relied upon by the German Government. The German Government states in particular that the Federal Republic of Germany, which is a very densely populated State, attaches special importance to ensuring that its population is protected from excessive noise emissions.

20. It is also settled case-law that national legislation which restricts or is liable to restrict intra-Community trade must be proportionate to the objectives pursued and that those objectives must not be attainable by measures which are less restrictive of such trade . . .

21. As regards the imposition of stricter standards than those laid down in the Directive, suffice it to state that, as the German Government has explained, limiting noise emissions from aircraft is the most effective and convenient means of combating the noise pollution which they generate. Without extremely costly investment, it is generally difficult to reduce noise emissions appreciably by carrying out works in the vicinity of airports.

22. Furthermore, the restriction, though stricter rules governing noise emissions from aircraft, on the possibility of registering an aircraft in Germany applies to all aircraft, new or used, irrespective of their origin, and does not prevent aircraft registered in another Member State from being used in Germany.

23. As regards, more particularly, the exemption from those stricter standards for aircraft registered in the Member State in question before the Directive was implemented, those aircraft must, as the German Government has explained, also comply with the stricter noise standards when they undergo technical modification, even if it has no bearing on noise emissions, or when they are temporarily withdrawn from service. Furthermore, their number can be determined by the German authorities.

24. The national authorities were thus entitled to consider that the number of aircraft not meeting the stricter noise standards was necessarily going to fall and, therefore, that the overall level of noise pollution could not fail to diminish gradually. Furthermore, the effectiveness of that policy of progressively eliminating from the national fleet aircraft not meeting the stricter noise standards would be undermined if their number could be increased, to an extent not foreseeable by the national authorities, by aircraft from other Member States.

25. Legislation of the kind at issue in the main proceedings therefore does not appear to be disproportionate.

Commentary

I. Free Circulation of Goods and National Noise Levels

(1) The Court's assessment whether the German refusal to register Aher's aero-plane in Germany was compatible with Directive 80/51, is limited to the few lines in paragraph 15: as Directive 80/51 fixes only minimum requirements concerning the noise level of aeroplanes, Germany was entitled to fix stricter limits and to refuse, on that basis, the registration of the plane.

(2) The rest of the judgment was used to examine whether the German meas-ure was compatible with Article 28 EC Treaty.[141] The fact that there was Directive 80/51 was of no concern, as it was not the compatibility of this Directive with Article 28 EC Treaty which the Court examined, but rather the German measures which went beyond the field of application of the minimum requirements of this Directive.

The Court started it examination with a repetition of the *Dassonville* formula[142] which was already mentioned in two preceding judgments in this book[143] and which stipulates that any national measure which is capable of hindering "directly or indirectly, actually or potentially, intra-Community trade" constitutes a meas-ure of equivalent effect under Article 29 EC Treaty. The Court had no difficulty in finding that the German provisions constitute such a measure of equivalent effect as a quantitative restriction, as they do not admit on the German market all aero-planes which comply with the requirements of Directive 80/51 (paragraph 18).

(3) In this case, when it examined the grounds for justifying the German meas-ures, the Court was less precise, and this cannot be but regretted. Indeed, it is easy to construct an argument that there has been a breach of Article 28 EC Treaty itself, as this provision is short, precise and clear. Where the legal construction of justification grounds is less precise, this leads to a *de facto* "superiority" of the arguments pleading in favour of the free circulation of goods, though the interests which justify the restriction of the free circulation of goods—for instance the pro-tection of human health, of the environment, the protection of commercial trans-actions against fraud, or the values mentioned in Article 30 EC Treaty[144]—might be of similar or even higher value for the society or, if one so wishes, the EC than the free circulation of goods.

---

[141] Art. 28 (ex Art. 30) EC Treaty: "Quantitative restrictions on iomports and all measures having equivalent effect shall be prohibited between Member States".

[142] Developed first in Case 8/74 *Procureur du Roi* v. *Benoît and Gustave Dassonville* [1974] ECR 837, para. 5.

[143] See pp. 242 and 267 *supra*.

[144] Art. 30 (ex Art. 36) EC Treaty: "The provisions of Arts. 28 and 29 shall not preclude prohibitions or restrictions on imports, exports or goods in transit justified on grounds of public morality, public policy or public security; the protection of health and life of humans, animals or plants; the protection of national treasures possessing artistic, historic or archaeological value; or the protection of industrial and commercial proerty. Such prohibitions or restrictions shall not, however, constitute a means of arbitrary discrimination or a disguised restriction on trade between Member States".

(4) The Court stated in general terms that a restriction on trade may be justified by considerations of public health or the environment, without indicating the provision of the Treaty on which this reasoning is based. Indeed, Article 30 mentions neither "public health" nor the environment as a ground for justifying a restriction of trade. And the Court has repeatedly stated that Article 30 is a derogation from Article 28 and must therefore be interpreted restrictively, which would exclude subsuming justifications other than those which are expressly mentioned under this provision.[145] Also, it follows on the one hand from Article 152 EC Treaty which deals with "public health" issues, on the other hand from Article 174 EC Treaty which mentions "human health" that these two notions are not necessarily identical.

(5) For that reason, it would have been preferable had the Court mentioned whether it intended to apply Article 30 EC Treaty or whether it concurred with the "*Cassis-de-Dijon*" doctrine, under which it had stated, for the first time in 1979 that obstacles to the free movement of goods within the Community resulting from disparities between the national laws had to be accepted in so far as such rules were applicable to domestic and imported products without distinction, and as they may be recognised as being necessary to satisfy mandatory requirements recognised by Community law.[146] In Case C–302/86, the Court had stated that the protection of the environment constituted such a mandatory requirement, capable of justifying a restriction of the free circulation of goods.[147]

(6) However, the Court had limited the application of the *Cassis-de-Dijon* doctrine to cases where there was no Community secondary legislation. In the present case, however, Directive 80/51 existed, and while it allowed Member States to adopt more stringent provisions, it is difficult to consider that the existence of a Community directive with minimum provisions is the same—as far as more restrictive national provisions are concerned—as the absence of any Community legislation. Indeed, Article 176 EC expressly allows the taking of more stringent national measures, where a Community environmental measure is based on Article 175 EC Treaty. But Article 80 EC Treaty does not contain a provision equivalent to Article 176 EC Treaty. *De facto*, therefore, in the present case the Court introduced Article 176 EC Treaty into Article 80 through the back door.

Nevertheless, in the end this solution seems the only reasonable one, as otherwise the minimum harmonisation intended by the Directive would prevent Member States from adopting more stringent provisions. However, as mentioned, one might have wished to see a less succinct elaboration of these aspects by the Court.

(7) Having found (paragraph 19) that high noise levels could constitute a problem for human health and for the environment, the Court had to examine whether the German provisions were discriminating or disproportionate. The Court did not examine the discriminating effect of the German measure. It is obvious that Aher's aeroplane which was presented for registration in Germany after Directive

---

[145] Court of Justice, Cases 7/68, *Commission* v. *Italy* [1968] ECR 633; 13/68, *Salgoil* [1968] ECR 679; 113/80, *Commission* v. *Ireland* [1981] ECR 1625; C–205/89, *Commission* v. *Greece* [1991] ECR I–1361.

[146] Court of Justice, Case 120/78, *Rewe* v. *Bundesmonopolverwaltung* [1979] ECR 649.

[147] Court of Justice, Case C–302/86, *Commission* v. *Denmark* [1988] ECR 4607.

80/51 and subsequent more stringent German legislation had entered into effect, was treated differently from aeroplanes of the same type which had been registered in Germany prior to that entry into effect. However, as Advocate General Cosmas has rightly pointed out,[148] this differentiation was expressly intended by Directive 80/51 which limited the application of Article 3 to the "first" registration in a Member State. Obviously, for the EC legislature, the underlying philosophy of such a provision was that no incitement should be created to register aeroplanes first in a Member State with a low noise level requirement and then have it registered—under the auspices of mutual recognition of registrations of another Member State—in a Member State with a strict noise level requirement.

As the two situations are thus not equal, the German provisions were not discriminating.

(8) The Court's examination whether the German provisions were proportionate to the targeted aim is convincing and requires only one comment: in Case C–473/98[149] the Court had considered a national ban on a pesticide as justified and proportionate. One of its main points as regards proportionality in that case was that the national provisions had foreseen the possibility of individual exemptions from the ban for reasons of the "undertakings' requirements in the matter of continuity". In the present case, the Court did not use one word to examine whether the German provisions should have provided for granting, in individual cases, exemptions from the general ban on noisy aeroplanes. Is such an "equity clause" part of the proportionality test, as the deliberation of the judgment in Case C–473/98, which was given by the full Court, suggests, or is it not, as the present judgment of the Court's Fifth Chamber makes one think? I see difficulties for the Court, in a future case, in rejecting a national provision which is otherwise justified on grounds of protection of the environment or of human health, just because such an equity clause for individual cases is lacking. Anyway, one might have wished some clarification on this point, too, by the Court.

II. Community Measures Concerning Noise

(9) Community policy on noise is not very coherent. While a strategy to reduce noise levels was announced as early as 1977,[150] it never was translated into a policy statement. In 1996, the Commission published a Green Paper on noise where it identified noise as one of the principal local environmental problems.[151] Following that, it submitted, in July 2000, a proposal for a directive on the assessment and management of environmental noise,[152] which has the aim "to define a common approach to avoid, prevent, or reduce harmful effects on human health due to expo-

---

[148] Advocate General Cosmas, Opinion in Case C–389/96 [1998] ECR I–4473, para. 14.
[149] Court of Justice, Case C–473/98, *Kemikalieinspektionen* [2000] ECR I–5681; see for a discussion of this case p. 225 *supra*.
[150] Second Community environmental action programme [1977] OJ C139/1, para. 67; see also Fourth Community environmental action programme [1987] OJ C328/1, para. 4. 5.
[151] Commission, Future noise policy, COM(96)540 of 4 November 1996.
[152] [2000] OJ C337E/251; explanatory memorandum in COM(2000)468 of 26 July 2000.

sure to environmental noise, by (a) assessment of environmental noise in Member States, based on common methods; (b) ensuring that information on environmental noise and its effects is made available to the public". It remains to be seen whether this proposal will be adopted by the European Parliament and the Council; anyway, it constitutes the first attempt to regulate noise exposure at Community level.

(10) For the rest, Community measures to reduce noise levels concern noise emissions from certain new products. The main objective of the different directives consists in assuring the free circulation of goods within the Community and to make sure that this circulation is not hampered by different noise standard levels in Member States. All noise levels fixed in the specific directives are based on the work of international or European standardisation organisations. They fix noise levels for products that are put on the market for the first time, but contain no provisions on noise emissions throughout the lifetime of a product. Member States may, of course, also provide for specific standards for the use of the products in sensitive areas.

Aircraft noise has been regulated, since 1979, by a number of directives which applied at Community level standards that were set by the Convention on International Civil Aviation; as mentioned, the Community directives do not fix emission limit values themselves, but refer to the provisions of the Convention. Directive 92/14 provided for a ban, as from 1995, of civil subsonic aeroplanes which did not comply with the Convention's "chapter 3" requirements, subject to certain derogations.[153] A number of aeroplanes from airline companies from third world countries were exempted from these provisions, because European airlines had sold these planes to the third world countries prior to 1995.

(11) In 1999, Regulation 925/1999 was adopted[154] which will prohibit the retrospective fitting of aeroplanes of Chapter 2 of the Convention in order to make them meet the stricter requirements of chapter 3 (the so-called hush-kitting). These restrictions were to take effect as from 1 April 2002. Derogations are possible for such aeroplanes that already operated, on 1 April 1999, in the territory of the Community.

This regulation provoked a violent controversy between the Community and the United States of America which claimed that the provisions of Regulation 925/1999 were protectionist and were in breach with the rules of the Convention on International Civil Aviation. The USA filed a complaint with the International Civil Aviation Organisation (ICAO). Following the terrorist events of 11 September 2001, the EU decided to repeal Regulation 925/1999 and to provide for the possibility of individual airports in the EU prohibiting the hush-kitted aircraft. This compromise is likely to lead to little improvement, as any airport which takes such measures, will be confronted with the argument that a prohibition of hush-kitted aircraft will lead to losses of jobs, business opportunities and competitive disadvantage.[155]

---

[153] Directive 92/14 [1992] OJ L76/21.

[154] Regulation 925/1999 on the registration and operation within the Community of certain types of civil subsonic jet aeroplanes which have been modified and recertificated as meeting the standards of volume I, Part II, Chapter 3 of Annex 16 to the Convention on International Civil Aviation, third edition (July 1993) [1999] OJ L115/1.

[155] See on this controversy also European Parliament, Resolution of 30 March 2000 [2000] OJ C378/70.

(12) Noise emissions from cars have been regulated since 1970, when noise emission limit values were introduced;[156] later amendments were introduced, mainly when technical progress had already led to a reduction of noise levels by those cars which were put on the market. The legal basis of these provisions was Article 94 EC Treaty, and since 1987 Article 95 EC Treaty. Progressive reductions of the noise levels for the individual car had limited effect—1 to 2 db(A)—on the overall reduction of noise from cars, due in particular to the significant growth in traffic and a slow replacement of older cars; furthermore, "the test procedure (ISO R 362) doesn't reflect realistic driving conditions and without a regular inspection procedure to ensure maintenance of the acoustical design features the noise levels of the vehicle may increase over time".[157]

For two-wheelers, emission limit values have existed since 1978, again limited to new motorcycles.[158] A directive on noise emission limits from tyres was adopted in 2001.[159] No legislation exists at the Community level on noise emission limit values of boats and railways, including high-speed trains.

(13) Noise from construction machinery has been regulated since 1979. The directives followed the general pattern. They applied to new machinery only, were based on internationally agreed standards and were agreed in reaction to technical development which had taken place beforehand. In 2000, a new directive was adopted which fixed noise emission limit values for "equipment for use outdoors" and which applies to 56 different types of equipment, such as chain saws, compaction machines, compressors, concrete breakers, hedge trimmers, lawnmowers, leaf collectors, loaders, shredders, tower cranes and water pump units.[160] The Directive, based on Article 95 EC Treaty, repeals earlier provisions, fixes emission limit values and tries to ensure the free circulation of outdoor equipment.

Household equipment—refrigerators, dishwashers etc.—is subject to another directive which leaves Member States the freedom to fix emission limit values, but fixes a framework for such requirements.[161] No Community-wide measures for noise emissions are fixed and also do not appear to be planned.

(14) Overall, Community measures which aim at the protection against excessive noise levels seem very inadequate. The two Court judgments on noise levels which were given by the end of the year 2000 concern the non-transposition of Community provisions on noise.[162] Never has there been a judgment which discussed the impact of noise on individuals. This shows rather clearly that the protection against noise is not yet really a serious objective of Community environmental policy.

---

[156] Directive 70/157 relating to the permissible sound level and the exhaust system of motor vehicles [1970] OJ L42/16.

[157] Commission (n. 151 *supra*), p. 7.

[158] Directive 78/1015 [1078] OJ L349/21; this directive was amended several times.

[159] Directive 2001/43, [2001] OJ L211/25.

[160] Directive 2000/14 relating to the noise emissions in the environment by equipment for use outdoors [2000] OJ L162/1.

[161] Directive 86/594 [1986] OJ L344/24.

[162] See, next to the present judgment, Court of Justice, Cases C–324/97, *Commission* v. *Italy* [1998] ECR I–6099; C–326/97, *Commission* v. *Belgium* [1998] ECR I–6107.

5

NATURE PROTECTION*

33. BIRD HABITATS

Judgment of the Court of 19 May 1998
in case C–3/96

Commission of the European Communities
v. *The Netherlands*
[1998] ECR I–3031

Facts and Procedure

Directive 79/409 on the conservation of wild birds[1] was adopted in 1979. Its objective was to protect all wild living birds in the Community. Its Article 2[2] contained a general obligation for Member States, while Articles 3[3] and 4[4] contained more specific obligations.

---

* For further judgments discussing nature protection issues see s. 1, chap. 1 *supra* (*Forests and Environment*), s. 16, chap. 2 *supra* (*Irish Bogs*), s. 31, chap. 4 *supra* (*Crayfish*) and s. 50, chap. 7 *infra* (*Leghold Traps*).

[1] Directive 79/409 on the conservation of wild birds [1979] OJ L103/1; amended by Directive 85/411 [1985] OJ L233/33.

[2] Directive 79/409 (n. 1 *supra*) Art. 2: "Member States shall take the requisite measures to maintain the population of all species of naturally occurring birds in the wild state in the European territory of the Member States to which the Treaty applies at a level which corresponds in particular to ecological, scientific and cultural requirements, while taking account of economic and recreational requirements, or to adapt the population of these species to that level".

[3] Directive 79/409 (n. 1 *supra*), Art. 3: "1. In the light of the requirements referred to in Art. 2, Member States shall take the requisite measures to preserve, maintain or re-establish a sufficient diversity and area of habitats for all the species of birds referred to in Art. 1. 2. The preservation, maintenance and re-establishment of biotopes and habitats shall include primarily the following measures: (a)creation of protected areas; (b) upkeep and management in accordance with the ecological needs of habitats inside and outside the protected zones; (c) re-establishment of destroyed zones; (d) creation of biotopes".

[4] Directive 79/409 (n. 1 *supra*), Art. 4(1): "The species mentioned in Annex I shall be the subject of special conservation measures concerning their habitat in order to ensure their survival and reproduction in their area of distribution. In this connection, account shall be taken of: (a) species in danger of extinction; (b) species vulnerable to specific changes in their habitat; (c) species considered rare because of small populations or restricted local distribution; (d) other species requiring particular attention for reasons of the specific nature of their habitat. Trends and variations in population levels shall be taken into account as a background for evaluations. Member States shall classify in particular

In 1989 the International Council of Bird Preservation, a private environmental organisation, completed a study for the Commission[5] where it established an inventory of all individual sites in Europe, including the Community, according to three categories of criteria which related to the number of species, the inclusion of the site on the list of the 100 most important sites in the Community for a vulnerable species or subspecies, or inclusion amongst the five most important sites for a vulnerable species or subspecies in a given region of the Community. The inventory, known as IBA 89, identified 70 sites in the Netherlands, covering an area of 797,920 hectares, as qualifying for classification on ornithological grounds. A list drawn up by the Netherlands' Ministry of Agriculture and Fisheries in 1991 identified 53 suitable sites covering 398,180 hectares.

The Commission was of the opinion that the Netherlands had classified an insufficient number of sites as special protection areas under Article 4 of Directive 79/409, as, by the date of application, the Netherlands had classified only 23 sites with a total area of 327,602 hectares. This constituted less than half of the sites listed in IBA 89.

The Netherlands was of the opinion that there was no legal obligation to designate special protection areas, as Member States, instead of designating such areas, could also have recourse to other conservation measures. Furthermore, the Netherlands' government argued that Member State had a margin of discretion in implementing Article 4(1) of Directive 79/409. Only the most suitable territories had to be designed and the Commission would thus have to prove, for each individual territory, that the non-designation constituted a breach of a legal obligation. Also, the Dutch government argued that, when drawing up its own list of suitable areas, it had used three criteria, which, however, led to different results from IBA 89.

Judgment (extracts)

55. It must first be observed that, contrary to the contention of . . . Netherlands, Article 4(1) of the Directive requires Member States to classify as special protection areas the most suitable territories in number and size for the conservation of the species mentioned in Annex I, an obligation which it is not possible to avoid by adopting other special conservation methods.

56. It follows from that provision, as interpreted by the Court, that if such species occur on the territory of a Member State, it is obliged to define *inter alia* special protection areas for them . . .

the most suitable territories in number and size as special protection areas for the conservation of these species, taking into account their protection requirements in the geographical sea and land area where this Directive applies".

[5] International Council for Bird Preservation, *Important Bird Areas in Europe* (International Council for Bird Preservation, Cambridge, 1989).

57. Such an interpretation of the obligation to classify special protection areas is moreover consistent with the system of specifically targeted and reinforced protection laid down by Article 4 of the Directive in respect in particular of the species listed in Annex I . . . , *a fortiori* since even Article 3 provides, for all the species of birds covered by the Directive, that the preservation, maintenance and re-establishment of biotopes and habitats is to include primarily measures such as the creation of protected areas.

58. Besides . . . if Member States could escape the obligation to classify special protection areas if they considered that other special conservation measures were sufficient to ensure survival and reproduction of the species mentioned in annex I, the objective of creation a coherent network of special protection areas, referred to in Article 4(3) of the Directive, might not be achieved.

59. Second, it must be pointed out that the economic requirements mentioned in Article 2 of the Directive may not be taken into account when selecting a special protection area and defining its boundaries . . .

60. Moreover, while Member States have a certain margin of discretion in the choice of special protection areas, the classification of those areas is nevertheless subject to certain ornithological criteria determined by the Directive . . .

61. It follows that the Member States' margin of discretion in choosing the most suitable territories for classification as special protection areas does not concern the appropriateness of classifying as special protection areas the territories which appear the most suitable according to ornithological criteria, but only the application of those criteria for identifying the most suitable territories for conservation of the species listed in Annex I to the Directive.

62. Consequently, Member States are obliged to classify as special protection areas all the sites which, applying ornithological criteria, appear to be the most suitable for conservation of the species in question.

63. Thus where it appears that a Member State has classified as special protection area sites the number and total area of which are manifestly less than the number and total area of the sites considered to be the most suitable for conservation of the species in question, it will be possible to find that that Member State has failed to fulfil its obligation under Article 4(1) of the Directive.

64. Consequently, the Netherlands Government's argument that the Commission must establish, territory by territory, specific infringements of that provision cannot be accepted.

65. Third, it should be observed, that the Netherlands Government, while not questioning the scientific reliability of IBA 89, contends that the application of the criteria on which that report is based cannot, in view of their general character, lead to unequivocal results as regards the classification of special protection areas. It has maintained that, although it applied the same criteria, as those on which IBA 89 is based, it arrived in its inventory of sites potentially classifiable as special protection areas at a result which was very different from that indicated by that report. At the hearing, however, it admitted that its criteria differed from those used in IBA 89.

66. In that regard, it is significant that . . . Netherlands has to this very day failed to produce a single document from the national procedure for classifying special protection areas which indicates the criteria which governed the designation of special protection areas in that Member State.

67. Moreover, throughout the pre-litigation procedure and also in its defence and rejoinder, it stressed that when designating special protection areas it had, under Article 2 of the Directive, to take account of economic and recreational requirements. That approach is inconsistent with the Netherlands Government's assertion that it applied exclusively ornithological criteria when designating special protection areas.

68. In this conncection, it must be pointed out that IBA 89 draws up an inventory of areas which are of great importance for the conservation of wild birds in the Community. That inventory was prepared for the competent directorate-general of the Commission by the Eurogroup for the Conservation of Birds and Habitats in conjunction with the International Council of Bird Preservation and in cooperation with Commission experts.

69. In the circumstances, IBA 89 has proved to be the only document containing scientific evidence making it possible to assess whether the defendant State has fulfilled its obligation to classify as special protection areas the most suitable territories in number and area for conservation of the protected species. The situation would be different if . . . Netherlands had produced scientific evidence in particular to show that the obligation in question could be fulfilled by classifying as special protection areas territories whose number and total area were less than those resulting from IBA 89.

70. It follows that that inventory, although not legally binding on the Member States concerned, can, by reason of its acknowledged scientific value in the present case, be used by the Court as a basis for reference for assessing the extent to which the . . . Netherlands has complied with its obligations to classify special protection areas.

71. It should be added that, even supposing that the application of the ornithological criteria in IBA 89 could lead different entitites to produce markedly different classifications of special protection areas, the mere possibility of this, which has not been shown to have occurred in the present case, cannot as such be taken into consideration in order to undermine the probative value of IBA 89 in this instance.

72. Since it thus appears that the Netherlands has classified as special protection areas territories whose number and total area are clearly smaller than the number and total area of the territories suitable, according to IBA 89, for classification as special protection areas, the requirements of Article 4(1) of the Directive cannot be regarded as satisfied.

73. Consequently, without there being any need to consider the other arguments which have been put forward, it must be held that by classifying as special protected areas territories whose number and total area are clearly smaller than the number and total area of the territories suitable for classification as special protection areas within the meaning of Article 4(1) of the Directive, . . . Netherlands has failed to fulfil its obligations under that directive.

Commentary

I. Designation of Habitats in the Netherlands

(1) This judgment was delivered 17 years after the adoption of Directive 79/409 and clarified—once more—two rather basic elements of that Directive: first, that Member States are under a legal obligation to designate, under Article 4(1) of Directive 79/409, special protection areas. The Court had decided on several occasions that Member States were obliged to designate special protection areas.[6] In view of the clear and unambiguous wording of Article 4(1), it is difficult to reach another conclusion. The Court also points quite rightly to Article 4(4) of Directive 79/409;[7] if there were no obligation to designate areas, Member States could escape the obligation of Article 4(4) just by omitting to designate.

(2) The second element is even more surprising. The Court stated that, contrary to the opinion of the Netherlands, the provisions of Article 2 could not be taken in consideration when special protection areas according to Article 4(1) of the Directive were to be designated. Again, this argument had been made by the Court many times before[8] and the only explanation why it was nevertheless raised by the Netherlands seems to be that the designation of habitats came, at the time of the judgment, under the responsability of the Ministry for Agriculture which was not very open to environmental arguments.

(3) This aspect would also explain the whole basis of the litigation. Indeed, under almost no circumstance was it possible to consider the designation of 23 sites as special protection areas as sufficient in order to comply with the Directive's requirements. Even the Netherlands had drafted a list of suitable sites which contained 53 sites—though the method used for the elaboration had been hidden from the Court of Justice. And it must not be forgotten that the designation of sites under Article 4(1) of Directive 79/409 should have been made by 1981; the Netherland was thus desperately late and desperately incomplete in its measures to implement Directive 79/409. This and further elements seem to show some lack of goodwill to follow the wording and the spirit of Directive 79/409.

(4) From the point of view of environmental protection, the most welcome part of the judgment is the one which comments on the inventory of suitable bird

---

[6] See for instance Court of Justice, Cases C–57/89, *Commission* v. *Germany* [1991] ECR I–883; in that case, the Court stated in para. 20 that Member States have a certain discretion when designating areas—which makes sense only if there is an obligation to designate; C–334/89, *Commission* v. *Italy* [1991] ECR I–93; C–355/90, *Commission* v. *Spain* [1993] ECR I–4221.

[7] Directive 79/409 (n. 1 *supra*), Art. 4(4): "In respect of the protection areas referred to in paras. 1 and 2 above, Member States shall take appropriate steps to avoid pollution or deterioration of habitats or any disturbances affecting the birds, in so far as these would be significant having regard to the objectives of this Article . . .".

[8] Court of Justice, Cases C–247/85, *Commission* v. *Belgium* [1987] ECR 3029; C–262/85, *Commission* v. *Italy* [1987] ECR 3073; C–57/89 (n. 6 *supra*); C–44/95, RSPB [1996] ECR I–3805 (see on this case p. 314 *infra*).

sites, IBA 89. The Court found that this inventory, while established by a private organisation and thus not having legally binding value for Member States, constituted an inventory which was established for the Commission, with the objective of furthering the application of Directive 79/409. It was based on transparent criteria which were ornithological. The Court therefore accepted IBA 89 as a valid scientific parameter for assessing Member States' compliance with the Directive. While Member States were allowed to contest the findings in that inventory, they had to base their arguments on the one hand on ornithological criteria, too, and on the other hand on scientific grounds.

(5) In this way, IBA 89—which in the meantime has been finetuned by the elaboration of IBA 94 in 1994—has become a guide for the designation of special protection areas throughout the Community. It is clear that Member States do not like this conclusion of the Court, and it came as no surprise that the Netherlands and also Germany as third party intervener in this case argued against the use of IBA 89. The more objective ornithological criteria exist which allow the identification of those sites which are suitable for designation as special protection areas, the more difficult it becomes for Member States not to designate these areas. It is clear, though—and the Court underlined this in paragraph 62 of its judgment—that Member States are not obliged to designate all suitable sites under Article 4(1), but only all most suitable sites, which is a fine difference.

II. The Designation of Birds' Habitats under Directive 79/409

(6) In the meantime, Directive 79/409 celebrated its twentieth anniversary in 1999. The sad part of this event was that Member States still have not yet fully complied with their obligations under Article 4(1). Thus, the "coherent whole" which Article 4 of Directive 79/409 tried to establish within and for the Community[9] is still not existent.

(7) The designation of habitats (special protection areas) under Article 4(1) of Directive 79/409 was a core obligation under that Directive. Some information on the progress achieved may be taken from the following table:[10]

---

[9] See Directive 79/409 (n. 1 *supra*), Art. 4(3): "Member State shall send the Commission all relevant information so that it may take appropriate initiatives with a view to the coordination necessaryto ensure that the areas provided for in paras. 1 and 2 above form a coherent whole which meets the protection requirements of these species in the geographical sea and land area where this Directive applies".

[10] See Commission, Second report on the application of Directive 79/409, COM(93)572 of 24 November 1993 p. 43 and 44; Commission, Natura 2000 Newsletter, December 2000, p. 6.

Designated special protection areas under Article 4(1) of Directive 79/409

Member State	Date	Number of area	Total surface km²	% of surface of Member State	State of designation
Belgium	31/12/1986				
	26/4/1991	36	4.313	14.1	
	14/11/2000	36	4.313	14.1	almost complete
Denmark	31/12/1986	111	9.601	22.3	
	26/4/1991	111	9.601	22.3	
	14/11/2000	111	9.601	22.3	almost complete
Germany	31/12/1986	117	2.910		
	26/4/1991	117	2.910		
	14/11/2000	617	21.672	6.1	incomplete
Greece	31/12/1986				
	26/4/1991	26	1.916		
	14/11/2000	52	4.965	3.8	incomplete
Spain	31/12/1986				
	26/4/1991	135	23.249		
	14/11/2000	260	53.602	10.6	incomplete
France	31/12/1986	20	1.520		
	26/4/2000	61	5.200		
	14/11/2000	117	8.193	1.5	obviously insufficient
Ireland	31/12/1986	16	0.367		
	26/4/1991	20	0.555		
	14/11/2000	109	2.236	3.2	incomplete
Italy	31/12/1986				
	26/4/1991	74	3.104		
	14/11/2000	342	13.707	4.6	incomplete
Luxembourg	31/12/86				
	26/4/1991	4	0.03		
	14/11/2000	13	160	6.2	incomplete
Netherlands	31/12/1986	5	0.077		
	26/4/1991	9	0.529		
	14/11/2000	79	10.000	24.1	almost complete
Austria	14/11/2000	83	12.080	14.4	incomplete
Portugal	31/12/1986				
	26/4/1991	34	3.189		
	14/11/2000	47	8.468	9.2	incomplete
Finland	14/11/2000	451	27.500	8.1	incomplete
Sweden	14/11/2000	394	24.647	5.5	incomplete
United Kingdom	31/12/1986	21	0.374		
	26/4/1991	40	1.289		
	14/11/2000	209	8.648	3.5	incomplete
Total	31/12/1986	309	14.518		
	26/4/1991	667	55.355		
	14/11/2000	2920	209.792		

(8) The table shows that, while there was some progress in the designation of habitats, this designation is still not complete more than 20 years after the adoption of the Directive. The five Member States having designated less than 5 per cent of their territory are France, Ireland, Greece, Italy and the United Kingdom. Three Member States have almost completed their designation, Belgium, Denmark—and the Netherlands. For this last Member State, progress since the judgment in the present case in May 1998 is remarkable: from 23 sites designated in 1996, covering about 8 km^2, this Member State passed 79 sites covering some 10.000 km^2. This again gives ground for the presumption that the Netherlands knew already at the time of the judgment in the present case which areas ought to be designated and that rather internal discussions had slowed down the designation of special protection areas. For once, therefore, the judgment of the Court of Justice seems to have had a rather immediate effect at the level of the Member State concerned.

34. HABITAT PROTECTION IN THE EC

Judgment of the Court (Fifth Chamber) of 6 April 2000
Case C–256/98

Commission of the European Communities v. *France*
[2000] ECR I–2487

Facts and Procedure

Directive 92/43 provides for the protection of habitats and of wild fauna and flora.[11] The Directive was adopted in 1992 and should have been transposed into national law by Member States by early June 1994. France transmitted circulars from 1993 and 1994, a law of early 1995 and a decree of the same year.[12]

---

[11] Directive 92/43 on the conservation of natural habitats and of wild fauna and flora [1992] OJ L206/7.

[12] Circular 38 of 21 January 1993, circular 24 of 28 January 1994; Law 95–101 concerning more stringent measures for the protection of the environment, of 2 February 1995, JORF of 3 February 1995, p. 1840; decree 95–631 on the conservation of natural habitats and habitats of wild species of Community interest, of 5 May 1995, JORF of 7 May 1995, p. 7612.

The Commission was of the opinion that France had not transposed Article 6[13] of Directive 92/43 into national law. It therefore applied to the Court of Justice. During the proceedings before the Court, France referred to a number of French legal provisions which, in its view, constituted an adequate range of measures for ensuring that the objectives of Directive 92/43, and in particular its Article 6, could be realised.

The Commission was of the opinion that nowhere in French law were the French authorities expressly obliged to apply conservation and protection measures to special areas of conservation, as required by Article 6(1) and (2) of Directive 92/43.

Judgment (extracts)

28. It is clear . . . that . . . in the application, the Commission essentially imputes to the French Republic a failure to establish a legal framework to accomodate the measures necessary to ensure the protection of special areas of conservation, such measures being understood in the sense of measures defined by the national legislation and designed to take effect at the same time as the adoption . . . of general measures necessary to ensure compliance with the Directive.

29. In its reply, the Commission amended its ground of complaint to focus on the question of the existence in Community law of an obligation incumbent on Member States to incorporate in their laws express provisions requiring the competent national authorities to apply the conservation and protection measures provided for in Article 6(1) and (2) of the Directive to special areas of conservation.

---

[13] Directive 92/43 (n. 11 *supra*), Art. 6: "1. For special areas of conservation, Member States shall establish the necessary conservation measures involving, if need be, appropriate management plans specifically designed for the sites or integrated into other development plans, and appropriate statutory, administrative or contractual measures which correspond to the ecological requirements of the natural habitat types in Annex I and the species in Annex II present on the sites. 2. Member States shall take appropriate steps to avoid, in the special areas of conservation, the deterioration of natural habitats and the habitats of species as well as disturbance of the species for which the areas have been designated, in so far as such disturbance could be significant in relation to the objectives of this Directives. 3. Any plan or project not directly connected with or necessary to the management of the site but likely to have a significant effect thereon, either individually or in combination with other plans or projects, shall be subject to appropriate assessment of its implications for the site in view of the site's conservation objectives. In the light of the conclusions of the assessment of the implications for the site and subject to the provisions of para. 4, the competent national authorities shall agree to the plan or project only after having ascertained that it will not adversely affect the integrity of the site concerned and, if appropriate, after having obtained the opinion of the general public. 4. If, in spite of a negative assessment of the implications for the site and in the absence of alternative solutions, a plan or project must nevertheless be carried out for imperative reasons of overriding public interest, including those of a social or economic nature, the Member State shall take all compensatory measures necessary to ensure that the overall coherence of Natura 2000 is protected. It shall inform the Commission of the compensatory measures adopted. Where he site hosts a priority natural habitat type and/or a priority species, the only considerations which may be raised are those relating to human health or public safety, to beneficial consequences of primary importance for the environment or, further to an opinion from the Commission, to other imperative reasons of overriding public interest".

30. It should be noted, however, that the amendment goes beyond a mere restatement, albeit in greater detail, of the initial complaints, thereby raising submissions before the Court which were not put forward during the pre-litigation procedure or in the application initiating the proceedings.

31. Those submissions are inadmissible because they are contrary to Article 38(1)(c) of the Rules of Procedure, under which the parties are required to state the subject-matter of the proceedings in the application initating proceedings. .

32. Since the Commission must be deemed to have withdrawn its complaints in relation to Article 6(1) and (2) of the Directive, as initially formulated, the application must to that extent be dismissed as inadmissible.

33. Consequently, there is no need to consider the question—which, moreover, was not addressed during the proceedings—whether Member States were under an obligation to transpose the provisions at issue, particularly Article 6(1) of the Directive, into national law before the Commission adopted the list of sites of Community interest pursuant to the third subparagraph of Article 4(2) of the Directive.

34. . . . as regards Article 6(3) of the Directive, the French Government admits that under the existing rules of French law relating to the prior assessment of the environmental implications of a development plan or project, the competent authorities are not able in all cases to refuse authorisation on the grounds that the findings of such an assessment were negative . . .

35. However, the French Government disputes the Commission's assertions that its legislation does not enable the competent national authorities to comply fully with the obligation laid down in Article 6(3) of the Directive to carry out a prior assessment of the implications for the environment of any plan or project not directly connected with or necessary to the management of the site but likely nevertheless to have a significant effect thereon, citing in that respect Law No 76–629 of 10 July 1976 on the protection of nature (JORF of 12 and 13 July 1976, p. 4203).

36. It is common ground that there has long been provision in French law, notably in the rules provided for by Law 76–629, for compulsory environmental impact assessments along the lines indicated by the Directive. Nevertheless, it is for the national authorities responsible for the transposition of the Directive into French law to make sure that those rules do indeed guarantee, with sufficient clarity and precision, the full implementation of Article 6(3).

37. However, as regards two of the three facets of French law as it stands which, in the view of the Commission, precludes full compliance with the obligations imposed by the Directive, the transposition into French law is not sufficiently clear and precise.

38. That does not apply to the first point raised by the Commission. As regards its assertion that the rules in force in France do not guarantee an assessment in the case of "plans" likely to have a significant effect on sites, the Advocate General has properly pointed out in paragraphs 32 to 34 of his Opinion both that the Directive fails to determine the term "plan" and that French law (Article 2 of Law 76–629) requires an environmental impact assessment in the case of both *"projets d'aménagement"* (development projects) and "*documents d'urbanisme*" (town planning). It cannot be regarded established, therefore, that the French legislation in force does not satisfactorily transpose into national law the term "plan" referred to in Article 6(3) of the Directive.

39. On the other hand, as regards the Commission's uncontested statement that, contrary to the Directive, the position in France is that the environmental impact assessment may be waived in the case of certain projects because of their low costs or their purpose, it should be noted that such exemptions cannot be justified in the terms of the discretion of Member States implied, according to the French Government, by the expression "likely to have a significant effect [on the site]". On this point, it is enough to note that, in any event, that provision cannot authorise a Member State to enact national legislation which allows the environmental impact assessment obligation for development plans to be waived because of low costs entailed or the particular type of work planned.

40. Lastly, as regards the Commission's statement that, contrary to the requirements of Article 6(3) of the Directive, there is no provision in French law which couples the obligation to make an environmental impact asessment with consideration of the site's conservation objectives, it should be noted that none of the provisions to which the French Government refers in its pleadings requires the assessment to determine the environmental impact of development plans in the light of the site's particular conservation objectives. It must be concluded, therefore, that those implications of Article 6(3) have not been transposed into French law with sufficient clarity and precision.

41. It follows that, as regards two of the three facets examined in paragraphs 38 to 40 above, Article 6(3) of the Directive has not been transposed into French law in a sufficiently clear and precise manner. Consequently, the action brought by the Commission is well founded in this respect.

42. . . . as regards the transposition into French law of Article 6(4) of the Directive, the Commission claims that the French Republic has not implemented substantive conditions laid down in that provision, concerning the carrying out of a plan or project notwithstanding a negative assessment of the impact on the site, in cases where there are no alternative solutions.

43. On that point, it is enough to note that the French Government acknowledges that it has not adopted the measures necessary to comply with Article 6(4) of the Directive.

Commentary

I. *Absence of or Incorrect Transposition of Directives*

(1) The judgment offers a good picture of the practical difficulties in transposing legal provisions which aim at nature protection into national law. In this case,

Article 6 of Directive 92/43 was in question. The Commission was of the opinion that France had not transposed this Article into national law. France then quoted a number of provisions of its national legislation which, it argued, allowed it to comply with the requirements of Article 6(1) and (2). The Commission accepted this, but nevertheless insisted that Article 6(1) and (2) needed an express transposition which required the French authorities to take special conservation measures according to Article 6(1) and to avoid deterioration and disturbances in habitats according to Article 6(2). And the Court considered that the Commission had changed the subject-matter of litigation so that its application was held inadmissible.

(2) Without knowing the wording of the application and of the subsequent submissions by the Commission which are, as it is normal, not reproduced in the judgment, it is impossible to assess whether the Court is correct in its decision. It may be mentioned that the Advocate General did not have the slightest doubt in this regard, did not even mention the possibility of a change of the subject-matter and considered the Commission's application well founded.

I am of the opinion that the problem of an express transposition of provisions contained in a directive is a neglected subject and deserves more attention. Many Community provisions, in particular definitions, statements on objectives, principles to follow and orientations to take, are quite frequently not transposed into national law.

(3) Article 6(2) is a good example. It makes a considerable difference whether the French legislation between 1976 and 1995 succeeds in avoiding deterioration or significant disturbance in habitats. It is submitted that for local and regional administrations, for economic operators, constructors, farmers and other persons, it is very relevant to find an express provision in national law which states "You shall not deteriorate habitats or provoke significant disturbance of species in habitats". Such an express provision makes negotiations easier, facilitates the knowledge of the legislation for all persons interested in activities concerning habitats and clarifies the state of the law for all citizens.

(4) As regards French legislation on Article 6(2), the Advocate General stated:[14] "France's transposition of Article 6(2) is . . . clearly insufficient. As noted above, this provision, in effect, contains a prohibition on activities which could lead to a deterioration of protected habitats or the disturbance of protected species. In the first place, France does not even claim that there exists in its law a provision which applies such a prohibition to special areas of conservation. While it does have rules prohibiting the destruction of the natural enviornment, these refer neither specifically to special areas of conservation nor generally to the objectives of the Directive . . .".

(5) When the Court declared the Commission's application inadmissible, it seems to have considered that the Commission first had claimed non-transposition of Article 6 by the France and that it claimed later that France had incorrectly

---

[14] Advocate General Fenelly, Opinion in Case C–256/98 *Commission* v. *French Republic* [2000] ECR I–2487, para. 25.

transposed the Directive into national law. It might well be argued that the lack of transposition by an express provision—supposing such an express transposition was required—is in fact a non-transposition of a provision. For the Commission, the advice can only be to consider national legislation, as far as is possible, to constitute a transposition of the Community provision and to base any claims on a bad— incomplete or incorrect or not "express" enough—transposition into national law.

After the adoption of a directive, the Commission regularly sends out standardised letters in which it asks Member States to show, by way of tables, how and where exactly they transposed the Directive's provisions into national law. In the past, Member States very regularly ignored these letters and hardly ever provided the tables. In the light of the present judgment, it might be advisable to revive the attempts to find out, via such tables, whether a Member States has not transposed or whether it has badly transposed the provisions of a Community directive— independently of the fact that one sometimes has the impression that the number of formal deficiencies is particular high in cases where the French natural environment is in question.

II. *Protected Habitats and National Derogations*

(6) No formal problems existed as regards the Commission's arguments that Article 6(3) and (4) had not properly been transposed, obviously, because these provisions had not been discussed in the pre-litigation stage. The Court was quite careful to examine whether French legislation complied with the Directive's requirements. Its conclusions are convincing, even where it does not follow the Commission's arguments as regards the French town and country plans and their impact on habitats (paragraph 38).

(7) As regards the "appropriate assessment" mentioned in Article 6(3), it should be noted that the Commission had tried twice to ensure that inside a designated habitat[15] all projects should be the subject of an environmental impact assessment according to Directive 85/337.[16] Twice, however, the Coucil had rejected this proposal[17] and the best which the Commission could obtain was the notion of "appropriate assessment"—whatever that means. The consequence is also that there is no mandatory consultation of the public concerned by a project, as provided for in Article 6(2) of Directive 85/337.

French legislation allowed environmental impact assessments not to be made where the total cost of a project was less than 12 million French francs or where they concerned electricity, gas or telecommunications networks.[18] As Article 6(3) provides that any plan or project which may have a significant effect on a habitat

---

[15] Commission, proposal for Directive 92/43 [1988] OJ C247/7, Art. 10; proposal for Directive 97/11 [1994] OJ C130/8.

[16] Directive 85/337 on the assessment of the effects of certain public and private projects on the environment [1985] OJ L175/50.

[17] See Directive 97/11 amending Directive 85/337 (n. 16 *supra*) [1997] OJ L37/5, recital 10.

[18] Advocate General Fenelly (n. 14 *supra*), para. 35.

shall be the subject of an "appropriate assessment", this derogation was considered unacceptable in the transposition of Article 6(3), though the Court did not specifically mention the French derogatory provisions.

As regards Article 6(4), the Court satisfied itself with the acknowledgement by France that this provision had not been transposed.

(8) In the light of this discussion of Article 6(3) and (4), it is not clear why the Court made the observation which was limited to Articles 6(1) and (2)[19] that it was doubtful whether Member States were under an obligation to transpose Article 6(1) and (2) into national law before the publication of the Community list of habitats. Clearly, if there is no obligation to transpose Article 6(1) and (2) before the Commission has published the Community list of habitats, then there is no obligation, at this stage, to transpose Article 6(3) and (4), as these provisions refer to the same habitats as Article 6(1) and (2).

Therefore, the Court should have examined whether there was an obligation for Member States to transpose Article 6 into national law before the Community list of sites of Community importance was published. The obiter dictum in paragraph 33 of the judgment is wrong, as there was a need for answering that question.

(9) In substance, Article 23 of Directive 92/43 requires Member States to transpose Directive 92/43 into national law within two years of its notification.[20] There is no specific provision to transpose Article 6, though it was clear at the time of adopting the Directive that the Commission's list of sites of Community importance could not be published immediately, since it depended on the establishment of the national lists. If the Court were correct that Member States had an obligation to transpose Article 6 only after the publication of the Commission's list, then no time would have been fixed for finishing the transposition.

From all this, I would conclude that the Council (Member States) had chosen to have Article 6 transposed into national law together with the other provisions though it could not become immediately operational.

(10) The transposition of Directives 79/409 on the conservation of wild birds[21] and of 92/43 posed considerable problems in France, on the one hand as regards the provisions on hunting, on the other hand as regards the provision on habitats. Before the Revolution of 1789, hunting in France was the prerogative of the nobility. This prerogative was abolished during the Revolution with the effect that hunting is perceived in France, at least in some circles, as a fundamental right and any restriction on this free right is perceived as a restriction of this fundamental right.

(11) Similar reflections influenced the attitude against the designation and protection of habitats. The populist movement, alimented in particular by farmers, fishermen, hunters and other groups and often also supported by vested local

---

[19] Para. 33 of the judgment.
[20] Directive 92/43 (n. 11 *supra*), Art. 23: "1. Member States shall bring into force the laws, regulations and administrative provisions necessary to comply with this Directive within two years of its noification. They shall forthwith inform the Commission thereof. 2. . . .".
[21] Directive 79/409 on the conservation of wild birds [1979] OJ L103/1.

interests, went so far as to form a political party/movement in defence of the rural form of living, arguing that the French rural traditions would be destroyed by the two Directives; since that movement had notable success in political elections, it influenced policy-makers, Parliament and public opinion quite considerably. In summer 1996, France went so far as to freeze its work on a national list of habitats under Directive 92/43 for several months, arguing that it was clear neither who would finance the managing of habitats nor exactly what activities would be forbidden within a habitat. Since then, the the co-operation between the Commission and France has been less tense; however, sufficient divergencies continue to exist and the management neither of Directive 79/409 nor of Directive 92/43 can be considered to be satisfactory in France at present.

35. PROTECTING SPECIFIC HABITATS

Judgment of the Court (Fifth Chamber) of 25 November 1999
Case C–96/98

Commission of the European Communities v. *France*
[1999] ECR I–8531

Facts and Procedure

The Marais Poitevin (Poitevin Marsh) is a large area in the west of France, in the departments of Vendée and Charente-Maritime, which has an overall surface of at least 80,000 hectares. It is of exceptional ornithological interest, as it contains natural wet prairies as well as many other habitats such as lagoons, dunes, polders, woods, peat bogs and waterways. The Marais is inhabited by large numbers of endangered wild bird species listed in Annex I to the Birds Directive,[22] and is used as a wintering area for more than 28 migratory species.

France had originally designated about 4,500 hectares of the Poitevin Marsh as a special protection area under Article 4(1) of Directive 79/409.[23] When the

---

[22] Directive 79/409 on the conservation of wild birds [1979] OJ L103/1.

[23] Directive 79/409 (n. 22 *supra*), Art. 4: "1. The species mentioned in Annex I shall be the subject of special conservation measures concerning their habitat in order to ensure their survuval and reproduction in their area of distribution . . . Member States shall classify in particular the most suitable territories in number and size as special protection areas for the conservation of these species, taking into account their protection requirements in the geographical sea and land area where this Directive applies . . . 4. In respect of the protection areas referred to in paras. 1 and 2 above, Member States shall take appropriate steps to avoid pollution or deterioration of habitats or any disturbances affecting the birds, in so far as these would be significant having regard to the objectives of this Article . . .".

Commission began, in December 1992, formal proceedings against France under Article 226 EC Treaty, France designated in total 26,250 hectares under Article 4(1).

The Comission was of the opinion that this area covered only about one third of the Poitevin Marsh which was of ornithological interest and that there was considerable pressure on the entire ecosystem because of systematic drainage, intensive cultivation of land and the construction of a new motorway. France designated a further 3,540 hectares, but contested any failure to act under Directive 79/409.

The Commission then applied, in April 1998, to the Court, raising four points against the French authorities: (a) failure to classify a sufficiently large area in the Poitevin Marsh as special protection area (SPA); (b) failure to confer sufficient legal status on the SPAs classified; (c) failure to take appropriate steps to avoid deterioration of the Poitevin Marsh; (d) declassification of part of a classified SPA in order to allow construction of a motorway.

Judgment (extracts)

[(a) the extent of the special protection area]

13. The Commission points out that 77,900 hectares of the Poitevin Marsh were recognised by the French authorities in 1994 as constituting an important area for bird conservation . . . (ZICO). In addition, 57,830 hectares of the Poitevin Marsh were included in the European ornithological inventory entitled "Important Bird Areas in Europe" published in 1989 ("the IBA"). According to the Commission, the entire ZICO of the Poitevin Marsh or, at the very least, the entire area featuring in the IBA inventory should be classified as an SPA.

14. The French Government contends that, in April 1996, the total area of the sites in the Poitevin Marsh classified as SPAs was 33,742 hectares . . . It points out in this regard that it intends in the near future to notify the further classification of almost 15,000 hectares considered relevant both in the light of ornithological criteria and at the operational level . . .

15. It should first be observed that it is common ground that the Poitevin Marsh is a natural area of very great ornithological value for many bird species covered by Article 4(1) and (2) of the Birds Directive and that the French Government does not, in substance, deny that the area of land in the Poitevin Marsh classified as SPAs is inadequate in the light of Article 4 of the Birds Directive.

16. Accordingly, without its being necessary to address the question as to the area over which the SPAs in the Poitevin Marsh ought to extend in order for the obligations under the Birds Directive to be satisfied, it must be held that the French Republic failed, within the prescribed period, to classify as SPAs, within the meaning of Article 4(1) and (2) of the Birds Directive, a sufficient area in the

Poitevin Marsh. The Commission's application must for that reason be upheld on that point.

[(b) the legal status of special protection areas already classified]

22. With regard to the . . . measures which according to the French Government, are intended to provide the SPAs with a sufficient protection regime, it must be borne in mind that, according to the Court's case-law, Article 4(1) and (2) of the Birds Directive requires the Member States to provide SPAs with a legal protection regime that is capable, in particular, of ensuring both the survival and reproduction of the bird species listed in Annex I to the Directive and the breeding, moulting and wintering of migratory species not listed in Annex I which are, nevertheless, regular visitors . . .

25. Even if it were to be assumed that the SPAs classified consist entirely of wetlands and that the Law on Water enable water resources in these areas to be preserved in an efficient manner, the fact still remains that, to the extent to which it includes only provisions relating to water management, the Law is not in itself such as to ensure sufficient protection for the purpose of Article 4(1) and (2) of the birds Directive.

26. So far as . . . agri-environmental measures are concerned, it must be held, as the Commission has argued . . . that these are voluntary and purely hortatory in nature in relation to farmers working holdings in the Poitevin Marsh.

27. Those measures cannot therefore, in any event, be capable of suplementing effectively the protection regime for the classified SPAs.

28. It must for that reason be held that, by failing to adopt measures conferring a sufficient legal protection regime on the SPAs classified in the Poitevin Marsh, the French Republic has failed to fulfil its obligations under Article 4(1) and (2) of the Birds Directive. The Commission's application must herefore also be upheld on this point.

[(c) the deterioration of the Poitevin Marsh]

29. The Commission . . . points out . . . that the natural meadows, which form the most important habitat for the conservation of wild birds in the Poitevin Marsh and which covered an area of 55,450 hectares in 1973, had an area of some 26,750 hectares in 1990, with approximately 28,700 hectares being placed under cultivation during the intervening period. With a view to facilitating agricultural activity, drainage was carried out, wetlands were reclaimed and ditches filled in.

30. According to the Commission, one of the important direct consequences of the reduction of wetlands has been the appreciable fall in certain bird populations such as wintering ducks and black-tailed godwits in the SPA of the Baie d'Aiguillon.

32. . . . The French Government . . . acknowledges that the protection regime for the area has not always been effective. However, it argues that the responsibility for the reduction in the wetlands rests primarily with the common agricultural policy ("CAP") and not solely with the French authorities.

33. Agri-environmental aid, the French Government submits, requires a considerable financial effort on the part of the State, whereas even aid for intensive agriculture, aid which is often more substantial, is financed entirely by the Community budget under the CAP. This difference in manner of implementation between the European policies on intensive agriculture and those supporting environmentally friendly agriculture lies, in the French Government's submission, behind the difficulties in conserving the Poitevin Marsh. Thus, the Community aid package for agriculture, which does not favour breeders, runs contrary to the policy of safeguarding wetlands.

35. It should first be pointed out in this regard that the first sentence of Article 4(4) of the Birds Directive . . . requires Member States to take appropriate steps to avoid, inter alia, deterioration of habitats in the SPAs classified pursuant to Article 4(1).

39. It is clear from an examination of, *inter alia*, the Fench Government's response of 11 June 1996 to the reasoned opinion, the reasoned opinion itself, and the maps placed on the case-file that the nature reserve of Saint-Denis du Payré and the common land of Poiré-sur-Velluire, which form part of the Marais Poitevin intérieur SPA, are at present drying out. So far as the SPAs of the Baie de l'Aiguillon and the Pointe d'Arcay are concerned, the documents before the Court show that marine-farming construction and embankment works have been extended in those areas, thereby disturbing bird life. Furthermore, the study by the Bird Protection League . . . indicates that the average population of wintering ducks in the Baie d'Aiguillon and the Pointe d'Arcay has fallen from 67,845 for the period 1977–1986 to 16,551 for the period 1987–1996.

40. It follows that the French Republic has failed in its obligation to take appropriate measures to avoid deterioration of the areas in the Poitevin Marsh classified as SPAs, in breach of the first sentence of Article 4(4) of the Birds Directive. As for the French Government's argument that Community aid measures for agriculture are disadvantageous to agriculture compatible with the conservation requirements laid down by the Birds Directive, it should be pointed out that, even assuming that this were the case and a certain lack of consistency between the various Community policies were thus shown to exist, this still could not authorise a Member State to avoid its obligations under that directive, in particular under the first sentence of Article 4(4) thereof.

41. Second, it must be pointed out that according to the Court's case-law, the first sentence of Article 4(4) of the Birds Directive requires Member States to take appropriate steps to avoid, *inter alia*, deterioration of habitats in the areas which are most suitable for the conservation of wild birds, even where the areas in question have not been classified as SPAs, provided that they should have been so classified . . .

43. It is thus necessary to consider whether the Court has sufficient evidence before it to find that the French Republic has failed, contrary to the first sentence of Article 4(4) of the Birds Directive, to adopt the measures necessary to avoid

deterioration of those areas in the Poitevin Marsh which should have been classified as SPAs.

44. It must be pointed out that there is nothing on the case-file to establish that all of the areas in the Poitevin Marsh which should have been classified as SPAs have suffered deterioration within the meaning of the first sentence of Article 4(4) of the Birds Directive. In particular, the fact that approximately 28,700 hectares of wetlands in the Poitevin Marsh were placed under cultivation between 1973 and 1990 does not constitute conclusive evidence in this regard. There is nothing to suggest, in any event, that these wetlands include all the areas in the Poitevin Marsh which should have been classified as SPAs. Furthermore, it appears that an unspecified portion of these wetlands was placed under cultivation before the Birds Directive entered into force.

45. It is clear, however, . . . that a number of areas suitable for classification as SPAs, such as, in particular, the common lands of Vouillé, Vix and Ille d'Elle, had been destroyed. .

46. It follows that the French Republic did not take the measures necessary to avoid deterioration of some, but not all, areas in the Poitevin Marsh which should have been classified as SPAs, and thereby failed to meet its obligations under the first sentence of Article 4(4) of the Birds Directive.

[(d) the declassification of part of the Poitevin Marsh]

55. . . . it is evident, as the French Government submits that the strip of land earmarked for construction of the motorway was mistakenly referred to as forming part of the Marais Poitevin intérieur SPA at the time when that SPA was notified to the Commission and that the declaration by the Minister for the Environment . . . did not involve a reduction in the surface area of the SPA classified but simply the rectification of an error in the particulars forwarded to the Commission.

Commentary

I. The Protection of Marais Poitevin and the Court

(1) It is submitted that the Commission, which prevailed in most of its arguments, hardly can use this judgment to preserve the Marais Poitevin. The reason for this is, in my opinion, that the Court misjudged the object of litigation which led to an unacceptable result as regards the first claim of the Commission. Subsequently, this led to an unsatisfactory decision as regards the third claim of the Commission.[24]

---

[24] As regards the four claims put forward by the Commission, see the end of "facts and procedure" above.

It is obvious from paragraph 13 of the judgment that the Commission wanted a statement by the Court that France was obliged to designate 77,900 hectares of the Marais Poitevin; "at the very least", the Commission wanted a statement that France was obliged to designate 57,830 hectares.

(2) The Court satisfied itself with the French indication that all areas which should have been designated had not yet actually been designated. It thus reached the conclusion that France had not designated "a sufficient area" in the Marais Poitevin. However, this is not what the Commission had asked for. The French ZICO in the Marais Poitevin had borders. Everybody thus knew precisely which areas had to be designated. Had the Court accepted the Commission's claim, then any future litigation on the exact borders of the special protection area of the Marais Poitevin would have been highly unlikely. The same argument would apply if the Court had indicated that France should have designated the area of the IBA inventory.

(3) In other words: the claim "77,900 hectares (minus 26.500 hectares already designated) must be designated" is not equivalent to the judgment that "a sufficient area must be designated".

The consequences of this difference must appear in the administrative procedure. Suppose that France was now designating the 15,000 hectares which it had announced, there would again be discussion with the Commission whether this constituted a "sufficient area" or not. Nothing can be taken from the judgment to answer that question. Had the Court decided on the Commission's claim—i.e. to classify all ZICO territory—this uncertainty could have been avoided. And it is small consolation that the Advocate General expressly advised the Court not to decide on the Commission's claim,[25] probably because the Advocate General had thought of being entitled to apply the findings of the general case on Dutch habitats[26] to the present, very specific case of the Marais Poitevin.

(4) In my opinion, therefore, the Court did not fully decide on the Commission's application. And the questions might well be posed, on the one hand, what the Commission must procedurally do in order to obtain a more precise judgment and, on the other hand, how the Commission can effectively protect natural habitats or special protection areas from progressive degradation. Indeed, the procedure under Article 226 EC Treaty was initiated in 1989, when the Commission received a complaint about the Marais Poitevin.[27] Ten years thus elapsed until the Court's judgment. It was shown in the table on page 289 *supra* that there are at present some 3,000 special protection areas in the Community which have been designated under Article 4(1) of Directive 79/409. To these must

---

[25] Advocate General Fenelly [1999] ECR I–8531, para. 11. "The Court is not required to rule on whether France was obliged to classify the totality of the ZICO area, as the Commission has in effect contended, though this question could arise in later proceedings. It suffices that France's failure to classify a sufficient area . . . is established".

[26] Court of Justice, Case C–3/96 *Commission* v. *Netherlands* [1998] ECR I–3031; see for a commentary p. 283 *supra*.

[27] Advocate General Fenelly (n. 25 *supra*) para. 3.

be added those areas which should be designated but have not yet been designated.[28] In view of this number of habitats, it is simply not possible to dedicate this amount of time and resources to each individual habitat, as the Commission has neither environmental inspectors nor any investigation competence. The practical consequence will be that the shrinking of habitats within the Community, in the Marais Poitevin and others, will continue.

(5) This assessment by the Court of the Commission's application regarding point (a) had consequences for the Commission's claim under point (c). Had the Court stated that France was obliged to designate the 77,900 hectares of ZICO, then it could have satisfied itself under point (c) that there was some deterioration in this area and could have concluded that France had not respected its obligations under Article 4(4) of Directive 79/409. In view of its statement on point (a), the Court found that a number of areas had been deteriorating, enumerating "in particular" some common lands (paragraph 45). Again, what can the European Commission do with this statement? Article 228 EC Treaty states: "If the Court of Justice finds that a Member State has failed to fulfil an obligation under this Treaty, the State shall be required to take the necessary measures to comply with the judgment of the Court of Justice". What kind of measures is France thus obliged to take?

(6) If ever the Commission were not resigned to the judgment, and trying to pursue the matter of Marais Poitevin further, there would most likely be long discussion with France about what measures were to be taken and at which exact places, in order to repair the damage.

If one looks at the core of the judgment one finds that the Court pronounced on issues which were undisputed between France and the Commission. This is not a very encouraging conclusion.

II. Court Actions on Specific Natural Habitats

(7) The Commission has frequently tried to ensure, by way of legal action under Article 226 EC Treaty, the protection of threatened habitats. However, few cases only were finally submitted to the Court. The first of these cases concerned the Leybucht on the German North Sea coast[29] which was affected by the construction of a dyke. The Court found that the construction of a dyke which aimed at the protection of life of humans could justify a restriction of a habitat, even when the exact lining of the dyke also took into consideration the interests of local fishermen.

---

[28] Court of Justice, Case C–355/90, *Commission* v. *Spain* [1993] ECR I–4221; Case C–166/97, *Commission* v. *France* [1999] ECR I–1719.

[29] Court of Justice, Case 57/89, *Commission* v. *Germany* [1991] ECR 883; see also Case C–57/89-R, *Commission* v. *Germany* [1989] ECR 2849, where the Commission had tried to see interim measures applied in the Leybucht.

The case of Santona concerned marshes, which Spain had not, but should have, designated as a special protection area under Article 4 of Directive 79/409.[30] The Court found that Spain had not fulfilled its obligations under Article 4 of Directive 79/409, by not designating the area and by allowing its deterioration. Case C–44/95 concerned a preliminary ruling regarding the Lappel Bank in the United Kingdom.[31] In Case C–166/97, the Court had to deal with the designation of the Seine estuary (France).[32] And in Case C–374/98, another French site, the Basses Corbières, was dicussed by the Court.[33]

(8) Thus, in about 20 years, the Commission has submitted only five cases on individual habitats for the judgment of the Court. As regards Directive 92/43 which was adopted in 1992 and which also concerns the protection of habitats,[34] there has not yet been any case on a specific habitat which was brought to the Court. This confirms the observation made above that court litigation for individual habitats will always remain exceptional.

36. DIRECTIVE 92/43 AND ITS HABITATS

Judgment of the Court (Sixth Chamber) of 7 December 2000 Case C–374/98

Commission of the European Communities v. *France*
[2000] ECR I–10799

Facts and Procedure

The French company OMYA had an authorisation, from 1968 to work a limestone deposit in the municipality of Tautavel in the French *département* of Pyrénées-Orientales. As that deposit became exhausted, the company requested, in 1994, an authorisation to exploit the limestone deposits in the neighbouring municipality of Vingrau. The two municipalities form part of the Basses Corbières natural site which hosts an important number of bird species protected by Annex I to Directive 79/409, in particular Bonelli's eagle, the honey buzzard, the black kite,

---

[30] Court of Justice, Case C–355/90 (n. 28 *supra*).

[31] Court of Justice, Case C–44/95, *RSPB* [1996] ECR I–3805; see also p. 314 *infra*.

[32] Court of Justice, Case C–166/97 (n. 28 *supra*).

[33] Court of Justice, Case C–374/98, *Commission* v. *France*, (2000) ECR I–10799 (see for this case also p. 304 *infra*).

[34] Directive 92/43 on the conservation of natural habitats and of wild fauna and flora [1992] OJ L206/7.

the kite, the Egyption vulture, the short-toed eagle, the marsh harrier, the hen harrier and Montagu's harrier. The French authorities had not designed the Basses Corbières as special protection area (SPA) under Article 4(1) of Directive 79/409.[35] However, they had recognised the site as a "*zone importante pour la conservation des oiseaux sauvages*" (ZICO) with an area of 47,000 hectares; within this zone, they had specially protected, by way of decrees, an area of 231 hectares in the municipalities of Tautavel and Vingrau and, furthermore, two other areas of 123 and 280 hectares respectively.

The Commission was of the opinion that the Basses Corbières should have been classified as an SPA under Article 4(1) of Directive 79/409 and that France had not taken sufficient conservation measures to protect the birds in Basses Corbièrees. Furthermore, the Commission considered that the French authorities had not taken appropriate steps to avoid disturbance of the species protected on that site, by allowing the opening and working of limestone quarries within the municipalities of Tautavel and Vingrau, in breach of France's obligations under Article 6(2) to (4) of Directive 92/43.[36] As the discussions with the French authorities led to no result, the Commission applied to the Court of Justice.

[35] Directive 79/409 on the conservation of wild birds [1979] OJ L103/1, Art. 4: "1. . . . Member States shall classify in particular the most suitable territories in number and size as special protection areas for the conservation of these species, taking into account their protection requirements in the geographical sea and land area where this directive applies . . . 4. In respect of the protection areas referred to in paras. 1 and 2 above, Member States shall take appropriate steps to avoid pollution or deterioration of habitats or any disturbances affecting the birds, in so far as these would be significant having regard to the objectives of this Article . . .".

[36] Directive 92/43 on the conservation of natural habitats and of wild fauna and flora [1992] OJ L206/7, Art. 6: " . . . 2. Member States shall take appropriate steps to avoid, in the special areas of conservation, the deterioration of natural habitats and the habitats of species as well as disturbance of the species for which the areas have been designated, in so far as such disturbance could be significant in relation to the objectives of this Directive. 3. Any plan or project not directly connected with or necessary to the management of the site but likely to have a significant effect thereon, either individually or in combination with other plans or projects, shall be subject to appropriate assessment of its implications for the site in view of the site's conservation objectives. In the light of the conclusions of the assessment of the implications for the site and subject to the provisions of para. 4, the competent national authorities shall agree to the plan or project only after having ascertained that it will not adversely affect the integrity of the site concerned and, if appropriate, after having obtained the opinion of the general public. 4. If, in spite of a negative assessment of the implications for the site and in the absence of alternative solutions, a plan or project must nevertheless be carried out forimperative reasons of overriding public interest, including those of a social or economic nature, the Member State shall take all compensatory measures necessary to ensure that the overall coherence of Natura 2000 is protected. It shall inform the Commission of the compensatory measures adopted. Where the site concerned hosts a priority natural habitat type and/or a priority species, the only considerations which may be raised are those relating to human health or public safety, to beneficial consequences of primary importance for the environment or, further to an opinion from the Commission, to otherimperative reasons of overriding public interest".

Judgment (extracts)

14. . . . it is undisputed that no part of the Basses Corbières site has been classified as an SPA . . .

15. . . . it is undisputed that the Basses Corbières site contains natural areas of particular ornithological interest, at least because of the presence of Bonelli's eagle, which is a species listed in Annex I to the birds directive.

17. Therefore . . . it must be concluded that the French Republic has not . . . classified any territory of the Basses Corbières site as an SPA within the meaning of Article 4(1) of the birds directive . . .

18. As regards the special conservation measures required by Article 4(1) of the birds directive, the Commission maintains that the measures adopted by the French authorities for the Basses Corbières site are insufficient. In particular, the three prefectoral decrees for conserving the biotope of Bonelli's eagle on that site, although they mention wild bird species other than Bonelli's eagle in their annexes, refer opnly to the latter species in their provisions and provide for specific measures only in respect of the latter.

20. . . . it should be noted in any event that, even though the three decrees for protecting the biotope are all aimed primarily at ensuring the conservation of the biotope of Bonelli's eagle, and thus the protection of that species, their provisions nevertheless benefit all wild birds frequenting the areas covered by that legislation, by laying down in some detail the prohibition of activities capable of adversely affecting the integrity of the biotopes in question.

21. Moreover, there is nothing in the documents before the Court to show that the regime established by the three decrees for protecting the biotope is insufficient in relation to the conservation requirements of any of the bird species present in the areas covered by those decrees.

23/24. As regards the complaint that the geographical extent of those special conservation measures is insufficient, it should be noted that the Groupe Ornithologique du Roussillon ("GOR") filed a proposal in March 1999 that the area extending over 950 hectares form the Serre de Vingrau-Tautavel to the Trou de Cavall . . . must be regarded as classifiable as an SPA particularly on account of the presence of large birds of prey . . .

25. It should also be noted that the inventory of areas which are of great importance for the conservation of wild birds, more commonly known under the acronym IBA (Inventory of Important Bird Areas in the European Community) includes the area in question . . .

26. It follows from the general scheme of Article 4 of the birds directive that, where a given area fulfills the criteria for classification as an SPA, it must be made the subject of special conservation measures capable of ensuring, in particular, the survival and reproduction of the bird species mentioned in Annex I to that directive.

27. . . . of the three decrees for protecting the biotope issued in relation to the Basses Corbières area, only one refers to the area indicated by the GOR as requiring classification as an SPA, and that the decree in question covers only part of that area. Moreover, the 231 hectares protected by that decree are not entirely included in that area.

29. In those circumstances, in the absence of any evidence capable of reopening the question whether the GOR's proposal that the 950-hectare area extending from the the Serre de Vingrau-Tautavel to the Trou de Cavall should be classified as an SPA is well founded, it must be held that, since a considerable part of that area does not benefit from a special conservation regime, the special conservation measures taken by the French authorities are insufficient in their geographical extent.

33. The Commission states that the realisation of the project to open and work limestone quarries in the territory of the Vingrau and Tautavel municipalities within the Basses Corbières site is likely to cause disturbance to the species present in that site and a deterioration of their habitat . . .

38. The French Government maintains that the Commission does not present any scientific or other evidence to demonstrate that the quarries create significant disturbance for the pair of Bonelli's eagles or for the other species . . .

43. It first needs to be considered whether Articles 6(2) to (4) of the habitats directive apply to areas which have not been classified as SPAs but should have been so classified.

44. In that respect, it is important to note that the text of Article 7 of the habitats directive expressly states that Article 6(2) to (4) of the directive apply, in substitution for the first sentence of Article 4(4)of the birds directive, to the areas classified under Article 4(1) and (2) of the latter directive.

45. It follows that, on a literal interpretation of that passage of Article 7 of the habitats directive, only areas classified as SPAs fall under the influence of Article 6(2) to (4) of that directive.

46. Moreover, the text of Article 7 of the habitats directive states that Article 6(2) to (4) of that directive replace the first sentence of Article 4(4) of the birds directive as from the date of implementation of the habitats directive or the date of classification by a Member State under the birds directive, where the latter date is later. That passage of Article 7 appears to support the interpretation to the effect that the application of Article 6(2) to (4) presupposes the classification of the area concerned as an SPA.

47. It is clear, therefore, that areas which have not been classified as SPAs but should have been so classified continue to fall under the regime governed by the first sentence of Article 4(4) of the birds directive.

48. The Commission's arguments to the contrary cannot be accepted.

49. Thus, the fact that, as the case-law of the Court of Justice shows, . . . the protection regime under the first sentence of Article 4(4) of the birds directive applies to areas that have not been classified as SPAs but should have been so classified does not in itself imply that the protection regime referred to in Article 6(2) to (4) of the habitats directive replaces the first regime referred to in relation to those areas.

50. Moreover, as regards the Commission's argument concerning a duality of applicable regimes, it should be noted that the fact that these areas referred to in the previous paragraph of this judgment are, under the first sentence of Article 4(4) of the birds directive, made subject to a regime that is stricter than that laid down by Article 6(2) to (4) of the habitats directive in relation to areas classified as SPAs does not appear without justification.

51. As the Advocate General points out in paragraph 99 of his Opinion, a Member State cannot derive an advantage from its failure to comply with its Community obligations.

52. In that respect, if it were lawful for a Member State, which, in breach of the birds directive, has failed to classify as an SPA a site which should have been so classified, to rely on Article 6(3)and (4) of the habitats directive, that State might enjoy such an advantage.

53. Since no formal measure for classifying such a site as an SPA exists, it is particularly difficult for the Commission, in accordance with Article 155 of the EC Treaty (now Article 211 EC), to carry out effective monitoring of the application by Member States of the procedure laid down by Article 6(3) and (4) of the habitats directive and to establish, in appropriate cases, the existence of possible failures to fulfil the obligations thereunder. In particular, the risk is significantly increased that plans or projects not directly connected with or necessary to the management of the site, and affecting its integrity, may be accepted by the national authoritites in breach of that procedure, escape the Commission's monitoring and cause serious, or irreparable ecological damage, contrary to the conservation requirement of that site.

54. Natural or legal persons entitled to assert before national courts interests connected with the protection of nature, and especially wild bird life, which in this case means primarily environmental protection organisations, would face comparable difficulties.

55. A situation of this kind would be likely to endanger the attainment of the objective of special protection for the wild bird life set forth in Article 4 of the birds directive, as interpreted by the case-law of the Court . . .

56. As the Advocate General has essentially argued in paragraph 102 of his Opinion, the duality of the regimes applicable, respectively, to areas classified as SPAs and those which should have been so classified gives Member States an incentive to carry out classifications, in so far as they thereby acquire the possibilitiy of using a procedure which allows them, for imperative reasons of overriding public interest, including those of a social or economic nature, and subject to certain conditions, to adopt a plan or project adversely affecting an SPA.

57. It follows from the above that Article 6(2) to (4) of the habitats directive do not apply to areas which have not been classified as SPAs but should have been so classified.

58. The complaint alleging infringement of Article 6(2) to (4) of the habitats directive must therefore be rejected.

Commentary

I. *The Habitat of Basses Corbières and the Court*

(1) "*Da mi factum, dabo tibi ius*" was an old Roman legal proverb. Persons who went to court had to submit the facts underlying their litigation, and the court then applied the rule of law applicable to the case. Reading the present judgment, one may wonder whether this proverb also applies to the Court of Justice. The Commission had applied to the Court because France had not designated the Basses Corbières site as a special protection area under Article 4 of Directive 79/409[37] and because the working of limestone quarries within the boundaries of that site constituted a deterioration in the site. The Commission had added that such a deterioration was contrary to the wording of Directive 92/43, Article 6(2) to (4).[38] Article 6(2) to (4) replaces, as from a certain moment, Article 4(4) first sentence of Directive 79/409.[39]

(2) The Court first found that the Basses Corbières site had not been designated under Article 4(1) of Directive 79/409, though it should have been designated. This omission was not in dispute between France and the Commission.

The Court then found that France had taken, in conformity with Article 4(1) of Directive 79/409, some conservation measures, but that these were not covering enough of the geographical area of the site. On this point, the judgment does not seem very convincing; indeed, the Court carefully avoids indicating exactly how big the special protection area of Basses Corbières is. It may be recalled that the IBA, mentioned in paragraph 25 of the Court's judgment, had given its size as of 150,000 hectares;[40] the French authorities had indicated an area of 47,400 hectares as ZICO (important zone for wild bird conservation); the French Association GOR had indicated 950 hectares as "classifiable as an SPA" (paragraphs 23/24); and the French authorities had taken special conservation measures for an area of 634 hectares which is about 1. 5 per cent of the surface of the ZICO! The Court's decision not to indicate to which area the omission of the French authorities refers means only that the discusion between the Commission and the French authorities on this point will continue. In administrative practice, this self-restraint by the Court will lead to minimal designations of the site. As at the time of the judgment, France was more than 19 years overdue with its obligations of designating Basses Corbières, it would have been highly desirable for the Court to indicate more

---

[37] Directive 79/409 (n. 35 *supra*), Art. 4.

[38] Directive 92/43 (n. 36 *supra*), Art. 6.

[39] See Directive 92/43 (n. 36 *supra*), Art. 7: "Obligations arising under Art. 6(2), (3) and (4) of this Directive shall replace any obligations arising under the first sentence of Art. 4(4) of Directive 79/409/EEC in respect of areas classified pursuant to Art. 4(1) or similarly recognised under Art. 4(2) thereof, as from the date of implementation of this Directive for the date of classification or recognition by a Member State under Directive 79/409/EEC, where the latter date is later".

[40] International Council for Bird Preservation (ed.), *Important Bird Areas in Europe* (International Council for Bird Presenation, Cambridge, 1989), p. 215.

clearly which area of Basses Corbières fulfilled the conditions of Article 4(1) of Directive 79/409.[41]

(3) Whatever the size of the classifiable SPA was, the Court was asked whether the limestone quarry work constituted a significant disturbance of the Annex I birds on the Basses Corbières site. However, the Court did not answer that question.

In order to understand the reasoning of the Court, it is necessary to recall the story of Article 4(4) of Directive 79/409 and of Articles 6 and 7 of Directive 92/43. In 1991, the Court had to decide the question what grounds could justify a deterioration or a significant disturbance of a site in the sense of Article 4(4) of Directive 79/409. The Court found that such grounds "must correspond to a general interest which is superior to the general interest represented by the ecological objective of the directive. In that context the interests referred to in Article 2 of the directive, namely economic and recreational interests, do not enter into considerations".[42]

To some Member States, this judgment seemed too far-reaching in favour of environmental interests. As at that time Directive 92/43 was negotiated in Council, Article 6(2) to (4) was inserted, with the express instruction in Article 7 that it were to replace Article 4(4) first sentence of Directive 79/409.

(4) In other terms, Directive 92/43 was intended to reduce the requirements of Article 4(4) of Directive 79/409. However, I conclude from the wording of Article 7 of Directive 92/43[43] and the fact that Articles 4(4) of Directive 79/409 and 6(2) to (4) of Directive 92/43 essentially cover the same ground, that in all cases where Article 6 of Directive 92/43 does not apply to a birds habitat, Article 4(4) of Directive 79/409 is (remains) of application.

The Court of Justice seems to be of a different opinion. It examines the application of Article 6 of Directive 92/43 and concludes, quite convincingly, that this provision does not apply. Consequently, it argues that Article 4(4) of Directive 79/409 applies (paragraph 47). And this ends its reasoning. It is not examined whether Article 4(4) applies in the specific case or not, nor is there the smallest justification why it is not examined. The only reason can be that the Commission had not expressly asked for this provision to be examined.

(5) *Da mi factum, dabo tibi ius.* What was in dispute between France and the Commission was the question whether the limestone quarry work constituted a significant disturbance of birds or not. This question remains unanswered. It is not clear whether the Court expects that, after its judgment, the Commission will begin new proceedings under Article 226 EC Treaty against France, this time based on the potential breach of Article 4(4) of Directive 79/409, and that in several years the Court will then answer the question whether the limestone quarry work does or does not constitute a significant disturbance of birds.

(6) From the administrative point, the judgment almost acts as a deterrent to bringing similar actions. The Commission has neither obtained an answer to its

---

[41] See also the criticism of the Court at p. 302 *supra.*
[42] Court of Justice Case C–57/89, *Commission* v. *Germany* [1991] ECR I–883, para. 22.
[43] Directive 92/43 (n. 39 *supra*), Art. 7.

question which area of the Basses Corbières qualifies as a special protection area nor received an answer whether the limestone quarry work constitutes a signif-icant disturbance or not. I submit that the Commission did ask these two ques-tions. The Court obviously was of the opinion that it did not.

II. The Protection of Non-designated Areas

(7) The Court's reasoning that Article 4(4) of Directive 79/409 also applies to areas that have not been classified as special protection areas but should have been so classified was developed in a case against Spain.[44] In that case, the Commission criticised Spain for not having designated the Santona marshes in the Autonomous Region of Cantabria and of not having taken appropriate steps to avoid pollution or deterioration of habitats in that area. Spain was of the opinion that Article 4(4) could apply only once an area had been designated under Article 4(1) of Directive 79/409. The Court was quite short on this aspect, stating in para-graph 22: "That line of reasoning must be rejected. The objectives of protection set out by the directive, as expressed in the ninth recital in its preamble, could not be achieved if Member States had to comply with the obligations arising under Article 4(4) only in cases where a special protection area had previously been established". The ninth recital of Directive 79/409 is hardly more expressive:[45] it permits the wide interpretation given to it by the Court, but certainly does not require it.

In the present case as well as in the case on the Marais Poitevin[46] the limits of this approach become visible: as long as the boundaries of the special protection area are not determined—and in the case of litigation between the national authorities of a Member State and the Commission the Court of Justice is the arbiter and may, it is submitted, not omit to assume this function and determine by judgment what constitutes a special protection area in a specific case—the use-fulness of the present judgment as a dispute settlement remains limited. After all, Advocate General Fenelly rightly stated in Case C–44/95: "in deciding to classify any area as an SPA, the Member State authorities must also fix its boundaries".[47]

(8) It is acknowledged that fixing the boundaries of a special protection area is delicate, may raise resistance with local people and national authorities and also touches principles of national sovereignty. However, the Court of Justice has to confront these problems many a time and there is no reason not to do so where economic and ecological interests are in confrontation. One such example is the

[44] Court of Justice, Case C–355/90, *Commission* v. *Spain* [1993] ECR I–4221.

[45] Directive 79/409 (n. 35 *supra*), ninth recital: "Whereas the preservation, maintenance or restora-tion of a sufficient diversity and area of habitats is essential to the conservation of all species of birds; whereas certain species of birds should be the subject of special conservation measures concerning their habitats in order to ensure their survival and reproduction in their area of distribution; whereas such measures must also take account of migratory species and be coordinated with a view to setting up a coherent whole".

[46] See p. 297 *supra*.

[47] Advocate General Fenelly, Opinion in Case C–44/95, *RSPB* [1996] ECR I–3805, para. 63.

above-mentioned application of Article 4(4) of Directive 79/409 also to areas which have not been designated as SPAs, but should have so been designated: the "fierce local controversy" of which the French government reported as regards Basses Corbières[48] becomes, in the light of this jurisdiction, without object, as the potentially negative impacts of the designation on the local economy also exist where a site is not designated, but should be designated.

III. Directive 92/43 and its Application

(9) Directive 92/43 was adopted in 1992 after several years of discussions; it was elaborated because the Berne Convention on the conservation of European wildlife and natural habitats 1979, to which the Community has adhered in 1981,[49] and which was also ratified by all Member States except Ireland, has not really proved efficient to protect the disappearance of habitats in Europe. Directive 92/43 asks Member States to draw up national lists of sites which are important for the conservation of habitat types of fauna and flora species. From these national lists, the Commission, in agreement with the Member State concerned, establishes a list of sites of Community importance. Member States shall then designate the sites on this list as Special Areas of Conservation, which, together with the habitats designated under Directive 79/409, form "a coherent European ecological network" or Natura 2000.

(10) The national lists had to be drawn up by June 1995. The state of affairs at the end of 2000 follows from the follwing table:[50]

List of sites proposed by Member States (as at 14 November 2000)

Member State	Number of sites suggested	area (km2)	% of surface of Member State	evaluation
Belgium	209	1.105	3.6	obviously insufficient
Denmark	194	10.259	23.8	incomplete
Germany	2196	20.434	5.8	obviously incomplete
Greece	234	26.522	20.1	incomplete
Spain	937	90.129	17.9	incomplete
France	1028	31.440	5.7	obviously incomplete
Ireland	317	6.140	8.7	obviously incomplete

[48] Para. 12 of the present judgment, not reproduced here.
[49] Decision 82/72 [1982] OJ L38/1.
[50] Commission, Natura 2000, Newsletter, December 2000, p. 7; a number of habitats in the present list were at the same time also proposed under Directive 79/409 (see the list on those proposals p. 289 *supra*). Therefore, the two lists may not be added together.

Member State	Number of sites suggested	area (km$_2$)	% of surface of Member State	evaluation
Italy	2507	49.364	16.4	incomplete
Luxembourg	38	352	13.6	incomplete
Netherlands	76	7.078	17.0	incomplete
Austria	127	9.144	10.9	incomplete
Portugal	94	16.502	17.9	incomplete
Finland	1381	47.154	13.9	incomplete
Sweden	2454	50.908	12.4	incomplete
United Kingdom	386	17.941	7.4	obviously incomplete
Total	12.178	384.472		

The table shows that no Member State has yet submitted a complete list of national sites. Belgium, Germany, France, Ireland and the United Kingdom in particular are lagging behind. The Community list, due for mid–1998, has not yet been published.

(11) Directive 92/43 has not very frequently been the subject of decisions by the Court of Justice. In 1997, the Court gave two judgments against Greece and Germany, because these two Member States had not transposed the Directive into national law.[51] The Directive was further discussed in a case where the Commission was of the opinion that France had not completely transposed Article 6(3) and (4) into national law,[52] and in a preliminary ruling which the Court gave at the end of 2000 and which concerned the criteria for establishing the national lists.[53]

If one goes back to the judgment in the present case for a moment, as the Court has ruled that Article 6(2) to (4) does not apply to sites which have not been designated as special areas of conservation by Member States, but should be so designated, does this mean that there is no obligation for Member States to avoid, in such areas, deterioration and disturbance of habitats? Of course, where such an area also comes under Article 4(4) of Directive 79/409, this latter provision will apply; but there are many other habitats which do not serve to host endangered birds that are listed in Annex I to Directive 79/409.

The result appears to be absurd and would certainly also be in contradiction with recitals 4 and 6 of Directive 92/43.[54] It therefore can only be hoped that the

---

[51] Court of Justice, Cases C–329/96, *Commission* v. *Greece* [1997] ECR I–3749; C–83/97, *Commission* v. *Germany* [1997] ECR I–7191.

[52] Court of Justice, Case C–256/98, *Commission* v. *France* [2000] ECR I–2487.

[53] Court of Justice, Case C–371/98, *Corporate Shipping*, (2000) ECR I–9235.

[54] Directive 92/43 (n. 36 *supra*), recitals 4 and 6: 4."whereas in the European territory of the Member States, natural habitats are continuing to deteriorate and an increasing number of wild species are seriously threatened; whereas given that the threatened habitats and species form part of the Community's

Court of Justice soon finds an opportunity to clarify he interpretation of Directive 92/43 on this point.

37. HABITATS AND ECONOMIC DEVELOPMENT

Judgment of the Court of 11 July 1996
Case C–44/95

Reference for a preliminary ruling in the case
Regina v. *Secretary of State for the Environment,*
ex parte Royal Society for the Protection of Birds
Intervener: The Port of Sheerness Limited
[1996] ECR I–3805

Facts and Procedure

The Medway estuary and marshes cover 4,681 hectares on the north coast of Kent. They are a wetland of international importance, used as a breeding and wintering area, by a number of wildfowl and wader species including the avocet and the little tern, two birds which are listed in Annex I to Directive 79/409.[55] Lappel Bank which comprises an area of about 22 hectares, falls geographically within the bounds of the Medway estuary and marshes. It shares several of the ornithological qualities of the area as a whole. It is an important component of the overall estuarine ecosystem and the loss of that inter-tidal area would probably result in a reduction in the wader and wildfowl populations of the Medway estuary and marshes.

Lappel Bank adjoins, at its northern end, the Port of Sheerness which is the fifth largest port in the United Kingdom for cargo and freight handling. The port, a florishing commercial undertaking and a significant employer, plans to extend its facilities; Lappel Bank is the only area into which the port can realistically envisage expanding.

When the United Kingdom Secretary of State for the Environment decided, in December 1993, to designate the Medway estuary and marshes as a special protection

natural heritage and the threats to them are often of a transboundary nature, it is necessary to take measures at Community level in order to conserve them". 6. "whereas, in order to ensure the restoration or maintenance of natural habitats and species of Community interest at a favourable conservation status, it is necessary to designate special areas of conservation in order to create a coherent European ecological network according to a specified timetable".

[55] Directive 79/409 on the conservation of wild birds [1979] OJ L103/1.

area (SPA), he considered that the need not to inhibit the viability of the port and the significant contribution which expansion into the Lappel Bank would make to the local and national economy outweighed the Lappel Bank's conservation value; he therefore decided to exclude that area from the Medway SPA.

In the subsequent court litigation, doubts were raised about the application of Directive 79/409. The House of Lords therefore asked the Court of Justice whether the grounds of Article 2 of Directive 79/409[56] could be taken into consideration when the boundaries of a special protection area were defined or whether other ways existed to take other than conservation interests into account in the classification process of a special protected area.

Judgment (extracts)

[classification of special protection areas under Directive 79/409]

23. Article 4 of the Birds Directive lays down a protection regime which is specifically targeted and reinforced both for the species listed in Annex I and for migratory species, an approach justified by the fact that they are, respectively, the most endangered species and the species constituting a common heritage of the Community...

24. Whilst Article 3 of the Birds Directive provides for account to be taken of the requirements mentioned in Article 2 for the implementation of general conservation measures, including the creation of protection areas, Article 4 makes no such reference for the implementation of special conservation measures, in particular the creation of SPAs.

25. Consequently, having regard to the aim of special protection pursued by Article 4 and the fact that, according to settled case-law... Article 2 does not constitute an autonomous derogation from the general system of protection established by the directive, it must be held ... that the ecological requirements laid down by the former provision do not have to be balanced against the interests listed in the latter, in particular economic requirements.

---

[56] Directive 79/409 (n. 55 *supra*), Art. 2: "Member States shall take the requisite measures to maintain the population of the species referred to in Art. 1 at a level which corresponds in particular to ecological, scientific and cultural requirements, while taking account of economic and recreational requirements, or to adapt the population of these species to that level".

Art. 4: "1. ... Member States shall classify in particular the most suitable territories in number and size as special protectection areas for the conservation of these species, taking into account their protection requirements in the geographical sea and land area where this Directive applies. 2. Member States shall take similar measures for regularly occurring migratory species not listed in Annex I, bearing in mind their need for protection in the geographical sea and land area where this Directive applies, as regards their breeding, moulting and wintering areas and staging posts along their migration routes. To this end, Member States shall pay particular attention to the protection of wetlands and particularly to wetlands of international importance. 3. ...".

26. It is the criteria laid down in paragraphs (1) and (2) of Article 4 which are to guide the Member States in designating and defining the boundaries of SPA's. It is clear . . . that, notwithstanding divergencies between the various language versions of the last subparagraph of Article 4(1), the criteria in question are ornithological.

[classification and overriding public economic interests]

29. In its judgment in Case C–57/89 *Commission* v. *Germany* [1991] ECR I–883, paragraphs 21 and 22 (hereinafter "Leybucht Dykes"), the Court held that the Member States may, in the context of Article 4(4) of the Birds Directive, reduce the extent of a SPA only on exceptional grounds, being grounds corresponding to a general interest superior to the general interest represented by the ecological objective of the directive. It was held that economic requirements cannot be invoked in that context.

30. It is also clear . . . that, in the context of Article 4 of that directive, considered as a whole, economic requirement cannot on any view correspond to a general interest superior to that represented by the ecological objective of the directive.

37. . . . Article 6(4) of the Habitats Directive as inserted in the Birds Directive, has, following Leybucht Dykes where the point in issue was the reduction of an area already classified, widened the range of grounds justifying encroachment upon SPAs by expressly including therein reasons of a social or economic nature.

38. Thus, the imperative reasons of overriding public interest which may, pursuant to Article 6(4) of the Habitats Directive, justify a plan or project which would significantly affect an SPA in any event include grounds relating to a superior general interest of the kind identified in Leybucht Dykes and may where appropriate include grounds of a social or economic nature.

39. Next, although Article 6(3) and (4) of the Habitats Directive, in so far as it amended the first sentence of Article 4(4) of the Birds Directive, established a procedure enabling Member States to adopt, for imperative reasons of overriding public interest and subject to certain conditions, a plan or a project adversely affecting an SPA and so make it possible to go back on a decision classifying such an area by reducing its extent, it nevertheless did not make any amendments regarding the initial stage of classification of an area as an SPA referred to in Article 4(1) and (2) of the Birds Directive.

40. It follows that, even under the Habitats Directive, the classification of sites as SPAs must in all circumstances be carried out in accordance with the criteria permitted under Article 4(1) and (2) of the Birds Directive.

41. Economic requirements, as an imperative reason of overriding public interest allowing a derogation from the obligation to classify a site according to its ecological value, cannot enter into consideration at that stage. But that does not, as the Commission has rightly pointed out, mean that they cannot be taken into account at a later stage under the procedure provided for by Article 6(3) and (4) of the Habitats Directive.

Commentary

I. *Classifying Habitats and Economic Reasons*

(1) The judgment deals with a rather common case of conflicting economic and environmental interests: when designating a special protection area under Directive 79/409, the Secretary of State for the Environment in the United Kingdom spared a specific part, the Lappel Bank, as a neighbouring port authority intended to enlarge its commercial port and the only realistic way of doing this was the use of the Lappel Bank area. The Court of Justice was asked whether Directive 79/409 or other rules of Community law allowed such practice.

The reasons for not including the Lappel Bank in the designation were economic. There was apparently no dispute on the facts that, ecologically, the Lappel Bank formed part of the Medway estuaries and marshes. The Court interpreted Article 4(1) and (2) of Directive 79/409[57] and found that according to these provisions only ornithological criteria could be taken into consideration when an area was to be deignated; economic considerations were not mentioned in that provision.

(2) The Court then had to deal with the argument that Article 2 of Directive 79/409 did provide for the taking into account of economic considerations.[58] The problem was that Article 2 was not mentioned in Article 4, though it was mentioned in Article 3.[59] The United Kingdom strongly pleaded in favour of extending the application of Article 2 also to situations which were covered by Article 4. The Court, however, did not follow this reasoning.

In the Court's opinion, Article 3 concerned general measures which concerned all birds that lived within the Community; Article 4 was much narrower, concerning only the birds listed in Annex I or migrating birds. Both these types of birds were particularly vulnerable: the birds of Annex I because that Annex included endangered species, and migratory birds because they changed their place of habitation so frequently. Furthermore, Article 3 concerned general conservation measures, whereas Article 4 addressed special conservation measures. The two Articles thus concern

---

[57] See the text of these provisions in n. 56 *supra.*

[58] See the text of Art. 2 in n. 56 *supra.*

[59] Directive 79/409 (n. 55 *supra*), Art. 3: "1. In the light of the requirements referred to in Art. 2, Member States shall take the requisite measures to preserve, maintain or re-establish a sufficient diversity and area of habitats for all the species of birds referred to in Art. 1. 2. The preservation, maintenance and re-establishment of biotopes and habitats shall include primarily the following measures: (a) creation of protected areas; (b) upkeep and management in accordance with the ecological need of habitats inside and outside the protected areas; (c) re-establishment of destroyed habitats; (d) creation of biotopes".

completely different situations; therefore, it was not possible to apply Article 2 in the context of the designation of special protection areas under Article 4.[60]

(3) The Court then had to answer the question whether its own judgment in Case C–57/89 could be used as a precedent for taking economic aspects into account.[61] In that case, an area which had been designated as a special protection area by the German authorities was to be narrowed down due to the construction of a sea dyke. The Court of Justice had decided that Article 4(4) of Directive 79/409 allowed such narrowing down only on exceptional grounds. "Those grounds must correspond to a general interest which is superior to the general interest represented by the ecological objective of the directive. In that context the interests referred to in Article 2 of the directive, namely economic and recreational requirements, do not enter into consideration".

In the present case, the Court confirmed that judgment in the sense that economic reasons could not be taken into consideration when there was question of deterioration or disturbance of a designated habitat.

Finally, the Court had to answer the question from the House of Lords whether Directive 92/43 had created a new situation and allowed the taking into account of economic grounds. The Court concluded that Article 6(3) and (4)[62] had been inserted into Directive 92/43, because the Council had found that the jurisdiction in Case C–57/89 which had enabled Member States to provide for disturbance of designated habitats under Article 4(4) of Directive 79/409 for important non-economic reasons, was too narrow; for that reason, they had inserted a provision that also economic considerations could justify a reduction of the size of a designated special protection area (paragraphs 37 and 38).

(4) However, this enlargement of the grounds referred to the impairment of a designated habitat, but not to the first classification of an area as a special protection zone, "even under the Habitats Directive, the classification of special protection areas must in all circumstances be carried out in accordance with the criteria permitted under Article 4(1) and (2) of the Birds Directive" (paragraph 40).

---

[60] See also Court of Justice, Case C–435/92, *APAS* [1994] ECR I–67, para. 20; Case C–355/90, *Commission* v. *Spain* [1993] ECR I–4221, paras. 17 and 18.

[61] Court of Justice, Case C–57/89, *Commission* v. *Germany* [1991] ECR I–883.

[62] Directive 92/43 on the conservation of natural habitats and of wild fauna and flora [1992] OJ L206/7, Art. 6(3) and (4): "3. Any plan or project not directly connected with or necessary to the management of the site but likely to have a significant effect thereon, either individually or in combination with other plans or projects, shall be subject to appropriate assessment of its implications for the site in view of the site's conservation objectives. In the light of the conclusions of the assessment of the implications for the site and subject to the provisions of para. 4, the competent national authorities shall agree to the plan or project only after having ascertained that it will not adversely affect the integrity of the site concerned and, if appropriate, after having obtained the opinion of the general public. 4. If, in spite of a negative assessment of the implications for the site and in the absence of alternative solutions, a plan or project must nevertheless be carried out for imperative reasons of overriding public interest, including those of a social or economic nature, the member State shall take all compensatory measures to ensure that the overall coherence of Natura 2000 is protected. It shall inform the Commission of the compensatory measures adopted . . .".

Thus, the Court concluded that the United Kingdom Secretary of State had not been entitled to exclude, for economic reasons, the Lappel Bank from the designation of a special protection area.

II. *Designating Fauna and Flora Habitats and Economic Considerations*

(5) Some years later, the Secretary of State in the United Kingdom considered proposing the Severn Estuary to the European Commission as a site eligible for designation as a special area of conservation under Article 4(1) of Directive 92/43.[63] The responsible port authority for the port of Bristol objected, as it saw its economic activity in and around the port affected. The port authority was of the opinion that the Secretary of State had to take into account, when designating an area, not only ecological grounds, but also economic grounds. The matter was discussed in court and another preliminary question was put to the Court of Justice, whether a Member State, when deciding which sites to propose to the Commission pursuant to Article 4(1) and/or in defining the boundaries of such sites, was entitled or obliged to take account of the considerations laid down in Article 2(3) of Directive 92/43.[64]

(6) The Court confirmed its line of argument in the present case by stating that "On a proper construction of Article 4(1) of Directive 92/43 . . . a Member State may not take account of economic, social and cultural requirements or regional and local characteristics, as mentioned in Article 2(3) of that directive, when selecting and defining the boundaries of the sites to be proposed to the Commission as eligible for identification as sites of Community importance".[65]

While I am of the opinion that the Court is completely right in its analysis, the practical reality should not be overlooked. In Case C–371/98, the Finnish government, which had commented in that case, stated that Member States were free to take into account economic considerations as long as they did not jeopardise the realisation of the objectives of Directive 92/43. In the present Case C–44/95, both the United Kingdom and French governments were of the opinion that economic considerations were to be taken into account when designations of special protection are as under Article 4(1) of Directive 79/409 were made; the United Kingdom wanted to interpret the notion of "'suitable" in a way that included such economic aspects. In Case C–374/98,[66] France had designated about 1. 5 per cent of a zone which it had, under national legal provisions, classified as an important area for

---

[63] Directive 92/43 (n. 62 *supra*), Art. 4(1): "On the basis of the criteria set out in Annex III (Stage 1) and relevant scientific information, each Member State shall propose a list of sites indicating which natural habitat types in Annex I and which species in Annex II that are native to its territory the sites host . . . .".

[64] Directive 92/43 (n. 62 *supra*), Art. 2(3): "3. Measures taken pursuant to this Directive shall take account of economic, social and cultural requirements and regional and local characteristics".

[65] Court of Justice, Case C–371/98, *First Corporate Shipping*, (2000) ECR I–9235.

[66] Court of Justice, Case C–374/98, *Commission* v. *France* [2000] ECR I–10799; see for a commentary of this case, p. 304 *supra*.

birds' protection, and it is difficult to see that it had any other than economic grounds for this attitude. In Case C–96/98,[67] there was again a small part only of the Marais Poitevin area which France had actually designated as special protection area, with little other ground than economic considerations.

(7) There is thus good reason to believe that the actual practice of Member States in designating habitats under Directive 79/409 or 92/43 does in fact consider economic aspects and is thus not in line with law. In some cases, environmental organisations as watchdogs help to prevent such practices, as was in the present case the Royal Society for the Protection of Birds. However, it must be feared that over a period of 30 to 50 years, these efforts will prove to be just not enough, in particular as regards Southern, Central and Eastern Europe.

(8) In paragraph 41 of its judgment, the Court made an obiter dictum which referred to the situation once a habitat has been designated. In that obiter dictum it was pointed out that a partial declassification of a designated habitat or the authorisation of works within the habitat could be authorised under the conditions of Article 6(2) to (4) of Directive 92/43 which also applied, according to its Article 7, to habitats designated under Article 4(1) of Directive 79/409.

In the case of the Lappel Bank, though, the obiter dictum was of no help. In the United Kingdom, the introduction of litigation has no suspensive effect on administrative decisions. And while the case of the Lappel Bank was pending, Swale Borogh Council gave, in June 1994, planning permission to the Port of Sheerness authorities to expand on to the Lappel Bank. By June 1995, about one third of the Lappel Bank was already used for the purposes of the port and the rest of work was, according to the port authorities, to be completed within some months.[68]

(9) Hitherto, the provisions in particular of Article 6(4) of Directive 92/43 have not often become relevant. The Commission has issued two opinions so far, both in the context of the construction of a motorway in Germany.[69] In both cases, it interpreted the provision of Article 6(4), in particular the requirement of overriding public interest, very widely, referring to the state of regional unemployment, economic weakness etc. In view of these opinions, it is not clear how it will ever be possible to contest the existence of an overriding public interest, in particular in Member States which are less wealthy than Germany. The Commission has issued a guidance document on the monitoring of Article 6 of Directive 92/43.[70] However, on the problem of Article 6(4), which is to reconcile Member States' interest to promote economic interests and the need to protect the environment, I share G. Winter's pessimism that the "Commission is no reliable pillar in this respect".[71]

---

[67] Court of Justice, Case C–96/98, *Commission* v. *France* [1999] ECR I–8531; see for a commentary on this case p. 297 *supra*.

[68] See Advocate General Fenelly, Opinion in the present case [1996] ECR I–3805, para. 9.

[69] Commission, Opinion of 27 April 1995 [1995] OJ C178/3; Opinion of 18 December 1995, [1996] OJ L6/14.

[70] Commission, *Managing Natura 2000 Sites. The Provisions of Art. 6 of the "Habitats" Directive*, 92/43/EEC (Office for Official Publications of the European Communities, Luxembourg, 2000).

[71] See J Harte, "Analysis on Case C–44/95" and G Winter, "Footnote on the case", n. 2 [1997] *Journal of Environmental Law* 139, 180.

38. HUNTING OF BIRDS

Judgment of the Court (Sixth Chamber) of 7 December 2000
Case C–38/99

Commission of the European Communities v. *France*
[2000] ECR I–10941

Facts and Procedure

In February 1999, the Commission applied to the Court for a declaration that France had failed to fulfil its obligations under Directive 79/409[72] by failing correctly to transpose Article 7 of that Directive.[73] The Commission was of the opinion (a) that France had set excessively early opening dates for hunting, (b) that it had set excessively late dates for the closing of hunting, (c) that it had not communicated all the provisions for tranposition in three Alsatian *départements* and (d) that it had not provided for a system of complete protection for birds during their migratory, breeding or nesting time.

France declared that hunting in France was regulated by Law 94–591 of 15 July 1994[74] and by Law 98–549 of 3 July 1998.[75] Furthermore, it indicated that the French Government had sent a report to the French Parliament in which it had stated that the various draft laws on early opening and closing dates for the hunting of migratory birds which Members of the Parliament had tabled before the adoption of Law 98–549, contained provisions which appeared to conflict with the obligations laid down by Directive 79/409 and that the French government could

---

[72] Directive 79/409 on the conservation of wild birds [1979] OJ L103/1.

[73] Directive 79/409 (n. 72 *supra*), Art. 7: "1. Owing to their population level, geographical distribution and reproductive rate throughout the Community, the species listed in Annex II may be hunted under national legislation. Member States shall ensure that the hunting of these species does not jeopardise conservation eforts in their distribution area. 2. The species referred to in Annex II/1 may be hunted in the geographical sea and land area where this directive applies. 3. The species referred to in Annex II/2 may be hunted only in the Member States in respect of which they are indicated. 4. Member Statres shall ensure that the practice of hunting, including falconry if practised, as carried on in accordance with the nationa measures in force, complies with the principles of wise use and ecologically balanced control of the species of birds concerned and that this practice is compatible as regards the population of these species, in particular migratory species, with the measures resulting from Art. 2. They shall see in particular that the species to which hunting laws apply are not hunted during the rearing season nor during the various stages of reproduction. In the case of migratory species, they shall see in particular that the species to which hunting regulations apply are not hunted during their period of reproduction or during their return to their rearing grounds. Member States shall send the Commission all relevant information on the practical application of their hunting regulations".

[74] Loi no. 94–591 [1994] JORF 10246.

[75] Loi no. 98–549 of [1998] JORF 10208.

not accept them; the government had expressed the opinion that it ought to be possible, in due course, to ensure that Law 98–549 was revised.

Judgment (extracts)

[(a) the opening dates for hunting]

23. ... Article 7(4) of the Wild Birds Directive seeks in particular to impose a prohibition of hunting of all species of wild birds during the rearing periods and the various stages of reproduction and dependency and, in the case of migratory species, during their return to their rearing grounds. Moreover, the Court has held that that article is designed to secure a complete system of protection in the periods during which the survival of wild birds is particularly under threat . . . Accordingly, protection against hunting activities cannot be confined to the majority of the birds of a given species, as determined by average reproductive cycles and migratory movements . . .

24. In this case, the French Government itself recognises that the early opening dates for the hunting of waterfowl indicated in the second paragraph of article L224–2 of the New Rural Code, as amended by Law No 98–549, do not enable all individuals of species which are rearing their young to be protected. That is tantamount to admitting that, for certain of the species concerned and in certain areas, hunting is opened too early.

25. Furthermore, it is clear from a study by the National Hunting Authority of February 1998 regarding two species of birds which may be hunted that the early opening dates for hunting given in the ministerial orders fairly frequently impinge upon the periods in which a significant number of young birds are dependant in so far as they are not yet able to fly. Thus, in the case of mallards, in eight departments no more than 80% of young birds were able to fly by the early opening date for hunting; on the same date, in 26 other departments, a maximum of 90% of young birds were able to fly. In the case of the coot, in eight departments, no more than 80% of young birds were able to fly by the early opening date of hunting; in 15 other departments, no more than 90% of young birds were able to fly by that date.

27. It follows that the system of early opening of the dates for the hunting of waterfowl, as established by Law No 98–549 amending Article L. 224–2 of the New Rural Code, is not capable of fulfilling the requirement laid down in Article 7(4) of the Wild Birds Directive, as interpreted by the Court, that there be a complete system of protection for wild birds over the period in which their survival is particularly threatened.

[(b) closing dates for hunting]

39. ... the French Government itself admits that the system at issue does not, in certain cases, satisfy the requirements of the Wild Birds Directive.

40. . . . it is clear from an examination of a table drawn up in accordance with information from the ORNIS database, produced to the Court, that, for 29 migratory species which may be hunted in France, the closing dates for hunting are fixed, depending on the species concerned, 10, 20 or even 30 days later than the date of commencement of return migration (also known as "pre-mating migration") of the species. The species concerned are mallard, lapwing, greylag goose, teal, coot, pintail, shoveler, wigeon, white-fronted goose, bean goose, scaup, stockdove, woodpigeon, moorhen, jack snipe, velvet scoter, curlew, grey plover, common eider, spotted redshank, redwing, blackbird, song thrush, fieldfare, black-tailed godwit, skylark, mistle thrush and snipe.

41. It follows that a greater or lesser percentage of birds, depending on the species involved, is not protected against hunting in the pre-mating migration period, during which the survival of birds is under particular threat.

42. As the Court has held, a method whose object or effect is to allow a certain percentage of the birds of a species to escape complete protection during the period of pre-mating migration, does not comply with Article 7(4) of the Wild Birds Directive . . .

43. As regards the staggering of closing dates for hunting, it must be borne in mind that the national authorities are not empowered by the Wild Birds Directive to lay down dates which vary according to species of birds unless the Member State concerned can adduce evidence, based on scientific and technical data relevant to each individual case, that staggering the closing dates for hunting does not impede the complete protection of species liable to be affected by such staggering . . .

44. The French Government has produced no such evidence.

45. It must therefore be held that, with regard to the choice of closing dates for the hunting of certain species of waterfowl and of migratory birds, the French Republic has not correctly implemented Article 7(4) of the Wild Birds Directive within the prescribed period. Consequently, the Commission's application must be upheld on this point as well.

[(c) Communication of transposition measures in three départements]

46. The Commission maintains that the French authorities have not communicated to it the dates of the hunting season for migratory birds in the departments of Lower Rhine, Upper Rhine and Moselle.

47. The French Government recognises that it had not forwarded any information of that kind . . .

48. Accordingly, it must be held that, by failing to notify within the prescribed periods the dates of the hunting season for migratory birds in the departments of Lower Rhine, Upper Rhine and Moselle, the French Republic has failed to fulfil its obligations under Article 7(4) of the Wild Birds Directive . . .

[(d) Transposition of Article 7(4) of Directive 79/409]

51. According to the French Government, the charge of failure to transpose the principle of complete protection into French law is purely formal since the "*travaux préparatoires*" for both Law No 94–591 and Law No 98–549 prove that the legislature wished to comply with Article 7(4) of the Wild Birds Directive, as interpreted by the Court, notwithstanding the fact that some of the dates adopted seem hardly compatible with that provision. In reality, the transposition of such a principle into national law is superfluous since the law in force ensures that it is actually applied. The French Government contends that, in any event, the Wild Birds Directive is a well-known measure—as well known as a provision incorporating a new principle in the Rural Code would be—and that citizens know that they are able to rely on it, as is demonstrated by the increasing number of administrative actions based on that measure. Moreover, the French courts have never declined to examine the compatibility of administrative measures with the Wild Birds Directive or, in particular, with the principle of complete protection.

52. In response to that submission, it must be observed, first, that it is common ground that the provisions of the second and third sentences of Article 7(4) of the Wild Birds Directive had not been formally incorporated into French law by the end of the period prescribed by the reasoned opinion.

53. Second, the Court has indeed held that the transposition of a directive into domestic law does not necessarily require the provisions of the directive to be enacted in precisely the same words in a specific, express provision of national law and that a general legal context may be sufficient if it actually ensures the full application of the directive in a sufficiently clear and precise manner. However, the Court has also held that faithful transposition becomes particularly important in the case of the Wild Birds Directive where management of the common heritage is entrusted to the Member States in their respective territories . . .

54. Third, with regard to the departments of Lower Rhine, Upper Rhine and Moselle, Article R. 229–2 of the rural Code provides: "The open season for hunting in general must be within the following dates:—general opening date, no earlier than 23 August;—general closing date, no later than 1 February".

Under the same code, it is the responsibilitiy of the prefect to make an annual order for opening of the hunting season.

55. In so far as domestic law contains no provision requiring the prefects of those departments to take account, in adopting the annual order for opening of the hunting season, of the prohibition of hunting any species of bird during the sensitive periods mentioned in paragraph 23 of this judgment, that law is subject to a degree of legal uncertainty as regards the obligations to be complied with by prefects in adopting measures. As a result, there is no guarantee that the hunting of wild birds will be proscribed during the rearing period or the various stages of reproduction and dependence or, in the case of migratory species, during their return to their rearing grounds . . .

56. It follows that essential provisions of the Wild Birds Directive, such as those of the second and third sentences of Article 7(4), have not in any event been completely, clearly and unambiguously transposed into the Fench rules . . .

57. It must therefore be held that, as regards the department of Lower Rhine, Upper Rhine and Moselle, the French Republic has not correctly transposed the second and third sentences of Article 7(4) of the Wild Birds Directive within the prescribed period . . .

On those grounds, the Court (Sixth Chamber) hereby:

1. Declares that, by failing correctly to transpose Article 7(4) of Council Directive 79/409 . . . , by omitting to communicate all the transposition measures relating to the whole of its territory and by failing correctly to implement the aforesaid provision, the French Republic has failed to fulfil its obligations under that directive;

2. Orders the French Republic to pay the costs . . .

Commentary

I. Hunters and Bird Protection

(1) This judgment examines a question of incomplete transposition of provisions of Directive 79/409 into French law, more than 20 years after the adoption of the Directive. It enumerates at least four pieces of French national legislation on the hunting of birds which were adopted since 1994.[76] These facts alone demonstrate the highly political nature of the question of bird hunting in France. Since the adoption of the Directive, French hunters have, in open defiance of Community and national law, practised hunting of birds outside the limits set. The "*chasse à la tourterelle*" has gained a certain reputation: here hunters in the Southwest of France hunt in springtime, outside each hunting period, and the French authorities have not contained this practice so far. In particular in French rural areas, hunting is considered to be a fundamental right and each attempt by public authorities—be it from local, regional, national or the Community side— to limit this right is considered an *excès de pouvoir* against which self-defence is legitimate. The fact that in 1999, France was condemned by the European Court of Human Rights because some of its hunting provisions were in conflict with the individual right of property, may, in future, slowly lead to some rethinking.

(2) French hunting methods came before the Court of Justice first in 1988 when the Court had to give a ruling on so-called "traditional" hunting methods, i.e. methods which were, generally, prohibited by Directive 79/409. In a number

---

[76] Apart from the Laws mentioned in nn. 73 and 74 *supra*, an order of 29 May 1997 of the Minister of the Environment [1997] JORF 8303; Law 2000–698 of 26 July 2000 on hunting [2000] JORF 11542. The date of adoptation of the New Rural Code and its subsequent amendments is not given.

of points which concerned the transposition of the Directive into French law, the Court found in favour of the Commission; however, as regards the traditional hunting methods, it found that the Commission had not submitted enough evidence and rejected the application,[77] a judgment which I would consider political.

In 1998, the Commission submitted the case to the Court a second time, as France had not yet complied with the judgment of 1988. The Commission asked, under Article 228 EC Treaty, that France should pay a fine of 105,000 Euros per day from the time of the second judgment until it fully complied.[78] The Commission, though, did not bring a new action against France as regards the traditional hunting methods, though, in a similar case, where it had been rejected by the Court in a first case against Italy, it had repeated the action.[79]

The present case is thus only the second case brought by the Commission which was bound to act, as the legislation of 1994 and 1998 deliberately and quite openly stated that the principles for opening and closing the hunting season, elaborated by the Court of Justice under Directive 79/409, should not be applied in France; the incompatibility of the new French provisions with Community law was even admitted by the French government in the present case.[80]

(3) However, the Court had, in a considerable number of cases, examined national hunting provisions and their compatibility with Directive 79/409.[81] In the present case therefore, its ruling was more concerned with the confirmation of earlier judgments than with breaking new legal grounds. The Court had in particular in Case C–157/89 established the basis of its interpretation of Article 7(4) of Directive 79/409. In that case, it had stated that Article 7(4) envisaged the complete protection of birds during the periods in which their survival is particularly threatened. This meant that national legislation was not allowed to limit the protection of birds to the majority of a specific species.[82]

(4) This jurisprudence was elaborated in the preliminary ruling in Case C–435/92. The Court repeated its interpretation that Article 7(4) intended to give complete protection to the birds. He then declared expressly that any method which would fix the end of the hunting season at a moment where the migration of birds had reached its peak was not compatible with Article 7(4); the same applied, according to the Court, to methods which were based on the system that a certain percentage of birds had started the migration or which fixed an average time for the beginning of the migration.

---

[77] Court of Justice, Case 252/85 *Commission* v. *France* [1988] ECR 2243.

[78] Commission, Sixteenth annual report on monitoring the application of Community law—1998, [1999] OJ C354/54.

[79] See Court of Justice, Cases 262/85 *Commission* v. *Italy* [1987] ECR 3073 on the one hand, 157/89, *Commission* v. *Italy* [1991] ECR 57 on the other hand.

[80] See paras. 11(not reproduced here), 24, 35 (not reproduced here), 39 and 51.

[81] See Court of Justice, Cases 247/85, *Commission* v. *Belgium* [1987] ECR 3073; 262/85 (n. 79 *supra*); 412/85, *Commission* v. *Germany* [1987] ECR 3503; 339/87, *Commission* v. *Netherlands* [1990] ECR 851; 288/88, *Commission* v. *Germany* [1990] ECR 2721; 157/89 (n. 79 *supra*); C–435/92, *Association des Animaux* [1994] ECR I–69; C–118/94, *WWF* v. *Veneto* [1996] ECR I–1223.

[82] Court of Justice, Case 157/89 (n. 79 *supra*), para. 14.

In that case, the Court also dealt with the staggering of the ending of the hunting season according to the different species of birds. The Court saw two essential disadvantages linked to such a method: on the one hand, hunting would lead to disturbance for other species for which the hunting season was already finished;[83] on the other hand, there was a risk of error between different bird species.[84] The Member State had, however, the chance to prove by appropriate scientific and technical data for each individual species that staggering the closing dates for hunting did not prevent the complete protection of those species of bird liable to be affected by such staggering.[85]

(5) Finally, the Court had to answer the question whether a Member State could fix different dates for the end of the hunting season. The Court answered in the positive; it also was of the opinion that the fixing of the date for the end of the hunting season could be subdelegated to local or regional authorities. In all cases, however, the legislation had to be drafted in such a way that complete protection of the birds during their migration remained ensured.

(6) The Commission was not always of the opinion that the hunting provisions of Directive 79/409 should be enforced. In 1994, it proposed itself to amend Article 7(4)[86] and to give greater freedom to Member States to regulate hunting provisions[87]—which, in practice, would apply in particular to France, furthermore to

---

[83] Court of Justice, Case C–435/92 (n. 81 *supra*), paras. 16 and 17: " . . . any hunting is liable to disturb wildlife and that it may in many cases affect the state of conservation of the species concerned, independently of the extent to which it depletes numbers. The regular elimination of individuals keep the hunted populations in a permanent state of alert which has disastrous consequences for numerous aspects of their living conditions . . . those consequences are particularly serious for groups of birds which, during the season of migration and wintering, tend to gather together in flocks and rest in areas which are often very confined or even enclosed. Disturbances caused by hunting force these animals to devote most of their energy to moving to other spots and to fleeing, to the detriment of time spent feeding and resting for the purpose of the migration. Those disturbances are reported to have an adverse impact on the level of energy of each individual and the mortality rate of all the populations concerned. The effect of disruption caused by hunting birds of other species is particularly significant for those species whose return migration takes place earlier".

[84] Court of Justice, Case C–435/92 (n. 81 *supra*), para. 18: "With regard to the second difficulty, namely the risk that certain species for which hunting has already closed will be subject to indirect depletion owing to confusion with the species for which hunting is still open, it must be emphasized that the third sentence of Art. 7(4) of the Directive is specifically intended to prevent those species from being exposed to the risk of depletion due to hunting during the period of pre-mating migration, requiring the Member States to take all necessary measures to prevent any hunting during that period".

[85] Court of Justice, Case C–435/92 (n. 81 *supra*), para. 21: "Fixing one single date for all species concerned for the closing of hunting, which is equivalent to that fixed for the species which is the earliest to migrate, guarantees in principle that the objective laid down in the third sentence of Art. 7(4) of the Directive is realized. However, it is possible that the Member State concerned may be able to adduce evidence, based on scientific and technical data relevant to each individual case, that staggering the closing dates for hunting does not impede the complete protection of the species of bird liable to be affected by such staggering".

[86] Commission, proposal for an amendment of Directive 79/409 [1994] OJ C100/7; explanatory memorandum COM(94)39 of 21 January 1994.

[87] Commission (n. 86 *supra*), which proposes to introduce a new Annex VI to Directive 79/409, reading: "The end of the hunting season shall be determined as follows: 1. for species whose conservation status is favourable and whose migration begins before 20 February, the hunting season closes at the lates within the 10-day period following the 10-day period when migratory passage begins; 2. for species whose conservation staus is favourable and whose migration begins after 20 February, or for

Italy and Spain. The Commission declared, in order to justify this change, that "the Member States are best placed to define the rules for the application of these principles—an observation which must be doubted on in the light of the different Court judgments mentioned above and in the light of the present judgment".

The Commission's proposal was rejected by the European Parliament whose chairman of the Environmental Committee declared that "the whole idea of shifting the hunting season under the principle of subsidiarity is ridiculous".[88] If one follows the concept of the Court of Justice that (migrating) birds are the common heritage of all Member States, it seems indeed that the proposal for amending Article 7(4) was motivated more by policy than by environmental reasons. Anyway, following the rejection by the European Parliament, the proposal was stranded in Council and was not adopted.

(7) In the present case, therefore, the Court just had to check French legislation against the background of these earlier judgments. It found that neither the opening nor the closing hunting dates in French legislation complied with these requirements. As regards the dates of the hunting seasons in the three departments of Lower Rhine, Upper Rhine and Moselle, France had recognised that it had not transmitted the dates of the hunting season for migratory birds to the Commission; legally, there was therefore no problem for the Court to find that France had not fulfilled its obligations under Directive 79/409. However, attention is drawn to the political side of this criticism: the oral hearing in the present case took place on 29 June 2000. This means that France had not yet communicated to the Commission the necessary transposition measure which it should have communicated by April 1981! The real problem of the European Union being a Union based on the rule of law lies in this deliberate, intentional and unpunished ignoring of legal rules which have been fixed by common consensus:[89] Indeed, it seems impossible to call a sanction the declaration by the Court, 19 years later, that France had not communicated all its transposition measures to the Commission.

II. Environmental Principles and Bird Protection

(8) The last point which the Court had to decide was the question whether the second and the third sentences of Article 7(4) had expressly to be transposed into

species whose conservation status is unfavourable and whose migration period begins before 20 February, the hunting season closes at the latest within the same 10-day period as that during which migratory passage begins; 3. for species whose conservation status is unfavourable and whose migration begins after 20 February, the hunting season closes at the latest within the 10-day period preceding that during which migratory passage begins".

It is unclear how hunters and birds would have been properly informed of these rules and how it would have been possible for anybody to monitor their practical application.

[88] Quoted from H Somsen, "Comment to Case C–435/92" [1994] *European Environmental Law Review* 174, 178.

[89] Of course, Directive 79/409 was adopted by unanimity. As it was adopted at a time when France held the Presidency in Council, it even bears the signature of M François-Poncet, the French President of the Council at that time.

French law. This was the Commission's request, as it was of the opinion that "although the early opening and closing dates for hunting are now fixed by the legislature, the latter has always allowed the administrative authorities a degree of latitude as determining such dates and laying down rules governing hunting within the legally defined periods".[90]

The Court first set out two general considerations on the transposition of Community provisions into national law (paragraphs 52 and 53). It then addressed the specific situation in the three departments of Lower Rhine, Upper Rhine and Moselle (paragraphs 54 and 55). Paragraph 56 seems to apply to French legislation in general. However, paragraph 57 again returns to the three departments and finds that "as regards the department . . ." France had not correctly transposed Article 7(4). Finally, the tenor of the judgment refers to France in general, not to the three departments.

(9) This part of the judgment is, to say the least, confusing. This becomes obvious when the question is posed whether France would have complied with its obligations flowing out of this judgment, if legislation in those three departments were to transpose the second and third sentences of Article 7(4) of Directive 79/409. This question is not merely hypothetical, as in many Member States— Spain and Italy, Belgium, Austria, Germany, the United Kingdom, Portugal (Madeira and Azores), Finland (Aaland Isles)—the regions have considerable legislative competence in environmental matters, in particular as regards nature protection. It is regrettable that the judgment, on this point, is not precise.

In substance, it is well known that a piece of law always has to be interpreted according to its general context, including the principles on which it is based. If such principles are expressly laid down in an environmental directive, there is a considerable risk that the practical, day-to-day application of the transposition measures loses the gist of the environmental Directive, where those general principles are not laid down in the transposing measure; "faithful transposition becomes particularly important in the case of the Wild Birds Directive where management of the common heritage is entrusted to the Member States in their respective territories".[91]

(10) In view of this situation, I am of the opinion that the tenor of the Court's judgment is correct and that France has to incorporate the full Article 7(4) into its national legislation; the situation in the three departments only is to be seen as an illustration of a more general situation.

It is submitted that the above-mentioned statement of the Court concerning the faithful transposition of Commmunity provisions into national law applies not only to the protection of wild birds, but rather to the protection of the environment generally. The protection of the water—of rivers and of seas—of air, of the natural environment, of the soil, of climate and of the ozone layer is entrusted to the Member States in their respective territories. There is no pan-European trustee

---

[90] Para. 50 of the present judgment, not reproduced above.
[91] Para. 53 of the present judgment.

for the European environment, and the same applies to the global environment. The protection of the environment is a common Community interest the management of which is entrusted to the Member States. It is they which adopt—and in the case of Community directives transpose—legislation and take numerous measures to preserve, protect and improve the quality of the environment. It is they alone which "shall finance and implement the environment policy" of the Community.[92] If Member States do not apply and ensure application, day by day, of the numerous provisions of environmental law in their territories, all political and legislative efforts at Community or international level remain dead letters. Environmental law becomes practical through application, and this is done at local, regional and national level first. It would be desirable for the Court to ensure that a more faithful transposition of Community environmental law into the national law takes place—and that the Commission becomes more conscious of this problem in the environmental sector.

---

[92] Art. 175(4) EC Treaty: "Without prejudice to certain measures of a Community nature, the Member States shall finance and implement the environment policy".

6

WASTE MANAGEMENT*

---

39. LOCAL MONOPOLIES IN WASTE

Judgment of the Court of 23 May 2000
Case C–209/98

*Reference for a preliminary ruling in the proceedings between
Entreprenoerforeningens Affalds/Miljoesektion /FFAD, acting for
Sydhavnens Sten & Grus Aps and Koebenhavns Kommune*
[2000] ECR I-3473

Facts and Procedure

In 1988, the Danish Ministry for the environment noted that approximately one
third of building waste, corresponding to 20 per cent of all waste for the whole of
Denmark, was produced in greater Copenhagen and that the facilities operating in
the Copenhagen area were capable of dealing with only a small portion of that
waste. The Ministry therefore asked the Metropolitan City Council of Copenhagen
to draw up a regional waste management plan. The Municipality of Copenhagen
found that in 1988 of the total amount of about 382,000 tonnes of building waste,
16 per cent was recycled, while the rest was landfilled. Therefore, it explored the
possibility of recycling more of the building waste. Together with the Danish
Environmental Agency, the Municipality set up the company RGS which became
responsible for managing the regional recycling centre at Groeften. Private
and public persons interested in participating in the project were invited to come
forward.

Subsequently, the Municipality of Copenhagen concluded contracts for the
receipt and processing of building waste produced within its boundaries with
three undertakings which operated sites for such waste, including RGS, the main
beneficiary. A municipal regulation from 1992, succeeded by another regulation
in 1998, expressly provided for the possibility of contracting agreements on building waste destined for recycling with a limited number of companies.

---

* For further judgments dealing with waste issues see cases in s. 3, chap. 1 *supra* (*Dusseldorp*) and
ss. 46 (*Kouroupitos*) and 49 (*Packaging Waste*) in chap. 7 *infra.*

Sydhavnens Sten & Grus, the applicant in the main proceeding, has, since 1983, been active in the recycling of building waste. In 1994 it received permission to set up a plant within Copenhagen for the sorting and crushing of building waste. When it applied to obtain building waste generated within the boundaries of the Municipality of Copenhagen, its application was rejected. The dispute was brought before a Danish court, which decided to have a number of questions put to the Court of Justice by way of a preliminary ruling.

Judgment (extracts)

[The restrictions on exporting waste]

32. . . . the national court is asking, essentially, first whether Article 34 of the Treaty precludes a system for the collection and receipt of non-hazardous building waste destined for recovery, such as that set up by the Municipality of Copenhagen, under which a limited number of undertakings are authorised to process waste produced in the municipality, and, if necessary, whether that system can be justified . . .

34. According to the settled case-law of the Court, Article 34 of the Treaty applies to national measures which have as their specific object or effect the restriction of patterns of exports and thereby the establishment of a difference in treatment between the domestic trade of a Member State and its export trade, in such a way as to provide a particular advantage for national production of for the domestic market of the State in question . . .

37. . . . the mere fact that an exclusive right to process the building waste produced in a municipality is granted to a limited number of undertakings does not necessarily have the effect of creating a barrier to exports contrary to Article 34 of the Treaty, provided that waste producers are still able to export it . . .

43. . . . It is for the national court . . . to ascertain whether the rules in question, whether resulting from the 1992 municipal regulations or from the 1998 municipal regulation, allow producers of non-hazardous building waste to export their waste using intermediaries if they wish.

44. Should it be held that the rules in question have the effect of restricting exports in a manner contrary to Article 34 of the Treaty, the national court raises the question whether those rules might be justified on the basis, on the one hand, of Article 36 of the Treaty and, on the other hand, of the protection of the environment as provided for, in particular, in Article 130(2) of the Treaty.

45. As regards the derogation provided for in Article 36 of the Treaty, it must be pointed out that such a justification would be relevant if the fact that building waste was shipped over a greater distance, as a consequence of being exported, and processed in a Member State other than that in which it is produced represented a danger to the health and life of humans, animals or plants.

46. In the present case, however, the waste in question is non-hazardous waste and nothing has been put forward to show that there is a danger to the health and life of humans, animals or plants; the participants in the proceedings before the Court have merely stated, on this point, that any infringement of Aricle 34 of the Treaty would be justified by virtue of Article 36 of the Treaty.

47. It follows that the derogation in Article 36 of the Treaty in relation to the health and life of humans, animals and plants cannot, in these circumstances, justify a restriction on exports contrary to Article 34 of the Treaty.

48. As regards the justification based on the protection of the environment, and in particular the principle referred to in Article 130r(2) of the Treaty that environmental damage should as a priority be rectified at source, it must be pointed out that the protection of the environment cannot serve to justify any restriction on exports, particularly in the case of waste destined for recovery . . . That is so *a fortiori* where, as in the case before the national court, environmentally non-hazardous building waste is involved.

49. Nowhere in the documents before the Court is it argued that the waste in question is harmful to the environment.

50. In those circumstances, restrictions on exports contrary to Article 34 of the Treaty, such as those alleged in the main proceedings, cannot be justified by the need to protect the environment, in particular by application of the principle referred to in Article 130r(2) of the Treaty that environmental damage should as a priority be rectified at source.

[Articles 82 and 86 (ex Articles 86 and 90) EC Treaty]

52. Second, the national court asks essentially whether Article 90 of the Treaty, read in conjunction with Article 86 of the Treaty, precludes the establishment of a local system, such as the system at issue in the case in the main proceedings, under which a limited number of specially selected undertakings can process environmentally non-hazardous building waste destined for recovery and produced in the area concerned, thus ensuring a sufficiently large flow of such waste to those undertakings, and excludes other undertakings even though they are qualified to process the waste.

53. It should be pointed out, first, that pursuant to the rules at issue in the main proceedings, three undertakings were authorised to receive building waste produced within the boundaries of the Municipality of Copenhagen with a view to recovering it and that other undertakings, including Sydhavnens Sten & Grus, are precluded from doing so. Apart from these three undertakings, no undertaking in Denmark can receive building waste produced in that municipality with a view to processing it.

54. It follows that those three undertakings must be regarde as undertakings to which the Member State concerned has granted an exclusive right within the meaning of Article 90(1) of the Treaty . . .

57/59/65. As regards the question of the existence of a dominant position, . . . it is for the national court to define the relevant market . . . Only if the national court considers that the undertakings concerned have a dominant position on a market . . . will it be necessary to consider the question of possible abuse.

66. It must be borne in mind that merely creating a dominant position by the grant of special or exclusive rights within the meaning of Article 90(1) of the Treaty is not in itself incompatible with Article 86 of the Treaty. A Member State is in breach of the prohibitions contained in those two provisions only if the undertaking in question, merely by exercising the exclusive rights granted to it, is led to abuse its dominant position or when such rights are liable to create a situation in which that undertaking is led to commit such abuses . . .

67. The Court has thus held that a Member State may, without infringing Article 86 of the Treaty, grant exclusive rights to certain undertakings provided they do not abuse their dominant position or are not led necessarily to commit an abuse . . .

68. In that regard, it should be pointed out, first, that the grant of an exclusive right over part of the national territory for environmental purposes, such as establishing the capacity necessary for the recycling of building waste, does not in itself constitute an abuse of a dominant position.

74. . . . it follows from the combined effect of paragraphs 1 and 2 of Article 90 that paragraph may be relied upon to justify the grant by a Member State, to an undertaking entrusted with the operation of services of general economic interest, of exclusive rights which are contrary to, in particular, Article 86 of the Treaty, to the extent to which performance of the particular task assigned to that undertaking can be assured only through the grant of such rights and provided that the development of trade is not affected to such an extent as would be contrary to the interests of the Community . . .

75. The management of particular waste may properly be considered to be capable of forming the subject of a service of general economic interest, particularly where the service is designed to deal with an environmental problem.

76. It is clear from the documents before the Court that the Municipality of Copenhagen, acting in accordance with national legislation, entrusted to three undertakings the task of processing building waste produced in that municipality and that those undertakings are required to receive such waste and process it so that it can be reused as far as possible. In those circumstances, it must be acknowledged that a task of general economic interest was entrusted to those undertakings.

77. Next, it is necessary to consider whether the exclusive right granted to the three undertakings is necessary for them to be able to perfom the task of general economic interest which has been assigned to them under economically acceptable conditions . . .

78. It is apparent from the evidence before the Court that when the Groeften centre was set up and an exclusive right was granted to a limited number of undertakings, the Municipality of Copenhagen was faced with what was regarded as a serious environmental problem, namely the burial of most building waste in the ground when it could have been recycled. Recycling was impossible owing to the lack of undertakings capable of processing the waste. In order to deal with he volumes of waste produced in the municipality and to ensure that it was recycled to a high standard, the municipality considered it necessary to set up a high-capacity centre; and, in order to ensure that this newly-established centre would be profitable, the municipality considered it necessary to ensure that the centre was guaranteed a significant flow of waste by granting it an exclusive processing right.

79. Admittedly, that exclusive right had the effect of excluding even qualified undertakings wishing to enter the market, such as Sydhavnens Sten & Grus. In the absence of undertakings capable of processing the waste at issue in the main proceedings, however, the Municipality of Copenhagen considered it necessary to set up a high-capacity centre. Furthermore, in order to ensure that undertakings would be interested in participating in the operation of a high-capacity centre, it was also considered necessary to grant an exclusive right, limited in time to the period over which the investment could foreseeably be written off and in space to the land within the boundaries of the municipality.

80. A measure having a less restrictive effect on competition, such as rules which merely required undertakings to have their waste recycled, would not necessarily have ensured that most of the waste produced in the municipality would be recycled, precisely because there was not sufficient capacity to process the waste.

81. In those crcumstances, it must be held that even if the grant of an exclusive right led to a restriction of competition in a substantial part of the common market, that grant could be regarded as necessary for the performance of a task serving the general economic interest.

82. Nor is there anything in the documents before the Court to suggest that the exclusive right granted in the present case is such that it will necessarily lead the undertakings in question to abuse their dominant position.

Commentary

I. Local Restrictions on the Free Circulation of Waste

(1) The municipality of Copenhagen had given to three undertakings the exclusive right to recycle construction and demolition waste (building waste) and, as another undertaking also wanted to take part in this business, the Court of Justice was asked by a Danish court which had to rule on the request whether the granting of exclusive rights was compatible with Community law.

(2) The Court of Justice had first to deal with the question whether the Copenhagen local provisions contained an export ban. It might be surprising to find such a question discussed in the context of local regulations; however the Copenhagen agglomeration generates about 380,000 tonnes of construction and

demolition waste, which is about 20 per cent of all waste generated in Denmark; and Copenhagen is some 20 minutes, truck drive away from Sweden, which might make the export of waste a profitable business.

The Court of Justice could not rule on the question whether the local regulations contained an export ban, as the parties in the main proceedings contradicted each other. Thus, it decided that it was up to the national court to state what the relevant rule of law was. However, the Court stated that, should there be such an export ban for construction and demolition waste, this would be contrary to Article 29 (ex Article 34) EC Treaty.[1]

(3) The Court then examined whether such an export ban could be justified by any provision of the Treaty. As the regulations expressly referred to non-hazardous construction and demolition waste, the Court was of the opinion that Article 30 (ex Article 36) EC Treaty, which allowed restrictions of export or import in order to protect the health and life of humans, animals or plants, could not apply. Furthermore, the Court ruled out recourse to Article 174(2) (ex Article 130r(2)) EC Treaty[2] and found "that the protection of the environment cannot serve to justify any restriction on exports, particularly in the case of waste destined for recovery" (paragraph 48).

(4) The Court's way of arguing and its conclusion are somehow surprising. Indeed, the Court has always held that Article 30 (ex Article 36) EC Treaty no longer applies where secondary Community legislation exists which addresses the problem in question. And in the case of the export of waste to other Member States (and to third countries), Regulation 259/93 exists to regulate such exports.[3] Therefore, the Court should have examined this Regulation and not so much Article 30 (ex Article 36) EC Treaty.[4] Even more surprising is the recourse to Article 174(2) (ex Article 130r(2)) EC Treaty. The principles laid down in that provision have, until now, never served as constituting possible autonomous justifications for restrictions on export or import of products or waste. Rather, they were constructed as *leitmotifs*, as guiding principles which could support the interpretation of legal provisions in primary or secondary Community law.[5]

(5) In my opinion, the present judgment of the Court cannot be understood as an attempt to change the past understanding of these principles, as the Court has not even undertaken the slightest attempt to explain any such change. Rather, it is presumed that the Court was motivated by the question of the Danish court which

---

[1] Art. 29 (ex Art. 34) EC Treaty: "Quantitative restrictions on exports, and all measures having equivalent effect, shall be prohibited between Member States".

[2] Art. 174(2) (ex Art. 130r(2)) EC Treaty: "Community policy on the environment shall aim at a high level of protection taking into account the diversity of situations in the various regions of the Community. It shall be based on the precautionary principle and on the principles that preventive action should be taken, that environmental damage should as a priority be rectified at source and that the polluter should pay".

[3] Regulation 259/93 on the supervision and control of shipments within, into and out of the European Community [1993] OJ L30/1.

[4] See also, for another case where the shipment of waste to another Member State was in question, Court of Justice, Case C–203/96, *Dusseldorp* [1998] ECR I–4075; the case is discussed at p. 22 *supra*.

[5] See in more detail p. 97 *et seq supra*.

had referred to that provision, though in a quite different context,[6] and as it intended to answer that question anyway in the negative, it did not attach primary importance to the proper construction.

(6) In substance, while it is clear that Article 30 (ex Article 36) EC Treaty would not have been applicable anyway, the proper examination following that would have been—Regulation 259/93 apart—Article 29 (ex Article 34) of the Treaty itself. This requires some explanation. As regards import restrictions, the Court has held that in the absence of Community secondary legislation, Article 28 (ex Article 30) EC Treaty allowed restrictions on the free circulation of goods by national provisions, where such provisions were necessary in order to satisfy mandatory requirements recognised by Community law;[7] in 1988, the Court recognised that environmental protection constituted such a mandatory requirement.[8] As yet, no such jurisprudence exists as regards Article 29 EC Treaty.

(7) The Court could thus have examined whether environmental protection requirements could also justify export restrictions. In Case 302/86, the Court had found that a deposit-and-return system for packaging—also a non-hazardous material—was necessary to promote the reuse of packaging which was a legitimate environmental objective, and that this could justify restrictions on the import of goods to Denmark. In the same way, it could be argued in the present case that the recycling of construction and demolition waste was an important objective of (local or national) environmental policy and could justify restrictions of exports. However, this line of thinking will not be pursued further, as the application of Articles 28, 29 and 30 to cases such as the present presupposes that there is no other secondary Community legislation. However, as mentioned, Regulation 259/93 deals with imports and exports of waste between Member States and should therefore have been the subject-matter of examination by the Court.[9]

(8) There is another judgment of the Court of Justice which may have caused the Danish court to formulate its question 1(c) and to refer to Article 174(2) (ex Article 130r(2)) EC Treaty. In Case C–2/90 the Court had held that an import ban on waste by the Belgian authorities was valid and did not discriminate against other Member States.[10] To justify the ban, the Court had used formulations which were somehow confusing[11] and led the majority of legal writers, including this author, to the opinion that the judgment in Case C–2/90 was politically motivated

---

[6] See Question 1(c) which was submitted to the Court (para. 29): "Does Art. 36 of the Treaty or any other valid consideration, such as the concern that environmental damage should be rectified at source and the establishment of any necessary treatment and disposal facility (see Art. 130r(2) of the Treaty), allow a municipal system as described in Question 1(a) to be established, where that system and the obligation for waste producers to use the system are based on the interest in promoting recovery of the waste covered by the system, including the interest in ensuring necessary treatment capacity?".

[7] Court of Justice, Case 120/78, *Rewe* v. *Bundesmonopolverwaltung* [1979] ECR 649.

[8] Court of Justice, Case 302/86, *Commission* v. *Denmark* [1988] ECR 4607.

[9] See also para. 4 of this commentary.

[10] Court of Justice, Case C–2/90, *Commission* v. *Belgium* [1992] ECR 4431.

[11] Court of Justice, Case C–2/90 (n. 10 *supra*), para. 34: " . . . The principle that environmental damage should as a priority be rectified at source—a principle laid down by Art. 130r(2) EEC for action by the Community relating to the environment—means that it is for each region, commune or other local

and not capable of generalisation. This being the case in the present action, the Court clarified that the principles laid down in Case C–2/90 do not apply to shipments of waste for recovery.[12]

II. Competition Rules and Restrictions on Trade in Waste

(9) Next, the Court examined whether the measures in Copenhagen raised problem with regard to competition rules. Before this part of the judgment is looked at, it should be noted that the Court referred to the waste management issue in Copenhagen as a "environmental problem" (paragraphs 75, 78 and 83). However, the disposal of construction and demolition waste or other waste on land is a disposal method which is a recognised way of handling waste that was generated. It is correct that Community waste management legislation, in the same way as waste management legislation of all Member States, favours the recycling and reuse of waste instead of its landfill, because in this way the economic value of waste is brought back to the economy.[13] If a Member State decides to reduce the waste that goes to landfill and undertakes rather to promote recycling and reuse of waste, this is certainly in line with Community environmental policy on waste. However, one should be aware that this is a deliberate political choice of a Member State, and it is doubtful whether this kind of situation really should be called an "environmental problem".

(10) Anyway, the Court first examined Article 86 (ex Article 90) EC Treaty.[14] It concluded that the three Danish undertakings had been granted an exclusive right within the meaning of Article 86(1). Not being able to determine, on factual grounds, whether the undertakings had a dominant position, the Court examined whether—if ever a dominant position could be ascertained—the undertakings had abused their position[15] or had been given so many exclusive rights that this led to an abuse of a dominant position. The Court found that the promotion of waste

entity to take appropriate measures to receive, process and dispose of its own waste. Consequently waste should be disposed of as close as possible to the place where it is produced in order to keep the transport of waste to the minimum practicable".

[12] Para. 48 of the judgment. The Court referred to its judgment in Case C–203/96, *Dusseldorp* (n. 4 *supra*).

[13] See in particular Directive 75/442 on waste [1975] OJ L194/47, as amended by Directive 91/156 [1991] OJ L78/32, Art. 3: "1. Member States shall take appropriate measures to encourage: (a) firstly, the prevention or reduction of waste production and its harmfulness . . . (b) secondly: (i) the recovery of waste by means of recycling, re-use or reclamation or any other process with a view to extracting secondary raw materials, or (ii) the use of waste as a source of energy".

[14] Art. 86 (ex Art. 90) EC Treaty: "1. In the case of public undertakings and undertakings to which Member States grant special or exclusive rights, Member States shall neither enact nor maintain in force any measure contrary to the rules contained in this Treaty, in particular to those rules provided for in Art. 12 and Arts. 81 to 89. 2. Undertakings entrusted with the operation of services of general economic interest or having the character of a revenue-producing monopoly shall be subject to the rules contained in this Treaty, in particular to the rules on competition, insofar as the application of such rules does not obstruct the performance, in law or in fact, of the particular tasks assigned to them. The development of trade must not be affected to such an extent as would be contrary to the interests of the Community. 3 . . . .".

[15] See Art. 82 (ex Art. 86) EC Treaty: "Any abuse by one or more undertakings of a dominant position within the common market or in a substantial part of it shall be prohibited as incompatible with the common market insofar as it may affect trade between Member States . . .".

recycling in the Copenhagen agglomeration was a task "serving the general economic interest". As there were no undertakings available in Copenhagen who were able to perform the task, the municipality was entitled to give exclusive rights to some undertakings, where such rights were limited in time to the period over which the investments could foreseeably be written off. Thus, Article 86 in conjunction with Article 82 EC Treaty would not apply.

(11) It is important to note that the Court started from the factual situation that there was no undertaking, in 1988, which was willing or able to recycle construction and demolition waste in Copenhagen. Danish public authorities were thus unable to perform the waste management policy which they had opted for. The granting of exclusive rights was preceded by an offer to all undertakings to join in the effort. At the end of the day, these exclusive rights were given to some undertakings and the wording of paragraph 79 seems to indicate that one of the reasons the Court accepted this system was that it was limited in time and in space. It is difficult to see, in retrospective, what else the Danish public authorities could have done in 1988, in order to get the construction and demolition waste of the Copenhagen agglomeration recycled.

(12) It is more interesting to consider whether local or regional or even national authorities in other Member States could follow the Copenhagen model and equally grant some undertakings—owned by the public authorities or private undertakings—exclusive rights. There are already at the political level candidates for this: in Italy, attempts were made in 1999/2000, to give a consortium for the collection of lead-containing batteries, COBAT, an exclusive right to collect, store and treat or dispose of such batteries. Following pressure for the European Commission which considered these provisions to be in conflict with the provisions on the free circulation of goods (waste), Italy amended its legislation, though the issue is still under discussion at Community level.[16]

In Cataluña (Spain), the regional authorities granted an exclusive right to an undertaking to collect, treat and dispose of, in Cataluña and to export to other parts of the Community hazardous waste. Also in this case, discussions are ongoing.

In Germany, local authorities complain that with the general reduction of waste generation and the general increase in waste recycling and recovery, they do not have waste enough properly to run their waste installations (waste incinerators with or without recovery of energy and landfills). At the political level, they argue therefore that local and regional authorities should have the right to orient certain types of waste—unsorted municipal waste as well as construction and demolition waste in particular—to the municipal waste installations and invoke, in support, the new provision of Article 16 EC Treaty.[17]

---

[16] See petitions 22/99 (Saraceno) and 231/99 (Rinaldi) to the European Parliament.

[17] Art. 16 EC Treaty: "Without prejudice to Arts. 73, 86 and 87, and given the place occupied by services of general economic interest in the shared values of the Union as well as their role in promoting social and territorial cohesion, the Community and the Member States, each within their respective powers and within the scope of application of this Treaty, shall take care that such services operate on the basis of principles and conditions which enable them to fulfil their missions".

(13) The difference in law between the Copenhagen system and this German policy demand is obvious: Copenhagen wanted to promote waste recycling, whereas the German local authorities do not have such an environmentally positive and desirable objective in mind. Copenhagen could not find undertakings to put the public policy—the recycling of construction and demolition waste—into practice, though it had tried to invite all interested undertakings to participate; Germany is confronted with more than enough undertakings and sees its problems at least in part caused by the increased recycling. Germany thus wants to exclude an environmentally desirable activity, recycling, and go back to a less desirable activity, the landfilling of waste or its incineration. Copenhagen has limited its system in time and in space; Germany wishes to have these local or regional monopolies restored as a permanent measure.

The Copenhagen system may not function—according to the Court—if it contains an export ban on waste; the German system could not function without an export ban on waste for recycling.

(14) The Court stated in 1992 that waste is a product, though of a specific nature, and therefore comes under the provisions of Articles 28 *et seq.* of the Treaty.[18] This means that private undertakings also have a right to see the free circulation of waste within the Community continue. A local or regional monopoly for certain types of waste would exclude these types of waste permanently from the provisions of Article 28 EC Treaty. In my opinion, this would require an amendment of the provisions on the free circulation of goods, all the more so as any risk to humans or to the environment that is created by the above-mentioned types of waste which are normally non-hazardous is not visible.

(15) Leaving the German political request aside, it would only in rather exceptional circumstances be possible for a local authority to follow the Copenhagen model and grant an undertaking exclusive rights to handle specific types of waste. Politically, however, it is likely that municipalities which wish to build an incinerator will try to take profit from this judgment, arguing that the incinerator will recover energy and is thus recovering waste. They will then try to give the operator of the incinerator exclusive rights during the amortisation of the building costs (20 to 30 years). This scenario is viable to the extent that exports of waste—and also shipments to other installations for recycling or composting in other local authorities or regions—are excluded. Again, the problem is thus raised of export bans for recyclable or recoverable waste.

(16) In my opinion, restrictions of exports of waste for recovery are possible, and only possible, under the conditions of Article 7(4)(a) of Regulation 259/93.[19]

---

[18] Court of Justice, Case C–2/90 *Commission* v. *Belgium* (n. 10 *supra*).

[19] Regulation 259/93 (n. 3 *supra*), Art. 7(4)(a): "The competent authorities of destination and dispatch may raise reasoned objections to the planned shipment:—in accordance with Directive 75/442, in particular Art. 7 thereof, or—if it is not in accordance with national laws and regulations relating to environmental protection, public order, public safety or health protection, or—if the notifier or the consignee has previously been guilty of illegal trafficking. In this case, the competent authority of dispatch may refuse all shipments involving the person in question in accordance with national legislation, or—if the shipment conflicts with obligations resulting from international conventions

It is true that this provision does not apply to non-hazardous waste which is listed in Annex II of the Regulation, as follows from Article 1(3)(a) of the Regulation.[20] However, construction and demolition waste is not mentioned in Annex II, but rather has to be subsumed under Annex III position AD 160 (municipal waste and domestic waste).[21] For that reason, the control and surveillance procedures of Regulation 259/93, applicable to Annex III waste, are relevant, including therefore also Article 7(4). As Community Regulation 259/93 is directly applicable in all Member States and prevails over national legislation, it is not possible for Denmark to classify construction and demolition waste, for shipment purposes, as waste which does not come under the control provisions for waste that is listed in Annex III.

40. CLEAN-UP OF SITES

Judgment of the Court of 9 November 1999
Case C–365/97

Commission of the European Communities v. *Italy*
[1999] ECR I–7773

Facts and Procedure

The San Rocco valley is a riverbed valley within the agglomeration of Naples. For some time, biological and chemical materials from a general hospital had been systematically discharged into that valley. One of the quarries which existed in that valley was used as an illegal landfill. This quarry was put under sequestration in May 1990; however, one year later, the quarry was again used as a landfill.

In June 1990, the Commission opened formal proceedings against Italy for omission to apply the Community provisions on waste to the San Rocco valley, by

concluded by the Member State or Member States concerned, or—if the ratio of the recoverable and non-recoverable waste, the estimated value of the materials to be finally recovered or the cost of the recovery and the cost of the disposal of the non recoverable fraction do not justify the recovery under economic and environmental considerations".

[20] Regulation 259/93 (n. 3 *supra*), Art. 1(3)(a): "Shipment of waste destined for recovery only and listed in Annex II shall also be excluded from the provisions of this Regulation except as provided for in subparas. (b), (c), (d) and (e), in Art. 11 and in Art. 17(1), (2) and (3)".

[21] There is no other insertion in Annex II or III where construction and demolition material would be better subsumed. If one were assuming that such waste is not listed at all, then Art. 10 of Regulation 259/93 would apply which stipulates that waste which has not yet been assigned to Annex II, Annex III or Annex IV shall be treated as if it were very hazardous, i. e. according to the control procedure for waste listed in Annex IV.

sending a letter of formal notice under Article 226 EC Treaty. The Commission was of the opinion that Italy had in particular failed correctly to apply Articles 4 and 8 of Directive 75/442.[22] As the Commission was not informed of measres by Italy to restore the environment in the San Rocco valley, in 1996, it sent a reasoned opinion to the Italian Government.

Italy answered by informing the Commission of a number of steps taken or envisaged to repair the situation. The Commission considered these measures to be insufficient and applied to the Court of Justice.

Judgment (extracts)

61. In the present case, the Commission is seeking a declaration that the Italian Republic has infringed the obligations imposed on Member States by Article 4 of Directive 75/442 . . .

62. It is true that the Court rules in Comitato di Coordinamento per la Difesa della Cava . . . with regard to the possibility raised by the national court of Directive 75/442 requiring the Member States to adopt appropriate measures in order to encourage the prevention, recycling and conversion of waste, rather than the tipping thereof, that Article 4 of Directive 75/442 does not create rights for individuals which the national courts must protect.

63. None the less, the question arising in the present case is whether the first paragraph of Article 4 . . . is to be interpreted as imposing the obligation contended for and whether that obligation was fulfilled in a given case. That is quite separate from the question whether the unconditional and sufficiently clear and precise provisions of an unimplemented directive may be relied upon directly by individuals as against the State . . .

64. Admittedly, Article 4 of Directive 75/442, which essentially repeats the terms of the third recital in the preamble thereto, set out the principal objective of that directive, namely the protection of human health and the environment against harmful effects caused by the collection, transport, treatment, storage and tipping of waste, which the Member States were obliged to observe in their performance of the more specific obligations imposed on them by Articles 5 to 11 of

---

[22] Directive 75/442 on waste [1975] OJ L194/47; amended by Directive 91/156 [1991] OJ L78/32, Art. 4: " Member States shall take the necessary measures to ensure that waste is recovered or disposed of without endangering human health and without using processes or methods which could harm the environment, and in particular:—without risk to water, air, soil and plants and animals,—without causing a nuisance through noise or odours,—without adversely affecting the countryside or places of special interest.

Member States shall also take the necessary measures to prohibit the abandonment or uncontrolled disposal of waste".

Art. 8: "Member States shall take the necessary measures to ensure that any holder of waste:—has it handled by a private or public waste collector or by an undertaking which carries out the operations listed in Annex II A or B, or—recovers or disposes of it himself in accordance with the provisions of this Directive".

the directive concerning planning, supervision and monitoring of waste-disposal operations . . .

65. However, in regard to the "necessary measures to be taken by the Member States under Article 4 of Directive 75/442, it was permissible for them to impose on operators requirements not prescribed by the other provisions of the directive in order to ensure attainment of the directive's essential objective . . .

66. Under the first paragraph of Article 4 . . . the Member States are to take the necessary measures to ensure that waste is recovered or disposed of without endangering human health and without using processes or methods which could harm the environment . . .

67. Whilst that provision does not specify the actual content of the measures which must be taken . . . it is none the less true that it is binding on the Member States as to the objective to be achieved, whilst leaving to the Member States a margin of discretion in assessing the need for such measures.

68. From the fact that a situation is not in conformity with the objectives laid down in the first paragraph of Article 4, then, the direct inference may not in principle be drawn that the Member State concerned has necessarily failed to fulfil its obligation under that provision to take the requisite measures to ensure that waste is disposed of without endangering human health and without harming the environment. However, if that situation persists and leads in particular to a significant deterioration in the environment over a protracted period without any action being taken by the competent authorities, it may be an indication that the Member States have exceeded the discretion conferred on them by that provision.

69. As to the territorial extent of the alleged infringement, the fact that the Commission's action is for a declaration that the Italian Republic has failed to fulfil its obligation to take the necessary measures only in San Rocco valley cannot have a bearing on any finding of such an infringement.

70. The consequences of non-compliance with the obligation under the first paragraph of Article 4 . . . are likely, by the very nature of that obligation, to endanger human health and harm the envionment even in a small part of the territory of a Member State . . .

79. It is . . . necessary to examine whether the Commission has established to the requisite legal standard, first, that the waste discharged into the San Rocco valley did not solely comprise waste waters and, secondly, that the Italian Republic failed to adopt the measures necessary to ensure that waste is disposed of without endangering human health and without harming the environment . . .

80. On the first point concerning the discharge of waste, on-the-spot investigations by the Nucleo Operativo Ecologico dei Carabinieri (Carabinieri environmental field unit) confirmed that the biological and chemical substances discharged into the watercourse of San Rocco valley did in fact endanger the health of nearby residents and was harmful to the environment, which is not denied by the Italian Government.

82. The results of the on-the-spot investigation, ordered by the Ministry of the Environment and carried out by the abovementioned field unit, show that rain

water and discharges from hospitals, a clinic and other establishments which could not be identified owing to the extent and inaccessibility of the San Rocco riverbed, flowed towards the watercourse which bisects the valley.

83. That result is corroborated by an investigation conducted by the Naples municipality that was referred to in Parliamentary Question No 4–24226 of 20 February 1991, from which it emerged that biological and chemical waste from the second general hospital were discharged into the San Rocco valley.

84. Accordingly, the Commission has adduced sufficient evidence to show that biological and chemical waste has been discharged into the watercourse which bisects the San Rocco valley.

85. Furthermore, it is primarily for the national authorities to conduct the necessary on-the-spot investigations, in a spirit of genuine cooperation and mindful of each Member State's duty under Article 5 of the EC Treaty(now Article 10 EC), to facilitate attainment of the general task of the Commission, which is to ensure that the provisions of the Treaty, as well as provisions adopted thereunder by the institutions, are applied.

87. Since the Italian Government has not adduced before the Court any evidence . . . , the facts alleged by the Commission concerning the discharge of waste into the watercourse bisecting the San Rocco valley must be regarded as proven.

105. . . . the Commission seeks a declaration that, by failing to take the steps necessary to ensure that, with regard to a tufaceous hollow in the San Rocco riverbed, which had in the past been used for fly-tipping, the quarry operator had the waste handled by a private or public waste collector or by a waste disposal undertaking, the Italian Republic has failed to fulfil its obligations in breach of the first indent of Article 8 . . .

106. Although fly-tipping would appear no longer to be carried on, the Commission points out that there is nothing to suggest that the Italian authorities have adopted the measures necessary to compel the operator of the unlawful tip to have the waste handled by a private or a public waste collector. Consequently, the Commission claims, the Italian Republic has failed to comply with its obligations under the first indent of Article 8 . . .

107. The Italian Government contends that the . . . complaint is unfounded. In its view, the fact that the quarry was used for fly-tipping demonstrates not that the Italian Republic infringed that provision but merely that the relevant Italian provisions were contravened. By placing the tip under sequestration, the Italian authorities took the steps necessary to put an end to the abuse.

108. In that connection, suffice it to state that, on receiving consignment of waste, the operator of an illegal tip becomes the holder of that waste. Article 8 of the amended directive accordingly imposes on the Italien Republic the obligation, in regard to that operator to take the steps necessary to ensure that that waste is handed over to a private or public waste collector or a waste-disposal undertaking, where it is not possible for that operator himself to recover or dispose of the waste.

109. Thus, by confining itself to ordering the sequestration of the illegal tip and prosecuting of that tip, the Italian Republic did not satisfy the specific obligation imposed on it by Article 8 of the . . . directive.

Commentary

I. Article 4 of Directive 75/442, a Cornerstone of Waste Handling Obligations

(1) This judgment has the potential of playing, in future, a very import role in waste management and in particular in the handling of old contaminated sites the number of which in the present Community is estimated to be about 750,000.[23] A key role in waste management will have to be played by Article 4 of Directive 75/442[24] and the interpretation given to this provision by the full Court will therefore have considerable weight.

(2) The interpretation of Article 4 in the present case posed some problems, as the Court had dealt with Article 4 already in an earlier judgment, in Case C–236/92.[25] In that case, some Italian citizens and an association had begun judicial action before an Italian court against the Regione Lombardia. This region had envisaged setting up, in Lombardia, several landfill installations. The applicants were of the opinion that Directive 75/442 provided for the obligation for Member States to promote, in the first line, the prevention of waste generation and in second line the re-use, recycling and recovery of waste.[26] They were of the opinion that neither the Italian Government nor the region had taken sufficient measures to prevent waste generation and to promote waste recovery. Under these circumstances, according to the applicants, the Region was prevented by Article 4 of Directive 75/442 to revert to the building of landfills, before first having gone in the direction of waste prevention and waste recovery. The Italian court asked the Court of Justice whether Article 4 had direct effect in the sense that it gave rights to private persons which the courts had to protect.

(3) The Court of Justice answered in the negative. In an extremely succinct judgment—overall, the judgment consists of 17 paragraphs only—it attributed to Article 4 programmatic character; that provision indicated, according to the

---

[23] European Environmental Agency, *Environment in the European Union at the Turn of the Century* (Office for Official Publications of the European Communities, Luxembourg, 1999), p. 192; the notion of "contaminated sites" includes old industrial sites, old waste sites and military sites.

[24] Directive 75/442 (n. 22 *supra*), Art. 4.

[25] Court of Justice, Case C–236/92, *Comitato per la Difesa della Cava* [1994] ECR I–483.

[26] Directive 75/442 (n. 22 *supra*), Art. 3: "Member States shall take appropriate measures to encourage: (a) firstly, the prevention or reduction of waste production and its harmfulness . . . (b) secondly: (i) the recovery of waste by means of recycling, re-use or reclamation or any other process with a view to extracting secondary raw materials, or (ii) the use of waste as a source of energy. 2. . . .".

Court, the objectives which Member States had to observe when implementing the planning, supervision and control measures flowing out of Articles 5 to 11 of Directive 75/442. As a justification, the Court mentioned that Article 4 repeated more or less the third recital of the Directive and referred furthermore to an earlier judgment which again concerned Member States' obligation and discretion to organise waste management structures.[27]

It is important to realise the litigation context in which the Court had made the remark on the programmatic character of Article 4; indeed, in Case C–236/92, there was no question of a specific problem for the environment in a given case. The applicants had tried to use Article 4 in order to influence waste management planning by the public authorities without a relation to a specific case.

(4) I had already in an earlier publication questioned not so much the conclusion of the Court in Case C–236/92, but rather the general statement that Article 4 only had programmatic character.[28] In the present case now, the Court nuances its earlier statement and concludes that Article 4 implies obligations for Member States, a conclusion which can only be welcome.

If one looks at Article 4, it is obvious that it also contains obligations in a given case. This follows, on the one hand, from Article 4 second subparagraph which prohibits the uncontrolled abandonment of waste.[29] In my opinion, it is obvious that Member States must introduce into their national legislation such a prohibition and even provide for criminal sanctions for cases of an uncontrolled abandonment of waste. Furthermore, the detailed enumeration of possible impairments in subparagraph 1 would have been unnecessary if there had only existed the intention to make a programmatic declaration; the statement that waste treatment and disposal should not harm humans and the environment would have been sufficient. Finally, the Court's affirmation of 1994 that Article 4 of Directive 75/442 had programmatic character was made under the validity of Directive 75/442 prior to its amendment in 1991. However, in 1991, Directive 91/156[30] amended Directive 75/442 and transformed it into the framework Directive for waste, to which numerous later directives and regulations in the waste sector referred.[31] Then it is more than normal that the framework Directive also lays down the basic substantive requirements on how waste shall be treated or disposed of. Denying such a substantive character of Article 4 would mean that for the most of Community waste legislation, there is no general, substantive requirement at all.

---

[27] Court of Justice, Case 372/85–374/85, *Traen* [1987] ECR 2141.

[28] L Krämer, "Droit à l'environnement et installation de déchets" in M Prieur and C Lambrechts (eds.), *Les hommes et l'environment; Etudes en Hommages à Alexandre Kiss* (Editions Prison-Roche, Paris, 1998), p. 353.

[29] The Court's remark, in Case C–236/92, had referred to Art. 4 in general and had not been limited to the first subpara.

[30] Directive 91/156 (n. 22 *supra*).

[31] See, for example, Directive 91/689 on hazardous waste [1991] OJ L377/20; Regulation 259/93 on the supervision and control of shipments of waste within, into and out of the European Community [1993] OJ L30/1; Directive 94/62 on packaging and packaging waste [1994] OJ L365/10; Directive 99/31 on the landfill of waste [1999] OJ L182/1.

(5) The Court is, in the present case, quite clear: Article 4 "is binding on the Member States as to the objective to be achieved, whilst leaving to the Member States a margin of discretion in assessing the need for such measures" (paragraph 67). This last criterion on the discretion in assessing the need for measures was obviously added by the Court, in order to prepare its subsequent conclusion that a breach of Article 4 may exist where a risk to human health or an environmental impairment "persists and leads in particular to a significant deterioration in the environment over a protracted period" (paragraph 68 and also paragraph 91). Indeed, it is clear that noise or odour or negative impact on the countryside caused by a landfill or a waste incinerator do not automatically constitute a failure to comply with the requirements of Article 4: as long as there is economic activity, there is some environmental impairment; zero emissions from human activities do not exist.

(6) The Court's interpretation of Article 4 may well help to find a balance between unavoidable impairments and failure to comply with the obligations flowing from Article 4. For instance, where a waste incinerator complies with all standards fixed by legislation and in its authorisation, a breach of Article 4 will normally not exist; however, where these emission limit values, noise levels etc. are not respected, that installation may well come under the scrutiny of Article 4.

II. Illegal Dumping of Waste: New Legal Solutions

(7) Perhaps even more important are the short remarks of the Court as regards Article 8 of Directive 75/442.[32] It may be remembered that in question was an illegal landfill. The Court found that the operator of that non-authorised landfill becomes the holder of that waste, so that the obligation to hand the waste over to a public or private waste collector is incumbent on him. However, Article 8 goes even further, as can be seen from the definition of "holder" in Article 1(c) of Directive 75/442: "'holder' shall mean: the producer of the waste or the natural or legal person who is in possession of it". In other words, the owner of land where waste is disposed of illegally or without authorisation becomes the holder of that waste. He is then obliged to remit that waste, under Article 8 of Directive 75/442, to an authorised waste collector—which means that he will have to pay for the collection of that waste.

(8) This construction opens up the possibility of holding owners of land much more responsible for unauthorised abandonment of waste than in the past. If these owners of land—including local authorities or other public bodies—become financially responsible for the clean-up of their land, they may become much more attentive to tolerating such unauthorised abandonment of waste on their land than in the past. Citizen groups, environmental organisations, local authjorities, but also police services and others have, through this judgment by the Court, obtained a very effective tool to fight against the tipping of waste.

[32] Directive 75/442 (n. 22 *supra*), Art. 8.

(9) There is another important aspect of the Court's judgment: where there is an illegal situation, in particular an unauthorised abandonment of waste or an unauthorised landfill, it is not enough, under Articles 4 and 8 of Directive 75/442, to fence the landfill in, to "close" it or to take similar measures. Indeeed, the environmental impairment which is mentioned in Article 4 normally continues in such a case, for instance the odour, the leeching of liquids into the soil, the waters or the groundwater, the air emissions, the attracting of rats, bird or other "pest" animals etc. The Court's judgment means that the consequences of such an illegal landfill have also to be eliminated, in particular by taking away the waste in question.

(10) The question may be raised how far this judgment could go. Two practical examples may serve as an illustration: in Ireland waste from extracting mineral resources was landfilled, prior to the entry in effect of Directive 91/156[33] and covered with water. The landfill was closed and progressively the water evaporated. At present, wind is taking away sand and dust from the landfill which is highly contaminated with toxic metals; that dust is causing damage to agriculture and, at least potentially, also to humans.

The second example concerns waste from the extraction of mineral resources in Germany, which was landfilled for some 200 years. The extraction finished about 50 years ago. At present, there is the intention to construct a motorway through the landfill and considerable quantities of the highly toxic materials will have to be moved.

(11) One may argue that Directive 75/442 is not of application, as in both cases the waste management process was terminated before the Directive came into existence.[34] However, I would take a different view. The waste which has been disposed of on land remains waste, as long as there are significant emissions from that material which go into the environment. It is only in this way that responsibilities can be established and the environmental impairment can be stopped. Therefore, in both cases I would argue that the owner of land is obliged to take the necessary measures to avoid environmental impairment: That owner may have recourse to the producer of waste or to other responsible persons. However, his initial responsibility remains.

It is very likely that in particular the old landfills—once called "ticking time bombs" by environmental organisations—will be the subject of considerable controversy as regards responsibilities for clean up. At the end of the day, public authorities may help owners to clean up their land in the form of public aid: however, such solutions are solutions which should be considered last. The first principle in environmental policy and law is that it is the polluter who should pay, not the taxpayer. If landowners were held responsible, they would undertake much more serious efforts to have the polluter—the waste generator, the industrial undertaking etc.—pay its share.

---

[33] Directive 91/156 (n. 22 *supra*).

[34] Waste from the extraction of mineral resources was not covered by Directive 75/442, but was included in the scope of application of it by Directive 91/156, which entered into effect in 1993.

III. On-the-spot Investigatons in Environmental Matters

(12) In paragraphs 80 *et seq.* the Court made a number of arguments regarding the on-the-spot investigation of specific cases. In concluding, it stated in paragraph 85 that Member States should make the necessary investigations and convey the results to the Commission, in the spirit of mutual co-operation. However, it is clear that Member States take almost all measures to keep investigation reports, surveys, inspection data etc. confidential and not to send such material to the Commission. They fear that the Commission, once in possession of such material, may use it "against" the Member State in question. Of course, this is erroneous, as the Commission's environmental action, also under Article 226 EC Treaty, is intended to protect the environment and not to impair Member States. However, the judicial construction of Court litigation under Article 226 EC Treaty is rather made in a way that the anxieties of the Member States are well-founded: Why must the Commission take action, in the present case, against Italy, when the authorities in Naples and/or Campania Region cannot or are not willing to take action in order to clean up the San Rocco riverbed? As the judicial system is organised in such a way that a Member State is brought to Court and, eventually, under Article 228 EC Treaty, has to pay a fine, it is comprehensible that Member States are reluctant to pass on data on on-the-spot investigations.

(13) In early 1990s, an attempt was made to separate the collection of data from policy-making by setting up the European Environmental Agency.[35] However, Member States successfully resisted any attempt, in particular from the European Parliament, to entrust the collection of data on the application of Community environmental legislation to the Agency. Nevertheless, the problem has not faded away. At present, the Commission only accidentally obtains reliable information on the local situation in a specific case, and its best source in that respect is individual citizens and environmental organisations. It cannot be expected that the Court's observations will change whatsoever at the present situation.

---

[35] Regulation 1210/90 [1990] OJ L120/1.

41. RECYCLING USED OIL

Judgment of the Court (Fifth Chamber) of 9 September 1999
Case C–102/97

Commission of the European Communities v. *Germany*
[1999] ECR I–5051

Facts and Procedure

Directive 75/439 on the disposal of waste oils[36] was adopted on 16 June 1975; it was the first environmental directive adopted by the Community. In its Article 3 this Directive provided: "Member States shall take the necessary measures to ensure that, as far as possible, the disposal of waste oils is carried out by recycling (regeneration and/or combustion other than for destruction)".

At the end of 1986, Directive 75/439 was amended by Directive 87/101.[37] The new Directive provided in its second recital: "Whereas regeneration is generally the most rational way of re-using waste oils in view of the energy savings which can be achieved; whereas, therefore, priority should be given to the processing of waste oils by regeneration, where technical, economic and organizational constraints allow it". Consequently, the new Article 3 read: "1. Where technical, economic and organizational constraints so allow, Member States shall take the measures necessary to give priority to the processing of waste oils by regeneration. 2. Where waste oils are not regenerated, on account of the constraints mentioned in paragraph 1 above, Member States shall take the measures necessary to ensure that any combustion of waste oils is carried out under environmentally acceptable conditions, in accordance with the provisions of this Directive, provided that such combustion is technically, economically and organizationally feasible. 3. . . .". Regeneration was defined as "any process whereby base oils can be produced by refining waste oils, in particular by removing the contaminants, oxidation products and additives contained in such oils" (Article 1).[38]

---

[36] Directive 75/439 on the disposal of waste oils [1975] OJ L194/23.

[37] Directive 87/101 [1987] OJ L42/43.

[38] Terminology in waste management law and policy has changed over recent decades. While in the mid-1970s "disposal" included the notions of recovery and of (final) disposal, at present there is a distinction between "disposal"—which includes landfilling and incineration without energy recovery—and "recovery"—which covers material recycling and the recovery of energy from incineration. The notion of "regeneration" is no longer used. In the present case, "regeneration" is thus to be understood as " [material] recycling".

Germany informed the Commission that Directive 87/101 had been transposed into German law by a number of legislative measures. The Commission, however, was of the opinion that these provisions did not give the recycling of waste oils priority, but merely parity with thermal processing of waste oils and began, in August 1992, formal proceedings under Article 226 EC Treaty. As the discussions with the German government did not lead to a solution, the Commission applied, in March 1997, to the Court.

Judgment (extracts)

32. . . . an examination of the German legislation has shown there to be no national provision expressly laying down that priority is to be given to regeneration in the processing of waste oils.

33. It is settled case-law, as the German Government points out, that the transposition of a directive into national law does not necessarily require the provisions of the directive to be enacted in precisely the same words in a specific express legal provision, and a general legal context may be sufficient if it actually ensures the full application of the directive in a sufficiently clear and precise manner . . .

34. However, while the provisions presented by the German Government as transposing Directive 75/439, as amended, form a legal context creating the conditions necessary for processing by regeneration—by organising the collection of waste oils and requiring that oils suitable for recycling be separated from other oils—and can be seen to attach greater importance to that type of processing, it is by no means apparent from that context that processing by regeneration is given priority over other types of processing, whether by means of compulsory measures or incentives.

35. It should be borne in mind in this regard that one of the objectives of Directive 87/101 was to give priority to the processing of waste oils by regeneration. That objective, expressed in the second recital in the preamble to Directive 87/101, is inspired by the fact that regeneration is the most rational way of re-using waste oils in view of the energy savings which can be achieved.

36. The existence in a Member State of technical, economic and organisational constraints which prevent priority from being given to processing by regeneration makes it necessary to give effect to the subsidiary obligation, laid down in Article 3(2) of Directive 75/439, as amended, to take the measures required to ensure that any combustion of waste oils is carried out under environmentally acceptable conditions, in accordance with the provisions of that directive. That obligation is itself made dependent on the condition "that such combustion is technically, economically and organisationally feasible", which appears at the end of Article 3(2).

38. With regard to the "technical, economic and organisational constraints" referred to in Article 3(1) of Directive 75/439, as amended, it should be noted that that expression forms part of a provision giving general expression to the obligation imposed on Member States and that, as such, it is not to be interpreted restrictively as proposed by the Commission.

39. It is clear from Article 3(1) of Directive 75/439, as amended that, by its reference to "technical, economic and organisational constraints", the Community legislature did not intend to provide limited exceptions to a rule having general application, but to define the scope and content of a positive obligation to give priority to the processing of waste oils by regeneration.

40. Contrary to the submission of the German Government, the definition of such constraints cannot be left to the exclusive discretion of the Member States. Apart from being contrary to the principle of the uniform interpretation and application of Community law, interpretation by the Member States alone would make the compatibility of processing by regeneration with technical, economic and organisational constraints a condition the fulfilment of which would depend entirely on the goodwill of the Member State concerned, which could thus render the obligation imposed on it worthless.

41. Accordingly, the provision relating to technical, economic and organisational constraints must be interpreted in the light of the other provisions of Directive 75/439, as amended, in order to ensure that the directive is effective in its entirety.

42. The provision relating to constraints must be understood as an expression of the principle of proportionality; accordingly, Member States are under an obligation to take measures appropriate and proportionate to the objective of giving priority to the processing of waste oils by regeneration, which is to say that the limit to that positive obligation is the existence of the technical, economic and organisational constraints referred to in Article 3(1) of Directive 75/439, as amended.

43. If, as the German Government contends, the technical, economic and organisational circumstances obtaining in a Member State were automatically to constitute constraints making it impossible to adopt the measures provided for in Article 3(1) of Directive 75/439, as amended, that provision would be deprived of all practical effect, since the obligation imposed on Member States would be limited by maintenance of the status quo, with the result that Article 3(1) would not impose a genuine obligation at all.

44. In the present case, the fact is that the Federal Republic of Germany has not adopted any specific measure aimed at giving priority to the processing of waste oils by regeneration and confines itself at present to referring to its own definition of constraints and to the circumstances obtaining in its territory in an attempt to justify the complete failure to introduce measures implementing Article 3(1) of Directive 75/439, as amended.

On the contrary, although an incentive used to exist in the form of the payment of an indemnity encouraging regeneration, and the principle of the payment of such an indemnity was in conformity with Article 14 of Directive 75/439, as amended, the indemnity was abolished by a recent law.

46. Similarly, the Federal Republic of Germany has chosen to continue to exempt oils used as heating fuel from the excise duty on mineral oils, thus encouraging the combustion of such oils, contrary to the objective pursued by Directive 75/439, as amended, notwithstanding that the levying of duty on those oils is prescribed within the general framework of Directive 92/81, and the principle of imposing a specific duty is also authorised by Article 15 of Directive 75/439, as amended.

47. In this connection it should be made clear that the possibility of continuing to apply an exemption from the excise duty on waste oils intended for combustion, approved by a Council decision of 30 June 1997, does not have the effect of precluding consideration of the fiscal measures which the Federal Republic of Germany could have adopted in order to comply with its obligations to implement Article 3(1) of Directive 75/439, as amended.

48. While it is not for the Court to determine the measures which a Member State should have taken in order to implement Article 3(1) of Directive 75/439, as amended, it none the less has a responsability, in determining whether there are constraints within the meaning of that article, to consider whether it was possible to adopt measures aimed at giving priority to the processing of waste oils by regeneration and satisfying the criterion of technical, economic and organisational feasibility.

49. Suffice it to say in this respect that there were a number of measures which could have contributed towards attaining the objective of giving priority to the treatment of waste oils by regeneration and whose adoption was technically, economically and organisationally possible, but the Federal Republic of Germany has not adopted any such measure; on the contrary, it has stopped one of them and has no other appropriate steps with a view to attaining the objective pursued by Directive 75/439, as amended.

50. It follows that, by failing to take the measures necessary to give priority to the processing of waste oils by regeneration, notwithstanding that technical, economic and organisational constraints so allowed, the Federal Republic of Germany has failed to fulfil its obligations under Article 3(1) of Directive 75/439, as amended.

Commentary

I. *Priority for Regeneration of Waste Oils*

(1) The judgment tried to give legal application to Article 3 of Directive 75/439, as amended, the wording of which reflected the political compromise of its draftsmen: on the one hand, there was the determination to strengthen the regeneration of used oil with regard to the 1975 version of Directive 75/439. On the other hand, the accumulation of possibilities of escaping from the obligation to give priority to regeneration was drafted in a very wide and general way: indeed, "technical, economic and organisational constraints" are words which allow many interpretations, and it might well be that Member States had thought that this clause would

hardly ever be checked by the Court of Justice. It is therefore also characteristic that the case was started because the Commission had received a complaint from a private person; the function as "guardian of the Treaty", so often attributed to the Commission by virtue of Article 211 EC Treaty,[39] was not sufficient to make the Commission act on its own initiative. On this point, there will be more said below.

(2) The Court could simply not find any specific measure in German law which gave priority to the recycling of waste oils over other types of processing, "whether by means of compulsory measures or incentives" (paragraph 34); the Court made this statement at three points in the judgment—paragraphs 32, 44 and 49—and this finding was obviously sufficient to dismiss the German defences. Previously, the Court had found that Article 3 did contain a legal obligation; in order to be effective, this provision could not be understood as leaving at the discretion of Member States, if they wanted to take measures in order to give priority to regeneration.

(3) As regards the existence of constraints, Germany had argued that technical constraints—insufficient production capacity and low quality of regenerated oil—economic constraints—non-profitability of secondary refining, disadvantage for economic operators such as independent oil-collectors or the cement industry and other undertakings which used waste oils as fuels—and organisational constraints—there existed only two undertakings in Germany and giving priority to regeneration presented the risk that they would obtain a monopoly—all justified the German decision not to give priority to the recycling of waste oils. These arguments which were more or less all economic were not accepted by the Court. The main argument used by the Court was that it was necessary to make Article 3(1) effective (paragraphs 41 and 43) and that therefore Germany had to take positive measures in order to give priority to it. The proportionality principle—this principle once more!—would not require Germany to do everything in order to promote regeneration. Where constraints became too great, Germany could perhaps invoke Article 3(1); however, as it had not done anything at all, it could not escape from being found to have breached its obligations under Directive 75/439.

II. Regeneration of Waste Oils—Reality and Law

(4) The judgment appears convincing in its legal reasoning and completely in line with the provision of Article 3(1) itself—if ever that provision was to have a content at all.

Until this point, the judgment does not offer specific characteristics which go beyond an ordinary environmental case. What do make this case so specific are two legal elements which are discussed hereafter. First, in 1992, the Council

---

[39] Art. 211 (ex Art. 155) EC Treaty: "In order to ensure the proper functioning and development of the common market, the Commission shall:—ensure that the provisions of this Treaty and the measures taken by the institutions pursuant thereto are applied; . . .",

adopted a directive on the harmonisation of the structures of excise of certain mineral oils.[40] This Directive, based on Article 93 (ex Article 99) EC Treaty,[41] introduced an excise duty for mineral oil that is intended for use, offered for sale or used as heating fuel or motor fuel. Member States were, however, allowed to apply for total or partial exemptions or reductions of the excise duty, where mineral oil was burned; a decision on such application was to be taken in the most extraordinary procedure.[42]

(5) Member States have extensively used the possibility of exempting waste oils from excise duties, where it they were used as fuel in cement industries or other production installations. As such exemptions were not limited in time and as it required a unanimous decision by the Council to terminate such an exemption, Member States were hardly restricted, if they wished to exempt waste oils from the excise duty. Overall, about 100 derogations existed at the end of 2000 under Directive 92/81, among them a derogation for waste oils for 12 Member States.

The formula used at present in the different Council decisions[43] for waste oils is: "[exemption for] waste oils which are reused as fuel, either directly or after recovery or following a recycling process for waste oils, and where the reuse is subject to duty". As such, this formula looks rather innocent; however, if one realises that any recovery or recycling process is an economic activity, it becomes clear that using waste oils directly is cheaper—and consequently more attractive—than after a recovery or a recycling process.[44] Each such exemption for waste oils thus promotes the incineration (combustion) of waste oils rather than their regeneration.

(6) Secondly, in mid-1998, the Commission published figures for waste oil management in the Community.[45] It appeared that 1994–95 37 per cent of collected waste oils (677,000 tonnes) were regenerated, while 63 per cent (1,150,300 tonnes) were used as fuels, without any prior treatment or after some treatment such as filtering reprocessing into fuel oil. For the different Member States, the following data were given:

---

[40] Directive 92/81 on the harmonisation of the structures of excise duties on mineral oils [1992] OJ L316/12.

[41] Art. 93 (ex Art. 99) EC Treaty: "The Council shall, acting unanimously on a proposal from the Commission and after consulting the European Parliament and the Economic and Social Committee, adopt provisions for the harmonisation of legislation concerning turnover taxes, excise duties and other forms of indirect taxation to the extent that such harmonisation is necessary to ensure the establishment and the functioning of the internal market within the time-limit laid down in Art. 14".

[42] Directive 92/81 (n. 40 *supra*), Art. 8(4): " . . . A Member State wishing to introduce such a measure shall . . . inform the Commission and shall also provide the Commission with all relevant or necessary information. The Commission shall inform the other Member States of the proposed measure within one month. The Council shall be deemed to have authorized the exemption or reduction proposed if, within two months of the other Member States' being informed . . . neither the Commission nor any Member State has requested that the matter be considered by the Council".

Thus, information to the Commission leads to a fictitious decision by the Council!

[43] See, for instance, Council Decision 1999/880 [1999] OJ L331/73.

[44] As regards the terminology, see n. 38 *supra*; the wording above thus does not follow the terminology that is common in waste management.

[45] Written Question E–3265/97 (Estevan Bolea) [1998] OJ C174/30.

Member State	collected waste oil in tonnes	Regenerated in tonnes	used as fuel in tonnes
Belgium	50.000		50.000
Denmark	40.000	20.000	20.000
Germany	600.000	360.000	240.000
Greece	5.000	5.000	
Spain	110.000	35.000	75.000
France	225.000	95.000	130.000
Ireland	14.000	14.000	
Italy	180.000	150.000	30.000
Luxembourg	2.300		2.300
Netherlands	60.000		60.000
Austria	38.000		38.000
Portugal	13.000		13.000
Finland	40.000	2.000	38.000
Sweden	90.000		90.000
United Kingdom	360.000	10.000	350.000
Total	1.827.300	677.000	1.150.300

Member State	collected waste oil	regenerated	combusted
Belgium	202.457	500	201.957
Denmark	36.337	0	29.327
Germany	485.000	298.000	187.000
Greece	5.000	5.000	0
Spain	110.000	35.000	65.000
France	242.000	80.813	168.571
Ireland	8.280	?	7.200
Italy	180.000	150.000	30.000
Luxembourg	3.477	3.477	0
Netherlands	49.000	0	49.000
Austria	33.700	0	37.400
Portugal	13.000	0	13.000
Finland	47.000	2.000	33.000
Sweden	72.000	?	58.500
United Kingdom	422.000	32.000	390.000
Total	1.809.231	606.790	1.269.945

(7) While these data stemmed from a study which the Commission had made, it published early in 2000 data which the Member States themselves had transmitted.[46] The figures referred to the period of 1995 to 1997: For the year 1997, the above figures were given.[47]

(8) The different figures must be interpreted with caution. The collection rate for waste oils varies considerably from one Member State to the other. Also, for instance, in Greece only 8 per cent of waste oil which is generated is legally collected separately and then regenerated. The residue of 92 per cent is collected illegally and sold untreated as fuel.[48] One might consider that roughly two thirds of the collected waste oil is incinerated and only one third is regenerated. The Commission report concluded:[49] "The main constraints on national level concerning the regeneration seem to be economic aspects such as that a minimum quantity of collected waste oil is needed for an economically profitable regeneration (. . . 60,000 to 80,000 tonnes per year . . .) and that there is a fierce competition between regeneration and combustion and no stimulating instruments. There are even grounds for the assumption that some Member States do not want to focus on regeneration. For instance, France expressed that in its point of view combustion is the environmentally better solution. In addition . . . the main constraints on European level are that there is no absolute priority for regeneration, no consistency in policy and no cooperation between Member States and that there is a general over-capacity of lubricants and poor competitiveness for regeneration".

(9) In legal terms, it is only reasonable to conclude that the large majority of Member States have not given priority to the regeneration of waste oil and are thus in a similar position to Germany. In view of the published data from the Commission itself, it is not understandable why the Commission, being the guardian of the Treaty, allows Member States provisions derogating from Directive 92/81 which must jeopardise any attempt to implement Article 3(1) of Directive 75/439; and why the Commission has not started formal proceedings under Article 226 EC Treaty[50] against all those Member States which are in a situation comparable to that of Germany. The prolonged, patent ignoring of the obligation flowing from Article 3(1) of Directive 75/439 is, in environmental matters, one of the worst legal problems the Commission is confronted with. Indeed, until the end of 2001, the Commission had not taken action against any other Member State for lack of compliance with Article 3(1) of Directive 75/439.

[46] Commission Report on the implementation of Community waste legislation, COM(1999)752 of 10 January 2000, pp. 57 to 59.

[47] Figures for Greece, Italy, Portugal and Spain were for 1994/5 and taken from the same study as the figures in the previous table.

[48] Commission (n. 46 *supra*), p. 48; see also Written Question E–3211/97 (Papayannakis) [1998] OJ C223/1.

[49] Commission (n. 46 *supra*), p. 50.

[50] Art. 226 EC Treaty: "If the Commission considers that a Member State has failed to fufil an obligation under this Treaty, it shall deliver a reasoned opinion on the matter after giving the State concerned the opportunity to submit its observations.

If the State concerned does not comply with the opinion within the period laid down by the Commission, the latter may bring the matter before the Court of Justice".

(10) The German philosopher Hegel once stated that if reality were not in line with his ideas, then that was a problem for reality. Paraphrasing this statement, one may think that if Community reality does not comply with Community law, legal action under Article 226 EC Treaty may have to be taken. However, the Hegel approach opens another perspective: there is also the possibility of adapting the law, in our case Directive 75/439, to reality. The longer the Commission hesitates to start taking action under Article 226 EC Treaty, the greater the probability becomes that Directive 75/439 will be amended and the priority for regeneration in Article 3(1) will be deleted. The problem is bound to be accentuated by the accession negotiations: in these negotiation with countries from Eastern, Central and Southern Europe, the Community insists on requesting that the candidate countries take over the *acquis communautaire*. But how can one seriously ask Poland or Hungary to adopt legal rules that give *de iure* and *de facto* priority to the regeneration of waste oil, when 12 of the 15 actual Member States do not do so? In the words of Hugo Grotius: "All evil starts when man departs from law".

(11) And the environment? There is little doubt that regeneration of waste oils is less expensive than recycling. However, environmental protection has little to do with finding, in all circumstances, the cheapest solution to a problem. Furthermore, the conditions under which waste oils are incinerated are anything but guaranteed to be environmentally sound. Indeed, while there are strict Community standards for the incineration of waste,[51] such strict standards are lacking at Community level—and it does not appear to be an exaggeration to say: also at the level of Member States—for production installations such as steel plants, power plants, chemical installations etc. Even for cement plants there are no Community-wide standards for the emission of pollutants into the air, the water or the soil.[52]

(12) From the point of view of the environment, the only logical request can be to require the standards for waste incinerators to become applicable as soon as one tonne of waste is incinerated—wherever such incineration takes place: indeed, for the environment it does not matter whether the pollutant stems from an incinerator or a production installation. However, such a policy is not capable of being realised at present, as Member States do not wish to be that strict with their economic interests.

(13) Directive 75/439, as amended, was several times discussed in Court. In Cases 30–34/81[53] and 70/81[54] the Court found that Italy and Belgium had not transposed the Directive into their national law. In 1990, Belgium was found to have breached its obligations in not having reported on the implementation of

---

[51] See, most recently, Directive 2000/76 on the incineration of waste [2000] OJ L332/91 which will, in 2005, replace the existing legislation on waste incineration.

[52] Directive 96/61 in the integrated pollution prevention and control [1996] OJ L257/26, very deliberately decided against Community-wide standards for installations; thus common standards for waste incinerators, (in part) for large combustion plants and for waste landfills are the exception, not the rule.

[53] Court of Justice, Cases 30–34/81 *Commission* v. *Italy* [1981] ECR 3379.

[54] Court of Justice, Case 70/81, *Commission* v. *Belgium* [1982] ECR 169.

Directive 75/439.[55] In 1993, the Court found that Italy had not yet complied with the judgment in Cases 30–34/81.[56]

In an early case, Case 21/79,[57] the Court of Justice had to determine the content of the financial incentive which Member States were allowed to give to undertakings according to Article 13 of Directive 79/439 (now Article 14).[58] Then, in three cases, Cases 172/82,[59] 295/82[60] and 173/83,[61] the Court had essentially to deal with the question whether French legislation which implemented Directive 75/439 contained a prohibition on export of waste oils to other EC Member States and whether such a prohibition was compatible with Community law. French legislation requested holders of waste oils to deliver their waste oils to approved collectors; these had received an exclusive collection right for a specific area. They had to deliver the waste oils to an approved disposal undertaking which had to treat the waste oils in its own plant.

The Court found that this system contained an implicit export restriction since it did not allow the export of waste oils to other Member States. While Member States were allowed to give exclusive collection rights, they were not, in the Court's opinion, allowed to restrict the export of waste oils. France was thus found to have infringed its obligations.

In its judgment in Case 240/83, delivered the same day as the judgment in Case 173/83, the Court found that the attribution of an exclusive area for collecting waste oils was compatible with the principle of freedom of trade. This principle was "not to be viewed in absolute terms but is subject to certain limits justified by the objectives of general interest pursued by the Community" and that "environmental protection . . . is one of the Community's essential objectives".[62]

---

[55] Court of Justice, Case C–162/89, *Commission* v. *Belgium* [1990] ECR 2391.

[56] Court of Justice, Case C–366/89, *Commission* v. *Italy* [1993] ECR 4201.

[57] Court of Justice, case 21/79, *Commission* v. *Italy* [1980] ECR 1.

[58] Directive 75/439 (n. 36 *supra*), as amended by Directive 87/101 (n. 37 *supra*), Art. 14: "As a reciprocal concession for the obligations imposed on them by the Member States pursuant to Art. 5, indemnities may be granted to collection and/or disposal undertakings for the service rendered. Such indemnities must not exceed annual uncovered costs actually recorded by the undertaking taking into account a reasonable profit.

The amount of these indemnities must be such as not to cause any significant distortion of competition or to give rise to artificial patterns of trade in the products".

[59] Court of Justice, Case 172/82, *Inter-Huile* [1983] ECR 555.

[60] Court of Justice, Case 295/82, *Rhone Alpes Huiles* [1984] ECR 575.

[61] Court of Justice, Case 173/83, *Commission* v. *France* [1985] ECR 491.

[62] Court of Justice, Case 240/83, *ADBHU* [1985] ECR 531.

42. PLANNING IN WASTE MANAGEMENT

Judgment of the Court (Fifth Chamber) of 28 May 1998
Case C–298/97

Commission of the European Communities v. *Spain*
[1998] ECR I–3301

Facts and Procedure

Directive 91/157 on batteries and accumulators was adopted in 1991.[63] It is based on Article 95 (ex Article 100a) EC Treaty and concerns batteries and accumulators which contain cadmium, mercury or lead. Member States are obliged to prohibit batteries, where the mercury content exceeds certain limits. They must provide for a separate collection of end-of-life batteries and accumulators. Article 6 of Directive 91/157 reads as follows:

"Member States shall draw up programmes in order to achieve the following objectives:
—reduction of the heavy-metal content of batteries and accumulators;
—promotion of marketing of batteries and accumulators containing smaller quantities of dangerous substances and/or less polluting substances,
—gradual reduction, in household waste, of spent batteries and accumulators covered by Annex I, promotion of research aimed at reducing the dangerous-substance content and favouring the use of less polluting substitute substances in batteries and accumulators, and research into methods of recycling,
—separate disposal of spent batteries and accumulators covered by Annex I.
The first programmes shall cover a four-year period starting on 18 March 1993. They shall be communicated to the Commission by 17 September 1992 at the latest.
The programmes shall be reviewed and updated regularly, at least every four years, in the light in particular of technical progress and of the economic and environmental situation. Amended programmes shall be communicated to the Commission in good time".

The Commission was of the opinion that Spain had not adopted programmes for batteries and accumulators and applied to the Court of Justice.

---

[63] Directive 91/157 on batteries and accumulators containing certain dangerous substances [1991] OJ L78/38. Directive 93/86 [1993] OJ L264/51 established a symbol—a crossed dustbin—for batteries falling under Directive 91/157. Directive 98/101 [1999] OJ L1/1 introduced a general ban for mercury-containing batteries.

Judgment (extracts)

9. . . . the Kingdom of Spain does not deny that it has not prepared or communicated the programmes in question to the Commission. It merely states that the Directive has been transposed into Spanish law by Royal Decree No 45/96, Article 6 of which incorporates the provisions of Article 6 of the Directive and specifies that it is the Autonomous Communities which are responsible for giving effect to he programmes in question.

10. The Kingdom of Spain goes on to state that it is endeavouring gradually to achieve the result pursued by the Directive, in accordance with Article 189 of he EC Treaty. It considers that the result defined in Article 6 of the Directive cannot be achieved merely by drawing up programmes, which, in its view, have no value in themselves unless they are accompanied by specific action facilitating the actual attainment of those objectives defined in that article as constituting the substance of the programmes.

11. That is why, in order to determine whether a Member State has actually fulfilled its obligations under Article 6 of the Directive, it is necessary, in the opinion of the Kingdom of Spain, to consider not whether or not it has drawn up the requisite programmes—which, even though they may be lawful, nevertheless remain theoretical—but rather whether it has undertaken specific action of a practical nature capable of enabling it to attain the objectives which those programmes are intended to achieve. To the extent to which those objectives are achieved, the result pursued by the Directive must be deemed also to have been achieved.

12. The Kingdom of Spain contends that specific action of that kind is taken in all the Autonomous Communities with a view to attaining the objectives set by Article 6 of the Directive. It cites by way of example a series of initiatives of various kinds undertaken on Spanish territory in order to attain those objectives, such as the *Ley Básica de Residuos* (Basic Law on Waste), which is a national statute, *Ley No 6/93 Reguladora de los Residuos de Cataluna* (Law on the Management of Waste in Catalonia), the agreements concluded between the autonomous administration of Castille-Léon and the municipalities for which it is responsible in order to provide for management of the collection, storage and processing of spent batteries and accumulators, the waste management plans drawn up in Aragon, Catalonia and Galicia, the studies carried out in order to determine the pollutant potential of the various types of batteries and to establish disposal and recycling systems for them, the decrees of the Community of Valencia governing grants for separate collection, storage and processing of spent batteries, the direct contracts concluded with specialised undertakings in Asturias, the Balearic Islands and the Rioja region and the public information campaigns carried out in all Autonomous Communities.

13. According to the Kingdom of Spain, those measures have resulted in specific action of a practical nature, in particular infrastructural investments making available to the population facilities for the effective collection of spent batteries. Those investments are intended not only to provide and distribute special containers for the collection of waste of that kind, but also to enable centres to be built for processing and recycling and safe storage sites to be provided for batteries that cannot be recycled. As a result of that action as a whole, which is being taken in all the Autonomous Communities, the objectives of Article 6 of the Directive are being achieved in practice.

14. According to settled case-law, a Member State may not plead provisions, practices or circumstances existing in its internal legal system in order to justify a failure to comply with the obligations and time-limits laid down in a directive . . .

15. It should be noted, moreover, as the Kingdom of Spain concedes in its defence, that the latter had not, by the date laid down in the Directive, namely 17 September 1992, either prepared or published a programme with a view to attaining the specific objectives laid down in the first paragraph of Article 6 of the Directive.

16. In that regard, incomplete practical measures and fragmentary legislation cannot discharge the obligation of a Member State to draw up a comprehensive programme with a view to attaining certain objectives, as required by Article 6 of the Directive.

17. It must therefore be held that, by not adopting within the prescribed period the programmes referred to in Article 6 of the Directive, the Kingdom of Spain has failed to fulfil its obligations under that article.

Commentary

I. *Programmes for Batteries*

(1) It takes the Court of Justice three phrases (paragraphs 14 to 16) to justify its judgment: 1. internal practices or measures may not justify failure to comply with obligations; 2. Spain had no programme; 3. incomplete practical measures and fragmentary legislation are not equivalent to the drawing up of a comprehensive programme. The breach of Spain's obligations under Article 6 of Directive 91/157 was obvious and one wonders why Spain had argued so strongly on the issue (paragraphs 9 to 13).

(2) The Court's judgments also have frequently stated that compliance in practice with requirements of Community environmental law was not enough and that specific measures had to be taken. This must be all the more true for a situation such as the present one, where Directive 91/157 explicity requires Member States to draw up programmes and where it describes the exact content and time-limit of such programmes. Contrary to Spain's opinion, Article 6 does not just ask Member States to reach certain objectives; this is obvious if one looks at the requirement to promote the marketing of certain batteries or to promote research: it is impossible to promote research by doing nothing.

(3) In the present case, the Court of Justice did not specify what constituted a "programme" in the sense of Article 6. However, in subsequent judgments it clarified this notion. In Case C–215/98,[64] the Court declared that a "study and the draft law relied upon by the Greek Government do not more than detail a number of programmes that may eventually be implemented". And the Court became even more specific in Case C–347/97.[65] In that case, the Belgian government had argued, similarly to the Spanish government in the present case, that it had taken a number of measures which corresponded to the requirements of Article 6, among others that it had concluded voluntary agreements with battery manufacturers at national and Community level. The Court then specified:

(a) Member States must draw up programmes and review and update them regularly;
(b) there must be a precise timetable;
(c) Member States must notify the Commission of the measures intended and the timetable envisaged, in order to allow the Commission to assess the measures;
(d) even if certain objectives have already been achieved, this does not excuse a Member State from drawing up the programmes required;
(e) "the agreements . . . do not provide that they must be reviewed and updated regularly, at least every four years, and communicated to the Commission"; as they do not constitute either a precise timetable for review, they do not constitute programmes;
(f) the positive measures taken by Belgium "constitute no more than a series of legislative provisions or ad hoc measures which do not possess the characteristics of an organised and coordinated system of objectives" which could be considered as a programme.

(4) The Court argued in a similar way when it had to assess whether France had adopted a programme for batteries under Article 6 of Directive 91/157.[66] It analysed the French measures and concluded finally in the same words as mentioned under (f) above that they constituted no more than a series of legislative provisions or *ad hoc* measures.

Not only were the programmes under Article 6 of Directive 91/157 established with difficulty and sometimes with delay, also Directive 91/157 and its amendment itself were translated with delay by some Member States. In Cases C–218–222/96,[67] the Court found that Belgium had not transposed Directive 93/86 into national law. In Case C–303/95,[68] the Court stated that Italy had not transposed Directive 91/157 in time; in Cases C–282/96 and C–283/96,[69] the

---

[64] Court of Justice, Case C–215/98, *Commission* v. *Greece* [1999] ECR I–4913.
[65] Court of Justice, Case C–347/97, *Commission* v. *Belgium* [1999] ECR I–309.
[66] Court of Justice, Case C–178/98, *Commission* v. *France* [1999] ECR I–4853.
[67] Court of Justice, joined Cases C–218–222/96, *Commission* v. *Belgium* [1996] ECR I–6817.
[68] Court of Justice, Case C–303/95, *Commission* v. *Italy* [1996] ECR I–3859.
[69] Court of Justice, Joined Cases C–282/96 and 283/96, *Commission* v. *France* [1997] ECR I–2929.

Court stated that France had not transposed Directives 91/157 and 93/86 into national law. The Court made the same statement in Case C–236/96[70] with regard to Germany.

II. Programmes and Plans in Community Environmental Law

(5) The difficulties regarding the drawing up of environment programmes by far exceed that of Directive 91/157. Generally, it is possible to distinguish between management plans and programmes. Neither the notion of plan nor that of programme is defined in Community environmental law. Article 175(3) EC Treaty speaks of "action programmes" which shall set out priority objectives that are to be attained, without describing the form and content of such programmes in any detail. The different environmental action programmes, adopted since 1973 at Community level, contained a timetable—normally four years—objectives to be attained and priorities to be initiated or achieved during the lifetime of the programme.

(6) In the area of waste management, only Directive 91/157 on batteries and accumulators requests, in Article 6, Member States to set up a "programme". The other legal instruments in the waste sector rather require the elaboration of "plans" which will be discussed below. An exception is Directive 1999/31 on landfills[71] which asks Member States for the elaboration of site-specific "conditional plans" in order to adapt existing landfills to the standards of Directive 1999/31; however, the significant feature is that such a conditional plan is to be elaborated for each individual landfill which needs adaptation. Furthermore, the competent authorities have to lay down a period for the completion of the plan. In substance, thus, there does not appear to be a significant difference between a "programme" and a "conditioning plan".

(7) In the water sector, Directive 76/464[72] requires in Article 7 that Member States establish programmes for the reduction of water pollution. These programmes must contain deadlines for their implementation and be notified to the Commission; some conditions are laid down for their content. Also Directives 78/659 on the quality of fishwater[73] and 79/923 on the quality of shellfish water[74] provide for pollution reduction programmes which must be implemented within a certain time-span. Where drinking water did not comply with the requirements of Directive 80/778, Member States had the ability to introduce a request for a longer compliance period than the one provided for in the Directive, they then had

---

[70] Court of Justice, Case C–236/96, *Commission* v. *Germany* [1997] ECR I–6397.

[71] Directive 1999/31 on the landfill of waste [2000] OJ L182/1, Art. 14.

[72] Directive 76/464 on pollution caused by certain dangerous substances discharged into the aquatic environment of the Community [1976] OJ L129/23 (see on this Directive p. 177 *supra*).

[73] Directive 78/659 on the quality of fresh waters needing protection or improvement in order to support fish life [1978] OJ L222/1 (see on this Directive p. 199 *supra*).

[74] Directive 79/923 on the quality required for shellfish water [1979] OJ L281/47 (see on this Directive p. 199 *supra*).

to submit an action plan with an appropriate timetable for the improvement of the waters.[75]

Terminology is shaky in the recent water framework Directive 2000/60.[76] This Directive will, at the end of 2013, replace Directives 76/464, 78/659 and 79/923, mentioned above. In Article 11, it requires Member States to establish, by the end of 2009 and for each river basin district, a "programme of measures" which must include a number of "basic measures" as minimum requirements and may contain "supplementary measures". Basic measures include controls of water and of dicharges as well as a number of other measures which also could figure in a plan. The programmes will be reviewed and updated, where necessary, every six years.

Furthermore, Article 13 of Directive 2000/60 provides, by the end of 2009, for the elaboration and publication of river basin management plans which must include specific minimum information, among others also "a summary of the programme or programmes of measures".[77] To complete the linguistic confusion, Article 13(5) indicates that such river management plans "may be supplemented by the production of more detailed programmes and management plans".[78] The plans shall be reviewed and updated every six years.

(8) In the sector of air pollution, Member States are obliged, under Directive 96/62,[79] to elaborate for those areas or agglomerations where the limit values for ambient air quality are exceeded without reaching the margin of tolerance a plan or a programme which also informs the Commission on the time within which the limit values will be achieved. Where a limit value including the margin of tolerance is exceeded, the Member State concerned has to elaborate an "integrated plan". There is a definition neither of "plan" nor of "programme". For large combustion plants, Member States had to establish programmes for the progressive reduction of annual emission from existing installations.[80] These programmes had to contain a timetable and specific minimum indications and had to be sent to the Commission.

(9) In some earlier directives, the Commission was under the obligation, once it had received the national programmes, to compare them in order to ensure "sufficient coordination in their implementation".[81] This requirement seems to have been abandoned for a number of years. Generally, it appears that the establishment

---

[75] Directive 80/778 relating to the quality of water intended for human consumption [1980] OJ L229/11, Art. 20 (see on this Directive p. 185 *supra*).

[76] Directive 2000/60 establishing a framework for Community action in the field of water policy [2000] OJ L327/1.

[77] Directive 2000/60 (n. 76 *supra*), Art. 13(4) and Annex VII, A(7).

[78] The same linguistic confusion is to be found in Art. 15(3) of Directive 2000/60 (n. 76 *supra*) which reads: "Member States shall, within three years of the publication of each river basin management plan or update under Art. 13, submit an interim report describing progress in the implementation of the planned programme of measures".

[79] Directive 96/62 on ambient air quality assessment and management [1996] OJ L296/55, Art. 8(3); this provision refers to Annex IV which fixes the content of such a plan or programme; however, the title of Annex IV only mentions "programmes".

[80] Directive 88/609 on limiting air emissions from large combustion plants [1988] OJ L336/1, Art. 3.

[81] Directive 76/464 (n. 72 *supra*), Art. 7(7); Art. 16(3) of Directive 88/609 (n. 80 *supra*) mentions "harmonised implementation at Community level".

and the content of national programmes is hardly ever monitored by the Commission, most likely for lack of resources.

(10) Community environmental law uses the term "plan" much less frequently. This is mainly the case in the area of waste management, where waste management plans must be elaborated for waste in general,[82] for hazardous waste[83] and for packaging waste.[84] The Member States may elaborate either separate plans or one single plan with different chapters; and, generally, they are free to decide whether they want to elaborate one national plan, several regional plans or even plans which cover only one municipality: as long as the whole territory is covered, this remains in the Member States' realm. The notion of "plan" is not defined. The Court of Justice requested, for waste management plans, that they must constitute "an organised and coordinated system" for the disposal and treatment of waste.[85]

The different directives give some information on the content of the waste management plans. Member States must send these plans to the Commission; only for hazardous waste is there an obligation for the Commission to compare these plans. The plans do not contain a timetable. Nor is there any obligation for Member States to review and update the plans.[86]

(11) This short examination of planning and programming in Community environmental law permits the conclusion that Community terminology is not consistent and even becomes more confusing in recent directives. Generally, programmes are rather to be seen as political instruments, whereas plans are more to be established as management plans. In directives, programmes normally are foreseen for a clean-up, for a specific political objective to be reached within a specific time-span. Programmes are more apt to be compared with each other and the absence of such comparisons cannot but be regretted. Programmes, in the words of the Court of Justice, form an organised and coherent system of objectives, since they are shaped and oriented to attain a result.

(12) It does not seem that the content of programmes is the subject of regular monitoring on the part of the Commission; the same is true for management plans. In view of this conclusion, it is remarkable that recent Community environmental legislation so much accentuates the establishment of plans or programmes. The new framework directive for water[87] which is likely to determine water policy and management in Western Europe for the next 20 years as well as

---

[82] Directive 75/442 on waste [1975] OJ L194/47; amended by Directive 91/156 [1991] OJ L78/32, Art. 7.

[83] Directive 91/689 on hazardous waste [1991] OJ L377/20, Art. 6.

[84] Directive 94/62 [1994] OJ L365/10, Art. 14.

[85] Court of Justice, Case C–387/97, *Commission* v. *Hellenic Republic* [2000] ECR I–5047, para. 76.

[86] An obligation to update waste management plans existed in Directive 78/319 on toxic and dangerous waste [1978] OJ L84/43, Art. 12(1); this requirement was deleted, when Directive 91/689 (n. 83 *supra*) replaced by Directive 78/319. Also Directive 85/339 on liquid beverage containers [1985] OJ L176/18, the predecessor of Directive 94/62 (n. 84 *supra*) had, in Art. 3, provided for the regular updating of the programmes which had to be drawn up.

[87] Directive 2000/60 (n. 76 *supra*).

the framework Directive on air[88] and the directives on national emission ceilings for certain atmospheric pollutants[88a] or on environmental noise—likely to be adopted during the year 2002—heavily rely on clean-up programmes and management plans.

It may well be that the reason for this is elsewhere: clean-up programmes and management plans are drawn up at local, regional or national, but not at Community level. Seen in this perspective, it may well be that the increased reliance on planning and programming is a veiled way of strengthening the role of Member States in the protection of the environment instead of strengthening Community integration.

43. EUROPEAN WASTE LISTS

Judgment of the Court (Sixth Chamber) of 22 June 2000 Case C–318/98

Reference for a preliminary ruling in the criminal proceedings against F. Fornasar, A. Strizzolo, G. Toso, L. Mucchino, E. Peressutti and S. Chiarcosso
[2000] ECR I–4785

Facts and Procedure

Police officers in Udine (Italy) made, in 1994, a routine inspection of a waste landfill and found a heap of waste, a number of tin cans and a drum, which had been discharged and been described as special waste, which was neither toxic nor harmful. They commissioned an expert's report to ascertain the nature of the waste. The expert charged found that the drum contained MDI, a substance that was extremely dangerous to human health. It is used for the manufacture of various synthetic resins and has a very broad range of uses for undertakings operating in different areas of manufacture. It turned out that the entire load of waste came from the Monfalcone works of Fincantieri, where various industrial activities are exercised. Neither could the exact origin within the works of Fincantieri be identified, nor was it possible to identify the actual use to which the MDI substance was intended.

During the proceedings before an Italian court, there were discussions on whether the substance could or should be classified as hazardous waste under Italian

---

[88] Directive 96/62 (n. 79 *supra*).
[88a] Directive 2001/81 on national emission ceilings for certain atmospheric pollutants [2001] OJ L309/22.

and Community law and, in particular, whether it would have to be considered "hazardous waste" under Community Directive 91/689[89] and the list of hazardous waste which had been established according to that Directive.[90] In this context, the national court put a number of preliminary questions to the Court of Justice.

Judgment (extracts)

[Member States' right to classify waste as hazardous]

34. . . . by its second, third, fourth and fifth questions . . . the national court is essentially asking whether Directive 91/689 prevents the Member States . . . from classifying as hazardous, waste other than that featuring on the list of hazardous waste laid down in Decision 94/904, and thus from adopting more stringent protective measures in order to prohibit the abandonment, dumping or uncontrolled disposal of such waste.

35. According to Messrs Mucchino and Peressutti, the Netherlands Government and the Commission, the list of "hazardous waste" within the meaning of Directive 91/689 and Decision 94/904 must be considered to be exhaustive. The Commission considers that Community law precludes that list being supplemented automatically solely on the basis that waste is ascertained to fall within the scope of the annexes to Directive 91/689. That approach is in line with the requirements to use a precise and uniform definition of hazardous waste.

36. The German and Austrian Governments, on the other hand, argue that, having regard to the wording of the second indent of Article 1(4) of Directive 91/689, the list of hazardous waste laid down by Decision 94/904 cannot be exhaustive. On the contrary, the second indent indicates that other waste may also be classified as hazardous by the Member States if it has one of the properties listed in Annex III to Directive 91/689.

43. As regards Directive 91/689, it must be borne in mind that the fifth recital of the preamble to that directive states that, in order to improve the effectiveness of the management of hazardous waste in the Community, it is necessary to use a precise and uniform definition of hazardous waste based on experience.

44. To that end, Article 1(3) of Directive 91/689 refers to the definition of waste laid down in Directive 75/442, and Article 1(4) defines hazardous waste. Decision 94/904 supplements Directive 91/689 and the annex thereto also refers to the definiton of "waste" in Article 1(a) of Directive 75/442.

45. The term "hazardous waste" in Article 1(4) of Directive 91/689 must be considered to mean the waste featuring in the list drawn up in accordance with the procedure laid down by Article 18 of Directive 75/442, and any other waste which

---

[89] Directive 91/689 on hazardous waste [1991] OJ L377/20.
[90] Decision 94/904 establishing a list of hazardous waste pursuant to Art. 1(4) of Directive 91/689 on hazardous waste [1994] OJ L356/14.

is considered by a Member State to display any of the proterties listed in Annex III to Directive 91/689.

46. In that connection, it must be observed that the Community rules do not seek to effect complete harmonisation in the area of the environment. Even though Article 130r of the Treaty refers to certain Community objectives to be attained, both Article 130t of the EC Treaty (now Article 176 EC) and Directive 91/689 allow the Member States to introduce more stringent protective measures. Under Article 130r of the Treaty, Community policy on the environment is to aim at a high level of protection, taking into account the diversity of situations in the vasious regions of the Community.

47. Furthermore, Article 7 of Directive 91/689 provides that in cases of emergency or grave danger, Member States are to take all necessary steps, including, where appropriate, temporary derogations from that directive, to ensure that hazardous waste is so dealt with as not to constitute a threat to the population or the environment. The Member States are to inform the Commission of any such derogations.

48. It follows from the foregoing that, pursuant to Article 1(4) of Directive 91/689, the list provided for by that directive entitles the Member States to classify any other waste which a Member State considers to display any of the properties listed in Annex III to that directive as hazardous. Thus, such waste is considered hazardous only in the territory of the Member States which have adopted such a classification.

49. In that event, the Member States are bound to notify such cases to the Commission for review in accordance with the procedure laid down in Article 18 of Directive 75/442, with a view to adaptation of the list of hazardous waste. Accordingly, on the basis of experience, the Commission is called upon to examine the extent to which it is appropriate to supplement the general list of hazardous waste applicable to all Member States of the Community by adding to it waste considered hazardous by one or more Member States pursuant to the second indent of Article 1(4) of Directive 91/689.

51. The reply to the second, third, fourth and fifth questions must therefore be that Directive 91/689 does not prevent the Member States, including, for matters within their jurisdiction, the courts, from classifying as hazardous waste other than that featuring on the list of hazardous waste laid down by Decision 94/904, and thus from adopting more stringent protective measures in order to prohibit the abandonment, dumping or uncontrolled disposal of such waste. If they do so, it is for the authorities of the Member State concerned which have competence under national law to notify the Commission of such cases in accordance with the second indent of Article 1(4) of Directive 91/689.

[knowing the origin of waste—a condition for classification?]

52. By its first question, the national court is essentially asking whether Article 1(4) of Directive 91/689 and Decision 94/904 must be interpreted as meaning that in a specific case it is a necessary precondition for waste to be classified as hazardous that its origin be determined.

53. The Commission contends that Article 1(4) of Directive 91/689 and Decision 94/904 must be interpreted as meaning that, in order for waste to be classified as hazardous, it is necessary to establish that that waste results from a manufacturing process or activity which appears on the Community list of hazardous waste.

54. The Netherlands Government, on the other hand, considers that, in order to classify waste as hazardous within the meaning of Article 1(4) of Directive 91/689 and Decision 94/904, there is no requirement for its exact origin to be established. The origin of waste is just one of the factors to be taken into consideration when deciding whether it is hazardous waste.

55. In that regard, suffice it to observe that, under Article 1(4) of Directive 91/689, the wastes on the list of "hazardous waste" must have one or more of the properties listed in Annex III of that directive and that that list is to take into account the origin and composition of the waste and, where necessary, limit values of concentration.

56. It is clear on the wording alone of that provision that the decisive criterion, as regards the definition of "hazardous waste", is whether the waste displays one or more of the properties listed in Annex III to Directive 91/689. Although the basis for inclusion in the list of "hazardous waste" is indeed the origin of the waste, that does not mean that it is essential for its exact origin to be determined for it to be classified as hazardous. The origin of the waste is not the only criterion for classifying it as hazardous but constitutes one of the factors which the list of hazardous waste merely "takes into account".

Commentary

I. *Community Lists on Waste*

(1) The classification of waste, and in particular of hazardous waste, is an extremely intricate problem of international, Community and national environmental law which would urgently need to be reformed. The considerable lack of transparency is probably one of the principal reasons for numerous illegal actions in the area of waste management and comparatively few criminal sanctions in this area.

The factual side of the present case was relatively clear: a highly dangerous substance had been discarded and had thus become waste. It was not possible to identify exactly where the material came from and which was its original intended use. Therefore, the Italian court wanted to know whether Italian authorities were entitled to classify the material as "hazardous waste".

(2) As regards Community law,[91] Article 1(4) of Directive 91/689 gives a definition of hazardous waste.[92] As the material was not, at least not explicitly, classified as hazardous waste in the list established by Decision 94/904,[93] the question was whether the Italian authorities were entitled to classify that material as "hazardous waste" under Italian law. The Court of Justice was quite short in its answer, confirming that the Italian authorities were so entitled.

It is difficult to consider how any other answer could be given. Decision 94/904 expressly mentions in number 4 of the introduction to the Community list of hazardous wastes: "In accordance with Article 1(4) second indent of Directive 91/689, any waste other than the ones listed below which is considered by a Member State to display any of the properties listed in Annex III to Council Directive 91/689 on hazardous waste is hazardous. All such cases will be notified to the Commission and will be examined with a view to amending the list in accordance with Article 18 of Directive 75/442".

(3) This wording is practically identical with the conclusion reached by the Court of Justice. The question whether the Community list of hazardous waste is exhausting—mentioned in paragraphs 35 and 36 of the judgment—is rather confusing, at least in the present case. Indeed, the Court rightly points out that Article 176 (ex Article 130t) EC Treaty allows Member States to introduce more stringent measures than those that were fixed at Community level[94] and the second indent of Article 1(4) is sufficiently clear to leave no ambiguity as regards Member States' rights.

---

[91] The present commentary is limited to Community law. As regards Community waste law and its implementation in Italy, see L Krämer, "La normativa comunitaria in materia di rifiuti e lo stato di attuazione in Italia" in *Rifiuti nel secolo XXI; il caso Italia tra Europa e Mediterraneo* (Edizioni Ambiente, Milan, 1999), p. 9 *et seq.*

[92] Directive 91/689 (n. 89 *supra*), Art. 1(4): "For the purposes of this Directive 'hazardous waste' means:

—wastes featuring on a list to be drawn up in accordance with the procedure laid down in Art. 18 of Directive 75/442/EEC on the basis of Annexes I and II to this Directive, no later than six months before the date of implementation of this Directive. These wastes must have one or more of the properties listed in Annex III. The list shall take into account the origin and composition of the waste and, where necessary, limit values of concentration. This list shall be periodically reviewed and if necessary (revised) by the same procedure,

—any other waste which is considered by a Member State to display any of the properties listed in Annex III. Such cases shall be notified to the Commission and reviewed in accordance with the procedure laid down in Art. 18 of Directive 75/442/EEC with a view to adaptation of the list".

[93] Decision 94/904 (n. 90 *supra*).

[94] Art. 176 (ex Art. 130t) EC Treaty: "The protective measures adopted pursuant to Art. 175 shall not prevent any Member State from maintaining or introducing more stringent protective measures. Such measures must be compatible with this Treaty. They shall be notified to the Commission".

It is not clear, though, why the Court mentions in para. 46 of the judgment that also Directive 91/689 allows "the member State to introduce more stringent protective measures". The only reason, why there is such a possibility is derived from the fact that Directive 91/689 is based on Art. 175 (ex Art. 130s) EC Treaty, and therefore also leads to the application of Art. 176 EC Treaty. In itself, Directive 91/689 does not contain any minimum clause; it rather states in Art. 1(1): "The objective of this Directive . . . is to approximate the laws of the Member States on the controlled management of hazardous waste". This wording rather points into the direction of a directive trying to establish uniform rules.

(4) Where the question of the exhaustive character of the Community list of hazardous waste would come into play, is when the Community expressly took a decision to consider a specific waste as non-hazardous (which was not the case in the present judgment): would then a Member State be able to invoke Article 176 EC Treaty or Article 1(4) of Directive 91/689 and classify this waste nevertheless as hazardous?

The answer would be more of a factual nature: if that specific waste displayed one of the characteristics of Annex III of Directive 91/689,[95] the Member State is right and entitled to have the waste classified as hazardous under its national law. If this is not the case, the Member State has no such right.

(5) Sometimes matters are more complicated, though. Recently, the Commission had to decide how old medicaments should be classified, whether as hazardous wastes or as non-hazardous wastes. It is clear that some medicament have properties mentioned in Annex III of Directive 91/689. However, other medicaments clearly do not have such properties. Differentiating between whether the medicaments have or do not have properties of Annex III is highly undesirable, as end-of-life medicaments are much better dealt with coherently: nobody is able to differentiate according to the medicament and the sorting and different treatment or disposal of such medicaments would be very time-, cost- and energy-consuming.

The majority of Member States were therefore in favour of classifying medicaments, apart from some obviously hazardous medicaments, as non-hazardous. However, in Finland end-of-life medicaments have been classified, for years, as hazardous and Finland pleaded, in application of the precautionary principle—"if you err, try to err on the safe side"—in favour of having all medicaments classified as hazardous. Suppose the Commission were deciding in the sense of the majority, would then Finland be allowed, under Article 176 EC Treaty, to maintain its legislation? I would think so, because end-of-life medicaments are rarely shipped around within the Community, the precautionary principle exists and neither solution is a completely "correct" solution.

In the present case, the question of the exhausting nature of the Community list of hazardous waste was irrelevant, as there was no Community decision yet on the material that had been discovered in Italy.

(6) The question which the Court had to decide next was whether it was indispensable for a Member State to know the exact origin of the waste in order to be able to classify it as hazardous. And the Court answered quite rightly that this was not necessary. Indeed, the criterion of the origin of the waste is one among others for the Community list of waste and is not mentioned at all as regards Member States' classification of wastes as hazardous under the second indent of Article 1(4) of Directive 91/689. This also is logical: indeed, where a Member State classifies a specific waste as hazardous, it has to notify the Commission. The Commission will then have to take the necessary measures in order to have the Community list of hazardous wastes completed: at this moment, the origin of the material can be

---

[95] Annex III of Directive 91/689 lists 14 types of properties which render wastes hazardous, such as H1 "explosive", H2 "oxidizing", H6 "toxic", H14 "ecotoxic" etc.

determined for the whole of the Community, as only some uses of the material might exist within the notifying Member State.

(7) At Community level, there existed two lists, established by Decision 94/3 for non-hazardous waste[96] and by Decision 94/904 for hazardous wastes. By Decision 2000/53, these two lists were brought together into one list,[97] which became effective from 1 January 2002. The new single list identifies "hazardous waste" with an asterisk. A further Commission decision, which was taken early in January 2001, brought further substantive amendments to the Community list.

II. Waste Lists in a Global Context

(8) Complications start where the shipment of waste comes in. Regulation 259/93 deals with the supervision and control of shipment of waste within, into and out of the European Community.[98] This Regulation introduced a control system for the shipment of waste that was based on a system elaborated by an OECD Decision of 30 March 1992. The shipment of green listed waste (Annex II to Regulation 259/93) underwent, in practice, no control system; the shipment of amber list waste (Annex III to Regulation 259/93) had a relatively strict control system and the shipment of red listed waste (Annex IV to Regulation 259/93) was the subject of very strict controls.

In general terms, green listed waste is not hazardous, whereas amber and red listed waste are hazardous. However, this is only a general division: in specific cases, non hazardous waste is classified in the amber list, in order to allow specific controls to be applied to movements of such waste. Examples of such classifications are: AC 260: liquid pig manure; faeces; AC 270 sewage sludge; AD 160 municipal/household wastes.

(9) The list of hazardous waste under Decision 2000/53 is thus not identical with the lists for the shipment of hazardous wastes (amber and red list wastes), and this complicates the application of a number of Community directives which provide for different provisions according to the hazardous or non-hazardous character of the waste. An example of this is Directive 85/337 on the environmental impact assessment; this Directive makes the environmental impact assessment obligatory for installations for the disposal of hazardous waste, but only in some specific cases for the disposal of non-hazardous waste.[99] A similar division is made in Directive 96/61 on the integrated prevention and pollution control.[100]

---

[96] Decision 94/3 establishing a list of wastes pursuant to Art. 1(a) of Council Directive 75/442/EEC on waste [1994] OJ L5/15.

[97] Decision 2000/532, replacing Decision 94/3/EC establishing a list of wastes pursuant to Art. 1(a) of Council Directive75/442/EEC on waste and Council Decision 94/904/EC establishing a list of hazardous waste pursuant to Art. 1(4) of Council Directive 91/689/EEC on hazardous waste [2000] OJ L226/3.

[98] Regulation 259/93 [1993] OJ L30, p. 1; amended by Decision 94/721 [1994] OJ L288/36; Decision 96/660 [1996] OJ L304/15; Regulation 120/97 [1997] OJ L22/14; Decision 98/368 [1998] OJ L165/20; Commission Regulation 2408798 [1998] OJ L298/19; Decision 1999/816 [1999] OJ L316/45.

[99] Directive 85/337 on the assessment of the effects of certain public and private projects on the environment [1985] OJ L175/40; amended by Directive 97/11 [1997] OJ L73/5, Annex I, nos. 9 and 10.

[100] See Directive 96/61 on the integrated prevention and pollution control [1996] OJ L257, p. 26., Annex I, nos. 5.1 and 5.3.

(10) The review of the lists of Regulation 259/93 is discussed and decided within the context of the OECD, and the European Community takes over the OECD review decisions,[101] as all EC Member States are also members of the OECD. As, however, OECD decisions are taken unanimously and the 29 OECD Member States do not always agree among themselves—there is a strong influence from trade-oriented countries such as United States, Canada and Australia—decision-making is slow within the OECD. Therefore, this procedure does not rule out the Community itself amending, under its own procedures, the annexes to Regulation 259/93.

(11) At worldwide level, the Basel Convention on the control of transboundary movements of hazardous wastes and their transposal of 22 March 1989 regulated the shipment of hazardous wastes.[102] In 1995, the Convention was amended and an export ban on hazardous waste shipments to non-OECD countries was introduced;[103] in 1997, two lists of wastes were introduced into the Basel Convention, one to which the export ban applied (List A) and the second one a list to which the export ban did not apply (List B), though they were considered hazardous. The European Community took over these lists by introducing a new Annex V into Regulation 259/93. However, as again the different lists of Basel, of the OECD and of the Community are not identical, it is extremely complicated to work out with precision which provisions should apply in a specific case.

It must also be remembered that the Basel Convention expressly provides that its contracting parties may adopt more stringent provisions.[104] Thus, the Community may classify specific types of waste as hazardous, which are not classified hazardous under the Basel Convention. And as the same provision applies, by virtue of Article 176 EC Treaty, within the Community, a harmonisation of the different lists will be a long-term objective.

(12) To these lists must be added the different lists which are established under Regulation 259/93 for the shipment of green listed waste to third countries,[105] the different provisions concerning the incineration of waste in different incinerators and the fact that Member States have at least in part maintained the existence of national waste lists. As, furthermore, the lists at the different level—States, Community, OECD, Basel—are not elaborated according to the same criteria, the overall picture is that of a rather non-transparent system.

---

[101] Regulation 259/93 (n. 98 *supra*), Art. 42.

[102] The Community has adhered to the Basel Convention by Decision 93/98 [1993] OJ L39/1.

[103] The Community took over this ban by Regulation 120/97 (n. 98 *supra*).

[104] Basel Convention, Art. 4(11): "Nothing in this Convention shall prevent a Party from imposing additional requirements that are consistent with the provisions of this Convention, and are in accordance with the rules of international law, in order to better protect human health and the environment".

[105] See Regulation 259/93 (n. 98 *supra*), Arts. 16 and 17. The Community undertook to ask each third country to indicate, for the shipment of green listed waste, whether it wanted to see the control procedures for green listed waste, for amber listed waste or for red listed waste applied—or whether it wanted to ban all shipments. The answers varied and—with changes of government, of policy, following pressure from interested bodies etc.—changed in time.

For hazardous waste, the Community has decided to adopt an export ban (see commentary, para. 10 *supra*).

44. RECOVERABLE WASTE: A PRODUCT?

Judgment of the Court (Sixth Chamber) of 25 June 1997
Joined Cases C–304/94, C–330/94, C–342/94 and C–224/95

Reference for a preliminary ruling in the criminal proceedings against
E. Tombesi, A. Tombesi, R. Santella, G. Muzi and Others and A. Savini
[1997] ECR I–3561

Facts and Procedure

E. and A. Tombesi are the proprietors of a firm which works marble. They were charged, *inter alia*, with the offence of discharging without authorisation marble rubble and debris from worked marble. R. Santella was charged with producing without authorisation toxic and dangerous waste consisting of pitch obtained from the emissions produced by electro-static filters used in cooking ovens. G. Muzi and others were charged with the offence concerning olive oil residues. A. Savini was charged with the offence of having transported, without authorisation, unsheathed copper left over from the manufacture of copper windings, fragments of cable, ferrous material, ferous scrap and mixed scrap. All defendants argued in court that the materials involved were no longer regarded as waste, but had to be considered as products.

Community legislation on waste[106] states that common terminology and a common definition of waste is necessary;[107] it defines waste as "any subject or object in the categories set out in Annex I which the holder discards or intends or is required to discard".[108] Directive 91/689 on hazardous waste refers to that definition.[109] Also Regulation 259/93 on the shipment of waste refers to that definition in Directive 75/442.[110]

As the Italian courts were in doubt whether the Italian provisions concerning the definition of waste were compatible with Community legislation, they asked the Court of Justice for a preliminary ruling.

---

[106] Directive 75/442 on waste [1975] OJ L194/39; amended by Directive 91/156 [1991] OJ L78/32.

[107] Directive 91/156 (n. 106 *supra*), third recital: " . . . common terminology and a definition of waste are needed in order to improve the efficiency of waste management in the Community".

[108] Directive 75/442 (n. 106 *supra*), Art. 1(a).

[109] Directive 91/689 on hazardous waste [1991] OJ L377/20, Art. 1(3): "The definition of 'waste' and of the other terms unsed in this Directive shall be those in Directive 75/442/EEC".

[110] Regulation 259/93 on the supervision and control of shipments of waste within, into and out of the European Community [1993] OJ L30/1, Art. 2(a): „Waste is as defined in Art. 1(a) of Directive 75/442/EEC".

Judgment (extracts)

41. By their questions which it is appropriate to consider together, the Preture Circondariali of Terni and Pescara seek to ascertain essentially whether the concept of "waste" referred to in the Community rules must be taken to exclude substances or objects capable of economic re-use.

44. . . . it should be borne in mind that Article 2(a) of Regulation No. 259/93, forming part of the Title I ("scope and definitions"), provides that, for the purposes of the regulation, "waste" means the substances or objects defined in Article 1(a) of Directive 75/442.

45. According to Article 1(1) thereof, Regulation No. 259/93 applies to shipments of waste within, into and out of the Community. Under Title III ("Shipments of waste within Member States"), Article 13(1) makes clear that Title II ("shipments of waste between Member States"), Title VII ("Common provisions") and Title VIII ("Other provisions") do not apply to shipments within a Member State.

46. Accordingly, it must be concluded that, in order to ensure that the national systems for supervision and control of shipments of waste conform with minimum criteria, Article 2(a) in Title I of Regulation 259/93, referring to Article 1(a) of Directivec 75/442 as amended, laid down a common definition of the concept of waste which is of direct application, even to shipments within any Member State.

47. As regards the intrerpretation of the Community legislation on waste, it must be borne in mind that, according to settled case-law, the concept of waste within the meaning of Article 1 of Directive 75/442, in its original version, and Article 1 of Directive 78/319 was not to be understood as excluding substances and objects which were capable of economic reutilisation. National legislation which defines waste as excluding substances and objects which are capable of economic reutilisation is not compatible with Directive 75/442, in its original version, and Directive 78/319 . . .

48. That interpretation is not affected either by Directive 91/156, which amended the first of those two directives, of by Directive 91/689, which repealed the second . . . , or by Regulation 259/93.

49. Thus, under Article 3(1) of Directive 75/442, as amended, the Member States are to take measures to encourage, first, the prevention or reduction of waste production and its harmfulness and, second, the recovery of waste by means of recycling, re-use or reclamation, or any other process with a view to extracting secondary raw materials or the use of waste as a source of energy. The sixth recital in the preamble to Directive 91/156 states that it is desirable to encourage the recycling of waste and the reuse of waste as raw materals and that it may be necessary to adopt specific rules for re-usable waste.

50. To that end, the system of supervision established by Directive 75/442, as amended, was reinforced by Directive 91/156. Pursuant to Article 8 of Directive 75/442, as amended, the member States are to ensure that any holder of waste either recovers or disposes of it himself in accordance with the provisions of the directive or has it handled by a private or public collector or an undertaking which carried out the operations listed in Annex II A or B. Annex II a concerns disposal operations, whereas Annex II B applies to operations which may lead to recovery and lists a series of processes such as use as a fuel or other means of generating energy, recycling or reclamation of materials and recovery of products.

51. According to Article 10 of Directive 75/442, as amended, any establishment or undertaking which carries out the operations referred to in Annex II B must obtain a permit. Moreover, under Article 12, establishments or undertakings which collect or transport waste on a professional basis or which arrange for the disposal or recovery of waste on behalf of others, where not subject ot authorisation, are to be registered with competent authorities. Finally, pursuant to Article 13, they are to be subject to appropriate periodic inspections by the competent authorities.

52. It follows that the system of supervision and control established by Directive 75/442, as amended, is intended to cover all object and substances discarded by their owners, even if they have a commercial value and are collected on a commercial basis for recycling, reclamation or re-use.

53. . . . a deactivation process merely to render waste harmless, landfill tipping in hollows or embankments and waste incineration constititute disposal or recovery operations falling within the scope of the Communiy legislation. The fact that a substance is included in the category of re-usable residues without any details being given as to its characteristics or use is irrelevant in that regard. The same applies to the grinding of waste.

54. The answer to the questions referred to the Court must therefore be that the concept of "waste" in Article 1 of Directive 75/442, as amended, referred to in Article 1(3) of Directive 91/689 and Article 2(a) of Regulation 259/93 is not to be understood as excluding substances and objects which are capable of economic reutilisation, even if the materials in question may be the subject of a transaction or quoted on public or private commercial lists. In particular, a deactivation process, intended merely to render waste harmless, landfill tipping in hollows or embankments and waste incineration constitute disposal or recovery operations falling within the scope of the abovementioned Community rules. The fact that a substance is classified as a re-usable residue without its characteristics or purpose being defined is irregular, in that regard. The same applies to the grinding of a waste substance.

Commentary

I. The Notion of "Waste" in Community Law

(1) The question when a material is to be called a "product" and when "waste" has occupied the Court of Justice on several occasions; and it is likely that cases

submitted to the Court in future on that question will increase in number. This is mainly due to the fact that economic operators do not like the Community definition of waste and want in particular those materials which are capable of being used economically (in form of reuse, material recycling or incineration with energy recovery) not to be called waste and thus not to come under the provisions which are applicable to waste.

(2) The Community adopted first in 1975 a directive on waste which defined waste as "any substance or object which the holder disposes of or is required to dispose of pursuant to the provisions of national law in force". "Disposal" was defined as "the collection, sorting, transport and treatment of waste as well as its storage and tipping above or under ground;—the transormation operations necessary for its re-use, recovery or recycling".[111]

(3) This definition was slightly amended by Directive 91/156, due also to international developments: the Basel Convention on the shipment of waste[112] understood the notion of "disposal" as covering disposal and recovery operations. This coincinded with the wording used by the OECD in different decisions concerning waste.[113] However, when the Basel Convention was elaborated, the OECD wished to maintain, for its members, specific provisions concerning the recovery of waste. This led to an OECD Decision of 1992 which limited the notion of "recovery" to recovery operations; at the same time, "disposal" no longer included such recovery operation and was thus narrowed in its sense.[114]

(4) As all Community Member States were also members of OECD, the Community thought it desirable to align its legislation as much as possible to the OECD provisions. Therefore, it introduced two different notions, "disposal" operations which were further specified in Annex IIA and "recovery" operations which were further specified in Annex IIB to the Directive. The common denominator to these activites became the notion "discard", in order to avoid the notion "disposal" being used as the common denominator and at the same time as the determining notion for operations which led to the final disposal of waste (IIA-operations).[115]

(5) The Court of Justice was first asked in 1990 about the definition of waste. In Cases C–206/88 and C–207/88[116] the Italian police had stopped some hauliers which were transporting (hazardous) waste without having a permit for such transport. In court, the hauliers argued that the material was to be incinerated and

---

[111] Directive 75/442 (n. 106 *supra*), Art. 1.

[112] Basel Convention on the control of transboundary movements of hazardous wastes and their disposal, of 22 March 1989. The Community adhered to this Convention by Decision 93/98 [1993] OJ L39/1

[113] See in particular OECD Decision C(88)90 of 1988, which understood "disposal" to cover final disposal operations as well as recovery and recycling operations.

[114] OECD Decision concerning the control of transfrontier movement of wastes destined for recovery operations, C(92)39 of 30 March 1992.

[115] It should be noted that this shift from "dispose" in Directive 75/442 (n. 106 *supra*) to "discard" in Directive 91/156 (n. 106 *supra*) only concerned the English version. The other language versions did not have the same linguistic difficulties and, therefore, did not change the wording of the two notions.

[116] Court of Justice, Cases C–206/88 and C–207/88, *Vessoso and Zanetti* [1990] ECR I–1461.

that the energy was to be recovered; thus, the material was capable of economic reutilisation and did not constitute "waste". The Court of Justice interpreted Directive 75/442 and found that "the concept of waste within the meaning of Article 1 of Directive 75/442 . . . is not to be understood as excluding substances and objects which are capable of economic reutilisation".

(6) In 1986, Germany adopted a new legislation on waste.[117] This legislation provided that material which could be recovered or recycled should be considered a secondary raw material and not as waste. The Commission took action against Germany and brought the matter before the Court of Justice which, in 1995, stated that Germany, "by excluding certain categories of recyclable waste from the scope of its legislation on waste" had failed to comply with its obligations under Community law;[118] the Court further declared that the notion of "waste" had not been affected by the amendment which Directive 91/156 had brought to Directive 75/442. It repeated this interpretation in the present case (paragraphs 47 and 48) and in a number of subsequent judgments.[119]

(7) In conclusion, it is thus clear and without doubt that the Community definition of "waste" also includes wastes which are capable of or destined for economic recycling or recovery. In particular economic operators accuse this notion of being too large; it is claimed that materials which, in one way or the other, are used or capable of being used for economic recovery operations should not be considered as waste, but rather as "secondary raw materials", "secondary products", "by-products" or obtain a similar classification.

The legal problem with this argument seems obvious: the notions of "economic value", economic reutilisation" or similar notions based on economic considerations are not notions which are linked to any specific national legal order. The "economic value" of material is independent from national borders, the European Community or industrialised countries. This means that each waste material has, somewhere in the world, some economic value. Thus, the consideration of "economic value" would lead to the deletion of the notion of "waste" altogether.

(8) Also, incineration with energy recovery is, in legal terms, a recovery operation.[120] Consequently, all materials that burn will have to be considered as "capable of economic reutilisation". Again, this would lead to abandoning the notion of waste altogether.

Nor is it possible to restrict the notion of "economic value" to economic activities in Community Member States or in industrialised countries. Indeed, this would mean, for instance, that waste which can be recycled in France, but not in Greece, would be considered secondary raw material in France, but not in Greece. What if Japan has developed a technology for the recycling of specific waste materials, which

---

[117] *Abfallgesetz* of 27 August 1986, BGBl. 1986, I, p. 2126.

[118] Court of Justice, Case C–422/92, *Commission* v. *Germany* [1995] ECR I–1097, para. 25.

[119] Court of Justice, Cases C–129/96, *Inter-Environnement Wallonie* [1997] ECR I–7411; C–418/97, *Arco Chemie*, (2000) ECR I–4475; C–318/98, *Fornasar*, (2000) ECR I–4785 (see also p. 350 *supra*).

[120] Directive 75/442 as amended by Directive 91/156 (n. 106 *supra*), Annex IIB, no. 1.

is not (yet) used in the European Community: should the material be considered waste or product?

II. Specifying the Notion of "Waste" and "Product"

(9) It is admitted that the notion of "waste" is not very precise. It will therefore have to be examined on a case-by-case basis whether material is discarded or whether there is an intention to discard. In this context, it should be clear that the above-mentioned definition of waste disposal also implies that material which has an economic value can be discarded: otherwise, there would for instance never be waste from the extraction or processing of precious metals, as here the residues of production clearly have an economic value.

(10) In 1998, the OECD tried to give some guidance for the distinction between product and waste, by listing a number of aspects which would have to be taken into consideration:[121]

"I. General considerations
   (1) Is the material produced intentionally?
   (2) Is the material made in response to market demand?
   (3) Is the overall economic value of the material negative?
   (4) Is the material no longer part of the normal commercial cycle or chain of utility?

II. Characteristics and specifications
   (5) Is the production of the material subject to quality control?
   (6) Does the material meet well developed nationally or internationally recognised specifications/standards?

III. Environmental impact
   (7) Do these standards include environmental considerations, in additional to technical or economic considerations?
   (8) Is the use of these material as environmentally sound as that of a primary product?
   (9) Does the use of the material in a production process cause any increased risk to human health or the environment greater than the use of the corresponding raw material?

IV. Use and destination of the material
   (10) Is further processing required before the material can be directly used in a manufacturing(commercial application?
   (11) Is this processing limited to minor repair?
   (12) Is the material still suitable for its originally intended purpose?
   (13) Can the material be used for another purpose as a substitute material?
   (14) Will the material actually be used in a production process?
   (15) Does the material have an identified use?
   (16) Can the material be used in its present form or in the same way as a raw material without being subjected to a recovery operation?
   (17) Can the material be used only after it has been subjected to a recovery operation?"

[121] OECD, Final Guidance Document for distinguishing Waste from non-Waste, ENV/EPOC/WMP (98) 1/Rev. 1 of 2 July 1998.

(11) The OECD underlines that this list must be used with care: "no particular weighting can be assigned to any of the above considerations. In order to evaluate the status of a material, comprehensively, all of the above considerations may be applied on a case-by-case basis. The fact that a material may have an identified use may be a valid consideration, but it should not be used in isolation to indicate the status of a material".[122]

Number (1) of this list clarifies, for instance, why the gold dust which is generated when golden rings or other jewellery is made and which is carefully captured, collected and sold nevertheless constitutes waste and not a product: if the jeweller could, he would produce no gold dust at all: his intention is rather to keep the quantity of gold dust generated as low as possible. In the same way, metal scrap is not intentionally produced: if its generator could avoid it, when making, for instance, a car body, he would do so. It is for this reason that the OECD lists which were established by Decision 92(39) enumerate both precious metal residues and metal scrap as waste.[123] The same applies to Community legislation.[124]

(12) The Community has not yet developed criteria in particular to determine when waste ceases to be a waste and becomes a product again. This borderline is important for the promotion of recycling and, to a lesser degree, of recovery (incineration) activities. The general point is that the recycling activity must be finished before the waste can be considered to be transformed into a product. For instance, where used paper (newspaper and other paper) is in question, the recycling process is finished when the paper enters the paper mill in order to be processed into (recycled) paper. Attempts from the economic side instead favour an approach according to which used paper could be considered to be a "product" when this paper is sorted according to different paper categories. The difference is not merely theoretical: indeed, the shipment between the place of sorting and the paper mill is in one case a shipment of waste, in the other case transport of goods. Furthermore, the holder of waste has certain obligations as regards the handling, storing, transporting and treating of the waste. In contrast to that, the owner of a product is, in principle, free to do with the product whatever he wishes; thus, there would be no obligation for him to bring the sorted paper—if this were qualified as a "product"—to a paper mill. He could bring it instead to an installation where it is burned, or anywhere else.

(13) The example of waste paper may appear trivial. However, where hazardous waste is in question, things become different. Indeed, the Community has adopted a Regulation which prohibits the export of hazardous waste to non-OECD countries, be it for recovery or be it for disposal purposes.[125] Where hazardous material

---

[122] OECD (n. 121 *supra*), para. 23.

[123] OECD Decision C(92)39 (n. 114 *supra*), Annex I.

[124] See in particular Decision 2000/532 replacing Decision 94/3 establishing a list of wastes pursuant to Art. 1(a) of Council Directive 75/442/EEC on waste and Council Decision 94/904/EC establishing a list of hazardous waste pursuant to Art. 1(4) of Council Directive 91/689 on hazardous waste [2000] OJ L226/3, chap. 10 02 (wastes from the iron and steel industry) and chap. 10 07 (wastes from silver, gold and platinum thermal metallurgy), etc.

[125] Regulation 120/97 [1997] OJ L22/14.

is in question, the classification of the material as "waste" or as "product" thus becomes very important. A similar application concerns the incineration of hazardous material: the incineration of hazardous waste is regulated by strict Community standards for installations which concern emission limit values, control and supervisory provisions and other issues.[126] The incineration of hazardous products is, in contrast to that, normally not regulated.

(14) In the present case, the Court of Justice was not asked whether the specific material which was transported or discharged by the defendants in the proceedings before the national court was waste or not. However, after what has been said above, there can be little doubt that the material constituted waste in all the different cases in question, though it is admitted that sometimes the borderline between "waste" and "product" is difficult to find.

45. THE LEGAL BASIS FOR WASTE MEASURES

Judgment of the Court of 28 June 1994
Case C–187/93

European Parliament
v. *Council of the European Union, supported by Spain*
[1994] ECR I–2857

Facts and Procedure

In February 1993, the Council adopted Regulation 259/93 on the shipment of waste.[127] This Regulation was adopted with a view to replacing Directive 84/631 on the shipment of hazardous waste within the Community[128] and to taking into consideration the Basel Convention on the shipment of hazardous waste,[129] the Fourth Lomè-Convention[130] and the Decision by the OECD on the shipment of waste for recovery operations.[131]

---

[126] Directive 2000/76 on the incineration of waste [2000] OJ L332/91.

[127] Regulation 259/93 on the supervision and control of shipments of waste within, into and out of the European Community [1993] OJ L30/1.

[128] Directive 84/631 on the supervision and control within the European Community of the transfrontier shipment of hazardous waste [1984] OJ L326/1.

[129] Basel Convention of 22 March 1989 on the control of transboundary movements of hazardous wastes and their disposal. The Community adhered to the Basel Convention by Decision 93/98 [1993] OJ L39/1.

[130] Fourth ACP–EEC Convention of 15 December 1989. The Community adhered to that Convention by Decision 91/400 [1991] OJ L229/1.

[131] Organisation for Economic Co-operation and Development (OECD) C(92)39 of 30 March 1992 on the control of transfrontier movements of wastes destined for recovery operations.

The Commission had based its proposal for Regulation 259/93 on Articles 95 and 133 (ex Articles 100a and 113) EC Treaty;[132] at that time, in 1990, Article 95 (ex Article 100a) provided for the procedure of co-operation between the European Parliament and the Council in the procedure for taking Community decisions, while Article 133 (ex Article 113) did not provide for any participation of the European Parliament. In its opinion on the proposal, the Parliament had agreed to that legal basis. However, the Council was of the opinion that the Regulation should rather be based on Article 175 (ex Article 130s) EC Treaty which provided, prior to May 1993, for unanimous Council decisions on which the Parliament had to be consulted. The Council consulted the European Parliament on the change of the legal basis; the Parliament was of the opinion that Articles 95 and 133 were the correct legal basis. The Council then adopted Regulation 259/93 and based it on Article 175 (ex Article 130s) EC Treaty.

The European Parliament applied to the Court as it was of the opinion that the Council had based Regulation 259/93 on the wrong legal basis.

Judgment (extracts)

14. ... an action for annulment brought by the Parliament against an act of the Council or the Commission is admissible provided that the action seeks only to safeguard its prerogatives and that it is founded only on submissions alleging their infringement.

15. In accordance with those criteria, the action must be declared inadmissible, inasmuch as it is founded on the exclusion from the legal basis of the Regulation of Article 113 of the Treaty. At the time when the Regulation was adopted, Article 113 did not provide for the European Parliament to be involved in any way in the drawing up of the acts envisaged in that article, so that its exclusion from the legal basis of the Regulation was not such as to prejudice the prerogatives of the Parliament.

16. However, in so far as it contests the fact that the Regulation is based not on Article 100a but on Article 130s of the Treaty, the application seeks to show that the prerogatives of the Parliament have been prejudiced by reason of the legal basis chosen and it is therefore admissible.

17. The Court has consistently held that, in the context of the organisation of the powers of the Community, the choice of the legal basis for a measure must be based on objective factors which are amenable to judicial review. Those factors include in particular the aim and content of the measure ...

18. As regards the aim, it is apparent in particular from the sixth and ninth recitals in the preamble to the Regulation that the system set up for the supervision and control of shipments of waste between Member States reflects the need to

---

[132] Commission [1990] OJ C289/9.

preserve, protect and improve the quality of the environment and is designed to enable the competent authorities to take all necessary measures for the protection of human health and the environment.

19. It follows from the seventh and tenth recitals that the organisation of the supervision and control of shipments of waste between Member States forms part of the package of measures taken by the Council in relation to waste management, as laid down in particular in Directive 91/156. Indeed, that directive itself states that movements of waste should be reduced and that Member States may take the necessary measures to that end in the waste management plans which they are obliged to draw up.

21. As regards the content of the Regulation, it should be noted that it sets out the conditions governing shipments of waste between Member States and the procedures to be followed for their authorisation.

22. Those conditions and procedures have all been adopted with a view to ensuring the protection of the environment, taking account of objectives falling within the scope of environmental policy such as the principles of proximity, priority for recovery and self-sufficiency at Community and national levels. In particular, they enable the Member States, for the purposes of implementing those principles, to take measures to prohibit generally or partially or to object systematically to and oppose shipments of waste which are not in conformity with Directive 75/442, cited above, as amended by Directive 91/156.

23. In those circumstances, it must be concluded that the Regulation falls within the framework of the environmental policy pursued by the Community and that it cannot be regarded, any more than Directive 91/156, as seeking to implement the free movement of waste within the Community. The Council could therefore validly exclude Article 100a of the Treaty from the legal basis of the Regulation and base it on Article 130s of the Treaty.

24. That conclusion is not invalidated by the fact that, by harmonising the conditions in which movements of waste take place, the Regulation affects such movements and thus has a bearing on the functioning of the internal market.

25. As the Court has consistently held . . . ,the mere fact that the establishment or functioning of the internal market is involved is not enough to render Article 100a of the Treaty applicable and recourse to that article is not justified where the act to be adopted has only ancillary effect of harmonising market conditions within the Community.

26. That is the position in the present case. As the Advocate General has pointed out in paragraphs 44 and 45 of his Opinion, the aim of the Regulation is not to define those characteristics of waste which will enable it to circulate freely within the internal market, but to provide a harmonised set of procedures whereby movements of waste can be limited in order to secure protection of the environment.

27. Nor can it be objected to the foregoing that the Regulation is intended to replace and repeal the aforementioned Directive 84/631, which was, for its part, based on Article 100 of the Treaty, in conjunction with Article 235.

28. The fact that the Regulation replaces another act which was based on Article 100 of the Treaty, relating to the approximation of the laws of the Member States having a direct bearing on the establishment or functioning of thec common market, does not necessarily mean that the Regulation must have recourse to Article 100 or Article 100a, which was introduced into the Treaty by the Single European Act and which provides for the adoption of measures for the approximation of the laws of the Member States which ave as their object the establishment and functioning of the internal market . . . The legal basis for an act must be determined having regard to its own aim and content.

29. It follows from all the foregoing that the application must be dismissed in its entirety.

Commentary

I. Waste and Products

(1) On page 1 *et seq* of this book, the Court's jurisprudence concerning the choice of the legal basis was discussed. While the present case appears, on its surface, to be in the tradition of the Court's jurisprudence, it has sufficient specific features to warrant a discussion of its own. These specific features are due to the fact that the material in question is waste.

Waste is a corporal object. Legislation on it is presumably as old as urban agglomerations, as the residues of human activity had to be taken care of in order to avoid environmental impairment. Industrialisation and the extension of economic activites have brought a massive increase in waste, as the residues from such production were included in the notion; at the same time, chemical inventions and the development of machinery increased the generation of hazardous waste.

(2) When the EC Treaty was elaborated, waste was not expressly included. And waste professions successfully managed to see, at least generally, waste materials excluded from the uniform customs code of the Community, arguing that waste was not a product since it had a negative economic value: it was the generator or holder of the waste who wanted to get rid of it and paid—or had to pay—a price for seeing his waste taken away.

This discussion, which is not to be reproduced here in all details, led a number of academics to consider that either waste did not come under the EC Treaty at all, since the Treaty dealt with "goods", whereas wastes were "bads", or that the waste services—the transport, security or handling services etc.—were only covered by the chapter on services, Articles 49 *et seq.*, of the EC Treaty.

(3) It was only on 1992 that the Court of Justice finally decided on that matter.[133] The Court first stated that where waste was to be recycled or recovered, this

---

[133] Court of Justice, Case C–2/90, *Commission* v. *Belgium* [1992] ECR I–4431.

was due to the economic value which the waste had and which was to be taken out of that waste by the different recycling or recovery processes. For this reason, recyclable or recoverable waste had to be considered as goods in the sense of the EC Treaty with the consequence that in particular Articles 28 *et seq.* (ex Articles 30 *et seq.*) EC Treaty were applicable.

(4) For waste which did not have such an economic value and which was just to be landfilled or otherwise disposed of, the Court had greater difficulties, as in an earlier case the Italian government had argued that antique goods did not come under the EC Treaty; the Court had countered that argument by stating that antique goods were "products which can be valued in money and which are capable, as such, of forming the subject of commercial transactions".[134] In Case C–2/90, the Court clarified that it was not the economic value but rather the possibility of being the subject of commercial transactions that was the decisive element. As waste recycling or recovery is dependent also on technology development, the price of raw materials, import possibilities etc. a differentiation of waste according to whether it had a positive or a negative market value was not practicable. For this reason, any waste material was covered by the provisions of the EC Treaty on goods, though the Court admitted that waste had "a special characteristic. The accumulation of waste, even before it becomes a health hazard, constitutes a threat to the environment because of the limited capacity of each region or locality for receiving it".[135] The classification of waste under Article 28 *et seq.* EC Treaty raised little objection and is now generally accepted.

(5) In Case C–155/91[136] the Court decided that Directive 91/156 which amended Directive 75/442 on waste[137] was rightly based on Article 175 (ex Article 130s) EC Treaty and was not to be based on Article 95 (ex Article 100a) EC Treaty, as the Commission had argued. The Court examined the aim and the content of the Directive and argued that it was the object of Directive 91/156 "to ensure the management of waste, be it of industrial or domestic origin, with a view to complying with the requirements of environmental protection"; the impact of the Directive on the internal market was only "ancillary".[138] The Commission had obviously considered that this judgment had brought the discussion on the legal basis for waste-related measures to an end; indeed, it withdrew an application to the Court related to Directive 91/689 on hazardous waste,[139] which the Council again had based on Article 175, while the Commission's proposal had been based on Article 95 EC Treaty.[140]

(6) This was the state of affairs when the present case was to be decided. It explains the obvious reluctance by the Court to re-enter into a discussion on the

---

[134] Court of Justice, Case 7/68, *Commission* v. *Italy* [1969] ECR 423.
[135] Court of Justice, Case C–2/90 (n. 133 *supra*) para. 30.
[136] Court of Justice, Case C–155/91, *Commission* v. *Council* [1993] ECR I–939.
[137] Directive 75/442 on waste [1975] OJ L194/39; amended by Directive 91/156 [1991] OJ L78/32.
[138] Court of Justice, Case C–155/91 (n. 136 *supra*), paras. 10 and 19.
[139] Directive 91/689 on hazardous waste [1991] OJ L377/20.
[140] Commission, proposal for a directive on hazardous waste [1988] OJ C295/8; amended [1990] OJ C42/19.

appropriate legal basis; the judgment contains, overall, about 12 paragraphs on this item (paragraphs 17 to 29) and makes extensive reference to the previous judgment in Case C–155/91, concluding that Regulation 259/93 "cannot be regarded, any more than directive 91/156, as seeking to implement the free movement of waste within the Community" (paragraph 23).

II. Trade in Waste

The general comments made above, page 1 *et seq*, on the distinction between principal objective and ancillary objective of a legislative measure need not be repeated here. Rather, the specific aspect of Regulation 259/93 may be raised, which concerns the shipment of waste; as such shipment is made for professional reasons, it seems justified to consider that the Regulation concerns the trade in waste by laying down conditions for such trade. These conditions include, as the Court mentions in paragraph 22, measures to protect the environment. However, it is far too short to conclude that they "all" were adopted with that purpose. Two examples may be given: non-hazardous waste, which is listed in Annex II to Regulation 259/93 may be traded, if it is traded for recovery purposes, practically without any restriction.[141] This means that Regulation 259/93 practically provides for such wastes unrestricted free circulation. It should be remembered that in 1990 "the total amount of waste generated in the 15 Member States purported to be about 910 million tonnes (exccluding agricultural waste); of those 22 million tonnes were hazardous".[142] Thus, for the great majority of all wastes, the provisions of Regulation 259/93 do regulate the trade with the objective of facilitating at least trade for recovery purposes.

(8) The second example concerns the shipment of waste for recovery within the Community. For such trade the possibility for Member States to raise objections based on environmental considerations are explicitly enumerated in Article 7(4)(a) of Regulation 259/93.[143] In Case C–203/96, the Court did not answer the question whether this constituted a final, exhaustive list of objections which may be raised against shipments of waste for recovery, but examined whether the Dutch authorities could furthermore also rely on Article 176 EC Treaty.[144] However, for the context of Regulation 259/93, it is undisputed that this enumeration is exhaustive. Thus, all the conditions and procedures which the Court mentions in paragraph 22 of its present judgment, are in fact rather limited in number. For the great majority of shipments of hazardous waste for recovery, the

---

[141] See Regulation 259/93 (n. 127 *supra*), Art. 1(3)(a): "Shipments of waste for recovery only and listed in Annex II shall also be excluded from the provisions of this Regulation except . . . (some minor exceptions are enumerated)".

[142] Commission, Communication on the review of the Community strategy for waste management, COM(96)399 of 30 July 1996, para. 17.

[143] See text of Art. 7(4)(a) on p. 28 *supra*, n. 90.

[144] Court of Justice, Case C–203/96 *Dusseldorp* [1998] ECR I–4075 (see p. 22 *supra*).

Regulation introduces the principle of prior informed consent requiring the agreement of national administrations before such waste shipments take place. However, this is not such a burden that the "other side" of these provisions can be neglected: shipments of hazardous waste for recovery may take place within the Community; Member States are not allowed to close their frontiers.

(9) Seen from this perspective, Regulation 259/93 has the objective of facilitating waste shipments within the Community, though it is true that it introduces, for hazardous waste, some specific procedures. However, that is normal and reasonable in order to reduce the risk which is inherently linked to the trade in any hazardous material, as far as possible. The Court does not discuss these aspects and thus gives the impression that the trade aspects of Regulation 259/93 were of no particular relevance for him.

(10) The Court may have been influenced by the Opinion of Advocate General Jacobs which argued, as regards the application of Article 95 or 175 EC Treaty, "a measure cannot be said to pursue an internal market objective merely because it is concerned with the movement of products between Member States . . . It must rather be asked whether the measure has the overall objective of promoting, rather than restricting, such movements. As the Council points out, it is clear in the present case that the overriding objective of the Regulation is to enable movements of waste to be prevented . . . The aim of the Regulation is not to define those characteristics of waste which will enable waste to circulate freely within the internal market; rather it is to provide a harmonised set of procedures whereby movements of waste can be prevented and controlled in accordance with national law and with the requirements imposed by the directive on waste".[145]

(11) In support of his opinion, the Advocate General quotes the case of alkaline manganese batteries the sale of which is prohibited in all Member States and concludes: "Such a restriction is imposed in order that batteries without an excessive level of mercury can circulate freely within the internal market".[146] In my opinion, this example reveals that the distinction is semantic and artificial and cannot be correct. Indeed, would then a total ban on mercury in batteries[147] be imposed "in order" to allow batteries without mercury to circulate freely within the internal market? And what would be the corresponding argument for a total ban on asbestos fibres, which was introduced for the whole of the Community in 1999?[148] It is submitted that EC-wide bans for substances or products are not decided to facilitate the free circulation of products not containing such substances or other

---

[145] Advocate General Jacobs, Opinion in Case C–187/93 [1994] ECR I–939, paras. 43 and 44.

[146] Advocate General Jacobs (n. 145 *supra*), para. 44.

[147] Such a ban was introduced in the meantime by Directive 98/101 [1998] OJ L1/1; as this Directive was a Commission directive, it did not expressly indicate the legal basis. However, as it was an amendment of Directive 91/157 on batteries [1991] OJ L78/38, which was itself based on Art. 95 EC Treaty, it may be considered that this ban was also based on that provision.

[148] Directive 99/77 [1999] OJ L207/18. This last Directive was an amendment of Directive 76/769 [1976] OJ L262/201 and thus did not indicate a legal basis.

products, but rather because such bans are product-related and therefore come under Article 95.[149]

(12) In conclusion of this point, it seems that the matter of the legal basis for waste measures was settled for the Court with Case C–155/91 and that the Court did not wish to re-open the discussion on this issue. It should not be forgotten that the choice of the legal basis also very considerably affects the delimitation of responsabilities for waste matters between the Community and Member States. It is obvious that Member States, by virtue of Article 175 EC Treaty, have greater possibilities for adopting national measures on waste management than they would have if Article 95 EC Treaty were the appropriate legal basis.

(13) The Court did not admit the Parliament's application as regards the legal basis of Article 133 (ex Article 113) EC Treaty. In this regard, it can be referred to the comments that were made concerning Parliament's prerogatives on page 1 *et seq supra*. Here only the following comment is to be added: suppose the correct legal basis for Regulation 259/93 is indeed Article 133 EC Treaty, would it not be rather embarassing if this were decided by the Court in a future case, which might occur some decades after the adoption of the Regulation in 1993? I had already referred to the principle "*da mi factum, dabo tibi ius*"[150] and it seems to me that it would make much more sense that, if the Court is asked to look at the correct legal basis of a legislative measure, all potential legal bases are examined. It is for this reason that, in my opinion, the Court should also have examined the application of Article 133 EC Treaty.

(14) The omitted examination is all the more regrettable as the Commission considered until very recently that, as regards international measures, trade-related environmental measures are to be based on Article 133 and not on Article 175 EC Treaty. For example, the Decision to adhere to the Cartagena Protocol on Biosafety which was adopted under the Convention on Biodiversity[151] must, in the opinion of the Commission, be based on Article 133 EC Treaty, as it constitutes a trade-related measure. Since the Member States are almost unanimously of the opinion that Article 175 EC Treaty is the appropriate legal basis, the Commission decided that it would ask the Court of Justice for an opinion on that matter;[152] the Court's opinion, however, came out against the opinion of the Commission.[153]

---

[149] See also the comments on p. 1 *et seq* above. In Case C–376/98, *Germany* v. *European Parliament and Council*, [2000] ECR I–8419, the Court again used its theory of "centre of gravity", this time, however, in order to state that Directive 98/43 which provides for a ban on tobacco advertising and sponsorship of tobacco products, cannot be based on Art. 95 of the Treaty. This judgment rather confirms my doubts about the theory.

[150] See p. 304 *supra*.

[151] Rio de Janeiro Convention on biological diversity of 5 June 1992; the Community adhered to this Convention by Decision 93/626 [1993] OJ L309/1.

[152] Art. 300(6) EC Treaty: "The Council, the Commission or a Member State may obtain the opinion of the Court of Justice as to whether an agreement envisaged is compatible with the provisions of this Treaty. Where the opinion of the Court of Justice is adverse, the agreement may enter into force only in accordance with Art. 48 of the Treaty on European Union".

[153] Court of Justice, Opinion 2/00 of 6 December 2001, not yet reported.

7

PROCEDURAL QUESTIONS

46. PENALTY PAYMENTS IN EC ENVIRONMENTAL LAW

Judgment of the Court of 4 July 2000
Case C–387/97

*Commission of the European Communities
supported by the United Kingdom* v. *Greece*
[2000] ECR I–5047

Facts and Procedure

On 22 September 1987, the Commission received a complaint on the waste disposal in the area of Chania (Crete). The complainant informed the Commission
that most municipalities of that region discharged their waste in an uncontrolled
way into a ravine of the river Kouroupitos close to Akrotiri village. This waste was
partly toxic and hazardous, as it included waste from military bases in the area,
hospitals and clinics, and production residues from salt factories, poultry farms,
slaughterhouses and all industrial sites in the Chania area.

The Commission informed the Greek government of these elements. The Greek
government answered on 15 March 1988; the facts were not contested. The government stated that work had started on the construction of waste disposal installations in the Chania area. The uncontrolled disposal of waste would end in
August 1988. The Commission took legal action against Greece under Article 226
EC Treaty,[1] arguing that Greece had not complied with its obligations under

---

[1] Art. 226 (ex Art. 169) EC Treaty: "If the Commission considers that a Member State has failed to
fulfil an obligation under this Treaty, it shall deliver a reasoned opinion on the matter after giving the
State concerned the opportunity to submit its observations.

   If the State concerned does not comply with the opinion within the period laid down by the
Commission, the latter may bring the matter before the court of Justice".

Articles 4 and 6 of Directive 75/442[2] and Articles 5 and 12 of Directive 78/319.[3] During the procedure before the Court, the Greek government confirmed that it would take all necessary measures to solve the problem. It would find an appropriate place for a waste landfill site, which also would be accepted by the population. Furthermore studies had been made on how the waste from the Chania region could be treated and disposed of.

The Court of Justice gave a judgment on 7 April 1992.[4] It found that pursuant to Article 145 of the Treaty of Accession, Directives 75/442 and 78/319 should have been implemented in Greece by 1 January 1981 at the latest and stated: "By failing to take the measures necessary to ensure that in the area of Chania waste and toxic and dangerous waste are disposed of without endangering human health and without harming the environment, and by failing to draw up for that area plans for the disposal of waste and of toxic and dangerous wast, the Hellenic Republic has failed to fulfil its obligations under Articles 4 and 6 of Council Directive 75/442/EEC of 15 July 1975 on waste, and Articles 5 and 12 of Council Directive 78/319/EEC of 20 March 1978 on toxic and dangerous waste".

On 21 September 1995, the Commission started new formal proceedings against Greece under Article 228(2) (ex Article 171(2)) EC Treaty,[5] as Greece had

---

[2] Directive 75/442 on waste [1975] OJ L194/39, Art. 4: "Member States shall take the necessary measures to ensure that waste is disposed of without endangering human health and without harming the environment, and in particular:—without risk to water, air, soil and plants and animals,—without causing a nuisance through noise or odours,—without adversely affecting the countryside or places of special interest".

Art. 6: "The competent authority or authorities referred to in Art. 5 shall be required to draw up as soon as possible one or several plans relating to, in particular:—the type and quantity of waste to be disposed of,—general technical requirements,—suitable disposal sites,—any special arrangements for particular wastes.

The plan or plans may, for example, cover:—the natural or legal persons empowered to carry out the disposal of waste,—the estimated costs of the disposal operations,—the estimated costs of the disposal operations,—appropriate measures to encourage rationalization, of the collection, sorting and treatment of waste".

[3] Directive 78/319 on toxic and dangerous waste [1978] OJ L84/43, Art. 5: "1. Member States shall take the necessary measures to ensure that toxic and dangerous waste is disposed of without endangering human health and without harming the environment, and in particular:—without risk to water, air, soil, plants or animals;—without causing a nuisance through noise or odours;—without adversely affecting the countryside or places of special interest. 2. Member States shall in particular take the necessary steps to prohibit the abandonment and uncontrolled discharge, tipping or carriage of toxic and dangerous waste, as well as its consignment to installations, establishments or undertakings other than those referred to in Art. 9(1)".

Art. 12: "The competent authorities shall draw up and keep up to ate plans for the disposal of toxic and dangerous waste. These plans shall cover in particular:—the type and quantity of waste to be disposed of;—the methods of disposal;—specialised treatment centres where necessary;—suitable disposal sites . . .".

[4] Court of Justice, Case C–45/91, *Commission* v. *Greece* [1992] ECR I–2509.

[5] Art. 228(2) (ex Art. 171(2)) EC Treaty: "2. If the Commission considers that the Member State concerned has not taken such measures it shall, after giving that State the opportunity to submit its observations, issue a reasoned opinion specifying the points on which the Member State concerned has not complied with the judgment of the Court of Justice. 3. If the Member State concerned fails to take the necessary measures to comply with the Court's judgment within the time-limit laid down by the Commission, the latter may bring the case before the Court of justice. In so doing it shall specify the amount of the lump sum or penalty payment to be paid by the Member State concerned which it

failed to comply with the judgment in Case C–45/91. As the discussions with the Greek government did not satisfy it, it decided to apply again to the Court. The Commission asked the Court to impose on Greece a penalty payment of 24,600 Euros for each day of delay in implementing the measures necessary to comply with the judgment in Case C–45/91.

The new application was registered on 14 November 1997.

Judgment (extracts)

[Admissibility]

42. . . . all stages of the pre-litigation procedure, including the letter of formal notice of 21 September 1995, occurred before[6] the Treaty on European Union entered into force. The letter of 11 October 1993 to which the Greek Government refers does not form part of that procedure. Second, the argument put forward by the Greek Government concerning the relevance, when setting the penalty payment, of factors and criteria relating to the past is indissociable from consideration of the substance of the case, in particular as regards the object of penalty payments under Article 171(2) of the treaty.

43. Accordingly, the plea of inadmissibility raised by the Greek Government must be rejected.

[Amendments of Directives 75/442 and 78/319]

51. . . . the obligations owed by the Hellenic Republic under Articles 4 and 6 of Directive 75/442 and Articles 5 and 12 of Directive 78/319 still apply as Community law now stands.

Scope of the obligations found not to have been fulfilled in the judgment in Case C–45/91.

55. It should be noted that, whilst Article 4 of Directive 75/442 did not specify the actual content of the measures to be taken in order to ensure that waste is disposed of without endangering human health and without harming the environment, it was none the less binding on the Member States as to objective to be achieved, while leaving to them a margin of discretion in assessing the need for such measures . . .

56. Thus the Court has held that a significant deterioration in the environment over a protracted period when no action has been taken by the competent

---

concerned which it considers appropriate in the circumstances. If the Court of Justice finds that the Member State concerened has not complied with its judgment it may impose a lump sum or penalty payment on it . . .".

[6] The judgment says "before"; however, it obviously means "after" (author's note).

authorities is in principle an indication that the Member State concerned has exceeded the discretion conferred on it by that provision . . .

57. The same analysis can be made as regards Article 5 of Directive 78/319.

58. In adition, the obligations flowing from Article 4 of Directive 75/442 and Article 5 of Directive 78/319 were independent of the more specific obligations contained in Articles 5 to 11 of Directive 442 concerning the planning, organisation and supervision of waste disposal operations and Article 12 of Directive 78/319 concerning the disposal of toxic and dangerous waste. The same is true of the corresponding obligations under Directive 75/442 as amended and Directive 91/689.

59. Accordingly, in order to determine whether the Hellenic Republic has satisfied the obligation to comply with the judgment in Case C–45/91, it must be established in turn whether each of the obligations found by that judgment not to have been fulfilled has, in so far as those obligations are mutually independent, since been complied with.

[Compliance with the obligations flowing from Article 171(1) of the Treaty]

62. It should be remembered that the present proceedings stem from a complaint received by the Commission on 22 September 1987, drawing its attention to uncontrolled waste disposal in the mouth of the river Kouroupitos, on the Akrotiri peninsula, by the majority of the municipalities in the prefecture of Chania. The waste included refuse from military bases in the area, hospitals and clinics, and residues from salt factories, poultry farms, slaughterhouses and all the industrial sites in the area.

63. In a study produced to the Court by the Greek Government entitled "Environmental Impact of Uncontrolled Solid Waste Combustion in the Kouroupitos Ravine, Crete", which was carried out in June 1996 by the Laboratory of Environmental Engineering and Management of the Technical University of Crete, in collaboration with the Institute of Ecological Chemistry, Munich, it is stated:

> ". . . The solid wastes are disposed of in the Kouroupitos ravine located approximately 30 km east of Chania, on the Akrotiri peninsula. The wastes are dumped into the ravine from the top at a distance of 200 m from the sea without any other care. The wastes have been uncontrollably burning for at least 10 years, while the burning is self-supporting due to the high levels of organic matter. The improper waste disposal combined with the uncontrolled burning of the solid wastes has resulted in an environmentally hazardous situation, with the leachate seeping into the (sea), and the products of the burning process being transferred both to land and sea".

64. As regards, first, fulfilment of the obligation imposed by Article 4 of Directive 75/442 to dispose of waste without endangering human health and without harming the environment, the Greek Government does not dispute that solid waste, in particular household refuse, is still tipped into the river Kouroupitos.

65. It is clear from the letters from the Prefecture of Chania to the Ministry of the environment of 7 and 18 August 1998, disclosed by the Greek Government, that most of the waste still ends up, in the same uncontrolled and unlawful manner, in the Kouroupitos ravine, which today receives all the household waste from the urban area of Chania.

66. The Greek Government concedes in its rejoinder that "in any event, only the definitive solution to the problem, that is to say discontinuing the operation at the river Kouroupitos and introducing a modern, lawful and effective system, could be regarded as fully satisfactory".

67. Moreover, it is apparent from paragraph 10 of the judgment in Case C–45/91 that the Greek Government had stated on 15 March 1988 in reply to the Commission that it was going to put an end to the operation of that tip after Augsut 1988 and create new disposal sites.

68. The fact remains that that has still not been done.

71. It must therefore be held that the Hellenic Republic has not complied with the judgment in Case C–45/91 inasmuch as it persists in failing to fulfil its obligations under Article 4 of Directive 75/442 . . .

72. As regards, second, fulfilment of the obligation imposed by Article 5 of Directive 78/319 to dispose of toxic and dangerous waste without endangering human health and without harming the environment, the Greek Government's assertion that toxic and dangerous waste have not been tipped into the river Kouroupitos since 1996 is supported by consideration of the file. Its assertion is disputed only partially by the Commission, which concedes that the quantities of toxic and dangerous waste have been reduced.

73. It is for the Commission in such circumstances to provide the Court, in the course of the proceedings, with the information necessary to determine the extent to which a Member State has complied with a judgment declaring it to be in breach of its obligations.

74. Since no such information is available, it has not been proved that the Hellenic Republic has failed fully to comply with the obligation to dispose of toxic and dangerous waste from the area of Chania in accordance with Article 5 of Directive 78/319.

75. As regards, third, fulfilment of the obligations to draw up waste disposal plans and to draw up, and keep up to date, plans for the disposal of toxic and dangerous waste, imposed by Article 6 of Directive 75/442 and Article 12 of Directive 78/319 respectively, it is settled case-law that incomplete practical measures or fragmentary legislation cannot discharge the obligation of a Member State to draw up a comprehensive programme with a view to attain certain objectives . . .

76. Contrary to the claims of the Greek Government, legislation or specific measures amounting only to a series of ad hoc normative interventions that are incapable of constituting an organised and coordinated system for the disposal of waste and toxic and dangerous waste cannot be regarded as plans which the Member States are required to adopt under Article 6 of Directive 75/442 and Article 12 of Directive 78/319 . . .

77. It therefore follows that the Hellenic Republic has likewise failed to comply with the judgment in Case C–45/91 inasmuch as it persists in failing to fulfil its obligations under Article 6 of Directive 75/442 and Article 12 of Directive 78/319 so far as concerns the drawing up of waste management plans and plans for the disposal of toxic and dangerous waste.

[Setting of the penalty payment]

84. In the absence of provisions in the Treaty, the Commission may adopt guidelines for determining how the lump sums or penalty payments which it intends to propose to the Court are calculated, so as, in particular, to ensure equal treatment between the Member States.

85. Memorandum 96/C 242/07 states that decisions as to the amount of a fine or penalty payment must be taken with an eye to their purpose, namely the effective enforcement of Community law. The Commission therefore considers that the amount must be calculated on the basis of three fundamental criteria: the seriousness of the infringement, its duration and the need to ensure that the penalty itself is a deterrent to continuation of the infringement and to further infringements.

86. Communication 97/C 63/02 identifies the matematical variables used to calculate the amount of penalty payments, that is to say a uniform flat-rate amount, a coefficient of seriousness, a coefficient of duration, and a factor intended to reflect the Member State's ability to pay while ensuring that the penalty payment is proportionate and has a deterrent effect, calculated on the basis of the gross domestic product of the Member State and the weighting of their votes in the Council.

87. Those guidelines, setting out the approach which the Commission proposes to follow, help to ensure that it acts in a manner which is transparent, foreseeable and consistent with legal certainty and are designed to achieve proportionality in the amounts of the penalty payments to be proposed by it.

88. The Commission's suggestion that account should be taken both of the gross domestic product of the Member State concerned and of the number of its votes in the Council appears appropriate in that it enables that Member State's ability to pay to be reflected while keeping the variation between Member States within a reasonable range.

89. It should be stressed that these suggestions of the Commission cannot bind the Court . . . However, the suggestions are a useful point of reference.

90. First, since the principal aim of penalty payments is that the Member State should remedy the breach of obligations as soon as possible, a penalty payment must be set that will be appropriate to the circumstances and proportionate both to the breach which has been found and to the ability to pay of the Member State concerned.

91. Second, the degree of urgency that the Member State concerned should fulfil its obligations may vary in accordance with the breach.

92. In that light, and as the Commission has suggested, the basic criteria which must be taken into account in order to ensure that penalty payments have coercive force and Community law is applied uniformly and effectively are, in principle, the duration of the infringement, its degree of seriousness and the ability of the Member State to pay. In applying those criteria, regard should be had in particular to the effects of failure to comply on private and public interests and to the urgency of getting the Member State concerned to fulfil its obligations.

93. In the present case, having regard to the nature of the breaches of obligations, which continue to this day, a penalty payment is the means best suited to the circumstances.

94. As regards the seriousness of the infringements and in particular the effects of failure to comply on private and public interests, the obligation to dispose of waste without endangering human health and without harming the environment forms part of the very objectives of Community environmental policy as set out in Article 130r of the EC Treaty (now, after amendment, Article 174 EC). The failure to comply with the obligation resulting from Article 4 of Directive 75/442 could, by the very nature of that obligation, endanger human health directly and harm the environment and must, in the light of the other obligations, be regarded as particularly serious.

95. The failure to fulfil the more specific obligations of drawing up a waste disposal plan and drawing up, and keeping up to date, plans for the disposal of toxic and dangerous waste, imposed by Article 6 of Directive 75/442 and Article 12 of Directive 78/319 respectively, must be regarded as serious in that compliance with those specific obligations was necessary in order for the objectives set out in Article 4 of Directive 75/442 and Article 5 of Directive 78/319 to be fully achieved.

96. Thus, contrary to the Commission's submissions, the fact that specific measures have been taken, in accordance with Article 5 of Directive 78/319, to reduce the quantities of toxic and dangerous waste cannot have a bearing on the seriousness of the failure to comply with the obligation, under Article 12 of Directive 78/319, to draw up, and keep up to date, plans for the disposal of toxic and dangerous waste.

97. In addition, account should be taken of the fact that it has not been proved that the Hellenic Republic has failed fully to comply with the obligation to dispose of toxic and dangerous waste from the area of Chania in accordance with Article 5 of Directive 78/319.

98. As regards the duration of the infringement, suffice it to state that it is considerable, even if the starting date be that on which the Treaty on European Union entered into force and not the date on which the judgment in Case C–45/91 was delivered.

99. Having regard to all the foregoing considerations, the Hellenic Republic should be ordered to pay to the Commission, into the account "EC own resources", a penalty payment of 20. 000 euro for each day of delay in implementing the measures necessary to comply with the judgment in Case C–45/91, from delivery of the present judgment until the judgment in Case C–45/91 has been complied with.

Commentary

I. The Kouroupitos Landfill

(1) This is the first judgment under the new Article 228 EC Treaty, in which the Court of Justice fixed a penalty payment. The judgment is thus likely to have considerable influence on the interpretation and handling of that Treaty provision.

The underlying case was relatively clear: considerable quantities of municipal and other waste had been discharged for years into a ravine of the River Kouroupitos in the Chania area of Crete (Greece). The Commission learned of the facts in 1987. The Greek government did not deny the facts and promised that the practice would end soon. This argument was repeated during the Court proceedings which the Commission initiated. However, when the Court gave its judgment in Case C–45/91 in 1992, the practice was still continuing. And when the second judgment was given, under Article 228 EC Treaty, Greece had still not complied with its obligations flowing from the Community Directive on waste management. At the request of the Commission, the Court thus ordered Greece to pay a daily penalty payment of 20,000 Euros.

(2) The first observation to make is on the discrepancy between the facts of the case and the claims made by the Greek government in the proceedings before the Court. Indeed, the Greek government never contested the fact that waste was discharged in an uncontrolled way and that such waste came from municipalities, hospitals and other installations which were either public or under public control or supervision. Yet, in Case C–45/91 it claimed that the Commission's application should be held inadmissible for formal reasons and, in any case, be rejected. And in the present case, Case C–387/97, Greece again was of the opinion that the Commission's application was inadmissible for formal reasons and, in any case, unfounded, despite the fact that Greece did not dispute that the uncontrolled tipping of waste in the Kouroupitos ravine continued.

(3) This way of handling the cases in Court must be a surprise. There does not seem to be consistency between the line of defence and the actual facts nor that the Greek government, which was also the defendant in the first case, Case C–45/91, undertook serious steps between the first and second judgments in order to arrange for the situation in the Chania region to be brought into line with Greece's obligations under Community law. It is well known that waste management in Greece suffers from a considerable number of deficiencies—the estimated figure of uncontrolled landfills which are in operation varies between 3,500 and 6,500—but at least the public awareness which is drawn to the situation of waste management in Greece by the different proceedings before the Court of Justice could have, one might think,

caused some further reflection on the need to improve waste management generally. As regards the present case, one might wonder what the waste management authorities of Chania, of the different municipalities, of Crete, and the police in Crete had done since 1986[7] in order to bring to an end a situation which was unhealthy, incompatible with any form of sound waste management, dangerous for the environment and hardly compatible with the provisions of Greek law.

Furthermore, the case is a model for the question to what extent governments can be believed when they affirm that a problem will "soon" be resolved or legislation "soon" be adopted. Action speaks louder than words.

(4) There is one specific problem which is of particular importance. The Greek government had argued in the present case that in particular toxic and dangerous wastes were no longer taken to the landfill[8] and the Court found that the Commission had not proven the contrary (paragraphs 73 and 74). However, the Commission does not send inspectors to Crete to examine the factual situation. Nor does it have the ability to have studies made or research executed on such factual situations, as this is too time-consuming—situations may change rather quickly—administratively too burdensome and as such studies would, in any case, depend on the co-operation of local or regional authorities. If one is serious about the factual application of environment law—whether it is Community or national environmental law—there is no option but to entrust independent bodies with the authority to investigate the practical application of the law within an undertaking, at local or regional or national level. The body can be an agency, the police or any other body, provided it has the minimum independence and the task of acting in the general (environmental) interest, in case of need also without the consent of local or regional authorities or administrations. As long as such inspections are not possible, the risk is high that many failures completely and correctly to apply environmental provisions remain unsanctioned because of lack of available data. This issue goes far beyond the application of Community environmental law, but concerns the application of environmental law generally.

(5) The judgment of the Court provided that Greece has to pay the penalty payment of 20,000 Euros per day "until the judgment in Case C–45/91 has been complied with". It is clear that Greece has thus to draw up management plans for waste and for hazardous waste for the Chania region. It is less clear, though, what Greece has to do about the illegal Kouroupitos landfill. The landfill will certainly have to be closed. However, this is not all, since waste has been tipped on this landfill for more than 15 years and, as the judgment reports in paragraph 63, continues to impair the environment. This continuing impairment of the environment would not be eliminated if the Kouroupitos landfill were closed: indeed, the odour, the risk of water pollution, of impairment of the landscape, will continue also after the closing.

---

[7] In the "Report for the hearing" of Case C–45/91, reproduced in [1992] ECR I–2509, it is mentioned, at 2510, that on 22 September 1986, heavy rainfalls had washed quantities of waste from the landfill into the sea.

[8] Para. 72 of the judgment; these arguments are further elaborated in paras. 60 and 61 of the judgment (not reproduced here).

For this reason, the only way of eliminating the risk to human health and to the environment which Article 4 of Directive 75/442 is intended to minimise, can only be taken away where the waste that was illegally dumped, is eliminated from the Kouroupitos landfill. One cannot seriously consider that Greece complies with the judgment of the Court of Justice by closing the landfill, and hundreds or thousands of tonnes of waste, among them hazardous wastes,[9] continue to lie around and perhaps to burn for a number of years. In a similar case of an illegal landfill in Naples (Italy), the Court of Justice decided that the closing of the landfill was not enough to comply with the requirements of Article 4 of Directive 75/442; as long as the wastes which had been deposited had not been taken away, the infringement of EC environmental law continued to exist.[10] This must also apply in the present case.

Therefore, compliance with the judgment in Case C–45/91 will be only achieved once the waste which is stored at present in the Kouroupitos landfill has been taken away and brought to an authorised landfill and where the site has been restored. The Commission, however, was of the opinion that a removal of the waste was not necessary, as it had not been requested by the Court of Justice. Therefore, it accepted that Greece stopped the payment of the penalty once the unauthorised landfill had been closed. Overall, Greece paid some two million Euro.

II. The Penalty Payment According to Article 228 EC Treaty

(6) The Commission had set up, in a memorandum of 1996[11] and in a communication of 1997,[12] its considerations for calculating the amount of the penalty payment which it would apply in its application under Article 228 (ex Article 171) EC Treaty. The memorandum of 1996 indicated in eight points which criteria the Commission intended to apply as regards its proposals for the fixing of a penalty payment. The Commission indicated that the seriousness of the infringement, its duration and the necessity of a deterrent effect were the three basic criteria which had to be examined in each case. The seriousness would also be measured with regard to the importance of the legal provisions which had not been respected and, furthermore, with regard to the consequences of the infringement for the general interest and for individual interests. The importance of Community provisions would not depend on their rank in the hierarchy of standards, but rather on their nature and effects. The consequences of the infringement were to be examined case by case. In any case, symbolic sanctions would not have a deterrent effect on Member States.

(7) The Communication of 1997 detailed the calculation method for the penalty payment. The Commission was of the opinion that there should be a fixed basic

---

[9] In para. 61 the present judgment indicates that the Greek government had stated that "toxic and hazardous waste from the American military base at Souda has not been deposited in the Kouroupitos ravine since 1996". This implies that such toxic and hazardous waste was deposited there until 1996.

[10] Court of Justice, Case C–365/97, *Commission* v. *Italy* [1999] ECR I–7773 (see on this case p. 341 *supra*).

[11] Commission, Communication 96/C 242/07 of 21 August 1996 [1996] OJ C242/6.

[12] Commission, Communication on the method of calculating the penalty payments pursuant to Art. 171 EC Treaty [1997] OJ C63/2.

amount of 500 Euros for each case. This amount had first to be multiplied by a figure that was fixed according to the seriousness of the infringement and varied, according to the importance of Community provisions at stake and the relevance of the infringement for general and individual interests, between one and 20. As regards the duration, a multiplication coefficient between one and three was to be applied.

Finally, the ability of each Member State to pay the penalty was to be taken into consideration. The Commission fixed, according to a specific calculation method, for each Member State a specific factor which had to be multiplied by the basic amount.[13]

Applying these criteria to the present case, the Commission considered that the seriousness of the Greek infringement rated six and the duration two. The formula to apply was thus: $500 \times 6 \times 2 \times 4.1$ which resulted in the Commission's application of 24,600 Euros.

(8) The Court confirmed that the criteria established by the Commission—the duration of the infringement, degree of seriousness and ability of the Member State to pay—are appropriate (paragraph 92), though it underlined that the Court of Justice was not bound by the method of calculation (paragraph 89). The Court did not specify how it reached the amount of 20,000 Euros per day. It may be assumed that the Court essentially followed the Commission's method of calculation and made a deduction, as the Commission had not proved that Article 5 of Directive 78/319 continued to be disregarded by Greece.

(9) Overall, the threat of having to pay a financial penalty under Article 228(2) appears to have a considerable preventive effect on Member States. The Commission has, in the past, decided to apply to the Court under Article 228(2) EC Treaty in the following environmental cases:

—Italy; non-compliance with the judgment in Case C–33/90 (absence of waste management plans in Campania);[14] 123,300 Euros per day;
—Germany; non-compliance with the judgment in Case C–131/88 (absence of legislation on groundwater protection);[15] 264,000 Euros per day;
—Belgium; non-compliance with the judgment in Case C–247/85 (incomplete transposition of Directive 79/409 on the protection of wild birds);[16] 7,750 Euros per day;
—Germany; non-compliance with the judgment in Case C–58/89 (failure to adopt legislation to transpose Directive 75/440 on the quality of surface water into German law);[17] 158,400 Euros per day;
—Germany; non-compliance with the judgment in Case C–288/88 (incorrect transposition of the hunting rules of Directive 79/409 on the protection of wild birds);[18] 26,400 Euros per day;

---

[13] Commission (n. 11 *supra*), para. 4: Belgium 6.2; Denmark 3.9; Germany 26.4; Greece 4.1; Spain 11.4; France 21.1; Ireland 2.4; Italy 17.7; Luxembourg 1.0; Netherlands 7.6; Austria 5.1; Portugal 3.9; Finland 3.3; Sweden 5.2; United Kingdom 17.8.

[14] Court of Justice, Case C–33/90, *Commission* v. *Italy* [1991] ECR I–5987.

[15] Court of Justice, Case C–131/88, *Commission* v. *Germany* [1991] ECR I–825.

[16] Court of Justice, Case 247/85, *Commission* v. *Belgium* [1987] ECR 3073.

[17] Court of Justice, Case C–58/89, *Commission* v. *Germany* [1991] ECR I–4983.

[18] Court of Justice, Case C–288/88, *Commission* v. *Germany* [1990] ECR I–2721.

—France; non-compliance with the judgment in Case C–252/85 (incomplete transposition of the provisions of Directive 79/409 on the protection of wild birds);[19] 105,500 Euros per day;

—United Kingdom; non-compliance with the judgment in Case C–56/90 (quality of bathing waters in Southport and Blackpool);[20] 106,800 Euros per day;

—Germany; non-compliance with the judgment in Case C–301/95 (partial transposition of Directive 85/337 on environment impact assessment;[21] 237,600 Euros per day.

With the exception of the case against France, none of these cases had actually been submitted to the Court until end of the year 2000, because either the case was resolved beforehand or the Commission's decision to apply to the Court has not yet been executed.

(10) Generally, environmental procedures under Article 226 EC Treaty take a long time.[22] For environmental procedures under Article 228 EC Treaty, the overall time practically has to be doubled, though the number of cases brought under Article 228 (ex Article 171) EC Treaty is very small. The Court has, since 1992, given judgments under Article 228 (ex Article 171) EC Treaty in five environmental cases.[23] The duration of the proceedings between the dispatch of the letter of formal notice under the procedure of Article 226 and the judgment in the procedure under Article 228 EC Treaty was 109, 106, 175, 120 and 134 months: as a minimum, the procedure thus took nine years. It is submitted that this is much too long, in particular, if one considers that between the obligation of the Member State to comply with Community environmental law and the beginning of formal proceedings under Article 226 EC Treaty, normally a considerable laps of time occurs; thus, in the present case, the Court of Justice rightly observed that waste should be treated and disposed of in the Chania area in conformity with Community environmental law since 1981. Either the Commission changes its working methods under Articles 226 and 228 EC Treaty, or only the most flagrant and persistent cases of failure to comply with Community environmental provisions will be caught by Article 228 EC Treaty.

(11) The financial sanction under Article 228 EC Treaty is the only sanction which the Community has at its disposal in environmental matters. In the year 2000, though, the Commission cautiously started to develop a new instrument: referring to the new Article 6 of the EC Treaty[24] it informed Member States that financial

[19] Court of Justice, Case 252/85, *Commission* v. *France* [1988] ECR 2243.

[20] Court of Justice, Case C–56/90, *Commission* v. *United Kingdom* [1993] ECR I–4109 (see also p. 53–4 *supra*).

[21] Court of Justice, Case C–301/95, *Commission* v. *Germany* [1998] ECR I–6135.

[22] Figures on the average length of environmental procedures are given above.

[23] Court of Justice, cases C–345/92, *Commission* v. *Germany* [1993] ECR I–1115; C–174/91, *Commission* v. *Belgium* [1993] ECR I–2275; C–366/89, *Commission* v. *Italy* [1993] ECR I–4201; C–291/93, *Commission* v. *Italy* [1994] ECR I–859; C–387/97, *Commission* v. *Greece* [2000] ECR I–5047(the present judgment).

[24] Art. 6 EC Treaty: "Environmental protection requirements must be integrated into the definition and implementation of the Community policies and activities referred to in Art. 3, in particular with a view to promoting sustainable development".

support under the Structural Funds and other Community instruments could not be made available, as long as the Member States had not sent in the lists of habitat sites which Member States should have drawn up by 1995 under Directive 92/43.[25] The Commission specified that it had to ensure that the financial funds made available by the different financial instruments did not lead to a destruction or deterioration of habitats which Member States had to protect under Community environmental legislation.[26] According to media report, this link led to a considerable acceleration of the establishment of the lists in some Member States.

47. ACCESS TO EUROPEAN COURTS

Order of the Court of First Instance (First Chamber) of 9 August 1995 Case T–585/93

Stichting Greenpeace Council (Greenpeace International) and 18 other applicants v. *Commission of the European Communities, supported by Spain*
[1995] ECR II–2205

Judgment of the Court of 2 April 1998 Case C–321/95P

Appeal by Stichting Greenpeace Council (Greenpeace International) and Others v. *Commission of the European Communities, supported by Spain*
[1998] ECR I–1651

Facts and Procedure

Council Regulation 2052/88 on the tasks of the Structural Funds and their effectiveness and on co-ordination of their activities between themselves and with the operations of the European Investment Banks and the other financial instruments

---

[25] Directive 92/43 on the conservation of natural habitats and of wild fauna and flora [1992] OJ L206/7.
[26] See Commission IP/00/266 of 16 March 2000: "*La Commission définit l'articulation entre la mise en oeuvre des actions structurelles et le respect des engagements Natura 2000*".

provides among others:[27] "Measures financed by the funds or receiving assistance from the EIB or from another existing financial instrument shall be in keeping with the provisions of the Treaties, with the instruments adopted pursuant thereto and with Community policies, including those concerning . . . environmental protection".

On 7 March 1991, the Commission adopted a decision by which it granted Spain financial assistance from the European Regional Development Fund up to a maximum of 108,578,419 ECU (Euros) for the construction of two power stations in the Canary Islands, on Grand Canaria and on Tenerife. By letter dated 23 December 1991, two of the applicants informed the Commission that the works carried out in Gran Canaria were unlawful, because no environment impact assessment according to Directive 85/337[28] had been undertaken; they asked the Commission to intervene to stop the works. At the end of 1992, another applicant informed the Commission that work had already started on both power stations without an environmental impact assessment having been made. On 3 December 1992, two declarations of environmental impact relating to the construction of the two power stations were issued which were, in February and March 1993, published in the *Boletín Oficial de Canarias.* Subsequently, several applicants brought legal proceedings before Spanish courts against the administrative authorisations for the two power stations and against the declarations of environmental impact.

At the end of 1993, the applicants applied to the Court of First Instance seeking annulment of a decision allegedly taken by the Commission to pay the Spanish Government a sum of 12 million ECU in reimbursement of expenses incurred in the construction of two power stations in the Canary Islands. The Commission raised an objection of inadmissibility, amongst others because the applicants lacked *locus standi.* The Court of First Instance declared the action inadmissible, as the applicants had no *locus standi* according to Article 230 (ex Article 173) EC Treaty.[29]

The applicants appealed against that judgment, arguing that the Court of First Instance erred in its interpretation of Article 230 EC Treaty.

---

[27] Regulation 2052/88 [1988] OJ L185/9, Art. 7.

[28] Directive 85/337 on the assessment of the effects of certain public and private projects on the environment [1985] OJ L175/40.

[29] Art. 230 (ex Art. 173) EC Treaty: "The Court of Justice shall review the legality of acts adopted jointly by the European Parliament and the Council, of acts of the Council, of the Commission and of the ECB, other than recommendations and opinions, and of acts of the European Parliament intended to produce legal effects vis-à-vis third parties.

It shall for this purpose have jurisdiction in actions brought by a Member State, the Council or the Commission on grounds of lack of competence, infringement of an essential procedural requirement, infringement of this Treaty or of any rule of law relating to its application, or misuse of powers.

. . . Any natural or legal person may, under the same conditions, institute proceedings against a decision addressed to that person or against a decision which, although in the form of a regulation or a decision addressed to another person, is of direct and individual concern to the former.

The proceedings provided for in this Article shall be instituted within two months of the publication of the measure, or of its notification to the plaintiff, or, in the absence thereof, of the day on which it came to the knowledge of the latter, as the case may be".

I. Order of the Court of First Instance (extracts)

[The *locus standi* of the applicants who are private individuals]

48. It has been consistently held that persons other than the addressees may claim that a decision is of direct concern to them only if that decision affects them by reason of certain attributes which are peculiar to them, or by reason of factual circumstances which differentiate them from all other persons and thereby distinguish them individually in the same way as the person addressed . . .

49. Before considering whether the conditions laid down in that line of authority are met in the present instance, it is appropriate to examine first the merits of the applicants' argument that when determining the admissibility of their action the Court should free itself from the restrictions those authorities impose, which are that third-party applicants must establish that they are affected by the contested measure in the same way as the addressee of the decision, and concentrate rather on the sole fact that they have suffered or potentially will suffer detriment or loss from the harmful environmental effects arising out of unlawful conduct on the part of the Community institutions . . . the applicants stress here that their interests affected by the contested decision are not economic, as has been the case in almost all the judgments delivered in relation to Article 173 of the Treaty, but of a quite different kind, relating to environmental and health protection.

50. The Court observes that whilst the abovementioned line of authorities comprises judgments given mostly in cases concerning, in principle, economic interests, it is none the less true that the essential criterion applied in those judgments—in substance, a combination of circumstances sufficient for the third-party applicant to be able to claim that he is affected by the contested decision in a manner which differentiates him from all other persons—remains applicable, whatever the nature, economic or otherwise, of those of the applicants' interests which are affected.

51. Consequently, the criterion which the applicants seek to have applied, restricted merely to the existence of harm suffered or to be suffered, cannot alone suffice to confer locus standi on an applicant, since such harm may affect, generally and in the abstract, a large number of persons who cannot be determined in advance in a way which distinguishes them individually in the same way as the addressee of a decision, in accordance with the case-law cited above. That conclusion cannot be affected by the fact, put forward by the applicants . . . that in the practice of national courts in matters relating to environmental protection locus standi may depend merely on their having a "sufficient" interest, since *locus standi* under the fourth paragraph of Article 173 of the Treaty depends on meeting the conditions relating to the applicants' being directly and individually affected by the contested decision . . .

52. The applicants' argument that their *locus standi* in this case should be assessed in the light of criteria other than those already set down in the case-law cannot, therefore, be accepted.

53. It must therefore be considered whether the applicants are in this instance individually concerned by the contested decision by reason of certain attributes which are peculiar to them, or by reason of factual circumstances which differentiate them from all other persons and thereby distinguish them individually in the same way as the addressee of that decision.

54. The applicants are 16 private individuals who rely either on their objective status as "local resident", "fisherman" of "farmer" or on their position as persons concerned by the consequences which the building of two power stations might have on local tourism, on the health of Canary Island residents and on the environment. They do not, therefore, rely on any attribute substantially distinct from those of all the people who live or pursue an activity in the areas concerned and so for them the contested decision, in so far as it grants financial assistance for the construction of two power stations on Gran Canaria and Tenerife, is a measure whose effects are likely to impinge on, objectively, generally and in the abstract, various categories of person and in fact any person residing or staying temporarily in the areas concerned.

55. The applicants thus cannot be affected by the contested decision other than in the same manner as any other local resident, fisherman, farmer or tourist who is, or might be in the future, in the same situation. . .

56. Nor can the fact that the second, fifth and sixth applicants have submitted a complaint to the Commission constitute a special circumstance distinguishing them individually from all other persons and thereby giving them locus standi to bring an action under Article 173 of the Treaty. No specific procedures are provided for whereby individuals may be associated with the adoption, implementation and monitoring of decisions taken in the field of financial assistance granted by the ERDF. Merely submitting a complaint and subsequently exchanging correspondence with the Commission cannot therefore give a complainant *locus standi* to bring an action under Article 173. As the Court of Justice has held, although a person who asks an institution, not to take a decision in respect of him, but to open an inquiry with regard to third parties, may be considered to have an indirect interest, he is nevertheless not in the precise legal position of the actual or potential addressee of a measure which may be annulled under Article 173 of the Treaty . . .

57. It follows that the circumstances on which the applicants rely are not sufficient to differentiate them from all other persons and thus distinguish them individually in the same way as the addressee of the decision.

[The *locus standi* of the applicant associations]

59. It has consistently been held that an association formed for the protection of the collective interests of a category of persons cannot be considered to be directly and individually concerned for the purposes of the fourth paragraph of Article 173 of the Treaty by a measure affecting the general interests of that category, and is therefore not entitled to bring an action for annulment where its members may not do so individually . . . Furthermore, special circumstances such as the role played by an association in a procedure which led to the adoption of an act within the meaning of Article 173 of the Treaty may justify holding admissible an action brought by an association whose members are not directly and individually concerned by the contested measure . . .

60. The three applicant associations, Greenpeace, TEA and CIC, claim that they represent the general interest, in the matter of environmental protection, of people residing on Gran Canaria and Tenerife and that their members are affected by the contested decision; they do not, however, adduce any special circumstances to demonstrate the individual interest of their members as opposed to any other person residing in those areas. The possible effect on the legal position of the members of the applicant associations cannot, therefore, be any different from that alleged hereby the applicants who are private individuals. Consequently, inso far as the applicants in the present case who are private individuals cannot, as the Court has held . . . be considered to be individually concerned by the contested decision, nor can the members of the applicant associations, as local residents of Gran Canaria and Tenerife.

65. Consequently, without there being any need to consider whether a decision capable of being challenged in an action under Article 173 of the Treaty exists in the present case and whether the applicants are directly concerned by the contested decision, the application must be declared inadmissible.

II. Judgment of the Court (extracts)

27. The interpretation of the fourth paragraph of Article 173 of the Treaty that the Court of First Instance applied in concluding that the applicants did not have locus standi is consonant with the settled case-law of the Court of Justice.

28. As far as natural persons are concerned, it follows from the case-law . . . that where, as in the present case, the specific situation of the applicant was not taken into consideration in the adoption of the act, which concerns him in a general and abstract fashion and, in fact, like any other person in the same situation, the applicant is not individually concerned by the act.

29. The same applies to associations which claim to have locus standi on the basis of the fact that the persons whom they represent are individually concerned by the contested decision. For the reasons given in the preceding paragraph, that is not the case.

30. In appraising the appellants' arguments purporting to demonstrate that the case-law of the Court of Justice, as applied by the Court of First Instance, takes no account of the nature and specific characteristics of the environmental interests underpinning their action, it should be emphasised that it is the decision to build the two power stations in question which is liable to affect the environmental rights arising under Directive 85/337 that the appellants seek to invoke.

31. In those circumstances, the contested decision, which concerns the Community financing of those power stations, can affect those rights only indirectly.

32. As regards the appellants' argument that application of the Court's case-law would mean that, in the present case, the rights which they derive from Directive 85/337 would have no effective judicial protection at all, it must be noted that, as is clear from the file, Greenpeace brought proceedings before the national courts challenging the administrative authorisations issued to Unelco concerning the construction of those power stations. TEA and CIC also lodged appeals against CUMAC's declaration of environmental impact relating to the two construction projects . . .

33. Although the subject-matter of those proceedings and of the action brought before the Court of First Instance is different, both actions are based on the same rights afforded to individuals by Directive 85/337, so that in the circumstances of the present case those rights are fully protected by the national courts which may, if need be, refer a question to this Court for a preliminary ruling under Article 177 of the Treaty.

34. The Court of First Instance did not therefore err in law in determining the question of the appellants' locus standi in the light of the criteria developed by the Court of Justice in the case-law set out at paragraph 7 of this judgment.

35. In those circumstances the appeal must be dismissed.

Commentary

I. Action in the General Interest and "Direct and Individual Concern"

(1) The proverb "*da mi factum, dabo tibi ius*" has already been quoted elsewhere in this book.[30] It needs to be quoted a third time. The discussion of the case must start with the Order of the Court of First Instance. In this regard it is submitted that the Court simply omitted to discuss Article 6(2) of Directive 85/337.[31] This provision deals with the procedure to be follwed in the case of an environmental impact assessment and reads:

"Member States shall ensure that:
— any request for development consent and any information gathered pursuant to Article 5 are made available to the public,
— the public concerned is given the opportunity to express an opinion before the project is initiated".

(2) Thus, the provision very clearly distinguishes between "public" and "public concerned". The latter has a specific right, namely the right to express an opinion before a project is initiated. And it may well be assumed that the appeal

---

[30] See pp. 309 and 389 *supra.*
[31] Directive 85/337 (n. 28 *supra*)

judgment of the Court of Justice which mentions "environmental rights" arising under Directive 85/337[32] also has this right of Article 6(2) in mind. This be as it may: the fact remains that for each project for which an environmental impact assessment has to be made, it is possible to determine with sufficient precision in advance which is the "public concerned" that has the right to express an opinion before the project is initiated. The persons belonging to the public concerned are differentiated from all other persons living on the Canary Islands. Directive 85/337 has singled them out and conferred on them a right which the other residents of the Canary Islands do not have.

(3) The provision of Directive 85/337, Article 6(2), is not mentioned at all in the whole Order of the Court of First Instance. It is true that neither of the applicants had raised it. However, it is submitted that the application of the relevant Community law provisions is up to the Court; the Court of First Instance should therefore have mentioned and discussed this provision.

I have no doubt that the provision of Article 6(2) gives persons and associations which belong to the "public concerned" a right the application of which can be enforced in courts.[33] Thus, in my opinion, the Court of First Instance erred in law by declaring the applicants' claim inadmissible using the arguments that it did. And the Court of Justice, having been made aware of that provision by the applicants during the appeal procedure as well as by the Advocate General's Opinion, was very succinct in its appeal judgment and discussed the question of *locus standi* in only seven paragraphs (paragraphs 27 to 33). It admitted that the applicants had "rights", but declared that these rights were affected only indirectly. Obviously, the Court of Justice did not wish to recognise that the Court of First Instance, by declaring that the applicants had no rights, had erred in law. Nor did it explicitly state that the argument for rejecting the applicants's claim had changed: while the Court of First Instance had declared "no rights", the Court of Justice argued: "well rights, but only indirectly affected".

One would have wished that the legal reasoning in such an important environmental case had been stated more clearly.[34]

---

[32] Judgment in Case C–321/95P, para. 30; paras. 31 and 32 mention "rights" which are derived from that Directive.

[33] See also Advocate General Elmer, Court of Justice, Case C–72/95, *Kraaijeveld* [1996] ECR I–5431, para. 70: "According to Art. 6(2) of the directive, it is for the Member States to ensure that any request for development consent and any information gathered are made available to the public and that the public concerned is given an opportunity to express an opinion before the project is initiated. The directive thus requires the Member States to introduce a consultation procedure to give individuals the right to express their opinion. Where a Member State's implementation of the directive is such that projects which are likely to have significant effects on the environment are not made the subject of an environmental impact assessment, the citizen is prevented from exercising his right to be heard. The Member State's own negligent implementation of the directive thus deprives the citizen of a right under the directive . . . In those circumstances my view is that Arts. 2(1) and 4(2) of the directive, in conjunction with Art. 6(2), confer rights on individuals". Advocate General Cosmas in the present appeal Case C–321/95P, paras. 59 and 60, agreed to that interpretation.

As regards Case C–72/95, see p. 42 *supra*.

[34] See J Jans, *European Environmental Law* (2nd edn., Europa Law Publishing, Amsterdam, 2000), p. 219: "The reasons given for the judgment are meagre and it is based on two fairly weak pillars";

(4) As the applicants had attacked the Commission's decision to finance the construction of the power stations and not the construction without environmental impact assessment itself, the question then is whether the applicants were affected directly or indirectly by the Commission's decision. The Court of First Instance did not discuss this question. The Court of Justice was of the opinion that the applicants' rights were (directly) affected by the Spanish decision to build the two power stations; then the Commission's decision could affect them only indirectly.

(5) However, the Commission's decision to finance the two projects which was taken in breach of the Commission's obligations under Article 7 of Regulation 2052/88[35] signalled to the Spanish authorities that the project could be initiated; its subsequent decisions to pay financial assistance signalled that Community law did not oppose continuation of the work. At least, it cannot be ruled out that the two projects had not been started and continued, if the Commission had assumed its obligations under Community law and had refused to pay or to continue to pay financial assistance. The Commission's decision has thus, in my opinion, affected the applicants in a direct way, and it is the lawfulness of this decision which is questioned, not the decision by the Spanish authorities to allow the two projects to be built.

(6) Jans[36] is right in comparing the applicants' situation with that of a third party in a case of state aid: a competitor is entitled under Article 230 EC Treaty to contest the legality of payment of state aid to another undertaking.[37] Thus, had the applicants been competitors with economic interests, they would have been regarded as directly affected. As they "only" have an environmental right under Article 6(2) of Directive 85/337, the Court of Justice considers them to be indirectly affected.

The Court of Justice considers that the applicants could find their right under Article 6(2) of Directive 85/337 in the proceedings before the Spanish courts, as in that procedure the legality of the decision to initiate the construction of the two power plants without environmental impact assessment was examined. However, first, not all applicants have filed such a case before the national court. Secondly, the question of the application of Article 230 EC Treaty cannot be made dependant on the question whether a case has been filed or could be filed before a national court. Finally, it is by no means ensured that a national court concludes that a project which was initiated without an environmental impact assessment is illegal; for instance, German courts consider the omission of an environmental impact assessment to be a procedural fault which is not of relevance for the pro-

---

L Krämer [2000] *Europäische Grundrechte Zeitschrift* 269: "rechtlich unrichtig und rechtspolitisch bedauerlich" (legally wrong and regrettable from the point of view of legal policy); N Gérard [1998] *Journal of Environmental Policy* 343: "parsimonious".

[35] Regulation 2052/88 (see n. 27 *supra*), Art. 7.

[36] J Jans (n. 34 *supra*), p. 219.

[37] See for the discussion of such a case p. 110 *supra*, Court of First Instance, Case T–150/95 *UK Steel* v. *Commission* [1997] ECR II–1433.

ject itself. Thus, it is by no means clear that the applicants' rights under Article 6(2) "are fully protected by the national courts", as the Court stated.

(7) From the point of view of legal policy the judgment must be regretted, as it shows that the financing of major projects by the Commission which are environmentally doubtful cannot really be challenged in a European Court. Member States and the project developer will hardly oppose the financing decisions, as they profit from them. How then shall environmental aspects be defended against financing decisions by the Commission or, for example, the European Investment Bank? Also financial institutions have environmental responsabilities.

II. Access to European Courts in Environmental Matters

(8) Until the end of the year 2000, all applications by individual persons or by environmental organisations which wanted to challenge a measure taken by the Community in order to defend the environment were declared inadmissible by the Court of Justice. Thus, in Case C–131/92,[38] a fisherman objected to the ban on drift-nets of more than 2.5 km length, which had been fixed by Regulation 345/92.[39] The Court found that the applicant was not directly and individually affected by the ban. Several years later, the Court of First Instance confirmed this assessment in another case where again drift-nets were in question.[40]

(9) In Case T–460/92,[41] the applicants opposed a decision by the European Investment Bank to cofinance a motorway project around Lyon (France). The Court of First Instance ruled that decisions by the Bank to grant loans could not be attacked by third persons who did not benefit from the loan. In Case T–475/93,[42] the applicants tackled the provisions of Regulation 259/93 on the shipment of waste,[43] arguing that these provisons destroyed their established business relationships with German waste holders. The Court of First Instance considered that the applicants were not individually and directly affected by the regulation. The Court did not consider whether a fundamental right of property of the applicants had been affected.

In Case T–461/93,[44] the applicants tackled the Commission's decision not to withdraw funds for the Mullaghmore tourist centre, given to Ireland under the Regional Fund system. The Court of First Instance held that the Commission had not taken a

---

[38] Court of Justice, Case C–131/92, *Arnaud and others* v. *Council* [1993] ECR I–2573.

[39] Regulation 345/92 [1992] OJ L42/15.

[40] Court of First Instance, Case T–138/98, *Armement Coopératif Artisanal Vendéen and others* v. *Council* [2000] ECR II–341.

[41] Court of First Instance, Case T–460/93, *Tate and others* v. *European Investment Bank* [1993] ECR II–1257.

[42] Court of First Instance, Case T–475/93, *Buralux and others* v. *Council*, not published in ECR; the appeal was rejected, Court of Justice, Case C–209/94P [1996] ECR I–615.

[43] Regulation 259/93 on the supervision and control of shipments of waste within, into and out of the European Community [1993] OJ L30/1.

[44] Court of First Instance, Case T–461/93, *An Taisce and others* v. *Commission* [1994] ECR II–733. The appeal was rejected: Court of Justice, Case C–325/94P [1996] ECR I–3727.

decision, so that the applicants could not tackle it. In Case T–117/94[45] a Commission decision under Regulation 1973/92, the environmental LIFE Fund[46] was attacked, which intended to promote nature protection measures in the Po valley. The applicants were considered not to be directly affected by the Commission decision.

The conclusion seems to be that financial decisions by Community institutions are not capable of being attacked by individuals, even if the money is used in disregard of existing Community environmental provisions. Access to justice against measures by Community institutions is underdeveloped.[47]

(10) In 1998, a United Nations Convention on access to information, public participation and access to justice in environmental matters was agreed in Aarhus (Denmark). It suggests that contracting parties give the public wide access to justice, and that non-governmental organisations "promoting environmental protection and meeting any requirements under national law" shall be deemed to have a sufficient interest to be concerned by an administrative decision affecting the environment or shall be deemed to have rights capable of being impaired where national law so requires. The Community and its Member States all signed the Convention. If the Community adheres to the Convention, it will have to adopt measures on access to justice in environmental matters, probably both to the European courts as well as to national courts.

48. PRELIMINARY JUDGMENTS

Judgment of the Court (Sixth Chamber) of 29 September 1999
Case C–231/97

Preliminary ruling in the proceedings between A.M.L. van Rooij
and Dagelijks Bestuur van het Waterschap de Dommel,
third party: Gebr. Van Aarle BV
[1999] ECR I–6366

Facts and Procedure

Directive 76/464 on pollution caused by certain dangerous substances discharged into the aquatic environment of the Community[48] was adopted in 1976 in the con-

---

[45] Court of First Instance, Case T–117/94, *Rovigo and others* v. *Commission* [1995] ECR II–455. The appeal was rejected: Court of Justice, Case C–142/95P [1996] ECR I–6669.

[46] Regulation 1973/92 [1992] OJ L206/1.

[47] See also L Krämer, "Public Interest Litigation in Environmental Matters before European Courts", in H Micklitz and N Reich (eds.), *Public Interest Litigation before European Courts* (Nomos, Baden-Baden, 1996), 297 *et seq.*

[48] Directive 76/464 [1976] OJ L129/23. On this Directive see also p. 177 *supra*.

text of Community measures to combat water pollution. It provided for the obligation of prior authorisation for any discharge into waters (Article 3) and requested Member States to establish pollution reduction programmes for certain dangerous substances (Article 7). Substances which were selected according to their toxicity, bioaccumulation and persistance were to be regulated at Community level (Article 6). Discharge was defined as "the introduction into the waters referred to in paragraph 1 of any substances in List I or List II of the Annex, with the exception of:—discharges of dredgings,—operational discharges from ships in territorial waters, dumping from ships in territorial waters" (Article 1(2)(d)).

The Dutch undertaking Gebr. Van Aarle BV operates a wood treatment business for improving the preservation of wood. During the wood impregnation process, steam is released which is then precipitated directly or indirectly on to nearby surface water, in particular a ditch at the back of the undertaking's premises which is dry for part of the year.

Mr. van Rooij lives next to the premises of the undertaking. He claimed that the steam is polluted by arsenic, copper and chromium and asked the competent authority to take measures with respect to the undertaking Van Aarle. This request was rejected. Mr. van Rooij brought the case to court, where he argued that both the direct precipitation of polluted steam and indirect introduction into surface water, via storm water drain, of steam which has been precipitated on to land or roofs in the vicinity of the Van Aarle undertaking must be regarded as discharges under Dutch legislation.

The Dutch court had doubts whether the decision on the dispute could be influenced by the meaning which Directive 76/464 gave to the notion of "discharge". Therefore, it stayed proceedings and referred the following questions to the Court of justice for a preliminary ruling:

"1. Must the term 'discharge' in Article 1(2)(d) of Council Directive 76/464/EEC . . . be interpreted as covering precipitation of contaminated steam on to surface water? Is the distance from which the steam in question is precipitated on to the surface water relevant in that respect?

2. Does the term 'discharge' cover steam which is first precipitated on to land and roofs and then reaches the surface water via a storm water drain, whether belonging to the establishment concerned or to residential or other buildings? Is it material to the reply to be given to this question whether the contaminated steam reaches the surface water via the storm water drain of the establishment concerned or via that of a third party?

3. If questions 1 and/or 2 are answered in the negative, is it permissible for national legislation to assign a different, more wide-ranging meaning to the term 'discharge' than that in the directive?"

Judgment (extracts)

23. As regards the facts of the main proceedings, it is common ground that the emission of steam is caused by an act attributable to a person, namely the process by which Van Aarle's employees impregnate the wood with a preservative by means of a steam fixation method; that the steam emitted contains arsenic, copper and chromium, which are substances mentioned in List II of the Annex to Directive 76/464; and that the steam is precipitated on waters which fall within the scope of the directive when the ditch behind Van Aarle's premises is not dry.

24. The French Government, however, disputes that in a situation such as that at issue in the main proceedings the emission of steam may be regarded as constituting a discharge within the meaning of Directive 76/464. It submits in particular that the directive, as shown by its title which refers to substances "*déversées*" (discharged) into the aquatic environment of the Community, applies only to pollution caused by discharges of liquid substances into another liquid environment. In the present case, however, the pollution is caused by steam, not by liquid substances.

25. It must be observed in this respect that while the term "*déversées*" used in the title of the French-language version of Directive 76/464 appears, in its generally accepted meaning, to support the interpretation put forward by the French Government, it is not, however, reserved exclusively to operations with liquids and may also be applied to solids. It is likewise the case that the Dutch, Danish and Greek version use the terms in the title of the directive—"*geloosd*", "*udledning*" and "*exchéontai*" respectively—which imply that the substance concerned is in the liquid state. However, the title of the directive in the other language versions does not support such an interpretation. The terms "discharged" (English version), "*Ableitung*" (German version), "*vertidas*" (Spanish version), "*scaricate*" (Italian version), "*lancadas*" (Portuguese version), "*utsläpp*" (Swedish version) and "*päästettyjen*" (Finnish version) do not necessarily imply that the substance in question is in the liquid state.

26. In view of those semantic differences, the Court must examine whether the interpretation put forward by the French Government is consistent with the purpose of the directive.

27. An interpretation which restricted the scope of Directive 76/464 to discharges of dangerous substances which are in the liquid state would run counter to the objective of the directive, which, as may be seen from the first recital in its preamble, is to protect the aquatic environment of the Community from pollution, particularly that caused by certain persistent, toxic and bioaccumulable substances.

28. It cannot be accepted that those substances, which are mentioned in the annex to the directive, are dangerous for the aquatic environment of the Community only if they are in the liquid state.

29. It follows that Directive 76/464 applies to discharges of all the dangerous substances mentioned in the annex thereto, whatever their state.

30. The French Government further submits that, in a situation such as that at issue in the main proceedings, pollution by steam first occurs in the atmosphere and only later reaches surface water. In those circumstances, it cannot be argued that there is a discharge within the meaning of Directive 76/464, and such a situation is instead one of those to which Council Directive 84/360 . . . on the combating of air pollution from industrial plants (OJ 1984 L188, p. 20) should be applied.

31. It is sufficient to observe here that the circumstance relied on by the French Government is not capable of precluding a phenomenon such as that at issue in the main proceedings from being classified as a discharge within the meaning of Directive 76/464, where there is pollution of surface water and that pollution is caused, directly or indirectly, by an act attributable to a person.

32. As regards the second part of Question 1, the distance between the surface water and the place of emission of the contaminated steam is relevant only for the purpose of determining whether the pollution of the waters cannot be regarded as foreseeable according to general experience, so that the pollution is not attributable to the person causing the steam.

34. By its second question the national court essentially asks whether the term "discharge" in Article 1(2)(d) of Directive 76/464 is to be interpreted as covering the emission of contaminated steam which is first precipitated on to land and roofs and then reaches the surface water via a storm water drain, and whether it is material in this respect whether the drain in question belongs to the establishment concerned or to a third party.

35. Having regard to the Court's interpretation of the term "discharge" in paragraph 22 above and to the facts of the main proceedings, it must be held that the circumstance that the contaminated steam, after being precipitated on to land and roofs, reaches the surface water via a storm water drain, belonging either to the establishment concerned or to a third party, is not capable of precluding the pollution of those surface waters from being the consequence of an act attributable to a person, namely the wood impregnation process carried out by Van Aarle.

37. In view of the answers to Questions 1 and 2, there is no need to answer Question 3.

Commentary

I. *Water Directive 76/464 and Air Emissions*

(1) The present judgment is illustrative of the potential of Community law for litigation which takes place before national courts. Before Dutch administration authorities, Mr. van Rooij did not succeed with his neighbourhood complaint, as the administration was of the opinion that "steam" could not constitute a discharge. The Dutch court, however, had doubts and asked the Court of Justice for an interpretation. And the Court of Justice interpreted the term "discharge"

broadly and included air emissions which precipitated into water into this term, in so far as such air emissions were attibutable to a person.

In a parallel case which was decided on the same day, the Court stated that the term "discharge" in Directive 76/464 "must be understood as referring to any act attributable to a person by which one of the dangerous substances listed in List I or List II of the Annex to the directive is directly or indirectly introduced into the waters to which the directive applies".[49]

(2) It is not known, whether it was Mr. van Rooij's lawyer or any other person who had the idea that Directive 76/464 could be applicable to steam or other air emissions. It remains, though, an ingenuous idea. Indeed, Directive 76/464 was conceived as a water directive and as I, myself participated in the making of that Directive, I can confirm that nobody thought of including steam or other air emissions into the field of application of Directive 76/464. The Community had not, in the mid-1970s, drafted legislation on air pollution, if one exempts directives on lead in petrol or sulphur in fuel. Such air pollution legislation was initiated for the first time in the early 1980s, when "*Waldsterben*" in Germany and a large public discussion in the United Kingdom on the impact of lead in the air on human health led to the first measures on air pollution at Community level.

(3) Of course, this historical aspect is of no relevance with regard to the objective text of Directive 76/464. However, it may be mentioned that the words "air", "air emission" or any similar term do not appear in Directive 76/464, either in the different Articles or in the recitals. Furthermore, Article 3(1) for List I substances[50] and Article 7(2) for List II substances[51] require prior authorisation for any discharge which may contain substances of List I or List II. Taking the Court's interpretation of the term "discharge", this means that Article 7(2) of Directive 76/464 also requires the fixing of air emission standards; water emission standards cannot be meant by this provision in such cases, where for instance a plant is far away from any water stretch and only emits into the air. And such air emission standards shall, as Article 7(2) and (3) provide, be based on the water quality objectives which Member States shall have fixed.

(4) All this is obviously not consistent. Air emissions may be generated far away from a stretch of water, so that a Member State cannot even know whether emissions into the air will later precipitate into the nearby river, lake, coastal water or elsewhere: which water quality objective should be determining? Recital 6 of

---

[49] Court of Justice, Case C–232/97, *Nederhoff* [1999] ECR I–6385, para. 37.

[50] Directive 76/464 (n. 48 *supra*), Art. 3: "With regard to the substances belonging to the families and groups of substances in List I . . . : (1) all discharges into the waters referred to in Art. 1 which are liable to contain any such substance shall require prior authorisation by the competent authority of the Member State concerned".

[51] Directive 76/464 (n. 48 *supra*), Art. 7: "2. All discharges into the waters referred to in Art. 1 which are liable to contain any of he substances within List II shall require prior authorisation by the competent authority in the Member State concerned, in which emission standards shall be laid down. Such standards shall be based on the quality oobjectives, which shall be fixed as provided for in para. 3.

3. The programmes referred to in para. 1 shall include quality objectives for water; these shall be laid down in accordance with Council Directives, where they exist".

Directive 76/464 expressly starts from the idea that List II substances are discharged into a nearby and not into whatever water.[52]

(5) Also, the Community fixed, for the first time, framework provisions for air emissions from industrial installations by virtue of Directive 84/360,[53] adopted in 1984 and which became applicable in 1987. However, this Directive only covered industrial installations which were expressly enumerated in its Annex I. The Community has not fixed rules for the air emissions of all installations, small and large, industrial, agricultural or municipal installations: it has limited itself in Directive 96/61 to some installations, which again are expressly enumerated in an annex.[54] In view of this, it is surprising to think that by virtue of Directive 76/464 any air emission which may, in a foreseeable way, lead to precipitation into a water shall be subject to an authorisation which fixes emission standards.

(6) Two final observations may round this consideration up: on the one hand, the substances of List II of Directive 76/464 are typically substances which are problematic when they enter the water;[55] however, neither the Community nor Member States have felt the need to fix air emission standards for them. And on the other hand, it must be stated that all 15 Member States, when transposing Directive 76/464 into national law, have not felt it necessity to fix standards for air emissions of List II substances, by way either of general provisions or of individual emission permits.

(7) In conclusion, while the wording of Directive 76/464 also allows air emissions which subsequently precipitate into water to be covered by the term "discharge", in my opinion a systematic interpretation of Directive 76/464 and its context with the different directives on air emissions clearly leads to the result that the term "discharge" is limited to discharges into the water and does not include emissions which first go into the air and later, by way of precipitation, into the water. The French Government was thus, in my opinion, right in its analysis of the Directive.[56]

The main purpose of the presentation of this case, however, is to demonstrate how Community environmental law may, in the hands of learned lawyers, become a very useful tool in legal disputes within Member States. Its interpretation by the Court of Justice in the present case appears to have changed an administrative practice in the Netherlands that had existed for more than 20 years.

---

[52] Directive 76/464 (n. 48 *supra*), recital 6: "Whereas . . . it is necessary to establish . . . a second list, called List II, containing substances which have a deleterious effect on the aquatic environment, which can, however, be confined to a given area and which depend on the characteristics and location of the water into which they are discharged". The Annex to Directive 76/464, List II, repeats this text word by word.

[53] Directive 84/360 on the combating of air pollution from industrial plants [1984] OJ L188/20.

[54] Directive 96/61 on integrated pollution prevention and control [1996] OJ L257/26.

[55] List II contains, among others, the following substances: zinc, copper, nickel, chromium, lead, selenium, arsenic, antimony, molybdenum, titanium, tin, barium, beryllium, boron, uranium, vanadium, cobalt, thalium, tellurium, silver, biocides, non persistent mineral oils, cyanides, fluorides, ammonia and nitrites.

[56] It should be pointed out that Advocate General Saggio reached the same conclusion that the Court of Justice subsequently did.

II. Preliminary Rulings on Environmental Matters

(8) The present case was submitted to the Court of Justice by way of a preliminary ruling under Article 234 (ex Article 177) EC Treaty.[57] Article 234 EC Treaty contributes to ensuring an interpretation of Community law which is consistent and reduces diverging interpretation of Community law by courts in Member States.

It is not intended to describe, in the context of this book, the object, effect and relevance of Article 234 EC Treaty in the judicial system of Community law. The reader is referred to specialised commentaries on this provision. In environmental matters, the Court of Justice has delivered, between 1976 and 2000, 61 judgments in total[58] which may be divided as follows:

National court	1976–1991	1992–1994	1995–1997	1998–2000	Total
Belgium	1	1	4	1	7
France	4	2	1	1	8
Italy	6	2	6	5	19
Germany	—	1	—	3	4
Netherlands	5	—	2	7	14
United Kingdom	—	—	1	2	3
Sweden	—	—	1	2	3
Finland	—	—	—	1	1
Denmark	—	—	—	1	1
Luxembourg	—	—	—	1	1
Total	16	6	15	24	61

(9) The number of preliminary rulings in environmental law is remarkably low, though there has been some increase in recent years.[59] Most of the rulings were given on requests from Italian and Dutch courts which count for half of all rulings. These figures demonstrate the greater openness—and also knowledge?—which courts from these Member States demonstrate with regard to Community

[57] Art. 234 (ex Art. 177) EC Treaty: "The Court of Justice shall have jurisdiction to give preliminary rulings concerning: (a) the interpretation of this Treaty; (b) the validity and interpretation of acts of the institutions of the Community and of the ECB; (c) the interpretation of the statutes of bodies established by an act of the Council, where those statutes so provide.

Where such a question is raised before any court or tribunal of a Member State, that court or tribunal may, if it considers that a decision on the question is necessary to enable it to give judgment, request the Court of Justice to give a ruling thereon.

Where any such question is raised in a case pending before a court or tribunal of a Member State against whose decisions there is no judicial remedy under national law, that court or tribunal shall bring the matter before the Court of Justice".

[58] Author's own calculation.

[59] During the last five years, the Court gave the following number of preliminary rulings: 1995: 251; 1996: 256; 1997: 239; 1998: 264 and 1999: 255. See Commission: Monitoring the application of Community Law. Seventeenth Report (1999). COM(2000)92 of 23 June 2000. Volume VI, p. 13.

environmental law: in both Member States, Community environmental law is not perceived as an impairment of or a threat to the national legal tradition, but rather as a supplementary opportunity to find justice.

Overall, only 10 Member States have hitherto, submitted cases for a preliminary ruling under Article 234 EC Treaty. It is hardly surprising that courts from Greece, Spain, Portugal and Ireland, four Member States which receive financial assistance for environmental projects from the Cohesion Fund, because of their "backwardness",[60] have not yet submitted any case for a preliminary ruling: rather, this must be seen as a sign that the protection of the environment by the judiciary is also linked to growing environmental awareness—which, in turn, is linked to economic development.[61]

(11) For a number of years, the Commission has published the results of an annual survey of cases where a court of a Member State should have asked for a preliminary ruling under Article 234 EC Treaty but did not do so. The survey, which is published at the end of the Commission's annual report on the monitoring of the application of Community law, puts the emphasis on judgments by supreme courts of Member States.

By way of example, the 1999 survey may be quoted. Here the Commission reported[62] that the Netherlands' Council of State (Raad van State) found, without making any request for a preliminary ruling, that the ban on exporting waste from one province of the Netherlands to another is not a measure having an effect equivalent to a restriction on exports within the meaning of Article 29 (ex Article 34) EC Treaty, although the Court of Justice had found, on the basis of Article 23 EC Treaty, that *ad valorem* charges on trade in goods between regions of the same Member State constituted charges having an effect equivalent to customs duties.

In another case before the Supreme Administrative Court of Sweden (Regeringsrätten) on which the Commission reported,[63] the question arose whether the withdrawal of a licence for operating the nuclear power plant of the Barsebäck power station and the demolition of the plant without an environmental impact assessment under Directive 85/337[64] was valid. The applicants had argued that also the demolition of the power plant could cause considerable environmental impairment. As an amendment of a project required an environmental impact assessment where it had significant effects on the environment, a complete demolition of a project would have to be seen as a form of amendment and treated equally. The Swedish Court held that the provisions of Directive 85/337 were not essential to the material outcome of the case and that there was therefore no reason to ask for a preliminary ruling.

---

[60] This is the wording of Art. 158 EC Treaty.

[61] See also J de la Fontaine, *L'agneau et le loup: Ventre affamé n'a pas d'oreilles.*

[62] Commission (n. 59 *supra*), p. 19.

[63] Commission (n. 59 *supra*), p. 20.

[64] Directive 85/337 on the assessment of the effects of certain public and private projects on the environment [1985] OJ L175/40; amended by Directive 97/11 [1997] OJ L73/5.

Overall, the dealings of the different courts and in particular their use of Article 234 EC Treaty demonstrates how far away the European Union is from being a Union of law. Different national interpretations of uniform standards must impair the legal cohesion of the European Union.

49. APPLICATION UNDER ARTICLE 226 EC TREATY

Judgment of the Court (Third Chamber) of 13 April 2000
Case C–123/99

Commission of the European Communities v. *Greece*
[2000] ECR I–2881

Facts and Procedure

Directive 94/62 deals with packaging and packaging waste.[65] It was adopted in 1994 and replaced Directive 85/339 on liquid beverage containers.[66] While Directive 85/339 had been based on Article 308 (ex Article 235) EC Treaty,[67] Directive 94/62 was based on Article 95 (ex Article 100a) EC Treaty.

Directive 94/62 fixes targets for the recovery and recycling of packaging waste which Member States had to achieve by mid-2001. These targets were to be revised by way of an amendment of the Directive at the latest by 1 January 2001, upon a proposal of the Commission. Furthermore, packaging had to comply with some essential requirements which were laid down in Annex II to the Directive and which were to be filled in in detail by technical standards that had to be elaborated by the European Standardisation Organisation CEN. Member States were not allowed to prohibit the marketing of packaging which complied with the requirements of Directive 94/62.

Member States had to bring into force the laws, regulations and administrative provisions necessary to comply with the Directive before 30 June 1996 and had to inform the Commission thereof. As the Commission had not received a notification of the transposition of the Directive into Greek law, it brought, under Article 226 EC Treaty, an action before the Court of Justice.

---

[65] Directive 94/62 on packaging and packaging waste [1994] OJ L365/10.

[66] Directive 85/339 on liquid beverage containers [1985] OJ L176/18.

[67] Art. 308 (ex Art. 235) EC Treaty: "If action by the Community should prove necessary to attain, in the course of the operation of the common market, one of the objectives of the Community and this Treaty has not provided the necessary powers, the Council shall, acting unanimously on a proposal from the Commission and after consulting the European Parliament, take the appropriate measures".

Judgments (extracts)

7. Referring to the Member States' obligations under Article 5 and the third paragraph of Article 189 of the EC Treaty (now Article 10 EC and the third paragraph of Article 249 EC), the Commission considers that the Hellenic Republic should have adopted the necessary measures to comply with the Directive within the prescribed period and notified it accordingly.

8. The Hellenic Republic does not dispute that it failed to fulfil its obligations as alleged. It states, however, that a draft law is currently before the competent ministers for signature.

9. Since the Directive has not been transposed within the period prescribed in the reasoned opinion, the action brought in this connection by the Commission is well founded.

10. On the other hand, the Court does not have to take account of the failure to provide information concerning the laws, regulations and administrative provisions necessary in order to comply with the Directive, since the Hellenic Republic did not adopt those provisions within the period prescribed in the reasoned opinion . . .

11. Therefore, the Court finds that, by failing to adopt the laws, regulations and administrative provisions necessary to comply with the Directive within the prescribed period, the Hellenic Republic has failed to fulfil its obligations under the Directive.

Commentary

I. *The Procedure under Article 226 EC Treaty*

(1) The legal questions of this judgment are trivial: Greece had not transposed Directive 94/62 on packaging and packaging waste within the time-span required by the Directive. At the request of the Commission, the Court found that Greece had not complied with its obligations under Directive 94/62. Article 228(1) EC Treaty expressly states that in procedures under Article 226 EC Treaty,[68] the Court may not go beyond the statement "that a Member State has failed to fulfil an obligation under this Treaty"; this includes, of course, an obligation under a directive, as the directive is based on the EC Treaty, too.

---

[68] Art. 226 (ex Art. 169) EC Treaty: "If the Commission considers that a member State has failed to fulfil an obligation under this Treaty, it shall deliver a reasoned opinion on the matter after giving the State concerned the opportunity to submit its observations.

If the State concerned does not comply with the opinion within the period laid down by the Commission, the latter may bring the matter before the Court of Justice".

(2) Between 1998 and 2000, the Court gave 45 judgments under Article 226 EC Treaty.[69] Of these, nine judgments dealt with the absence of national legislation to transpose Community directives into national law; 14 judgments concerned the incomplete or incorrect transposition of Community directives into national law and 22 judgments dealt with poor application of the transposed legislation. Whether the Commission initiates a procedure under Article 226 EC Treaty against a Member State is entirely up to the Commission. It is true that the wording of Article 226 EC Treaty reads different: at least as regards the pre-judicial part of the procedure, the discussion between the Commission and Member States, in particular the issuing of a reasoned opinion, there is, according to the wording of that provision, an obligation of the Commission which is also, under Article 211 EC Treaty, obliged "to ensure that the provisions of this Treaty and the measures taken by the insititutions pursuant thereof are applied".

(3) However, the Court has constantly held that Article 226 EC Treaty does not oblige the Commission to initiate formal proceedings against a Member State; and neither another Community institution nor a Member State or an individual person has standing, under Article 230 or 232 EC Treaty, for attacking the Commission, because it has failed to initiate proceedings under Article 226 EC Treaty.[70] The reason for this, according to the Court, is that Article 226 EC Treaty has the objective of ensuring that the legal order of the Community is preserved, and this task is given to the Commission. The procedure of Article 226 does not aim at protecting interests of Member States or of Community institutions. This objective function of Article 226 EC Treaty also explains why the Court does not admit the defence by a Member State that an action was brought too late.[71]

(4) The procedure under Article 226 EC Treaty consists of three stages:

(a) formal notice of breach of obligations to the Member State;
(b) issue of a reasoned opinion;
(c) application to the Court of Justice.

Steps (a) and (b) jointly constitute the pre-judicial procedure which has the objective of enabling the Member State to comply with its obligations under Community law or to present its arguments to the Commission on why there is no breach of Community law. For this reason the Commission is obliged to specify clearly the basis on which it considers the Member State's breach to have occurred.[72]

(5) The formal notice does not require a specific form. In practice, however, the notice is given in the form of a letter addressed to the Member State in question. However, in particular in urgent cases, the Commission may also give oral notice,

---

[69] All figures hereafter are my own calculations. See in detail, for the years 1998 and 1999 and for previous years L Krämer, "Die Rechtsprechung der EG-Gerichte zum Umweltrecht 1998 und 1999" [2000] *Europäische Grundrechte Zeitschrift* 265.
[70] Court of Justice, Cases 48/65, *Lütticke* [1966] ECR 28; C–247/87, *Star Fruit* [1989] ECR 291; C–87/89, *Société nationale* [1990] ECR I–1981.
[71] Court of Justice, Case C–96/89, *Commission v. Netherlands* [1991] ECR I–24.
[72] Court of Justice, Case C–266/94, *Commission v. Spain* [1995] ECR I–1975.

for instance during a meeting, though this practice has become extremely rare. The decision to give formal notice is taken by the Commission, after detailed preparation of the Commission services. The letter of formal notice is agreed word by word at administrative, legal and political level, before it is transmitted to the Member State. This careful preparation is also a result of the view held by the Court of Justice that the Commission's letter of formal notice defines the object of litigation for any subsequent Court proceedings:[73] thus, the Commission cannot, in any subsequent part of the procedure under Article 226 EC Treaty, include any additional point of complaint against a Member State, since that Member State would not have had "the opportunity to present its observations" on such points; in other words, the right of the Member State to be heard would not be respected in such a case.

(6) Normally, the Member State has two months to reply to the Commission's letter of formal notice. However, since the Commission discusses and decides on cases under Article 226 EC Treaty only once every six months, the time available to Member States for a reply is almost always much longer. In the present case, Directive 94/62 was to be transposed into national law before 30 June 1996. The Commission sent the letter of formal notice on 16 January 1997. It received no answer and thus issued a reasoned opinion on 2 October 1997 which gave Greece, *de facto*, almost eight months to react.

(7) A reasoned opinion is issued where the Commission either has not received an answer or is not satisfied with the Member State's answer. The reasoned opinion is produced in the same way as the letter of formal notice. It gives a detailed and comprehensive description of the case as it presents itself in the opinion of the Commission, indicates its legal assessment and describes in detail by which measure Community law has been breached. Should proceedings subsequently be initiated before the Court of Justice, the facts—this, at least, is the concept of the reasoned opinion—no longer need clarification; therefore, normally, the dispute before the Court can be confined to legal issues.[74]

On average, the timespan between the decision to send a letter of formal notice and the application to the Court in environmental matters was 35 months between 1992 and 1994, 33 months between 1995 and 1997, and 48 months—thus a full four years—in 1998 and 1999.[75] In the present case, which did not raise any factual or legal problem, this time-span was 27 months, still a rather long time.

(8) The Commission occasionally publishes a press release on those disputes which it considers politically or environmentally important. The impact of such

---

[73] Court of Justice, Case C–279/94, *Commission* v. *Italy* [1997] ECR I–4743, para. 14: "the purpose of the letter of formal notice at the pre-litigation stage of the procedure for establishing a State's to fulfil its obligations is to delimit the subject matter of the dispute and to indicate to the Member State asked to submit its observations the factors enabling it to prepare its defence"; see also Case C–337/89, *Commission* v. *United Kingdom* [1992] ECR I–6103.

[74] Court of Justice, Case C–279/94 (n. 73 *supra*), para. 15: "the reaonsed opinion provided for in Art. 169 of the Treaty must contain a coherent and detailed statement of reasons which led the Commission to conclude that the State in question has failed to fulfil one of its obligations under the Treaty".

[75] L Krämer (n. 69 *supra*), p. 267.

press releases is sometimes considerable, depending on the sensitivity of the media to the issue. However, the Commission does not make public either the letter of formal notice or the reasoned opinion. This practice, for which no explanation can be found in Article 226 EC Treaty, is justified with the argument that the confidentiality of the relations between Member States and the Commission would otherwise be disturbed and a smooth solution to the problem made more difficult.[75a] This attitude seems to be in the interest neither of the environment nor of the citizen and it is not conducive to an open society.[76] And Article 255 EC Treaty[77] hardly allows such a restriction, as it cannot be seen that such a restriction is in the public or private interest.

(9) The Commission has a very wide discretion to apply to the Court of Justice and, in practice, less than 10 per cent of cases where the procedure under Article 226 EC Treaty was initiated are actually submitted to the Court. There is no delay required in submitting the application to the Court, nor need for the Commission to demonstrate a specific legal interest in order to obtain a judgment.

Between 1976 and the end of 2000, the Court of Justice decided 98 environmental cases under Article 226; for the 37 cases which were decided, in 1998 and 1999, on that legal basis, the average timespan between the dispatch of the letter of formal notice and the judgment of the Court was 68 months, thus over five and a half years. The procedure between the Commission and the Member States took, on average, 48 months, the procedure before the Court 20 months.[78] In the present case, the timespan between the dispatch of the letter of formal notice and the judgment was 39 months. And the Court's statement that Greece had failed to fulfil its obligation came 46 months after the time—30 June 1996—when Greece should have complied with its obligations.

II. Packaging and Packaging Waste in the Community

(10) Directive 94/62 on packaging and packaging waste was not the first packaging legislation adopted at Community level. In 1985, the Community adopted Directive 85/339 on liquid beverage containers.[79] This Directive, adopted after long

---

[75a] In Case T–191/99 *Petrie and others* v. *Commission*, judgment of 11 December 2001, not yet reported, the Court supported the Commission's position.

[76] See Written Question E–1106/98 (Lambrias) [1998] OJ C354/62, where the Commission explains its policy under Art. 226 EC Treaty, arguing also that it normally publishes the reasoned opinion. This appears not to correspond to normal practice.

[77] Art. 255 EC Treaty: "Any citizen of the Union, and any natural or legal person residing or having its registered office in a Member State, shall have a right of access to European Parliament, Council and Commission documents, subject to the principles and conditions to be defined in accordance with paras. 2 and 3.

2. General principles and limits on grounds of public or private interest governing this right of access to documents shall be determined by the Council, acting in accordance with the procedure referred to in Art. 251 within two years of the entry into force of the Treaty of Amsterdam.

3. Each institution referred to above shall elaborate in its own Rules of Procedure specific provision regarding access to its documents".

[78] L Krämer (n. 69 *supra*), p. 267.

[79] Directive 85/339 on liquid beverage containers [1985] OJ L176/18.

and passionate lobbying in particular from Anglo-Saxon trade organisations, asked Member States to establish programmes for the reduction of packaging for liquid beverage containers. These programmes could be implemented, among others, by voluntary agreements. There were hardly any other obligations for Member States laid down in this Directive. Nevertheless, the Directive was not particularly successful, as a considerable number of Member States did not establish programmes. In 1993, the Commission reported that six of the then 12 Member States had not set up such programmes;[80] in some cases, the Court gave judgment.[81]

(11) Other Member States adopted rather far-reaching national measures to promote the reuse and recycling of packaging. In Italy, some legislation was introduced to prohibit non-biodegradable plastic bags.[82] Denmark introduced a system to promote the reutilisation of bottles and linked it to a deposit-and-return system. The Commission considered the Danish system to be incompatible with Article 28 (ex Article 30) EC Treaty, but the Court, in a landmark decision, held that the Danish system was, in essence, compatible with that provision.[83] Denmark had also introduced a ban on metal cans for certain drinks and the Commission decided not to apply to the Court against that legislation. Instead it announced in 1989 that it would propose Community-wide legislation for plastic packaging (in order to cover the Italian situation) and metal packaging (in order to cover the Danish situation).[84] While it was preparing its proposals, Germany adopted legislation for packaging which introduced, among others, quota for returnable bottles. As this affected the trade, in particular in mineral waters, beer and juice, which also relied on one-way or plastic bottles, the Commission decided, under strong pressure from trade and industry, to propose a directive which covered all packaging and to base it on Article 95 (ex Article 100a) EC Treaty. This proposal, submitted in 1992, was adopted in 1994, shortly before the accession of three new Member States to the Community; Directive 85/339 was repealed.

(12) The new Directive 94/62 tried to reconcile economic and ecological considerations. It declared that reuse and material recycling of packaging should have priority over other forms of recovery (incineration), as long as there was no new scientific information demonstrating the need for other priorities. However, the

---

[80] Commission, Tenth annual report on monitoring the application of Community law—1992 [1993] OJ C233/1 (164).

[81] Court of Justice, Cases C–252/89, *Commission* v. *Luxembourg* [1991] ECR I–3973; C–192/90, *Commission* v. *Spain* [1991] ECR I–5933; C–255/93 *Commission* v. *France* [1994] ECR I–4949.

[82] Court of Justice, Case 380/87, *Cinisello Balsamo* [1989] ECR 2491; the Court held that Directive 75/442 on waste [1975] OJ L194/39 did not prohibit such bans. The Court did not pronounce on whether such a ban was compatible with Art. 28 (ex Art. 30) EC Treaty, as the Italian judge, under the procedure of Art. 234 EC Treaty, had not put a corresponding question to the Court.

[83] Court of Justice, Case 302/86, *Commission* v. *Denmark* [1988] ECR 4607.

[84] Commission, Communication on "A Community Strategy for Waste Management", SEC(89)934 of 18 September 1989, no. V: "Following the Court's judgment in case 380/87, Community action on plastic waste is an urgent necessity. Proposals to ban metal containers have already been introduced in some Member States, thus jeopardizing the free movement of goods. Community action is needed in this field too".

provisions on prevention of packaging waste (Article 4) and reuse of packaging (Article 5) are formulated in a very vague form and hardly push Member States into the direction of prevention and reuse of packaging.

The core of the Directive is Article 6 which fixes recovery and recycling targets for packaging. By 2001, Member States had to recover at least 50 and as a maximum 65 per cent of packaging material. For each individual packaging material— glass, paper and cardboard, metal, plastic etc.—between 25 and 45 per cent had to be materially recycled and each individual material had to reach a quota of 15 per cent. Greece, Ireland and Spain obtained less strict targets and a longer period for reaching them.

(13) Furthermore, the Directive requested that Member States set up collection systems for packaging, fixed essential requirements for the safety and environmental performance of packaging which was to be supplemented with industrial standards, limited the concentration of heavy metals in packaging, provided for extensive data collection schemes for packaging, asked Member States to establish management plans, provided for the adoption of economic instruments at Community level (which were never even proposed by the Commission) asked Member States to notify any draft legislation on packaging and to report every three years on the implementation of the Directive. It also stated that packaging which complied with the requirements of the Directive should be allowed to circulate freely within the Community. As regards a revision of the targets, the Directive provided that Council and the European Parliament would decide, before 1 January 2001, on a significant increase in the targets for the period 2001 to 2006 and, later on, fix the targets for each new five-year period.

(14) Directive 94/62 took off only with difficulty. Economic operators welcomed the provisions on the free circulation of packaging, but were largely opposed to the recycling and recovery targets. Multinational companies set up specialised lobby groups in order to combat the Directive and succeeded in preventing the Commission, until end 2001, to submit new proposals for targets, thus preventing the fixing of such targets in time for the period 2001 to 2006. Council and European Parliament remained silent on this.[84a] The Commission took legal action against Denmark for not allowing metal cans on the Danish market.[85] And while the Member States seem on track, at the moment of writing these lines, to reach the targets for 2001, the future of this Directive appears uncertain, in view of the opposition of economic operators, in particular from the United Kingdom and the Anglo-Saxon world, and the lowered enthusiasm of public authorities in several Member States to pursue a continued, active policy to promote prevention, reuse and recycling of packaging. The future enlargement is likely to further increase the difficulties.

[84a] A proposal was finally made in December 2001, COM [2001] 729 of 15 December 2001.
[85] See Case C–246/99, *Commission* v. *Denmark*; this case and a parallel case, C–233/99, *Haugsted Hansen*, is likely to be decided in 2002; i n spring 2002, Denmark announced that it would abandon the ban of cans. This policy change came after political elections which brought a conservative government to power.

(15) From the environmental point of view it must be underlined that Directive 94/62—perhaps together with some other waste provisions—is almost the only Community piece of legislation which requires the active participation of individual persons and households by separately collecting packaging waste, to become active in order to protect the environment. While water and air directives mainly address public authorities and ask them to follow certain provisions, packaging and packaging waste provisions ask individuals to contribute to the achievement of the commonly fixed objectives. The individual person may thus have the feeling that he/she can also help, by his/her proper behaviour, to combat environmental impairment.

The foreseeable fate of Directive 94/62 is that the Community institutions will not pursue the objectives, principles and priorities which they fixed themselves in the Directive's text at the moment of its adoption. As, however, this observation leads into the area of speculation, the subject is not further pursued.

50. INTERIM MEASURES FOR THE ENVIRONMENT

Order of the President of the Court of First Instance of 12 February 1996 Case T–228/95R

S. Lehrfreund Ltd v. Council of the European Union and Commission of the European Communities [1996] ECR II–111

Facts and Procedure

In 1991, the Council adopted Regulation 3254/91[86] which prohibited the use of leghold traps and provided for provisions to prohibit the import of pelts of 13 animal species[87] from countries which did not have adequate standards for prohibiting the use of leghold traps or which did not have internationally agreed humane trapping standards[88]. In 1994, the Commission decided, based on Article 3(2) of

---

[86] Regulation 3254/91 prohibiting the use of leghold traps in the Community and the introduction into the Community of pelts and manufactured goods of certain wild animal species originating in countries which catch them by means of leghold traps or trapping methods which do not meet international humane trapping standards [1991] OJ L308/1.

[87] These are: beaver, otter, coyote, wolf, lynx, bobcat, sable, raccoon, musk rat, fisher, badger, marten and ermine.

[88] Regulation 3254/91 (n. 86 *supra*), Art. 2: "1. The introduction into the Community of the pelts of the animal species listed in Annex I . . . shall be prohibited as of 1 January 1995, unless the Commission, in accordance with the procedure laid down in Art. 5, has determined that, in the country where the pelts originate: *cont./*

Regulation 3254/91, that the prohibition on the import of pelts was to enter into force on 1 January 1996[89] and that it would decide, before 1 September 1995, which countries met the conditions of Article 3(1) of Regulation 3254/91. A draft list of such countries was made public, but never adopted by the Commission.

In December 1995, the Commission informed Member States that it considered the implementation of Regulation 3254/91 "impracticable"; it asked Member States to ensure that even after 31 December 1995 trade in pelts would not be disrupted.

The applicant is a company which buys, processes and sells furs. It was of the opinion that Regulation 3254/91 affected its interests and applied to the Court of First Instance to order the Council and the Commission to pay damages. At the same time, the applicant asked, under Articles 242 and 243 EC Treaty,[90] that Regulation 3254/91 be suspended and that any further interim measures should be taken which the Court considered appropriate. The Council asked the Court to make a declaratory statement in the sense that Regulation 3254/91 did not require Member States to implement import restrictions under Article 3(1) of Regulation 3254/91.

Order (extracts)

14. Article 104(1) of the Rules of Procedure of the Court of First Instance specifies that an application for . . . suspension is admissible only if the applicant is challenging the measure in question in proceedings before the Court of First Instance. Under Article 104(2), applications for any of the interim measures . . . must state the circumstances giving rise to urgency and the pleas of fact and law establishing a prima facie case for the interim measures applied for. The measures sought must be provisional in that they must not prejudice the decision on the substance . . .

—there are adequate administrative or legislative provisions in force to prohibit the use of the leghold trap; or
—the trapping methods used for the species listed in Annex I meet internationally agreed humane trapping standards.

The Commission shall publish in the Official Journal of the European Communities a list of the countries which meet at least one of the conditions set out in the first para..

2. The prohibition referred to in para. 1 shall be suspended for one year, expiring on 31 December 1995, if the Commission, in accordance with the procedure laid down in Art. 5, has determined before 1 July 1994, as a result of a review undertaken in cooperation with the competent authorities of the countries concerned, that sufficient progress is being made in developing humane methods of trapping in their territories"

[89] Regulation 1771/94 [1994] OJ L184/3.
[90] Art. 242 (ex Art. 185) EC Treaty: "Actions brought before the Court of Justice shall not have suspensory effect. The Court of Justice may, however, if it considers that circumstances so require, order that application of the contested act be suspended".
Art. 243 (ex Art. 186) EC Treaty: " The Court of Justice may in any cases before it prescribe any necessary interim measures".

20. The applicant considers that there are two possible interpretations of the consequences of the failure to adopt, by 1 January 1996, the implementing measures mentioned in Article 1(2)(a) of Regulation 1771/94 . . .

The first is that a total import ban for all the relevant species comes into effect on that date for all non-member countries, irrspective of whether or not a particular country satisfies the conditions of Article 3(1) of Regulation 3254/91 (an "absolute ban").

The second is that no ban comes into effect in the absence of implementing measures. It will only do so once the Commission has adopted the measures provided for, that is to say once it has determined the countries from which imports are authorised, and will only apply to countries not on that list (a "deferred ban").

58. It is clear from its explanations at the hearing that the forms of order which the applicant is now seeking are, primarily, a declaration to the effect, essentially, that Article 3(1) of Regulation 3254/91 is to be interpreted as laying down a "deferred ban" . . .

[The applicant's request for a declaration as to interpretation]

60. This request must be dismissed as inadmissible because it is incompatible with both the specific nature of interim proceedings and, more generally, the system of remedies of which it forms a part.

61. The EC Treaty distinguishes between direct actions before the Community judicature and the procedure for seeking a preliminary ruling under Article 177. Only in the latter case may the Court of Justice be asked to give a decision whose operative part itself relates directly to the interpretation of a rule of Community law. Such a decision cannot, therefore, be obtained in interim proceedings, which are necessarily an adjunct to a direct action . . . As regards the imports envisaged by the applicant, moreover, the rules contested in the present case are applied not by the defendants but by the authorities of the Member States. There is thus no legitimate interest for the applicant's main claim since the effects of any order granting it would, prima facie, be confined to the parties to the present interim proceedings. An interpretation by the Court of Justice, on the other hand, could be obtained in the context of proceedings before a national court and apply by virtue of a decision of that court to the relations between the applicant and a national authority which had issued a decision on the basis of the ban in issue.

[The application for suspension of the operation of Regulation 3254/91]

62. The application for interim measures alleges several types of damage which the applicant has suffered or may suffer.

63. The applicant has not put forward the damage which it claims to have suffered already, and to be likely to suffer in the future, as a result of the legal uncertainty which it alleges, as constituting serious and irreparable harm and thus giving rise to a situation of urgency requiring the ordering of interim measures before judgment is given in the main action . . . In any event, the requested suspension could not remedy damage which has already occurred. The damage referred to above cannot, therefore, justify the adoption of such an interim measure.

64. As regards the future damage which the applicant claims it will suffer because the contested ban will prevent it from importing certain products, a distinction must be drawn, as proposed by the applicant itself on the basis of the two possible interpretations in that regard, between the hypothesis of an absolute ban and that of a deferred ban . . .

If Article 3(1) is assumed to lay down a deferred ban, in principle it cannot itself place the applicant in a situation of urgency until the Commission adopts the implementation measures for which provision is made. The applicant has not produced any prima facie evidence that such measures . . . would have irreversible effects as soon as they came into force, before any judicial decision could be obtained . . . In any event, even if it were established that such a situation were imminent, that would not justify suspending the operation of Article 3(1) as the legal basis for such implementing measures but merely, at most, adopting interim measures regarding the operation of those provisions themselves.

67. If Article 3(1) is to be interpreted as laying down an absolute ban, it must first be considered what effects would ensue from a suspension of its operation, in order to define more precisely the legal conditions on which the granting of an order for suspension is dependent. The suspension requested would irremediably deprive the contested ban of its effect for as long as the interim order remained valid, and to the extent that goods of the kind referred to in Regulation No 3254/91 were brought into free circulation in the Community by the applicant or any other importer. It cannot therefore be granted unless there are exceptional circumstances which demonstrate that, despite the effects identified above, it would be disproportionate to dismiss the applicant's request. However, such a conclusion . . . is in any event not supported by the arguments and evidence put forward as regards either the applicant's statements seeking to establish the urgency of the application for interim measures or the *prima facie* case in the main action.

68. . . . the applicant has not sufficiently established that it is likely to be forced into liquidation before judgment is given in the main action.

71. In the absence of more detailed information on the applicant's financial and economic situation, therefore, it is not possible to conclude at present that the threat of its being forced into liquidation is so serious and pressing as to justify, exceptionally, granting the relief sought.

72. Nor do the pleas in law and arguments put forward in support of the main action establish the existence of an exceptional situation justifying such relief. No obvious conclusions can be drawn from them in these interim proceedings as to the lawfulness of the measure in question or the liability of the Community. In particular, the arguments concerning the choice of legal basis and the alleged direct effect of GATT raise complex questions which cannot be examined here without prejudging the decision of the Court on the substance. Similar consider-

ations apply to the arguments relating to the principle of proportionality, since they involve applying that principle to a measure of Community legislation and it is necessary to determine precisely to what extent each of the alleged breaches is capable of affecting the applicant's position. This latter observation applies also to the extent that the applicant, manifestly assuming that the law at present lays down an absolute ban, accuses the Commission of having failed in its duty to adopt implementing provisions in respect of Regulation No 3254/91. In that regard, it may be concluded from the applicant's explanations concerning urgency in the hypothesis of a deferred ban that, following the adoption of such provisions in line with the draft submitted by the Commission, that prohibition would have appreciably the same effects for the applicant as an absolute ban, since it would prevent imports from the United States and Canada . . . In the absence of specific information from which it might be concluded that, on the basis of the present text of Regulation No 3254/91, the Commission should have authorised imports from those countries, even though they do not prohibit the use of leghold traps and there are as yet no internationally agreed humane trapping standards, it is not possible in these proceedings to discern in what way the Commission's failure could have affected the applicant.

73. The application for interim measures must therefore be dismissed, without there being any need to examine the question of admissibility raised by the defendant institutions.

Commentary

I. Interim Measures in Environmental Cases

(1) Until end of the year 2000, only very few cases had been decided where interim measures were asked for. In no case has the Court decided to provide for such interim measures. In Case C–57/89R,[91] the Court refused to stop the construction of a dyke in a protected area. In Case T–219/95R,[92] the applicant tried to stop, by application for interim measures, French nuclear tests in Mururoa. Its application was rejected as inadmissible, since the Court considered that the applicant, a citizen of Mururoa, was not directly and individually concerned by the tests. The present case was thus only the third environmental case on interim measures.

(2) The problem of interim measures is addressed in Articles 242 and 243 EC Treaty.[93] One of the reasons for the small number of cases is, without doubt, due to the fact that only the Court of Justice and the Court of First Instance can take

[91] Court of Justice, Case C–57/89R, *Commission* v. *Germany* [1989] ECR 2849.
[92] Court of First Instance, Case T–219/95R, *Danielsson* v. *Commission* [1995] ECR II–3051.
[93] See the text of these Arts. in n. 90 *supra*.

interim measures, and only in cases which are before them. The Commission has no possibility of taking interim measures. In view of the length of the duration of the procedure under Article 226 EC Treaty[94] the urgency of interim measures has often disappeared when the case reaches the Court.[95]

(3) Articles 242 and 243 EC Treaty deal only with proceedings on interim measures in a rudimentary form. The Rules of Procedure of the Court of First Instance[96] added a number of further requirements: the measure in question must be challenged before the Court of First Instance, the circumstances which give rise to urgency must be stated, and the applicant must makes pleas of fact and law establishing a *prima facie* case for the interim measure. The Court of First Instance further added that the "measures sought must be provisional in that they must not prejudge the decision on the substance".[97]

(4) I have some doubts whether all these supplementary requirements are really covered by the Treaty provisions. For instance, an interim measure may also be justified where there is no "urgency", but where the applicant would, without the interim measure, be left without any financial means. I fail to see why there must be pleas "of law" establishing a *prima facie* case for the interim measure; I would submit that the plea of fact is sufficient. And finally, I fail to see why the measure sought "must not prejudge the decision on the substance": it could well be that the provisional payment of damages—as in the present case—is justified by virtue of the interim decision, but that a more thorough examination would, in the judgment, lead to the rejection of the application. Contrary to what the present Order seems to indicate,[98] such opposite decisions seem perfectly compatible with the nature of an interim measure: the defendant may claim in the main proceedings damages and interests for having to pay, by virtue of the interim order, a sum of money to the applicant.

(5) The Order does not seem altogether clear. In paragraph 2 it states that the applicant requested the Court "to order suspension of the operation of Regulation 3254/91". The Council argued that the application should be dismissed as inadmissible or, in the alternative, as unfounded and, furthermore, proposed that the

---

[94] See on the duration of procedures under Art. 226 EC Treaty p. 421 *et seq supra.*

[95] In Case C–42/89, *Commission* v. *Belgium* [1990] ECR I–2821, there was a serious contamination of drinking water with lead in the Belgian city of Verviers. This had led even to fatalities. The Commission considered asking the Court for interim measures, but refrained from that, since the fatal cases dated several years back. The legal advice was that interim measures would be possible if a new fatal accident occurred!

[96] The present Order carefully avoids giving a reference for these Rules. They were published in [1991] OJ L136/1; amendments in [1994] OJ L249/17; [1995] OJ L44/64; [1997] OJ L103/6 and [2000] OJ L322/4. The Rules of Procedure of the Court of Justice are published in [1991] OJ L176/7; amendments [1995] OJ L44/61; [1997] OJ L103/1; [2000] OJ L122/43 and [2000] OJ L322/1.

[97] See para. 14 of the present Order.

[98] See para. 65 of the present Order (not reproduced above): "All the parties to these interim proceedings interpret the provision as laying down only a deferred ban. Although the arguments put forward in support of that interpretation do not appear prima facie to be clearly unfounded, nevertheless, as the applicant itself points out . . . , a literal analysis of Art. 3 of Regulations 3254/91 might lead to the conclusion that the ban is absolute. The President cannot, therefore, give a decision on such a complex question without prejudging the decision of the Court on the substance . . .".

Court make "a declaratory order . . . stating that . . . the regulation does not require Member States to implement import restrictions" under Article 3(1) of Regulation 3254/91 (paragraph 11). The applicant then stated that such a declaration would satisfy its interest; however, "in case the President of the Court should consider himself unable to make such a declaration, the applicant maintained its request for suspension of operation" (paragraph 12). The Order concluded from that that "the applicant is to be deemed to have abandoned its initial, general request for the adoption of any further interim measure" (paragraph 58), a conclusion which I would not necessarily draw from the written statements reproduced in the Order.

(6) A legal analysis of the Order is complicated by the reproduction of the facts and pleas which in my opinion are not altogether comprehensible. Probably, the outcome of the interim proceedings was also influenced by the evolution of Regulation 3254/91 which is a real "saga" and a model of how Community legislation should not be made. Suffice it therefore to say for the interim procedure that the overall conclusion of the Order is correct: the applicant cannot really request a suspension of Regulation 3254/91 with the argument that its application would create economic difficulties for the applicant.

II. Leghold Traps in Community Law

(7) The use of leghold traps to catch animals is considered non-selective— about 10 per cent of all animals caught are caught unintentionally—and cruel; the use of such traps is forbidden in more than 60 states all over the world. Induced by a petition by 272 members of the European Parliament, the Commission had not only proposed a ban on leghold traps but also an import ban on the fur of animal species. from those countries which continued to use leghold traps. And the Council—doubtless also under the influence of the personal appearance of Brigitte Bardot, a committed defendant of animals' rights—had adopted this proposal and had stated that the ban was to come into effect in 1995, unless the Commission made a specific statement; the Council expected that by then internationally agreed "humane trapping standards" would exist.[99]

(8) As the Commission did not make such a statement before 1 July 1994, the date provided for in Article 3(1) of Regulation 3254/91, the ban became effective on 1 January 1995. Commissions Regulation 1771/91 was adopted only on 19 July 1994; furthermore, the content of that Regulation—prolonging the entry into effect of the import ban—was not covered by any provision of Regulation 3254/91.[100]

[99] See the wording of Art. 3(1) of Regulation 3254/91 (n. 88 *supra*).

[100] See Regulation 1771/94 (n. 89 *supra*), Art. 1: "1. The prohibition on the introduction into the Community of the pelts of the animal species listed in Annex I to Council Regulation (EEC) No 3254/91 and of the other goods listed in Annex II to that Regulation, shall enter into force on 1 January 1996.

2. The Commission shall . . . determine before 1 September 1995: (a) which countries meet the condition of Art. 3(1) of that regulation and (b) the appropriate forms for certification referred to in Art. 4 thereof".

The reason for this Commission decision was probably that international "humane trapping standards" were nowhere elaborated and that in partcular the United States, Canada and Russia heavily opposed the Community import ban, arguing that it was contrary to the rules of GATT on free trade and that it disadvantaged indigenous populations. In view of this, the Commission proposed, in December 1995, to replace the import ban by a mandate to be given to the Commission in order to negotiate an agreement with third countries on humane trapping standards.[101] The Council did not adopt this proposal, but agreed to negotiations.

(9) In 1997, the Commission reached agreements with Canada and Russia on the one hand, with the United States on the other hand, which the Council agreed to in the form of decisions.[102] From an environmental point of view, it may well be doubted whether the "standards" which are laid down in both agreements really are "humane trapping standards", or whether they are not, instead, standards which more or less describe the factual situation. Legally, however, there can be no doubt that these standards are not "internationally agreed". Rather, they are agreed bilaterally or trilaterally, and had the Council really meant such negotiated agreements between the Community and other countries, it would certainly have used another expression.

(10) The Council had adopted, in 1997, a list of those countries for which the import ban would not be applicable;[103] also in the light of the conclusion of the two agreements, it modified that list in 1998.[104] The import of pelts from all animals listed in the annex to Regulation 3254/91 from Canada and the United States was authorised—with the exception of the sable (*martes zibellina*); as "*zibellina*" indicates the Siberian origin of this animal, it may be concluded that this animal does not exist in the wild in North America. For Russia, the import of five animals was allowed.

(11) Overall, it appears that the core of Regulation 3254/91, the ban on leghold traps, has been reached for the Community without the international trade in pelts or furs being significantly hampered. The legal constructions and reconstructions around Regulation 3254/91 are, however, quite impressive. It may be hoped that these rules did not seriously affect the applicant's economic activity.

---

[101] [1996] OJ C58/17.

[102] Decision 98/142 concerning the conclusion of an Agreement on international humane trapping standards between the European Community, Canada and the Russian Federation and of an Agreed Minute between Canada and the European Community concerning the signing of the said Agreement [1998] OJ L42/40; Decision 98/487 concerning the conclusion of an International Agreement in the form of an Agreed Minute between the European Community and the United States of America on humane trapping standards [1998] OJ L219/24.

It should be noted the United States had only agreed to an "Agreed Minute" not to a formal "Agreement".

[103] Decision 97/602 [1997] OJ L242/64.

[104] Decision 98/596 [1998] OJ L286/56.

INDEX

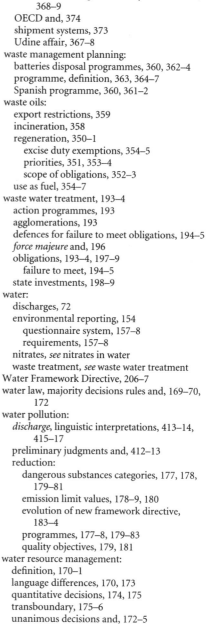

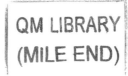